ALSO BY JOHN EGERTON

A Mind to Stay Here (1970)

The Americanization of Dixie (1974)

Visions of Utopia (1977)

Nashville: The Faces of Two Centuries (1979)

Generations (1983)

Southern Food (1987)

Side Orders (1990)

Shades of Gray (1991)

SPEAK NOW AGAINST THE DAY

SPEAK NOW AGAINST THE DAY

The Generation Before the
Civil Rights Movement
in the South

John Egerton

ALFRED A. KNOPF   NEW YORK

1994

THIS IS A BORZOI BOOK
PUBLISHED BY ALFRED A. KNOPF, INC.

Grateful acknowledgment is made to the Southern Regional Council for permission to reprint an excerpt by William Faulkner from *The Segregation Decisions* published by the Southern Regional Council, Atlanta, Georgia, in 1956.

Library of Congress Cataloging-in-Publication Data

Egerton, John.
Speak now against the day: the generation before the civil rights movement in the South/John Egerton.—1st ed.
    p.   cm.
ISBN 0-679-40808-8
1. Civil rights workers—Southern states—History—20th century. 2. Civil rights workers—Southern states—Biography. 3. Civil rights movements—Southern states—History—20th century. 4. Afro-Americans—Civil rights. 5. Southern states—Race relations. I. Title.
E185.61.E28   1994
323'.092'275—dc20   93-47491
                                                                CIP

Manufactured in the United States of America
First Edition

For Harry Ashmore, John A. Griffin, and Johnny Popham, elder statesmen of the mythical and whimsical Southern War Correspondents and Camp Followers Association, and in memory of Harold Fleming, their late and esteemed fellow penman and prince of bon mots.

And for Ann, first and last.

We speak now against the day when our Southern people who will resist to the last these inevitable changes in social relations, will, when they have been forced to accept what they at one time might have accepted with dignity and goodwill, will say, "Why didn't someone tell us this before? Tell us this in time?"

—WILLIAM FAULKNER

Contents

SPEAK NOW AGAINST THE DAY

Prologue: Hinge of History

Tuesday, August 14, 1945: When the word finally came at six o'clock that evening, downtown Atlanta exploded in a clangorous din of pent-up anticipation and excitement. Unleashed by President Harry S. Truman's radio announcement that Japan had surrendered and World War II was over, tens of thousands of Georgians erupted into the streets. They poured out of offices and stores, emptied theaters and restaurants, brought traffic to a standstill. Sirens blew, horns blasted, bells rang; people screamed, kissed, danced, drank. In spontaneous and simultaneous unison with their fellow citizens from New York to Los Angeles and practically every town and hamlet in between, the ecstatic Atlantans shook the ground with a wild and deafening celebration.

Before sunset brought the sidewalk temperature down out of the nineties and lowered the steambath humidity by a few points, sweating, shouting newsboys were hawking extras of the Atlanta *Constitution* and the Atlanta *Journal* up and down Forsyth and Peachtree Streets and all over the business district. The papers were literally hot off the press, their ink still damp and smudgy, their page-one headlines and stories hastily thrown together. The message they delivered amounted to physical confirmation, virtual proof, of a reality that seemed almost too good to be true.

WAR-WEARY WORLD AT PEACE
AS BEATEN JAPS SURRENDER

proclaimed the *Constitution's* banner headline. Just one week earlier, the paper had reported the destruction of Hiroshima, a Japanese city of more than 300,000 people—roughly the size of Atlanta—by the first atomic bomb ever used in warfare. Editor Ralph McGill, quoting Revelations in a column called "The Smell of Fire and Brimstone," hailed the harnessing of the atom as "easily the greatest story that has happened in our lifetime"—but with deeply mixed emotions, he said the use of atomic power as a weapon of mass destruction was "a great and terrifying thing."

McGill wrote an editorial-page column seven days a week in a style that blended sagacity, humor, righteous indignation, and melancholy fatalism.

Two days after the Hiroshima blast, he told his readers that Hitler had turned Germany into "one great big Ku Klux Klan Klavern," but now justice had finally prevailed, because it was Jewish refugees and other exiles fleeing from the Nazi dictator who had come to America and created the A-bomb that won the war. "God is not mocked," the Atlanta editor declared. Other commentators on the page with McGill shared his sense of moral vindication in the war's outcome. The Nazi idea of a master race was utterly demolished by Hitler's defeat, wrote columnist Robert Quillen, and the same fate had befallen the Japanese; victorious America, on the other hand, was not a superior race but "a mixture, an idea, a way of life, an attitude."

In the August 15 *Constitution*, under the headline CITY THUNDERS INTO POSTWAR ERA, celebrating Atlantans expressed their elation at the end of a long war (three years, eight months, and seven days, McGill reminded them) and their nervous anticipation of what lay ahead. The war had interrupted the New Deal programs aimed at rescuing the nation—and especially the South—from economic quicksand, said one observer; now it was time to face the challenges of peace.

Those challenges took many forms. The economic stimulation that the war had brought to the depressed South in the form of military bases and defense industries had to be converted to the peacetime creation of consumer goods and services. Per capita income in the region was still under four hundred dollars a year (closer to two hundred dollars for blacks), and that was barely more than half the national average. One out of every three adults had left school by the end of the sixth grade. Millions of men and women, white and black, would be returning from the military or from wartime jobs in the North; they would need education and job training, employment, housing, medical and legal help.

A new generation of young leaders, bringing back with them visions of a better life elsewhere, was already showing an eager readiness to help lift the South out of its eighty-year nightmare of post–Civil War stagnation. The black thirty percent of the region's thirty million citizens were especially hungry for change; in the view of Atlanta-born Walter White, leader of the National Association for the Advancement of Colored People, the victory for freedom and democracy abroad was a prelude to the battle for those ideals at home.

With more finality than any occurrence since the end of the Civil War, the American triumph in World War II appeared to mark the conclusion of an old and outdated era in the South—or so it seems now, with the benefit of a half-century of hindsight to sharpen our vision. In the blissful aftermath of that historic conquest, the American people reached a rare state of consensus that momentarily obscured the age-old barriers between them. They were, in that fleeting instant, truly We the People, eager to form a more perfect Union, and the Southerners among them were as caught up in that contagious spirit of righteousness and invincibility as any of their countrymen.

Here, surely, was a rare and momentous turning point in American history, and especially in the checkered history of the South: a crossing from darkness into light, a hinge of time swinging shut on a constricted past and opening to an expansive future. Yesterday—an almost endless ordeal of reconstruction, colonial exploitation, caste and class divisions, segregation, isolation, poverty, depression, and wartime sacrifice—was finally on the wane, if not yet altogether finished. Tomorrow—an age of opportunity, growth, prosperity, recovered self-esteem, national parity, and full citizenship—seemed ready and waiting to be born.

When I was waiting to be born at Crawford W. Long Hospital in Atlanta on a sultry June evening in 1935, Tomorrow was not yet visible on the Southern horizon. An occasional mule-drawn wagon still clopped and rattled over the streetcar tracks in the heart of the city, leaving the stark afterimage of enduring peasantry to linger in its wake. As close as Atlanta came to being the South's leading metropolis, it was in those lean days not much more than a big county-seat town with an indelible stain of red clay on its sidewalks. In the cities and towns as in the cotton fields and piney woods, the South was still caught in the paralyzing grip of the Great Depression. To make matters worse, the states were plagued with a bumper crop of political demagogues adept at turning the region's misery to their personal advantage. Georgia was a prime example. Under the cankered copper dome of the state capitol in downtown Atlanta, Governor Eugene Talmadge, a vociferous foe of President Roosevelt and his New Deal programs of relief and recovery, used an iron hand and an acid tongue to rule the state like a feudal baron.

Atlanta's population had almost quadrupled since the turn of the century as a steady influx of families from the hardscrabble farms of the South, driven out by the boll weevil and a host of man-made ravages, turned in desperation to the city as their only hope for survival. Though it was not as large as New Orleans or Houston or Louisville, Atlanta was widely regarded as a showcase of the progressive South, a thriving hub of state government, higher education, religion, and commerce. Even so, more than a third of its households in 1935 were without indoor plumbing or electric lights or both, and the generally wretched living conditions caused thousands to suffer and die of illnesses now virtually unknown to us, from hookworm, scurvy, and pellagra (the diseases of poverty and malnutrition) to the epidemic infections of typhoid fever, smallpox, tuberculosis, and polio.

In the "separate but equal" operation of hospitals, schools, housing projects, and public transportation, whites got the lion's share of funds that were in reality pitifully inadequate for one system of services, let alone two. Civic and religious leaders fervent for social reform generally steered clear of race and class issues, focusing instead on winning souls to Christ, reducing violent crime, and attacking the evils of alcohol. Prohibition had been repealed nationally, but Georgia and most of the South remained legally dry. Atlanta teemed with moonshine-makers, bootleggers, gamblers, and prostitutes; by one informed estimate, forty percent of the city's policemen had profit-sharing ties with the illicit liquor trade.

Atlanta was also a hotbed of the Ku Klux Klan, and thousands of white men (including, it was reported, a majority of the police force) belonged to the secret society as proudly as to the Masons or the Shriners or the Rotary—looked upon it, in fact, as a charitable organization dedicated to the perpetuation of Victorian morality and white Protestant supremacy, two of the prevailing dogmas of the time. (Another reactionary group, the Black Shirts, also had a broad base of popular support; they used a Fascist political message to rally unemployed whites against black workers during the depression.)

Against these currents of reaction, Mayor James L. Key battled to make progressive improvements, especially in the areas of education and welfare. He managed to legalize Sunday baseball and "picture shows" in the 1930s, but for those successes and his outspokenness (he had called Prohibition a failure, criticized the Klan, and supported voting rights for blacks), he was pushed out of the Methodist Church and finally, in 1936, out of office, losing to a young and ambitious Talmadge-backed candidate named William B. Hartsfield.

I knew none of this, of course, being only an infant at the time. My father was a traveling salesman, and Atlanta was a temporary outpost in our family's nomadic migration across the depression-wracked landscape. As I think of him now, it occurs to me that my father had a lot in common with Ralph McGill: a rural Tennessee birth in the twilight of the nineteenth century, an opportunity to discover wider vistas as a young man, a fondness for Southern country folks, a way with words and a sense of their power, a jumble of contradictory emotions on the subject of race, and a troubled mind masked by hail-fellow good cheer. They even looked a lot alike—five-ten or so and stocky, with dark, wavy hair and glasses. As I have peered into the shuttered recesses of regional and personal history, McGill and my father have taken on an almost interchangeable persona in my mind's eye.

Before the summer of 1935 was over, we had moved again—my father and the three older children by car and my mother with me, the squalling infant, by train—up through north Georgia and across Tennessee to the little western Kentucky village of Cadiz, where my mother's parents lived. The family needed a safe harbor in which to ride out the economic storm that was battering the entire country, and Cadiz was the only real choice open to them. Luckily, it turned out to be a good move and a permanent one, the last for my mother—and, in a homing sense, for all of us.

My older sisters years later would recall how shocked they had been by the experience of ending their youthful sojourns in the urban South (Washington, Richmond, Jacksonville, Atlanta) and settling into an impoverished rural environment where malnutrition, disease, and illiteracy were so commonplace as to be largely unnoticed and unremarked. The contrast made a profound impression upon my siblings, even though their comparison was only white to white and South to South; the relative disadvantage of blacks in both settings was enormous, as was the South's status vis-à-vis the rest of the country, but segregation and isolation rendered such contrasts virtually invisible in the eyes of little children.

Still and all, the prostrate South that Franklin Roosevelt inherited from Herbert Hoover in 1933 had at least risen to its knees when World War II ended. By almost every measure, it was still dead last among the regions—in education, employment, income, health, home ownership, and political participation—but its soldiers had gone to Europe and Asia and Africa to fight a war for human freedom, many of its women had left home to work in factories and stores, and its economy had been stimulated by wartime production; now the spoils of victory would soon be up for grabs.

Television was coming, and jet airplanes, and air-conditioning, and a sparkling showcase of consumer goods, from high-powered V-8 Fords and Chevrolets to electric "iceboxes" with inside lights, and nylon hose with seams up the back. There were GI loans for new houses, and GI Bill benefits to pay for education, and from the farm to the factory there were jobs waiting to be filled. The South had a multitude of chronic ills—Mr. Roosevelt himself had called the region in 1938 "the Nation's No. 1 economic problem"—but its people, white and black, looked to the postwar period as the long-awaited time of salvation and redemption, the time when second-class citizenship would finally end. At long last, the South had a future worth striving for.

It was five o'clock in the afternoon, Cadiz time, when President Harry Truman's peace message came over the floor-model Zenith radio in our living room on August 14, 1945. As a boy of ten, I had no sense of what that dramatic announcement might mean for me or my family or our town, let alone the South and the nation; I only knew that it meant victory for our side. In my delight with that, I was momentarily (albeit unknowingly) bonded in common cause with the newsboys on the streets of Atlanta, the milling throngs in Times Square and Harlem, the Japanese-Americans in internment camps as near to us as Arkansas, the weary Allied troops far across the Pacific Ocean, and the millions of other citizens of the One Nation Indivisible. Safe and secure in my little cocoon of rural tranquillity, I had only to think of adding decibels to the clamorous celebration. Grabbing a long-handled aluminum pan and a big spoon from my mother's kitchen, I ran out to join the impromptu victory parade on the sidewalk in front of our house.

From the perspective of the nineties, the Southern landscape of the thirties and forties seems dreamily distant and remote to me, and yet altogether familiar. I marvel at the countless ways in which remembrance and discovery blend into a seamless tapestry of that now-vanished time and place. Like a William Faulkner novel or the photographs of Dorothea Lange or the movie version of *The Grapes of Wrath*, yesterday's South evokes memories in which imagination and reality are fused and inseparable. By 1945, Atlanta had undergone vast changes from just one decade earlier, but the passing years since then have tended to flatten the contours and allow a broader perspective that diminishes the differences. Time and space themselves lose their limiting powers when we leave the here and now on a mental journey into the past.

It all connects. That's the first thing you need to remember, and the last. Anywhere you start, you're walking into the middle of something. There's no way you can go back to the actual beginning, because there *is* no beginning, and no end. History is not a straight line but a rolling wheel; it's a perpetual story, and all the spokes of it eventually tie together. This particular story—more precisely, this reconstruction of some scenes from the twentieth-century South—commences more or less arbitrarily with the election of Franklin D. Roosevelt and ends with the United States Supreme Court's *Brown* v. *Board of Education* decision. Between those two dates—Tuesday, November 8, 1932, and Monday, May 17, 1954—the South left Yesterday and entered Tomorrow, and the day the war ended in 1945 may have been the invisible hinge, the imperceptible moment of turning from the one to the other.

To glimpse that moment at street level in the joyful heart of Atlanta seems especially fitting, for the city was—and still is—the urban epicenter of the South, not just in a geographical sense but also historically, symbolically, philosophically. Its lofty and enduring status was assured when it rose from the ashes to more than double its former size just six years after General William Tecumseh Sherman's Union army torched two-thirds of the buildings in the landlocked community of ten thousand people on November 16, 1864. Almost from the time of its rebirth, Atlanta has beckoned to Southerners as the region's gateway, its crossroads, its meeting place. By the 1940s, all of the jarring contrasts that made up the culture and character of the South were vividly illuminated there—caste and class and color, wealth and poverty, hope and despair, tradition and change, *Gone With the Wind* romance and *Tobacco Road* reality.

Atlanta in 1945 was between Talmadges; father Gene's heyday was all but over, and son Herman's had not quite begun. Standing between them was thirty-eight-year-old Governor Ellis Arnall, a liberal Democrat who had led the Georgia legislature to abolish the poll tax and extend voting privileges to eighteen-year-olds. Arnall and his allies had even coaxed the electorate into approving a new state constitution. A newly formed non-profit organization in Atlanta, the Southern Regional Council, had begun an interracial search for solutions to the region's vexing social problems. A spirit of renewal was in the air, and Governor Arnall sought to feed it, frequently writing articles for national magazines in which he proclaimed the dawning of a glorious day of liberalism and equality and prosperity for the New South.

But events were conspiring to hold back the day. By law, Arnall could not succeed himself in office, and before the end of 1946, the Talmadge dynasty had been resurrected and plans were afoot to ensure that the all-white Democratic primary would effectively and perpetually bar most blacks from voting. South Carolina, Alabama, and other Southern states devised similar measures of defense and retaliation as yesterday's rulers girded for battle against the harbingers of tomorrow.

In July 1946, while Arnall was still governor, an organized band of more than two dozen unmasked white men ambushed and executed four blacks—two young men, one of them an army veteran, and their wives—in broad daylight in a rural county not fifty miles from the state capitol. Many Georgians recoiled in horror from the brazen atrocity, but weeks and then months slipped by with no criminal charges filed and no arrests made. An ominous wave of lynchings and other terrorist crimes against blacks rolled across the South that summer. Ralph McGill assailed the perpetrators in thunderous outrage—but refused to endorse a federal anti-lynching law, saying the Southern states had to work the problem out themselves. Even in Atlanta, the prospects for such reform seemed poor; the postwar strength of white supremacy and the pervasiveness of Jim Crow laws and customs dictated that black citizens of the city could not even serve as jurors or be employed as policemen.

Overlaid upon the exposure of the South's ingrained patterns of racial discrimination in the mid-forties was another powerful force in the American drama of that volatile time: an obsessive anticommunism. A combination of real and imagined threats from the Soviet Union and other Marxist societies had given birth to a rigid orthodoxy of political and social thought. People who criticized authority or resisted conformity raised suspicions; they were accused of being unpatriotic and disloyal "fellow travelers," or enemy agents enmeshed in the "Communist conspiracy" to overthrow the government of the United States.

Those who questioned the widely accepted "Southern way of life" and tried to reform its racial laws and customs were certainly challenging established authority. It took only a small step from that self-evident conclusion for the reactionary rulers and opinion-shapers of the postwar South to view the proponents of racial integration and the followers of communism as two inseparable sides of a single coin. According to that line of logic, anyone who advocated "race mixing" was by definition at least pink if not red, a Communist sympathizer if not a card-carrying Communist.

So much of this relatively recent history seems wildly improbable now, looking back on it, but here's what's truly amazing to me: This is not about another time and place far removed from my own experience; it's about what has happened in my lifetime, in just a little over half a century, here in the Southern states of America, where I have lived the whole of my life. In a very specific and substantial way, this is *my* history. I haven't witnessed everything, of course—no one person could be in so many places and hear so many voices and recall it all fifty years later. But in the hope that I might know and understand it better, I have gone back and scoured the written record, sought out as many once-active participants as I could find, and searched my own memory—and from the accumulated mass of words and pictures and artifacts, I have put together this verbal and visual account, this imperfect representation of what the historians call the recent or modern or contemporary South.

One of the things I have come to see in retrospect is how favorable the conditions were for substantive social change in the four or five years right after World War II. It appears to have been the last and best time— perhaps the only time—when the South might have moved boldly and decisively to heal itself, to fix its own social wagon voluntarily. But it didn't act, and the moment passed, and all that has happened in the tumultuous decades since—the federal court decisions, the minority quest for civil rights, the actions of presidents and congressional bodies, of governors and legislatures, of mayors and city councils and law-enforcement officials—has followed from that inability to seize the time and do the right thing, not simply because it was right, but because it was also in our own best interest.

In a manner of speaking, there are essentially three kinds of history: what actually happened, what we are told happened, and what we finally come to believe happened. The first is infinitely expansive and beyond retrieval; if you doubt that, try to write down everything you said and did yesterday. The second pours forth in a ceaseless torrent of verbal and visual and audible documents that constitute the public and private record, and in myriad volumes of expansion and comment upon that record. The third, derived from the first two, is filtered through the experiences and reasoning powers of each receiving reader and viewer and listener, and is the ultimate shaper of our individual and collective understanding, belief, and identity.

It is the third of these that I confront and grapple with in these pages. A brief period in the life of my homeland has attracted my interest, aroused my curiosity, and finally claimed my undivided attention. At the beginning of it, in 1932, a political initiative launched in response to a desperate economic crisis brought hope to a beleaguered populace mired in colonial dependency. At the end, in 1954, a union of two hallowed American constitutional principles—equal justice under the law and the right of citizens to petition their government for a redress of grievances—brought to robust life a movement toward freedom that now, forty years later, still energizes people and nations around the world.

I have concentrated on the time between those two momentous turning points to ponder why things happened as they did, and what it would have taken to bring about a more amicable and equitable result. Who were the prophets of Tomorrow in the South? What was their vision? How did the institutional pillars of the society—religious and academic, political and journalistic—respond to that better vision? How did the North respond? Why was the moment of opportunity after the Second World War not realized and captured and converted to the South's advantage? Why did it take a virtual revolution in the courts and in the streets, and another generation of time, to bring us to a point that was almost within our reach when America—"a mixture, an idea, a way of life, an attitude"—won the war and took the lead in the international crusade for freedom and democracy?

And so I come forward, a middle-aged, middle-class, white Southern male with moderately liberal biases in this, the last decade of the twentieth century, five hundred years downstream from Columbus and forty years after *Brown* v. *Board of Education*, to report the answers I have found to these questions and to relate a story that I believe needs to be told about a time that needs to be remembered. The story doesn't include everything that happened, of course, or even necessarily what the record and its earlier interpreters have told us happened; it is simply my partial and subjective account of what I believe happened in the South's fading days of opportunity before *Brown* came down and brought with it a social revolution.

It has taken me a long while—almost sixty years—to get here, to get my mind focused and my eyes open and my ears attuned. But now, finally, I can feel the movement of Yesterday's South in the throes of change, and I can see the faces and hear the voices—and so, step by step, the story proceeds to unfold.

I

1932–1938:
A Feudal Land

I had never really seen plantation country, save in passing, until after I came to Georgia in the spring of 1929. It was a bad time to see it. It was struggling with the boll weevil plague which had come with the twenties. And it was soon to fall into the demoralization of land and people which the depression of the thirties brought. A second cotton kingdom died then. The cabins began to empty, their doors and shutters sagging. Looking back at it now, I know that segregation began to die then too, though it was twenty-odd long years until May 17, 1954.

—RALPH McGILL,
The South and the Southerner

1. *The Cruelest Year*

When America caught cold, the South got pneumonia, and when the nation was really sick, as it was in the Great Depression, its colonial states below the Mason-Dixon Line were on their deathbed. (I call them colonial not because they harked back to the era before the American Revolution, though some of them did, but because they were still wards of the national government 150 years after the revolution had ended British dominion.) It was exceedingly rare for citizens and their leaders, North or South, to agree on much of anything, but on the night of Tuesday, November 8, 1932, they rose in overwhelming majority to anoint a fifty-year-old paraplegic who had promised them a "New Deal." God knows how desperately they needed one; the old deal had bankrupted tens of thousands of businesses, tripled the suicide rate, and driven millions of theretofore-functional citizens to a nomadic search for their very survival. Historian William Manchester called 1932 "the cruelest year," and he was right. It was the year the United States of America almost went belly-up.

At the Biltmore Hotel in midtown Manhattan, where the Democrats had their national headquarters, Franklin Delano Roosevelt was compelled to wait until past midnight for Herbert Hoover to throw in the towel. There was never any doubt about the outcome, but the counting of hand-marked ballots stretched out the inevitable conclusion, and the results trickled in by radio and telephone. Like a slow-motion avalanche, the mountain finally fell on the incumbent President. Roosevelt carried forty-two of the forty-eight states and had a popular-vote margin of seven million out of forty million cast. When his son Jimmy at last lifted him gently into bed in the wee hours of Wednesday morning and left him to his own thoughts, the President-elect must have wondered what on earth was in store for him and his besieged and beleaguered nation. Though he would soon assure us we had nothing to fear but fear itself, he acknowledged in that private moment of sober reflection his own fear that he might not have the strength to handle the enormous job he had just been given.

The eleven states of the old Confederacy favored him with sixty to ninety percent of their votes. Four years earlier, Hoover had broken the so-called Solid South by winning five of those states over the Democratic nominee, an anti-Prohibition Irish Catholic Yankee urbanite named Al

Smith, but FDR, a New York patrician himself (and a wet, too), got them back with a smile and a promise. Even if Hoover had been a great man and a great president—and he was neither—he still would have had to answer for the failed banks and the five-cent cotton and the endless lines of hungry, destitute people on relief.

So the election of Roosevelt was one of those deeply significant shifts in American history that come along only once in a generation or a century— and if it was that important for the nation, you can imagine what it meant for the South. Even some of the state and local plutocrats who would soon be cursing the very name of Roosevelt and assailing his liberal programs— people like Senator Carter Glass of Virginia, Governor Eugene Talmadge of Georgia, Senator "Cotton Ed" Smith of South Carolina—endorsed him and voted for him. You might say Huey P. Long of Louisiana rode to the Senate on Roosevelt's coattails (though in truth he didn't need them), and Theodore G. Bilbo, having just completed a scandal-ridden term as governor of Mississippi, would win election to the Senate in 1934 as an ardent New Dealer. Most nonwhite Southerners were locked out of the electoral process, and those who did get to vote went for the Republican Hoover purely from force of habit, but a dramatic turning away from the party of Lincoln was about to begin among black voters North and South.

When you consider what desperate shape the South was in at that time, it's easy to understand why so many people in the region looked to Roosevelt for their deliverance. Some even thought of him as one of them, a part-time Southerner by virtue of his country estate at Warm Springs, Georgia, where he had been going periodically for a decade to rest and soothe his polio-stricken legs. Roosevelt didn't shy away from that Southern identity; in fact, he delighted in being called "a Georgia farmer-politician."

Not many people knew that he also had an indirect interest in some Kentucky real estate. His mother's people, the Delanos, were involved in a turn-of-the-century acquisition of mineral rights in a vast coalfield in Harlan County, and in 1908, Franklin went there with his uncle, Warren Delano, to take a look at the holdings. They traveled to southwest Virginia by railroad and continued on horseback into a pristine Kentucky valley of sparkling streams and virgin forests that looked to the young man like a Garden of Eden. In letters to his wife, Eleanor, he described these "magnificent views" in great detail. It was twenty-three years later, just a year and a half before the 1932 election, that war broke out in Harlan County between hired gunmen of the coal companies and miners seeking union representation.

Franklin Roosevelt made a connection in his mind between the idyllic wilderness he had seen in 1908 and the coalfield killing ground at the

Battle of Evarts in 1931; he also recognized that it was people like the Delanos—estate-building, laissez-faire capitalists—who were largely responsible for the plight of what he called "the forgotten man at the bottom of the economic pyramid." The nation, and especially the South—from the coalfields to the cotton mills, from the tenant farms to the grim, gray interior cities (small though they were)—was overwhelmingly populated with such forgotten men and women and children, and everywhere they seemed to be headed toward either violent revolution or total collapse.

While Roosevelt was waiting for President Hoover to concede defeat, Southerners of every rank and station waited too. In a sense, the entire region was in a state of suspension, for no one else in the country had more riding on that election than the people of the South. Their perceptions of the economic crisis and its far-reaching consequences no doubt differed greatly from one to the next, but few among them could have failed to realize that something momentous was happening.

The rising generation of young adults would retain especially durable memories of that changing of the guard. Time and circumstance summoned them as messengers, as heralds; they were the leading wave of what was to become a twentieth-century social revolution more sweeping than anything since the Civil War. Some of them would eventually fall back into the ranks of the silent majority, but others would be thrust into prophetic roles that they could not have imagined at the time Franklin Roosevelt came to power. Either way, none of them would ever forget Election Day, 1932.

Near the University of Mississippi campus in Oxford on that rainy November day, shy, reclusive William Faulkner, at thirty-five an Ole Miss dropout and former postmaster of the university (fired for his careless handling of the mails), showed little interest in politics, but a passion— and a genius—for fiction rooted in his own time and place. *Light in August,* the latest of his half-dozen novels, was just out, and the literary critics were generous in their praise of it. If they failed to plumb the depths of his vision, they could certainly be excused, for so did his family, his friends, his neighbors—and, in all probability, Bill Faulkner himself.

In Richmond, thirty-one-year-old Virginius Dabney worked late but enthusiastically on his *Times-Dispatch* editorial trumpeting the Roosevelt victory. In Shelby, North Carolina, thirty-two-year-old W. J. Cash was just beginning a ten-year exploration of the enigmatic Southern psyche. In Birmingham, Virginia Foster Durr, twenty-nine, and other members of her family were celebrating not only the triumph of FDR but the reelection of her brother-in-law, Hugo L. Black, to the U.S. Senate. In Nashville, the literary clique of traditionalists at Vanderbilt University who called themselves Agrarians was momentarily heartened by Roosevelt's interest in subsistence farms. At nearby Fisk University, sociologist Charles S. Johnson, thirty-nine, was cautiously optimistic that the new administration would enlist social scientists as allies in a broad attack on the nation's domestic problems. Another young Nashvillian, twenty-eight-year-old Howard A. Kester, was a Socialist Party candidate for Congress that day. (He ended up with only 677 votes—but even so, he ran ahead of his party's presidential candidate, Norman Thomas, in the district.)

Thurgood Marshall of Baltimore was a twenty-four-year-old senior at the Howard University law school in Washington that fall; one of the first jolts in his political awakening was his startled discovery that the District of Columbia code barred all of its citizens from voting. In New York, a younger (twenty-two) but more politically conscious black student named Pauli Murray, Maryland-born and North Carolina–raised, cast her first presidential vote for the Socialist Thomas.

Erskine Caldwell, a native Georgian, had just been catapulted to fame and notoriety as the author of a grotesquely comic novel, *Tobacco Road*. James Agee of Knoxville was writing for the magazines of Henry Luce in New York, and John N. Popham, a young Virginian, was a fledgling reporter for the *New York Times*. Walking past the Paramount Theater at Broadway and Forty-third Street on his way to work, Popham sometimes exchanged greetings with a tall, gangly doorman who spoke with a thick Southern drawl. They would meet again in 1947 when the reporter interviewed six-foot-seven James Elisha Folsom, the newly elected governor of Alabama.

The Roosevelt victory would also make a lasting impression on the very young. Far to the south of Manhattan, on a dusty country road in Amite County, Mississippi, light-years distant from the glitter of Broadway, eight-year-old Will Davis Campbell climbed onto the school truck the morning after the election and heard his uncle, Luther Campbell, the driver, exclaim, "Roosevelt won! The depression's over!" The youngster was puzzled. What was the depression, he wondered, and what did Uncle Luther mean by saying it was over?

2. *The State of the South*

Uncle Luther was wrong, of course; it wasn't over, not by a long shot. The South at that moment resembled nothing so much as a bleak and ravaged wasteland, a depleted colonial territory mired in isolation, help-lessness, ignorance, and utter despair. Only in the eyes of little children did it look "normal"—and only to them because they had nothing but more desolation to compare it to.

This is a hard point to get across. The entire country was in desperate straits, not just the South, and the pervasiveness of deprivation made it seem more ordinary and natural than it was. (People who remember those times can acknowledge now how little they had, but often say, "I never thought of us as being poor.") Disparities of race and social class were so much a part of the culture that it was rare to hear them challenged. And, when you consider the region's ameliorating qualities—the strengths of character and personality, the sheltering arms of church and family, the warmth of many personal relationships, the fertility of the fields, the yield of woods and waters, the healing warmth of winter, and all the rest—it's not surprising that some Southerners remember the thirties and forties with nostalgic fondness. But hardship there was, and plenty of it, from top to bottom—and the closer you were to the bottom of the economic and social ladder, the worse it got.

There is no way to convey now an explicit sense of the look, smell, sound, and feel of the South in that somber autumn of 1932, but in its practical effect, if not literally and historically, this was a feudal land, an American-ized version of a European society in the Middle Ages. It was rural, agri-cultural, isolated. It had its ruling nobles, its lords of the plantation manor—and its peasants, its vassals. Its values were rooted in the land, in stability and permanence, in hierarchy and status, in caste and class and race. The highest virtues were honor and duty, loyalty and obedience. Ev-ery member of the society—man and woman, white and black—knew his or her place, and it was an unusual (not to say foolhardy) person who showed a flagrant disregard for the assigned boundaries and conventions.

There were almost thirty million people living in the eleven states of the old Confederacy, a vast area generally separated from the rest of the country by an imaginary line stretching eighteen hundred miles from the eastern shore of Virginia to the tip of west Texas at El Paso. (There is a much larger South, in the eyes of many people, variously defined as embracing, in addition, part or all of Oklahoma, Missouri, Kentucky, West Virginia, Maryland, Delaware, and the District of Columbia—and, as we will see subsequently, some ways of defining the region take in even more territory—but for the moment, the boundary of the Confederate states serves our purposes.) Almost all of the nine million blacks and a substantial majority of the twenty-one million whites in this sweeping expanse were so lacking in resources and creature comforts—by our modern-day standards, at least—that it seems elementally fair and honest to call them dirt-poor. Many of them didn't like that phrase, and still don't, but it fits.

And yet, it wouldn't be right to leave the impression that everyone was in the same boat. There was definitely a pecking order, a vertical framework—the "economic pyramid," as FDR called it—with all the nonwhites on the bottom and the poorest of the poor whites just above them. If you were white and had some status in politics or agriculture or business or education or the church, you were better off than the struggling majority of resident Southerners. To be more specific, if you held elective office you were in a position to get more than your share of privileges, or if you were a big planter you had a distinct advantage over the yeoman farmers of the land; a mill owner's life was conspicuously easier than the lives of his workers, and a college graduate had a lot more going for him than an adult whose formal schooling had ended after the fourth grade; an Episcopalian generally was better fixed than a "holy roller" or even a regular Baptist. To be sure, there was such a thing as better and worse—but the bigger truth was that the whole country was in pain, and the South, by almost any measure you could apply, was suffering much more than the rest of the United States (which, for the sake of brevity, if not literal accuracy, I'll label as the North).

More than three-fourths of all Southerners had a standard of living in the fall of 1932 that would certainly qualify them as paupers, as we would define that term today. Two-thirds of them lived on farms or in small villages, and close to two-thirds of the farmers were sharecroppers or tenants. The average gross income of farm families didn't reach $1,000 a year in nine Southern states, casting them to the bottom of the agriculture heap—but lest you think those were the poorest of the poor, keep in mind that they at least were employed and had a bare minimum of food and clothing and shelter to sustain them; millions of others were vagabonds with no resources at all.

City life may have offered some advantages to poor Southerners, but in truth, the cities were little more than oversized country towns where the problems of employment, health, education, and safety were often just as acute as in the rural areas. The largest city in the South in 1930 was New Orleans, with 459,000 people; half a dozen others had between 200,000 and 300,000, and a mere ten more topped the 100,000 mark.

Malnutrition was rampant—and often worse, ironically, in the urban areas, simply because it was not possible to live off the land there. But the farms were not much better, for what they grew—mainly cotton and tobacco—you couldn't eat. The same was true in the mountainous coalfields, where almost everyone was severely undernourished.

To be a sharecropper or a tenant farmer in the South in 1932 was to be caught up in an existence that often was nothing more than peonage or forced labor—just one step removed from slavery. You rented the land from its owner, and made the crop for him with his furnish of seed and fertilizer and mules and tools; he sold you food and other necessities on credit at high interest in his commissary; he kept the books, handled the sales, and divided with you at harvest time. You were lucky if you broke even; some went in the hole, and not one in ten actually came away with a few dollars in profit. So when I say the average farm income was between, say, $500 and $1,000 a year, that means the landlords got a little something and the sharecroppers got next to nothing.

Rural housing for all but the fortunate few was primitive—no running water or electricity, no appliances, no telephone, no insulation, no window screens (maybe not even windows), no paint, no privacy. Clothing was anything but adequate; shoes were a luxury, coats and hats an absolute extravagance. Food was a monotonous repetition of what little there was available: salt pork, lard, sorghum molasses, corn pone, biscuits, grits, white gravy, and a narrow selection of boiled vegetables—field peas, cabbage, sweet potatoes, greens. Supplies were so limited that a family was considered fortunate if it had enough for two meager meals a day.

In such severely limited circumstances, poor health was inevitable, and doctors to combat it were few and far between. Mothers and babies were twice as likely to die during childbirth in Alabama or Louisiana as in Connecticut or Nebraska or Washington State. Those who survived childhood were still very much at risk; people got sick, stayed sick, and died with grimly predictable frequency. They suffered from diseases of the environment, diseases brought on by poor diet, exposure, overwork, stress. Even their few channels to simple pleasure—tobacco, whiskey, sex—were often deadly, giving them lung cancer, alcoholism, venereal disease. The more abstemious among them were not spared, either; like everyone else, they were vulnerable to pellagra, hookworm, malaria, tuberculosis, and a dozen other crippling or killing diseases. An image of this Southern peasant emerged and persisted, and finally became a grotesque caricature more to be scorned than pitied: a ragged, dirty figure, slow-footed, dim-witted, lazy, illiterate, toothless, crippled in mind and body. The distorted image provided both Northerners and the better-off white Southerners with a handy scapegoat for the South's ills: lazy niggers, dumb hillbillies, black scum, white trash.

Almost nobody had money. The South could count a quarter of the nation's population but only a tenth of its wealth. No more than five hundred people in the entire region had incomes of $100,000 or more in 1929, and three years later that list was reduced to a tiny handful; probably no more than a hundred or so people per state earned even $10,000 in 1932. The ones with the lowest earned income of all were those who actually did the hardest work. Cotton pickers were paid twenty cents for a hundred pounds—so little that even the strongest and swiftest of them had less than a dollar to show for a backbreaking day's work. Coal miners got thirty cents a ton and could make as much as two dollars a day for a twelve-hour shift with a pick and shovel, but it was part-time work. In the textile mills, women and children worked seventy-two hours a week for fifteen to twenty-five cents an hour. And, no matter how much or how little the faceless thousands of workers ended up with, the company store quickly relieved them of it.

The desperation of unorganized miners and textile workers and the imperious manner of the mine and mill owners, most of whom had their headquarters in the North, sparked some violent clashes in the late twenties and early thirties. The coal-mine wars attracted national attention; so did the textile strikes, particularly a major one in Gastonia, North Carolina, in 1929. These were ideological as well as economic struggles, pitting not just liberals and progressives but more radical leftists—Socialists, Communists—against the robber barons of capitalism. Blood was spilled, people died—and, since most of the mine and mill workers and all of their bosses were white, the conflicts gained added visibility in the white press. Workers were no less exploited in the cotton fields, but most of them were black—as were about half of the sharecroppers and tenant farmers—and their landlords lived close by and kept tight control of them, so there was not as much open conflict on the farms, and when there was, outsiders didn't pay much attention.

Cotton was more than just the primary source of employment in the South—it was a symbol of all that the region represented, the best and the worst. Cotton was king, or had been; it built the fortunes, the sprawling plantations, the white-pillared mansions, the romantic myths. Before the depression, cotton was planted over a staggering forty-five million acres of the South, and in the bumper-crop years, almost everyone got at least a taste of the trickle-down milk and honey. But there was another side, a darker reality. Cotton used up people and land, consumed and then discarded them. The big planters were like gamblers, betting their soil and their seed and their field hands against the weather, the weevils, the market, the foreign competition. Historically, through the slavery era and beyond, the planters had won more often than not, and won big—but times were changing, and the signs were everywhere that they were headed for a fall.

In 1919, a golden year of postwar prosperity, cotton soared to thirty-five cents a pound on a big crop of about fifteen million bales; the following year, plummeting demand and a huge stockpiled surplus sent prices crashing to fourteen cents and triggered a major agricultural depression nine years before the Big One. The bottom dropped out of the tobacco market, too, and the price of prime cultivated land fell to ten dollars an acre or less.

All through the twenties, cotton careened up and down the scale, driven by one uncontrollable force after another. The mind-set of the planters was to keep gambling. Oblivious to the warning signs—the loss of foreign markets, the rise of synthetics, the massive surplus, the insect scourge, the vagaries of flood and drought and tornadoes, the depletion of the soil, the pain and anguish of a captive labor force—they blindly rolled the dice again and again, risking everything for one more strike, one more bumper crop.

A reckless, greedy, all-or-nothing approach to economic activity seemed to characterize the American mood in the Roaring Twenties, and the South was especially susceptible to it—not just the cotton barons, but others as well. The last of the region's magnificent stands of virgin timber were almost exhausted by 1930; historian Thomas D. Clark, a native Mississippian, writing of this mindless tragedy years later, said the timber companies "did more economic harm to the South than Grant, Sherman, and the carpetbaggers put together." The railroads, having finally reached the coalfields, were hauling black gold away as fast as they could mine it, and the same take-the-money-and-run attitude prevailed around the oil and gas wells in Texas and Oklahoma, where big strikes had the ironic effect of flooding the market and imposing a giveaway price of two or three cents a barrel. The Florida land boom of the 1920s was a greed-driven mirage that evaporated almost as quickly as it had blossomed. Manufacturing was still in its infancy in much of the South, but the makers of textiles and steel and other products were already operating with an arrogant disregard for their workers, the environment, and the jurisdictions in which they were located.

The big owners of industries, utilities, natural resources, and agricultural lands felt they had a perfect right to maximize their profits by whatever means necessary—to extract, exploit, use up, and throw away at will. There were no government regulators to stop them, no investigative reporters, no powerful labor unions, and even a suggestion of such intrusions was denounced as nothing less than Bolshevism. Most but not all of the men who controlled the Southern economy were absentee owners with no real interest in the region except its quick-profit potential. Among the homegrown exceptions were the planters—of course, and a few of the textile manufacturers and railroad owners, but they were, in the main, even more hostile to prying outsiders, would-be regulators, and union organizers than were their Northern counterparts.

And so, with utter disdain for the consequences, the captains of commerce applied their exploitative philosophy to the South. As they saw it, the natural resources were there to be used, not preserved and protected;

the South wasn't a homeland or an integral part of the nation so much as it was a colony, a resource to be exhausted. It needed little in the way of schools and other institutions to strengthen it, because it had no long-term future—and besides, the children of the wealthy could be sent away to school much more cheaply, and be better served in the process. The native people were seen as either racially or culturally inferior, or both, and their only value was as a plentiful labor source. With the same language slave traders had once used to describe chattel ("docile, obedient, abundant, cheap"), the boosters of industry and agriculture characterized the Southern workforce in the 1930s.

It was this way of thinking that produced the South of the Great Depression, the South that Franklin D. Roosevelt and the Southern-dominated, majority-Democratic Congress took over from the Republicans after the 1932 election: a ravaged land, its timber stripped, its hills eroded, its worn-out fields barren and dusty, its rivers filling with topsoil and trash and raw sewage, its air thick with a pall of soot and coal smoke, and tens of thousands of its people in flight, driven north in a desperate search for a better life.

Between 1900 and 1930, nearly three and a half million more people moved out of the South than into it. Slightly more of them were white than black. Two kinds of people led the exodus—those from the bottom and those from the top. Farmworkers, day laborers, the unskilled and unemployed and uneducated masses, white and black, left in droves. Countless thousands of competitive, creative, gifted young people of both races also fled in search of greater opportunities. (Look through any dictionary of twentieth-century American biographies and you will be startled to see how many journalists, authors, broadcasters, artists, musicians, entertainers, athletes, and other professionals were born in the South but made their mark elsewhere.)

These were signs that something was drastically wrong in the land of cotton, but not much notice was taken. Sixty-five years after the Civil War ended, the South was still traumatized by its catastrophic defeat. It looked to the North with envy, resentment, hatred, defiance, and an apparently incurable inferiority complex. Far from exhibiting a desire to be free from the burden of history, the South seemed instead to cling obsessively to its past, to relive it and even rewrite it. The glorious Lost Cause had instilled a sense of pride and honor and moral superiority in many whites, but the hard truth was that the South in the 1930s was itself a lost cause, a downtrodden region haplessly nursing wounds that were as much self-inflicted as administered from without.

Consider its isolation. A case could be made that the restoration of trains and ships for freight and passenger service in the South never caught up to the North after the Civil War simply because the capital was not available to finance it. And, since Northern industrialists produced all the cars, trucks, buses, and tractors—and the Southern states couldn't afford to build roads—the disparity continued into the automotive age. There were five million mules in the South in 1932, but only fifty thousand tractors— one for every fifty farms. Northerners had twice as many automobiles per capita as Southerners, and a far more modern and extensive network of roads. Trains and buses were the modes of public transportation in this pre-airline era, and they too provided better service in the North than in the South. The isolation of the South, so the argument goes, was a direct consequence of its economic disadvantage.

But there is another kind of isolation, more mental than physical, and in this realm the South seemed intent on raising the walls around itself. Radio was knitting the nation more closely together (television, of course, had not been introduced), but the rural South was hardly tuned in at all, because electricity had only reached one in every twenty-five farms. There were some pretty good newspapers in the region, and even some small-circulation magazines and journals, but only a tiny percentage of families was able to nurture regular reading habits. The South had by far the highest illiteracy rate in the nation (five times as high in South Carolina as in Pennsylvania or Illinois or California), and it was dead last in the number of libraries and in the frequency of their use.

Schools also lagged far behind. Only about four million Southern children—half the ones under age eighteen—were enrolled at all; the rest spent their days working on the farms and in the factories (that is, if they were lucky enough to be occupied at all). The school days per year were fewer by a month or more in the South than in the North, and the annual state and local expenditures were so low (thirty-five to seventy-five dollars per pupil, less than half the national average) that the fourteen lowest slots in the national rankings were all occupied by Southern and border states. Since federal funds for schools were negligible to nonexistent, this was the extent of public education. No wonder only sixty thousand young people graduated from high school in the South in 1930.

In the private sector, Northern philanthropy provided most of the educational opportunity available to whites in the isolated mountains of Appalachia and to blacks throughout the South until the 1930s. The Rockefellers and Peabodys, Julius Rosenwald, John F. Slater, Anna T. Jeanes, and the Congregational Church appear to have done almost as much for the education of the Southern poor in the seventy-five years following the Civil War as all of the South's state and local governments combined.

Higher education in the pre-depression years was a luxury that only a relative handful of Southerners could experience. More contributions from wealthy Northerners and federal appropriations under the Morrill Land-Grant Act had created close to seventy-five public and private colleges for Negroes between the end of the Civil War and the beginning of the Great Depression, but they could offer their limited curricula to only a few hundred students each—and many were, in reality, little more than high schools and vocational schools. There were about 250 public and private colleges and universities for whites in the region by 1930—and they too were, by and large, an undistinguished lot. Only the state universities of Texas, North Carolina, and Virginia had graduate programs or libraries of any magnitude, and among private institutions, only Emory, Duke, Vanderbilt, Tulane, Rice, and perhaps one or two others were remotely comparable. In the entire South in 1930, only 186,000 students, white and black, were enrolled in college. Among the 30,000 or so who graduated—quite literally, one in a thousand of the South's people—were a substantial number who quickly sought greener pastures beyond the magnolia curtain.

The elite nature of higher education and the classical construction of its curriculum further widened the gap between the privileged few and the needy many, but another form of mental isolation was almost as destructive. Within the colleges and universities themselves, a rigid orthodoxy of thought and opinion governed virtually every discipline and field of study. Scholars who dared to broaden the prevailing historical, scientific, political, religious, or racial perspectives of their communities were forced out of one institution after another across the South in the first three decades of this century. Both the politicians who indirectly controlled public colleges and the religious and civic stewards of private institutions tended to see themselves more as guardians of established truth and righteousness than as leaders in a search for enlightenment. With rare exceptions, academic freedom was perpetually endangered, if it existed at all.

Colleges and universities, hardly less than the other principal institutions of Southern society, reinforced and extended a circumscribed culture defined by the prevailing interpretations of history, religion, the arts and sciences, socioeconomic class, race, politics. The manifestations of this narrow view reached far beyond the academy. They could be seen in the bigotry and intolerance of all religious people toward the nonreligious (of whom there were precious few admitted ones); of Christians toward Jews (there being only about 150,000 of the latter); of Protestants toward the million or so Catholics; and even of Baptists and Methodists (about fifteen million total) toward Presbyterians and Episcopalians—who were, of course, reciprocally disdainful. They could be seen in the frequency of official acts of censorship against books, movies, plays, and other forms of artistic expression. They could be seen in common reactions of suspicion, fear, and hostility toward critics, outsiders, or anyone else whose speech, appearance, or behavior was perceived to be "different." Since almost everyone in the South was of either Anglo-Saxon or African descent, others were easy to spot.

Massive contradictions were bred by this self-imposed posture of intellectual isolation. The South embraced Prohibition with righteous fervor long before Congress approved the Eighteenth Amendment in 1917 and long after it was repealed in 1933—but from start to finish, Southerners drank as much liquor as anyone else, and made more illicit moonshine than everyone else. Two-thirds of the fourteen thousand whiskey stills and the half-million gallons of busthead booze seized and destroyed by federal revenue agents in 1931 were uncovered in the South—and yet, more bootleg whiskey reached the market from this region than from any other sectional cluster of states. (Incidentally, the South also supplied most of the nation's cigarettes and soda pop.)

Gambling and other vices, and lawlessness in general, thrived in a shadowy Southern landscape hidden from public scrutiny. Even as the South was sending the highest percentage of people to church and displaying in other ways an abundance of piety, it was spilling its own blood as if the region were at war. Only a couple of states in the so-called Wild West came close to matching the South's proclivity for violent crimes. Kentucky and Tennessee had ten times more armed robberies and aggravated assaults per 100,000 people than Wisconsin, and North Carolina had a rate of murders and killings eight times greater than New York's. (A murder, someone Southern once explained, is a capital offense committed by one stranger against another; a killing is a homicide resulting from conflict between parties known to, perhaps even kin to, each other.)

Lynching, a damning measure of any society's tolerance for violent behavior, had always been a problem in the United States, and especially in the South. Tuskegee Institute in Alabama tried for many years to keep records of this crime, in the hope that exposure would compel society to abolish it. According to the institute's figures, there were 2,771 lynchings (defined as mob violence against a person in custody, or one being pursued for an alleged crime) in the United States between 1890 and 1930, and the victims in the vast preponderance of these illegal executions were black men in the South. Not included in the Tuskegee count were large numbers of fugitives hunted down and killed by deputized posses (not officially mobs) and many others reported as "escaped from custody." Lynch victims almost always died slow, agonizing, tortured deaths by hanging, burning, beating, dragging, butchering, or some other sadistic means.

More than five hundred blacks were lynched in Mississippi during that forty-year period; more than four hundred died in Georgia, and more than three hundred each in Louisiana and Texas. About two hundred whites were lynched in those four states combined during the same years. Congress almost enacted a federal anti-lynching statute in 1922, but a filibuster of Southern senators killed the bill after it had passed by a wide margin in the House—and Southern lawmakers managed from then on to block all such attempts to punish lynchers. Left to their own crime-solving devices, the Southern states were totally ineffective in prosecuting lynchers; not even one atrocity in a hundred ended with a participant's being tried and convicted.

As the decade of the 1930s began, the number of reported lynchings had diminished to a range of ten to twenty a year, but a related problem— violence *within* the criminal justice system—was receiving more national attention, and it was notoriously excessive in the South. Conditions and practices inside state prisons were widely understood to be—even accepted as—medieval and Draconian in nature; any form of punishment, including torture, could be administered without strong objection from the outside. Convict leasing had finally been outlawed, but local and state officials still found surreptitious ways for farmers, factory owners, and others to keep prison inmates in a state of virtual slavery while they "worked off" payment for their crimes. Chain gangs were common in every Southern state. And, since virtually all police officers, judges, lawyers, jurors, and jailers were white males, the potential for routine injustice to all blacks—and to white women as well—was constantly present. All that saved white women—and occasionally black women—from the worst possible fate was the white male's Freudian fear of, and latent guilt concerning, women in general. Nothing saved the black male; he bore the brunt of pain and suffering in every Southern state's approach to crime and punishment.

A revealing indicator of the extent to which Southern blacks were at the mercy of the law-enforcement system was contained in a pamphlet called "Burnt Cork and Crime." It was written by Robert B. Eleazer, a white researcher at the Commission on Interracial Cooperation, an Atlanta-based agency founded after World War I. In it, Eleazer documented dozens of cases in which whites had disguised themselves as blacks and committed crimes that innocent blacks were subsequently arrested for— and often convicted.

Criminal justice was by no means the only segment of society in which blacks were vulnerable in the depression-era South, of course. Any thorough review of conditions in the region during that period is bound to turn up one example after another of social and economic problems that were essentially racial in nature. State and local laws mandating segregation of the races didn't become widespread until the 1890s, but in less than forty years they had raised barriers between whites and blacks in the region that were practically impenetrable. In essence, the ruling whites had managed to nullify virtually all of the basic civil and political rights of black citizens—and both houses of Congress, a succession of Democratic and Republican presidents, and the United States Supreme Court (in the historic *Plessy* v. *Ferguson* case of 1896) had actively aided in the dismemberment.

It doesn't seem in any sense an overstatement to say that racial mores finally became the single most prominent characteristic that set the South apart from the rest of the country. In 1910, when the segregation laws were almost fully in effect, more than eighty percent of all black Americans lived in the eleven Old South states. Oppressive social and economic conditions eventually drove millions of them out of the region; a half-century later, in 1960, almost as many blacks would live outside the South as in it. And, since the segregation laws have been repealed, visible evidence of regional differences in racial prejudice has just about disappeared.

In the thirties, though, such evidence was everywhere. All of the border states, from Delaware and Maryland to Missouri and Oklahoma, mandated some forms of segregation by law, and even a few states not contiguous to the South (Kansas, for example) permitted segregation in the public schools. If you go back far enough in American history, you'll find racial discrimination in the laws and practices of every state. As recently as the late 1940s, fourteen states far away from the South, including Michigan, Colorado, Oregon, and California, had laws prohibiting racial intermarriage. But primarily, it was the eleven states of the old Confederacy that built compulsory segregation and blatant white supremacy into their laws and customs across the board, and that's what made them seem so different from the rest of the country in the 1930s.

Segregation was defended by whites as part and parcel of the age-old "Southern way of life," but in truth the practice was a post-slavery, post–Civil War, post-Reconstruction scheme to isolate the black citizenry from the democratic process and to reestablish and perpetuate white supremacy. For more than a decade after the Civil War ended, states and local communities attempted with varying degrees of success to reorder their societies in such a way that citizens of whatever race or class could enjoy basic civil rights and participate in the political process. This was in part coerced by decree of the governments installed under the Reconstruction laws, but there were some white Southerners who approved of the philosophy of inclusion, or at least accepted it as a matter of enlightened self-interest. It was not unheard of in that period for blacks to vote, run for office, be elected, and serve; to testify and serve on juries; to enjoy restaurants, saloons, parks, and other public gathering places; to sit where they pleased in theaters and trains; and to live wherever they could afford to buy housing.

But then, after Reconstruction ended, the old guard of powerful white planters and others—the so-called Bourbons—began to regain control and reassert their authority over blacks and low-income whites. When friction developed between the races—competition for jobs, for political office, and such—the ruling whites found it expedient to keep the working-class whites in line by giving them certain privileges and immunities that were denied to blacks. At first through informal manipulation and then, gradually, through ordinances and laws, blacks were removed from the mainstream of Southern life and relegated to "their place" on the periphery.

And so, over the next couple of decades (from the mid-1880s until about 1906), Jim Crow was born—or, to be more precise (and ironic), I should say *adopted*, for in fact the practice of racial separation that came to bear the Jim Crow tag was modeled after procedures widely used in Northern cities before the Civil War. (In *The Strange Career of Jim Crow*, historian C. Vann Woodward documented the systematic exclusion of blacks from public and political life in Boston, New York, Philadelphia, and other cities in the decades before the Civil War.) The Populist Party's short-lived reform movement of the 1890s was to be the last manifestation of an enlightened democratic spirit in the South; after that failed and the Republicans abandoned the region to the Bourbons, the "Solid South" of white supremacy was reestablished.

Jim Crow was one more Yankee invention of dubious benefit to the South, but the whites in charge seized upon it with uncritical haste. First they segregated the railroads, ordering blacks into the front coaches nearest the sooty engine and coal car. (When buses came along, blacks were sent to the back; no system was ever devised to segregate seating on airplanes.) Segregation spread rapidly through the entire fabric of the society. The franchise was taken away, and elective office went with it; the last black politician on the national scene, Congressman George H. White of North Carolina, left the House of Representatives in 1901, and no other blacks from the South would serve again in Congress until 1972, when Andrew Young of Georgia and Barbara Jordan of Texas were elected. (In the North, Illinois and New York were the only states to elect an African-American congressman in the first half of this century.) Poll taxes, white primaries, literacy tests, and other rules designed to remove blacks from voting had precisely that effect. The only exceptions were in more moderate border cities such as Louisville, or in places like Memphis and San Antonio, where machine bosses controlled the black vote and used it to stay in power.

In courtrooms, where black lawyers were exceedingly rare and black judges nonexistent, new restrictions were placed on the status of blacks as plaintiffs, witnesses, and jurors. Hospitals, where black doctors and nurses could not practice, denied admission to black patients. (Even blood was segregated.) Churches, which had split along racial lines before the Civil War, reaffirmed their separateness, as did schools and colleges. All types of public accommodations, from parks and theaters to restaurants and libraries, adopted segregation policies, and the same applied to toilets and water fountains. There were white and black newspapers. There were jobs and unions and even entire industries that catered to one race or the other, but not both. Cemeteries were either black or white. Interracial dating and marriage, of course, were strictly forbidden. In public discourse and in public print, blacks were commonly denied the courtesy of personal or professional titles (*Dr., Mr., Mrs., Miss*). In polite company, they were called colored people or Negroes (*black* was then considered a derogatory term, and so was *African; African-American* was not in the white lexicon). The most common and hated word was *nigger;* only slightly less cutting was *negro,* uncapitalized (and pronounced *nig-ra*), for it was a visible and explicit denial of any status as a person. (Among the whites who persisted in the use of the lowercase *n* were the Vanderbilt Agrarians in their 1930 manifesto, *I'll Take My Stand,* and James Agee a decade later in *Let Us Now Praise Famous Men.*)

During the first three decades of this century, segregation so permeated the laws and customs and daily activities of the South that it did, in fact, seem as though it had been in place forever. Northerners appeared not to be bothered by the South's peculiar new institution—if, indeed, they took note of it at all—but as the pace of black migration into their cities quickened, they turned more and more to informal practices of separation similar to those the South was imposing overtly through the force of law.

The racial arrangement that the white South had chosen was riddled with paradox and contradiction. People who advocated out-migration of blacks as the ultimate solution had no satisfactory answer to the question they always heard in response: Who'll do all the hard work? It was mostly blacks who picked the cotton and worked the tobacco, who cooked and cleaned, who nursed the babies and cared for the sick and elderly. Without them, the "Southern way of life" would have been impossible.

And there was another profoundly sobering irony, one that few people seemed to think about, or at least to talk about. It was this: The ultimate cost of a segregated Southern society was perpetual disadvantage and second-class colonial status vis-à-vis the North. Simply put, the South was too poor to support dual and overlapping institutions and services—schools, hospitals, universities, park systems—and it couldn't catch up without using all of the human resources it possessed. The South in its relationship to the North was uncomfortably similar in many ways to blacks in their relationship to whites: cast down, taken for granted, ridiculed, exploited, robbed of assets and of self-esteem. It would take bold, courageous, sacrificial initiatives to break the old pattern and build a new and more equitable society. Until that happened, the South was doomed to languish in the swampy backwaters of American life.

Almost no one was thinking such thoughts in 1932, least of all the politicians who were largely responsible for the South's ironclad system of segregation and for its low standing in the nation. Of all the factors, internal and external, that contributed to the shaping of the Southern character at that point in its history, none could have been more central than its political leadership—or lack thereof.

It goes without saying that they were all white, all Democrats, and almost all males (the one notable exception being Miriam "Ma" Ferguson, governor of Texas—a stand-in for her husband, zany Jim Ferguson, who sold the electorate on a package deal: "two governors for the price of one"). These were the days when politics provided the best live entertainment around, and elections were the South's number-one spectator sport. Theodore G. Bilbo had just finished a disgraceful term as governor of Mississippi and would soon be elected to the U.S. Senate, and Georgia voters chose Eugene Talmadge, a bombastic planter-lawyer, to be their governor. The Senate was already pretty much dominated by some shrewd operators, including Carter Glass of Virginia, "Cotton Ed" Smith of South Carolina, Kenneth McKellar of Tennessee, Pat Harrison of Mississippi, Walter George of Georgia, Joseph Robinson of Arkansas, Josiah Bailey of North Carolina, and virtually the only progressive in the lot, Hugo Black of Alabama. Joining them after the 1932 election would be Harry F. Byrd of Virginia, Huey Long of Louisiana, Richard Russell of Georgia, Robert R. Reynolds of North Carolina, James F. Byrnes of South Carolina, and John H. Bankhead, Jr., of Alabama. Speaker of the House John Nance Garner of Texas would be tapped as FDR's vice president.

These were, by and large, the men who controlled Southern politics by controlling their electorates, their legislatures, the governors' offices—and even, to a substantial degree, the two houses of Congress. Collectively they had more than enough seniority, tenure, and key committee chairmanships to command the attention of whoever happened to be occupying the White House. Participatory democracy was of no interest to most of them; they were more concerned with limiting the vote to manageable size. In Virginia, only about ten percent of all the people age twenty-one and older could be expected at the polls, even for a crucial election like the one in 1932; in the region as a whole, fewer than three in ten adults voted.

With all the restrictions that either kept blacks, women, and the poor away from the polls or used them as pawns in a game of power, and with the almost total absence of an opposition party, the Democrats who controlled the South were an oligarchy, a loose confederation of feudal lords answerable to no one. In personality, style, appearance, and philosophy they differed greatly one from another, but as a group they were recognizably related, and even the rare exceptions like Hugo Black were few enough in number to be tolerated by the others as eccentrics. Like the Bourbons who preceded them and the men of like mind who would follow in their wake, the South's political rulers of the early 1930s built and maintained their empires by drawing from the same sources of energy: cotton, conservative Protestantism, laissez-faire capitalism, and white supremacy.

Suspicious of outsiders, distrustful of Yankees, reflexively resistant to change (except the kind that jingled in their pockets), the lords and their lackeys, whether in Washington or in statehouses and courthouses from Richmond to Austin, looked upon the coming of Franklin Delano Roosevelt as a mixed blessing. At least he was a Democrat, they said—but he was a Yankee, and a left-winger (compared to them), and he kept dropping hints about the need for big changes. That made them nervous. Still and all, conditions were bad, really bad, and something had to be done—some federal aid to the farmers and the schools, some relief, maybe a little business stimulus. The last thing in the world they wanted to tamper with was segregation and white supremacy. As best they could tell, race was the furthest thing from FDR's mind, too. They would just have to watch and wait, just bide their time and see how radical this smooth-talking New Yorker really was.

3. *Bourbon Legacy*

How did this condition of extreme desperation come about? What was it that sent the South, once a spawning ground of national wealth and power and leadership, provider of nine of the first twelve presidents of the

United States, plummeting into a bottomless quagmire of poverty, help-lessness, and defeat? When and where and why did the fall begin? There are so many answers to these questions that no single explanation can possibly suffice, and no consensus is ever likely to emerge. You can start with the Spanish explorations in the fifteenth century, or the English colonial outposts in the seventeenth century, or the slave ships from Africa, or the revolutionary birth of the nation, or the war that divided the states and almost destroyed the country in the nineteenth century. You can start anywhere you like, and still you will end up in the 1930s with a nation in desperate straits and its Southern region on the brink of total collapse—and the effects will be much more obvious and unmistakable than the causes.

The events that fill these pages took place primarily in an era that began with the Roosevelt years in the early 1930s, but a prelude to set the stage for their retelling seems almost essential. More or less arbitrarily, then, I look back to the aftermath of Union victory in the Civil War as my point of departure, and for the sixty-five-year period between the war's end and the onset of the Great Depression, I have drawn up a chronological se-quence of generalized assertions. These are statements of probable truth for which there is, among scholars and students of history, a broad con-sensus:

• The victors, like all victors throughout history, followed military con-quest with economic and political rule. Northern Republicans—officials of the Union government and other so-called carpetbaggers—moved south into positions of power after the war, imposing a program of federal oc-cupation and supervision in the region. The stated political purpose was to prepare the rebellious states for reentry into the nation and to extend citizenship rights to all male residents, including former slaves; the un-stated economic objective was to exploit the region's natural resources and its supply of cheap labor.

• In 1877, after more than a decade of this Reconstruction—during which the radicals and reformers of both major political parties in the North gradually lost interest in the people and problems of the South—a bargain was struck between Republicans and Democrats to end federal domination and day-by-day administration of the Southern state govern-ments. The North thus relinquished political power within the region, but kept a tight grip on economic power.

• The Southern white men who gained control of those governments were variously characterized as Bourbons, Redeemers, Conservatives (all terms of confused meaning and limited utility now). Much like their an-tebellum predecessors, they were mostly noblesse-oblige paternalists identified with the landed gentry—planters, bankers, merchants. They sought at first not so much to deny civil rights to blacks as to contain and control the black vote and lure it away from the national Republicans. But the Southerners and the Republicans, though they were political rivals, had much in common: a patronizing interest in the black masses and a similar disdain for the white poor; a class-oriented vision of the economic and social structure; mutual preference for a government more oligarchic than democratic in nature; and an agreement in principle that the North should build more factories and let the South remain primarily a land of cotton and farms. In the boardrooms of the North, where Yankee money did most of the talking, Republican lenders and Bourbon borrowers made the decisions that perpetuated the colonial status of the South.

• The Populist revolt against the upper-class oligarchy in the 1890s was a radical uprising of grassroots workers, mostly farmers, against both the Southern patricians and their Northern allies. At first the movement sought to unite working-class whites and blacks, but when the ruling Democrats, with help from the North, stymied the rebellion, the Populists in frustration turned their reactionary fury against the blacks, whom the planter Democrats were already in the process of disenfranchising and abandoning. Thus, by the beginning of the twentieth century, all of the factions in the Southern power struggle—the Northern Republicans and Democrats, the Southern Redeemers, the Populists—had first exploited and then cast aside the millions of powerless Southern blacks, leaving them ignored and helpless at best, and at worst prey to the violent frustrations of their white neighbors.

• For the next three decades, as whites in the region outdid one another in zealous pursuit of legalized segregation and white supremacy, the South slipped deeper and deeper into the morass of isolation, inferiority, defensiveness, and self-delusion—and that is essentially where it was when the depression fell upon the United States and Franklin D. Roosevelt answered the call for a rescuer to take command. The alienation felt by white former Confederates toward the national government—the Union—had not by any means abated when FDR came in. By the same token, the federal government had shown little concern for African-Americans since the Reconstruction era ended—and not all that much for Southern whites. What was new and different about the New Deal, insofar as the South was concerned, was its interest in economic—not political—reform.

To encompass two eventful generations of American history in a few brief summary statements such as these seems like too much of a shortcut to the New Deal years. It should be helpful—if not absolutely necessary—to go back and take a closer look at some pivotal and transitional people in that earlier period, and to pick up a few amplifying historical details.

Inviting the congressmen and senators and governors of the Southern states to take part in a mission of domestic economic and social reform in 1932 was a little bit like summoning a pack of foxes to help clean up the henhouse. (No doubt, in the proprietary view of the South's political leaders, it was Roosevelt who was the fox, and the South was first on his list of chicken coops to be cleaned.) The politicians were the heirs of a shrill and potent breed of reactionary extremists who held political power at the beginning of the twentieth century, and they in turn had been handed control by the white planters and former Confederate generals who took over the states after Reconstruction ended in the late 1870s.

Some of those who ruled the states at the end of the nineteenth century, such as Tom Watson of Georgia, had started out on a Populist crusade to organize the poor, white and black, against exploitation by the reestablished planter class. Watson had the makings of a genuine reformer, a charismatic leader outraged by the injustices he saw all around him. Others, like "Pitchfork Ben" Tillman of South Carolina, a raving, half-blind zealot (living proof of the old adage that in the land of the blind, the one-eyed man is king), were devoted from the start to unrelenting white supremacy. In the end, virtually all of these Southern radicals, including Watson, were so infected by the virus of racial hysteria that it became their legacy, a chronic infection wracking the South in body, mind, and spirit.

Look from ex-General John B. Gordon, a Bourbon senator and governor, to the volatile Watson, who served in both houses of Congress, to his adversary-turned-ally Hoke Smith, and on to Eugene Talmadge in the Roosevelt years, and you can see the disease being transmitted in Georgia. Or witness the transfer of it in South Carolina from General Wade Hampton to Ben Tillman to Cole Blease and "Cotton Ed" Smith—an unbroken line spanning almost a century. Likewise in Mississippi, you can observe the degeneration from the reconciler L. Q. C. Lamar to James K. Vardaman to Theodore G. Bilbo. In one Southern state after another, ranting demagogues subverted the rule of law and the democratic process to disastrous effect in the first half-century after the Civil War—and in most of the states, the subversion continued for another forty or fifty years after that.

Off and on from about the mid-1880s until World War I, white voices of opposition or anguished doubt were occasionally raised against extreme racial subjugation. George Washington Cable, a New Orleans writer, took up the issue in his 1885 book, *The Silent South*, published in New York. Segregation laws, he declared, amounted to a "stupid firing into our own ranks," not only wrong but ineffective. No one was advocating social equality, he asserted; the real issue was the denial of civil rights, of elementary justice. Various churchmen, most of them Methodists and Episcopalians, joined the cause at about the same time. Among them were Edgar Gardner Murphy, an Episcopal priest in Alabama, and Atticus G. Haygood, a Georgia educator and minister (later to become a Methodist bishop), who in 1881 wrote a book called *Our Brother in Black: His Freedom and His Future.* Some respected journalists of the period, most notably Henry Watterson, editor of the Louisville *Courier-Journal,* tried to come to grips with the problem, as did some businessmen, such as Lewis Harvie Blair of Richmond, who in 1889 wrote *A Southern Prophecy: The Prosperity of the South Dependent upon the Elevation of the Negro.*

In education, James Hardy Dillard of Tulane University and John Spencer Bassett of Trinity College (later Duke University) were among those calling for fairness. Another was Thomas Pearce Bailey, former superintendent of schools in Memphis and dean of the department of education at the University of Mississippi, who in 1914 wrote *Race Orthodoxy in the South,* a book calling for full political, civil, and economic rights for blacks. "The real problem is not the negro," concluded Bailey, "but the white man's attitude toward the negro." There were other dissenters scattered about the region, but even in chorus they raised no more than a whisper against the shouts of the politicians.

Occasionally, expressions of dissent by blacks were heard, but they came mainly from afar, because outspoken candor by nonwhites in the South was known to be reckless, even suicidal. When Ida B. Wells, born a slave in Mississippi in 1862, dared to write critically of unequal funding of schools and of lynching in Memphis in the early 1890s, she was fired from her teaching job, her small newspaper was destroyed by fire, and her life was threatened; thereafter, she waged her crusade for equality from Chicago.

After the Populist uprising fizzled, the Progressive movement ushered in some modest reforms in a variety of areas, but race relations was not chief among them. The last quarter of the nineteenth century, wrote the historian Rayford W. Logan years later, was the nadir for black Americans, the Dark Ages; Jim Crow, he said, was permanently enthroned at the center of Southern life and culture as the twentieth century commenced, and "second-class citizenship for Negroes was accepted by Presidents, the Supreme Court, Congress, organized labor—indeed, by the vast majority of Americans, North and South, and by the 'leader' of the Negro race, Booker T. Washington." And yet, as bad as those times were for blacks in particular and the South in general, they would not get much better in the "progressive" years ahead.

Booker T. Washington was the best-known black American of his time, having founded Tuskegee Institute in Alabama in 1881, when he was just twenty-five years old, and later having told his remarkable story to the world in an acclaimed autobiography, *Up from Slavery*. Washington gained immeasurable stature and approval from whites throughout the country in 1895 when he declared, in his famous Atlanta Compromise address, that the Negroes of the South should stay in the region, accept segregation and disenfranchisement, work hard, and look to the charity of whites for help in securing a subservient role in agriculture and industry. "Cast down your bucket where you are," he advised his listeners. In effect, he strategically conceded the superiority of whites, commended their behavior toward blacks in the post–Civil War years, and endorsed the U.S. Supreme Court's "separate but equal" doctrine *in advance*, a year before its articulation in *Plessy* v. *Ferguson*. Perhaps he was simply trying to buy some time for his race to get on its feet—but looking back, it appears that he played directly into the hands of the white oligarchy that was just then beginning to chisel segregation and white supremacy into the stone tablets of the law.

From that declaration, delivered when he was still a young man (thirty-nine), Booker T. Washington went on to twenty more years of influential service before his death in 1915. He was the unofficial "Secretary of Negro Affairs" for Presidents Theodore Roosevelt and William Howard Taft, and a favored recipient of Northern philanthropy from such self-made men of wealth as John D. Rockefeller and Andrew Carnegie. None of his white admirers was able, though, to fulfill the one request he included in his Atlanta Compromise speech: that blacks be given a truly fair and equitable share of public support within the framework of segregation. "Separate but equal," from the very first, was an empty and meaningless phrase.

Nine years earlier, another young Southerner, thirty-six-year-old Henry W. Grady, a white journalist and "New South" booster who was part-owner and managing editor of the Atlanta *Constitution*, had made a speech in New York that, like Washington's address, had a curious staying power. Grady was already heralded as a colorful orator for his incisive commentaries on the South's colonial poverty. (Once, describing a fellow Georgian's funeral, he noted that the dead man was dressed in a New York suit and shoes from Boston, laid out in a Cincinnati casket, and buried under a Vermont marble tombstone; all the South furnished, he said, was "the corpse and the hole in the ground.") In his 1886 address to an overflow audience of wealthy and conservative New York businessmen (one of whom was retired General William Tecumseh Sherman, drolly recognized by Grady as a man "slightly careless with fire"), the Atlanta speaker lived up to his advance billing.

The South must have economic growth and development in order to recover fully from the Civil War, he said, and the way to get it was to put the memory of war behind them, court Northern capital and industry, and treat their fellow citizens of color in a fair and honorable way. In the satisfied manner typical of whites of his class, Grady maintained that the race problem was virtually solved, and needed no further assist from the North. He made no apology for his belief in white supremacy, and his audience appeared not to expect or even want one; they and the Northern newspapers that spread the word of his appearance in days to come were full of uncritical praise for the dynamic journalist's vision of a New South.

The welter of state laws and local ordinances mandating segregation of the races thus received affirmation and even a certain validity not only from the swelling ranks of political opportunists and demagogues but from the mouths of two earnest and presumably well-intentioned young Southern spokesmen, one black and the other white. Public opinion in the North, from the business leaders to the philanthropists to the man on the street, tended to seize upon the good news and ignore the bad. They had heard enough from Booker T. Washington and Henry W. Grady to be persuaded that the South was returning to the national fold, rejoining decent society. They could dismiss the rantings of Ben Tillman and Tom Watson as meaningless political diatribes; the New South, the Real South, was bright with promise and no longer a menace or a nagging concern. A comforting thought, no doubt—but unfortunately a long way from the truth.

More than a thousand blacks were lynched, almost all of them in the South, in the decade between Grady's speech and Washington's, and several hundred whites met the same fate; the death toll continued at a rate of about a hundred victims a year right on into the first decade of the new century. A rising tide of white extremism was sweeping through the South as the ruling majority, armed with a welter of new segregation laws, moved to complete the resubjugation of former slaves whose tenuous hold on freedom had been slipping since the end of Reconstruction.

Urban riots reflecting the growing hostility of whites toward blacks erupted in Wilmington, North Carolina, in 1898 and in New Orleans in 1900; in 1906, martial law was imposed to halt such outbursts in Brownsville, Texas, and in Atlanta. Two witnesses to the latter event were William Edward Burghardt Du Bois, a thirty-eight-year-old New Englander who taught at Atlanta University, and Walter White, a thirteen-year-old boy who lived in the heart of the city, where the four-day rampage of lawlessness took place. In later years, Du Bois and White would serve together in New York as officers of the National Association for the Advancement of Colored People (hereafter referred to by its well-known initials—NAACP), and would eventually part company in strategic and philosophical disagreement over policy issues. But in 1906, before they even knew of each other, the Atlanta riot gave permanent shape and meaning to their understanding of the South and of the deep complexities of race.

Du Bois didn't literally witness the riot—he was out of town when it erupted—but he saw the destruction and death that it caused, and felt the intensity of white radicalism that fueled the outburst. The effect was to strengthen in him a conviction that already showed through in his writing and would remain a central focus throughout his influential life—namely, that meek submission and accommodation to whites in the manner of Booker T. Washington would be disastrous and ultimately fatal to all people of African descent in America.

Du Bois was already recognized as a direct and dissenting rival of Washington. He had written *The Souls of Black Folk,* an incisive volume of essays on black culture, in 1903, and had organized a reformist task force of twenty-nine national (mostly Northern) black leaders at the Niagara Falls Conference in 1905. Largely in response to urban riots such as the one in Atlanta, he helped to found the NAACP in 1909, serving as the only black on its initial slate of officers; a year later he left Atlanta for New York to launch and edit a hard-hitting monthly magazine, the *Crisis,* for the new civil rights organization. There he was to remain for twenty-four years, solidifying his reputation as an outspoken advocate of black pride and racial justice.

W. E. B. Du Bois—balding, goateed, somberly formal in manner and appearance—was in every sense a formidable figure. Born and raised in small-town Massachusetts to parents of mixed African and European descent ("not Anglo-Saxon, thank God!" he always said), he got his first look at the South and its large African population when he enrolled in 1885 as a seventeen-year-old freshman at Fisk University in Nashville. Before he graduated three years later, he had discovered the strength and beauty of an oppressed race, and the revelation inspired him permanently. Three particular remembrances from his Nashville experience surfaced in his writing years later. One was the rigorous and challenging quality of his formal instruction. Another was the eager receptivity to learning shown by black children in the impoverished rural Tennessee schools where he taught each summer. And the third was the breathtaking beauty of a Fisk coed, Lena Calhoun—who later saw her good looks replicated in her talented and famous grandniece, Lena Horne.

But Du Bois had little time for socializing. He went on to take another degree at Harvard, to study further at the University of Berlin, and to return to Harvard and earn a Ph.D. in 1895. Unable because of his race to get a teaching post at any of the major universities in the North, he taught briefly at Wilberforce, a black college in Ohio, and then conducted a research study on Negro life in the city of Philadelphia. In 1897 he returned to the South to direct a new program in the social sciences at Atlanta University.

One day in the spring of 1899, as he was on his way to keep an appointment with Joel Chandler Harris, an editor of the *Constitution* and creator of the Uncle Remus tales, Du Bois was jerked to a halt by something he saw in the front window of a grocery store. There on display was the twisted hand of a recently lynched black man. The heinous symbolism of that exhibit struck him with such force that he turned around and went home, convinced that not even the "better sort" of Southerner, like Harris, could mitigate the deep-rooted sickness in the souls of white folks.

Temperamentally an abrasive and cantankerous man—some said cold and arrogant—Du Bois more than compensated in scholarly and journalistic brilliance for whatever he may have lacked in personal charm. Walter White, who was known to some as a rather difficult man himself, more than met his match in Du Bois, and their time together at the NAACP was seldom tranquil.

"I am a Negro," wrote White in his 1948 autobiography, *A Man Called White*. "My skin is white, my eyes are blue, my hair is blond. The traits of my race are nowhere visible upon me." Both of his parents were very light-skinned, and he could easily have passed undetected into the freer and more comfortable life of the white majority. But the reign of anarchy and violence that gripped Atlanta during four oppressively hot Indian summer days and nights in September 1906 caused him to know, "in terror and bitterness of soul," that he would forever choose to fight for the rights of racial minorities.

In the fever of an explosive gubernatorial campaign between two factions of Democrats trying to "outnigger" each other, Atlanta had worked itself into an emotional frenzy as the oppressive summer heat dragged on into autumn. The candidate of the party regulars was Clark Howell, who ran Henry Grady's old *Constitution*. A faction of insurgents headed by Hoke Smith, a former part-owner of the rival *Journal*, had joined forces with the volatile Tom Watson, and the two sides slugged it out daily on the stump and in the pages of their papers. Egging them on were two even more sensational and extreme dailies—the *Georgian*, edited by John Temple Graves, Sr., and the *News*. All were addicted to yellow journalism and incendiary language on matters of race and politics.

The already-besieged black masses quickly became pawns in the political campaign, and by late September, when fabricated rumors of murders and sexual assaults by blacks against whites were blaring daily in the headlines, a violent outburst seemed unavoidable. At about that time, the North Carolina novelist Thomas Dixon, celebrated for his fictional incitements to Negrophobia, showed up in Atlanta with a fiery stage version of *The Clansman* (the same story that D. W. Griffith would put on film as *The Birth of a Nation* in 1915, setting off another reactionary wave).

Walter White was with his father, a mail carrier, in a horse-drawn cart on Peachtree Street in the early-evening shadows of a sultry Saturday— the date was September 22, 1906—when a casual acquaintance of theirs, a lame Negro bootblack, hobbled past them with a white mob in pursuit; he was quickly caught and clubbed to death. Stunned and shaken by the sight of this vicious attack, George White and his son retreated, barely managing to get to their home on Houston Street without being assaulted themselves. All through the night and the next day, they waited in fear of more violence.

At dusk on Sunday, a white mob gathered on the street outside their house. "That's where that nigger mail carrier lives!" Walter White heard someone shout. "Let's burn it down!" He and his father were at the front window with pistols, frozen with fear and excitement, and as the mob began to move toward them, the young teenager experienced a terrifying and indelible moment of truth. "In that instant," he later wrote, "there opened up within me a great awareness: I knew then who I was. I was a Negro, a human being with an invisible pigmentation which marked me a person to be hunted." At what seemed like the last moment, a volley of shots from nearby distracted the mob, and they dispersed, but the memory stayed with Walter White for the rest of his life.

About two dozen blacks and at least five whites were killed in the Atlanta riot, and close to a hundred people were injured. The message to the Southern black minority was crystal clear: If such unrestrained lawlessness and violence could happen here, where many middle-class blacks in business, academia, the church, and the professions were living, then no place was safe.

In the overheated and explosive atmosphere of the time, the South appeared to have lost whatever forward motion it had, and had begun to slip backward. Blacks in particular sensed the falling, for they were the objects of the violence and the discriminatory laws. They were rapidly losing their elected representatives in government, too, as whites systematically stripped them of their right to vote. The few Southern whites who acknowledged the problem publicly and tried in their own limited ways to address it were a tiny minority swimming against the tide, and even the best of them were hardly heard from at all until the Jim Crow laws of disenfranchisement and usurped civil rights were firmly in place throughout the South.

If there was any institutional base at all for the promotion of better living conditions for the region's masses of poor people, white and black, it was in the churches. Then as always, religion was a powerful controlling force among all classes of Southern people; it was the one institution that almost everyone turned to for aid and comfort in times of distress. The overwhelmingly conservative and orthodox emphasis of the churches was on individual salvation in the hereafter, but simple Christian charity compelled them to acknowledge the needs of suffering people in the here and now.

Elsewhere in the nation at the turn of the century, a social gospel movement was emerging in response to a multitude of problems associated with the shift from an agricultural to an urban-industrial society. The North was in turmoil over long and punishing work hours, the exploitation of women and children in industry, unsafe workplaces, paltry wages, the lack of benefits for workers, slum housing, poor to nonexistent health care, and a general disregard for laboring people. (These, incidentally, were essentially nonracial issues. About nine million of the seventy-six million people living in the United States in 1900 were identified as Negroes, and of them, fewer than one million lived outside the South; their relatively small numbers and the informal barriers to employment they faced as a racial minority made blacks only a minuscule fraction of the workers in Northern industries.)

The leaders of the social gospel movement felt a greater need to make the world around them a better place for their church members to live in than to help lift souls up to heaven one by one. While Southern churches were holding revivals to rescue sinners from the devil, the mainline Protestant denominations of the urban North were bringing moral pressure to bear on the sins of capitalism. The more conservative of those congregations simply wanted a greater show of charity from the industrial barons, but their more radical counterparts longed to replace capitalism with an altogether different social order in which wealth and power would be more widely distributed. What emerged and defined the social gospel movement was a moderate fusion of the two, a reform-minded union of denominational groups interested in progressive, socially conscious Christianity.

They were largely responsible for the founding in 1908 of the Federal Council of Churches of Christ in America, an ecumenical body drawing primarily from seven Northern denominations: Baptist, Congregational, Disciples of Christ, Episcopal, Lutheran, Methodist, and Presbyterian. There were separate organizations of some of these churches in the South—lingering vestiges of the secessionist impulse that had precipitated the Civil War—and still others that were all black, but none of them took part in the formation and early mission of the Federal Council. Even so, a scattering of prominent Southerners, leaders within the churches and other institutions, kept a close eye on the Northern movements of religious and political progressivism, and tried in modest ways to apply them to the overriding issues of race and poverty in the South. One of these quiet reformers was Willis D. Weatherford, a Texas-born religious educator.

His middle-class family of Methodist and Baptist regulars had given Willis Weatherford a solid grounding in church and school by the time he transferred as a twenty-two-year-old junior to Vanderbilt University in Nashville in 1897. Five years later, armed with a Ph.D. in classical studies and theology, he moved directly into a Nashville-based job as a student secretary covering colleges in fourteen states of the South and Southwest for the Young Men's Christian Association. The International YMCA, a nondenominational organization founded in England, had been active in the religious mainstream of the United States for about fifty years when Weatherford embarked on his mission to help spread its programs of evangelism and youth-support services throughout the South.

Traveling by train, the energetic young organizer spent the next seventeen years covering his territory, and then, from 1919 to 1936, he presided over a Nashville graduate school of Christian education, another endeavor sponsored by the YMCA. A tall, rugged, forceful man with a commanding presence, Weatherford gained stature and influence (and a certain paternalistic formality) as the years passed. Well connected to the philanthropic families and institutions of the North, he was to be a skillful fund raiser for a succession of institutions: Blue Ridge Assembly, a YMCA summer conference center in the mountains of North Carolina; the Southern Sociological Congress, an organization that studied racial and social issues; the YMCA college in Nashville; the Commission on Interracial Cooperation in Atlanta; and two higher-education institutions with which he maintained close ties—Fisk University in Nashville and Berea College in Kentucky.

As the twentieth century progressed, the South found it harder and harder to ignore all the reforms that characterized the social gospel and political progressivism in the North. The same forces that spawned those reforms—industrialization, population density, ethnic conflict, extreme divisions of wealth and poverty—were clearly evident in the Southern region, and people were gradually being compelled to acknowledge them. Then too, of course, the South was burdened with its own peculiar curses, from the evils of peonage and convict leasing to illiteracy, malnutrition, and the ever-worsening state of race relations.

Willis Weatherford was a moving force in the small circle of indigenous leaders who gave their time and energy to these matters. He organized a conference of white and black educators in Atlanta in 1908 to discuss "what college men can do to improve the racial situation." He wrote a book in 1910—*Negro Life in the South*—that served as a college text on race relations. At the Blue Ridge Assembly beginning in 1912, he convened steady streams of college students, academicians and administrators, church officials, politicians, and leaders of business and industry to reinforce their Christian faith and to contend intellectually with social issues. More and more as the years went by, these groups included both whites and blacks, Protestants and Catholics, progressives and conservatives, even Southerners and Northerners. In a spirit of brotherhood and good intentions, they dealt earnestly but gingerly with the segregation issue, sometimes observing it in the breach but never, until years later, insisting openly that Jim Crow laws be removed from the statute books.

Probably the most visible and far-reaching effort by Southerners to confront their social dilemmas in this period was the Southern Sociological Congress, a regionwide assembly that first convened in Nashville in 1912 and continued annually for eight years. Weatherford was one of the moving forces behind it. The effort began when Tennessee's Republican governor, Ben W. Hooper, was persuaded to host the first conference and issue the call to delegates. About seven hundred ministers, educators, social workers, government officials, and others attended the four-day meeting to discuss a wide range of Southern social issues. (The few blacks who came—mostly ministers and college administrators—were assigned to segregated seats in accordance with the Jim Crow laws.) There was a strong religious flavor to these proceedings, underscored by the presence of numerous representatives of the Federal Council of Churches and of the Southern denominations that were by then entering a cautious liaison with the council.

A spin-off group, the University Commission on Southern Race Questions, was created at the first congress by representatives of eleven white state universities who viewed the subject "with sympathetic interest." In years to come, they and other white Southerners, including the indefatigable Willis Weatherford, would call repeatedly upon a small cadre of black college and university presidents for advice and assistance, among them Robert R. Moton, Booker T. Washington's successor at Tuskegee; John Hope, the first black president of Atlanta's Morehouse College and later president of Atlanta University; and Mordecai Johnson, who in time would become the first black president of Howard University in Washington.

After 1912, as the Southern Sociological Congress reconvened annually in Atlanta, Memphis, Houston, and other cities, the segregation of delegates was made an issue—and resolved, finally, in favor of ignoring the law and letting people sit where they pleased. This act of defiance was played down by all in attendance, but most of them must have felt privately that it was too radical for comfort; in any case, by 1919 the number of delegates had diminished to a remnant too small to keep the organization alive.

The congress and its satellite assembly of university officials never formally came to grips with the segregation issue. All of the whites, including Weatherford, paid lip service to the separate-but-equal doctrine, and by the time the First World War was over, segregation was so deeply entrenched in the South that the best the white liberals could muster was a professed "understanding of and friendship with the Negro" and a commitment to push for improvements in the status of blacks within the bounds of the segregation laws. Nothing could have shown more clearly than this cautious response just how ineffectual the religious and academic institutions were against the prevailing forces of racial and political orthodoxy in the South.

It was at about this time that communism and socialism swept from Russia and Western Europe into the bubbling cauldron of American political thought and action, there to maintain a controversial presence for decades to come. But the isms that immobilized the South in those years were far more ancient: medievalism in agriculture and industry, fundamentalism in religion, traditionalism in academia, racism in the laws and customs of white supremacy. Forty years after their return to national politics, Southern congressmen and senators were building empires on a base of unchallenged seniority that promised to put them soon in complete control of Congress. Woodrow Wilson, the first Southern-born president in fifty years, offered little or no opposition to the forces, North and South, that kept the region barefoot and bigoted. Even his Republican predecessors, William Howard Taft and Teddy Roosevelt, had seemed relatively more sensitive to the problems of race and class. (It took the Republican presidents of the 1920s, behaving like the storybook trio of monkeys that heard, saw, and spoke no evil, to make Wilson seem—undeservedly—a tiny bit better by comparison.)

It could be argued that World War I helped race relations a little, providing as it did a unifying surge of patriotism and opportunities for blacks to excel as soldiers (albeit in segregated units). The South got an economic boost, too, from war industries and military bases and rising cotton prices. But as soon as peace was declared, war against the black minority broke out at home, not just in the South but in the urban North as well. James Weldon Johnson, a Floridian of many talents who was then serving as acting secretary of the NAACP (with Walter White of Atlanta as his handpicked assistant), labeled the time as "the Red Summer of 1919"— red with the blood of hundreds of people killed or injured in race riots from Longview, Texas, and Elaine, Arkansas, to Tulsa, Knoxville, Washington, and Chicago. Twenty-six riots erupted in that one year alone (more than half of them outside the South); seventy Southern blacks, some still wearing the uniform of their country, were shot, beaten, or burned to death by lynch mobs.

Acute anxiety over the uncontrolled violence and the rumors of worse racial conflicts to come spurred a small group of prominent white Southerners, including Willis D. Weatherford and a thirty-five-year-old Methodist minister named Will W. Alexander, to meet in Atlanta and at the YMCA's Blue Ridge retreat in North Carolina for extended discussions of the crisis. They assembled a team of staff field-workers—two men, one white and the other black, in each Southern state—and sent them into communities where tensions were highest, offering their services as mediators and as organizers of concerned citizens willing to work for improved race relations.

All through 1919 and into 1920 the cadre of planners worked, bringing other whites and several blacks into the circle with them. The group had first informally called itself the Interracial Committee; in time, with Will Alexander as director and John J. Eagan, a progressive industrialist, as president, the organization was officially incorporated as the Commission on Interracial Cooperation.

4. *A Stirring of New Voices*

Will Alexander was ordained into the Methodist ministry while he was still a Missouri farm boy, almost a decade before he earned a degree from the Biblical Department at Vanderbilt in 1912. He spent about a dozen years in Nashville, first as a student and then as pastor of a church near the campus, where Willis Weatherford, nine years his senior, was a member of his congregation. The two men teamed up on a mission of social service in the winter of 1914, organizing a charity fund for unemployed people in the city. That was the beginning of a close personal and professional association that would continue for forty years.

With Weatherford's help, Alexander got a job during the First World War in a YMCA program at army camps in the South, serving as a sort of chaplain and social worker. Much of his time was spent soothing overheated tempers in an atmosphere made volatile by continued acts of hostility and aggression toward blacks and by such highly publicized events as a dramatic cross-burning on Stone Mountain near Atlanta in December

1915 to herald a "rebirth" of the Ku Klux Klan. (Kentuckian D. W. Griffith's motion picture *The Birth of a Nation* was the torch that lit the cross.) At war's end, Alexander felt a calling to continue his work in race relations rather than return to the ministry, and it was he, with the advice and assistance of Weatherford, who came up with the plan to create the Commission on Interracial Cooperation. (For the remainder of the twentieth century, that organization and its eventual successor, the Southern Regional Council, would typify indigenous liberal initiatives to promote racial harmony.)

Throughout the 1920s, the commission was just about the only Southern organization with any influence or effectiveness at all in opposing racial violence in the region. It sought out and brought together people who were concerned about the destructive consequences of continuing hostility. Hundreds of local groups—some white, some black, some biracial—and statewide affiliates in thirteen states (the old Confederacy plus Kentucky and Oklahoma) gave the CIC a grassroots base. Men and women of both races came into the organization from churches, schools and colleges, agriculture and industry, the press.

If any single common interest bound them together, it was their abhorrence of violent and abusive treatment of law-abiding black citizens. The whites who predominated in the organization saw themselves as liberal friends of the black minority in the South, but not necessarily as enemies of segregation; as a matter of fact, none of them publicly expressed any interest in challenging the Jim Crow system, and in general they looked upon the CIC as an instrument of fairness and conciliation vital to the maintenance of "separate but equal" segregation. Most of the funds needed to support the commission's staff and programs came from Northern philanthropists—who likewise avoided direct opposition to Southern laws and customs.

It was Will Alexander's special talent that he could hold together so large an aggregation of diversely motivated people. Once, in 1926, he expressed his personal belief that segregation laws were unjust to blacks and thus indefensible morally, but when that opinion almost cost him his job, he discreetly avoided repeating it. Instead he tried to meet people where he found them, giving patient counsel to the conservatives who feared social change and quiet encouragement to the progressives who yearned for it. As a consequence, the CIC developed a curious image of liberal activism within the bounds of cautious and proper respectability.

Such men as Weatherford, industrialist John Eagan, and M. Ashby Jones, pastor of a large Baptist church in Atlanta—all patrician gentlemen of the "father knows best" school—dominated the board. Robert Moton, R. E. Jones, and a few other black members tended to be paternalistic and authoritarian toward other blacks but deferential to the white leaders. A women's division of the organization, first headed by Carrie Parks Johnson and then by Jessie Daniel Ames, was able from the start to present a biracial example of progressive thought and action that generally exceeded that of the men.

Alexander had been quick to grasp the importance of enlisting women in the cause of improving race relations. Even though they held a superior status over the blacks they employed in their homes, white women were themselves considered subservient to white men, so they had an inkling of what it felt like to be low-rated. What's more, many of them knew to their shame that a prime excuse for lynching was the perpetrators' vow "to protect the purity of white womanhood." As for black women—deemed inferior by both race and sex—Alexander had enough common sense to see that they were in fact a rock of stability for families on both sides of the color line.

Speaking at a meeting of Southern Methodist women in 1920, the CIC director set in motion an idea that promptly led to the creation of a race-relations committee headed by Carrie Johnson of Georgia. Soon the women went to Tuskegee Institute in Alabama to meet with a similar group of black women that included Charlotte Hawkins Brown, Mary McLeod Bethune, and Margaret Washington, widow of Booker T. (Charlotte Brown, a North Carolina native educated in Massachusetts, was the founder and headmistress of a private academy in Sedalia, North Carolina, for black girls; Mrs. Bethune, raised in a South Carolina sharecropping family, had prepared for missionary work in the North before founding a college in Florida for black students.)

The Tuskegee gathering was quickly followed by another pathfinding event: a biracial conclave of a hundred women in Memphis. Many of them would remember years later the electrifying moment when the white women, seated in the meeting hall, rose in unison in a spontaneous act of courtesy as the black women marched in. They remembered, too, the tears of emotion when Belle Harris Bennett, leader of the whites, sang "Blest Be the Tie That Binds." It was these women, white and black, who sparked the formation of the CIC's Division of Women's Work under Carrie Parks Johnson.

But the CIC was hardly a radical force. Though it was an outspoken foe of the Klan, lynch mobs, and various forms of intolerance, it didn't urge and wouldn't endorse a federal statute outlawing lynching—that, the leaders insisted, was a local and state responsibility—nor did it challenge in any way the entrenched laws and customs of segregation. Its administrative staff included, in addition to Alexander and the director of the women's division, a research director (first Thomas J. Woofter and then

Arthur F. Raper, both of whom had Ph.D.'s in sociology) and an experienced writer and editor, Robert B. Eleazer. All were white; no black staff member ever worked in the Atlanta office of the commission.

In sum, the CIC in its first decade of existence was a reflection of the times, a moderate response to a festering social problem that the vast majority of white Americans preferred to ignore. Will Alexander and his associates were benign and honorable men and women of high motivation and goodwill, seeking, in the words of one of them, "some plan by which the two races may be able to live in friendliness and mutual respect"—but separately, leaving the thorny question of segregation to be resolved "by the wisdom and justice of oncoming generations."

The South—and all of America—was in no mood to settle much of anything in the roller-coaster decade of the Roaring Twenties. The 1918 constitutional amendment prohibiting the manufacture or sale of alcoholic beverages had set off an epidemic of defiance and gangsterism, and all kinds of lawbreakers seemed to catch sparks from it: lynchers, urban rioters, Klan vigilantes, Communist agitators, the shock troops of management and organized labor's guerrilla fighters. Women got the vote by constitutional amendment in 1920, but that had no immediately discernible moderating or humanizing influence on the white men who made up the lion's share of the electorate.

Blacks had begun to flee the South by the tens of thousands annually, and wherever they went—New York, Chicago, Detroit—white hostility tended to follow. White Southerners couldn't decide whether the exodus was a good sign or a bad one. Some argued that reduced numbers of blacks would lessen white fears and improve race relations; others said it would only cause a shortage of hired help and make matters worse. In general, Southern blacks perceived that many Southern whites held warm personal feelings for them as individuals but thought of African-Americans in general as an inferior race, while Northern whites tended to support the principle of justice for the black race but had no personal contact with any of its people. There was a common expression for this anomaly: In the South, it doesn't matter how close Negroes get, as long as they don't get too high; in the North, it doesn't matter how high they get, as long as they don't get too close. Segregation was not the law up North, but it was the fact—nothing like as oppressive as in the South, of course, but bad enough to make a mockery of the Promised Land image held out to northbound emigrants. And the Klan was there too, almost as virulent and menacing in, say, Indiana as it was in Georgia or Alabama.

On every side, the walls were pressing in. The South was not working its way out of the old problems that had precipitated the Civil War, or the newer ones that had arisen in the postwar years of Reconstruction and redemption and radicalism. In the graphic image of the farmer, the region was still sucking hind tit on the national hog, still acting and reacting like the runt of the litter.

One of the oldest and most complex dimensions of the racial dilemma was sexuality. It hung like an albatross about the neck of the South. During slavery, virtually all of the racial intermixing was occasioned by white men—slave masters, in the main—availing themselves of powerless black women who were theirs for the taking. (The 1860 census counted a half-million "mulattoes," practically all of them descended from white paternal roots.) Emancipation drastically reduced that source of sexual favors, or cut it off altogether. In the decades that followed, all sorts of weird psychological reactions bubbled to the surface. The final, terrible consequence was that black men were envisioned as the demons responsible for every outrage, from alienation of affections (both white and black) to white male guilt to the worst offense of all: rape and dethroning of the queens of white purity. For those largely imagined transgressions, they were dismembered and murdered in the cruelest ways imaginable.

Novelists sometimes ventured into the forbidden chamber of race-sex horrors, but not until after World War II would many social scientists get past the taboos and begin to ask blunt and painful questions. Until then, it was as if no one with a voice to protest could see clearly what was happening and summon the courage to condemn it. In blind defiance of reality, the orthodox view before and after slavery was that white males were not guilty of any significant crossing of the sexual line; there were occasional transgressions, yes, but not many. When the lynching of Southern black men became epidemic in the 1890s and early 1900s, the white "man on the street" no doubt believed that the vast majority of such incidents occurred in reaction to the rape of white women by sexually crazed black men. Careful studies subsequently showed that fewer than one-third of all lynchings involved even a claim of rape, and the number in which a black assailant was positively identified came to only a minor fraction of the total. Numerous writers, including some Southerners, laid out these facts in print time after time, but they were no match for demagogic manipulators of public opinion. The devastating truth was that all along—even in the twentieth century—by far the most incidents of interracial sex in the South were initiated by white males with black females. Whether by terror, force, coercion, enticement, persuasion, or mutual consent, white men were the primary instigators of physical union between the races in the generations after the Civil War, just as they had been in the generations before.

No one was in a position to understand these truths as profoundly as the offspring of interracial unions. The culture ordained that they were colored people, Negroes, blacks, mulattoes—members of an inferior and subjugated race—regardless of the fractional proportions of their racial makeup. (If people of mixed racial heritage in the United States were now to be officially classified as "colored," as they are in many other cultures, they might well constitute close to a majority of the population.) In the restrictive era of segregation, countless thousands of Americans whose ancestry embraced two or more racial and ethnic identities transcended the confining labels of society and, with great generosity of spirit, made significant contributions to both the white and black strands of American history. Some of them attached particular importance and high priority to defending the rights of racial minorities and attacking such atrocities as lynching. Walter White was one such person; James Weldon Johnson was another.

Johnson was born in 1871 in Jacksonville, then a primitive little port town on the east coast of Florida. His mother, who was part French and a schoolteacher, was from the Bahamas; his father, a Virginia-born freeman, also had Caribbean roots. Both were musically talented and drawn to books, though the elder Johnson, a hotel waiter, had no formal education. James and his younger brother Rosamond remembered their childhood years as a serene and happy time unclouded by any complications of poverty or segregation. They went as children on trips by sea to visit relatives in New York, and sat anywhere on trains without restrictions in the pre–Jim Crow days, and they grew up with as many white friends as black. It was not until he was seventeen and a freshman at Atlanta University that Jim Johnson was rudely awakened to the harsh realities of racism.

In Atlanta, two things stood out to him: a hostile and menacing climate of white supremacy in a drab, landlocked sea of red clay, and an island of black intellectual refinement in the middle of that—the latter a heady concentration of class and culture embodied in a multicolored black elite. Johnson chafed against the sea, but thrived on the island. When he graduated in 1894, after six years of combined study and work, he was primed mentally and temperamentally for a career of creative achievement. Cool and clever, stylish and sporty, tall, tan, gray-eyed, and handsome, he seemed bound for a life of visibility that no amount of discrimination could obscure.

First, though, he went back to Jacksonville and spent seven years as principal of a school for black children, living with his parents and exploring a variety of creative ventures in his spare time. He and others started a newspaper, and he contributed articles and poems to it; he studied law independently, and passed the exam admitting him to the Florida bar; he and Rosamond wrote tunes and lyrics together (among their accomplishments by the turn of the century, besides many songs for Broadway plays, was "Lift Every Voice and Sing," commonly referred to as the Negro national anthem).

All along the way, James Weldon Johnson seemed to have a knack for rising above the stings and cuts of racism, floating past and escaping them with a smile and a clever turn of phrase. When he moved to New York early in the new century, he looked forward to a career in music with his brother and a good-humored, free-spirited life of productivity and pleasure.

It was just then, though, that segregation and white supremacy were being imposed with malice across the South, and the virus reached out into the country. On the road in cities of the North and Midwest and West, Johnson was enraged to find petty discrimination and gratuitous insults on the rise; even in the restaurants and theaters of Manhattan these things were happening to him, and he reacted with uncharacteristic bitterness and rage. He met W. E. B. Du Bois during these years, and was inspired by the force of his ideas. He campaigned for Teddy Roosevelt's election in 1904, and was rewarded with a series of appointments as a U.S. consul in Latin America, during which time he wrote a novel (*The Autobiography of an Ex-Coloured Man*) and a long poem commemorating the fiftieth anniversary of Abraham Lincoln's Emancipation Proclamation.

Then, briefly back in Jacksonville while Woodrow Wilson was in office, Johnson was forcefully struck by the iron grip of Jim Crow and the violence that was readily used to enforce it. By the fall of 1916 he had moved again to New York, hoping to establish himself as a writer. The travails of the African-American population troubled him deeply, though, and so he was predisposed psychologically to say yes when Joel E. Spingarn, chairman of the board of the National Association for the Advancement of Colored People, asked him to join the staff as field secretary.

For the next fifteen years, Johnson was the NAACP's leading staff officer. He organized almost 250 new chapters around the country in his first three years on the job; the South, which had only three local branches when he started, had close to fifty by the end of 1919. One of the newest and strongest was in Atlanta, and it was through it that Johnson met Walter White and recruited him for the national staff. As riots and lynchings increased after the war, White proved to be an expert field investigator, posing as a white man to gather incriminating evidence on the perpetrators. Soon, Johnson replaced John R. Shilladay as executive secretary, and thus became the first black staff director of the organization, with White as his assistant.

Throughout the 1920s, the NAACP and the National Urban League, another race-relations organization of somewhat similar origin and focus, represented the emergence of an insistent black voice of protest against white supremacy and Jim Crow discrimination. Booker T. Washington's deferential tone of conciliation and submission seemed to have gone to the grave with him in 1915. Though they were founded in the North and led initially by whites, the NAACP and the Urban League in the twenties got most of their reformist energy and their moral outrage from black Southerners who saw the new problems of the urban North and the old problems of the rural South as two sides of a single coin. James Weldon Johnson of Florida and Walter White of Georgia were eloquent in their condemnation of racial injustice, and *Crisis* editor W. E. B. Du Bois—not a native Southerner, true, but tempered by the blue flame of segregationist heat during his Atlanta days—gave the NAACP an unmistakably black but also Southern accent. The Urban League's magazine, *Opportunity*, was edited by another black Southerner, Charles S. Johnson, and it too was unequivocal in its denunciation of racial discrimination.

Charles Spurgeon Johnson was still in his twenties when he moved to New York from Chicago in 1922 to become research director of the Urban League and editor of its magazine. His father was a Baptist minister whose mother had received rare educational advantages as a favorite slave on a Virginia plantation, and young Charles grew up in a Southern black family stimulated by books and intellectual activity. He was sent away to high school in Richmond and went on to earn degrees at Virginia Union University and the University of Chicago. First as a student and then as a valued colleague of the famed Chicago sociologist Robert E. Park, Johnson quickly made a name for himself as an outstanding social scientist. What he referred to as his "living laboratory" included, in addition to his unusual childhood and youth, a year of World War I combat service in France and directorship of a research team commissioned to investigate the disastrous 1919 Chicago race riot, in which some two dozen blacks and about fifteen whites were killed.

When he got to New York, where he was to stay for six years, Charles Johnson found himself in the vortex of a black intellectual struggle for influence and leadership. The time was long since past when a single individual—a Frederick Douglass, a Booker T. Washington—could speak for the entire race; various factions now sought to exercise political leverage and define racial identity, and they disagreed on methods as well as objectives.

Marcus Garvey, the flamboyant founder of the Universal Negro Improvement Association, had inspired a large following for his plan to lead the African-American masses out of their subservience and into liberty and freedom in Liberia. (Internal problems within his organization eventually led him instead to the federal penitentiary in Atlanta, and he was subsequently deported in 1927 to his native Jamaica.) The NAACP was variously seen as liberal or progressive, reasonable or radical, depending on the viewer and the point at issue; a large and multifaceted confederation of mostly middle- and upper-class blacks and their white allies, the organization sought justice for the African-American minority primarily through political and legal action. The Urban League, in its pursuit of the same basic goal of racial equality, differed more in style than substance; its approach was less confrontational than the NAACP's, and it was generally perceived as a slightly more conservative or middle-of-the-road complement to the association.

Charles S. Johnson was the perfect embodiment of that cooler image. Urbane and sophisticated, he was a scholar and diplomat whose quiet efficiency and unthreatening professional manner won him the admiration of his black associates and the support of many influential whites. He lacked the abrasive militancy of Du Bois, but not the stern scholar's controlled intellect; his ego was no match for Walter White's, but his energy and courage were; he was in no sense a stylish bon vivant like James Weldon Johnson, but he understood and appreciated and promoted the value of black literature, music, and the arts. Both Johnsons, Du Bois, and White stood together opposite Marcus Garvey in the 1920s on the question of where the African-Americans would find their destiny; they stood far less united, though, on the question of how.

While these men sought in their various ways to chart a path to equality for the black minority, events continued to demonstrate the white majority's determination to ambush and defeat the effort. Beginning in the spring of 1921, James Weldon Johnson spent the better part of two years lobbying Congress to pass a federal anti-lynching law, only to see the attempt finally stalled by a Southern-led filibuster in the Senate. The bill was introduced in the House by Congressman L. C. Dyer of St. Louis, whose district included a large black population. After months of parliamentary maneuvering and rancorous debate, it passed there by a margin of more than a hundred votes, but the victory echoed like a warning alarm in the Senate, and there, in December 1922, a solid phalanx of Southerners aided by Henry Cabot Lodge of Massachusetts and other conservative Republicans prevented the measure from coming to a vote.

Death snatched old Tom Watson of Georgia out of the arena while that debate was going on, as it had taken South Carolina's Ben Tillman before it started, and defeat at the polls prevented Mississippi's James K. Vardaman from taking part. But there was no shortage of arch-conservatives still on hand to stand and fight. Pat Harrison of Mississippi, Tom Heflin of

Alabama, Tom Connally of Texas, Carter Glass of Virginia, and "Cotton Ed" Smith of South Carolina were the shock troops in a solid Southern victory, and all of the many subsequent attempts to outlaw lynching by federal statute suffered the same fate.

Walter White wrote a blistering denunciation of the practice, entitled *Rope and Faggot*, in 1929, and Arthur F. Raper's 1933 book, *The Tragedy of Lynching*, based on a study by the Commission on Interracial Cooperation, brought sympathy to the victims and shame to the South, but changed nothing. Probably the most effective weapon against lynch mobs in the 1930s was the Association of Southern Women for the Prevention of Lynching, an activist network of white and black churchwomen and others organized by Jessie Daniel Ames of the CIC; paradoxically, though, even Mrs. Ames was opposed to a federal anti-lynching law, taking instead the position of most white Southerners that the problem could best be dealt with internally, without Northern interference. This was the same states' rights argument that had been the rallying cry of secessionists in 1860; even the region's progressive reformers seemed mesmerized by its putative power.

There is a school of thought that says the correlation between creative ferment and parlous times is no coincidence; the former is a direct outgrowth of the latter. I'm inclined to believe that. Bad times make good literature, good art, good theater. Most of the reasons given for this anomaly are complex, but one is simple and obvious: There's so much good material to work with.

The 1920s are a case in point. In a time of diminishing opportunity and fading hope for black Americans and for the South, a time of depression and oppression, artistic experimentation and productivity blossomed for African-Americans in New York's Harlem and for a white literati in several locales around the South. Both phenomena were commonly referred to as "renaissance" movements, as if they were revivals of earlier manifestations of creativity. It may be closer to the truth to think of them as original and unprecedented.

The swelling exodus of blacks from the South more than tripled New York City's black population (to 180,000-plus) between 1910 and 1923, and by far the majority of them lived in Harlem, a section rapidly being vacated by whites. After the rise and fall of the charismatic and ebony-hued Marcus Garvey, it was the "tan intelligentsia" of college-educated professionals—the "Talented Tenth," as Du Bois called them—whose response to racism was not so much political or economic as it was literary and artistic. Foremost among the leaders, to no one's surprise, were the

NAACP–Urban League quartet of Johnson, Johnson, Du Bois, and White. Charles Johnson in particular fostered the movement; he was "the entrepreneur of the Harlem Renaissance," the one, said the poet Langston Hughes, "who did more to encourage and develop Negro writers during the 1920s than anyone else in America." He and Du Bois gave the renaissance prominence in the pages of *Crisis* and *Opportunity.* One of James Weldon Johnson's contributions to the movement was a classic volume of sermons in verse called *God's Trombones,* and Walter White found time to dash off a couple of fair-to-middling novels.

The extent to which the South provided the raw talent for the Harlem Renaissance is remarkable, to say the least. Expatriates from the Southern and border states—migrants, refugees, exiles—were the main contributors to the outpouring of novels, poetry, nonfiction, drama, and visual art (as well as music, a movement all its own) that defined the renaissance. In addition to the quartet above, there were such talented contributors as the aforementioned Langston Hughes, who came from Missouri; novelist Jean Toomer and poet Sterling Brown, both born in the District of Columbia; poet-novelist Arna Bontemps of Louisiana; novelist-folklorist Zora Neale Hurston of Florida; visual artists Aaron Douglas of Kansas and William H. Johnson of South Carolina; and poet Countee Cullen of Baltimore. Poet Paul Laurence Dunbar of Ohio and critic-chronicler Alain Locke of Philadelphia were just about the only two pure Yankees in the lot. The South's loss, once again, was the North's gain. Altogether, the creative output from Harlem in the middle years of the twenties included more than forty major works of fiction, poetry, and drama, and numerous other artistic creations.

By 1928, friction within this "New Negro" movement and economic hard times everywhere began to drain off the energy and talent of the renaissance, and Harlem slowly lost its luster as a fountain of creativity. Charles S. Johnson, still only in his mid-thirties, left for an academic career at Fisk University, and within a few years he had lured James Weldon Johnson there too, along with Aaron Douglas and Arna Bontemps and, briefly, Langston Hughes and Sterling Brown. Some, like Du Bois and White, stayed in New York, but most of the others scattered across the country or went to Europe.

Still others were gaining recognition in what might be called the music division of the renaissance: classical-concert singers Roland Hayes of Georgia and Paul Robeson of New Jersey, jazz genius Duke Ellington of Washington, D.C., blues musicians W. C. Handy and Bessie Smith up from Tennessee, and the forerunners of all these, King Oliver and Jelly Roll Morton and a whole passel of New Orleans jazz musicians—the heralds of Louis Armstrong—who moved upriver to St. Louis and Chicago and then to points east, Harlem being the eventual rainbow's end. But all of this creative energy was finally overwhelmed and tossed to the winds by much more powerful forces: the dispiriting grip of the Great Depression and the obliterating dominance of white supremacy.

The Caucasian literary renaissance in the South was more diffuse and thus harder to describe or assess. It had to count among its losses some Southern expatriates, notably Thomas Wolfe of North Carolina, whose *Look Homeward, Angel* was a major American novel of 1929, and Georgia native Erskine Caldwell, who would create a sensation with two "poor white trash" Southern novels, *Tobacco Road* and *God's Little Acre*, in the early 1930s. Mostly, though, the whites stayed at home—James Branch Cabell and Ellen Glasgow in Virginia, DuBose Heyward and Julia Peterkin in South Carolina, T. S. Stribling in Tennessee, Elizabeth Madox Roberts in Kentucky, Paul Green in North Carolina. Mississippian William Faulkner enjoyed an early stretch of bohemian camaraderie in New Orleans with fellow Southerners Hamilton Basso, Lyle Saxon, Roark Bradford, and David L. Cohn; with them, too, was a Northern expatriate, Sherwood Anderson of Ohio, who would soon move to the mountains of southwest Virginia and spend the rest of his life there. Faulkner, returning to his native Oxford, came out with two novels in 1929 (*Sartoris* and *The Sound and the Fury*) and another (*As I Lay Dying*) in 1930.

From these writers and others active in the South in the 1920s came some justly famous books and some Pulitzer Prize winners (not necessarily one and the same), and also several literary journals: *Sewanee Review* and *South Atlantic Quarterly*, both well established by then, and such newly launched publications as the *Virginia Quarterly Review*, the *Reviewer*, the *Double Dealer*, and the *Southwest Review* in Dallas. In this new wave of writing and criticism there was a clear break with the romantic past; although Margaret Mitchell's *Gone With the Wind* was yet to come, most of the Southern writers of the 1920s were more interested in realism and in contemporary themes than in the sweet magnolia moonbeam mythology of gallant colonels, delicate but headstrong ladies, and happy, obedient darkies. Several of the renaissance writers were particularly interested in probing beyond the social barriers of race and class. Heyward's novel *Porgy*, Peterkin's *Scarlet Sister Mary*, Stribling's *Birthright*, and Green's plays (*In Abraham's Bosom* and others) all reflected this shift. Gothic realism marked Faulkner's earliest novels, which dealt mainly with rural Mississippi whites.

Two other currents of intellectual stimulation in the twenties that attracted broad public notice were especially important to the South, and their effect was long-lasting. One was generated by the H. L. Mencken school of iconoclasts and debunkers emanating from Baltimore. The other was a running battle between social scientists at the University of North Carolina in Chapel Hill—the so-called Regionalists—and a band of poets and critics in and around Vanderbilt University in Nashville who called themselves first the Fugitives and then the Agrarians.

As a second-generation German-American who spent his entire life in Baltimore, a tightly segregated border-South city below the Mason-Dixon line, Henry Louis Mencken could and often did lay legitimate claim to both Southern roots and Northern sensibilities. Notwithstanding his common-folk immigrant heritage and his polytech education, he was heart and soul an intellectual, an elitist, an aristocrat, a brilliantly bombastic and slashing social critic whose printed assaults struck their intended targets with the indiscriminate force of a Gatling gun.

Before he was thirty, Mencken was an established and respected writer for the Baltimore *Evening Sun,* and from that base (which he would maintain for fifty years), he gained further influence beginning in 1914 as the guiding spirit and leading editor of two national magazines, *Smart Set* and *American Mercury.* Other newspapers and magazines also loved his pugnacious style and sought his byline avidly, so that by 1920 the prolific "sage of Baltimore," a wartish, cigar-chewing character with the vocabulary of a Harvard-educated street fighter, was one of the best-known journalists in America, revered by some and reviled by others, but read by almost all.

In 1917, Mencken had written a critical essay for a New York paper on the emptiness of the Southern cultural landscape. Three years later he expanded the piece substantially and included it in the second volume of what he proudly called *Prejudices,* his collected journalistic output. His essay "The Sahara of the Bozart" (a play on the French *beaux arts* of high culture) was a frontal attack on the South, which, in Mencken's acerbic view, had become "almost as sterile, artistically, intellectually, culturally, as the Sahara Desert." With ruthless and derisive glee, he stained the region with a poison pen as deadly as Sherman's sword, citing real or invented examples of social-cultural-political degradation. Along the way, he made clear his utter disdain for small-*d* democracy, large-*P* Prohibition, the Ku Klux Klan, Methodists (by which he meant practically all religious faiths), Anglo-Saxons, romantic writers of the old school, and pretense in any form. Practically no one, white or black, Southerner or Yankee, Gentile or Hebrew, escaped his wrath unless he or she had demonstrated creative ability.

A great aristocratic culture of superior men had once ruled the Old South, Mencken declared, but the region had since been "drained of all its best blood" by hordes of "poor white trash" driven by phony Puritanism, political demagoguery, and ignorant hostility toward the arts and letters.

His relentless diatribe went on for pages; in its wake, the meager and fragile cultural institutions of the defenseless South lay in ruins.

Though he had been writing critically about Southern literature and culture for well over a decade, Mencken was hardly prepared for the double-barreled reaction that followed his "Sahara" indictment. There was a more or less predictable scream of outrage at first from various aggrieved parties—but then, from all over the South, whispers of acknowledgment and affirmation and even appreciation began to be heard. He was taken aback, rendered almost speechless—but only momentarily. Soon Mencken was saying to the scholars, writers, and others who had found bracing truths in his broad-brush screed that they must become the critics of their own society, for that was the primary role and calling of every serious literary artist. To that end, he helped to open the pages of his magazines and of several influential newspapers to a far-flung regiment of Southern writers who dared to take his advice, and all through the 1920s these grateful disciples of the Baltimore bomber slowly raised their voices.

The excessive and outrageous richness of Mencken's language was so mesmerizing that neither his detractors nor his defenders tended to get beyond his attack and into a consideration of remedies. Style simply overwhelmed substance. So much *was* wrong with the South, and so much of it had been ignored for so long, that a cataloging of the sins, whether overstated or not, was bound to get attention. Spelled out with Mencken's gift for invective, the catalog drove his enemies into almost incoherent rage and dazzled his liberated allies into uncritical obedience.

It was this second group—the prisoners he freed—that was so surprising and so remarkable. In one way or another, to one degree or another, for a short while or for the rest of their lives, dozens of Southern writers, including some who went on to distinguished careers, got a tremendous psychological and artistic boost from H. L. Mencken. This is just a partial list: novelists James Branch Cabell, Ellen Glasgow, Thomas Wolfe, Julia Peterkin, DuBose Heyward, Frances Newman, and Walter White; poets Langston Hughes, James Weldon Johnson, and Countee Cullen; critics Hunter Stagg, Addison Hibbard, John McClure, and Nell Battle Lewis; playwright Paul Green; scholars Archibald Henderson, William L. Poteat, and Howard W. Odum; journalists Joseph Wood Krutch, W. J. Cash, Julian Harris, Julia Collier Harris, Grover C. Hall, Gerald W. Johnson, Virginius Dabney, George Fort Milton, John Temple Graves, and Louis I. Jaffé.

Mencken gave encouragement and aid to the little magazines, too—especially the *Reviewer* in Richmond and the *Double Dealer* in New Orleans. Even many writers who had no direct contact with him were inspired by the potency of his pen. Ralph McGill, a football player and

English major at Vanderbilt in 1921, spoke of him reverently as "our knight in shining armor." In Memphis in 1926, eighteen-year-old Richard Wright, a refugee from rural Mississippi, read a thundering denunciation of Mencken in the local paper and decided that he had to know what this white man had said to cause such an outburst of rage. Using a library card he had borrowed from a sympathetic white man where he worked, Wright went to the segregated public library with a note that said, "Dear Madam: Will you please let this nigger boy have some books by H. L. Mencken?" Thinking Wright was a messenger for the white patron, the librarian gave him a volume of *Prejudices*—and thus began the future novelist's education in the use of words as weapons of liberation.

The curious little cluster of faculty members, students, and townsmen around Vanderbilt who kept up a running literary discussion as self-styled Fugitives between 1915 and 1925, and who published a poetry journal, the *Fugitive,* in the latter years of that period, were certainly aware of Mencken, and he of them. English teachers John Crowe Ransom and Donald Davidson were the instigators of the Fugitive group, and two of their rising young compatriots were students Allen Tate and Robert Penn Warren. They all agreed with Mencken that orthodox Old South romanticism was a literary dead letter—but beyond that, there was almost nothing to draw the two camps together.

Mencken was intent on recruiting activist prose critics to deliver a self-conscious new literary style to the South; the Fugitives were not activists, not prose writers, and not even all that interested in the South. What they cared about was the craft of poetry and the intellectual stimulation they derived from writing it and discussing it. Tate admired Mencken, corresponded with him, and submitted poems to *Smart Set* and *American Mercury* (none were accepted); Davidson also sought to write for the magazines, but no warmth developed between him and the Baltimore iconoclast. No doubt Mencken perceived that he would find no sycophants in this den of bards, and no renegade South-bashers; for their part, the Nashvillians saw that Mencken knew little and cared less about poetry. They must have winced at his crude and incendiary manner, and felt a twinge of jealousy at its effectiveness. In any case, their contact remained formal—and turned downright hostile after a Mencken foray into the backwoods of Tennessee in 1925.

The scene was different at the University of North Carolina in Chapel Hill. There, something close to a new school of social criticism blossomed in response to the Mencken bombardment. Archibald Henderson, biographer of George Bernard Shaw, was among the first Southerners to praise

"The Sahara of the Bozart." Addison Hibbard, author of a widely distributed column on books, called "Literary Lantern," was another early and enthusiastic Mencken adherent. Other Chapel Hill scholars, including historians Fletcher M. Green and Frank Porter Graham, looked with quiet favor on the dust stirred up by the wind out of Baltimore. Mutual admiration had long bound Mencken and UNC playwright Paul Green, and those ties grew stronger in 1924 when the *Reviewer* moved from Richmond to Chapel Hill and Green became its editor. In that same year, Gerald W. Johnson of the Greensboro *Daily News*, a devoted Menckenite who mimicked the master's acerbic style, moved over to Chapel Hill to teach journalism and work on a fledgling journal called *Social Forces*. And, probably most important of all, the founder and editor of that journal, sociologist Howard W. Odum, overcame some initial hesitancy to form a close professional and personal bond with Mencken.

Odum, a native Georgian with two doctoral degrees from the North and ten years of experience in research, teaching, and administration, was called to Chapel Hill in 1920 to establish the social sciences in the UNC curriculum, and in short order he started the Department of Sociology, the School of Public Welfare, the Institute for Research in Social Science, and *Social Forces*, the quarterly journal. Those entities also generated a major portion of the manuscripts that found their way into print at the University of North Carolina Press and helped that academic publishing enterprise, the South's first of any consequence, make an early and influential name for itself. For reasons that never were entirely clear, the university had moved to the forefront of Southern higher education early in the twentieth century under the leadership of Harry Woodburn Chase, and during Frank Porter Graham's tenure as president from 1930 to 1949 it flowed like a fountain of progressive teaching, research, and public service—unquestionably the region's leading academic institution, and one of the nation's best as well.

Howard Odum's contribution to UNC's lofty reputation was substantial. His roots in the rural South and his scholarly training combined to give him an authoritative perspective on social and cultural issues that tended to substantiate and legitimize the deficiencies cited in Mencken's catalog of horrors. Odum neither looked nor acted the part of a bullying agitator; in fact, he disliked Mencken's abrasiveness and gently chided him for ascribing broadly to poor people the blame for what political demagogues and assorted other reactionaries had done to the region. But if Mencken was crudely indiscriminate in his snide salvos, he was at least firing in the right direction, and Odum was impressed when the shots fell with such telling effect.

Mencken had great respect for science and scholarship, neither of which were part of his own experience, and he deferred to those qualities in Odum. The two men settled into a complementary relationship that made a one-two punch of activist bombast and scholarly criticism, and Gerald Johnson, a marksman skilled at shooting both from the hip and from the shoulder, was their connecting link. (In 1926, Johnson left Odum's shop to join Mencken at the *Sun*, and remained there for nearly twenty years.) Odum also aspired to be a novelist, and in the late 1920s he penned a trilogy of folk chronicles built around a road-wise black Ulysses named John Wesley "Left Wing" Gordon. Mencken had high praise for the work.

The sheer volume of Odum's written contribution to scholarship and literature—like that of Mencken's to journalism—was impressively vast. Its quality may have been overrated, if the tendency of it to fade with time is any indication, but the quiet and cautious scholar had other strengths that earned him a lasting reputation. One was his ability to attract outstanding colleagues to his faculty, people like Rupert B. Vance and Guy B. Johnson; another was his influence on a long line of graduate students, from Arthur F. Raper in the 1920s to John E. Ivey in the 1940s. Considering all the people he influenced through his teaching, writing, and research, Howard W. Odum was one of the pivotal figures of the twentieth-century South—and in that respect, once again, he and H. L. Mencken stood together in very select company.

They also stood side by side physically once in a while—as, for example, in the summer of 1925, when they both went to the east Tennessee town of Dayton for the sensationally publicized trial of John T. Scopes, a high-school science teacher accused of violating the state's law against teaching the theory of evolution. The famed attorney Clarence Darrow and a team of Yankee lawyers defended Scopes, and thrice-failed Democratic presidential candidate William Jennings Bryan headed the prosecution. Odum was there as an observer, and saw in the event a tragedy for all concerned; Mencken, covering it for his paper, ridiculed it as a comic spectacle, a "Monkey Trial" that made monkeys and boobs of the people of Tennessee and the South.

Across the mountains in Nashville, the remnant of Vanderbilt Fugitives—particularly Donald Davidson and John Crowe Ransom—at first looked away in detached indifference and then in embarrassment from the courtroom antics of the attorneys, the spectators, and the grandstanding H. L. Mencken, who slandered the state and the South as "the bunghole of the United States" and "a Holy Land for imbeciles," and damned its people as "gaping primates" and "yokels of the hills" and "fundamentalist bigots." As time went by, the Nashvillians felt their anger rising in reaction to the smug self-righteousness of all outside critics. Finally they decided to strike back.

5. Eve of the New Deal

The Fugitives had declared themselves to be in flight from "the high-caste Brahmins of the Old South," from sentimentality and self-delusion, from the substance as well as the form of poetry and fiction as it was written and revered in the nineteenth-century South. In their intensely cerebral pursuits, they were thus a part of the modernist breeze that wafted ever so gently through the region in the early 1920s. If any single individual could be said to have started that wind, it would have to be H. L. Mencken, with Howard Odum joining in and the black and white Southern expatriates in New York adding something from afar. (To keep all of this in perspective, remember that the "literary talk" of writers was essentially an intellectual exercise touching only a relative handful of participants and a larger but still elite and limited audience; meanwhile, the political and economic forces that drove life in the South and the nation continued apace, finding nothing compelling in the debate.)

But Mencken's trashing of the Southern icons, highlighted by his Monkey Trial dispatches, and his successful enlistment of so many native Southern social critics had direct consequences in Nashville. Building on an impulse that predated the Scopes trial and reverberated far beyond Baltimore and Chapel Hill, the veteran Fugitives still at Vanderbilt, together with Allen Tate, who had moved to New York, began in the months and years after Scopes to articulate a defensive Southern self-consciousness that culminated in 1930 with a new fellowship of true believers—the Agrarians—and a book of essays defiantly called *I'll Take My Stand: The South and the Agrarian Tradition.*

It was, in the most profound sense, a reactionary document, a lashing out at foreign forces (industrialization, communism, the North) and a defense of hoary Southern virtues, real and imagined. The discovery of those virtues had come late to most of the contributors to the manifesto—in fact, none of them were on record in, say, 1920 as ardent devotees of Confederate or antebellum sentiment—but latter-day conversion seemed only to heighten their devotion. The twelve men whose essays made up the book were actually quite different from one another in temperament and philosophy, and their essays reflected those differences to some extent. But the title (a line from the Confederate anthem "Dixie"), the introductory statement of principles (written mainly by John Ransom), and the polemical tone of the book itself were enough to assure that it and the authors would be heard as one loud voice of defiance.

The intellectual energy to produce the manifesto came primarily from Ransom, Davidson, and Tate, who had some significant differences among themselves but a galvanizing desire to start a movement of rebellion against the Menckenesque literary current they saw racing across the country. These three recruited the other nine (they were turned down by several more) and tried with only limited success to mold them into a cell from which a body of adherents could grow. The book's introduction described the Agrarians as "Southerners well acquainted with one another" (hardly the case, since some of them had never met) and declared that "all tend to support a Southern way of life against what may be called the American or prevailing way." That distinction could best be characterized, the statement said, with the phrase "Agrarian *versus* Industrial."

Industrialism was the paper tiger that all the writers were exhorted to confront with whip and chair, and most of them dutifully did so, calling up criticisms from as far back as the Iron Age. The Agrarian alternative was also an idea of convenience more than of conviction, for this was not a book by farmers about farming. By indirection and by determined avoidance of an overtly reactionary motive, the organizers of the Agrarian rebellion thus challenged an enemy they couldn't defeat with an ideal they couldn't defend, and the result was as predictable and decisive as it had been when their spiritual forebears first tried it in the 1860s.

Contradictions and gaping inconsistencies abounded throughout. The twelve writers (all but two of whom had ties to Vanderbilt, either as former students or as faculty members) were products of the rural South, with only one marginal exception in the case of John Gould Fletcher, born in the small city of Little Rock, Arkansas, in 1886. But none of them (again, with the possible exception of Andrew Lytle) could claim farming as a livelihood, then or previously—and some, like Tate, knew absolutely nothing about the soil. Lytle's contribution was the only chapter specifically on agriculture, and it was a soft-handed scholar's sweeping diatribe against paved roads, ledger books, radios, store-bought clothes, motorized machinery (which he crudely branded "the nigger in the woodpile"), and sundry other manifestations of modernism. Progressive farming, he concluded, "is the biggest hoax that has ever been foisted upon a people."

Fletcher, a wealthy product of private schools who had spent most of his adult years in England, wrote the chapter on education, and it turned out to be a lament for the old private academies of classical instruction for the rich. He launched a fusillade of abuse against public education, calling it "a disaster of the first magnitude." If it cannot be destroyed, he declared, it should be reserved for the intellectual elite, with perhaps a little manual instruction made available to the lower classes. "It is simply a waste of money and effort to send . . . an unspoiled country boy or girl" or "the negro" to high school or college, said Fletcher. "The inferior, whether in life or in education, should exist only for the sake of the superior."

Robert Penn Warren's essay was the only one to address race as a dimension of Southern life; in it, he invoked Booker T. Washington in calling for agricultural and vocational training for blacks, equal justice before the law, and a modicum of fairness within the prevailing system of segregation. (Davidson found the piece to be offensively progressive and wanted to leave it out of the book, but Tate, who was Warren's close friend, prevailed in opposing the rejection.) H. C. Nixon, a political scientist at Tulane University, approached the question of industry versus agriculture from an economic perspective, and concluded that the South must limit industrial expansion—not eliminate it—and take pains to preserve and protect its farmers from industrial exploitation. (This essay, too, was adjudged weak and deviant by Davidson.)

Others, including Stark Young (the eldest of the group, at forty-nine), John Donald Wade, and Frank L. Owsley, drew from their understanding of the Southern past an implied or expressed vision of the future that reflected their longing for a culture of privilege such as the white landed gentry once enjoyed. John Crowe Ransom took a similar tack, praising what he called the "squirearchy" and a life of leisurely pursuits built upon a strong agricultural system, with industry decidedly secondary. Allen Tate's contribution was a complex treatise on Southern religion that seemed curiously unfocused and shed no light on the then-current debates over fundamentalism and the social gospel movement.

Finally, there was Donald Davidson. As he saw it, the rich folk art of the Old South—storytelling, humor, oratory, crafts, writing—was in grave danger of succumbing to the impersonal and smothering threat of industrialism. The new wave of socially conscious writers had sold out to the Yankee dollar, he charged; DuBose Heyward and Paul Green were latter-day abolitionists, and T. S. Stribling was trying to be another Harriet Beecher Stowe or Clarence Darrow, and James Branch Cabell and Ellen Glasgow were similarly tainted. Their duty, Davidson clearly felt, was to forswear these sins and become once again Southern and provincial—and make "a last stand in America against the industrial devourer." Davidson made no mention of Mencken or Odum, but their shadows fell oppressively over him as he wrote.

I'll Take My Stand was professed by its planners to be a spirited defense of yeoman farmers and other salt-of-the-earth white folks—their work, their play, their religion, their art. Mencken had assailed these very people unmercifully, and unfairly; they certainly deserved better. But what they got from the Agrarians was a paean to farm life that celebrated the plantation squirearchy and glossed over contemporary realities of tenant farming and sharecropping and peonage. The book was a pedantic outpouring of philosophical ideas from an intellectual elite, rather than anything that even hinted at practical or political solutions to the plight of the agrarian South. These nonfarming dilettantes had almost nothing to say to the yeoman farmers who struggled to survive on Southern soil. Even in their condemnation of industrialism the Agrarians were sadly off target, seeing far more danger in the evils of communism, which had no economic power at all in the region, than in capitalism, which ran the textile mills and turpentine camps and coal mines with such utter disdain for their laborers.

The Agrarians claimed to be standing up for the South against the hordes of invaders from beyond; in truth, they were a tiny clutch of middle- and upper-class white males from the mid-South who spoke, by and large, for themselves—and even there encountered points of serious disagreement. Finally, as writers, they utterly failed to define or demonstrate what they had to offer to the South, agrarian and industrial, that was better than, or even different from, the prescriptions of writers in the Old South, the New South, or the Mencken-Odum schools of contemporary Southern social criticism.

From faraway Baltimore, H. L. Mencken single-handedly commanded the attention of writers in every corner of the South, and others who had left the region in despair. He somehow found Olive Tilford Dargan (a.k.a. Fielding Burke) in the mountains of Appalachia, and Charles J. Finger in the Ozarks, and struggling advocates of social change such as Will Alexander in Atlanta, and expatriates black and white, from James Weldon Johnson to Thomas Wolfe, and scores of academicians and journalists all the way to Texas.

Mencken turned fifty at about the time the Agrarians were publishing their manifesto in 1930, and by then his muckraking attacks on the South had almost run their course. That same year he married Sara Haardt of Montgomery, Alabama, a former coed at Goucher College in Baltimore and a liberated Southern belle whose stories he had published in the *American Mercury*. The old curmudgeon's views on the South seemed to soften after that—or perhaps it was just that he lost interest in the subject.

Mencken had a limited and distorted view of Southern history and almost nothing in the way of a blueprint for social change, but his paint-peeling style of invective and the dreadful conditions that undeniably existed in the region were an irresistible combination. Howard Odum had a much more realistic historical view of the South and a better vision of remedies too. Those assets did much to overcome the pedestrian quality of his writing and his deep dislike of activism and conflict; as different as Odum was from Mencken, he too built a following that dwarfed that of the Agrarians.

I'll Take My Stand was widely reviewed in the South and beyond, and debates between one or more Agrarians and their critics took place before large audiences in Richmond, New Orleans, and elsewhere in the months after publication. But if the debates were spirited and close, the reviews were overwhelmingly critical, and the book sold barely more than two thousand copies before it went out of print in 1941, eleven years after it first appeared. Not until it was reissued more than twenty years later (by which time several of the contributors had gained fame and there was a general revival of interest in Southern letters) did the book enjoy a measure of success.

The Southern response to the Agrarian manifesto strongly suggests that people in the region who read books and thought about social issues at the beginning of the 1930s were generally more progressive in their outlook than the authors of the reactionary collection. An incident involving Allen Tate underscores that conclusion.

Twenty-seven-year-old Thomas D. Mabry of Clarksville, Tennessee (where Tate was living with his wife, Caroline Gordon), enrolled in 1931 at Vanderbilt for a master's degree in English. His interest in race relations led him to make the acquaintance of James Weldon Johnson, who had just joined the English department at nearby Fisk University, and Langston Hughes, who was temporarily teaching there. Hoping to build some informal ties between black and white writers in Nashville, Mabry decided to ask the Fisk luminaries and some of the Agrarians to a social function at his home; among those he invited were Tate, Johnson, Hughes, and Donald Davidson.

Johnson attended, and he and Mabry subsequently formed a strong friendship. Hughes and Davidson apparently weren't there. As for Tate, he not only spurned the invitation; he took offense at it, and used his response to lecture Mabry on racial etiquette, putting forth his theory that "there should be no social intercourse between the races unless we are willing for that to lead to marriage." The rules of Southern civilization didn't permit writers of the white and black races to meet socially, he said; maybe in New York or London or Paris, but not here—and furthermore, he added, he wouldn't lift a finger to break the taboo, for that was "probably beyond my powers and . . . certainly outside my inclinations."

Mabry fired back a letter expressing contempt for Tate's "vacuous and insulting essay on racial relations." He accused him of "moral lassitude" and "intellectual dishonesty," as well as "the sophistry so common among nigger-baiters." Unfazed, Tate wrote back again, admitting his "moral lassitude" and acknowledging that Johnson and Hughes were "my intellectual equals." But the thirty-one-year-old poet concluded that his refusal to meet with them was rooted in a desire not to see them "insulted or humiliated" by whites.

Aside from such personal exchanges as this, it was rare for the literary, academic, artistic, and journalistic principals in the Southern renaissance of the twenties and thirties to engage in candid discourse on the thorny issue of race. They had little or nothing to say about white supremacy, the once and future problem that burrowed like a mole into the subconscious soul of the South. For all their differences, neither Mencken nor Odum nor the Agrarians came close to addressing the problems of segregation and discrimination and inequality. At best, they were paternalistic and patronizing; at worst, they were deeply racist believers in the innate superiority of Caucasians—and no matter where they fell on that spectrum, they rationalized their views and avoided facing the issue that could not be wished away.

Mencken could cheerfully and honestly encourage—and publish—black writers from Harlem, but have no interest whatever in the conditions of the black masses, whether they were in the cotton fields of Alabama or the slums of Baltimore. The University of North Carolina liberals were proud to feature James Weldon Johnson in a week-long forum of lectures and seminars on "Negro life" in 1927, and Langston Hughes in a public reading of his poetry in 1931, but they couldn't figure out how to hire a black faculty member or admit a black graduate student for another twenty years. Some of the Agrarians, notably Robert Penn Warren and H. C. Nixon and even Allen Tate, came in time to a more equable view of race in America, but most of the others—Donald Davidson foremost among them—remained defiantly unreconstructed rebels to the bitter end.

By the time the Agrarians took their stand against industrialism, the South was already flattened; it had been the first to fall under the lumbering steamroller of the depression. Herbert Hoover, the third straight Republican in the White House, seemed helpless and immobilized against the economic forces that were pulling the country down. Only deepest Dixie—Mississippi, Alabama, Arkansas, Georgia, Louisiana, and South Carolina—had voted against him, and even they were torn. All of the other Southern and border states, in the first major desertion from the Democratic Party in fifty years, had chosen Hoover, whom they considered "damp," over Al Smith, who was not only openly "wet" but a Yankee and a Catholic to boot. Hoover, also a Yankee, rewarded the Dixie renegades by deferring to their racial views (when he didn't share them outright); beyond that, he had precious little to offer them.

Industrialism did figure significantly in the problems the South faced in the 1920s and beyond, of course, and a number of issues the Agrarians alluded to—materialism, impersonality, environmental damage—eventually became vital and pressing concerns. But by and large, the economic and social issues of paramount importance to the South and the nation in the late twenties and early thirties concerned matters the Agrarians virtually ignored: labor-management relations, race relations, laissez-faire capitalism, exploitation of natural and human resources.

Some industrial giants had invaded the Southern states much earlier, in response to the New South boosterism of Henry Grady and others in the late nineteenth century. For the most part, they were extractive and exploitative—and worse, in a land full of hungry people, they produced little or nothing edible, not to say nourishing. They removed the iron ore and coal and timber, hauling it away on their railroads. They refined sugar in south Florida, made steel in Alabama and wood products in North Carolina, turned out textiles and tobacco products in the Piedmont region that stretched from Virginia to Alabama; later they struck oil and natural gas in Louisiana and Texas.

In all of those industrial ventures, it would be hard to point to a single community where the lives of ordinary people were measurably improved by the industry's presence. These enterprises did put a little money in some people's pockets, it's true, but in terms of upgrading health and housing and education, or raising the quality of social and cultural life, or reducing race and class divisions, they did almost nothing. Those were the failings the Agrarians should have zeroed in on, instead of simply decrying another Yankee invasion; after all, some of the industries were Southern in origin, and all of them required the active cooperation of the region's powerful leaders.

Tobacco was first among those industries, and the one most invigorated by Southern money. At the heart of it was the American Tobacco Company, an empire created by Washington Duke of North Carolina and his son, James Buchanan "Buck" Duke, in the decades after the Civil War. Their monopoly, enhanced by automatic cigarette-rolling machines (a Southern invention), was broken up by the U.S. Supreme Court in 1911, but the Dukes were hardly impoverished thereby. They had dominated not only the industry that manufactured tobacco products but also the network of farmers that supplied the raw materials; when their iron grip was broken, Buck Duke had enough resources left to build another fortune (in hydroelectric power development) and to create an endowment that transformed little Trinity College in Durham into Duke University.

By 1930 the factories that turned out packaged cigarettes and other tobacco products were just about the only industry in the South, and one of the few nationwide, that remained profitable. The product was virtually depression-proof: dirt-cheap (you could buy a pack of twenty smokes for a nickel or a dime) and habit-forming too. And still at the top of the industry pyramid was the American Tobacco Company. Its president by that time was George Washington Hill, Buck Duke's spiritual heir. He received well over a million dollars in salary and bonuses in 1930. Few if any of his factory workers—and probably none of the growers and harvesters of Southern tobacco—then earned as much as a thousand dollars a year.

The other major industry that stood figuratively on the edge of the growing fields was textiles. Cotton (and later synthetic fibers) made mill owners in the South as profit-hungry and as exploitative of labor as their New England predecessors were before the mills moved south, and when times got tough, a familiar and predictable pattern of conflict developed between management and workers. It had happened before, in the South and elsewhere, but virtually all efforts to establish collective bargaining for Southern workers had ultimately failed. Desperate conditions in the depression gave birth to another wave of attempts.

The first major clash occurred in some German-owned rayon mills at Elizabethton, Tennessee, in March 1929, when a group of women workers who were making about nine dollars a week decided to strike for higher pay. The plants were closed, and violence hovered over the dispute. The strikers had the support of the American Federation of Labor; the plant owners got the governor of Tennessee to send in a force of state militiamen—at company expense—to maintain order. In time, the mill owners succeeded in dividing the workers and breaking the strike.

Across the mountains in Gastonia, North Carolina, meanwhile, strikers shut down the Loray Mill, the largest of many plants in the area and thus the trendsetter on wages, working hours, and other labor issues. Though it was owned by a Rhode Island corporation, Loray had been founded in 1900 with local capital, and it maintained a position of paternalistic dominance in the community. Massive layoffs and wage cuts precipitated the strike, and in the months that followed, the management-labor dispute grew into a struggle that involved, among others, the state militia, the entire textile industry, the Communist-backed National Textile Workers Union, several religious denominations, outside pressure groups supporting both sides, and a corps of newspaper reporters from North Carolina, the South, and the rest of the country. The owners broke the strike, but not before two people died—Gastonia's police chief, Orville Aderholt, and a martyred worker, Ella May Wiggins. (Five years later, a general strike in the textile industry would come to a similarly tragic and fruitless conclusion.)

Liston Pope, a North Carolina mill owner's son and Duke University graduate who later became dean of the Yale University Divinity School, went to Gastonia a decade after the strike to gather material for what turned out to be a classic of social history, *Millhands and Preachers*. In it he described a conflict reminiscent of eighteenth-century Europe, with the captains of industry, supported by leaders of the churches and other local institutions, maintaining privilege in the depression at the expense of the millhands and laborers. It was, as Pope recognized, a class struggle among whites, since discrimination kept blacks out of all but a handful of the most menial jobs, but it cut to the heart of the South's economic crisis; a pervasive and crippling vestige of feudalism still characterized the region's economy.

Even as the strikes in Gastonia, Elizabethton, and other communities took place, voices in favor of better treatment of workers were raised in several quarters of the press, the church, the university, and industry itself. Howard Odum's *Social Forces* and the *Virginia Quarterly Review* were among these; so were such newspapers as the Macon *Telegraph* under Mark Ethridge, the Chattanooga *News* under George Fort Milton, Josephus Daniels's Raleigh *News & Observer*, the Montgomery *Advertiser* edited by Grover Hall, Sr., and the Norfolk *Virginian-Pilot* under Louis Jaffé. President William L. Poteat of Wake Forest College and M. Ashby Jones, a charter member of the Commission on Interracial Cooperation—both of them Baptist ministers—also took a progressive stance on the issue, as did textile manufacturer Donald Comer of Alabama and others. Frank Porter Graham got more than four hundred prominent North Carolinians to sign a forthright statement of support for new laws and policies to protect workers from exploitation and abuse.

In the coalfields of Appalachia, other laborers struggled for fair treatment. Even before 1920, the United Mine Workers of America had tried to organize workers in the Southern coalfields, but it was not until 1931 that the followers of John L. Lewis, in a pitched battle with coal company forces that included state and local police, won the right to collective bargaining in eastern Kentucky. At Evarts, in Harlan County, Communist organizers tried to squeeze between the UMWA and the company chiefs to win the loyalty of the miners, but they failed. Harry M. Caudill, an eloquent chronicler of Appalachia (and also a native and lifelong resident), described the Harlan County miners as "unswervingly patriotic"—but, he said, "the operators, their lawyers and a large segment of the press raised the hysterical cry that the workers were Communists whose demands were written for them in the Kremlin. To the everlasting shame of every Kentuckian, Governor Flem D. Sampson repeated this slanderous nonsense."

Among the people who came to Harlan County with the support and encouragement of the U.S. Communist Party were a group of writers called the National Committee for the Defense of Political Prisoners. The novelist Theodore Dreiser headed the group, which included Sherwood Anderson (then living in Virginia) but no others who could be even remotely identified as Southerners. So great was the number of American intellectuals professing a passion for communism and socialism at that time that it is impossible to say whether the writers—and specifically any Southern-born writers who identified with their cause—were in fact members of the Communist Party, which was then a legally constituted body. In any case, Caudill's conclusion rang true: The miners themselves were unswayed by either the coaxing of the Communists or the accusations of the coal operators.

The Socialist Party had been represented on the U.S. presidential election ballot since 1900 (though not always in the Southern states), and the Communists, under various banners, had been active politically in the country (but again, mainly in the North) since 1919. At about the time of the stock market crash in America, the international Communist Party was pursuing ways to exploit social and racial unrest in this country, and particularly in the South. Increasingly in the 1930s, conflicts between labor unions and company bosses, workers and the unemployed, blacks and whites, poor and affluent people—and between Socialists and Communists—spilled out into public view. Two of the most visible incidents— the case of the "Scottsboro boys" in Alabama and the trial of Angelo Herndon in Atlanta—brought the Communists squarely into the center of things. Like the coal and textile strikes before them and the Scopes trial before that, these were cases that broke out of regional isolation and onto a national stage—reinforcing, in the process, the South's unflattering image as a place of bigotry and intolerance.

The Scottsboro tragedy unfolded in March 1931 when two teenage white girls hoboing on a freight train in north Alabama told the police that they had been raped by several blacks. Nine young black males, age thirteen to twenty, soon were arrested as suspects and then charged with the crime. In the space of just fifteen days, the youths were indicted, tried, convicted, and sentenced (except for the youngest) to die in the electric chair. In the mob atmosphere that prevailed, the nine became pawns in a complex struggle between their defenders and attackers: on the one side, the NAACP, the Communist-supported International Labor Defense, and a variety of liberal and progressive groups and individuals, all of whom were convinced of the innocence of the defendants and determined to win their release; and on the other side, local and state prosecutors and various white supremacy groups, all of whom wanted the executions to be carried out. None of the youths were ever electrocuted, but it took until 1950 to win final release from prison for the last of them.

A year after the Scottsboro arrests, trouble caught up with Angelo Herndon, a nineteen-year-old black youth from Ohio. A member of the Communist Party, he was arrested in Atlanta in June 1932 and charged with insurrection for organizing an interracial protest demonstration by a group of unemployed people. Herndon was convicted and given a sentence of up to twenty years in prison. Again, diverse factions of defenders and detractors carried on a battle in the case (among the former: Benjamin J. Davis, Jr., a black Georgia Republican who subsequently became a Communist; Elbert P. Tuttle, a white Georgia Republican who later became a federal judge; and C. Vann Woodward, a young professor at Georgia Tech who went on to become the South's most prominent twentieth-century historian). Finally, in 1937, the Georgia law under which Herndon was convicted was declared unconstitutional by the U.S. Supreme Court, and he was freed.

In all of these cases and causes and clashes that rumbled like distant thunder through the South in the years after World War I—the intellectual conflicts, the strikes, the trials—the most notable new development was the emergence of a legitimate inside voice of dissent (albeit sometimes selective, faint, and ineffectual) against the political-economic-social status quo. H. L. Mencken and Howard Odum and their followers led the way, moving forward from the modest beginning of W. D. Weatherford and others before him. To theirs were added the voices of academicians, journalists, novelists, ministers, women, labor leaders, blacks in exile, and some regionally based black lawyers and educators.

Not only was it tolerable for people to show an interest in communism; it was also acceptable—even intellectually fashionable—for people to speak positively of themselves and others as liberals. (One of the most notable books of 1932 was Virginius Dabney's *Liberalism in the South*, published by the University of North Carolina Press.) In a multitude of ways, the new progressives were calling on their homeland to abandon the myths of the Old South, to surrender false pride and complacency, and to begin the task of self-renewal that could finally restore it to its rightful and equitable place in the nation.

It must be acknowledged that this dissenting expression was hardly more than a faint echo in the beleaguered South of the early 1930s. The sober reality was that political demagogues retained their power not in spite of the church and the press and the universities, but because of them; it was the folks in those institutions, after all, who made up a substantial part of the truncated electorate, and who were so instrumental in the shaping of public opinion. The mainstream churches leaned heavily in favor of Hoover and Prohibition and segregation, and so did most of the newspapers. The universities—North Carolina notwithstanding—were too much under the thumb of their political or religious guardians to stake out a position of their own. And as for the politicians themselves, they were conspicuously absent from the thin ranks of the critics and the reformers; in fact, when I try to think of senators or congressmen or governors of the period who were advocates of or spokesmen for or even followers of social reform, Hugo Black of Alabama is just about the only one who comes to mind.

Whether or not they acted consciously and deliberately, most white Southerners effectively sought to expel the black minority from every station of life except menial jobs in the fields and kitchens. The primary intent and consequence of segregation was to retain black manpower and womanpower for the hard and heavy work, the essential labor. In almost every other dimension of daily life, from neighborhoods to schools and from politics to history, African-Americans were slowly receding from view.

Black historians were too few in number and their audiences too small to have much impact. Carter Woodson, foremost among them, was a Virginian educated at Berea College in Kentucky (before it was segregated), at Chicago and Harvard, and at the Sorbonne. He wrote *The Negro in Our History* in 1922, and at about the same time founded the Association for the Study of Negro Life and History and the *Journal of Negro History*. Overshadowing his influence was that of the preeminent white historian, Georgia-born Ulrich B. Phillips. Though he received his doctorate from Columbia University and enjoyed a long tenure at universities in the North, he was one of the last of the Old South mythologists, a benevolent paternalist whose view of blacks as an inferior race was apparently as acceptable at Wisconsin and Michigan and Yale as it would have been at any university in Georgia or Mississippi. In an essay summing up his understanding of the central theme of Southern history in 1928, Phillips declared that one thing above all else permanently united and bonded white Southerners of every class and station: a deeply rooted conviction that the region would always be "a white man's country."

Without a doubt, Phillips spoke for the vast majority of the white South. Two and a half centuries of slavery and seventy years of segregation, broken only briefly and ineffectively by Emancipation and Reconstruction, had conditioned them to believe that the ideals and principles spelled out in the Declaration of Independence, the Constitution, and the Bill of Rights were by some mysterious interpretive twist meant to apply only to them, the white majority. But language is an independent force, having within itself the power to instruct and inspire and exhort. The African people who endured slavery, who took hope from Emancipation and Reconstruction, who resisted segregation, found in the language of America's cherished documents some immortal words that energized them and gave them the will to fight on: *liberty . . . freedom . . . union . . . justice . . . equality.* During and after the time of slavery, there were blacks who attached the aspirations of their race to these exalted ideals.

In the twentieth century, the words of those visionary African-Americans reached beyond the grave to inspire new generations. W. E. B. Du Bois, James Weldon Johnson, and a host of others carried the light from the old century to the new, and lit the way for the ones who would come later, still looking for the South and the nation to fulfill the promises of American life. Some few would pursue total assimilation into the dominant white culture of America; others, celebrating their Africanness, would follow a separatist route based on an exclusive black heritage and culture; and all the rest, like every other element in the polyglot culture that has always defined and described the people of the United States, would eventually insist upon political, civil, and social equality in every dimension of their lives. For blacks most especially, Du Bois defined the split identity in *The Souls of Black Folk* in 1903. "Twoness," he called it—the African and the American in one body, inseparable, the one incomplete without the other.

Not every white Southerner was comfortable with U. B. Phillips's vision of the region. The social critics inspired by Mencken and Odum took mild or extreme exception to the various manifestations of status-quo conservatism that retarded the region and kept it in a perpetual state of dependence and poverty. But with only a few exceptions, the critics stopped short of any outward hint that the prevailing racial mores needed to be reexamined. The black prophets of a new social order spoke in the main from exile in New York and elsewhere, and soon they would embolden a few men and women in the black churches and schools of the South to stand and deliver a similar message of change. It was almost as difficult—though not as dangerous—for white Southerners to espouse radical notions about the human worth of the descendants of Africans who lived among them. The social and cultural proscriptions were as deep as they were broad, and for thirty years they had been reinforced by written laws affirmed all the way to the top of the federal government; it took a special kind of courage—or madness—to speak and act against such overwhelming force.

And yet, some did. Mildly radicalized by their religious and educational experiences, a handful of young people born within five years or so of the turn of the century stepped forward in the twenties to advocate a new course of action in the South, a way of living that would uplift the poor, unite the races, and bring peace and prosperity to the region, the nation, and the world. Coming as they did at the tail end of the social gospel movement, this activist remnant was a spontaneous and unexpected phenomenon, a delayed germination and sprouting of seeds sown years earlier.

Even in its most radical form in the North, the social gospel had paid scant attention to racial discrimination, and by the time the movement finally reached into the South, its advocates in the mainline churches seemed more concerned about the pros and cons of evolution theory and Prohibition repeal than they did about matters of color, caste, and class. But a few people, driven by an evangelical Protestant impulse to give missionary aid to the exotic poor—in the South no less than in, say, China—did begin to think and speak and write about racial matters before World War I. Through the YMCA and its counterpart, the Young Women's Christian Association, or in some cases through their denominations, such people as W. D. Weatherford, Will Alexander, Mabel Katherine Howell, and Sara Estelle Haskin took the first small steps. These four, coincidentally, were all Methodists, and their careers in religious work were either launched or boosted forward in Nashville in the beginning decades of the twentieth century. And, to take the coincidence of proximity one step further, there were in Nashville and elsewhere in Tennessee by the early 1930s no less than a dozen white social activists who turned out to be prophets of Southern social change—and at least half of them were contemporaries (though in no sense compatriots) of the reactionary Agrarians on the campus of Vanderbilt University.

The School of Religion at Vanderbilt had appointed to its faculty in 1928 a fifty-seven-year-old Disciples of Christ minister and social gospel reformer from Iowa named Alva W. Taylor. He had been a lecturer in the school's popular summer workshop for ministers of rural churches, and his skill at raising money (including a sizable sum from John D. Rockefeller, Jr.) had allowed the Vanderbilt chancellor, James H. Kirkland, to be persuaded that Taylor would make a fine addition to the permanent faculty. Kirkland found the Fugitives and Agrarians too unorthodox for his tastes, but he soon grew downright alarmed and alienated by Taylor, a gentle and mild-mannered social activist who saw the role of the church as a reconciling force serving, among others, those who occupied the bottom rungs of the economic ladder. It took the chancellor eight years to get rid

of the popular and respected professor, but before that, numerous of
Taylor's students went out into the South with an urgent sense of mission
to change the social order.

Four in particular, all of whom were in his classes in 1930, just as *I'll
Take My Stand* made its appearance, were destined to be key figures in
the coming battles for regional reform: Howard A. Kester, a Presbyterian
from Virginia, a YMCA stalwart with interracial interests, a budding Socialist, an organizer of left-wing activists, an investigator of lynchings for
Walter White of the NAACP; Ward Rodgers, a Texan come east by way of
Oklahoma, a Methodist, later to be a parish minister, an organizer of
tenant farmers, also a Socialist; Don West, a mountain boy from Georgia,
a radical young poet, a preacher in the fundamentalist tradition, a labor
activist, a cofounder of the Highlander Folk School, a man who would be
branded a Communist because of his perception of Jesus as a working-class
revolutionary; and Claude C. Williams, a Tennessee sharecropper's son, a
God-haunted teenage preacher in the Cumberland Presbyterian Church,
a World War I veteran, later a labor organizer, educator, and preacher in
Arkansas and Alabama and, like West, accused of being a member of the
Communist Party.

Other native or adopted Tennesseans were contemporaries and occasional allies of the Alva Taylor disciples. Three of them—Myles Horton,
James Dombrowski, and John B. Thompson—first met at Union Theological Seminary in New York, where they were immersed in Christian Socialism by two noted theologians, Harry F. Ward and Reinhold Niebuhr.
Horton, a son of west Tennessee tenant farmers, had been guided to
Union by a Congregationalist minister named Abram Nightingale; he returned to Tennessee and teamed up with Don West to establish the
Highlander Folk School, an unorthodox center for adult education, soon
after Will Alexander brought the two young men together. Thompson,
another Tennessean and a Presbyterian, and Dombrowski, a Methodist
from Tampa, Florida, followed Horton to Highlander.

To this list could be added H. L. Mitchell, a radicalized west Tennessee
poor white farmer's son, who went from high school almost directly into a
lifetime of organizing work with tenant farmers; and three remarkable
young women—Alice Harris, Constance Adams, and Joyce King—who
joined with the men they married (Howard Kester, Don West, and Claude
Williams, respectively) to form partnerships based on full equality more
than a generation before that principle took root in the South. (Zilphia
Mae Johnson was another, before and after she married Myles Horton in
1935.)

All of this social ferment in one state before the end of 1930 suggests the
probability, if not the certainty, of similar underground currents flowing

elsewhere in the South. But by their very nature, these were the dissenting voices of such a small minority that they could barely be heard in the
vast wilderness of social inertia. Most of the mainline Protestant churches
in the region (indeed, in the entire country) had been for Herbert Hoover
in 1928 when his opponent was a Catholic, and would be for him again in
opposing Franklin Roosevelt in 1932 (and for Roosevelt's next Republican
rival, Alf Landon, in 1936); many newspapers displayed the same loyalties, except for those dyed-in-the-wool partisans with their unshakable
devotion to the Democratic South and its segregationist convictions. Almost all of the universities were bastions of social rest, pillars of devotion
to the status quo, and such administrators and faculty members as dared
to contemplate a more active posture could look about them and see
enough casualties to make them think twice. Even the renowned Howard
Odum was so circumspect in his personal commitments that he studiously
avoided joining the Commission on Interracial Cooperation for eight years,
until his friend and admirer Will Alexander more or less shamed him
into it (ten years later, in 1937, Odum would become chairman of the
organization).

These were the institutions that gave the South its identity and its
stature, such as it was, in the pivotal election year of 1932—the church,
the press, the universities, and three more: the Democratic Party, the
planter class, and the barons of industry. Together they ruled a colony
shot through with contradictions—a land saddled with the burden of
military defeat, and choosing in spite of it to live with a self-delusive
myth of moral superiority; a land rich in nature's bounty, but living
hand-to-mouth with imported food, building materials, tools, and even
cotton clothing; a land so desperate to retain racial segregation and
white supremacy that it was willing to accept regional segregation and
inequality in the bargain.

And yet, miraculously, there were saving graces in the South and in its
people—strengths of family and community that manifested themselves in
manners and fellowship, in generational continuity and respect for history,
in richly original music and art, and in the indigenous gifts of language and
cookery; strengths of religion that went deeper into faith and belief and
devotion than the institutional church could fathom; strengths of nature
that returned with seasonal regularity to bless the people and their place.
These were not the exclusive property of the well-to-do—they belonged
to rich and poor, white and black, old and young.

A fiercely loyal attachment had grown up around this diverse place, this
vast kingdom between the mountains and the sea. It yielded a livelihood,

albeit sometimes grudgingly. It had God-power, it was holy—you put down seeds and things grew. It held memory, so much of it that many people could not leave, and many of those who did were forever seized by a compulsion to come back. The South was sorely troubled, but it was not without universal and abiding virtues—not in the long ago, or in the thirties, or later. What the region lacked most grievously was honest, dedicated leadership. Its long-suffering people certainly deserved far better than they got.

When it finally came Franklin Delano Roosevelt's turn to govern, he had a mandate to chart a new course of economic and psychological recovery for the nation, and the South got a sympathetic friend in court. He had spent enough time on his Georgia farm to gain a genuine liking for the people, and he saw how desperately they needed help. They had nothing to tax—not a pot to piss in or a window to throw it out of, as their earthy humor told it—but they were generous to a fault, bringing the patrician Mr. Roosevelt possums to eat and corn liquor to drink (he did both), and generally making him feel at home, and he was deeply touched by their kindness.

Earlier, before he was crippled with polio, he had served his federal apprenticeship as an assistant secretary of the navy in the administration of Woodrow Wilson. His boss there was Josephus Daniels, who owned the Raleigh *News & Observer*, and Roosevelt learned Southern ways from him no less than from the likes of Ben Tillman and James K. Vardaman and Tom Watson, all of whom held sway in the U.S. Senate. (I like to think that the future president may also have learned something about the South from my father's father, an obscure Tennessee lawyer who, for reasons that I have never understood, was plucked out of the Dickson County courthouse in 1913 and awarded a top legal post in the Navy Department. He kept the job for eight years, during which he and FDR were colleagues and close companions. I remember that one of my father's proud possessions, passed down to him in the family, was a framed photograph of the young Roosevelt, signed in 1918 to "my dear friend Judge Egerton, with sincere best wishes.")

If recovery had been all that the South and the nation needed in 1932, both they and the President might have succeeded spectacularly. But recovery was only part of what Roosevelt wanted, only the beginning. In the long view, he was most interested in bringing about basic reforms, and it was precisely this that the Southern oligarchy feared, for their feudal kingdoms were built upon constancy and control.

For decades after the Civil War, an unending public debate had held center stage in Dixie: Old South versus New South, agriculture versus industry, rural and small-town life versus city life, adversarial versus cooperative relationships with Yankees, the need for tradition versus the need for change. Sometimes it made good theater, but it was at bottom a bogus debate, a set of distinctions without real differences. Older, conservative white men of power and privilege controlled both sides of the argument, and their basic attitudes and beliefs were essentially the same on all the subjects that really mattered—the place of blacks, the status of women, the separate and limited powers of church and state. To a man, they were far more Democratic than democratic, and believed—like their conservative forebears—that the fewest possible voters should oversee the least possible government, serving the "best sort" of people first and dividing the rest among all the others. If that sounds more Republican than Democratic, remember that the two parties were not all that different philosophically before FDR came on the scene.

The great contribution of the New Deal to the cultural and political life of the South was that it turned a mock debate into a real one and offered a genuine alternative to the Old South/New South philosophy. The liberal agenda of Franklin Roosevelt and his administration called for a massive economic reformation to bring higher living standards to all; far-reaching new programs in support of labor, education, health, housing, and the general welfare; major reforms in agriculture and industry; and an opening of the democratic political process to virtually all adults as an alternative both to the oligarchic status quo and to the threat of state control under socialism or communism. Of necessity, these changes would bring about more federal government planning and regulation, more collectivism, more bureaucracy. It was not a perfect blueprint by any means, but it did bring hope to small farmers, wage earners, racial and ethnic minorities, and others in desperate straits. Eventually, inevitably, such transforming changes would challenge the continued existence of white supremacy and extreme socioeconomic class stratification. It was the realization of this prospect, more than anything else, that energized and mobilized a permanent resistance among Southerners in the President's own Democratic Party.

If Roosevelt could have accomplished his goals simply by carrying the people with him, he would have realized his highest ambition—but in order to remake the South, he had to have the cooperation of its despots. In his first administration he managed to keep most of them in camp, partly by observing an informal and unspoken rule of mutual consent that the laws and customs of white supremacy would not be challenged. As time passed, though, it became clear that neither the President nor the Southerners could hold that position indefinitely.

6. *The Fireman Cometh*

Franklin D. Roosevelt was elected four times to the presidency of the United States; had he lived, he would have served sixteen years in the White House. His New Deal for the American people was considerably shorter. It lasted no more than about six years, from the date of his first election in November 1932 to somewhere around the midterm congressional elections of November 1938. From that time forward, the reactionary opposition was powerful enough to stymie reform; in fact, had it not been for World War II, his enemies probably would have succeeded in dragging Roosevelt himself down to defeat.

In a way, he must have welcomed the diversion of war, grimly serious as it was, for even though his popularity remained high with a great majority of ordinary citizens, and his party continued to dominate the political landscape, he had essentially lost control of the Congress to a conservative coalition of Republicans and breakaway Southern Democrats. As the political mastermind of the most massive program of emergency relief and economic recovery ever undertaken by this or any other country, the President had commanded the support not only of his legions of ardent disciples but also of the reluctant denizens of conservatism in the Democratic Party. But by the beginning of 1939, so much opposition was mounting against him and his domestic programs that the unifying consequences of a global threat to national security effectively served as a timely shift of focus and a jolt of new energy for his flagging administration.

The supremely confident new President and his coterie of advisers, cabinet officers, and staff assistants had started with feverish haste and boundless enthusiasm in March 1933. All through the campaign and in the days between election and inauguration they had been making plans, and on Sunday morning, March 5, the day after his swearing-in, Roosevelt calmly and decisively began to generate a succession of sweeping actions that would save the nation from disaster.

By executive order, he commanded a shutdown of all banks—those not padlocked in panic already—and called the forced closure a "holiday." He set the Treasury Department's presses to work printing new money. He called the new Congress into extraordinary session, and when the lawmakers arrived, he had their work laid out for them. An emergency banking bill was pushed through both houses and signed into law on the very first day they met. In what came to be known as the Hundred Days, thirteen major pieces of legislation went on the books before the exhausted representatives and senators adjourned in mid-June. Direct relief of human misery, work-relief programs, bank deposit insurance, home mortgage refinancing, regulation of the stock market, new labor laws, and public housing legislation were among the measures approved. (There was even an act authorizing the sale of low-alcohol beer and wine, this in anticipation of speedy ratification by the states of a new constitutional amendment repealing Prohibition. Both houses of the lame-duck Congress had overwhelmingly approved it just a month earlier—concluding, apparently, that if there ever was a time when a body needed a drink, this nerve-racking season of depression and despair was surely it.)

A rush of new programs and agencies proliferated in an alphabetical epidemic—AAA (Agricultural Adjustment Act), CCC (Civilian Conservation Corps), TVA (Tennessee Valley Authority), FERA (Federal Emergency Relief Act), NIRA (National Industrial Recovery Act), and so on. NIRA then gave birth to PWA (Public Works Administration), and FERA spawned another work-relief effort, CWA (Civil Works Administration)— neither of which should be confused with the WPA (Works Progress Administration), which would come along under the Emergency Relief Appropriation Act of 1935. As they said out at the ballpark, you couldn't follow the game without a program—and even then, it was easy to get confused. Such acronymic initiatives as these were to become virtually a trademark of the New Deal, and a few of them would survive as permanent legacies of the Roosevelt era.

Partly in contrast to the stiffly conservative Herbert Hoover and partly because of his own personal and political skills, Franklin Roosevelt clearly displayed from the start his enormous capacities as a leader. It was not his specific program ideas so much as his personality that captured people's minds and hearts; more pragmatic than ideological, he was a consummate politician, a large, handsome man with a big smile, a memory for names and faces, a gift for gab, a sense of humor, and a sensitivity to human suffering. He turned his physical handicap into an asset simply by rising above it. He could explain complicated things in simple language, like a good teacher or a preacher, and he used that gift masterfully to hold the people he had won to his side, whether he reached them directly in public appearances or indirectly in his "fireside chats" on the radio and in his innovative press conferences with working reporters. He could say "my old friend" in a dozen languages. With all of these gifts, FDR conveyed a vivid image: Here was an energetic and resourceful man who genuinely liked people and wanted to help those in need by whatever means necessary; if anyone could pull America to safety from its raging house fire, surely it was this sincere, plucky, courageous, gimpy-legged volunteer fireman leading the bucket brigade.

With more enthusiasm than they had shown for any Yankee since well before 1860, the people of the South took President Roosevelt to their hearts, and he remained there throughout his tenure in the White House. Far ahead of their leaders—and generally ahead of the rest of the country as well—Southerners white and black gave him their overwhelming support early and late, in peace and in war, and nothing ever destroyed their faith in him. Even though there were no Southerners in the inner circle of presidential advisers and staff assistants and only one of note in his cabinet (Secretary of State Cordell Hull, a longtime Tennessee congressman), Roosevelt drew on his own credentials as a part-time Georgian and his generally good relations with the Southerners in Congress to make certain that the region was not slighted in the overall plan of relief and recovery.

The people who headed cabinet-level departments and administrative offices for the President included several whose influence on the fortunes of the South would be pervasive and enduring, and all of them were from the East or Midwest. Harry L. Hopkins, a top aide to Roosevelt when FDR was governor of New York, wore a variety of hats, foremost of which was as chief administrator of New Deal relief programs. Hopkins and three cabinet secretaries—Henry A. Wallace of Agriculture, Harold L. Ickes of Interior, and Frances Perkins of Labor—were probably the figures in the executive branch who affected the South the most (except for the President himself, of course, and for Eleanor, his wife and distant cousin, whose unofficial role may have been the most significant of all).

Mrs. Perkins, the first woman ever to receive a federal cabinet appointment, had served FDR as industrial commissioner of New York, and she was a loyal administrator of New Deal labor programs during all of his years in the White House. Wallace, a longtime agricultural journalist in his native Iowa—and a Republican until 1928—headed the Department of Agriculture for eight years and served four more as Vice President. Ickes, a Chicago journalist and lawyer and a former president of that city's NAACP chapter, was also an ex-Republican. He not only ran the Department of the Interior from 1933 to 1946 but headed the Public Works Administration as well, and did more than any other New Deal cabinet officer to bring black Americans and liberal white Southerners into the government.

Of all his many talents as a politician and public figure, Franklin Roosevelt's strongest suit was surely his ability to motivate people—to take them into his confidence, to inspire them, to win their loyalty, to play them one against another. He was a manipulator, pure and simple, and that side of his nature inevitably reinforced the convictions of his devotees, who saw him as an angel of mercy, and his detractors, who thought of him as the devil incarnate. He said yes to practically everyone, left and right, stroking and flattering and gently prodding them to bring out their best, like a great conductor before an orchestra, or a manager handling an all-star team. In one respect, his manner was almost the opposite of manipulation, giving free rein to every participant in the faith that competition would produce excellence—but the catch was that each of the players often felt that he or she had a green light to move ahead, when in fact the same liberties had also been bestowed upon others. Among his closest aides and associates, it was thus not uncommon for brooding animosities and latent conflicts to hover just beneath the surface, concealing a wide range of ideological and psychological differences.

Roosevelt's relationship with the legislative and judicial branches of the federal government also showed signs of presidential manipulation, but with a twist: The lawmakers and judges often had a sense of self-importance every bit as large as the President's, and they were as apt to try to shape his thoughts and actions as he was to mold theirs. The separation-of-powers principle of the U.S. Constitution has never been more severely tested than in the New Deal era—and the most contentious and volatile manifestations of the conflict arose when the strong-willed President found his way blocked by the Southern leadership in Congress.

The Bourbon-Redeemer Democrats who forged a regional oligarchy—the so-called Solid South—in the post-Reconstruction era had needed almost no time at all to take control of the old Confederacy, and just fifty-five years to win virtually complete dominion over the U.S. Congress. When the Roosevelt landslide in 1932 reestablished the Democrats as the majority party (they outnumbered Republicans 60 to 35 in the Senate and 310 to 117 in the House), it was the Southerners who gained the most. They didn't have numerical superiority on the party roster of senators and representatives, but they had so much seniority that two-thirds of the thirty most important committees of both houses in the first New Deal Congress were chaired by Southerners, all experienced men who knew how to get what they wanted.

One of Roosevelt's rivals for the presidential nomination, House Speaker John Nance Garner of Texas, had been given the vice-presidential spot on the ticket in return for his concession, but the party leadership was so loaded with Southerners-in-waiting that it would keep the speaker's chair filled with them for the next thirty years, first with Joseph Byrns of Tennessee, then with William B. Bankhead of Alabama, and finally with Sam Rayburn of Texas. In the Senate, floor leadership was held by Joseph T. Robinson of Arkansas from 1923 until his death in 1937 (meaning, of course, that he was majority leader from 1933 on), and his replacement was another Southerner, Alben Barkley of Kentucky, who edged out Pat Harrison of Mississippi by a single vote in a closed-door power struggle among Democrats of the upper chamber.

How did the Southerners get such a stranglehold? To begin with, they had succeeded in building an inner unity around an ideology of Southern nationalism—the Lost Cause lament, the heartbreak of defeat, the code of honor, hatred of Yankees, and so forth. They maintained a monolithic society, the four corners of which were politics (Democratic), religion (Protestant), race (Caucasian), and livelihood (cotton), and through physical and intellectual isolation they shielded it from outside influences. They kept taxes low and public services at a minimum, and deflected criticism by pitting working-class whites and blacks against each other, thus leaving the middle and upper classes in positions of relative but perpetual advantage. And, finally, they controlled the political process so completely through malapportionment, poll taxes, and other limitations on voting that blacks, women, urban dwellers, and the generality of low-income people were either depreciated or left out of the process altogether. Incumbents thus could return themselves to office with the blessing of as little as ten percent of the age-eligible voting population.

Once ensconced, the Southerners, already well versed in the etiquette of social relations, quickly mastered the rules of the legislative club. As well as any and better than most, they honed the skills of parliamentary procedure, oratory, horse trading, and hospitality. They instinctively grasped the subtle distinctions between appearance and reality, betting and bluffing, party loyalty and personal ambition. As different as they were from one another—and they were indeed vastly different in many ways—they were so close together ideologically and so determined to stay that way that they almost begged to be caricatured and stereotyped as bucolic Foghorns.

Some, like Senator Ellison D. "Cotton Ed" Smith of South Carolina, tried hard to cultivate an outrageous image—and succeeded. Born during the Civil War and groomed by such classic Rebels as Wade Hampton, Ben Tillman, and his longtime colleague Cole Blease, Smith seemed to personify in dress and mannerisms the very essence of a stereotypical retired Confederate colonel and cotton-country gentleman. To all that he added a gift for rhetoric that made him a walking, talking showpiece throughout six full terms in the Senate. A lawyer and the son of a Methodist minister, he seemed intent on overcoming the implied respectability of his background. He was a profane and unrelenting racist of the old school, a man who could equate a decent wage for cotton-pickers with intermarriage and "black contamination of the pure white race." He had favored federal assistance to farmers for almost a quarter of a century before FDR came along, but despite his claims to constituents that he was a loyal New Dealer, Smith was, from 1933 on, an obstructionist foe of almost every legislative initiative the White House attempted. Although he was chairman of the Senate Agriculture Committee, the administration had to turn for leadership to another committee member, John H. Bankhead, Jr., of Alabama, in order to get its massive farm relief legislation, the Agricultural Adjustment Act, safely through the Senate.

In contrast to the excessively flamboyant Smith was the aristocratic and parsimonious Carter Glass of Virginia, a tightly wound little man whose three decades in Congress had left him with a self-righteous certitude that bitterly disdained the very notion of broad-based democracy. At the age of seventy-five—six years Smith's senior—he was the oldest member of the Senate, and he would still be there when Roosevelt died. Hoping to blunt his opposition by co-opting him in 1933, the President tried to get Glass to be his treasury secretary, but the cantankerous old senator refused the bait. Although he never deserted the Democratic Party, he acted from the start of the New Deal as if FDR were the deserter, a socialistic tinkerer whose policies would destroy white supremacy and deliver the nation to communism.

Glass and Smith anchored a solid rock of Southern intraparty rebels who seldom could be found in the New Deal's corner. With them most of the time were Harry Flood Byrd of Virginia, Josiah Bailey of North Carolina, Walter George of Georgia, and Tom Connally of Texas. To a man, they were latter-day Tories and states' rights royalists—terms aptly descriptive of their economic and social conservatism, their racial views, their abiding belief in class privilege, and their clever control of the folks back home. Paradoxically, their election-day allegiance to the machinery, if not to the platform and principles, of the Democratic Party kept them perpetually in power. Many Southern politicos such as these served in Congress for thirty years or more.

Also in solid opposition to Roosevelt—but from the left, and only briefly—was Huey Long of Louisiana. If the Tories thought FDR was a dangerous left-wing radical, they shuddered at the very mention of "the Kingfish" and his "Share Our Wealth" program. (The President understood their alarm; he considered Long one of the most dangerous men in America.) Here was a self-styled "dictator for the people," a ranting zealot whose ambition transcended ideology and whose political compass gyrated wildly around the dial. In Louisiana he controlled the legislature, the courts, the schools, the banks, the police, the press. To the menace of Ku Klux Klan terrorism, he offered cold comfort. "Quote me as saying that Imperial bastard will never set foot in Louisiana," he told reporters in reference to one particular hooded nemesis. "When I call him a son of a bitch, I'm not using profanity—I'm referring to the circumstances of his birth." Long was probably more a friend of the black and poor masses than any other member of the Senate, and more an enemy of the privileged classes, but his closest lieutenants, including Shreveport preacher Gerald L. K. Smith and legislator Allen J. Ellender, who followed him to the Senate, tended to be right-wing extremists of a more predictable stripe. Long himself was busily plotting a serious challenge to Roosevelt's reelection plans when an aggrieved constituent shot the senator dead in a corridor of the Louisiana State Capitol on September 8, 1935.

A few Southern senators were not only party loyalists but enthusiastic supporters of the early New Deal relief and recovery programs, and even of many of the more far-reaching reforms. Hugo Black of Alabama was the most liberal of them, by almost any measure, and FDR rewarded him with the first vacant seat on the Supreme Court in 1937. By then, Claude Pepper of Florida had come into the upper house, and he became the foremost Southern liberal there when Black left. Others were consistent New Dealers throughout their careers, among them Alben Barkley of Kentucky, Morris Sheppard of Texas, and Hattie Caraway of Arkansas, the first woman ever elected to the Senate from any state. John Bankhead of Alabama and Joe Robinson of Arkansas, the majority leader, were more conservative in their personal views than these others, but their loyalty to the President and the party usually kept them from straying off the New Deal ranch.

The same could hardly be said of half a dozen others: Richard Russell of Georgia, Kenneth McKellar of Tennessee, Pat Harrison of Mississippi, James F. Byrnes of South Carolina, Robert R. Reynolds of North Carolina, and the most enigmatic of them all, Theodore G. Bilbo of Mississippi. More conservative on most issues than the loyalists but also less class oriented than the royalists, these few were constantly working to maintain good standing in both camps. In Roosevelt's first term, when race issues were by mutual consent kept out of the equation of governmental activism, a boilerplate racist like Bilbo or more paternalistic white supremacists like the others could indulge in a moderate or even radical approach to economic problems; thus, on almost all the major legislative acts passed into law in 1933 and 1934, Southern opposition in the Senate was confined to the half-dozen or so unreconstructed rebels of the Carter Glass persuasion. If race relations had been made a central issue in that first term, it is doubtful that any Southern or border-state senator, with the possible exception of Hugo Black, would have deviated at all from the rigidly orthodox catechism of white supremacy. The Yankees, if the truth were known, might not have voted much differently.

In its own way, the House of Representatives showed a similar if less visible pattern of ideological and strategic division among its Southern Democrats. But there the party's margin over the Republicans was nearly two hundred seats, and with the Democratic right wing small and not well organized, the administration had an easier time getting its program through. Men like Howard W. Smith of Virginia and Martin Dies of Texas were early and vocal opponents of the New Deal, but their notoriety as reactionaries would not truly blossom until later. Meanwhile, from the safe center to the more adventurous but still moderate left, several Southern congressmen would make names for themselves as early New Deal supporters, among them William B. Bankhead (brother of Senator John Bankhead) and Lister Hill, both of Alabama; Maury Maverick (a 1934 election winner) and Marvin Jones of Texas; Robert Lee "Muley" Doughton of North Carolina; and Edward H. "Boss" Crump, the kingpin of Memphis (and, in years to come, ruler of the entire political domain of Tennessee).

With his mandate from the people and his huge party margins in both houses of Congress, Franklin Roosevelt was in an ideal position to gamble for far more than relief and recovery. When the midterm congressional elections of 1934 brought the Democrats not a technical and customary adjustment downward but a surprising increase of nine seats in each house, the administration unleashed another whirlwind of new proposals—and in that "Second New Deal," both the reach of Roosevelt and the resistance of his adversaries exceeded their 1933 levels.

Before the end of summer, 1935, another dozen or so pieces of major legislation had cleared Roosevelt's desk. Two new programs were established under the Federal Emergency Relief Act: the Works Progress Administration (WPA), a massive public-works effort aimed at tapping the skills and talents of the unemployed, and the Resettlement Administration (RA), a diversified attempt to help farm families displaced by the depression. Other legislative innovations soon followed: the Rural Electrification Administration (REA), the National Youth Administration (NYA), the National Labor Relations Act, the Social Security Act, the Soil Conservation Act, and various additional laws affecting banking, taxation, interstate commerce, farm mortgage protection, and regulation of public utilities.

The sweep and scope of the New Deal offensive and its bold vigor in comparison to the demoralized lassitude of the Hooverites were like an invasion of spring air and sunlight into a dismal winter den. Across the land, people responded with enthusiasm and rising hope to their hearty, smiling new President and to the cornucopia of programs spilling forth in his name and that of the Democratic Party. The "forgotten man" of FDR's victorious campaign was no longer forgotten; the factory laborer, the share-cropper, the tenant farmer, the immigrant, the neglected mother, the exploited child, the unemployed city dweller—these and many others who bore the brunt of the Great Depression and all its extreme contrasts of wealth and poverty were beginning to experience some relief from their pain and suffering, and they showed their approval with an outpouring of gratitude and affection.

That response energized and uplifted the New Deal architects, and they were emboldened even more when the American voters dramatically re-affirmed the Roosevelt mandate in the 1936 elections. FDR swept to an eleven-million-vote victory over his Republican opponent, Governor Alf Landon of Kansas. The electoral margin was 523 to 8, with only Maine and Vermont in Landon's column, prompting one pundit to quip, "As Maine goes, so goes Vermont." The Democrats all but vanquished the GOP in Congress, too, attaining majorities of 76 to 16 in the Senate and 331 to 89 in the House (minor parties won the few remaining seats). The same pattern prevailed all over the nation; forty of the forty-eight state gover-nors were Democrats, and so were the vast majority of legislators.

In 1937 and 1938 the Roosevelt administration pushed still more new legislation through Congress, including the National Housing Act (for slum clearance and low-cost public housing), the Fair Labor Standards Act (to regulate wages, hours, and child labor), and the Bankhead-Jones Farm Tenancy Act—named for its chief sponsors, Senator John Bankhead of Alabama and Congressman Marvin Jones of Texas—under which was es-tablished the Farm Security Administration (FSA) to consolidate the gov-ernment's response to issues involving sharecroppers and tenant farmers.

From the earliest signs of the oncoming depression in the 1920s and throughout Franklin Roosevelt's quest for national leadership, the plight of tenant farmers and sharecroppers had symbolized all that ailed Amer-ica. This was still an agricultural nation, by and large, and its millions of small farmers stared failure squarely in the face. It was a nationwide problem, of course, but it was nowhere more acute than in the rural South, where practically everyone's livelihood was tied in one way or another to the soil. The first Agricultural Adjustment Act in 1933 was partially invalidated by the U.S. Supreme Court three years later, and a new act was written to replace it in 1938. During those same years, several other laws affecting farmers were enacted, and more than one cabinet-level official had a hand in trying to fix the agriculture problem. To follow the winding path of some of those efforts and other New Deal initiatives

of a similar nature is to see how complex and unpredictable, how incidental and accidental, the ponderous machine of government truly is, and
how much it depends for energy and direction on the whims and impulses
and imperfect judgments of those who sit at the controls.

In 1935 the University of North Carolina Press published a critical
study of Southern agriculture that had an immediate impact on government policy. *The Collapse of Cotton Tenancy* was praised by FDR himself
(though it was in fact a sharp indictment of early New Deal policies), and
it directly influenced the reformist shape and substance of the Bankhead-
Jones Act and the second Agricultural Adjustment Act. The book was
coauthored by three men with deep Southern roots: Charles S. Johnson of
Fisk University, Edwin R. Embree of the Rosenwald Fund, and Will W.
Alexander of the Commission on Interracial Cooperation.

Almost as significant as the book itself was the personal dynamic among
its three authors. Johnson and Alexander we have encountered before in
this narration—the one a black Virginian trained in sociology at the University of Chicago and groomed for his return south by service to the
Urban League and the Harlem Renaissance in New York; the other a
Missouri-born white man with a Tennessee education and many years of
Atlanta-based experience in race relations. Embree was, in a sense, the
link between them, a Midwesterner by birth but a Southerner by virtue
of the fact that he had been raised in the Kentucky home of his grandfather, John G. Fee, who had founded Berea College as an interracial
school in the 1850s on land donated by the abolitionist firebrand Cassius
Marcellus Clay. Embree went to Berea himself before the turn of the
century, only a few years before Kentucky lawmakers forced the college to
expel its black students and operate thereafter under new segregation
laws. He went on to Yale and then into philanthropic work with the
Rockefeller Foundation, and in 1928 he was asked by Julius Rosenwald,
head of the Sears, Roebuck empire in Chicago, to take charge of the
Rosenwald family's charitable investments. Embree was keenly interested
in public policy, in the South, and in race relations (he was, among other
things, the author of a farsighted book, *Brown America*, "the story of a
new race," in 1931). As president of the well-endowed Rosenwald Fund,
he was in a favorable position to act substantially on his interests.

At the CIC, Alexander had benefited directly from the charitable resources managed by Embree, and in 1930, when he was invited to become
a trustee of the Rosenwald Fund, he accepted readily. Both Embree and
Alexander knew Charles Johnson well and admired his record of scholarship and diplomacy in Chicago, New York, and Nashville; they recruited

the Fisk sociologist to serve part-time as the fund's director of research. For nearly twenty years the three men would work in close harmony, making many significant contributions to the long-range resurrection of the South with funds drawn from the well-feathered Rosenwald nest in Chicago. By no means the least of their efforts was the role they played in the desegregation of the New Deal.

Soon after Roosevelt was inaugurated, they devised a plan to make certain that the needs and interests of black Southerners would be taken into consideration by federal policymakers. They wanted someone in a position of authority in the administration to be an advocate for African-Americans, someone who would see to it that they weren't left to the pitiless mercies of Southern white supremacists and Yankee reactionaries. The Rosenwald team proposed to pay the salary of this "adviser on Negro affairs" with foundation funds, in order to keep the position out of the firing range of members of Congress. They managed to get the proposal into the White House for consideration, and it was quickly approved by FDR himself, in keeping with his inclination to encourage almost anyone with fresh ideas.

Embree and Johnson then turned to Secretary of the Interior Harold Ickes, whom they had known in Chicago as a tough, aggressive lawyer and public-spirited advocate of social justice. Ickes liked their idea and agreed to appoint an advocate, but he felt strongly that the first appointee should be a white man, the better to face up to white critics of Negro opportunity. He got no resistance from the Rosenwald men; they already had a white candidate in mind. Thirty-one-year-old Clark H. Foreman, a grandson of Clark Howell, the arch-conservative founder of the Atlanta *Constitution*, had impeccable academic credentials (including a Ph.D. from Columbia University)—but more to the point, he had worked for a couple of years each at the CIC under Alexander and at Rosenwald under Embree. They knew and trusted him as a charming but hard-driving liberal who would stand up to the Southern reactionaries. The irascible and combative Ickes liked those qualities, and he gave Foreman the job in August 1933.

Initial resistance came not from white Southerners but from the NAACP and the black press. W. E. B. Du Bois and Walter White were insulted by the paternalism implicit in the appointment. Veteran publishers Robert S. Abbott of the Chicago *Defender* and Robert L. Vann of the Pittsburgh *Courier*, both of whom were native Southerners and militant critics of racial discrimination in all its forms, echoed a similar cry of outrage. The complaints were short-lived, though, for not only did Foreman prove to be effective, but he was soon joined by a black assistant, twenty-six-year-old Washington, D.C., native Robert C. Weaver, a Harvard-educated economist. And Ickes then went further to appoint a black assistant solicitor,

William H. Hastie, another bright, under-thirty Washingtonian with a Harvard degree.

Ickes was the leading standard-bearer for social change in the early Roosevelt years, breaking the segregationist ice in the Interior Department and in the Public Works Administration, which he also headed (and into which Clark Foreman moved in 1934). Other cabinet-level administrators followed the lead of Ickes in appointing black assistants and race-relations advisers, and by the late 1930s about a hundred such posts had been filled. The number seems insignificant in a bureaucracy as vast as the federal government, but at the time the appointments symbolized a major break with the past and a promise of greater changes to come. Blacks had worked for the national government before 1933, of course, but rarely in positions of authority; furthermore, segregation in the various agencies and departments had always prevailed as a matter of course, and the District of Columbia was as thoroughly divided racially as any city in the Deep South.

The New Deal didn't exactly change those conditions overnight—in fact, even the ostensible signs of progress sometimes turned out to be false indicators. Robert Vann, the black publisher from Pittsburgh, had made an early break from the Republican Party to support FDR, telling African-American voters to "turn Lincoln's picture to the wall" and make the switch with him. But Vann (whose ancestral lineage included some of the same eastern North Carolina roots as that of the white historian C. Vann Woodward) lasted only two years as an assistant attorney general in the Department of Justice, and he left the government embittered by his experiences. So did Forrester Washington, an Atlanta dean of social work who went, on Will Alexander's recommendation, to a post in the Federal Emergency Relief Administration. The essence of their complaints was that the administration was not truly committed to equal opportunity, and that token signs of black inclusion in government departments concealed the reality that they had no real influence or authority to reduce racial discrimination.

Out in the precincts where federal laws were supposedly being implemented, there was often an enormous gap between lofty ideals and commonplace realities. Take the Tennessee Valley Authority, for example. The TVA was a pathfinding and controversial New Deal agency created in 1933 to bring navigation and flood control to the wild Tennessee River and hydroelectric power to its impoverished valley residents. Headquartered in Knoxville, far from the governmental mainstream in Washington, the TVA was directly exposed to the ingrained and remorseless prejudices of the South. In spite of its bold image as a model of social planning and its stated policy of nondiscrimination in hiring, the agency (directed and managed in the main, incidentally, by Midwestern progressives) repeatedly yielded to its area congressmen and senators in excluding blacks from its benefits.

The TVA's model town of Norris, Tennessee, was for whites only. Not even one in every twenty-five salaried positions in the agency went to black applicants, and most of those were for maids, cooks, and janitors; from 1933 to 1950, only two blacks were hired in professional positions—and both of them were to supervise other blacks. Between 1934 and 1938, the NAACP sent Charles H. Houston, John Preston Davis, and Thurgood Marshall into the Tennessee valley to investigate the agency's discriminatory practices, but neither Congress nor the press paid much attention to their findings. The TVA may have been the most radical of all the New Deal's agencies (critics called its economic planning initiatives "socialistic"), but in its overall handling of racial and socioeconomic issues, it seldom rose above the conventional biases of its Southern environment.

In spite of such shortcomings, however, the Roosevelt administration was no replay of the Hoover-Coolidge-Harding years—or, for that matter, of Woodrow Wilson's. Nonwhite minorities, the economically distressed, and Southerners of every class and color who had endured a perpetually inferior status vis-à-vis Northerners could find in the New Deal's promises and programs sound reason to hope that they were headed for better times.

Agriculture, the enterprise at the heart of the economic peril when FDR took office, commanded the undivided attention of a multitude of New Deal administrators, bureaucrats, and members of Congress from 1933 on. Together they tried just about everything—price supports, production limits, commodity protection, soil conservation, crop diversification, easier credit, tax reforms, farm mortgage refinancing, reciprocal trade pacts, scientific and technological improvements, even land redistribution. It might have been argued in, say, 1940 that eight years of government intervention had not rescued agriculture from distress, but no one could seriously claim that the New Dealers had simply sat on their hands.

The restructuring and transformation of the American (and especially Southern) farm economy in the decades of the thirties and forties have been impressively documented by numerous historians and others. Collectively, they have recorded a sprawling, multidimensional tale of mechanization, electrification, migration, and technological innovation that has dramatically changed the size and character of farms and affected the lives of millions of people. Much of this might have happened eventually in any case, but there is no doubt that government intervention was the single most potent and effective stimulus to what has become an ongoing revolution.

Throughout most of his eight years as the first director of this effort, Secretary of Agriculture Henry A. Wallace performed, as expected, more or less like the moderate and cautious Midwesterner that he was, and not in any sense like the left-wing radical he was widely thought to be by the time he mounted a third-party campaign for president in 1948. Coincidental with his tenure as the administration's top farm hand, fierce ideological debates on agriculture policy raged just beneath the surface. In a way, this was just another replay of the classic struggle between the hands-on and hands-off philosophies of public policy.

The American agriculture establishment, made up of federal and state bureaucrats, university agriculturists, traditional organizations of farmers, and the larger planters and corporate executives to whom they catered, wanted to maintain the independent and unregulated free-market traditions that had served their interests; they were challenged by insurgent groups of reformers pressing for more equity, more government intervention to help the working class, and more planning of a cooperative nature. Wallace did not become strongly identified with either side of the argument; like FDR, with whom he was very close, he gave encouragement to both camps.

Far more of an interventionist and a reformer than Wallace was his undersecretary, Rexford G. Tugwell, a Columbia University economist whose friendship with Franklin and Eleanor Roosevelt preceded by several years their move to the White House. Introverted and temperamental, Tugwell lacked FDR's charm, but his skills as a social planner and his interest in the welfare of those hardest hit by the depression made him a valuable member of the President's inner circle of advisers.

In April 1935, Roosevelt signed an executive order naming Rex Tugwell director of the Resettlement Administration, an independent new agency with a broad mandate to rehabilitate communities in depressed rural areas and to relocate displaced families into newly created rural and suburban villages. Previous efforts along these lines by the Federal Emergency Relief Administration and the Division of Subsistence Homesteads in Harold Ickes's Interior Department were incorporated into the new agency. Knowing that a substantial majority of its community efforts would be in the deeply impoverished South—and having observed that Will Alexander was an influential advocate of the interests of poor Southerners, black and white—Tugwell prevailed upon Alexander to become his deputy director.

Short, portly, convivial "Dr. Will" (his common tag with practically everyone who knew him) was by then fifty-one years old and widely hailed as the dean of liberal white Southerners. His imprint was all over the region. He had directed the Commission on Interracial Cooperation in

Atlanta for sixteen years; he had coordinated the effort to start a new black institution, Dillard University, in New Orleans, and served briefly as its first president; at his suggestion, the Rosenwald Fund had established a fellowship program that was sending dozens of bright young Southern men and women, white and black, out into the wider world for advanced study. His connections and influence were legendary, not only among white and black progressives but also with radicals and reactionaries of the left and right. Never one to seek glory for himself, he quietly downplayed the press notice of his Resettlement Administration appointment—but his name was also in the news because the critical study of farm tenancy that he had coauthored with Charles Johnson and Edwin Embree was just beginning to reverberate through Washington.

By his own admission, Will Alexander had neither the temperament nor the desire to administer a large bureaucratic organization; his style ran more to personal charm and folksiness, more to storytelling over drinks and dinner than to writing memos and chairing meetings. But Tugwell convinced him that his services were desperately needed, and so, out of a sense of duty, he left his wife and family in Atlanta, left the CIC in the care of its small cadre of faithful staffers, and took up residence in the Cosmos Club in Washington for what he thought would be a brief sojourn. In fact, it lasted five years.

Tugwell's visionary ideas about easing credit for beleaguered tenant farmers and sharecroppers, and resettling many of them on misused and wasted land acquired by the federal government, appealed to Alexander's continuing concern for Southern social problems. The New Deal's first attempts to address agriculture issues had more or less ignored the chronic plight of farm laborers—yet in the South alone in the mid-thirties, there were nearly two million tenant families, totaling about nine million people, and those numbers didn't include the tens of thousands of day-wage laborers who drifted from farm to farm, or the countless migrant agricultural workers who followed the harvest. Displaced coal miners and other rural laborers stranded by the depression also added to the backcountry crisis.

Although most of the money appropriated on their behalf was spent on loans and grants to individuals rather than on developing homestead villages for a dozen to several hundred families each, it was these communities that attracted the most attention and opposition. Between 1933, when planning was begun on the first two subsistence homesteads (one in West Virginia, the other in Tennessee), and 1946, when a hostile Congress finally abolished the program, about a hundred new communities were created, two-thirds of them in Southern or border states. Some Southerners in Congress—including Maury Maverick, in whose home state of Texas ten of the villages were built, and the Bankhead brothers, who helped land eight of them in Alabama—initially gave enthusiastic support to Tugwell and Alexander in their efforts to lift the rural poor out of serfdom.

But far more vocal were the opponents, led by Senators Harry Byrd of Virginia and Kenneth McKellar of Tennessee and House members E. E. Cox and Malcolm C. Tarver of Georgia. They railed against the inclusion of new communities for blacks, even though rigid segregation was maintained throughout the program and only a token few all-black communities were ever built. They also complained of collectivism, waste and extravagance, social experimentation, and big-brother intrusion by the federal government. They vilified Rex Tugwell as a reckless radical, if not a Communist, and his arrogant disdain for such critics had the effect of confirming their negative opinions. But even genial Southerners like Alexander were sometimes spattered with the same brush, as in a 1939 House debate when Congressman Cox called him an "off-color politician" (by which he presumably meant pink, if not red), and in 1942, when C. B. Baldwin, a Virginian and successor to Tugwell and Alexander, was bluntly tagged a Communist by Senator McKellar.

As time went on, "Dr. Will" proved to be better suited to the give-and-take of program-tending in Washington than the more abrasive Tugwell, who was long on planning but short on selling or implementing his ideas. By the fall of 1937, the Resettlement Administration had been transformed into a new agency, the Farm Security Administration, within the Department of Agriculture, and Tugwell had moved on to other challenges. Will Alexander moved up to the top job, working for the secretary, Henry Wallace. The new Bankhead-Jones Farm Tenancy Act preserved many of Tugwell's ideas under the FSA banner, but shifted the emphasis from democratic empowerment in cooperative communities to individual tenant purchase of subsistence farms. Still, controversy dogged the program until the very end, when all of the nearly eleven thousand housing units were either bought by their residents or sold at public auction. The liquidation was essentially completed in 1948, by which time both Tugwell and Alexander were long gone.

One of Alexander's legacies was his persuasive appeal to idealistic young Southerners, white and black—and others beyond the South—to give of themselves for the betterment of the region and the nation. The roster of his recruits to government service included Clark Foreman, George S. Mitchell, Horace Cayton, Mark Ethridge, Brooks Hays, Ira De A. Reid, John Fischer, Julia Waxman, Skip Hudgens, Gordon Parks—a few of the many who went on to prominence. In addition, scores of Rosenwald fellows were among the multitude who heeded Dr. Will's Pied Piper call to public service.

Rex Tugwell left some deep tracks too, not least of them being in the Farm Security Administration's photographic documentation project. A onetime Colorado cowboy named Roy Stryker, who had been Tugwell's graduate assistant at Columbia, was summoned to Washington by his former mentor in 1935 to organize a team of photographers and record what Tugwell called "as complete a record as [possible] of an agonizing interlude in American life." Stryker was not a photographer himself, but he had a knack for finding and motivating such professionals, and the dozen or so individuals who did the bulk of the work for him—among them Ben Shahn, Walker Evans, Russell Lee, Dorothea Lange, Jack Delano, and Marion Post Wolcott—left a collective body of work that is universally acclaimed as a timeless and classic example of photographic excellence. None of the main FSA photographers were from the South (Walker Evans of St. Louis came closest) and none were black (though Stryker, on direct orders from Alexander, did reluctantly take on Rosenwald fellow Gordon Parks as an apprentice); nonetheless, almost half of the more than 120,000 images they left in their "complete record" were Southern scenes of revelation and timeless poignancy.

It is surprising how much the fine arts figured in the programs and philosophy of the New Deal—not through endowments of independent creativity, as we have now, but through direct government employment of creative artists. In addition to the FSA photographers, there were four arts projects (for writers, actors, artists, and musicians) in the Works Progress Administration—and even mural painters in the Treasury Department, their role being to "embellish Federal buildings with the best contemporary American art." The esthetic sensibilities of public officials may have had something to do with fund allocations for projects such as these, but the more likely explanation is probably the one given by relief czar Harry Hopkins, who said of his WPA artists: "They've got to eat just like other people." (And not sirloin and caviar, either; top pay was $103.50 a month.) Providing creative work for creative people was actually an inspired idea; it not only attacked the unemployment problem in an original way, but also gave the viewing, reading, and listening public a panorama of useful, often excellent, and at times inspirational fare.

The WPA's Federal Writers' Project is especially noteworthy for the sheer volume of its output: more than three hundred publications, including a hundred books, in just four years—from the fall of 1935, soon after the WPA was established by executive order, to the fall of 1939, when Hopkins moved over to the Commerce Department and the projects were broken up.

Each state and some large cities had Writers' Project offices, and their staffs—novelists, poets, journalists, editors, and other professionals who were unable to find employment elsewhere—turned out a diversity of informative and well-written materials on everything from folklore and narratives of ex-slaves to contemporary interviews and travel information. The American Guide Series of state and city resource books drew widespread praise for both their content and the quality of their prose.

Henry G. Alsberg, a fifty-seven-year-old ex-journalist and theater producer from New York, directed the Writers' Project for Hopkins with just the right mix of political savvy and artistic sensitivity. In the constant tension between creative free expression and government propaganda— and between the idealism of a nation trying to rise to its promise and the reality of a nation beset by gangsterism in the North, racism in the South, and poverty everywhere—Alsberg somehow managed to steer a steady course. Loudly clashing ideologies were vying for attention: liberalism and conservatism, New Deal optimism and Old School skepticism, communism and socialism and fascism. Rumors and frontal attacks mixed with occasional praise swirled around Alsberg throughout his tenure, until he was finally fired by Hopkins's successor.

Some soon-to-be-noted or already well-known Southern writers got valuable exposure in the state-based projects, among them novelist Lyle Saxon in Louisiana, folklorist and novelist Zora Neale Hurston in Florida, dramatist Paul Green in North Carolina, folklorist Vance Randolph in Arkansas, and aspiring novelist Eudora Welty, who took photographs for the Mississippi guidebook. But once again, racial and social taboos held the South back. Even though Alsberg encouraged the state directors to enlarge the role of blacks, most were unwilling to do so (Hurston, a veteran of the Harlem Renaissance, was one of the top writers in the Florida project, but she was a singular exception). Most of the African-Americans who participated in the Writers' Project made their contributions in New York, Chicago, Washington, and other cities; included on that list were Sterling Brown, Richard Wright, Arna Bontemps, Margaret Walker, Frank Yerby, Ted Poston, and Ralph Ellison.

Two of Harry Hopkins's top aides, Aubrey Williams of Alabama and Ellen S. Woodward of Mississippi, were staunch advocates of the creative artists' projects, and both of them would eventually feel the heat of Southern congressional criticism. Once, after a Writers' Project party in Washington, an outraged Senator Theodore Bilbo, having seen a snapshot of white and black staff members casually socializing, thundered on the Senate floor that such "crimes" were punished in Mississippi by "hanging from the highest magnolia tree." (He later had the remark stricken from the *Congressional Record*.)

Another critic, Texas congressman Martin Dies, expressed alarm about what he said were subversive ties more than racial ones. His newly created Committee on Un-American Activities held hearings for weeks in the summer of 1938, during which he and other members characterized the writers' and artists' projects as "a hotbed of Communists." Typical of the know-nothing recklessness of the committee's probe was the attack by Representative Joe Starnes of Alabama on "a Communist by the name of Christopher Marlowe." (The famed British playwright had been dead since 1593.) But the hearings took their toll. Within a year, President Roosevelt had transferred Harry Hopkins, and the dismantling of the WPA creative projects soon followed.

Aubrey Williams didn't have a lot to do with the artistic ventures of the WPA, but he was a lightning rod for Hopkins from the day he joined him at the Federal Emergency Relief Administration in May 1933—and a stormy decade in Washington did nothing to lessen his notoriety. Williams was soon to become one of the foremost liberal advocates of social change in his native region. Many a Southern member of Congress listened in openmouthed disbelief to the Alabamian's drawling, soft-spoken radicalism and concluded that he was a traitor and a menace to the Southern way of life. Naturally, Williams didn't see himself that way at all, but he was definitely a threat to the traditions that gave exclusive advantage to white, upper-class Southern males, and he was never hesitant to say so.

From early on, Williams had lived an unconventional life. Born and raised in meager circumstances in the rural orbit of Birmingham, where his father was a blacksmith and wagon builder, young Aubrey got most of his early education through the Cumberland Presbyterian Church, to which his hardworking mother was deeply devoted. He went to work before he was ten, and in 1911, when he was twenty-one, he was admitted to ministerial study at Maryville College, a Presbyterian institution in Tennessee, even though he had finished only one year of formal schooling. The formative experiences of his early life pointed him toward service to people in need, and by the time he got to Maryville, he had earned his spurs as a skillful helper and advocate for exploited Southern millhands and miners.

Over the next decade or so, Williams studied at Maryville and at the University of Cincinnati, went to France to work for the YMCA, saw combat with the French Foreign Legion and then with the U.S. Army, returned to finish a degree in social work at Cincinnati, pastored a Lutheran church in Kentucky, got married, became a Unitarian, aimed for further study at Harvard Divinity School, and turned at the last minute in a different career direction to become executive secretary of the Wisconsin Conference of Social Work. After ten years in that job, he got into public-relief assistance as a government social worker during the Hoover depression years, and that brought him to the attention of Harry Hopkins in the spring of 1933. It didn't take the two men long to discover their common interests and outlook.

Williams was assigned to oversee the federal relief effort in six Southern states, and as he immersed himself in the gritty reality and the grimy politics of those jurisdictions, his unflinching determination to reach the needy with direct assistance quickly got him in hot water with the likes of Senators Huey Long of Louisiana and Joe Robinson of Arkansas and Governor "Alfalfa Bill" Murray of Oklahoma. When both Hopkins and President Roosevelt gave him support and encouragement, Williams proceeded with growing confidence to assert his vision of government activism. He and Hopkins sold FDR on the concept of work relief, as opposed to direct handouts, and it was his proposal that led in late 1933 to the establishment of the Civil Works Administration, which was something of a forerunner of, and model for, the Works Progress Administration of 1935.

By then, Williams had moved his family to the Washington area and settled into a fast-paced life of hard work and occasional play, making friends with other New Deal liberals—including fellow Alabamians Clifford and Virginia Durr of Montgomery and Senator Hugo Black—and building a firm link with FDR and an even closer relationship of mutual admiration and collaboration with Mrs. Roosevelt. The creation of the WPA and the National Youth Administration within three months of each other in mid-1935 was a sign of even greater responsibility for Williams, since he was not only second in command at the WPA for a time, but also executive director of the NYA.

Throughout his New Deal years, Aubrey Williams openly exhibited a populist idealism that accorded to minorities and the poor a full measure of equality in every aspect of the programs he administered. Remembering the lean years of his own youth and the desperate circumstances of so many Southern peasants—and seeing most of them worse off in the depression than they had been thirty years earlier—he was driven with a zeal rooted in his Alabama past to come to their aid, and when critics blasted him as a "screwball planner" or a meddlesome troublemaker or a Communist, he was all the more determined to stand and fight. Particularly in the NYA, which was his alone to direct, he went out of his way to ensure that blacks and other demonstrably needy groups were fully represented. In that respect, the program was a model of fairness—everything that such agencies as TVA and the Civilian Conservation Corps were not.

The purpose of the NYA was to provide employment and education support services to young people whose opportunities for personal development were sharply curtailed by the depression. Hopkins, Williams, and Eleanor Roosevelt were united in their belief that children and youth were innocent and unnecessary victims of the nation's economic and social calamity, and they wanted to give high priority to programs aimed at that population group; NYA was their primary vehicle. All three of them were also aware that the South had a disproportionately large number of such young people, white and black. Considering that, Mrs. Roosevelt encouraged Hopkins to include a black representative, sixty-year-old Mary McLeod Bethune, on the NYA's national advisory committee. The appointment was made, and shortly thereafter, in the late summer of 1935, Williams put Mrs. Bethune on his staff as head of the NYA Office of Minority Affairs. From then until she returned to her home in Florida ten years later, she was the most visible and influential African-American in the New Deal.

Practically everything about Mary McLeod Bethune seemed to have a heroic quality, a larger-than-life dimension. Born during Reconstruction on a plantation near Mayesville, South Carolina, she was the fifteenth of seventeen children in a family of illiterate sharecroppers; her parents and some of her older siblings had been born in slavery, and no one before her had spent a day in school. The arrival of a Presbyterian mission for blacks gave her that opportunity, and with missionary help she went on to a church-supported high school in North Carolina and then to the conservative Moody Bible Institute in Chicago. Her dream was to be a missionary to Africa, but the Presbyterian mission board thought it somehow inappropriate to send a young black American woman to the service of black Africans, and they refused to appoint her. Undaunted, Mary McLeod dedicated her life to the education of African-American children.

After teaching for nearly a decade in Southern mission schools, she started an institution of her own—for girls—in Daytona Beach, Florida, in 1904. It became Bethune-Cookman College after a merger in 1923, and Mrs. Bethune (having married and separated) served as its president until 1942. She also founded the National Council of Negro Women in 1935, heading it until 1949, and was a longtime board member of the NAACP and the Urban League. During her government service in the Roosevelt years, she was the convenor, host, and "mother superior" of the Federal Council on Negro Affairs (or, as it was popularly called, the Black Cabinet), in which the first black administrative appointees in the New Deal established an influential presence, not only with the Roosevelt executive branch but with leading civil rights activists outside the government.

As the first black woman ever to hold a position of any significance in the federal government, Mary Bethune established a lofty precedent for all who followed. From a childhood in the cotton fields, she had blossomed into a dedicated, intelligent, fearless, forceful, eloquent figure—a large and imposing woman, dark and serious and redoubtable, resplendently outfitted in regal attire that often included a flowing cape and scepter. She had the stately bearing and demeanor of an African queen, and even Washington's resident white supremacists were a bit in awe of her. They knew little or nothing of her background; what they saw and heard was a supremely confident individual whose very presence seemed to make color irrelevant.

That must have been what Eleanor Roosevelt thought when she first met Bethune at a social function in the 1920s. Their acquaintance evolved into a close friendship that eventually gave the Florida educator access to the White House and influence with both Eleanor and Franklin. For her part, Mrs. Bethune revered the President and the First Lady, and steadfastly defended them from critics on the right and left for the rest of her life.

And with good reason, particularly in the case of Mrs. Roosevelt. First among the towering figures of the New Deal, from her husband on down, the President's wife was committed in her heart and soul to the ideals and the documentary icons of American democracy. She was forty-eight years old when the New Deal began, a conspicuously tall, ungainly woman with a fluttery, high-pitched voice that belied a fighting spirit. Born to privilege but not contentment, she had left her unhappy childhood behind when her Uncle Teddy Roosevelt gave her away in marriage to her cousin Franklin in 1905.

The couple's relationship was tinged with heartbreak before and after he was stricken with polio in 1921. "Back of tranquillity lies conquered unhappiness," she liked to say, quoting someone now forgotten; her conquest involved boosting her husband back into politics, becoming his eyes and ears and feet, traveling thousands of miles a year for him, broadcasting radio commentaries and writing newspaper columns, establishing her own identity as a champion of the underdog, and giving of her time and money and energy to a multitude of charitable and progressive causes.

The Roosevelts never put limits on each other. As her interest in the desperate plight of blacks and poor whites deepened, Eleanor used her great influence to help them—exhorting administration officials and members of Congress to step up their efforts, bringing her friends Mary Bethune and Walter White to the executive residence for chats with her husband, making phone calls or visits in behalf of the organizations and issues and concerns that filled her lengthy care list. She tried to persuade her husband to be more outspoken in his support of the underclass, and when he declined to do so, she endeavored to work around him. "Well, what about me? Do you mind if I say what I think?" the historian Frank Friedel quoted Eleanor as asking the President. He reportedly replied, "No, certainly not. You can say anything you want. I can always say, 'Well, that's my wife. I can't do anything about her.' "

She was vilified by the right wing—by Southern reactionaries in particular—as a meddlesome do-gooder and bleeding-heart liberal, but most Americans, including most Southerners, knew better. They recognized genuine human decency when they saw it, and they returned their admiration and affection for her care and concern. Marquis Childs, writing about Eleanor Roosevelt years later, said hers was "the story of the ugly duckling who at last came into the life of a swan and yet remembered what it was like to be an ugly duckling."

In the domestic realm, Franklin Roosevelt's political rocket had risen from ground zero in 1932 to its apogee in 1936, and then had started its long descent. The South benefited more than any other region from that flight of hope and glory, and the vast multitude of its people saw in FDR a public servant deserving of their undying love and respect. Never before had so many Southern men and women and children put such faith in a politician (nor have they since). Tragically, though, it was Southern politicians—white men in the legislative branch of the federal government and others in the states—who led the opposition against the President, his wife, his cabinet officers, and the Democrats' own New Deal. What mattered to them more than economic recovery, more than democratic reform, more than anything, was the preservation of their own privilege and advantage and power, and of the fabled Southern way of life. To keep all that, they willfully opposed their President and neglected their people—the Southerners and other Americans they were sworn to serve.

7. *Thunder on the Right*

It took the whole of the first Roosevelt administration for the leaders of the American black minority population to be persuaded that their best hope for social reform and equal opportunity lay not with the Republicans but with the New Deal Democrats. And, coincidentally or not, it took about the same amount of time for the Southern political opposition to coalesce across party lines with other strands of right-wing thought and form a militant national resistance movement against Franklin Roosevelt and his allies.

The landslide of 1936 was so overwhelming that it lulled FDR and his brain trust into a false sense of confidence. Public-opinion polls, a new tool of the social scientists, had forecast a close election, but they were wildly and embarrassingly inaccurate. Three-fourths of the citizens over age twenty-one in the East, Midwest, and West had voted, and they favored Roosevelt over Alf Landon by about three to two. In the South, poll taxes and other voting restrictions kept three-fourths of the adults from participating at all (in South Carolina, Georgia, Alabama, and Mississippi, not even one citizen in five cast a ballot), but those who did vote gave the President an even greater margin of victory. Most of the black vote, small though it was, went to Roosevelt, dramatically reversing the three-to-one cushion they gave to the Republicans in 1932. Focusing on the still-needy segment of the population in his second inaugural address, FDR declared that one-third of the nation still lacked decent food, clothing, and shelter, and barely two of every hundred families had disposable income of as much as $5,000 a year.

A solid national coalition had united behind the popular image of FDR and the liberal programs he espoused. Those who benefited most from the federal government's activism—small farmers, the urban poor, labor union members, blacks and other minorities, Southerners in general—swelled the rank and file of troops marching to the Democratic drummer. Catholics and Jews along with Protestants, intellectuals and creative artists as well as the workaday masses, and women as much as men found hope and promise in the pronouncements of their leader and the policies of his administration.

There was only one black member of Congress (Democrat Arthur W. Mitchell of Chicago), and there wouldn't be more than one until after World War II, but white Democrats from outside the South had begun to show more sensitivity to social issues, including race; back in 1922, only eight of them had voted for the Dyer anti-lynching bill, but 171 of 185 would split from their defiant Southern colleagues in 1938 and support a similar bill—and still the Southerners would filibuster it to death.

Party politics and public office below the White House level were not exactly on the cutting edge of social reform, but neither were they entirely without signs of change. In Kentucky, Charles W. Anderson, Jr., a black attorney, was elected to the state House of Representatives from Louisville in 1933 and was subsequently reelected several times. And in Congress, it was at least possible by 1936 for white Southerners to run as unabashed New Deal liberals and get elected, as witness the presence of Alabama's Hugo Black and Florida's Claude Pepper in the Senate and

Maury Maverick of Texas in the House. Alabama's House delegation in 1937 included at least four men firmly allied with FDR: Speaker William Bankhead, Lister Hill, Luther Patrick, and John Sparkman. Border-state senators like Alben Barkley of Kentucky and Harry S. Truman of Missouri also voted consistently as liberals, and there were others similarly inclined.

Truman was bound for higher glory, of course, and Black was FDR's first appointee to the Supreme Court; Pepper would last until 1950 as the Senate's lone-wolf Southern liberal; and Maverick—well, Maury Maverick lived up to his name. His range-riding grandfather's unbranded cattle had come to be called mavericks, and the word entered the language as a descriptive term for free-roaming, independent, outspoken individuals. Congressman Maverick was most assuredly one of those.

Born and raised in San Antonio around the turn of the century, Maury Maverick was deep-dipped in the rough-and-tumble politics of frontier Texas. A brash, earthy, undisciplined hell-raiser—and withal, exceptionally intelligent—he prided himself in claiming that he had never earned a diploma in his life (though he did attend Virginia Military Institute and the University of Texas, and passed the state bar exam after only a year of law school). For all his he-man antics, Maverick was from boyhood a sensitive champion of the underdog—of which Texas had an inordinate number. He went into World War I a patriot (seriously wounded, he won a Silver Star) and came out a pacifist; he declared himself an implacable foe of the wealthy elite that exploited the labor of impoverished Mexicans, blacks, and Anglos; as San Antonio's tax collector from 1920 to 1934, he fought for social reforms and against the corrupt political machine that dominated the city's politics.

The New Deal was a dream come true for Maverick, and when he won a seat in Congress in 1934, his liberal reputation preceded him onto the floor of the House. "In the South are my people," he declared, "neither worse nor better than any other Americans," and that egalitarian point of view was the sum and substance of his public life. He said of the South: "With all her faults, I love her still. But this will not keep me from telling the truth and lambasting her when she needs it, and she needs it plenty."

A squat, pudgy brawler with bulging eyes and a bullfrog voice, the iconoclastic Maverick attacked pretense and pomposity with the ferocious intensity of a hungry dog on a bone. Among his lasting contributions was a new word, *gobbledygook*, to ridicule high-flown bureaucratic and academic jargon. He quickly became the spokesman of a clutch of House liberals who backed most of the New Deal's programs—except those they deemed too timidly conservative—and FDR was delighted to have such articulate pressure from the left. "I'm so liberal I say *chigro* instead of *chigger,"* the irreverent Texan joked, and though he, like virtually all white progressives, stopped short of attacking segregation, he was foremost among his House colleagues in demanding equal treatment and dignity for minorities and the poor. Roosevelt was ecstatic on election night in 1936 to learn that among the many Democrats who would return to Washington with him was Maury Maverick.

But a small band of liberal knights errant in Congress, together with others in the executive branch and literally millions of enthusiastic followers across the country, were not enough to assure the New Deal of permanence. The 1936 landslide may have proved to FDR that he no longer needed the South to win the White House, but he still had to have the support of Southerners in Congress to get his programs approved. At the beginning of his quest for national leadership, he had tacitly struck an unholy bargain with the Dixie bloc: their support of his programs in exchange for his accommodation to their racial and social biases. He had no deep convictions on the subject. In his eyes, this was strictly a political trade-off, the kind of deal he handled so adroitly, and he used it to push them much further to the left than anyone might have expected. He could laugh at their "nigger" jokes, look the other way when blacks suffered public indignities, even withhold his endorsement of anti-lynching legislation—all of which he did—and at the same time give support and encouragement to liberal administrators, jurists, lawmakers, activists, and intellectuals who attached high priority to social reform in the South. Somehow the bargain had held through four years of relief and recovery—but reelection and the start of a second term for the President proved to be the warning buzzer for a monumental intraparty clash.

Roosevelt had been careful not to exclude arch-conservative Democrats from the New Deal; in fact, he earnestly courted the favor of some, with notable success. Bernard Baruch, the South Carolina–born wizard of Wall Street, was brought into FDR's inner circle of advisers by Senator James F. Byrnes, and he remained a close associate of the President. Boston financier Joseph P. Kennedy, whom critics branded a speculator and an isolationist, held three different high appointive positions during the first two administrations, and even wrote a book in 1936 called *I'm for Roosevelt* (in which he declared emphatically, "I have no political ambition for myself or my children").

Still, the overwhelming majority of reactionary Republicans and Southern Democrats were filled with fear and panic by the direction in which FDR was steering the nation, and so were many others atop the economic and institutional totem pole—corporate and industrial barons, big planters, doctors and lawyers, religious leaders, newspaper publishers. What they objected to, in broadest terms, were government initiatives that weakened their long-established economic advantage: land and income reforms in agriculture, collective bargaining, regulation of wages and hours, production controls, price supports, regional planning, and government-owned utilities like TVA.

The Southern States Industrial Council, headed by John E. Edgerton, a Tennessee manufacturer (and no kin of mine), sounded the reactionary alarm against unions, foreign labor (including Yankees), and "dilution of racial purity" in the workforce. The council opposed wage and hour regulations, and even fought to perpetuate regional pay differentials that discriminated against the South's own workers. Such unmitigated advocacy of economic privilege was by no means confined to the South's wealthy elite. It was from the ranks of these upper-echelon critics, North and South, that the anti–New Deal Liberty League was established in 1934, claiming among its sponsors the two previous Democratic presidential nominees, Al Smith and John W. Davis.

The federal courts loomed as an even more immediate New Deal stumbling block. By the end of 1935, lawsuits against New Deal legislation had resulted in more than a thousand injunctions, and the Supreme Court subsequently invalidated almost a dozen major laws, including significant portions of the National Industrial Recovery Act and the Agricultural Adjustment Act. Increasingly, conservatives throughout the nation saw the Supreme Court as the last hope for keeping state and local solutions ahead of federal remedies and business interests ahead of individual rights and liberties in the traditional American scheme of things. The strain on the court's four conservative, three liberal, and two moderate justices revealed itself clearly in the high number of five-to-four decisions they rendered.

The South was squarely in the center of the spreading opposition to the New Deal. Even as they voted for relief and recovery programs, Southern members of Congress saw to it that pay scales remained lower in the South than elsewhere, and lower for blacks than whites—all in the interest of perpetuating the cheap-labor/white-supremacy status quo. A $2-billion infusion of federal funds in the South in the first six years of the Roosevelt era brought tens of thousands of jobs and countless physical improvements to the region, raising the standard of living substantially—but also raising the ire of planters, businessmen, and even homemakers who complained of the loss of low-paid employees. They were outraged that relief was taking away the field hands and janitors and cooks who had previously found no other choice except to work from sunrise to sunset, from can to can't, for fifty cents a day.

Georgia Governor Eugene Talmadge never took a neighborly liking to Roosevelt; on the contrary, he was among the first to proclaim belligerent opposition to the man and his programs. Rumor had it that Huey Long, just before his assassination, was plotting an anti–New Deal alliance with Talmadge. As unlikely as that seems, given their conflicting viewpoints, they did share an overweening ambition for higher office and for Southern, if not national, dominion. Roosevelt stood directly in their way—and furthermore, he was rapidly winning the allegiance of the South's people—so it's not hard to imagine that a conspiracy to stop him was in the works.

In January 1936, a few months after Long's death, Talmadge joined with Louisiana preacher and Kingfish loyalist Gerald L. K. Smith and North Carolina novelist Thomas Dixon to stage a "Grass Roots Convention" in Macon, Georgia. John H. Kirby, an arch-conservative Texas lumberman, put up most of the money for the gathering, and such wealthy Northerners as Alfred P. Sloan and Pierre S. du Pont also contributed. The anti-Roosevelt rhetoric was loud and reckless, but ineffectual; invitations to "Jeffersonian Democrats" from Maryland to Texas attracted only a few hundred people, and even some of them were put off by the extremist tone of the event. That fall, Talmadge tried to unseat Senator Richard B. Russell, a lukewarm New Dealer at best, but a dependable party loyalist. Predictably, Russell gave him a sound thrashing.

Certain tactics always seemed to work for the demagogues: blame the Yankees, blame the Republicans, blame the foreigners, the Communists, the Catholics and Jews—and if all else failed, blame the "niggers." Nobody could pluck those strings more adroitly than Gene Talmadge. Snapping his bright red suspenders, ringing spittoons with unerring accuracy, spouting outrageous slanders against every obstacle in his path to a Fascist dictatorship, the "Wild Man from Sugar Creek" parlayed a University of Georgia law degree and a labor-intensive south Georgia plantation into an income base for his entertain-the-rubes rise to power. Elected governor in 1932 as a New Deal tub-thumper and reelected in 1934 under similar pretenses, he promptly jumped ship to organize the abortive grassroots revolt in Macon. When he failed in 1936 to unseat Russell and in 1938 to defeat Georgia's other senatorial incumbent, Walter George, the undaunted Talmadge got himself elected governor again in 1940, and remained a force to be reckoned with until his death in 1947.

In the final analysis, though, it was not court decisions or right-wing pressure groups or even rabble-rousing governors like Gene Talmadge that dealt such crippling blows to Roosevelt and the New Deal; rather, it was the veteran Southerners in Congress, men as outwardly proper and respectable as Senator Russell and as unapologetically bigoted as his colleagues Cotton Ed Smith and Theodore Bilbo. Together—and with the acquiescence of their Northern lodge brothers in the House and Senate—

they kept democracy at bay in the South for another generation. The people of this region have never spoken more clearly than they did at the polls in 1936—they gave FDR over seventy-five percent of their votes—but their voices have never been so effectively nullified as they were in the years that followed.

The signs of incipient revolt were clearly visible before the 1936 election, but apparently no one took them seriously. At the Democratic Convention in Philadelphia that summer, Cotton Ed Smith had stalked out of the meeting hall when a black minister was called upon to open a session with prayer. "By God, he's as black as melted midnight!" roared the South Carolina senator, quivering with rage. "Get out of my way! This mongrel meeting ain't no place for a white man!" Others dutifully trailed him into temporary self-exile. Then, to compound the Southerners' outrage, the convention delegates threw out their long-standing "two-thirds" rule and allowed a simple majority to nominate the party's presidential candidate, thus depriving the Southern bloc of minority control over the process. Clearly, the Northern liberal coalition was in charge, and FDR was openly aligned with them. His overwhelming victory in November, far from causing resigned acceptance among Southern conservatives and their like-minded allies, only served to escalate their alarm and hostility.

Shortly after Congress returned to work in early 1937, Roosevelt began to make known his conviction that major reform of the federal judiciary was the only way to ensure final approval and implementation of the New Deal. Too many new laws were being overturned by judges who held a narrow view of federal authority, the President believed. In a February message that few of his advisers had been consulted on, he asked both houses to act promptly on a sweeping proposal to create up to fifty new federal judgeships, including six on the Supreme Court—one for every sitting jurist who, having served ten years or more, refused to retire after age seventy. Six of the nine sitting justices, including all four of the conservatives, happened to fit that description.

The "court-packing plan," as the press came to call it, hit Capitol Hill like a clap of thunder, and the storm of controversy that followed lasted six months. Generally speaking, the President got most of his Southern support in the Senate from Florida's Pepper, Alabama's Black, Bilbo and Harrison of Mississippi, Robinson and Caraway of Arkansas, Kentucky's Barkley, and Sheppard of Texas—but the much more vocal opposition was led by Byrd and Glass of Virginia, Bailey and Reynolds of North Carolina, Smith of South Carolina, George of Georgia, and Connally of Texas. Vice

President Garner, another obstructionist foe, worked behind the scenes to torpedo the bill.

In the House, Maury Maverick quickly signed on as a sponsor of the legislation, and Lyndon B. Johnson actually won his seat there in a close election in the Texas hill country that year by making his support of the plan a pivotal issue. But even in the Texas delegation Maverick and Johnson were outnumbered, and House opponents from throughout the South easily managed to dodge the heat, forcing the Senate to take the matter up first.

It was this issue that finally brought the anti-Roosevelt Southerners out into the open. Those who had mumbled their discontent in private now shouted it to any who would listen—and many did. The court-packing plan smacked of executive reprisal; it was an audacious scheme that seemed to toss aside age-old constitutional principles. The debate dragged on through the spring. The Supreme Court, meanwhile—apparently taking heed of its vulnerability—gave signs of having discovered new justifications for upholding controversial legislation (including the Social Security Act, which in January 1937 began withholding a maximum of $30 a year— one percent of the first $3,000 of income—from workers' paychecks). Each succeeding decision the court rendered in favor of the New Deal was widely viewed as further proof of the effectiveness, for good or ill, of the Roosevelt power play. "A switch in time saves nine," one wit noted; another observer called the court's action "self-salvation by self-reversal."

In May, conservative Justice Willis Van Devanter made a timely announcement of his retirement, and Senate Majority Leader Joe Robinson, having been promised the first vacancy on the court, prepared to move up, with Pat Harrison of Mississippi in line to take his Senate post. Indeed, it was their anticipation of these promotions that kept Robinson and Harrison in line as proponents of court reform. At that point, Roosevelt could have dropped the plan and still had what he wanted: a court more receptive to the New Deal philosophy. But the President, cockily overconfident, wanted total victory, and he leaned hard on his troops to deliver it.

With each passing week, though, support for the legislation seemed to fade, and the opponents sensed victory. The FDR coalition was coming apart, although Roosevelt himself seemed unable to see it, and no one was able to impress the fact upon him. He didn't help his cause when he pointedly refrained for weeks from telling Joe Robinson that the court vacancy was his. As pressure mounted on all sides, the temperature in both houses of Congress followed the Washington summer thermometer straight up to the boiling point.

On July 13, while Senator Josiah Bailey of North Carolina was deep into a diatribe against the court bill, Robinson got up and left the chamber, exhausted and in pain. The next morning he was found slumped on the floor in his apartment, dead of a heart attack. The court-packing plan, already in grave danger, quickly died its own anticlimactic death without ever coming to a vote; a week later, the Senate sent the bill back to committee.

In his thirty-three years of congressional service, Joe Robinson had represented Arkansas in both houses, and he had also been Al Smith's vice-presidential running mate in 1928. He was no liberal, certainly, but he was a loyal team player for FDR and the Democrats, and his departure destroyed the administration's defenses. A bruising battle for his leadership post ensued between Pat Harrison and Alben Barkley, and the President further alienated the conservatives by letting it be known that he supported the more liberal Kentuckian. Insult was heaped on injury when Theodore Bilbo, Harrison's hostile Mississippi colleague and a man whose loyalty had often gone to the highest bidder, cast the decisive vote that gave Barkley the victory by a cliff-hanging majority of one.

In August, when Roosevelt nominated fifty-one-year-old Hugo La-Fayette Black to fill the Supreme Court vacancy, some of the senator's Southern colleagues, including Bilbo, George of Georgia, McKellar of Tennessee, Connally of Texas, and Reynolds of North Carolina, quickly joined the liberals in voting sixty-three to sixteen to confirm him. (Was this simply senatorial courtesy? Southern pride? Did they want most of all to remove him from their midst? Were they setting him up for some sort of surprise attack? Even now, their motives remain a mystery.) The die-hard Virginians, Glass and Byrd, were the only two Southerners to vote no; several others, including Cotton Ed Smith and Josiah Bailey, managed to be absent from the chamber when the vote was recorded.

A month later, journalist Ray Sprigle of the Pittsburgh *Post-Gazette* reported what had long been common knowledge in Alabama and even among the members of the Senate: that Black had joined the Ku Klux Klan in the mid-1920s, and had used the secret society's endorsement to help launch his career in politics. In the resulting uproar, the new justice finally decided to go on national radio to defend himself. He acknowledged the former membership, but cited his Senate record as proof that he had repudiated the Klan. Few were placated on either side of the issue, and a cloud of suspicion followed Black to the bench.

It didn't linger for long. Black, a largely self-educated man whose parents had been country storekeepers in Alabama, proved to be one of the Supreme Court's most learned and articulate defenders of civil liberties and civil rights, a liberal in the truest and best sense of that much-abused word. In one of his first cases he sided with the majority in declaring that the University of Missouri must offer equal opportunity in its higher-education system to qualified applicants such as Lloyd Gaines, the Negro plaintiff in the suit at issue. That 1938 case, *Missouri ex rel. Gaines* v. *Canada*, was the first race-and-education decision ever handed down by the Supreme Court.

One signpost after another revealed the first two years of Roosevelt's second administration to be the parting of the ways between him and most of his former allies in the Southern congressional delegation. In 1937 and 1938 he lost the allegiance of both Mississippi senators, Bilbo and Harrison, of Tennessee's McKellar, and of North Carolina's Reynolds, to name just four; by 1939, even his principal first-term adviser in the Senate, James F. Byrnes of South Carolina, was cleverly undercutting the President at almost every turn. In the House there were a few bright lights, but not enough: Maury Maverick was defeated in 1938, just as Martin Dies, a reactionary east Texan, was rising to notoriety with the quiet encouragement of Vice President Garner; Lister Hill of Alabama left the House to run successfully for Black's Senate seat; and in the Deep South states of Louisiana, Mississippi, Georgia, and South Carolina, progressive or moderate or even mildly conservative congressmen were as scarce as hens' teeth.

It is worth remembering that until the late 1930s, when Franklin Roosevelt appeared ready to attempt a fundamental realignment of the Democratic and Republican parties along ideologically distinct liberal and conservative lines, his difficulties with the Southern conservatives, all of whom were Democrats, had little to do with such principles as states' rights and federal authority, and practically nothing to do with the issue of race. In fact, men as different in demeanor and outlook and personality as Bilbo and Jimmy Byrnes were reliable supporters of New Deal legislation until 1937, apparently seeing little if anything in FDR's personal behavior to make them fear that he was going to spark an economic or racial revolution in the South.

But the court-packing battle changed all that, and Black's appointment, his Klan history notwithstanding, served notice to the Southern bloc that a monumental fight for liberal social change—possibly even including racial change—was on the horizon. The outbreak of world war would cause most of the Southerners to put aside their differences with the President, but the realignment would be limited and temporary; on domestic issues, they never trusted him again. Two who had been with him from the first were Bilbo and Byrnes; their sharply contrasting styles of subsequent opposition showed how infinitely diverse and inventive were the ways of Southern politicians.

A compassion for the rural poor among whom he was born and a raging fear and hatred of all things alien to his understanding struggled constantly for dominance inside the fertile personality of Theodore G. Bilbo—and most of the time, the fear and hatred won out. Raised in a pious Baptist family of modest means on a farm near Poplarville in southeast Mississippi, he tried theology school briefly before studying law at Vanderbilt University in Nashville, and then spent twenty-five years in public office in his home state—including two terms as governor—before being elected to the U.S. Senate at the age of fifty-six in 1934.

Scandal trailed him like a skunk's scent from the very start of his political career. He was accused of bribe-taking, conflict of interest, stealing, lying, and abuse of women, among other things; in one breach-of-promise case he was sent to jail, and the state senate narrowly missed expelling him for "his established bad character and lack of credibility." But Bilbo—whose axiom was "The voters will always forget"—had that peculiar Southern knack for stump oratory, and he beguiled and blustered his way to the top. Like Gene Talmadge and Cotton Ed Smith, he could masquerade convincingly as a poor white country boy put upon by the big delta plantation colonels and the corporate barons on one side, and by the "niggers" on the other. Blacks were a slight majority of Mississippi's two million people in 1930, but only a token few hundred of them were permitted to vote. "I'm calling on every red-blooded American who believes in the superiority and integrity of the white race to get out and see that no nigger votes," he exhorted campaign crowds, "and the best time to do it is the night before!"

The name *Theodore* means "God's gift," he was fond of declaring, and *Bilbo* means "a two-edged sword—and I'm both edges." (There was another dictionary meaning, chillingly symbolic: a *bilbo* in Spanish was "an iron bar with shackles, originally used to confine the feet of slaves aboard ships.") During his second term as governor, "The Man," as he liked to call himself (and be called by others), kept Mississippi in the Democratic column behind Al Smith, a Catholic and a whiskey-drinker—"and me a dry, a Baptist, and a Ku Klux Klansman," Bilbo boasted. He seemed almost pleased when writers referred to him as "a Mississippi Mussolini"; others, less charitable, dubbed him "the Bilbonic Plague." He left the state government in shambles in 1932, and then promptly entrained for Washington, where he talked Senator Pat Harrison into getting him a New Deal post in the Department of Agriculture. After less than two years in that sinecure, he turned on Harrison and his elderly colleague, Senator Hubert Stephens, and went home to challenge and defeat Stephens. And so, from 1935 on, the amiable and easygoing Harrison had Bilbo as his senatorial cross to bear.

During his first term in Washington (and sporadically after that), the explosive Mississippian displayed a paradoxical affinity for Franklin

Roosevelt and many of the New Deal programs. Both the President and most of Bilbo's colleagues in the Senate humored "The Man," indulged him, tolerated him. When he embarrassed them with his extreme Negrophobia, they pretended not to be listening—as when, for example, in both 1938 and 1939, he praised Nazi Germany's racial policies and introduced legislation calling for the federal government to spend a billion dollars on the deportation of twelve million African-American citizens to colonial lands in Africa.

But when the Southerners joined forces to resist social change, Bilbo was their friend and ally—as when, again in 1938, the Dixie senators staged a grueling seven-week filibuster to defeat another anti-lynching bill. Every one of them—including the liberal Claude Pepper of Florida, who was running for reelection—closed ranks under the banner of "states' rights" in this obstructionist fight. Pat Harrison put aside his gentler nature and his hostility to Bilbo and joined his junior colleague barb for barb in a double-barreled blast at "this treason against the South." Jimmy Byrnes of South Carolina, smooth and urbane beyond a hint of his humble origins, vowed that he and his Southern brothers would talk on for a century, if necessary, to prevent the majority from imposing its will upon them.

Of all the men in the Dixie bloc, from the simplest to the most complex, none was more fascinating or puzzling than Byrnes. In sharp contrast to the colorful extremists and fanatics who had dominated South Carolina politics for the better part of a century—Ben Tillman, Cole Blease, Cotton Ed Smith—the little Irishman, James Francis Byrnes, was a model of respectability and cool restraint. Born a Catholic in Charleston shortly before his father died in 1882, he was nurtured by his hardworking mother, a struggling dressmaker, and by an aristocratic lawyer who hired him at age thirteen to be an errand boy and subsequently became his mentor. Jimmy didn't go far in school, but he rose quickly from runner to office clerk to court stenographer to attorney, passing the bar in 1904 without benefit of formal instruction.

By 1910, when he was elected to the U.S. House of Representatives, Byrnes had married and gravitated to the church of his Episcopalian wife, had made a name for himself as a lawyer and editor in Aiken, near the Georgia line, and had cast himself as a moderate reformer on the bridge between the old South and the new. Thoroughly immersed in the racial mores of the region, he believed unquestioningly in the total supremacy of the Caucasian race; like many so-called progressives of his time, he saw Jim Crow laws and black disenfranchisement as positive reforms that would make it easier for paternalistic whites to deal fairly and benignly with "their negroes."

Tillman and Smith were in the Senate and Blease was in the governor's office when Byrnes got elected; in their shadow, he must have looked and sounded like a meek little do-good lawyer spouting pious platitudes about "duty" and "fairness." Indeed, in his first reelection race, he was challenged by an opponent who called him a "nigger lover"—and after that he concluded that outspoken white supremacy was essential if he wanted to be successful in politics. The strategy worked for fourteen years, during which he was such a dependable Southern guardian of white privilege that the Congress-watchers at the NAACP took disparaging note of his "militant white racism." But even when he tried, he was no match for the sulfurous Blease, who "outniggered" him to victory in a race for the Senate in 1924. Six years later, Byrnes tried a softer tack, appealing "to the reason and intelligence of the people instead of their passions and prejudices," and he came away with a narrow upset victory.

As a loyal Democrat, he had campaigned for Al Smith in 1928, and long before the New Deal was invented he was courting favor with Governor Roosevelt, whom he had known for at least a decade. In fact, the term *New Deal* itself could well have come from Byrnes, because he worked for FDR as a speechwriter and strategist in the 1932 campaign. Though he was only a first-term senator, the crafty Carolinian was a Capitol Hill veteran who knew well the ways of the Club, and he soon gained added stature as the President's unofficial point man in the Senate. The two had much in common: ambition, pragmatism, a knack for control by indirection, a consuming passion for the political game. Ideology was secondary to them; winning was always first.

Not least of the favors that endeared Byrnes to Roosevelt was his introduction of Bernard Baruch into the White House inner sanctum. The celebrated Wall Street wonder boy and freewheeling financier had enjoyed a comfortable South Carolina boyhood as the son of a Prussian-born Jewish surgeon famed for his service to Robert E. Lee and the Confederacy. By the time he was thirty years old, young Baruch had acquired a huge Carolina plantation retreat, and over the years he frequently entertained his political friends there, including FDR. For social as well as financial reasons, Roosevelt treasured his association with Baruch, and he gave Byrnes full credit for having brought them together.

Senator Byrnes was especially valuable to the President as a middleman between the liberals and conservatives on Capitol Hill. He could go either way with ease, moving so quietly and inconspicuously that his influence was often unnoticed—and all the more effective for that. Practically every bill that became law in Roosevelt's first term got a helping hand at some crucial moment from Jimmy Byrnes. Other Southerners held the leadership posts and the committee chairmanships, but no one

Florida agricultural workers waiting to draw a day's pay during the Great Depression

Convict laborers under guard in rural Georgia in the 1930s

Picketers at a mill in Georgia during the textile industry general strike, 1934

Delegates to the first Southern Tenant Farmers Union convention,
Marked Tree, Arkansas, 1935

A coworker watches as Melvin Swinea fills out his application for membership in the Southern Tenant Farmers Union at a rally in Parkin, Arkansas, 1937.

Trustees of Providence, an interracial cooperative farm in Mississippi, 1938. From left, front row: Sam Franklin, Sherwood Eddy, Arthur Raper; middle row: John Rust, Reinhold Niebuhr, Charles S. Johnson; back row: James Causey, William Scarlett

Willis D. Weatherford (front, center) and others, including Samuel Chiles Mitchell, behind him, at Weatherford's Blue Ridge YMCA Assembly in the mountains of North Carolina

This 1935 experimental model of the mechanical cotton picker designed by brothers John and Mack Rust presaged a time soon to come when machines would displace millions of laborers in the fields.

Some Southern Democrats of the 1930s:
Above: *Senators Carter Glass of Virginia (left) and Tom Connally of Texas*
Below: *Senator Huey Long of Louisiana*
Opposite, inset: *Senate Majority Leader Joseph T. Robinson of Arkansas*
Opposite, right: *Congressman Maury Maverick of Texas*
Opposite, bottom: *Senators Walter George (left) and Richard Russell of Georgia meet
President Franklin D. Roosevelt on the campaign trail, 1938.*

Langston Hughes, Charles S. Johnson, and E. Franklin Frazier (from left) with friends in New York during the Harlem Renaissance of the 1920s

Atlanta Daily World *editor Frank Marshall Davis at his desk in 1934*

Opposite, above: *Thurgood Marshall with client Donald Murray (center) and mentor Charles H. Houston at a state court hearing on Murray's plea for admission to the University of Maryland law school, 1935*

Opposite, below: *Charlotte Hawkins Brown (center) with four of her teachers at Palmer Memorial Institute, a private girls' school founded by her at Sedalia, North Carolina, in 1904*

Above, left: *"Lone-wolf liberal" Senator Claude Pepper of Florida*

Above, right: *Jessie Daniel Ames, founder of the Association of Southern Women for the Prevention of Lynching*

Attorney William H. Hastie was thirty-two when President Roosevelt appointed him in 1937 as the first African-American to be a federal judge.

Robert C. Weaver, an economist with a Ph.D. from Harvard, was the first of about a hundred blacks appointed to administrative and advisory positions in the New Deal during the 1930s.

Texas Congressman Martin Dies (center), chairman of the first House Un-American Activities Committee in 1938, with fellow Democrat and committee member Joe Starnes of Alabama (left) and J. B. Matthews, a Kentucky native and ex-Communist who was HUAC's chief investigator

University of North Carolina sociologist Howard W. Odum

Opposite, below: *Mississippi novelist William Faulkner (left) and Milton Abernethy, owner of the Intimate Bookshop in Chapel Hill, North Carolina, photographed there in 1931*

Florida-born novelist and folklorist Zora Neale Hurston

James Weldon Johnson went from Jacksonville, Florida, to an illustrious career as a writer, diplomat, teacher, and NAACP leader.

Social critic H. L. Mencken of the Baltimore Sun was an inspiration to many Southern writers of the 1930s.

Liberal activist Howard "Buck" Kester (front), relaxing with two strike-idled coal miners at Wilder, Tennessee, in 1933

Southern Tenant Farmers Union leaders H. L. Mitchell (left) and Howard Kester (right) with Norman Thomas, U.S. Socialist Party leader, in Tyronza, Arkansas, 1934

At about the time he cofounded the Highlander Folk School with Myles Horton in 1932, twenty-six-year-old Don West had a degree in theology, a reputation for radicalism, and a shiny black motorcycle.

Inset: Herman C. Nixon, an Alabamian, moved from right to left to center in the 1930s—first as a Vanderbilt Agrarian, then as an organizer of the Southern Conference for Human Welfare, and finally as an academician.

Georgia's once and future governor, Eugene Talmadge, on a campaign stop in rural Telfair County during his unsuccessful 1938 campaign to unseat U.S. Senator Walter George

in the Senate had more of an inside track than he did. Cautiously skirting controversial issues, including race, he went home to run for reelection in 1936 with the admiration and respect of his colleagues and the strong support of his Democratic constituents. His opponents tried to brand him and the President as Socialists "who consort with colored people," but the ploy was a spectacular failure; Roosevelt got ninety-eight percent of South Carolina's votes in 1936, and Byrnes lost only one precinct in the entire state.

You might think that such an overwhelming mandate would compel a politician to keep moving in the direction he was going. Byrnes seemed perfectly positioned: to the right of Black and Pepper, to the left of Glass and Bailey, a dignified cut above such knee-jerk bigots as Bilbo and Cotton Ed—and most important of all, right in the center of the White House, where real power was supposed to reside. But it was precisely here, at the moment of his and Roosevelt's greatest triumph, that Byrnes fell once again under the hypnotic spell of the ancient Southern bugaboo of race.

With his blood brothers in the Dixie bloc leaning heavily on him, and with his own emotional convictions reinforcing their insistent pleas, the junior senator from South Carolina took a racial turn to the right as soon as Congress convened in 1937. For the next two years—until Roosevelt himself put the domestic agenda on ice and sought refuge in the pressing concerns of foreign policy—Jimmy Byrnes acted more like Cotton Ed than like "the President's favorite senator" (as he had been described in the press in 1933). Suddenly he was hostile to strikes by the industrial unions, to certain staff decisions within the Farm Security Administration, to minimum wage provisions in the Fair Labor Standards Act, to appropriations for the Works Progress Administration—and beneath each criticism was a racial angle, a caveat based on skin color.

When the anti-lynching bill was placed at the top of the Senate's 1938 agenda by Majority Leader Alben Barkley, Byrnes angrily blamed the NAACP and Walter White. "Barkley can't do anything without talking to that nigger first," the senator was quoted as saying. In the ensuing filibuster, Byrnes escalated his attack on White, charging that Congress had become his puppet. The Democratic Party, he declared, had fallen under the control of "the Negroes of the North," and the South "has been deserted by the Democrats."

In reality, Walter White had precious little influence in Washington, and neither did any other minority figure in American public life. What Byrnes and the other Southerners truly feared was that as soon as Roosevelt and the white liberals finished recruiting Northern blacks and making room for them in the Democratic Party, they would turn their

attention to the South. But such convulsive changes were far in the future—and in the meantime, the Southerners still had the filibuster. In the
legislative arena, it was The Bomb, the ultimate weapon. With it, they
stopped the anti-lynching bill cold once again, while President Roosevelt
sat uneasily in his office, intently gazing in another direction.

Jimmy Byrnes was not the only Southern senator to ride back to Washington on the Democratic tidal wave in 1936; Carter Glass, Pat Harrison,
and John Bankhead rode with him, and so did Josiah W. Bailey. A pious
Confederate of the old school, Bailey had first arrived from North Carolina
with the unbeatable blessings of the Baptist Church and Buck Duke's
electric power company, and he never did anything to cause either pillar
to shake beneath his feet. Along with religion and business he was also
devoted to white supremacy, and that holy trinity was enough to plant
Bailey in the Glass house of righteous resistance to the New Deal almost
from the start. Once in a while he strayed over to the Roosevelt camp, and
like Cotton Ed Smith and a few others, he was not above telling the voters
that he was a New Deal Democrat—sort of. But by 1937, when he was
safely back in Washington for six more years, you could confidently expect
to find old Josh Bailey spewing hot coals on the heads of FDR and the
liberals.

The court-packing episode was the catalyst for a bipartisan effort by
Senate conservatives to mount a semiformal counterrevolution, and the
sixty-five-year-old Bailey was one of its ringleaders. He and ten others,
including four Southerners, started meeting early in the year to map
strategy. Buoyed by the failure of the court reform plan and alarmed by
the onset of an economic recession in late summer, the group—enlarged
by then to about thirty, equally divided between Republicans and Democrats, and including more than a half-dozen Southerners—came close to
formally uniting behind a "conservative manifesto" that emphasized five
major governmental imperatives: to reduce taxes, to balance the budget,
to curb labor violence, to promote free enterprise, and to honor states'
rights. Bailey was the chief draftsman and editor of the document.

Their movement had begun as an alarmed reaction against what they
perceived as Roosevelt's intention to convert the Democratic Party into an
ideological base for all liberals; the aim of Bailey and his allies was to form
the nucleus of an opposition party, a conservative resistance. But then, as
the President's fortunes sagged, some of the plotters began to think they
might be able to defeat him without a drastic realignment of the two
parties (failure, they knew, would mean the loss of their party privileges).
Soon they were mired in partisan wrangling while their grand strategy

disintegrated. In December the story of their secret pact broke in the papers, and the plotters were widely suspected of fronting for the Liberty League, an elite nest of ultra-right-wing reactionaries. Amid finger-pointing and denials, Josh Bailey was left to take most of the heat for what looked like an underground resistance plan, if not some sort of bungled party coup.

It was right after this incident that the disruptive and mean-spirited filibuster against the anti-lynching bill broke out, ushering in 1938 on a somber and jarring note of raw hostility. The gloves were off now. With the midterm congressional elections in the offing, the President decided in June to single out certain philistines who were up for reelection, and to bring the weight of his personal popularity to bear against them. Two of the senators on his hit list were Walter George of Georgia and Cotton Ed Smith of South Carolina.

With the opinion polls showing more than two-thirds of the American people—and an even higher proportion of Southerners—still solidly in favor of him and the New Deal, Roosevelt went to Barnesville, Georgia, on August 11 for a campaign speech and declared, while Senator George sat stone-faced on the platform with him, that he and the staunchly conservative ex-judge "do not speak the same language." The President urged his stunned audience not to send George back to Washington. The senator, with an admirable display of manners, shook hands with him at the end and said tersely, "Mr. President, I want you to know that I accept the challenge."

A few days later, in another town, George sagely avoided a direct hit at Roosevelt but launched a scathing attack on alien others he associated with him, including Tommy Corcoran (a Yankee Catholic), Benjamin Cohen (a New York Jew), the labor leader John L. Lewis, and James Ford, the black vice-presidential nominee of the Communist Party. Turner Catledge of the *New York Times*, a native Mississippian, listened to the crowd erupt with cheers and knew that George's blatant hate-mongering was going to work. "It reminded me," he wrote later, "of what Pat Harrison used to say—that he could be a statesman for five years, but on the sixth—election year—he went back home to 'sling the shit.' " George slung it with pinpoint accuracy, and it landed right on FDR's spats. Four weeks later the senator won the Democratic primary in a landslide over the bombastic Eugene Talmadge and a little-known party functionary.

By the time Roosevelt got to South Carolina he had almost lost his taste for hand-to-hand combat, but he couldn't resist a parting jab at Cotton Ed, who was being challenged by Governor Olin D. Johnston. The senator was primed and ready, itching for a fight. His walkout at the 1936 Democratic convention had made him a folk hero among his white constituents, so he played the racial tune again—and won reelection with ease. Even worse from FDR's perspective must have been the knowledge that Smith got behind-the-scenes help from none other than Jimmy Byrnes.

As in the court-packing fight, Roosevelt had overplayed his hand, and the costs to his prestige and his program were enormous. The "Dixie Demagogues," as writers Allan A. Michie and Frank Ryhlick dubbed the Southern congressional clique in a 1939 book, had slyly provoked the President into snatching defeat from the jaws of victory. In the November general election, the Democrats lost seven seats in the Senate and seventy in the House. And there was more bad news: The white press was lambasting FDR for his liberal programs and his high-handed manner with Congress and the courts, while the black press was attacking him for the lack of substance in his civil rights record and his soft-pedaling of Southern racists. Nazis, Fascists, and Communists were seen increasingly as a menace to the nation, and in the House of Representatives, the newly formed Committee on Un-American Activities was pursuing "foreign agents and disloyal citizens" with reckless abandon. The economy was still stalled, the budget deficit was ballooning, and the multiple problems of chronic poverty still plagued an alarming number of Americans, including a majority of Southerners.

When he boarded a train for Georgia and a much-needed Thanksgiving holiday in November 1938, the President could only look back in puzzlement and dismay at the string of frustrating defeats that had followed directly in the wake of his greatest election victory. War was about to envelop Europe, and the debate over how much or how little the United States should do to help its allies there had already begun. With an increasing sense of urgency—and not a little relief—Franklin D. Roosevelt quietly laid his domestic agenda aside for the duration. For all practical purposes, the New Deal was over.

8. *Shaking the Pillars*

Measured in political terms, the impact of the New Deal on America in the 1930s was enormous; it was, after all, a political movement, if not more extensively a nonviolent revolution in which one ideology replaced another and power changed hands across the board. (That may be an overstatement of the case if you consider how substantially the Southern Democratic elite retained its authority—but on a national scale, the results really did seem revolutionary.)

Political transformation was not all that was happening in those years, though, even if it was the primary force at work in the society. Too much concentration on what politicians say and do can cause you to discount the activities of people and institutions outside the center ring of politics. I'm thinking particularly of what could be called, for want of a better umbrella term, the intelligentsia: scholars, academicians, thinkers; teachers and preachers; journalists and authors; activists on behalf of a cause, an issue, a social goal. The pillar institutions—church, press, university—and the special-interest associations of agriculture, industry, and labor were all profoundly affected by New Deal politics, but they in turn also had a powerful impact on the political process. In the spread of ideas, thoughts, impressions, and opinions into the public mind, the intelligentsia was probably at least as influential as the much more visible cadre of mainstream politicians. And in the South most especially, those who thought and spoke out, who wrote and took action, were vitally important figures in the 1930s, whether they were identified with the heralds of social change or the bedrock of resistance to it.

Religious motivation accounted for some of the movement on both sides of the fence. The thirties were years of such desperation that social experimentation was inevitable, and yet the very presence of conservative institutions intent on protecting their material possessions and their power foreordained a high level of social paralysis. In an indirect way, the Northern social gospel movement and the activist interests of the Federal Council of Churches did cause some Southerners to be mindful of the needs of the less fortunate among them—but in the main, their search for avenues of service led them to stations outside the institutional church.

Circumspection and a certain diplomatic caution marked the activities of most Southern Protestant denominations in those years, and the same was true of the relatively small number of Catholic parishes in the region and the far smaller congregations of Jews. The Protestant churches of the African-American minority were also quiescent; so surrounded and isolated were they by the power of white supremacy and segregation that aggressive agitation for social reform could only have struck them as a foolhardy notion. And, in the seminaries and colleges and secondary schools that operated with church support, it was exceedingly rare for people who advocated controversial deviations from the status quo to hold on to their positions, let alone make modest advances up the institutional ladder.

There were individual exceptions in almost every denominational body, of course. William L. Poteat, an ordained minister who served as president of Wake Forest College, an esteemed Baptist institution in North Carolina, was perhaps the most noted of a number of Southern Baptists who took a liberal or progressive view on most theological and social questions. Methodists, Presbyterians, Episcopalians, and Congregationalists in the South also had some leaders who held moderate or left-of-center views on such issues as biblical literalism, evolution, militarism and war, race relations, Prohibition, worker rights, lynching, the Ku Klux Klan, and the welfare of the poor. The long ordeal of the Scottsboro boys in Alabama rallied many denominational forces—Northern, mostly, but not entirely—to mount a defense that saved the youths from hanging, and support groups were also organized on behalf of striking miners and textile workers. In the main, though, religiously inspired people who worked for social change in the South did so either as individuals or as members of organizations not officially tied to the mother church.

Two of the oldest such organizations were the Christian student associations, the YMCA and YWCA. Willis D. Weatherford's work among male students had begun early in the century, and in the mid-1930s, the two institutions founded under his leadership—the Blue Ridge Assembly in North Carolina and the YMCA Graduate School in Nashville—were still operating. Weatherford was a race-relations pathfinder in the first phase of his career, but the brotherly progressivism of his youth seemed more like paternalistic caution as he grew older; he resisted efforts to break down segregation in the student movement, not only between whites and blacks but between male and female associations as well. Though he maintained personal ties with a number of black college presidents and other minority figures of his generation (he coauthored a book on race relations with Charles S. Johnson in 1934), and even invited them on occasion to functions at Blue Ridge or in Nashville, the formal and somewhat imperious Dr. Weatherford saw to it that the laws and conventions of racial and sexual separation were strictly observed throughout his tenure at the two institutions.

The YMCA Graduate School was forced to close in 1936, a victim of the depression. Negotiations between Weatherford and Vanderbilt University, which held the mortgage on the school's physical plant, finally broke down, and Weatherford, then past sixty, was disappointed to learn that Vanderbilt, his alma mater, wouldn't make a place for him on its faculty. Fisk University hired him, though, to head its department of religion and philosophy, and he remained there until 1946. It was also in the mid-forties that Weatherford retired as director of the Blue Ridge Assembly, which he had started back in 1912. Always a man of enormous energy, he then gave two more decades to Berea College as a fund raiser and special consultant, not finally retiring until after his ninetieth birthday.

It is difficult to assess the numerous and diverse contributions of a man like Willis Weatherford. His career spanned almost three-quarters of a century; given such a lengthy tenure, it is hardly surprising that his views and actions should seem so advanced when he began, but lagged ever further off the pace of change as the decades passed. His inability to move beyond a paternalistic acceptance of segregation and the "separate but equal" myth underscores the complexity of achieving basic reform in a tightly controlled society. Even so, he began softly calling the white South to task for its racial misdeeds earlier than almost anyone of his race. Such notable Southern progressives as Will Alexander and Frank Porter Graham publicly praised Weatherford for awakening them to careers of public service—and he deserved the credit.

The Young Women's Christian Association in the South generally stayed ahead of its male counterpart in pressing for cooperation and equality across the barriers of race and sex, but joint conferences and united programs didn't become a reality until after World War II. Throughout the thirties and most of the forties, however, the Y's were the nearest thing to a student social-issues movement then existing in the colleges and universities of the South.

Will Alexander's primary institutional base, the Commission on Interracial Cooperation, stayed in business until 1944, but its activities were sharply curtailed after he took permanent leave in 1935 to work for the Roosevelt administration. The CIC (another case of religious motivation finding an outlet beyond the confines of the church) made its most valuable contributions in the 1930s with well-researched studies of lynching, tenant farming, and other problems prevalent in the South. The churches were largely silent on these issues, but groups such as the Association of Southern Women for the Prevention of Lynching got most of their strength from dedicated churchwomen. Jessie Daniel Ames of the CIC was recognized as the foremost activist and organizer in that movement.

The Southern Commission on the Study of Lynching was formed under CIC auspices in 1930 and chaired by George Fort Milton, the progressive young editor of the Chattanooga *News*. Charles S. Johnson and three other prominent blacks joined six whites on the ten-member commission, and investigative research was carried out by Arthur Raper of the CIC and a black sociologist, Walter Chivers of Morehouse College. Raper authored the 1933 final report, which was published by the University of North Carolina Press.

But in spite of the efforts of the women's association and the study commission, lynchings, near-lynchings, and various other vigilante killings continued to plague the South. On an average of more than once a month throughout the thirties, the terror of such lawless acts was imposed with deadly effect, nine times out of ten on someone black. Beyond the "official" statistics on lynching, many additional deaths of blacks at the hands of whites were classified as disappearances or accidents, or as some "legal" form of homicide such as involuntary manslaughter or self-defense. The end result was the same: death without due process. Southerners were left with the frustration and shame of an antisocial crime that their courts refused to punish and their congressmen seemed to excuse or even defend.

Tenant farming and sharecropping, another of the South's glaringly visible problems, drew the concerned attention of many progressives besides those who worked in the New Deal—and here again, religiously inspired groups and individuals played an active part. Numerous variations on the theme of cooperative farming and community renovation were orchestrated in the 1930s. Sometimes the crosscurrents of several initiatives could be found in a single community—Crossville, Tennessee, for example.

Timber cutting, subsistence farming, and coal mining were the primary occupations around Crossville, a remote village on the Cumberland Plateau between Knoxville and Nashville. Missionaries from the Congregational and Presbyterian churches had been coming to the area since the late 1800s, bringing churches, schools, and medical services to the scattered communities of white settlers there. Edwin Wharton, a former settlement-house worker in Cleveland, Ohio, was the schoolmaster at Pleasant Hill, a few miles out of Crossville, beginning in 1917; his wife, May Cravath Wharton, a physician, started a medical facility there and stayed on through a long and useful career as the celebrated "doctor woman of the Cumberlands." A "Yankee missionary" of the Congregational Church named Abram Nightingale arrived in Crossville in 1924 and served for thirty-two years as a selflessly devoted minister to all who came in need—and many did, particularly in the lean years of the depression.

Nightingale attained legendary status for his good works, which he pointedly valued more highly than pious expressions of faith. One of his disciples was a country boy named Myles Horton, a YMCA student who worked under his direction for a couple of summers in the 1920s; Horton went on to Union Theological Seminary in New York and then returned to Tennessee and started the Highlander Folk School. In 1933, Nightingale was among a handful of Crossvillians who purchased land near the town and persuaded federal authorities to start a relief community, Cumberland Homesteads—one of the very first of the new communities created by the Farm Security Administration and its predecessor agencies. Among those who joined Nightingale in providing help on the project were Arthur Morgan, a director of the Tennessee Valley Authority; Dagnall F. Folger of Nashville, who was hired to select (from thousands of applicants) the 250 families who would live in the new community; Howard "Buck" Kester, a YMCA radical from Vanderbilt who recruited destitute families of stranded coal miners idled by a strike in a neighboring county; and, eventually, Alva W. Taylor, mentor of Kester and numerous other religious activists at Vanderbilt before his mild-mannered radicalism cost him his job there.

And if all those busy individuals were not enough to enliven the little village of Crossville and sparsely populated Cumberland County, there was also Eugene Smathers, a Presbyterian missionary who came in 1932 to serve four small country parishes. The twenty-three-year-old son of a Kentucky sharecropper had a seminary degree, an Arkansas wife, and a call to service from the Northern Presbyterians—a more liberal body than their Southern brethren. While the Cumberland Homesteads were struggling to build a new community on an economic base of subsistence farming and cottage industries, Smathers went quietly to work establishing a similar "force for good" on a smaller scale (about fifty families) in the Big Lick community.

A church was built, and a school, and a community center; there was also a health clinic, where a visionary preventive-medicine program was developed with small monthly "prepayments" from each family; most of the farming was done on a cooperative basis, and marketing was planned along the same lines; summer work camps brought a variety of outsiders to the community, including the first black people ever to stay overnight in the county. Big Lick became a small-scale model of what a cooperative community could be, and of what could be done to improve life in the rural South. And Gene Smathers in time became a noted figure in the United Presbyterian Church; thirty-five years after his arrival in Tennessee—and twenty years after the last of the Farm Security Administration homesteads got the political ax from Congress—the gentle shepherd of Big Lick was elected moderator (president) of his church's national governing body.

Buck Kester's odyssey in search of a more just and equitable South was destined to continue. From the days of his youth in Virginia and West Virginia, he had exhibited a deep revulsion to bigotry and discrimination. Under the auspices of the Presbyterian Church and the YMCA, he traveled widely in the United States and abroad, and while still in his early twenties he was involved in interracial conferences with numerous activists, including black leaders Channing Tobias, Mary McLeod Bethune, George Washington Carver, Mordecai Johnson, and Benjamin Mays. As a result of his views and actions, Kester was fired from his YMCA job at Vanderbilt in 1926; he and his like-minded bride, Alice Harris of Decatur, Georgia, then moved to New York, where he was hired as youth secretary of the Fellowship of Reconciliation, an organization of religious pacifists. Before he returned to Nashville in 1929 for graduate study in religion under Alva Taylor at Vanderbilt, Kester was a self-described "Norman Thomas Socialist," and three years later he would carry the party banner in a brief and unsuccessful try for a seat in Congress.

In the summer of 1934, Kester was in the forefront of a small group of religiously motivated Southerners who convened at Monteagle, Tennessee (where Myles Horton and Don West had established the Highlander Folk School two years previously). After hearing a rousing call to action by the Christian Socialist Reinhold Niebuhr, the group chartered the Committee of Younger Churchmen in the South—later to be renamed the Fellowship of Southern Churchmen. They took as their mission the preaching and practicing of brotherhood all over their sorely troubled homeland. "I had lost faith in the promises of politics, unionism, and the organized church," Kester explained later. The kind of healing the South and the nation needed desperately, he felt, had to be "based on the teachings of Jesus and the principles of democracy." Among those who joined him in the new fellowship (which he was to serve as a one-man staff for ten years) were some now-familiar names: Alva Taylor, Abram Nightingale, Gene Smathers, James Dombrowski of Highlander, and James Weldon Johnson of Fisk University, the former executive secretary of the NAACP.

Buck Kester, then only thirty years old, was a fearless and passionate believer in racial and social justice—"an idealist with revolutionary tendencies," as one of his admirers described him. It would be difficult to name any white Southerner of the time who had more contacts across racial lines than he did, or more of a clear-eyed vision of the crippling effects of segregation on blacks and whites alike. Throughout the thirties, in his post with the Fellowship of Southern Churchmen and in his work with the NAACP and the Southern Tenant Farmers Union (the latter an Arkansas-based interracial cluster of field hands organized by H. L. Mitchell, the militant son of a Tennessee sharecropper), Kester never wavered from his commitment to Christian Socialism. Ironically, his bitterest battles were to be fought not against reactionaries on the right but against what he saw as a Communist threat from the left.

Two more men in the meeting with Niebuhr at Monteagle in 1934 were Eugene Cox and Sam Franklin. Within two years they had used a financial stake from Sherwood Eddy of the national YMCA to buy more than two thousand acres of delta farmland in Bolivar County, Mississippi, and to begin planning an interracial cooperative farm there. The land proved to be unfit for cotton farming, so in 1938, Cox, a Texan, and Franklin, an east Tennessee native, managed to shift to another site of twenty-eight hundred acres near Tchula, Mississippi, in Holmes County. Before the Civil War, it had been a prosperous spread known as Providence Plantation; in the deep tracks of the depression, it was a fallow, desolate terrain of weed-choked fields and falling-down tenant shacks where black peasants who had missed the migration to Chicago and points north waited in stranded silence for any sign of hope.

Providence Cooperative Farm was meant to be such a sign. Cox and his wife, Lindy, Franklin and his wife, Dorothy, and another couple, David and Sue Minter (he a physician with roots in North Carolina and Texas), formed the nucleus of the management team, with Franklin overseeing the farming operations and Cox running the commissary and credit union. They were six idealistic young Christian Socialists, backed by a board that included Niebuhr and Eddy, black educators Charles S. Johnson and F. D. Patterson, and two transplanted Texas populist cotton farmers, brothers John and Mack Rust, inventors of a cotton-picking machine that within ten years would symbolize the mechanical revolution that all but emptied the cotton fields of the black belt. Living and working with the white families for nearly twenty years—until their alarmed and fearful neighbors reacted violently against the rise of civil rights activism in the 1950s—would be scores of black families desperate for any chance to improve their miserable lot.

There were numerous other endeavors launched by native Southerners to create cooperative schools and communities in the 1930s, places like Tom Alexander's Springdale School at Cruso in the mountains of western North Carolina, and the Macedonia community, founded by Morris Mitchell near Clarkesville in north Georgia. Earlier, the Llano Cooperative Colony in Vernon Parish, Louisiana, spawned Commonwealth College, a radical labor school; it was moved in the mid-twenties to a new site at Mena, Arkansas. And still later, in 1942, a Georgia Baptist minister named Clarence Jordan would begin an idealistic effort to unite white and black farmers in a common quest for economic security. Their Christian community, called Koinonia, took root a few miles down the road from a large peanut-farming operation owned by the family of Jimmy Carter, another Georgia Baptist who would in time make his own niche in history.

Religious and philanthropic motivations had generated by far the most educational ferment in the South for decades after the Civil War—so much so that even as late as 1930, Christians with Northern roots and capitalists of similar origin had given more to the cause of education in this struggling region than some entire states had managed to invest. The New England–based American Missionary Association and such philanthropists as Julius Rosenwald, Andrew Carnegie, John D. Rockefeller, and Georgia-born George Foster Peabody often set the pace in spending for schools, students, and libraries. Rockefeller's General Education Board, for example, invested over $125 million in Southern schools in the first four decades of this century (and spent many millions more, incidentally, in eradicating communicable diseases and creating networks of public health service systems in the region). It was the General Education Board, more than any other single group, that pushed and prodded the states to develop public schools.

An obsessive preoccupation with race and class was the central cause of the South's tragic neglect of public education. All too many of the white men who dominated political and cultural life in the region for decades after Reconstruction viewed education as a privilege reserved primarily for their sons and others of the same station; they had little concern for the schooling of women and almost no interest at all in the education of blacks or poor whites. Every Southern state was laggard in imposing taxes to support schools and in passing compulsory-attendance laws; as late as 1935, eight of the eleven ex-Confederate states had no laws providing free textbooks to schoolchildren. Then, to compound the neglect, when the states finally did accept primary responsibility for education, they did so within the rigid confines of segregation and "separate but equal" duality, imposing a costly double burden that was bound to leave them ever further behind the North.

Colleges and universities more or less followed the same pattern. Private institutions generally got more attention and support than public ones (or at least enjoyed more freedom from political domination), schools for men were more privileged than those for women, and opportunities for whites were infinitely greater than for blacks. This ancient curse of race-class bias grew more intense as the level of schooling increased; many of those who conceded that elementary training for girls or blacks or the poor might be a social necessity were strongly opposed to its extension beyond high school, even though such institutions were always segregated by race, often by sex, and, as a practical matter, by economic status.

All eleven Southern states eventually opened one or more public colleges for blacks (as did Pennsylvania, Ohio, and the six states bordering the South), but until the 1940s, most of those institutions—about three dozen total—were as much like high schools as colleges. Even the private colleges for blacks (most of them supported by Northern religious bodies) offered only limited instruction above the bachelor's level. By 1930, fewer than fifty African-Americans nationwide had earned doctoral degrees (almost all of them at such schools as Harvard, Columbia, and the University of Chicago), and even though the number quadrupled in the 1930s and doubled again in the 1940s, there were still no more than five hundred blacks with doctorates in the entire country. The South (which would have a black population of over ten million in the 1950 census) awarded only a small fraction of those degrees through such black institutions as Meharry

Medical College in Nashville—and none at all, of course, through any of its white universities.

The white schools of higher learning not only failed to serve blacks, women, and working-class people; they shortchanged their enrollees in a variety of ways, too. Political intrusions in the public colleges and religious dogma in the church-supported ones went hand in hand with the limiting preoccupations of race and class. Early in the 1900s, private colleges such as Trinity (now Duke) and Emory demanded a level of religious and social and racial orthodoxy that forced out independent thinkers, and the pattern they set was followed time and again by Vanderbilt, Tulane, and other top-of-the-line schools in the private sector.

Public higher education was even more vulnerable to ideological and political manipulation. Back in 1913, the University of South Carolina's president, Samuel Chiles Mitchell, had been pushed out of office by Governor Cole Blease for not toeing the political line. (Mitchell, a historian, was a vocal Southern religious and social activist of the early twentieth century, as his three sons, Morris, Broadus, and George, would also be in the next generation.) Thereafter, the governors seemed almost to dominate the academic campuses at will. Before he left the Mississippi governor's office in 1932, Theodore Bilbo booted 179 faculty members and administrators out of the state's colleges, put political hacks in top campus posts, and caused the University of Mississippi and four other institutions to lose their accreditation. Governor Eugene Talmadge did much the same thing in Georgia in the early 1940s, with the same disastrous result. In the wake of the Huey Long era, the president of Louisiana State University, James M. Smith, was one of several public officials who went to prison for malfeasance of office. J. William Fulbright, a former Rhodes scholar serving as president of his alma mater, the University of Arkansas, was fired by his governor in 1941 for exhibiting a generally uncooperative attitude on political matters. When a similar fate befell President Homer Rainey of the University of Texas five years later, he was even more roughly handled by the governor, the legislature, and his own trustees, some of whom tagged him an infidel and a Communist.

Southern universities in the 1930s had precious little to commend them. A 1934 report of the American Council on Education found that only seven institutions in the region had even one department adequately staffed and equipped to produce doctoral candidates, and only two of those faculties (genetics at the University of Texas and sociology at the University of North Carolina) were classified as eminent. By 1938 the prestigious Association of American Universities had only four Southern members—the universities of Virginia, North Carolina, and Texas, along with Duke—in its selective ranks.

The foremost of the black institutions often had some distinguished faculty members—Fisk, for example, had the noted sociologist Charles S. Johnson and a host of Harlem Renaissance and WPA artists and writers, including James Weldon Johnson, Arna Bontemps, and Aaron Douglas— but their financial and physical resources were so limited that their realistic status was at best only that of a small liberal-arts college. (Most black colleges did have one feature the white institutions lacked: integrated faculties. Charles Johnson's mentor at the University of Chicago, Robert E. Park, was one of several white scholars who subsequently taught at Fisk; W. D. Weatherford was another. Indeed, the school didn't even have a black president until Johnson himself was named to the post in 1946.)

The single most glowing exception to broad-based mediocrity in the Southern academic world was the University of North Carolina at Chapel Hill. Over its long history (it was chartered in 1789), the university had acquired a level of independence and quality that kept it in the front rank of public and private schools in the region. It was during the administration of Frank Porter Graham, though, that UNC became the light of the South and a place of national significance. In a twenty-year golden age under his leadership, the institution established a record of productivity and a tradition of unfettered intellectual inquiry that was the envy of scholars throughout the nation.

UNC's singular eminence, though widely recognized, was puzzling to many people, and its success in deflecting the intrusions of politicians was also something of a mystery. The senators and congressmen, governors, legislators, and university trustees of North Carolina in the Graham years were not great statesmen by any means, nor were faculty salaries at the school particularly attractive, nor did any appreciable number of students, professors, or administrators come to Chapel Hill from distant and privileged backgrounds. On the contrary, the cast of characters there was not all that different from that to be found in Florida or Alabama or Texas. The school was small, too; only about 2,500 students and fewer than 250 faculty members were on the campus when Graham was drafted out of the history department in 1930 to assume the presidency. He took over an institution that seemed intent on steering a moderate and cautious course in perilous times. Paul Green and Howard Odum and a few others had already achieved a measure of literary and scholarly notice, but for the most part, UNC was probably closer to the model of a typical Southern university than it was to the fountainhead of American intellectual life.

Under the steady hand of Frank Graham, though, it blossomed like a desert flower. Whatever the achievements and contributions of others, Graham was the single most significant factor in the university's success. He set the tone, the productive climate; more than that, his own life was a largely admirable and inspiring blend of scholarly devotion, social commitment, personal integrity, and political shrewdness. To his legions of admirers, he was an exceedingly popular Mr. Chips. Along with his warm manner and liberal convictions, he was a Tarheel through and through, and he cleverly put his Southern credentials to use whenever they seemed called for. It helped immensely with all sorts of folks that he could claim with becoming pride and modesty to be a native of Fayetteville, a Phi Beta Kappa graduate of the university (class of 1909), an ex-marine, and a seasoned UNC staff member (YMCA secretary, then dean of students, then professor). The trustees quickly coalesced around him as an ideal choice for the presidency.

Graham's disarming friendliness, generosity, humor, and magnanimity were his greatest strengths. He and his wife, Marian, having no children of their own, more or less adopted the student body. Open house at their home on campus was a regular Sunday-night ritual, and "Dr. Frank," who had an uncanny grasp of names and backgrounds, could make every student feel like his personal friend. The same mental filing system worked wonders at the legislature in Raleigh, where he navigated the halls of government with all the understated skill of a masterful lobbyist. Keeping well-mended fences on the political range gave the UNC president and his institution a degree of freedom that other universities could only envy—as, for example, in 1931, when two faculty members, playwright Paul Green and sociologist Guy B. Johnson, hosted the black poet Langston Hughes for a well-publicized reading and lecture before a packed house in the campus theater.

To be sure, Graham's well-known personal sympathies for laboring people, tenant farmers and sharecroppers, disadvantaged minorities, and underdogs in general outraged some people, and he had enemies who loathed him and longed to depose him. But he was no reckless radical; ever sensitive to lurking political dangers, he managed twice in the 1930s to dodge the explosive issue of racial desegregation in the university student body. When Thomas R. Hocutt, a graduate of North Carolina College for Negroes at Durham, sought admission to the UNC school of pharmacy in 1933, he was stopped by a state court ruling that his application was technically invalid—and Graham stayed discreetly silent. Five years later, when North Carolina resident Pauli Murray presented her credentials from a prestigious New York City women's college and applied for admission to the UNC graduate school, Graham became personally involved, pleading with her in a remarkable exchange of letters to give the state time to make segregated educational opportunities truly equal.

In 1935, Thurgood Marshall, then an NAACP staff attorney, had won a state verdict ordering the admission of a black applicant to the University of Maryland law school. Another state bordering the South, West Virginia, acted voluntarily in 1938 to remove race as an automatic barrier of admission to state-supported graduate and professional schools, and soon thereafter the U.S. Supreme Court ruled that Missouri must either admit an academically qualified applicant to the law school at its state university or establish a separate and equal law school for blacks elsewhere in the state. Missouri chose to attempt the latter course, quickly opening a small law college at all-black Lincoln University. Without addressing the "separate but equal" issue directly, the nation's highest court had thus indicated for the first time that racial segregation might not stand a constitutional test in the light of mid-twentieth-century reality.

Such momentous legal and philosophical questions were hardly in the forefront of any Southerner's thinking in the late 1930s, though, and in those years Frank Porter Graham gave his university unexcelled progressive leadership without directly confronting the volatile issue of segregation. He was certainly a thorn in the hide of right-wing reactionaries—of which North Carolina had plenty, from the halls of Congress right on down—but the breadth and depth of his popularity kept him securely in office for two decades, and his faculty enjoyed the unique safety of having a leader who was more of an activist and a liberal than they were.

Howard Odum was to be a principal beneficiary of that progressive atmosphere. In ten years at Chapel Hill, he had parlayed his role as a Southern social critic into a prestigious entrepreneurial empire of research and publishing backed by large foundation grants. Stung by occasional heavy criticism of his progressive pronouncements in the 1920s, he had retreated somewhat into scholarly ambiguity when Frank Graham took over, but his prolific output of books and articles continued, most notably in the 1930s with *An American Epoch*, an impressionistic portrait of Southern folk culture, and *Southern Regions of the United States*, a monumental (though maddeningly disorganized) statistical analysis of the South's assets and liabilities.

Odum saw the big picture of the South—the old and the new, the pieces and the whole—and he was widely regarded as the preeminent expert on the subject. But, particularly in comparison with Graham, who had a far greater tolerance for dissent and a talent for political infighting, the once-controversial sociologist seemed meek and moderate, if not downright conservative. Ever skeptical of political solutions to social problems, he never had much involvement with the New Deal; he even kept his distance from the Tennessee Valley Authority, where regional planning along the lines Odum had long advocated was considered a cardinal principle.

After *Southern Regions* appeared in 1936, Odum headed a committee to explore the feasibility of forming a permanent regional research group, and the following year he was made president of the Commission on Interracial Cooperation. His long-range hope was to lead in the development of a private and independently supported comprehensive organization devoted to Southern regional planning and policy-making, and he was dismayed to see rival efforts proliferate along those same lines in the late 1930s—TVA and other New Deal initiatives, something called the Southern Policy Committee, and a curiously eclectic venture, the Southern Conference for Human Welfare, which was scheduled to convene in Birmingham in November 1938. More bruising yet to Odum's ego was his discovery that the Birmingham gathering would feature a keynote address by none other than his own president, Frank Porter Graham.

Others on the Chapel Hill campus were also active in the social arena of the South—and some, like Graham, were more adventuresome than Howard Odum. One whose youthful audacity and aggressiveness irritated Odum at times was William T. Couch, who was barely past thirty when he was named director of the UNC Press in 1932 (an appointment that actually confirmed his de facto status for the five previous years). Couch, son of a Virginia Baptist preacher, was a UNC graduate who had impressed Graham and others with his grasp of publishing and his liberal social philosophy. Before he came, the press under Louis Round Wilson had focused mainly on esoteric titles for a narrow scholarly audience; under Couch's leadership, it tripled the annual output of new books, and a substantial proportion of them addressed contemporary political, economic, social, and racial issues.

In truth, the UNC Press was the nearest thing the South had to a general-interest book publishing company. Before W. T. Couch left to direct the University of Chicago Press in 1945, he brought about 450 titles into print; about one in ten of them were by or about blacks, and twice as many more addressed other aspects of the South and its conditions, problems, and needs. Books on sharecropping, lynching, criminal justice, labor problems, and mill towns were issued (and generally well received by critics and the reading public). Black writers Charles S. Johnson, Arthur H. Fauset, J. Saunders Redding, Horace Cayton, and Benjamin Brawley were among those who made strong contributions to the list; so did many progressive whites, including Virginius Dabney, Clarence Cason, Herman C. Nixon, and the brothers Broadus and George S. Mitchell. And of course, the authors also included several with UNC ties: Odum, Guy B. Johnson, Gerald W. Johnson, Paul Green, Rupert Vance, and Arthur Raper. Couch edited a couple of important volumes himself, and served for two years as North Carolina director of the WPA Writers' Project and three more as the agency's Southern regional director.

Against the pervasive Northern stereotype, whether in New York books or Hollywood films, of the Southerner as primitive beast—as wounded animal to be feared or pitied but always kept at bay—W. T. Couch and the UNC Press struggled to present a more intelligent and realistic picture of human beings deserving of attention, respect, and (sometimes) help. In this endeavor they were joined by virtually no other academic or commercial press in the South until well after World War II. Throughout Couch's tenure, he was the only Southern book publisher interested in racial and social issues affecting the region.

When he was a young man, Couch seldom ducked an issue. One of the Agrarians snidely called him a "parlor Bolshevik." He frequently spoke out in anger in support of striking industrial workers and against their bosses. In 1936 he came forcefully to the defense of a UNC professor under fire for having dined in an interracial group that included James W. Ford, the Communist Party's black candidate for Vice President of the United States. Jonathan Daniels, editor of the Raleigh *News & Observer*, wanted the professor fired, but Couch and Frank Graham staved off the attack.

Howard Odum found Couch's public actions disturbing, and he was even more concerned when Graham enlisted the press director to play a prominent role in the Southern Conference for Human Welfare in Birmingham. Odum and Couch were never close personally. Historian Daniel Joseph Singal described them as "two prima donna competitors vying with each other for national attention and financial support." Ironically, though, they were very much alike in their opposition to communism, their concessions to white racial mores—and, eventually, their distrust of the radical activists who emerged from the Birmingham meeting. Despite their differences, Couch and Odum were central figures in the large and influential body of Southern wordsmiths—novelists, poets, dramatists, essayists, journalists, scholars, editors, and publishers—who sought throughout the 1930s and beyond to describe and explain what was happening to their land and their people.

9. *Pens and Swords*

To be candid, it is probably an overstatement to call the writers and the rest of the intelligentsia influential, though I have characterized them as such more than once in this narrative. For all their countless words of liberal attack and conservative defense, of admonition and exhortation, of analysis and interpretation and prophecy, there is not much evidence that they ever persuaded the political and religious and educational leaders, the barons of industry and the press, or the bosses of organized labor to take the South in a new direction. Nobody who had the power to lead, so far as I can tell, was truly influenced by the South's writers to depart from the old and discredited pattern of leadership.

But homage must be paid. The word-makers left behind a body of work in the permanent record providing incontrovertible proof that someone in the South in the 1930s saw and recognized what was really wrong with the region—and, in a few rare cases, even spelled out the remedies that would eventually and inevitably be necessary. (Their legacy also included readers and students with changed perceptions and broadened visions.) To read them now, in the light of all that has happened subsequently, is to realize that the creative process is sometimes reflective of its environment, and literature—any good writing, fictional or factual—can be viewed (in retrospect, at least) as a sort of social barometer, an imprecise but revealing indicator of what is coming down the road.

When he authored *Liberalism in the South* in 1932, Virginius Dabney, editorial writer of the Richmond *Times-Dispatch,* concluded that "the press of the South equals, if indeed it does not surpass, that of any other section of the United States in forthrightness and in liberalism." He cited as evidence of that assertion four Southern papers and their editors who had won Pulitzer Prizes in the 1920s for their attacks on lynching and the Ku Klux Klan: C. P. J. Mooney of the Memphis *Commercial-Appeal;* Louis I. Jaffé of the Norfolk *Virginian-Pilot;* Grover C. Hall, Sr., of the Montgomery *Advertiser;* and the Columbus (Georgia) *Enquirer-Sun* under Julia Collier Harris and her husband, Julian Harris (son of famed folk-tale spinner Joel Chandler Harris). Another editorialist, Robert Lathan of the Charleston *News & Courier,* was also named by the Pulitzer judges for his criticism of Southern political leadership.

Dabney cited several other publishers, editors, and papers that he felt were deserving of praise for their progressiveness, including Adolph S. Ochs of the Chattanooga *Times* (also owner of the *New York Times*); editorial writers Mark Ethridge of the Macon (Georgia) *Telegraph,* Gerald W. Johnson of the Greensboro (North Carolina) *News,* and Douglas Southall Freeman of the Richmond *News Leader;* and the leading papers of South Carolina (the *State* in Columbia) and Arkansas (the *Gazette* in Little Rock). In the spirit of their patron social critic, H. L. Mencken, these papers and their editors had abandoned Old South romanticism and called their region to task for its failings, and Dabney heartily approved. (Curiously, the papers he criticized for being too conservative—the Charlotte *Observer,* the Louisville *Courier-Journal,* the Atlanta *Constitution*—were later to be regarded as among the most progressive in the region.)

On into the 1930s, newspapers in the South continued to give voice to writers of a muckraking or crusading bent. The *Constitution* won a Pulitzer in 1931 for exposing graft in city government (Julian Harris was in on that one, too, having come up from Columbus the year before), and the paper turned more aggressive editorially later in the decade under its new editor, Ralph McGill. The *Courier-Journal* rose to the front rank of American newspapers under publisher Barry Bingham, whose father, Robert Worth Bingham, had taken leave to serve as President Roosevelt's ambassador to Great Britain; editor Mark Ethridge had left Macon for the Richmond newspapers before moving on once more to Louisville, where he drew on his earlier connections to assemble a "Georgia Mafia of journalists" that included Tarleton Collier of the Atlanta *Georgian* and James E. Pope of the Atlanta *Journal*. Another publisher-turned-diplomat who left his paper in younger family hands and saw it gain stature was Josephus Daniels of the *News & Observer;* his son Jonathan (like Collier and numerous others, a minor novelist in his spare time) returned to Raleigh to edit the paper after his father became FDR's ambassador to Mexico in 1933.

Still more father-to-son legacies marked the maturing of Southern journalism. The son and namesake of John Temple Graves, a turn-of-the-century editor in Atlanta, had a large following in the Roosevelt years as a syndicated columnist with the Birmingham *Age-Herald;* editor Grover C. Hall, Jr., of the Montgomery *Advertiser* was a successor to his father there, as was George Fort Milton, Jr., at the Chattanooga *News;* in Florida, Paul Poynter's son Nelson took over the reins of the St. Petersburg *Times*.

Also in the 1930s, papers in Dallas, Houston, New Orleans, and Miami showed encouraging signs of growth and maturity. In Nashville, Silliman Evans, a New Deal liberal from Texas, took over as publisher of the morning *Tennessean*. Hodding Carter, a hard-hitting reformer from Louisiana, started a progressive tradition at the *Delta Democrat-Times* in Greenville, Mississippi. Another Menckenite, W. J. Cash of the Charlotte *News* and other papers, worked for most of the decade on his singular volume of regional interpretation, *The Mind of the South*.

Often, even the journalists who left their native turf made contributions that reflected well on the quality of the region's papers. Among those who went north to sparkling careers were Arthur Krock of the *Courier-Journal* and Turner Catledge of the *Commercial-Appeal* in Memphis, both of whom ended up at the *New York Times*—Catledge by way of the Baltimore *Sun*. Gerald W. Johnson left the Greensboro paper to work for Howard Odum at Chapel Hill, and then joined Mencken at the *Sun*. The younger George Milton wrote history and biography on the side, before and after his Chattanooga days. Douglas Southall Freeman stayed at the

Richmond *News Leader* until he retired, but gained national fame as a Civil War historian; he won a Pulitzer Prize in 1935 for his definitive four-volume biography of Robert E. Lee.

Virginius Dabney stayed in Richmond, too, and by the mid-1930s he was editor of the *Times-Dispatch*, a post he would hold for almost thirty-five years. Identified as he was with the philosophy of liberalism even before the New Deal began, Dabney was one of the most prominent figures on the long and impressive list of notable Southern journalists of the thirties. In the later years of his career, the rush of events left him stranded in the rearguard ranks of conservative resistance, but through most of the Roosevelt era he was something of a symbol of progressive opinion in the region.

As yellow-dog Democrats in the one-party South, the editors and publishers of the region's major daily newspapers may have seemed more liberal than they really were. Almost all of them endorsed Roosevelt four times, while a solid majority of their Northern counterparts remained steadfastly Republican. But beyond their knee-jerk party partisanship and their lingering tendency to regard Yankees with defensive suspicion, the Southern journalists as a group did tend to be a little to the left of center on many public issues. Virginius Dabney's background and his evolving editorial profile put him in close company with almost all of his regional contemporaries; his views and actions prior to World War II cast revealing light on the strengths and weaknesses of Southern liberalism in those years.

Dabney was an "old family" Southerner with living elders who had endured the suffering of the Civil War; he had a classical education (at the University of Virginia, where his father taught history); his responsibility at the paper was for opinion, not news, and for him and his able assistants, the ambience was reflective, almost leisurely; at home, he had a dutiful wife and loyal black servants to relieve him of most family and domestic duties, and even his religious obligations could be met with a certain Episcopalian detachment. It was Dabney's good fortune to be almost entirely free, from the very beginning of his career, to focus intently on an intellectual life of writing, reading, and conversation, and he, like most of his journalistic fellows of the same station, made the most of it. (I cite these conditions not to be judgmental about the exalted status of editors in that less frenetic time, but to try to explain how they could turn out as much copy as they did.) Not only did Dabney and many other editors write editorials and columns almost every day; they also wrote authoritative volumes of history and current affairs, articles for some of the leading national magazines of the day, an abundance of correspondence, and even some works of fiction. In those days, when letter-writing was a widely practiced art not yet atrophied by long-distance telephoning, and reading was not yet threatened by television, the prodigious output of the journalists was not considered extraordinary.

Dabney seemed to come quite naturally to his personal brand of enlightened progressivism. The women's suffrage fight had been won, and he was glad of it; the pro-evolution/anti-fundamentalism battle, highlighted by the Scopes trial, had shifted public opinion in a more liberal direction, and he was glad of that, too. Baptized in Mencken's acidic ink, he had a reputation as a Southern realist, a member of the intellectual elite, and an incisive social critic. He supported Al Smith in 1928, favored the repeal of Prohibition, and denounced the verdicts against the Scottsboro boys in Alabama and Angelo Herndon in Atlanta. In his paper no less than in his personal associations, he was unfailingly courteous to blacks; they were *Mr.* or *Mrs.* or *Dr.* to him, and they were Negroes with a capital *N*, which was considered quite liberal and advanced for a Southern newspaper. The struggling black press in the South, made up almost entirely of small-circulation weeklies, looked to white editors like Dabney with a certain respect and envy, and in a small way he returned the compliment, cultivating a professional relationship with such men as P. B. Young, who had founded the Norfolk *Journal & Guide* in 1910 and would remain its editor and publisher until after World War II.

Dabney endorsed the right of workers to organize unions, scorned the Republicans as the party of wealth and privilege, and defended the free-speech rights of Communists and other radical activists; when critics painted him pink, he seemed more amused than disturbed. Beyond all that, he also regularly and forcefully expressed his editorial disgust with lynching and the Klan, and he gave strong support to the anti-poll-tax and anti-lynching movements. Even Walter White of the NAACP was impressed; in 1937 he mounted a personal campaign—unsuccessful, as it turned out—to get for Dabney the Pulitzer Prize. (The award did finally come to him in 1948.)

Because of his prominence as a spokesman for progressive change in the South, Virginius Dabney hoped for—even, it seems fair to say, expected—the gratitude of blacks and others in distress. As he saw it, he represented an enlightened class of whites who were the Negro's best friends, and he wanted them to show their appreciation by waiting patiently and politely for gradual improvements in their status. The white South, he believed, would have to be allowed time to solve its own problems; even lynching and the poll tax could best be eliminated by state, not federal, action. Communist agitation of the black masses and laboring whites worried him, and he stayed away from the Southern Conference for Human Welfare in Birmingham in 1938 to avoid association with such political radicals. For all his liberalism, Dabney had no serious quarrel with Jim Crow segregation, but only with its demeaning and patently unequal aspects. When the impulse for reform finally caught up with him, he proved to be a cautious and restrained moderate, and as the currents of political and social activism slowly began to gather speed in the late 1930s, he was distressed to discover that moderation and gradualism in the quest for democratic equality would not be enough to see him through.

In the atmosphere of ferment that the New Deal spawned and that elements of the church, the university, and the press gingerly nourished, the South also gained notice in magazines and books that rode the new wave of literary realism. While Hollywood continued to feed on the stereotypical myths of the Old South, novels and documentary books of nonfiction made a significant shift toward hard reality. (*Gone With the Wind* was a gigantic exception, of course—a romance novel that the movies ballooned into a phenomenon of cultural immortality.)

National magazines such as Mencken's *American Mercury, Scribner's, Harper's, The Atlantic Monthly, The Nation, The New Republic, Life, Look, Collier's, Time, Newsweek,* and *The Saturday Evening Post* would gradually show an awakening interest in the South, and in time those periodicals would include a significant number of Southern-born writers and editors on their staffs. The two major black journals, the *Crisis* and *Opportunity,* were heavily manned from the start with native Southerners.

Inside the region, the most substantial twentieth-century magazines were literary quarterlies, beginning with the *Sewanee Review* and the *South Atlantic Quarterly* around the turn of the century. A rash of new magazines broke into print in the 1920s, among them Howard Odum's *Social Forces,* the *Virginia Quarterly Review,* the *Southwest Review* (successor to Stark Young's *Texas Review* and heir to the well-traveled *Reviewer* of Richmond and Chapel Hill), and the short-lived publications of the Nashville and New Orleans literati, the *Fugitive* and the *Double Dealer.* Another journal of note, the *Southern Review,* got its start at Louisiana State University in 1935.

The magazines were, by Southern standards, stylishly avant-garde, but in no sense radical; Odum's journal and the *Virginia Quarterly* were probably nearest to the national mainstream of New Deal progressivism. The *VQR,* edited through the thirties by Stringfellow Barr and Lambert Davis, kept abreast of the writings and public pronouncements of liberal whites, but rarely reviewed books by or about blacks and almost never invited black authors or reviewers to contribute to its pages; *Social Forces,* like the UNC Press, showed more of an inclination toward race-class issues.

At the movies, social realism was all but invisible in the steady flow of escapist entertainment that continued unabated throughout the thirties. Hollywood had bolted out of the silent era, but not out of the mentality that fed on Old South stereotypes. From *Hearts in Dixie* in 1929 to *Gone With the Wind* a decade later, motion pictures seldom looked at the South with anything approaching historical accuracy. In one film after another, colonels and cavaliers and assorted other aristocratic white knights bestowed honor and courtesy upon their delicate ladies and spirited belles while banjo-plunking darkies sang and danced in the background. This mythic South was a pastoral land of harmony and contentment, a nostalgic and sentimental throwback to a time of innocence that never was.

And, on the rare occasions when filmmakers did have in mind a social message, not just idle entertainment, the result was often heavy-handed and sensationalized (as with *I Am a Fugitive from a Chain Gang* in 1932) or thinly disguised New Deal propaganda (as with *Our Daily Bread*, a subsistence farm melodrama produced by King Vidor, a native of Galveston, Texas, in 1934). The first of Erskine Caldwell's "poor white trash" novels, *Tobacco Road*, went from the printed page in 1932 to a long run of over seven years on Broadway and finally to the silver screen in 1941—and all the way to the bank, Caldwell was hounded by irate critics who accused him of cynically exploiting the degenerate underclass he had grown up with in rural Georgia. Whether or not that was his intent, it was certainly true that America's moviegoers and book buyers (by far the most of whom lived outside the South) were willing to spend their money for Southern mythology, be it romantic or grotesque—and filmmakers and publishers, observing how easy it was to collect on the formula, continued to pander to that gullible public.

The pattern in fiction was a lot more complicated than that. Scores of novels in the thirties explored the themes of race and class in the South, and they ranged across the spectrum from romantic and patronizing to crudely comic to serious and penetrating. Whatever it was that brought the South to the magnetic center of American literary creativity in the 1920s and kept it there at least until the fifties, the fact is that those were years of extraordinary fruitfulness for many writers with Southern roots— and unlike most of their predecessors prior to World War I, they wrote about a South that was much closer to the hard-edged truth than to the Dixie fable.

Earlier Southern winners of Pulitzer Prizes for fiction or drama—Julia Peterkin, T. S. Stribling, Paul Green—were joined before the thirties ended by Georgia novelist Caroline Miller (*Lamb in His Bosom*); Arkansas-born poet John Gould Fletcher (one of the Agrarians); *Gone With the Wind* author Margaret Mitchell of Atlanta; and Marjorie Kinnan Rawlings of Florida, who wrote *The Yearling*. South Carolinian DuBose Heyward's earlier novel, *Porgy*, found new life on the stage and then, in 1935, was transformed by George and Ira Gershwin into a classic American folk opera, *Porgy and Bess*.

Not celebrated by the prize-givers until much later was William Faulkner, who quietly continued writing in Mississippi—and, periodically, in Hollywood, where his screenplays were much more generously compensated than his light-selling novels. Writing obsessively, he produced ten books in the 1930s (seven novels, two collections of stories, and a volume of poems), and though he was by no means thought of as a "social protest" novelist, his stories were certainly not sentimental fairy tales, and his motley troop of rural Mississippi characters were anything but romantic props. By the late 1940s, Faulkner would be filling the minds of those characters with thoughts and insights and questions that the South was only beginning to articulate.

During his brief bohemian sojourn in New Orleans in the 1920s, Faulkner had fraternized with a little clique of writers that included Lyle Saxon and Roark Bradford—like him, about thirty years old and just beginning their literary careers—and fifty-year-old Sherwood Anderson, famed for his bittersweet *Winesburg, Ohio* stories. Anderson, having drifted south from Chicago, befriended Faulkner and helped steer his first novel to a publisher. Despite his Midwestern identity, Anderson had Southern roots, and he had gone to New Orleans hoping to settle there. The close kinship he felt with the South came through his father, a North Carolinian who had left the region in his youth and ended up in the Union Army. But the Louisiana summers were too oppressively humid for Anderson, and soon he was on the lookout for a cooler place to work. One of his Georgia friends, newspaper editor Julian Harris, told him about a country place in the mountains of southwest Virginia where his father had sometimes gone to write and fish. And so it was that Sherwood Anderson finally found a home in the South; he ended up running a weekly newspaper in Marion, Virginia, and spending the last fifteen years of his life there.

It was from Marion that Anderson went to Harlan County, Kentucky, in 1931 with a group of leftists, the Communist-backed League of American Writers, to investigate labor-management problems in the coal mines. His sympathies were clearly with the working class, and he was an outspoken critic of lynching, poll taxes, anti-labor laws, and other denials of due process and democratic opportunity. His novels reflected his social consciousness, and so, especially, did *Puzzled America,* a 1935 collection of character sketches; in it, Anderson combined his skill as a storyteller with the talents of a keen-eyed reporter to portray working-class people struggling for something to believe in and hope for in the drab and cheerless pit of the Great Depression. Most of his stories were from the South—from one-mule farmers, factory workers, coal miners, dispossessed wanderers. Like the Agrarians, Anderson blamed their plight primarily on the mindless and impersonal forces of modern Yankee industrialism; unlike his conservative brethren, though, he saw federal action as the only hope for their rescue. Approvingly, he quoted a mill worker as saying that with the government's help, "we might be able to make the South into something gorgeous."

Native Southerners with a burning desire to write fiction on the central themes of social conflict in the thirties were not numerous, but there were more of them than you might expect. Harry Harrison Kroll, son of a Tennessee sharecropper, wrote books of unblinking realism (*Cabin in the Cotton* and *I Was a Sharecropper*) based on his own experiences; Grace Lumpkin's *To Make My Bread* probed the exploitation of mill workers in the big textile strike at Gastonia, North Carolina, in 1929, and so did books by some other Southern novelists, including Olive Tilford Dargan (using the pen name Fielding Burke) and Myra Page. Hamilton Basso, a young protégé of the New Orleans literary set, wrote several novels, including *Court House Square,* a story about race relations in a small Southern town; James Saxon Childers called his 1936 book *A Novel About a White Man and a Black Man in the Deep South,* and that's exactly what it was. Arna Bontemps, a Louisiana native and one of the promising young writers of the Harlem Renaissance, expressed his social views through poetry and historical novels such as *God Sends Sunday* and *Black Thunder.*

Other black authors came to the fore in those years, many of them through the Federal Writers' Project. Langston Hughes, best known as a poet, scored with a collection of stories, *The Ways of White Folks,* in 1934 and a play, *Mulatto: A Tragedy of the Deep South,* the following year. Zora Neale Hurston of Florida created characters of depth and complexity in her books—particularly her 1937 novel, *Their Eyes Were Watching God*—and though she would die penniless and forgotten in a Florida welfare home in 1960, the distinctiveness of her work would eventually bring her belated but well-deserved recognition. Sterling Brown and Frank Marshall Davis, two more poets of the thirties, proclaimed in starkly different styles the enduring strength and will to survive of African-Americans. Brown's primary tool was dialect; Davis, a key figure in the early 1930s at the Atlanta *Daily World,* the nation's only black daily newspaper, fired bullets of hot anger in such poems as "Snapshots of the Cotton South" and "My Christ Is a Dixie Nigger" (the latter reminiscent of Langston Hughes's "Christ in Alabama").

Richard Wright's main impact on the literary and social consciousness of the South would be felt in the 1940s, but he sent up a signal of things to come with a story, "The Ethics of Living Jim Crow: An Autobiographical Sketch," published in a 1937 Federal Writers' Project book called *American Stuff*. A first-person remembrance of his early life in Arkansas, Mississippi, and Memphis, the story was later combined with other stark descriptions of Southern racism in *Uncle Tom's Children*, Wright's first book.

Critics have often disagreed in their assessment of the social and literary motivations of three well-known white Southern writers from this era—Thomas Wolfe, James Agee, and Erskine Caldwell—and their divergent careers do present some absorbing similarities and contrasts. They came up in the new post–Civil War middle class; all three left the South as young men and never returned to live there (though Wolfe tried, briefly, shortly before his death). Further, they all became famous by writing about the people and places they had left behind. Beyond that, they had little else in common.

Thomas Wolfe went from his mother's Asheville boardinghouse to the University of North Carolina, and then to Harvard for graduate study; in the late 1920s, while living in New York City, he wrote *Look Homeward, Angel*, a long and penetrating autobiographical novel that won the praise of literary critics and the condemnation of Ashevillians stung by his unflattering depiction of them. (Jonathan Daniels, a classmate of his at UNC, charged in the Raleigh *News & Observer* that Wolfe had "spat upon" North Carolina and the South.) At the age of twenty-nine, the expatriate author was, without realizing it, at the apex of his career; though he wrote voluminously, his remaining years were an unending struggle to exceed the critical acclaim and personal satisfaction he had gotten from his first success.

Wolfe's private life (his professional life too) was clouded with conflict and brooding self-absorption; he never outgrew the narrow provincialism of his upbringing, never escaped the feeling of inferiority he got from being a white Southerner in Manhattan, or the sense of superiority he felt toward Americans of African descent. (One of the few times he was able to identify positively with a black person's achievement was at the 1936 Olympics in Berlin, when he stood and cheered as Alabama-born Jesse Owens triumphed spectacularly over Adolph Hitler's "master race" athletes.) On the face of it, you might think that Wolfe would have been a compatible ally of the Vanderbilt Agrarians, critical as he was of Yankee "progress" in the South—but he had no time for the Nashville clique, and they could not forgive his desertion of the South for New York or abide the magnitude of his celebrity there. After he died of a rare tubercular infection in 1938, his editors got several more books out of the vast body of his unpublished work. One of them, brought out in 1940, bore a title that seemed to characterize Wolfe's eternal dilemma and that of many a self-exiled Southerner: *You Can't Go Home Again.*

James Agee envied Wolfe's literary success. He too was born and raised in a Southern mountain city (Knoxville), studied at Harvard, and went on to a writing career in New York before his death at an early age (forty-five). The two books for which he is best known, *Let Us Now Praise Famous Men* and *A Death in the Family*, were both about the South. The latter, a novel published two years after his own death in 1955, was set in the Knoxville of his youth, and was awarded a Pulitzer Prize; the former, a documentary book about tenant farmers, was written on assignment for *Fortune* magazine in 1936, published by Houghton Mifflin in 1941 (with photographs by Walker Evans, one of the Farm Security Administration lensmen), and ignored by all but a handful of readers and critics until Agee's posthumous fame resurrected it.

Unlike Wolfe, who was nine years his senior—but very much like so many other writers of the time—Agee was caught up in the political and social currents of the thirties. He was intellectually attracted to Marxism (though never a member of the Communist Party), and when he went to Alabama with Evans to work on the story that would become his belatedly celebrated book, he was motivated by the impulses of a liberal activist, a reformer. The result was a document that is as much about Agee's grappling with his own heritage as it is about the three white tenant-farming families with whom he and Evans spent a total of six weeks in the summer of 1936. A certain nobility of purpose and a hint of paternalistic protectiveness—common flaws among reformers—are not hard to discern in *Let Us Now Praise Famous Men.* Although those qualities may not diminish it as a work of art, they do limit it as a political and social documentary. "Agee isn't really imaginatively concerned with [the families] in their own right," concluded the critic Louis D. Rubin, Jr., forty years after the book was published. "It is *his experience there* that fascinates him." (The judgment may be too harsh; there is no denying the force and power of Agee's descriptive language.)

At the time all this happened, Agee certainly felt deeply committed to the people about whom he had written, and he had no patience with anyone who failed to appreciate that. In 1937, after *Fortune* had rejected their story and a famous writer from the South, Erskine Caldwell, had upstaged them with a polemic on farm tenancy, Agee and Evans reacted with outrage, accusing Caldwell and his collaborator, Margaret Bourke-

White (the star photographer of *Fortune*'s flashy new sister magazine, *Life*), of exploiting the hapless and downtrodden sharecropper for propaganda and profit. It didn't help at all that the photo-documentary by Caldwell and Bourke-White, *You Have Seen Their Faces*, was a hit with critics and book buyers alike.

In just five years of public exposure, Erskine Caldwell had acquired a multiplicity of detractors. He was best known for two ribald, low-comedy novels of Deep South degeneracy, *Tobacco Road* in 1932 and *God's Little Acre* the following year. The first soon became a Broadway hit, making Caldwell rich as well as famous and giving both books the exposure to soar into the stratosphere of multimillion-copy sales. There was embedded in the novels a strand of social criticism, but the grotesque absurdity of his mindless and amoral characters left many people convinced that his cynical objective was to make money at the expense of the South's poor whites.

Caldwell at first did little to correct that notion. Ever since his boyhood days as a Presbyterian minister's son in rural Georgia, he had been a rebel, bouncing from school to school, taking with him some of his father's social gospel liberalism and playing it back as left-wing radicalism. The first of his four marriages, in the mid-1920s, brought him a quiet place to write (in Maine) but also three children, and he was not one to take up the domestic role cheerfully. With the Broadway success of *Tobacco Road* and the subsequent popularity of both of his early novels came heavier complaints that he had no serious purpose at all, but only an unprincipled willingness to shock and titillate his readers. The charge may have troubled Caldwell; in any case, he responded with two 1934 articles in the *New Masses*, a magazine of the Communist Party, exposing a wave of unreported lynchings in Jefferson County, Georgia, his former home and still the home of his parents.

The following year, Caldwell attacked the evils of sharecropping and tenant farming in two four-part clusters of articles published by the New York *Post*. White and black families alike were being victimized by a dehumanizing system of economic slavery, he declared, and government at every level was guilty of helping to perpetuate the system. The stories stirred controversy in the national press, in Congress, and throughout the South. Then, in the summer of 1936, Caldwell and Bourke-White met in Wrens, Georgia, where his parents lived, and began the first of two trips through the rural South to gather the material for *You Have Seen Their Faces*.

Their book received widespread and generally favorable comment when it was published in November 1937. *Time* magazine, the *New York Times*, *The Nation*, and other Northern publications credited Caldwell for the "force and conviction" of his essay, and for his documentation of conditions in the Cotton Belt. Southern reviewers, including W. T. Couch in the *Virginia Quarterly Review* and Donald Davidson in the *Southern Review,* were much more critical. ("He does not want a solution," fumed Davidson. "He wants a fight. He wants an uprising. He is a Marxian.") Almost all the reviewers, including the Southerners, were highly complimentary of Margaret Bourke-White's photographs, calling them "superb" and "nearly perfect"; even Davidson was moved to judge them "excellent" and "far more romantic than realistic"—an assessment he intended as favorable.

The photographs, akin in style and quality to the Farm Security Administration collection, still evoke an emotional response after all these years. As for the essay, it is weakened by a hand-wringing conclusion devoid of fresh or imaginative proposals for breaking up the sharecropping system. But even so, Caldwell's denunciation of that system—not of the victims, or of the South, but of the exploitation of both—is eloquent and powerful.

"The South has always been shoved around like a country cousin," he began. "It buys mill-ends and wears hand-me-downs. It sits at second-table and is fed short-rations." The South "works harder than anybody else, chopping its cotton and sawing its wood from dawn to dusk. In return for its labor it does not expect much, does not ask much, never receives much." The South "is the place where anybody may come without an invitation and, before the day is over, be made to feel like one of the home-folks. Scientists with microscopes and theologians with Bibles come to the South to tell it what is wrong with it, and stay to buy a home and raise a family. Gaping tourists come to pick its flesh to pieces, and remain to eat fried chicken and watermelon for the rest of their lives."

But, Caldwell wrote, "the South has been taking a beating for a long time, and the pain and indignity of it is beginning to tell." He sketched a culture of profit-grasping plantation lords, rabble-rousing politicians, platitudinous preachers, and detached experts (sociologists, economists) whose actions—or inactions—had caused race and class discrimination to flourish. The South, he said, is "a retarded and thwarted civilization," a "worn-out agricultural empire," a reactionary land that has "purposely isolated itself from the world" and "taken refuge in its feeling of inferiority." Supposedly, it has been cured of slavery, hookworm, high tariffs, and boll weevils, but it is "still sick," still holding ten million people, white and black alike, in conditions "just short of peonage." Mark against the South, he declared, "its failure to preserve its own culture and its refusal to accept the culture of the East and West. Mark against it the refusal to assimilate the blood of an alien race of another color or to tolerate its presence."

It was a blistering indictment, the kind of attack that most white Southerners hated with a raging passion, particularly when it came from one of their own—and in the case of Caldwell, they found plenty to fire back at. His standing as a critic was compromised by his prior etching of bestial Southern characters whose greed, cunning, and sexuality were more evocative of comedy and ridicule than revelation and sympathy. Even in the broad middle range of Southern critics and writers, from Virginius Dabney to the increasingly reactionary Margaret Mitchell, there was a nose-holding dismissal of Caldwell for his "excursion into the cesspools of Southern crime, degeneracy, and lust." (Faulkner often got the same harsh treatment.)

Furthermore, others charged, Caldwell was a "deserter to the North," a "profiteer of poverty," a radical with Communist leanings, if not party membership—and, worst of all, in the eyes of many, an adulterer. (He had left his wife and family to move in with Margaret Bourke-White at a Manhattan hotel, and she eventually became, for a few stormy years, his second wife.) He had the instincts of a reformer, but not the character, not the staying power, not the commitment. The words and pictures of *You Have Seen Their Faces* still have a resonant potency, but Erskine Caldwell, one of Georgia's prodigal sons, couldn't sustain his role as social critic, and in the crucial years to come, his was not an effective voice for change.

You Have Seen Their Faces is exemplary of a genre of books that emerged in the mid-1930s and found a permanent place in the literature: documentary combinations of essays and photographs conveying a face-to-face, you-are-there sense of contemporary life. The South was a popular theme and subject for such books, and they poured forth from resident and expatriate Southerners with steady regularity.

During a ten-year period beginning in 1933, at least a dozen volumes of illustrated regional interpretation appeared. Among them, in addition to the Caldwell and Agee books, were Julia Peterkin's *Roll, Jordan, Roll*, a descriptive study (with Doris Ulmann's photographs) of black residents on some old South Carolina plantations; Clarence Cason's *90° in the Shade*, a native Alabamian's gentle but forthright call for social reform (photographs by James Edward Rice); H. C. Nixon's *Forty Acres and Steel Mules*, an ex-Agrarian's late-thirties acknowledgment of the necessity for modernization; Richard Wright's *12 Million Black Voices*, subtitled *A Folk History of the Negro in the United States;* and Arthur Raper's *Tenants of the Almighty*, another account of the plight of sharecroppers. The Nixon, Wright, and Raper books all featured Farm Security Administration photographs.

Numerous other books of Southern introspection and analysis, without photographs, rolled from the presses in the same period. Raper, the North Carolina sociologists (Howard Odum, Rupert Vance, Guy B. Johnson), and Fisk's Charles S. Johnson were among the most prolific authors, producing more than a dozen volumes among them. W. T. Couch edited a WPA volume of personal histories from the Carolinas and two other states called *These Are Our Lives*. J. Saunders Redding described the lives of black Southerners in *No Day of Triumph*. Jonathan Daniels (*A Southerner Discovers the South*) and Virginius Dabney (*Below the Potomac*) produced journalistic travelogues, Muriel E. Sheppard described mountain life in *Cabins in the Laurel*, Carl Carmer offered a transplanted New Yorker's perspective in *Stars Fell on Alabama*—and W. J. Cash, of course, published what was destined to be the most renowned of these interpretive works, *The Mind of the South*.

And there was more. Considering all the books of fiction and nonfiction written by Southerners about the South in the New Deal era, it seems fair to say that self-examination of the region and its manifold problems was more advanced and more extensive than ever before—exceeding, perhaps, what any other American region's writers had attempted. The historians had not yet accepted the challenge to reconsider and revise the Old South myth, and the politicians seemed hopelessly blind to the impending crises of race and class, but an appreciable number of the men and women who regularly put their thoughts and ideas on paper managed with varying degrees of specificity and clarity to give warning of the coming storms of change.

High among them was James Weldon Johnson, a renaissance man in the broadest sense of that term. He had retired from the NAACP leadership in 1930 and gone at age sixty to teach at Fisk University in Nashville, beginning yet another phase in his richly varied career. In light of his many contributions to music, theater, literature, diplomacy, and race relations, his relative obscurity in the late twentieth century is puzzling, even disturbing. Had he done nothing else at all, he should be favorably remembered for an essay he wrote at Fisk in 1934. Called *Negro Americans, What Now?*, it was first published as a softcover pamphlet and then in New York as a book. In essence, it was a candid assessment of the Southern/American racial dilemma and what must be done about it. Johnson was addressing the contemporary scene, but he had a keen sense of history and a clear vision of the future; his words even now echo with the bell-clear ring of prophecy.

Looking back on nearly half a century of active involvement in racial and social matters, he was less sanguine than he had been as a younger man. The twelve million African-American people of the United States faced a narrow range of options, Johnson said; he reviewed them one by one. Exodus to Africa—Marcus Garvey's folly—or to some exclusively black state or territory on this continent was hopelessly impractical and unrealistic ("we and the white people may as well make up our minds definitely that we, the same as they, are in this country to stay"). Insurrection was equally futile, not for moral or pacific reasons but for practical ones; it was foolish to think physical force could liberate blacks from the "lawless, pitiless, brutish mob." Revolution aided by Communists or other outside forces was a naive and dangerous idea, doomed to failure—and was, in any case, no assurance of freedom from racial prejudice.

Blacks had only two viable choices, Johnson concluded: acceptance of segregation, isolation, and perpetually inferior status, or an all-out effort to achieve integration. His deep commitment was to the latter: "The only salvation worth achieving lies in the making of the race into a component part of the nation, with all the common rights and privileges, as well as duties, of citizenship." It would be a long and difficult struggle, he warned. In spite of centuries of striving, blacks were "still Jim-Crowed, discriminated against, segregated, and lynched," still shut out of jobs, schools, politics; sometimes the most persistent integrationist grew weary and became resigned to isolation and separate development (he cited W. E. B. Du Bois as a prime example).

But separation, Johnson said, would not be easier or more feasible; it would require duplicating the basic economic and social machinery of the nation—and there would still be the racist white majority to deal with. No, he said, the best long-term option—for whites as well as blacks—was to "use all our powers to abolish imposed segregation, for it is an evil *per se* and the negation of equality." He called on African-Americans to put aside their petty jealousies and rivalries and become a united force for across-the-board integration. "White America cannot save itself if it prevents us from being saved," he said. "No self-respecting Negro American should admit even tacitly that he is unfit to be associated with by fellow humans. Each one can stand manfully on the ground that there should be nothing in law or opinion to prevent persons whose tastes and interests make them agreeable companions from associating together, if they mutually desire to do so."

This quintessentially American believer in the democratic icons of justice and equality had emerged from a lifetime of struggle with his self-respect intact. He had an unassailable sense of dignity, as revealed in what he described as a "pledge to myself which I have endeavored to keep: I will not allow one prejudiced person or one million or one hundred million to blight my life. I will not let prejudice or any of its attendant humiliations and injustices bear me down to spiritual defeat. My inner life is mine, and

I shall defend and maintain its integrity against all the powers of hell."

James Weldon Johnson, a largely unheralded prophet of America's better self, would have made a persuasive elder statesman for the postwar nation's journey toward union, but he was not to be there. On June 26, 1938, the author's car was struck by a train at a crossing near his summer home in Maine. His wife, Grace Nail, was critically injured in the crash; Jim Johnson was killed. His funeral, at a Methodist church in Harlem, brought together more than twenty-five hundred people representing every tint and shade in the human rainbow.

10. *Lightning on the Left*

In its thirty years of existence up to the time of James Weldon Johnson's death, the National Association for the Advancement of Colored People had never found an easy road to strength and influence in American life. From the beginning, its leaders had discovered how complicated it was to build an activist force for black uplift in a predominantly white culture; perhaps inevitably, there were always nitpickers on the left who judged the effort to be too weak and timid, and naysayers on the right who saw it as too aggressively radical. In his role as executive secretary, Johnson had led the NAACP through the twenties and into the depression years. As soon as he departed for Fisk in 1930, his successor, Walter White, and the editor of the *Crisis*, W. E. B. Du Bois, began to attack each other in what was to become a crippling internal battle for power and control.

White, speaking for what the sociologist E. Franklin Frazier called the black bourgeoisie, kept a single-minded focus on the problems of segregation and discrimination; Du Bois, representing the leftist intellectual elite to which he belonged—and bidding also to speak for the aggrieved masses of lower-class blacks—came to the more radical position that African-Americans had to have economic independence before they could achieve equality. Blacks must push for integration at every level of society, said White; no, Du Bois shot back, they must first unite as a race in voluntary segregation from the white majority and build an economic defense against discrimination and inequality. (James Weldon Johnson had tried not to take sides in the debate, saying that either option would be acceptable to him, as long as there was steady progress toward one or the other; if not, he predicted in 1934, the African-American minority eventually would resort to "the making of its isolation into a religion and the cultivation of a hard, keen, relentless hatred for everything white.")

Here was the classic and perpetual schism within black America, the basic conflict from which no escape seemed possible. Walter White expressed one side as official NAACP policy; Du Bois contradicted it in the pages of the *Crisis*. Worse yet, the two men could barely contain their personal dislike for each other, and that made their differences over philosophy and strategy all but insurmountable. Du Bois said White was "absolutely self-centered and egotistical"—and too light-skinned in any case to identify with the victims of racial discrimination. (Marcus Garvey had issued a similar put-down of Du Bois a few years earlier.) Finally, in 1934, with White in firm control, Du Bois resigned from the NAACP staff and accepted a teaching and research post at Atlanta University, whence he had come in 1910; he steeled himself for what he referred to sardonically as "the cold douche of a return to life in the South."

Notwithstanding his dread of reentry, Du Bois was extraordinarily productive in the years that followed. Between 1934 and 1940, he founded *Phylon*, a social science research journal focusing on race, and published three of his most important books: *Black Reconstruction in America*, a pathfinding revisionist history; *Black Folk, Then and Now*, a study of the African role in world history; and *Dusk of Dawn*, an autobiographical perspective on America's racial problems.

Others within the NAACP, notably Howard University professors Ralph Bunche and Abram Harris, kept up the criticism of White's administration after Du Bois departed. But it was the association's expanding presence in the courts that made it increasingly a force for change, and the man most responsible for that was the dean of Howard's law school, Charles Hamilton Houston.

Raised in an upper-middle-class Washington family (his father was also a lawyer) and educated at Amherst College and the law school of Harvard University, Charles Houston accepted the Howard deanship in 1929, when he was thirty-four years old. Within five years he had guided the law school to full accreditation with the help of such bright young faculty members as Tennessee-born William H. Hastie and James M. Nabrit, Jr., a native of Atlanta.

From the days of his youth, Houston had bristled under segregation, and he had grown to adulthood with an angry determination to fight it—not physically but mentally, with the Constitution and American jurisprudence as his sword and shield. In the law school, he looked for bright young students to be his spear-carriers. Thurgood Marshall of Baltimore turned out to be one such candidate. Houston thought he detected a good mind that was largely undisciplined and unchallenged; by the time he signed the lanky young man's law diploma in 1933, he had stoked him with anti–Jim Crow zeal. And, to make sure the fire was lit and burning, the dean took his star pupil on a driving trip into the South that summer. Marshall never forgot the shock of their constant confrontation with raw prejudice.

A year later, just as W. E. B. Du Bois was heading back to the South himself, Houston agreed to help the NAACP set up an activist legal program focused on fighting segregation in court. Soon after he was settled in the association's New York office, he brought Thurgood Marshall and a New Deal lawyer, William H. Hastie, up to join him. Their long-range objective, Houston wrote in a *Crisis* article, was "the abolition of all forms of segregation in public education." Their initial strategy was to compel the states to equalize educational opportunity for blacks and whites in graduate and professional schools, either by establishing expensive new programs in the black colleges or by desegregating the white institutions.

Marshall had come a long way in a hurry. Born in Baltimore in 1908, the year before Du Bois and others founded the NAACP, he had gone to Lincoln University, an all-black, all-male school in Pennsylvania, as a fun-loving, seventeen-year-old freshman in 1925, and emerged five years later as a slightly more serious but still uncommitted young man. (One of his classmates at Lincoln was Kansas-born Langston Hughes, six years older than he and already a poet with exposure to Africa and Europe and the Harlem Renaissance; it was Hughes who prodded Marshall into joining a student campaign to desegregate Lincoln's all-white faculty.) Though he entered Howard's graduate program with the thought of becoming a dentist, Marshall soon came under the influence of Charles Houston, and thereby found the discipline and motivation that would characterize his long and distinguished career in law.

While briefly engaged in private practice in Baltimore, Marshall in 1934 took the case of Donald Murray, a Maryland native and Amherst graduate whose application for admission to the University of Maryland law school had been denied because he was black. Charles Houston served as co-counsel with Marshall at the trial in a courtroom in Annapolis; he listened with pride as his former student told the judge that the case involved not just the right of his client but "the moral commitment in our country's creed." They won a directed verdict, later to be affirmed by a state court of appeals. In the fall of 1936, Donald Murray entered the University of Maryland School of Law; he graduated three years later in the top third of his class.

Thurgood Marshall became chief legal counsel of the NAACP in 1938 after Houston, his mentor and friend, returned to private practice. Before parting, they marked the rite of passage with another significant victory: The U.S. Supreme Court, in the *Gaines* v. *Missouri* case, said the state law school must admit Lloyd Gaines or set up a "separate but equal" law school to serve black students. Marshall and the NAACP had crafted a simple but effective strategy that the association would follow for more than a dozen years: If the states insisted on keeping opportunity separate, they would be pressed to make it equal—and pay a punishingly high price in the process.

During his tenure as the NAACP's chief executive in the 1930s, Walter White sought to carve out a niche for himself that neither the Du Bois/ *Crisis* faction nor the legal initiatives of Houston, Marshall, and Hastie would overshadow. White liked the limelight, and he was not only an outgoing individual but a fearless social activist as well. His efforts as a lobbyist in the halls of Congress and as an investigator of lynchings in the rural South had won him high marks for skill and courage, but in neither arena was his bold performance rewarded with spectacular results. Like James Weldon Johnson before him, he tried repeatedly to prod the Congress into action on such issues as lynching, poll taxes, Negro voting rights, peonage, tenant farming, and labor unions. Also like Johnson, he was not easily discouraged by failure.

To help him in his undercover investigations of lynch-mob activities, Walter White enlisted the help of Howard Kester, the Tennessee-based white activist whose interracial experience had brought him to the attention of the NAACP. Kester had several close scrapes as an investigator, most notably in Marianna, Florida, where his life was threatened in October 1934 as he documented (for later publication by the NAACP) the gruesome details of a frenzied lynch mob's torture and dismemberment of a black field hand thought to have been the lover and murderer of a young white woman.

Taking into account the virulence of Southern racism in those years and the dangers that faced anyone, black or white, who was bold enough to question it, the wonder is that men and women like Buck and Alice Kester could survive at all in such an oppressive climate. Those who did take exception, no matter how mild or vigorous, to the temper of the times were automatically branded as radicals—unwanted troublemakers at best, and at worst, aliens and Communists and traitorous enemies of the people. Most amazing of these native Southern pariahs were the ones who stayed in the region and worked independently, without the protection of such established forces as the university and the church. Sometimes they banded together in little organizations of their own creation. Kester's Fellowship of Southern Churchmen was one such group; two others of note were the Southern Tenant Farmers Union in Arkansas and the Highlander Folk School in Tennessee.

The Fellowship of Southern Churchmen was never anything more than a loose confederation of like-minded believers in a general philosophy of Christian brotherhood and populist democracy. All of its members had primary duties elsewhere, most of them in church or university jobs. With the support and encouragement of Reinhold Niebuhr, the Fellowship of Reconciliation, and other Christian Socialist groups and individuals, the Fellowship of Southern Churchmen brought together a small group of men and women, white and black, who were committed to social reform. For ten years after it was organized in 1934, Buck Kester was its leader, but only in the last three of those years was that a full-time job. Prior to 1934—the year he turned thirty—Kester had attracted considerable notoriety in and out of the South for his Socialist politics, his clashes with institutional forces as disparate as Princeton and Vanderbilt universities and the Communist Party, his work on behalf of striking Tennessee coal miners, and his extensive interracial activities. As it turned out, the soft-spoken Virginian was just getting started.

In the last half of the 1930s, Kester found time to lead the Fellowship of Southern Churchmen, continue his lynching investigations for the NAACP and the American Civil Liberties Union, be ordained as a Congregational Church minister, and write a book (*Revolt Among the Sharecroppers*). Still another of his significant contributions during that period was his involvement with H. L. Mitchell and others in a pathfinding labor organizing venture, a biracial alliance of field hands called the Southern Tenant Farmers Union.

For all their similarities as young white men working for the social and economic betterment of poor people in their native South, Howard Kester and Harry Leland Mitchell had come to their activism by two very different routes. Kester was a middle-class, college-educated Virginia town boy with Presbyterian and Quaker roots and an evangelical pacifistic commitment to Christian ethics; Mitchell was a country boy born in a two-room tenant shack next to a cotton field and raised among sharecroppers and timber cutters by hardworking parents who moved from job to job in the vast bottomland farming region of Tennessee, Mississippi, and Arkansas.

H. L.'s people were loyal Confederates who found their faithfulness rewarded with little more than the specious promise that even in the most abject poverty they were better than "the niggers." His father was a self-trained barber who sharecropped cotton on the side and still found time to preach and proselytize as a Baptist evangelist. The boy was a field hand himself by the age of eight, and he grew to young manhood knowing what it was like to work sixteen-hour summer days for his family's paltry crop, or for fifty cents' worth of credit at the plantation commissary.

In December 1917, when he was eleven years old, young Mitchell rode an excursion train from his home village of Halls to nearby Dyersburg in west Tennessee to witness a lynching. With hundreds of other white people drawn to the site by advance billing of the event, he looked on as a black grocery-store delivery boy named Scott Lignon was chained to an iron stake in the courthouse yard. A white woman to whom he had delivered groceries had accused Lignon of making sexually suggestive remarks to her, and on her word alone, the young man was dealt a swift and fatal penalty. Scraps of wood were piled around him, soaked with kerosene, and set afire. H. L. Mitchell saw the flames, caught the nauseating odor of burning flesh, heard the victim's screams of suffering and the cheers of the morbidly excited throng. Sickened and terrified, he bolted out of their midst and fled. The atrocity was branded in his memory for life.

A high school graduate by the skin of his teeth, Mitchell married young and went off in rebellious search for a more fulfilling lot than fate had given his parents. Rejecting their Baptist piety, he abandoned the Christian faith altogether, and he also gave up on Democratic Party politics to become a follower of Norman Thomas and the Socialists. But the pull of his family and the South was too great for him to overcome, and for nearly seven years he ran a dry-cleaning business in the back of his father's barbershop in the east Arkansas cotton field village of Tyronza.

His closest friend in Tyronza was Clay East, a hardworking gas-station operator who liked to talk politics. After the stock market crashed in 1929 and the depression set in, East came around to Mitchell's view that socialism was America's best hope for salvation. Mitchell went to a Socialist conference in Washington in 1933—meeting Howard Kester of Nashville while there—and the following February he persuaded Norman Thomas to come and see how little the New Deal's vaunted agricultural recovery programs were doing to help the burdened sharecroppers and tenant farmers of Arkansas. The appearance of the fifty-year-old Socialist warhorse in the high school auditorium in Tyronza effectively lifted Mitchell and East to the forefront of Arkansas socialism. A few months later, in July 1934, a delegation of eleven white and seven black farmworkers evicted from a nearby plantation for protesting low pay and poor working conditions called on the two Tyronza mavericks for help. Their coming together marked the beginning of the Southern Tenant Farmers Union.

Mitchell and East recruited several Socialists from within two hundred miles or so of the Arkansas delta to aid in the movement. Kester came from Nashville, and two of his Alva Taylor–trained classmates at Vanderbilt, Ward Rodgers and Claude Williams, reported in from west Arkansas; brothers John and Mack Rust (soon to perfect their mechanical cotton picker) answered from across the river in Mississippi, and a self-styled Arkansas hillbilly named J. R. Butler, toughened by years of labor in the oil fields, sawmills, and cotton patches, brought his experience to the fray. Within the ranks of the aggrieved tenant farmers themselves, strong leadership came from whites like Alvin Nunnally and Bill Stultz, and from Isaac Shaw, E. B. McKinney, and other blacks.

In just four years the Tyronza-born STFU would have more than thirty thousand members in seven states. They boldly confronted not only the planter-banker-politician power structure in the Cotton Belt, but the New Deal liberals as well, demanding from the former a minimum wage (ten cents an hour or a dollar a day) and accusing the latter of rescuing landlords while the serfs languished in the depths of poverty. The national press came to investigate, and helped the union win sympathy and support from outside the South; Norman Thomas came back again, and though he was run off by a hostile white mob, he used the incident to gain more attention for the STFU. The John L. Lewis–led Committee for Industrial Organization, soon to split from the American Federation of Labor, took a special interest in the revolt of the Arkansas farm laborers; even Congress and the White House showed increasing concern for the plight of sharecroppers and tenant farmers.

But for all this newfound attention, the STFU was made to pay dearly. Powerful planters brought down the wrath of state and local authorities on the union. Some of their leaders were arrested, and virtually all were physically threatened; mass evictions put thousands of field hands out of work and out of their homes; acts of violence—beatings, house-burnings, terrorist killings—multiplied. (Clay East was attacked by a mob in one Arkansas town and run out of the state, and Buck Kester was hauled out of a mass meeting in a little country church and almost lynched before his captors relented and let him walk to safety across the Mississippi River bridge.) The federal government's efforts to address the issues raised by the union were simply inadequate, and the support of national labor groups was even less helpful. The very idea of farmworkers organizing to bargain collectively was radical enough, but the black-white unity within the STFU was more than even most of their potential supporters could understand or accept.

When he first arrived in Arkansas, H. L. Mitchell had brought with him the conventional racial views of most Southern whites, at least to the extent that he outwardly abided by the customs and laws of segregation. But he soon came to see that the landlords used racial bias to divide laboring people and thus make easier the economic exploitation of both whites and blacks. Responding to the firm conviction of most of the sharecroppers that they must stand together or lose all, Mitchell became a committed believer himself, declaring publicly: "There are no 'niggers' and no 'poor white trash' in the Union. These two kinds of people are all lined up with the Planters. We have only Union men in our organization, and whether they are white or black makes no difference."

An all-black underground union of sharecroppers in Alabama known to have support from the American Communist Party sought to make common cause with the STFU, but Mitchell and Kester, on the advice of Norman Thomas, avoided them. Then, in 1937, the STFU tried to affiliate with the Congress of Industrial Organizations, only to be diverted into an unwanted subordinate merger with UCAPAWA—the United Cannery, Agricultural, Packing and Allied Workers of America—a CIO union headed by Donald Henderson and rumored to be Communist-dominated. Over the strenuous objections of Mitchell and Kester, both of whom were openly distrustful of the tactics and objectives of the Communist Party, the members of the STFU followed the advice of Claude Williams and voted to affiliate with UCAPAWA. Two subsequent years of bitter wrangling within the new alliance brought the STFU members around to agreement with Mitchell and Kester, but it was too late to undo the damage; by the time the tenant farmers managed to sever the relationship, their union was in disarray.

The Southern Tenant Farmers Union had won friends afar, but no real victories in the cotton fields at home. Times were almost as tough for the serfs of Southern agriculture in 1939 as they had been five years earlier, when H. L. Mitchell and Clay East first answered the pleas of the Tyronza field hands. But the courageous efforts of the long-suffering sharecroppers and their union were not wasted. With their help, about fifty evicted farm families moved to Mississippi and resettled on the cooperative farm established there by Sherwood Eddy and his followers; many more found homes in the Farm Security Administration's cooperative New Deal communities—indeed, the federal government's concern for farmworkers on the bottom of the economic heap was generated in part by the STFU's attention-grabbing activities. And finally, because of its ability to put aside racial bias in order to confront larger economic and social issues, the STFU created a model of interracial cooperation in the mid-1930s that would still be relevant decades later.

The curious case of Claude Williams provides something of a footnote to the saga of the Southern Tenant Farmers Union. Williams had made his way from central Tennessee to the west Arkansas town of Paris in the mid-1930s, and was pastor of a Presbyterian church there for a few stormy years before moving to Mena to work at—and eventually head—Commonwealth, the radical labor college. (Among the "Arkansas leftists" who preceded him there, enrolling for classes in the spring of 1935, was a young student named Orval Faubus, later to become notorious as one of the South's confrontational segregationist governors.) Williams was to be Commonwealth's last leader; state officials, saying the school fomented anarchy, seized its property and closed it in 1940.

Always, it seemed, the unorthodox and enigmatic preacher was leaving his post under a cloud of suspicion—and always, his response to criticism was the same: "I have taken my stand with Jesus of Nazareth," Williams replied stoically. "If I believe in him, I cannot believe in race prejudice or class antagonism and exploitation." On the wall above his desk, he kept framed pictures of his heroes—Jesus, V. I. Lenin, and Eugene V. Debs—to watch over him in silent approbation.

No less controversial was Williams's quixotic venture into the Arkansas farmworkers' dispute. In one widely publicized incident, he and Willie Sue Blagden, a young white woman from a prominent Memphis family, were beaten with leather straps by a vigilante mob for protesting the killing of a black farmworker. So closely did controversy and disruption trail Williams into the union that Mitchell and Kester became convinced, after he sided with UCAPAWA, that he had been sent to Tyronza by the Communist Party to disrupt or perhaps take over the STFU. The farm union's executive council voted in 1938 to expel him from the organization; he appealed the decision, but it was overwhelmingly confirmed by the general membership. No one seemed to trust Claude Williams, not even the South's known Communists—but he was a man to be reckoned with, and he would be heard from again.

The Highlander Folk School, like the Southern Tenant Farmers Union and Commonwealth College, was another homegrown Southern venture of the 1930s that departed in unorthodox and controversial ways from the prevailing dogma on labor, race, class, and other fundamental issues. It got its start in the fall of 1932 when Myles Horton and Don West leased a house and two hundred acres near Monteagle, Tennessee, from Lilian Johnson, a wealthy native of Memphis with a Ph.D. from Cornell University "up East" and an abiding interest in programs of political and social cooperation.

Though still in their twenties, both men had acquired education and experience that far transcended their youth and their simple rural origins. Along the way from his west Tennessee boyhood to the Monteagle folk school venture, Horton had studied and traveled in his own state, in New York and Chicago, and in Denmark and elsewhere in Europe, and had picked up the support of such men as Abram Nightingale, Reinhold Niebuhr, Harry F. Ward, Robert E. Park, Norman Thomas, and Sherwood

Eddy. West, the oldest of nine children in a Georgia mountain farm family, had stayed in the South for his education, but after completing his theology degree under Alva Taylor at Vanderbilt in 1931, he, like Horton, had gone to observe the folk school movement in Denmark.

Horton's ambition, when he returned to the South early in 1932, was to establish an institution of education and social activism for working-class adults in the mountains of Appalachia. During a visit with Will Alexander at the Commission on Interracial Cooperation in Atlanta, he learned of Don West's similar interests, and a few days later he caught up with West at W. D. Weatherford's Blue Ridge YMCA assembly. They traveled together to Tennessee, first to see Abram Nightingale in Crossville and then, at his suggestion, to meet Lilian Johnson at her summer home near Monteagle. By the time of Franklin Roosevelt's election victory that fall, Horton and West had leased the property from Johnson and started their venture—which they christened the Highlander Folk School—on a $1,300 nest egg that Niebuhr, Eddy, Thomas, and other Socialists had raised for Horton.

The two young men had lofty ideals. They wanted "to educate for a new social order," said Horton, "and to conserve and enrich the indigenous cultural values of the mountains." But their early achievements fell far short of their ambitions. Highlander's interest in labor, race, and left-wing causes drew immediate and continuous fire from state and local officials, industry bosses, the press, and even some New Deal bureaucrats. The school was chronically plagued with budget problems, too, and its enrollment of resident adults seldom numbered above a dozen. Red-baiting by outside detractors and dissension within the school's thin internal ranks also took their toll. Don West was more politically and ideologically motivated than Horton, and the two men soon were locked in a quiet struggle for authority; Horton won, and in the spring of 1933, barely six months after they had begun, West packed up and left the mountain school.

He went first to Atlanta to aid in the defense of Angelo Herndon, and then to North Carolina for a similar effort on behalf of arrested workers in the Burlington textile mill strike (UNC staff members W. T. Couch and Paul Green were among the people he enlisted in that cause). Next, West spent several years in Kentucky pursuing an eclectic succession of left-wing causes, mainly in the coalfields, before he and his family were forced by his notoriety and their personal needs to take refuge in north Georgia. He had been arrested and jailed a few times, but more often than not he had stayed on the move, hiding from the law or fleeing on his motorcycle just one jump ahead of the cops—and either way, the handsome and intense young radical gained near-legendary status as a sort of phantom revolutionary who left a trail of radical poems and sermons in his wake.

Like his former classmate Claude Williams, he was widely accused of being a Communist; also like Williams, he was to continue his independent and solitary odyssey, moving in and out of sight on the margins of Southern activism for another two or three decades to come.

Myles Horton, on the other hand, had found his calling at Highlander, and it would remain his only mission in life. Through his ties to New York's Union Theological Seminary and the University of Chicago, where he had studied, he persuaded several native Southerners to return and join the school's staff, among them James Dombrowski of Florida and Tennesseans John Thompson and Ralph Tefferteller. Some women with close ties to the region's rural laboring class also became early members of the Highlander family: May Justus, Vera McCampbell, Lucille Thornburgh, and Zilphia Mae Johnson, an Arkansas student who came recommended by Claude Williams in 1935 (and married Myles Horton a few months later). Horton rounded out the Highlander staff with a few of his Northern friends, principally Elizabeth "Zilla" Hawes, Franz Daniel, and Ralph Helstein.

Jim Dombrowski was the steadying influence among them, a quietly efficient and religious man in his mid-thirties whose reserved manner hid a passionate belief in social justice. While Horton and others were making as big a public splash as they could, Dombrowski served for almost ten years as Highlander's dependable manager of day-to-day operations. A grandson of Polish Lutheran immigrants, he became a Methodist during his high-school years in Tampa, Florida, and went on to academic distinction in Georgia and New York, earning degrees at Emory, Union Theological Seminary, and Columbia. It was during his Union days that Harry F. Ward awakened him to the plight of miners and mill workers in the South, and his subsequent arrest during the 1929 textile strike in Elizabethton, Tennessee, marked the real beginning of Dombrowski's career as an activist reformer. More of a Christian than Horton and most of the others, he was at the same time every bit as much a Socialist and idealist as they; the class-conscious and class-divided South would soon collapse under the weight of its own inequities, he believed, and a reformed society based on cooperation and equal opportunity would rise to replace it.

As Highlander struggled to make its presence felt in the early years, it sought support from various New Deal agencies—emergency relief, the TVA, subsistence homesteads. But the mainstream political parties, government bureaucracies, and institutions such as the university and the church soon came to see the school as an adversarial body not subject to their control, and one by one they chose to distance themselves from it. As time went by, Highlander became more and more closely identified with the embryonic labor movement in the South, and with radical methods of social change.

The basic operating philosophy of Horton and his colleagues—that ordinary working people, no less than the privileged, could find within themselves and their neighbors the solutions to whatever problems they faced—was generally interpreted by alarmed observers as an expression of populist radicalism, if not communism or anarchism. What kind of school was this, they wanted to know, that taught its students to walk picket lines and sing protest songs, that gave them reading lessons out of the polemical works of Socialists, that stirred them to a frenzy with raucous Saturday-night square dances? The all-white surrounding community could note with some relief that no black students were enrolled there, but blacks were invited to visit occasionally, and in 1934 a black professor from Knoxville named J. Herman Daves was hired as a part-time instructor. His arrival was followed quickly by anonymous threats of death and destruction.

Highlander didn't aggressively challenge racial segregation in the thirties, as the Fellowship of Southern Churchmen and the Southern Tenant Farmers Union did; its primary focus was on the rights of laboring people in the mountains, the vast majority of whom were white—and that alone was more than enough to keep the school in hot water. On those occasions when race did enter the picture, it was simply one more red flag flying in the face of those who saw Highlander as a disruptive force in their midst. With or without that flag, the school still suffered from sensationalized and distorted exposure, even in such moderately inclined newspapers as the Chattanooga *News,* the Chattanooga *Times,* and the Nashville *Tennessean.*

As small and resource-poor as it was, Highlander had a surprising degree of visibility during the depression. In November 1932, even as the school was enrolling its first students, Horton joined with Buck Kester, Alva Taylor, and others in support of coal miners at Wilder, Tennessee, who were striking in protest against shrinking wages and miserable living conditions. Horton was arrested during the long and sometimes violent strike, and Barney Graham, the miners' leader, was shot and killed by company-hired gunmen. That was the first in a continuous chain of efforts by Highlander people to help organize coal miners, timber cutters, textile workers, and even local employees of the federally funded Works Progress Administration. Horton and his colleagues were also involved in an abortive attempt to convene the All-Southern Conference for Civil and Trade-Union Rights in Chattanooga in 1935; the biracial meeting of laboring people was broken up by an ad hoc posse of Chattanooga policemen and American Legion zealots, but the delegates eluded their attackers and reconvened at Highlander. Such exploits as these were given wider visibility in *People of the Cumberlands*, a Hollywood drama about Highlander and the unions produced by the noted filmmaker Elia Kazan.

Throughout the thirties, Highlander saw itself as far less traditionally academic than the usual run of colleges and schools, but also less doctrinaire than an institution like Commonwealth College. Horton's way of avoiding an ideological tag (more precisely, Dombrowski's way, adopted by Horton) was to extend a welcoming hand to one and all—Socialist, Communist, New Deal Democrat, Southerner, Northerner, or whoever would meet him halfway. Few except Highlander's closest allies were satisfied with that stance, though; right-wing antagonists still equated the school's radicalism with communism, while others on the left complained that Horton and his staff were either too close to, or too far from, the New Deal, the black minority, the labor movement, or the impoverished hordes of destitute Southerners. This was the same kind of constant political and ideological hairsplitting that kept the fragile network of liberal Southerners from coalescing in opposition to the dominant forces in the region.

In 1937, when the CIO underscored its breakaway independence from the American Federation of Labor by launching a major union-building campaign focused on the textile industry, the Highlander Folk School committed its meager resources to the effort. A half-dozen or more of its staff members and as many as forty of its former students were among the more than six hundred organizers who took part in the Southern phase of the two-year, $2-million campaign. After scoring some impressive gains in the early stages, the labor offensive was slowed by a national economic downturn, the so-called Roosevelt recession of 1938. There was an eventual payoff, though: the formation in 1939 of the Textile Workers Union of America, a potent new national organization in the industry that rose from the ashes of two failed attempts in the previous decade. It was an important victory for labor—especially Southern labor—on the eve of World War II.

But the triumph, following fifty years of frustrating defeats, still was only one battle, albeit a big one, in an ongoing war for the rights of working people. Most unions, North as well as South, were still functionally segregated by race—and, in spite of new federal laws covering collective bargaining, wage and hour regulation, and the employment of women and children, white and black workers alike still found themselves largely at the mercy of a laissez-faire employment system. What's more, those like the Highlander people who voiced strong criticism of the status quo in labor relations and advocated reforms, whether modest or radical, soon discovered to their dismay that the price of advocacy was to be publicly condemned for disloyalty and branded with the rose tattoo of communism.

Before the New Deal, the American labor movement had done precious little for Southern workers, and virtually nothing for blacks—so little, in fact, that those who shaped black opinion were much more favorably responsive to the Republican capitalists in management than to the bosses of labor. Barely fifty thousand African-Americans nationwide were union members—one in a hundred of the rank and file—and half of them belonged to the all-black Brotherhood of Sleeping Car Porters, which was unrecognized by the Pullman Company and treated as an unwanted stepchild by the American Federation of Labor. Big corporations and industries often recruited unemployed blacks as strikebreakers, and generally saw it as being in their interest to keep white and black workers segregated. Labor leaders North and South were slow to realize that by going along with that divide-and-conquer tactic they were blindly playing into the hands of the labor movement's bitterest enemies.

Exceptions to the pattern of rigid segregation would first be seen in a small number of unions—some mine workers' locals, the trowel trades, the longshoremen, timber workers in certain parts of the South, and the fledgling Southern Tenant Farmers Union—but by and large, organized labor in the early 1930s benefited only whites. It helped if you were a man and a Northerner, too; few women belonged to recognized unions, and men in the steel mills of Pittsburgh and the cotton mills of New England had more status and more security than their counterparts in Birmingham and Gastonia.

The initial recovery and reform programs of the New Deal necessarily and inevitably opened labor-management issues to careful scrutiny. Early in the new administration, passage of the National Industrial Recovery Act of 1933 established the right of non-farm workers "to organize and bargain collectively" through their own chosen representatives. In the South, where unions were weak or nonexistent, this had the effect of exposing all sorts of labor problems. Wages were too low (barely two-thirds what they were in the North); the workday was too long; women and children were exploited; working conditions were often dangerous and unhealthy.

Efforts to address these inequities in the textile industry had been stymied repeatedly by imperious and dictatorial mill owners. The Gastonia strike in 1929 had shattered the National Textile Workers Union. As soon as the first New Deal labor legislation became law four years later, another organization, the United Textile Workers Union, launched an organizing drive in the mills. By the late summer of 1934, it had more than a quarter of a million members, most of them in the Southern piedmont region stretching from the Carolinas to Alabama and Mississippi. A general strike was called on Labor Day weekend, and it quickly spread throughout the industry; more than 375,000 millhands in the South and New England walked off the job. But industrialists brought in armed guards and pressured state authorities to send militia units into the mills. After more than two weeks of violent confrontations, during which at least seven strikers and a police deputy were killed and thousands of families were evicted from company housing, the strike was finally broken.

In the emotional aftermath, an air of failure bordering on disaster hung over the episode, but in the longer view, the strike served an important purpose. It helped to spark the 1937 CIO organizing drive, and it also gave inspiration for the passage of new federal legislation, particularly the Fair Labor Standards Act of 1938, which regulated wages and hours and protected the rights of women and children in the workplace. What's more, all of these events and initiatives brought to a head a monumental conflict within the labor movement that had to do mainly with strategy, politics, power—and, just beneath the surface, with race.

At the 1935 convention of the American Federation of Labor, the industrial unions led by John L. Lewis, head of the mine workers, clashed with the trade unions led by William "Big Bill" Hutcheson of the carpenters. The debate turned nasty; Hutcheson denigrated Lewis's ancestry in crudely explicit language, and Lewis, who looked like a lion, roared and then struck like one, leaving the felled chief carpenter in a pool of blood. Lewis calmly straightened his tie, lit a cigar, and walked out of the hall, resigning from his AFL vice-presidency as he departed. The new Committee for Industrial Organization that he and others subsequently formed had in 1938 become the permanent Congress of Industrial Organizations, a fierce rival of the AFL.

One of the many ways in which the two warring factions differed was on the question of race. The AFL, despite its general pronouncements of nondiscrimination, was in practice overwhelmingly a white man's family of unions. The CIO had a direct interest in Southern industries—mines, textiles, oil and gas, garment-making, tobacco—all of which employed a substantial number of black workers. John L. Lewis and his CIO allies, such as Sidney Hillman of the Amalgamated Clothing Workers, knew from long experience that their effort couldn't muster the necessary strength of numbers to succeed unless it was united across racial lines. From the beginning they pragmatically pursued a policy of racial equality, and though it took years for this monumental social change to be fully embraced and implemented by the rank and file, the CIO nonetheless became the first major institutional segment of American society to adopt such a philosophy.

The AFL continued in place as the conservative wing of the labor movement; they were the representatives of the crafts and trades, mainly Northern and overwhelmingly white. The CIO took its stance as the scrappy new liberal wing, serving as agents for industrial workers North and South, and they were openly interracial. By the end of the decade, the Young Turks had achieved some success in organizing the Southern textile workers—and in the process they had converted thousands of hostile and suspicious laboring people into committed allies. They were still a long way from achieving job and wage security and a place of genuine appreciation and respect in the larger society, but they had made a good start.

The richest elements of personality and human interest are scarcely accommodated in this brief account of organized labor's New Deal renaissance and its march into the South in the thirties. The arresting image of John L. Lewis punching out Big Bill Hutcheson is enough to suggest that much more could be said to show how vigorous and colorful labor's main characters of that time truly were. The contributions of Myles Horton and his Highlander associates in the textile campaign are illustrative. So, too, are the exploits of two remarkable individuals, both native Southerners: Lucy Randolph Mason of the CIO and Asa Philip Randolph of the Brotherhood of Sleeping Car Porters.

Just as the CIO's Southern organizing drive was beginning in June 1937, Lucy Mason conspired to get a personal audience with John L. Lewis and Sidney Hillman; in short order, she persuaded them that their labor confederacy should hire her as its troubleshooter and roving ambassador in the South. On the face of it, the idea was almost laughable: Into a clamorous arena where men's emotions were bound to produce coarse and even violent behavior, the unions would be sending a prim, petite, fifty-five-year-old, white-haired little lady wearing pince-nez, hat and gloves, a gentlewoman's proper suit, and sensible shoes. She was the unmarried daughter of an Episcopal clergyman, the epitome of blue-blooded Virginia refinement and gentility, a descendant of the Masons, Randolphs, Marshalls, and Lees who stood among the giants of history in the Old Dominion.

But what her disarming appearance concealed was crystal clear in her demeanor and in the performance of her duties. In more than twenty years as an executive with the YWCA in Richmond and the National Consumers League in New York, "Miss Lucy" had demonstrated a shrewd and analytical mind, an abundant reservoir of independence and self-confidence, and a deep commitment to the elevation of women, blacks, and working-class people in American life. She had courage and determination, boundless energy, an innate sense of justice and fair play, and a passion for grassroots democracy. Like a Helen Hayes movie character, she was a dynamo posing as a sweet little lady, and for sixteen years she gave the CIO a weapon its foes were powerless to repel. All they had to fight back with was men, just ordinary Southern men; they didn't stand a chance. As one of them told her in utter frustration, "Whatever the CIO pays you, I'm sure you're worth it."

Driving thousands of miles a year in her black Chevrolet coupe, she prepared the way for organizers to land safely in countless small towns and mill villages. She could converse as easily with preachers, editors, sheriffs, and mill owners as with exploited workers, strikers, and the unemployed. She was a public-relations expert, a persuasive speaker, a mediator, and a valuable liaison, not only to her union superiors but also to New Deal agencies in Washington and to other liberal groups operating in the South, including Highlander, the Southern Conference for Human Welfare, and the Southern Summer School for Women Workers in Asheville, North Carolina.

As a genteel Southern white lady who broke out of the confinement of her class to serve others, Lucy Randolph Mason was an inspiration to many women of similar station—writers and activists Katharine Du Pre Lumpkin, Lillian Smith, Virginia Foster Durr, and Josephine Wilkins, to name a few. If these women approached the volatile subject of race with circumspection in the beginning—and most of them did—they eventually moved faster than the generality of white liberals to a rejection of Jim Crow segregation and a committed belief in racial equality.

For people like A. Philip Randolph, arbitrarily consigned by skin color to an inferior status in the society, the emotions of angry rejection and determined commitment came much sooner. Early in his childhood in a small north Florida town, he saw his father, an African Methodist Episcopal preacher, risk life and limb to rescue another black man from a lynch mob. The elder Randolph raised his sons in the nurture and admonition of Jesus and Shakespeare, both of whom they learned to read aloud with deep feeling and conviction. Young Philip went north to New York City as a teenager in about 1905, attended City College for a while, and then finished his education in the school of hard knocks. By 1917, when he was twenty-eight, he and a friend had started a magazine, the *Messenger*. They called it "the only radical Negro magazine in America."

Tall, slender, handsome, and eloquent, Randolph was an effective advocate—both as a writer and as a speaker—for pacifism, socialism, labor unions, and the rights of African-Americans. Once he made an unsuccessful run for Congress. His visibility brought him an invitation in 1925 to organize and direct the Brotherhood of Sleeping Car Porters, a scattered contingent of overworked and underpaid black men who did all the hard labor on a chain of rolling hotels operated by the Pullman Company. Against the fierce opposition of management, Randolph forged a union of over two thousand members before the depression struck—and then, when the New Deal gave unions a new lease on life, he resumed the campaign to win recognition and status from both Pullman and the American Federation of Labor.

At about the time John L. Lewis was punching his way out of the AFL, Randolph was shoving his way in. His was an expatriate Southerner's rich voice thundering through the Northern union halls, insisting that organized labor could never win a decent life for white workers until it first opened its own house to the free and equal service of all workers. Before the end of the 1930s, he had won his fight with Pullman and the AFL, but bigger battles lay ahead. In the years to come, A. Philip Randolph would remain a beacon of strength in labor, race relations, and the reformation of the South.

11. *Birth of a Notion*

As different as they all were, each from the next, practically every one of the writers, activists, and intellectuals produced by the South and brought to the fore in the 1930s had one thing in common: At some time or other, they were publicly branded as sympathizers with the alien doctrines of communism, if not as fellow travelers or card-carrying members of the Communist Party itself.

The onus fell not just upon those who openly proclaimed such ties—Richard Wright in his youth, for example, or vice-presidential candidate James Ford—or on radicals like Claude Williams and Don West, who sometimes gave even their friends cause to wonder; it also shadowed Aubrey Williams, a liberal public servant, and Walter White, a middle-class reformer, and Frank Porter Graham, who spoke from a prestigious institutional base, and Myles Horton, who found political ideology a boring subject, and Howard Kester, whose devotion to Christian socialism actually made him an archenemy of communism. No less an establishment liberal than Virginius Dabney had the charge thrown at him, too, and so did Ralph McGill and Will Alexander, and even the demure Miss Lucy Mason.

What was to become in time a wave of red hysteria didn't start out as an exercise in reckless name-calling. During the period between the Russian

Revolution in 1917 and the fade-out of New Deal reforms some twenty years later, communism and its older political cousin, socialism, were very much in vogue in the United States. As time went on, however, arch-conservative defenders of the status quo throughout the country seemed to assume more or less automatically that all those who advocated a different social order must have violent revolution ultimately in mind. If you wanted to give the laboring majority or the black minority or women or children or the unemployed a better shake, you were an agitator, a troublemaker—and when the Communists and Socialists included these ameliorating objectives in their political platforms, that confirmed the worst suspicions and fears of a substantial segment of the nation's socioeconomic elite and their vigilant guardians on the right.

The Socialists under Eugene V. Debs had championed the cause of the American laboring class for almost a quarter of a century before Norman Thomas emerged as the party's leader and presidential candidate in 1928. Thomas ran a total of six times, finally bowing out after the triumph of Harry Truman and the Democrats in 1948. His high-water mark came in 1932, when he got almost 900,000 votes. The Communists first entered the electoral process as the Workers Party in 1924, and stayed on the ballot for five consecutive elections. William Z. Foster headed their ticket the first three times, and Earl Browder was the candidate in 1936 and 1940. The Workers Party became the Communist Party in 1932 and also made its best showing that year, with 102,000 votes.

Before 1932, the Socialists had looked upon the South with its racial problems as simply one manifestation of a floundering national economic system; replace dog-eat-dog competition and greed-driven profiteering with a cooperative spirit of sharing, the Socialists seemed to say, and all these problems of domestic injustice, including race and class discrimination, will soon fade away. Over the years, socialism had become a familiar (though minor) fixture on the American political scene, a bit player in the quadrennial drama of interparty warfare. The Democrats and Republicans had their alternative philosophies of representative government with which to woo voters; the Socialists had yet another philosophy, but they went about campaigning and politicking to win converts and build a grass-roots constituency in much the same way as the major parties did.

But the international Communist movement didn't even give lip service to such libertarian notions as free and open political expression. From top to bottom the Communist Party was a rigid hierarchy controlled by a dictator and his handpicked comrades, who (not unlike the feudal lords of the Old South) weren't the least bit interested in bringing more people into the political process. Their economic theory was actually a variation on the philosophy of socialism—a fact that confused most Americans—but it was also the antithesis of representative government, just as was the dictatorial state socialism (fascism) that Benito Mussolini brought to Italy in the 1920s and Adolph Hitler subsequently imposed in Germany. Japan, under Emperor Hirohito, followed a similar model. Though the differences among them were substantial, all these ideologies were marked by superpatriotic nationalism, aggressive militarism, antidemocratic despotism, and racial homogeneity.

Communism was first and last a totalitarian ideology, a party line scripted in Moscow and passed down from the Kremlin in edicts that were neither debatable nor negotiable. While the Socialists in this country looked to Norman Thomas for leadership, and he in turn strove to win their trust and keep their support, Communists in the United States, like Communists everywhere, gave their unwavering allegiance to the international party apparatus based in Moscow, and to Joseph Stalin, the Soviet dictator who had seized power after V. I. Lenin died in 1924.

As the Communists developed plans for international expansion in the late 1920s, they began to focus on racial discrimination in this country as a weakness to be exploited. Initially the party took as its inspiration and model the earlier black nationalist strategy of Marcus Garvey and his "Back to Africa" program. Later the Communist Party declared that there should exist somewhere in this country a separate "Negro Republic," an all-black nation-state; come the revolution, it would of course be recognized as a Communist satellite. In the summer of 1932 the party recruited twenty-two young African-Americans (Langston Hughes, Ted Poston, and a few other writers among them) to make a movie in Moscow "documenting the manner in which capitalist America discriminates against and oppresses its colored citizens." The blacks, who were not themselves Communists, did make the journey to Russia and stayed for nearly two months, but the ill-fated project never got off the ground. Before returning home, some of the disillusioned recruits embarrassed their hosts by firing parting shots of criticism at what they saw as the oppressive character of Stalinist Russia.

In part because of such impractical ventures as these, the Communist Party floundered in the United States and utterly failed to attract a sizable following among blacks. But before the mid-1930s the strategy had begun to shift. Building on the miscarriage of justice against African-Americans exemplified in the cases of the Scottsboro boys in Alabama and Angelo Herndon in Atlanta, the Communists mounted a prolonged and highly visible campaign to defend the accused blacks. Not only did they outmaneuver the NAACP and various other liberal groups (including the Socialists); they also drew public opinion to their side and effectively forced the left wing of American activism to affirm and support their efforts.

Those endorsements and the eventual victories their lawyers won for the Scottsboro boys and Herndon in the U.S. Supreme Court gave the Communist Party a degree of legitimacy it had been unable to achieve by other means.

Not coincidentally, it was at just this time in the mid-1930s that the Communist International, the party's world congress, decided to delay for a while its go-it-alone plan of world revolution in order to build antiracist, antifascist alliances of convenience with left-wing groups in America and Europe. This so-called Popular Front was to be the interim vehicle for the Communist Party's drive against capitalism—and in short order, it recorded some impressive achievements. In addition to financing the International Labor Defense campaign that took the Scottsboro and Herndon cases to the Supreme Court, the party supported the American Writers' Congress in its probes of labor abuses in the mines and mills of the South; it helped blacks and other workers establish unions, including some in the South; and it put its resources behind the National Negro Congress, an activist organization that sought to challenge and undercut the NAACP. Among other things, the National Negro Congress launched the Southern Negro Youth Congress to organize young blacks, whom the NAACP had largely ignored.

The Communists also won the backing of some prominent individuals. Paul Robeson, the celebrated black athlete turned actor and concert singer, spent almost four years in the Soviet Union in the latter half of the thirties, and when he came home, his was the foremost American voice of militant black anger against racism and fascism. Richard Wright, the expatriate Mississippian, joined the Communist Party in Chicago in the thirties, while using his tenure in the WPA Writers' Project to produce the stories of Southern racism that made up his first book, *Uncle Tom's Children*. From there he went on to New York to write for the Communist *Daily Worker* and to produce his most famous novel, *Native Son*, before leaving the party in disillusionment in 1942. While some college-educated blacks were making their way into the New Deal, others, like Harvard Law School alumni Benjamin J. Davis, Jr., son of Atlanta's leading black Republican, and John Preston Davis, director of the National Negro Congress, were gaining notoriety (and Communist support) as harsh critics of racial injustice wherever they found it, from New Deal agencies to Southern statehouses and courthouses.

It was not uncommon in the mid-thirties for some Southern activists— intellectuals, labor leaders, editors of black newspapers, and others—to compliment the Communists for their outspoken opposition to Jim Crow segregation and white supremacy. Southern white resistance to communism in these years actually had much less to do with economic theory, which was poorly understood at best, than with the more emotional issues of race and religion. The Communists were atheists who advocated social equality without any racial distinctions, and that was more than enough reason to make them unwelcome in the God-fearing, churchgoing land of Jim Crow.

American Communist Party leader William Z. Foster's vice-presidential running mate in 1932—and also Earl Browder's during his two campaigns—was an expatriate black Southerner, thirty-nine-year-old James W. Ford, son of a Birmingham steelworker. As a teenager he had labored in the mills himself, but somehow managed to finish high school and go at age twenty to Fisk University, from which he eventually graduated after serving in France as a World War I soldier. Ford got a job in Chicago, joined a labor union, and was fired for his involvement in a militant anti–Jim Crow protest. He joined the Communist Party in 1926. From then until his death, thirty years later, he worked openly and actively for the party, for the labor movement, and especially for the constitutional rights of African-Americans, in whose behalf he consistently voiced the same aspirations as generations of Americans before and after him: in Ford's words, "a decent and secure livelihood, human rights, and an equal, honorable, and respectable status in social life." His fellow Alabamians gave the Foster-Ford ticket 726 votes in the 1932 election.

The travails of the Communist Party in Alabama are illustrative of just how much of an uphill climb the movement faced in the South. When it first entered Southern politics in the late 1920s, the party attempted to exploit the volatile labor-management climate in Birmingham, where the capitalist barons of coal and iron ore and steel manufacturing had for fifty years been running the economic, political, and social machinery of Alabama pretty much as they pleased. A relatively small number of black workers and a tiny handful of whites in Alabama subsequently joined the party or one of its units, such as the sharecroppers union; they literally risked their lives to participate in what they believed was the best and, as far as they knew, the only real initiative to win economic justice for Southern laboring people in mining, manufacturing, and agriculture. At most, the movement enlisted no more than a few thousand people before it peaked and subsided in an atmosphere of unrelenting hostility. By the end of 1938, the Communist Party in Alabama had only a few hundred members—and virtually everywhere else in the South, it could claim even less of a presence than that.

The Communists were busily trying to infiltrate and subvert the leftist and antifascist organizations of this country when Stalin abruptly undercut and destroyed the Popular Front in the summer of 1939 by signing a mutual nonaggression pact with Hitler. The confusion thus generated was to be compounded further in less than two years when Hitler's troops invaded Russia anyway. The Soviets and their brand of socialism thus automatically became allies with the Americans in a war against Hitler and his brand of socialism—and neither version was compatible with the socialism of Norman Thomas and his party in the United States. Throughout the war years, American propagandists managed simultaneously to portray communism as an international menace—and the murderous Premier Stalin as kindly "Uncle Joe."

By the beginning of the 1940s, the net result of all these national and international developments was that instability reigned in the political arena of the United States, North and South, as surely as it did in the world at large. The New Deal had lost much of its popular mandate, and conservatives, Democrat as well as Republican, were rising up in retaliation. Right-wing extremists—Fascists, Nazi sympathizers, the German-American Bund, the Brown Shirts and Black Shirts and Silver Shirts, the homegrown Ku Klux Klan—were more numerous and more disruptive of the political process than was the left-wing conglomeration of Communists, Socialists, and sundry other radicals. Hitler probably had a bigger following in the United States than Stalin; certainly he did in the South. Illustrative of the depth and pervasiveness of political confusion was the crypto-Fascist Union Party, a motley assortment of American oddball kooks and extremists, North and South, right and left; they got almost 900,000 votes in 1936—more than three times as many as the Communist and Socialist Party totals combined.

Here in the South, where political participation of any kind was low and political sophistication was even lower, few people could grasp such hair-splitting ideologies as Socialist anticommunism. H. L. Mitchell could refuse to ally the Southern Tenant Farmers Union with the Communist-backed union of Alabama sharecroppers, as he did, and Howard Kester could keep Claude Williams and Don West, old friends he suspected of being Communists, out of the Fellowship of Southern Churchmen, as he did, but those were just empty gestures in the eyes of most white Southerners. The more telling point to them was that Mitchell and Kester were outspoken interracialists—and in the South, no philosophy or ideology was more dangerously radical than that.

F̲ew people in public life were more aggressively opposed to raising the status of blacks in American society—especially Southern society—than Martin Dies, Jr., the Democratic congressman from east Texas. Like his father (also a congressman) before him, Dies was an arch-conservative Anglo-Saxon purist whose political furnace was stoked with an all-consuming hatred of immigrants and people of color. Like many outspoken American isolationists in the thirties (including Senator Robert R. Reynolds of North Carolina and several other Southern members of Congress), the Texas lawmaker harbored a deep admiration for Hitler that was in large measure tied to the German dictator's philosophy of Aryan racial purity.

In 1937, Martin Dies enlisted the aid of Congressman Sam Dickstein of New York, a Jew alarmed by Hitler's anti-Semitism, to advance the idea of a House investigation of American extremist groups associated with the Nazis, Fascists, Bolsheviks, and other foreign interests. Republicans and Southern Democrats went along with the proposal, and in May 1938 the House Committee on Un-American Activities was established, with Dies as its chairman. He was joined by another like-minded Southerner, Joe Starnes of Alabama, and five others, including two Republicans. (Dickstein was not one of them; he had been cleverly maneuvered to the sidelines.) In an introductory statement of intent, Dies declared that the committee "will not permit any character assassination or smearing of innocent people." Neither the public nor the Congress, he said, "will have any confidence in the findings of a committee which adopts a partisan or preconceived attitude."

For the post of chief committee investigator, Dies hired forty-four-year-old J. B. Matthews, a Kentucky native who sequentially had been a Methodist missionary in Asia, a college professor (at Nashville's Scarritt College and elsewhere), a radical pacifist and racial equalitarian, a Socialist, and finally a hard-line Communist. Then, in what he described as a dramatic conversion—and his erstwhile comrades called an opportunistic betrayal—Matthews had offered his services to the right-wing opposition. Not only was he a valuable red-hunter by virtue of having been one himself; he was also a skilled propagandist who in short order produced *The Trojan Horse in America*, an anticommunist call to arms ghost-written for the byline of Martin Dies.

The House Un-American Activities Committee—HUAC, as it came to be known—never showed much interest in hunting for Nazi sympathizers; it was the reds they were after. Before the summer of 1938 was over, a parade of carefully chosen witnesses had grabbed headlines with sensational testimony charging that the Communists secretly controlled the CIO and other labor organizations, the movie industry in Hollywood, and a wide range of liberal and progressive social-action groups. Matthews himself supplied most of the names of suspects, including those of many individuals active in the New Deal.

In its beginning phase before and during the Second World War, HUAC seldom focused its attention on the South or on the issue of race; the

right-wing concept of "un-American" behavior was more broadly construed then. Not until racial equality became a pressing right-wing concern in the Cold War years would the zealots in the House and Senate
elevate Southern integrationists to the top of their "disloyalty" list. By that
time, Dies and a few other key Southerners, including Representative
John Rankin and Senator James O. Eastland of Mississippi, would have
effectively fused their opposition to racial equality with the anticommunist
hysteria orchestrated by Senator Joseph McCarthy of Wisconsin and other
Northern Republican reactionaries. Seldom if ever had such a cooperative
alliance between North and South been seen. In the frantic hunt for
subversives and traitors, the Southerners had no hesitation about following the McCarthy line. For their part, the Northern right-wingers just as
willingly joined forces with the Southerners in a false alchemy that made
a mix of black and white come out red.

Dies had welcomed the election of Franklin Roosevelt in 1932, and had
gone along for a time as a loyal Democrat and New Deal partisan; even as
late as 1937 he was still on good personal terms with the President, though
he sometimes made disparaging references to the "idealists, dreamers,
politicians, and professional do-gooders" in the administration. But along
the way, Dies decided that the Democratic Party was slipping away from
its Southern power base and into the hands of Yankees, Catholics, Jews,
city bosses, immigrant ethnics, Negroes, laborites, liberals, radicals—in
short, the very people he hated. HUAC gave him a base from which to
fight back against this alien wave, and against FDR himself. Throughout
the war years, Dies and J. B. Matthews and their bipartisan Northern and
Southern colleagues on the committee would stand vigilantly in the watch-
towers, searching for Communists in every nook and cranny of American life.

As the struggle between left and right intensified in the political
theater of the thirties, the neutral zone between them was gradually
reduced to a narrow corridor where moderates and conciliators crowded
together and paced nervously. People of a more radical persuasion at
either end of the spectrum were usually easy to identify. (This was particularly true in the South, where liberals and progressives were few in
number and right-wing reactionaries made no bones about their extremist
views.) But those in the middle were harder to recognize, having as they
did a more even-minded outlook. And, to complicate things further, they
often appeared to step out of the neutral zone and cross the line to one side
or the other.

Mainstream Democrats dominated the moderate ranks in the South (there being no Republicans to speak of), but they, too, were outnumbered by conservative extremists in their own party. New Dealers may have been criticized for leaning too far to the left or right, but their sensitivity to pressure from both sides virtually ensured that they would remain in the middle. Leaders in the church, the university, and the press, almost by the nature and definition of their positions, likewise tended to slide toward the center. Even such organizations as the Commission on Interracial Cooperation, the various Northern philanthropies that funded Southern reforms, and the NAACP were usually outflanked by someone on the left, and the same was true of the Agrarians and others on the right.

From a Southern perspective, one of the more curious of these moderate initiatives was started in April 1935 when Francis Pickens Miller of Virginia, working under the auspices of a national public-interest group called the Foreign Policy Association, invited about three dozen prominent citizens (all of them white males) to Atlanta to explore setting up a committee to work on the region's manifold problems. Miller was a well-traveled, forty-year-old, middle-class liberal with a strong interest in international religious and social issues. A Presbyterian minister's son, he had been a YMCA worker (one of Willis Weatherford's protégés), a Rhodes scholar, an administrator in the World Student Christian Federation, and a cofounder (with Reinhold Niebuhr and others) of the magazine *Christianity & Crisis*. He had recently joined the Foreign Policy Association as a field secretary, organizing public-interest forums and study groups around questions of national policy.

In Atlanta, Nashville, Birmingham, and elsewhere, Miller found some thoughtful Southerners who shared his interest and concerns. He and a handful of others—chiefly Chattanooga editor George Fort Milton, Tulane University professor Herman C. Nixon (the onetime Vanderbilt Agrarian), and Brooks Hays, an Arkansas lawyer working for the Farm Security Administration—called the Atlanta conference to discuss several topics of primary interest to the South: agrarian policy, democratic institutions, social objectives, economic planning. Twenty-nine invitees from nine Southern states attended.

Within a year, Miller and his companions had formally established the Southern Policy Committee as an organization loosely tied to the national association from which it sprang, but having its own officers (Nixon, Hays, Miller) and study groups in several Southern locales. On Nixon's initiative, they also managed to breach the wall of race and sex segregation by bringing Charles S. Johnson and Lucy Randolph Mason into the group (after which a few of the white men promptly resigned in protest). The planners were cheered when about seventy-five people showed up for a general conference at the Lookout Mountain Hotel, near Chattanooga, in May 1936.

From all appearances, the SPC was an established reality, even though it had no reliable source of funds for an ongoing mission of any substance. But exactly what was it to be, anyway—a legislation and policy center? an academic discussion forum? a research and education group? a political action committee? Were they actually going to do something, or was this just to be more endless talk? Predictably, the delegates couldn't agree. They had begun with lofty pronouncements about helping the South and the nation regain a sense of direction, but their debate soon lapsed into ideological quarreling over thorny philosophical and social issues.

To Nixon, the exercise had a depressingly familiar ring; every time Southern intellectuals tried to work together, it seemed, they ended up in contentious dispute. Among the Lookout Mountain delegates were some of his former Agrarian colleagues—Donald Davidson, Frank Owsley, Allen Tate—still preaching their reactionary sermons against government intervention and Yankee industrial invaders. Since parting company with them earlier in the decade, Nixon had taken up with their critics, Howard Odum and the Chapel Hill social scientists, who had their own "Southern regional committee" study group going. But they too were so engrossed in intellectualizing that they never got around to the nuts and bolts of regional reform. Labor organizers and others of a more radical bent were also meeting around the region, but none of these groups had yet become a catalyst for change.

Francis Pickens Miller would keep up his organizing effort for a couple of years or so before turning his mind to foreign policy and the Nazi threat, thus leaving the remnant of Southern Policy Committee stalwarts to find their own ways of addressing the South's woes. While they were together, though, Miller and his friends, particularly Nixon and Hays, did manage to assemble periodically a cadre of leaders who had been trying since the advent of FDR to point their impoverished homeland toward a new and better day. In this group were journalists such as Milton, Virginius Dabney, Jonathan Daniels, and Mark Ethridge; academicians Nixon, Frank Porter Graham, W. T. Couch, and Arthur Raper; New Dealers Hays, Will Alexander, Aubrey Williams, and Clark Foreman. The few blacks and women who participated in the discussions from time to time had limited roles to play, but their presence was at least a token reminder that the region's crises concerned more than just the white male population.

Howard Odum was conspicuous once again by his absence. As he had done with the various regional initiatives of the New Deal, and as he soon would do with regard to the Southern Conference for Human Welfare, Odum chose not to be an active player in the deliberations of the Southern

Policy Committee. The Chapel Hill sociologist's dream was to merge his study group with the Commission on Interracial Cooperation (of which he had just been chosen president), thus creating a powerful and comprehensive new Southern regional research and development council. For a brief time he entertained the hope that Miller would be willing and able to roll the SPC into the same big ball, but when that became problematic, Odum dropped the idea. His own ambitious strategy was complex enough; he hardly had time for the grand plans of others.

Two spin-off groups created by the Southern Policy Committee turned out to be more important than the SPC itself. One was the Alabama Policy Committee, a Birmingham-based gathering of industry and labor leaders, academics, journalists, and public officials; the other was a highly informal and constantly shifting aggregation of Washington-based Southerners in the New Deal who met irregularly under the SPC banner at a popular riverside restaurant-saloon not far from Capitol Hill. H. C. Nixon, an Alabamian himself, had a lot to do with the vitality of the Birmingham group; Francis Pickens Miller, who with his journalist-wife, Helen Hill Miller, lived in the Virginia suburbs, was the chief convener of the District of Columbia group. Joining the Millers, Brooks Hays, and Will Alexander for dinner at Hall's Restaurant periodically were such rising young public servants as Maury Maverick of Texas, Lister Hill and John Sparkman of Alabama, Estes Kefauver and Abe Fortas of Tennessee, Claude Pepper of Florida, and others (among them once or twice a lanky Texan named Lyndon B. Johnson). The chief significance of the Washington group was that it provided a private forum for moderately progressive Southerners in the federal government to explore ideas about social change in the region. As for the assembly in Birmingham, it would perform a much more specific and functional service in the late thirties.

By 1938, there existed in the South a loose confederation of groups and individuals within hailing distance, right or left, of Roosevelt's New Dealers. It would be an overstatement to call them a network or an alliance. They were not all of one mind, or of the same political, economic, religious, social, or ideological persuasion; they weren't even all acquainted. At best they were a loose scattering of activists who knew of one another by reputation. They had two things in common: their Southern heritage, and a critical perspective that made them believe the South could do better, had to do better, for itself and its citizens. Some of them had met occasionally, shared ideas, and tried in a variety of ways to influence the course of events. Most of them dreamed longingly of a South peacefully transformed from its feudal past to a freer, more prosperous, and more democratic future.

Shortly after the general election that November, a substantial number of them met under one roof to consider how they might work together for the greater good of their native land. In the very act of meeting they did something memorable, something that had not happened before (and would not happen quite that way again). For numerous reasons, the Southern Conference for Human Welfare in Birmingham never lived up to its promise—but few of those who were present at the creation ever forgot the singular significance of that historic occasion and the part they played in it.

Countless threads of thought and association and cooperation went into the weaving of this tapestry. It was to be the most diverse gathering of Southerners anywhere, for any purpose. People were there from every level of government, from management and labor, from the churches and the universities and the press, from the radical left to the moderate right, from plantations and tenant farms, from the ranks of blacks and women so often excluded. Indeed, so many different factions were involved that it seems almost impossible now to sort out the various sources of cause and effect.

One of the principal contributors to the birth of the conference was Joseph S. Gelders, a young, middle-class liberal from Birmingham's small but solid Jewish community. In the tradition of intellectual accomplishment that has long been a hallmark of Southern Jewry, Gelders reached maturity with a quick mind and an active interest in social issues. He went to public school in Birmingham, attended the University of Alabama and Massachusetts Institute of Technology, and served in the army during World War I, all with respectable ease if not flying colors. He held several jobs in Birmingham before returning to the University of Alabama in 1929 to finish his bachelor's and master's degrees, and he remained there to teach physics until 1935.

By then more interested in politics and economics than in the sciences, Gelders was deeply troubled by the pervasiveness of poverty and racism in the depression-wracked South, and because of his outspokenness on such matters, the university declined to renew his contract. Upon moving to New York, he became active in the National Committee for the Defense of Political Prisoners, an organization that rallied intellectuals to the support of working-class people and victims of racial oppression. In years to come it would be listed repeatedly as a Communist front; in the summer of 1936, when Gelders returned to Birmingham as its Southern representative, the committee was viewed with alarm as one more among many militant pro-labor organizations in that teeming center of industrial strife.

Almost immediately he took up the cause of a local Communist Party official in jail for possessing literature deemed by the authorities to advocate the violent overthrow of the government. Not long after Gelders and others staged a public protest of the man's treatment, their dissent was answered with a terrorist reprisal. Late one September evening, as Joe Gelders was returning home from a meeting, three men abducted him at gunpoint, drove him into the rural Alabama countryside, stripped him naked, and beat him to within an inch of his life. When he finally recovered, a grand jury heard him positively identify two of his assailants as former strikebreakers at a local steel mill; instead of returning indictments, the jury seemed almost to applaud the assault on a "red" who deserved what he got.

If Gelders had been a militant revolutionary bent on destroying the established order, his treatment might not have seemed so shocking; after all, Birmingham was a tough town in those days, and violence there was commonplace. But the thirty-seven-year-old activist was no flamethrower; he was a respectable member of the community, a man whose convictions were appreciated and even endorsed by a number of important people in the Birmingham power structure. Joe Gelders was a familiar hometown fellow to those people, not a clandestine Communist; even if they disagreed with his tactics, they acknowledged that his motives and his methods were open for all to see, and they admired his commitment to the poorest of the poor.

Undeterred by his own vulnerability to danger, Gelders continued to work for social reforms, and at every opportunity he promoted an idea that had become important to him: a regionwide conference aimed at drawing a broad panoply of Southern progressives to the cause of civil liberties. In 1937 he met H. C. Nixon when the two men served on a committee investigating a labor-management conflict in Gadsden, Alabama. Early the next year, at the scene of a worker strike in Tupelo, Mississippi, Gelders and Lucy Randolph Mason of the CIO discovered that they had a mutual interest in such issues as voting rights and equal protection of the law. Back in Birmingham, where the CIO leadership was forging alliances with black workers and the local NAACP chapter, Gelders helped to organize a right-to-vote club to register black voters in advance of the May 1938 Democratic primary.

That same spring, Gelders spent five weeks drumming up support in New York and Washington for his dream of a Southern conference. He had gone in part because Lucy Mason had offered to discuss the proposal with her friend Eleanor Roosevelt and, if possible, to get Gelders an audience with the First Lady. As it turned out, she did better than that; early in June, Mason took Gelders to the Roosevelts' home in Hyde Park,

New York, for a meeting with both Mrs. Roosevelt and the President.

This was the time when FDR was planning his frontal attack on Senator Walter George and several other anti–New Deal Southern reactionaries in Congress who were running for reelection. All through the late winter and early spring, he had been conferring with his trusted advisers, plotting retaliation. Georgia native Clark Foreman, a Harold Ickes aide in the Public Works Administration, had helped the President find a candidate to run against George. During their conversations, Foreman passed on to FDR an idea that had surfaced at one of the Southern Policy Committee dinner sessions at Hall's Restaurant: A document enumerating the South's major economic problems should be prepared and circulated as a call to battle against the feudal oligarchy that was killing New Deal reforms and keeping the region in paupery.

The idea appealed seductively to Roosevelt's Machiavellian taste for political maneuvering. Here was a new and promising Southern strategy. This could be a document by Southerners about the South's problems and needs, a sort of reformers' manifesto that calmly and judiciously stated the grim facts without directly waving such emotionally charged red flags as race relations, union organizing, and land reform. With it, the President could go directly to the people, over the heads of their entrenched leaders. If there was a liberal opposition in the South, surely this was the time to call it out—and if the effort failed, there would at least be some Southern shoulders to bear the defeat with him. (The historian Harvard Sitkoff later offered a blunter assessment of FDR's stake in the conference: "If it succeeded, he would have a liberal, united party supporting him; if it failed, he would be free of the campaign's taint and would still be able to work with Dixie politicos.")

Roosevelt sent Foreman to Lowell Mellett, director of the National Emergency Council, a governmental policy-planning agency, with instructions to prepare the document. Quickly they set up a working group of scholars and writers (most of them recruited through the Southern Policy Committee) to produce the chapters, and a twenty-two-member task force of Southerners to oversee their work. The drafters, with input from Arthur Raper, George S. Mitchell, H. C. Nixon, and numerous others, rushed to complete the job by early summer; often they ended up in late-night sessions at Mellett's home or that of Clifford and Virginia Durr, nearby. An Alabamian and a New Deal lawyer active in the SPC, Cliff Durr wrote one of the report's fifteen chapters, as well as the President's cover letter of introduction, which included this now-famous line: "It is my conviction that the South presents right now the Nation's No. 1 economic problem—the Nation's problem, not merely the South's."

The blue-ribbon task force, which was called the Committee on Economic Conditions in the South, included only a few known liberals: Frank Porter Graham of the University of North Carolina, Barry Bingham of the Louisville *Courier-Journal*, H. L. Mitchell of the Southern Tenant Farmers Union, and the sole female, Lucy Randolph Mason. All of the members were white. In July they delivered to President Roosevelt the *Report on Economic Conditions of the South*, a lean (sixty-four pages), dry, dispassionate summary of the region's chronic and crippling poverty.

The South, the report stated, was richly endowed with natural and human assets, yet it was perpetually at the bottom of almost every indicator of national productivity. Its topsoil was eroding away; its people were either leaving in search of greater opportunity or abiding on starvation wages; its education and health care and housing were not even remotely adequate to meet minimum needs. Southern people worked just as hard as their fellow Americans, but earned only half as much (on average, only $315 a year); they desperately required the most basic things: food, fuel, clothes, housing, jobs, schools, transportation, medical attention.

There was barely a mention of the beleaguered black minority, and none at all of labor unions or land redistribution or political participation. All the emphasis was on the region's acute disadvantage in comparison with the rest of the nation. The facts were undeniable, yet no fingers were pointed at the perpetrators of Southern economic distress.

When Joe Gelders and Lucy Mason visited the Roosevelts, the report on economic conditions was nearing completion, and FDR was loading his guns for the coming duels with Walter George, Cotton Ed Smith, and other Dixie naysayers. When he heard Gelders talk of calling a regional conference to discuss civil liberties, the President deftly reshaped and enlarged the idea. How about a conference of Southerners responding to the report on economic conditions? he asked. And not just an elite white male response, his wife added—there should be some women and blacks and union members among the delegates, and tenant farmers too, and the agenda ought to include such topics as the poll tax, lynching, equal justice, and the rights of laboring people.

At the time, Eleanor was showing *People of the Cumberlands*, Elia Kazan's new movie about Appalachia, to White House visitors, and she was filled with enthusiasm for the Highlander Folk School and its services as a cultural center and labor college. People like Myles and Zilphia Horton and James Dombrowski should take part in this conference, she said—and for her part, she would be glad to come and speak herself.

Gelders and Mason floated into Washington on cloud nine. They met briefly with Mellett and Foreman, with Cliff and Virginia Durr, and with Mrs. Durr's brother-in-law, Justice Hugo Black, who tentatively agreed to make a major address at the Southern conference. Back in Birmingham, Gelders arranged a preliminary meeting with members of the Alabama Policy Committee, and they showed enthusiasm. One of them was H. C. Nixon, who was winding up a six-month project in Birmingham while on a leave of absence from the Tulane University faculty. Nixon's new book, *Forty Acres and Steel Mules*, published by the University of North Carolina Press, was an impassioned call for equal opportunity and economic security for the Southern working class, white and black, and it placed him squarely in the forefront of what was shaping up as a generally positive and constructive response to the government report on economic conditions in the South.

As he listened to Gelders's expansive description of the proposed conference—a huge affair, probably taking place there in the Alabama industrial capital and drawing from all walks of Southern life—Nixon may have finally decided on a course of action he had been contemplating for some time. Soon thereafter, he resigned his Tulane post (where he had been under fire from President Rufus C. Harris and local right-wing elements for his liberal involvements) and threw in with Gelders to help plan and organize the conference.

There followed a summer flurry of committee meetings at which some basic decisions were made: The event would take place in Birmingham after the November elections; it would be called the Southern Conference for Human Welfare; U.S. Commissioner Louise O. Charlton of Birmingham, a member of the Alabama branch of the Southern Policy Committee and also a state Democratic Party official, would preside as temporary chairman; the three most prominently featured speakers would be Frank Porter Graham, Eleanor Roosevelt, and Hugo Black; and subcommittees would be established to respond to each section of the economic-conditions report.

In many ways, Birmingham was an ideal location for an all-Southern summit meeting on social issues. Delegates from such far-flung places as Richmond, Miami, and San Antonio would see it as a central crossroads, but it had more than geography to recommend it; from its violent and explosive birth as an industrial hub, the city had evolved into something resembling a continuous production of socioeconomic drama, a morality play throbbing with heroes and villains, victims and perpetrators, and a cast of thousands.

In its short life—less than seventy-five years—Birmingham had risen in a burst of flame and fury befitting a city watched over by an iron statue of Vulcan, the Roman fire god. It was at once everything Henry Grady dreamed of and everything the Agrarians feared in their conflicting visions of an industrialized New South. Rich deposits of coal, limestone, and iron ore were there for the taking, and the railroads had come to get them, running on rich Northern capital and cheap Southern sweat. By the early years of the twentieth century, huge enterprises manufacturing steel and iron products filled the valley with a rosy furnace glow and a perpetual pall of smoke.

Nothing was small-scale in Birmingham. The population climbed from almost zero to nearly forty thousand in the thirty years before 1900; in the next thirty years it ballooned to more than a quarter of a million, and continued to grow rapidly in the depression years (Jefferson County would have almost a half-million people by 1940). Absentee capitalists, itinerant speculators, resident entrepreneurs, and calculating politicians held a tight grip on the city; together, they voraciously consumed the natural and human resources—the latter a voiceless multitude, desperate for paying jobs, flowing in a steady stream from the ravaged Alabama outback. This volatile combination begat all sorts of excesses—pervasive deadly violence, political reactionaryism, extremes of wealth and poverty, moral certitude, religious intolerance, racial and ethnic bigotry.

The barons of Birmingham industry, soon to be dubbed the "Big Mules" by Alabama populists and the press, were masters of consolidation. They may have damned Charles Darwin and the theory of evolution, but survival of the fittest was a notion that warmed their hearts. Repeated attempts to organize workers in the mines and mills had yielded little except blood and frustration for more than half a century, but finally, with the coming of the New Deal and its support for organized labor, the contest between Mules and men evened out a bit.

John L. Lewis and the United Mine Workers, under the organizing rights granted by the National Industrial Recovery Act, built their Alabama membership to about twenty thousand by the end of 1934. The massive national textile strike that same year started in Alabama and spread across the South. The Mine, Mill, and Smelter Workers had some success in the Birmingham area, and so did the Steel Workers Organizing Committee. By 1938, with leadership from people like William Mitch of the mine workers' union and numerous white and black organizers in the union locals, the Birmingham labor force, some fifty thousand strong, had established a beachhead within the barony.

It was nothing revolutionary, to be sure; they weren't about to cause an outbreak of democracy. Only about sixty thousand people—one-fifth of the voting-age population—were registered in Birmingham and Jefferson County (including no more than three or four hundred blacks), and less than half of them bothered to vote regularly, in part because of the punitive poll tax. There was also a nagging friction in the workplace between whites and blacks, and the corporations worked overtime to turn white

workers against both blacks and the Communist organizers who had surfaced among them.

And yet, against the most formidable opposition, organized labor did
make some inroads. The Birmingham unions, operating from a pragmatic
and democratic belief in the strength of numbers, made a start toward
racial integration; they raised the level of political involvement (and gave
liberals a little backbone); they helped to reduce wage disparities (regional, racial, and sexual); they led the way to improvements in the administration of justice and in the recognition of civil liberties. No other
organization in Alabama showed as much of a willingness to take on the
colonial lords—or as much promise of success—as did the CIO unions.
And, compared to other institutions in the South in the late 1930s, labor
unions clearly showed the most interest in racial accommodation and in
across-the-board participation in the political process. For all these reasons, labor was bound to be a key player in the Southern Conference for
Human Welfare, and Birmingham was thus a good choice as a meeting
site.

In addition to H. C. Nixon and Louise Charlton, several other members
of the Alabama Policy Committee played an active role in the SCHW
preparations, among them Birmingham Congressman Luther Patrick and
Postmaster Cooper Green, labor leaders Mollie Dowd and William Mitch,
industrialist Donald Comer, and columnist John Temple Graves II of the
Birmingham *Age-Herald*. Clark Foreman was active behind the scenes as
chief liaison between the conference and the Roosevelt administration.

And Joe Gelders was there too, of course; he, more than anyone else,
had persuaded the Southern Policy Committee members, the New Deal
Democrats, and leaders of labor, the press, academia, and the religious
community to cooperate in this venture. If any of them were nervous
about working with a notorious left-winger like him, they didn't show it.
Either they disbelieved the rumors that Gelders was a card-carrying Communist, or they didn't care, because they knew him, liked him, trusted
him. As the planning proceeded, it was clear that the SCHW hierarchy
viewed itself—Gelders included—as a Southern progressive movement,
neither radical nor reactionary but essentially moderate in its aims and
purposes.

As the time for the conference drew near, enthusiasm was high all
across the South. One ominous note that preceded it, however, was President Roosevelt's failure to defeat Walter George and Cotton Ed Smith
and their reactionary colleagues in the primaries. Worse still, he had seen
more than six dozen Democrats in Congress lose their seats in the general
election, and now even his former supporters in the Southern press were
lambasting him for his clumsy purge attempt. Just as the Birmingham

gathering was about to convene, FDR was packing for a train trip to Warm Springs and a somber Thanksgiving retreat in the Georgia backcountry, there to lick his wounds and ponder what the Dixie demagogues had done to his cleverly crafted Southern strategy.

12. *Revival in Birmingham*

Picture yourself as an observer in the midst of this scene: It is Sunday evening, November 20, 1938, in Birmingham, Alabama. The South has baked through a seemingly endless, bone-dry summer, only recently relieved by just enough rain to settle the dust. Birmingham and all of Alabama, indeed all of the South, still lie prostrate and exhausted in the smothering embrace of the Great Depression. Here in the South's Pittsburgh, its scruffy, brawling industrial vortex, the steel mills and coal-burning enterprises once spewed so much soot and smog into the air that you could barely see well enough to read the street signs; now the primary atmospheric color is a dingy shade of gray, and an eerie, muffled stillness hovers over the city.

From somewhere in the downtown darkness, a belltower clock tolls seven times. The opening session of the Southern Conference for Human Welfare is just half an hour away, and upwards of fifteen hundred delegates from thirteen states, progressive sons and daughters of the Mother South, are expected to come here to take up a monumental task. On the broad Eighth Avenue sidewalk and the lawn in front of the Municipal Auditorium, a swelling throng of men and women is moving slowly toward the open doors. There is energy in the very air around the eager delegates; they feel it and show it with a nervous hum of excitement that suggests anticipation, uncertainty, dread, anxiety, hope. Some in the crowd are dressed as if for church or the theater—the men in dark suits and hats, the women in dresses and coats with ankle-length hems and fur throws at the shoulders. Others seem shy and uncomfortable in their ill-fitting Sunday-go-to-meeting clothes. A few wear simple print dresses and faded bib overalls and brogans—the uniform of factory workers and farmers across the South.

Aside from this noticeable and rather curious blend of social classes, there is something else unusual about the crowd: Though most of them are white, a substantial minority are Negroes. As they move toward the doors, the two races feign nonchalance while they discreetly steal fleeting glimpses of one another. The doors marked COLORED ENTRANCE are up a flight of stairs on the Twentieth Street side of the auditorium, and most of the blacks are moving in that direction. But the main portals are standing open to the lighted foyer, and no ticket-takers are there, no guards, and so some of the arriving nonwhites are simply filtering through with the rest of the throng.

Pulling up at the curb is a limousine with a little Alabama flag on the fender. Out steps Governor Bibb Graves with his wife, Dixie. (Graves and James H. Price of Virginia have been called the only two bona fide New Deal governors in the South.) And here come Alabama's two senators, John H. Bankhead and Lister Hill, and Birmingham Congressman Luther Patrick, and Florida Senator Claude Pepper, and the governor-elect of South Carolina, Burnet R. Maybank. Maury Maverick, the recently defeated congressman from Texas, is also present. Numerous state and local officials from Alabama, with their wives, are among the hosts here; earlier in the afternoon, the women led a motorcade of visiting dignitaries on a tour of Birmingham "beauty spots."

This is also an Alabama homecoming for such New Deal officials as Aubrey Williams, once a Birmingham store clerk, and Helen Fuller, a local schoolgirl who grew up to become a Justice Department lawyer. In a couple of days the conference spotlight will fall on the nation's First Lady, Eleanor Roosevelt, when she appears for a major address, and after that another celebrated native son, Supreme Court Justice and former Alabama senator Hugo Black, will be here to receive the conference's Thomas Jefferson Medal. Other Southerners in the administration who are expected to take part in these deliberations are Will W. Alexander, Brooks Hays, Mary McLeod Bethune, George S. Mitchell, and Clark Foreman.

But public officials make up only a fraction of the delegates. Southern newspapers are represented by such well-known editors and publishers as Barry Bingham and Mark Ethridge of Louisville, George Fort Milton of Chattanooga, Jennings Perry of Nashville, and Birmingham's own John Temple Graves. George C. Stoney, a young North Carolinian, is here on assignment for *Survey Graphic* magazine in New York. The numerous emissaries from organized religion range from Rabbis Jacob Kaplan of Miami and Julius Mark of Nashville to Father T. M. Cullen of the Catholic archdiocese of Mobile and the Reverend F. Clyde Helms, pastor of a large Baptist church in Columbia, South Carolina.

The labor movement may have the most delegates of all. John L. Lewis of the United Mine Workers is not present, but most people here have heard the story that his union is the largest financial backer of the conference. William Mitch of the UMW and Mollie Dowd of the Women's Trade Union League, two Birmingham-based labor officials, are among the principal organizers of the conference. Also here are Lucy Randolph

Mason and Witherspoon Dodge of the CIO, H. L. Mitchell and Howard Kester and other members of the Southern Tenant Farmers Union, Stanton E. Smith of the American Federation of Teachers, and Manuel Garcia of the Cigar Makers Union in Tampa. Not just leaders, either, but rank-and-file stalwarts like Hosea Hudson, a black foundryman and organizer from Birmingham; twenty-seven-year-old Eula Mae McGill, an Alabama textile mill worker recently fired for her union organizing efforts; and eighty-two-year-old Brush Smith, a longtime Tennessee coal miner.

The Socialists are here in the person of Mitchell and Kester and a few others, like Frank McCallister of the Southern Workers Defense League, and there are a handful of Communists too, including Donald Burke of Virginia and Rob Hall of Alabama. Myles Horton and Jim Dombrowski have come from the Highlander Folk School. Francis Pickens Miller of the Southern Policy Committee is on hand, as are native Alabamians Clifford and Virginia Durr of Washington. Also present are John P. Davis of the National Negro Congress; a South Carolina labor lawyer, John Bolt Culbertson; the Birmingham industrialist Donald Comer; and even Prentiss Terry of the arch-conservative Southern States Industrial Council.

The university community is represented by a host of people, including Cortez Ewing of Oklahoma, H. C. Nixon of Tulane (until recently), Charles W. Pipkin of Louisiana State, W. T. Couch of North Carolina, F. D. Patterson of Tuskegee, Charles S. Johnson of Fisk, C. Vann Woodward of Florida, Arthur Raper of Agnes Scott, Benjamin Mays of Morehouse, nineteen delegates from Alabama Polytechnic Institute (better known as Auburn), and at least as many from the University of Alabama. Another scholar in the crowd is the Swedish social economist Gunnar Myrdal, who is beginning work on a massive research project concerning race relations in America.

There has never been such a gathering as this in the South, such a diverse convocation of progressives from every stratum of the society. As dissimilar as they are, the people who comprise this racially and economically and professionally variegated multitude are all seeking ways to make their region a healthier, better educated, better paying, less violent, more charitable, more equitable, more democratic place. Are they a symbol of hope a-borning, a harbinger of the much-debated and long-awaited New South? Most of them want desperately to believe that.

Inside the cavernous hall, about two thousand seats are set up on the main floor facing the stage, and thirty-five hundred more are tiered in a horseshoe around them. Custom still has its heavy hand on the crowd; it dictates that whites move to claim the best seats from the floor up, leaving the blacks to take what's left—the notorious "crow's nest," remote and removed from the action. But this is not a customary event; this is a happening, and there is a subtle relaxation of the old rules. The racially mixed crowd gravitates to the auditorium floor, filling the seats there and spilling over into the rim of the horseshoe. The segregation protocol breaks down; people sit wherever they find empty seats. No one seems distressed or uneasy in the informal, friendly atmosphere.

This first session of the Southern Conference for Human Welfare is billed as a "devotional service." Judge Louise O. Charlton presides. A local minister opens with prayer, and several stirring songs by a local industrial high school chorus warm up the crowd; the revival mood continues as H. C. Nixon introduces the featured speaker for an "inspirational address." Frank Porter Graham, the charismatic North Carolina educator and spear-carrier for Southern liberalism, steps to the podium. Dignified, handsome, articulate, compelling, he sounds the trumpet of dedication and sacrifice and service.

We have so much work to do, he declares. We must catch up with the nation. We desperately need the aid of the federal government—to equalize educational opportunity, to improve wages, housing, and health care, to allow full political participation, to close the economic, social, and cultural gaps between the South and the nation.

These are dark times in the world, he tells the raptly attentive throng. Dictators strut with impunity, persecuting Jews, Catholics, Negroes. Frank Graham's voice quivers with power and passion and sincerity: "In this day when democracy and freedom are in retreat everywhere in the face of totalitarian powers and their regimentation of youth and persecution of minorities, let us raise the flag of freedom and democracy where it counts most," here in our own land. Driving the point home to his listeners and to the South, he is electrifyingly specific: "The black man is the primary test of American democracy and Christianity. The Southern Conference for Human Welfare takes its stand here tonight for the simple thing of human freedom. Repression is the way of frightened power; freedom is the enlightened way. We take our stand for the Sermon on the Mount, the American Bill of Rights, and American democracy."

Ovations, spontaneous and thunderous, punctuate his words. Blacks lead the cheers and applause, but they are not alone. At the end, Graham and his idealistic Christian-Democratic vision inspire a prolonged and vociferous standing tribute. Not everyone joins in, but most do—the academics, the laborites, the Communists and Socialists, the ministers and priests and rabbis, Southern Democrats of almost every stripe and tint, and even some of the hard-bitten cynics in the press.

More than half a century later, there would be a few still living, like Eula McGill and Stanton Smith, who remembered that night as a singular moment of Southern hope and promise. For Virginia Durr, one more in that surviving remnant, the memory was vivid and indelible. "It was a love feast," she said. "We had a feeling of exhilaration, like we had crossed the river together and entered the Promised Land. It was one of the happiest experiences of my life."

The Birmingham newspapers gave extensive advance notice of and continuing coverage to the Southern Conference for Human Welfare, and favorable editorial comment as well. Like the delegates themselves, the papers seemed to take the *Report on Economic Conditions of the South* as an accurate summary that called for a constructive and cooperative response from within the region. The conference was, in effect, a Southern answer to the report. With a friend in the White House and Southerners in many positions of importance throughout the federal government, declared the Birmingham *Post*, the South must seize the moment: "If ever we are to make progress, now is the time."

Muted warnings were voiced against labeling the SCHW a political movement, yet most acknowledged that nothing short of massive and sustained political action was likely to lift the South out of the morass of poverty. If the involvement of so many Southern Democrats and New Deal figures in the conference and the presence of Mrs. Roosevelt on the program were not enough to underscore the political dimension, FDR himself did the job with a message read to the delegates at the opening session Monday morning. The long struggle by liberal leaders of the South for human welfare had borne fruit in the New Deal, the President said, but the battle for parity with the rest of the nation was far from over; many interrelated human and economic problems remained. "You know from years of trying the difficulties of your task," he concluded, "but if you steer a true course, and keep everlastingly at it, the South will long be thankful for this day."

More than twelve hundred registered delegates from all eleven former Confederate states plus Kentucky and Oklahoma paid the conference registration fee of one dollar and took part in the three days of discussions; countless hundreds more attended the sessions that were open to the public. Blacks made up about a fourth of those who registered, and several of them took part in the program as panelists or speakers. Working through more than a dozen committees (on education, housing, labor relations and unemployment, farm tenancy, capital and credit, constitutional rights, prison reform, voting rights, race relations, problems of youth, and other topics), the delegates quickly set out to make their generally liberal feelings known.

But in the very breadth of their liberalism were the seeds of their own undoing, for then as now—as always—such political labels as *liberal* and *conservative* could not adequately accommodate the multiplicity of special interests or the shades of opinion and commitment within the group. Some were eloquent in condemning discriminatory freight rates affecting Southern businesses, but weren't opposed to wage differentials between Northern and Southern labor markets. Some wanted federal action to outlaw lynching and poll taxes and to open up the political process, while others thought these were reforms best left to the states. Some wanted more government control of wages and hours, child labor, and opportunities for women and blacks in the workplace, but others felt these economic matters should be worked out by management and labor. The delegates were introduced to some visionary ideas—"birth spacing" clinics, public defenders to represent the poor in court, inclusion of Negro history and culture in school textbooks—but few seemed ready to implement these farsighted notions.

Some notable and quotable statements rang out. Virginia Durr launched what one newspaper called "a witty and caustic attack" on big business, the press, and the House Un-American Activities Committee for their efforts to "smear and destroy" the labor union movement. John P. Davis of the National Negro Congress presented detailed and damning proof of racial inequities in education (black schools in the region getting eleven cents for every dollar spent on white ones, and over four hundred counties having no black high schools at all). And Aubrey Williams, never one to speak guardedly, had to call a press conference to clarify a flippant remark he had made about "class warfare" that Congressman Martin Dies, listening from Washington, branded as a subversive statement. (Even before the SCHW conference began, Dies told reporters he had inside information that the Communists were trying to convert black Americans to their cause in Birmingham and other cities of the South, and he vowed that his committee would go there soon to investigate. Later he claimed that one of his undercover agents had attended the SCHW meeting to gather evidence on Communist activities.)

These were just a few of the emotions generated by the Southern liberals who showed up in Birmingham; equally as complex and intriguing were the feelings of those who stayed away. Ralph McGill and Virginius Dabney were originally listed among the sponsors of the conference, but neither of them came, in part because Communists were to be present. Several other well-known journalists, including W. J. Cash, Jonathan Daniels, Louis I. Jaffé, Gerald W. Johnson, and Hodding Carter, also skipped the event; so did Lillian Smith, editor of the progressive *North Georgia Review*, and P. B. Young, editor of the influential *Journal & Guide*, a black weekly in Norfolk, Virginia. Don West, the radical leftist who had helped to start the Highlander Folk School, was another no-show. Walter White and W. E. B. Du Bois were absent too, apparently uninvited; their outspoken hostility toward segregation no doubt made them too hot to handle, even for the bravest liberals.

Jessie Daniel Ames, still an official of the Commission on Interracial Cooperation and a leader in the anti-lynching movement, was disdainful of the SCHW, calling it a "lunatic fringe" harmful to race relations; her absent leader at the CIC, Will Alexander, three years gone from the organization and never to return, was not openly critical of the Birmingham effort, but he too declined to participate. Both Ames and Alexander may have taken their negative cue from their colleague Howard Odum (as two of Odum's Chapel Hill faculty associates, Guy Johnson and Rupert Vance, surely did). Whatever the case, it would have been awkward at best for any of them to have gone to Birmingham after the eminent sociologist had made disparaging remarks about the conference and its aims.

The journalists had a variety of reasons to be suspicious of the SCHW. Though in general they had applauded the report on Southern economic conditions, they were outraged by FDR's bumbling attempt to purge his Dixie detractors in Congress, and most of them saw the conference as another example of behind-the-scenes manipulation by the President. They also reacted negatively to the choice of Hugo Black to receive an award named after Thomas Jefferson—whether because of the jurist's right-wing past as a Klansman or his left-wing record as a senator, it's hard to say. And, too, the participation of Communists and Socialists certainly influenced some of the newspapermen to stay at home.

Odum's motives were also multiple and complex. His long-term effort to create a Southern regional research and planning council was clearly jeopardized by initiatives such as the SCHW—"it and twenty other groups that are literally taking the lead to do what the council ought to do," he complained—and he stood back in frustration from it. He shrugged off W. T. Couch's involvement, but found Frank Graham's hard to take, and it widened the breach between them. "As usual," observed the historian Michael O'Brien, "Odum and Graham had diametrically opposed views of social reform."

No doubt the Southern Conference for Human Welfare provided all sorts of critics, right and left, with a large and stationary target. One hostile sharpshooter who fired on it early and often was Birmingham's police commissioner, forty-year-old Theophilus Eugene "Bull" Connor, then in the early years of a long and controversial career in local politics. As one of the conference committees was meeting in the Municipal Auditorium on Monday afternoon, Connor and a contingent of police officers walked in and told the startled group that they were sitting in violation of a city ordinance banning racially mixed meetings, and they would have to move or face arrest. H. C. Nixon was presiding. After conferring with others, he reluctantly and apologetically asked the participants to separate, whites to the right side of the aisle and blacks to the left, and they did so.

Within minutes the word had spread to other committee meeting sites and to delegates elsewhere. At a session later that evening, local participants said police enforcement of the Jim Crow law at recent public meetings had been selective, arbitrary, and punitive. The angry conferees then adopted a resolution condemning the action and expressing "regret that local laws and ordinances seriously inconvenience the conference, which is interracial in its approach to the problems of the South." They would affirm their indignation twice more before the conference adjourned, finally instructing their elected officers not to book future meetings in cities where segregated seating would be required.

Eleanor Roosevelt arrived in Birmingham before dawn Tuesday morning, on a train from Atlanta. Her speech to the League of Women Voters in the Georgia capital had prompted an admiring Ralph McGill to call her "a grand person" who had "done more for the cause of democracy and patriotism than all the patriotic associations rolled into one." (The First Lady also had gently chided Atlanta's official censorship board for voting to ban a stage production of Erskine Caldwell's *Tobacco Road*, and McGill used even stronger words to condemn the board's decision. What was truly profane, vulgar, and dirty, he wrote, was not the theatrical fantasy but the economic reality of the South's many Tobacco Roads, including those in Fulton County—Atlanta—where "8,000 people are living on less than $3 a month.")

In addition to lengthy reports on the welfare conference and editorials praising Mrs. Roosevelt, Birmingham's Tuesday papers carried several stories of interest to the delegates: The city commission had sent the President a telegram of thanks for his condemnation of Nazi persecution of the Jews; fund cutbacks were forcing the Works Progress Administration to drop at least 400,000 workers from its rolls nationwide; in Birmingham and Jefferson County, more than four thousand families with no employment and no job prospects were "facing starvation" unless emergency relief could be found; a front-page feature told of a family of ten living on about a dollar a day in a lean-to shack made of sawmill slabs. Too bad they can't make it over to the welfare conference, the writer opined; they could give the scholars there some fine points on economic distress.

A story from Washington analyzing the heavy Democratic losses in the 1938 elections showed that the defeats were all in the North and West, so Southerners would actually increase their already firm control of the party machinery in both houses. And from Wiggins, Mississippi, came a grim reminder of the ancient curse of racist violence: There, the day before, a mob of two hundred white men had tracked down and lynched a twenty-four-year-old black laborer they suspected of attacking and robbing an elderly white woman.

Aubrey Williams spent the morning whisking Mrs. Roosevelt from one stop to the next on a crammed schedule of appearances. In midafternoon they hurried to the First Methodist Church, where the conference committee on youth problems was in session and a heated debate was raging over the decision to enforce the city's segregation ordinance. Not noticing that the assembled crowd was racially divided, Mrs. Roosevelt walked to the front row with Williams and sat down, as she later put it, "on the colored side." When someone hesitantly brought the new protocol to her attention, she was reluctant to move. "Rather than give in," she explained, "I asked that chairs be placed for us with the speakers facing the whole group."

Criticism of the ordinance inevitably focused on Bull Connor and the city commission. "They praise FDR for speaking out against persecution of the Jews in Germany," said one delegate, "but what about persecution of blacks here, such as yesterday's lynching in Mississippi?" Others declared that there should be a federal anti-lynching law, and Congressman Luther Patrick jumped to his feet to explain why he opposed such legislation. Only the Southern mob slayings would be targeted, he said, not the urban gang killings in the North; the South always gets singled out.

Mrs. Roosevelt challenged Patrick. "I'm wondering why the solution doesn't lie in the hands of the people of the South," she said. "Why isn't it at your door to frame a law that you think meets the needs and is satisfactory to the people of the South? Has there ever been a real effort by Southern lawmakers to pass an anti-lynching law that would apply everywhere?"

There was a burst of applause; when it subsided, Patrick replied in a low voice, "As far as I know, there has not been."

Mrs. Roosevelt's part in that afternoon episode would be talked about for years to come, and the story of her seating would be so embellished in the telling and retelling that the truth would slip away and myth would replace it. Most accounts would paint a stirring picture of a boldly rebellious First Lady—some even had her defiantly placing her chair astraddle a chalk line in the aisle between the white and black segments of the audience. In point of fact, however, she didn't seize upon the opportunity to make an issue of local laws and customs; in general, it was not her inclination to challenge segregation directly. After she spoke in the Municipal Auditorium that night to a massive crowd (divided racially), she took a question from the audience on the subject, and gave this answer:

"What do I think of the segregation of white and Negro here tonight? Well, I could no more tell people in another state what they should do than the United States can tell another country what to do. I think that one must follow the customs of the district. The answer to that question is not up to me but up to the people of Alabama."

It was not her diplomatic skirting of the issue that people would recall, though, but rather her plea for equal educational opportunity, for "oneness in America," and for a society in which "no one is pressed down by his brothers." The auditorium was filled to overflowing with more than six thousand people (about equally divided, white and black), and another thousand or more had to be turned away. In a dramatic gesture, Mrs. Roosevelt first went out to the main entrance to greet those who couldn't get in. Then, back on the stage with Congressman Patrick, Senator Pepper, and Judge Charlton, she captured the audience with her warmth and sincerity. Even after listening to her thirty-minute speech and an hour of responses to questions, they were reluctant to let her go.

Finally, by midnight, eighteen hours after she had arrived, Eleanor Roosevelt was back on a train bound for Warm Springs and the Thanksgiving holiday with her family. Birmingham had been cheered and charmed by her presence—but the glow that lingered in her wake was no panacea for what ailed the city, the South, or the Southern Conference for Human Welfare.

There are those who say that the late 1930s in the South—or, more precisely, the last months of 1938 in Birmingham—represented a fleeting moment of opportunity for regional deliverance from the grip of the feudal past. To be sure, the depression was slowly winding down, and the New Deal had raised the hopes of many, and labor unions were finally gaining a measure of respect, and blacks were perhaps a little less besieged than they had been in the twenties or earlier, and the attitude of white resistance to social change was not as hostile and hardened as it would in time become.

But the euphoria that filled Municipal Auditorium when Frank Graham welcomed the Southern conference delegates on November 20 and when Eleanor Roosevelt thrilled a turn-away crowd two nights later obscured the hard reality of conservative and reactionary power that had controlled the South from one end to the other for generations. Nothing that happened in those four days in Birmingham altered that imbalance of power in any significant way.

Those who took part in the conference were the most visible segment of a liberal and progressive minority of undetermined size and strength. It's conceivable that behind them were hundreds of thousands of like-minded Southerners waiting for constructive leadership to emerge; it's also possible, and perhaps even likely, that the Municipal Auditorium crowd was the heart and soul—and most of the body—of progressive opposition in the region. What marked them as liberal, in comparison with other Southern leaders, was their willingness to appear in public and acknowledge that the South had problems, and to accept some responsibility for addressing them. And yet, even among those in attendance, there were deep disagreements and animosities.

No one waved militantly anti-labor banners in the hall, but some parlor Democrats were shocked to see so many union members in attendance—and that note of class division was minor compared to the bitter feelings that separated the AFL partisans from the CIO. Blacks were treated respectfully by the organizers until someone decided to make segregation an issue, and then the conference split into quarreling factions, one that resented the enforcement, and the other that resented the resentment; neither side, though, offered any challenge to the "separate but equal" philosophy that perpetuated black inferiority to whites and Southern inferiority to the North.

The Democrats who controlled the conference (there being no admitted Republicans present) looked on the handful of Communists and Socialists as a single bothersome faction to be courted or tolerated or hated; few could grasp or appreciate the political and ideological differences that made the Socialists and Communists despise each other. Most of the women in attendance wanted government at every level to guard against sex discrimination in the workplace, but some of the ladies and a good many men disapproved of the very notion that a woman's place was anywhere but in the home.

John Temple Graves of the Birmingham *Age-Herald* chipped in with a tongue-clucking put-down of those who strayed from the prevailing racial orthodoxy. Writing in praise of Tuskegee Institute President F. D. Patterson for his failed effort to halt debate on the segregation ordinance, the patrician columnist declared: "With all that needs to be done for our Southern Negroes, those who raised this question of seating practice rendered no service to improved race relations and cast a damper on the whole conference."

And so it went. Governor Bibb Graves, for all his New Deal credentials and his CIO support, declared himself "surprised and shocked" when the conference passed resolutions against segregated seating and in favor of a federal anti-lynching law. He was also embarrassed and angered by another motion, this one urging him to pardon the five Scottsboro boys still in prison—less than two weeks after he had emphatically refused to take such action.

On the last day of the conference, a nineteen-member committee on permanent organization chaired by W. T. Couch (and including only one black delegate) put forth a plan of organization that called for a slate of general officers and a council made up of seven representatives from each of the thirteen member states. When it became obvious that all of the general officers would be white, the plan was amended to add several delegates at large, to ensure that at least a few blacks would be included.

Debate on the structure and the various nominees was lengthy and rancorous. Frank Porter Graham, though he was not present and had begged not to be nominated, was elected permanent chairman over Judge Louise Charlton, who also asked that her name be withdrawn (she was given the ceremonial post of honorary chairman). Mollie Dowd was chosen secretary, though she complained of manipulative shenanigans in the nominating caucuses and told the bickering conferees that she "would not consider it an honor to serve in that office." Clark Foreman was named treasurer and H. C. Nixon was chosen to be executive secretary—the only full-time, salaried post in the organization. Representatives of religion, education, labor, industry, government, the press, and nonprofit agencies made up the larger council.

As the final session of the conference approached—the Wednesday-night finale honoring Justice Black—the weary delegates seemed at least as divided among themselves as they were from the conservative society around them. On one point, though, they appeared to be united, and that was in the selection of Frank Graham as their leader. "Of all the people in the South," Lucy Randolph Mason declared in a subsequent letter to the University of North Carolina president, "you are the one first choice to lead any progressive southern movement." The only way the Southern Conference for Human Welfare could hope to succeed, she said, was with Graham at the wheel. With deep reservations but an abiding sense of duty, he would eventually agree to assume the responsibility.

Finally, just as the last session of the conference was about to begin in the half-filled auditorium, one more sensational incident was played out behind the stage curtain. Seventy-year-old William E. Dodd, noted historian and former U.S. ambassador to Germany, had to be escorted forcibly from the backstage area after his invitation to present the Jefferson Medal to Justice Hugo Black was rescinded and Dodd was told at the last minute that John Temple Graves would speak in his place. The late-night postmortem sessions buzzed with two conflicting rumors about the reason for Dodd's removal: One was that his pro-war stance displeased the Communists; the other was that his anti-liberal views displeased Hugo Black. The official reason given in the press was that Dodd was ill. No doubt, by the end, he was.

Senator John Bankhead introduced Graves ("a liberal Southerner and a helpful thinker in a troubled age"), and the journalist presented Justice Black with a plaque honoring him as "the Southerner who has done most to promote human and social welfare in line with the philosophy of Thomas Jefferson." A quotation from Jefferson's 1801 inaugural address was also inscribed on it: "Equal and exact justice to all men, of whatever state or persuasion." (The same words were chiseled in stone above the main entrance to the Jefferson County Courthouse in Birmingham.)

The justice tried his best to recapture the spirit of the previous nights. He focused on Jefferson and his ideals, and drew deeply from the Virginian's own words (rendering the pertinent quote as "equal and exact justice under the law to all men of whatever *race* or persuasion"). But after so much high drama and controversy and excitement, the remaining delegates, in a state of near exhaustion, could only muster perfunctory applause. The evening was an anticlimax, and when it ended, no one hung around to talk much longer.

The Southern Conference for Human Welfare, a four-day call to service that gently but insistently shook the South to consciousness from decades of slumber, was far and away the most significant attempt by Southerners, up to that time, to introduce a far-reaching agenda of change and improvement to their native land. It would long be remembered, not for what it achieved, but for what it aspired to and what it attempted.

In the early morning hours after the delegates had departed, a frigid blast of winter air plunged temperatures in north Alabama into the twenties, and large, heavy snowflakes blanketed Birmingham with its first white Thanksgiving in memory. The forecast was already written: It would be a long, cold winter in Dixie.

II

1938–1945:
Road of Hope

We black folk, our history and our present being, are a mirror of all the manifold experiences of America. What we want, what we represent, what we endure is what America is. If we perish, America will perish. . . . The differences between black folk and white folk are not blood or color, and the ties that bind us are deeper than those that separate us. The common road of hope which we all have traveled has brought us into a stronger kinship than any words, laws, or legal claims. Look at us and know us and you will know yourselves, for we are you, looking back at you from the dark mirror of our lives.

—RICHARD WRIGHT,
12 Million Black Voices

1. A *Liberating War*

It lingers still, in the memory of many, as the last "good war"—a justified pursuit of a noble cause by "the Allies," a heroic aggregation of Yanks (pardon the expression) and their fighting pals. As America stood on the threshold of World War II, "We the People" were far from united in our support of the undertaking—and yet, even then, the moral imperatives seemed clearly to outweigh the practical reservations. All over Europe and Asia, we saw innocent victims being ground under the boots of marauding imperialists. It would be ethically indefensible for us to ignore such wanton slaughter—and careless in any event, since we would surely be the next prey of the aggressors. And, not least to be considered, it was apparent long before the shooting started that the war would also be an economic, political, and social shot in the arm for "the patient": the sickly American nation, afflicted with chronic anemia and depression.

Nowhere was that inoculation more beneficial than in the South. The New Deal, for all its blessings, had barely scratched the surface of Southern need, and the region was still the mudsill on which the rest of the nation stood. World War II ushered in an economic boom that not only ended the Great Depression in Dixie but finally blew away eighty years of stagnation dating all the way back to the beginning of the Civil War. For the first time in its history, the South experienced a genuine bloom of economic opportunity, a broad-based and sustained flowering that brightened virtually every corner of the society. Industry, agriculture, and government fed this surge with new facilities, new crops, new services. The war effort opened up millions of new jobs for both uniformed and civilian personnel; more than that, it transported hundreds of thousands of them out of the narrow confines of their native environment and into a wide world of exotic people, places, and ideas. At last, Southerners were no longer hopelessly stranded, isolated, idle, and broke; they were on the move, and the general direction was up.

It would have taken no persuasion at all to convince me that it was a good war; I was a pint-sized GI Joe commando from day one. Three months after my formal education commenced at Cadiz Graded School in my Kentucky hometown, the Japanese bombed Pearl Harbor and burned the "day of infamy" forever in my memory. In my eyes, this was no far-off conflict; it struck home in numerous ways. My father went to sea with the navy for the second time (he had also served in World War I), and others I knew and loved also left, some never to return. A new army base, Camp Campbell, was rising swiftly along the Kentucky-Tennessee border just thirty miles from Cadiz, and convoys of soldiers in battle dress passed frequently through our town. Twice, in fact, I remember watching in openmouthed awe as war games filled the horizon with paratroopers, and men with hand grenades and rifles and drawn bayonets dashed from house to house in a grand display of mock combat. No bombs fell, no blood was spilled, no enemy threatened our comfort and safety. When it's sanitized like that, war can be a very uplifting and unifying experience.

It wasn't long before surplus equipment became available, allowing boys like me to wear helmet liners, carry ammo belts and mess kits, pass spy messages in homemade code, and imagine waves of enemy soldiers falling like flies in the withering sweep of our machine-gun fire. The Kentucky Theater, across the street and two doors up from my house, kept us amply supplied with blood-and-guts battle movies throughout the war—Gary Cooper as Sergeant York, John Wayne and Errol Flynn as courageous leathernecks and dogfaces, scores of other Hollywood heroes as fighter pilots and down-with-the-ship sailors. Charging out into the Saturday afternoon sunlight from that dark, cavernous propaganda pit, we could almost see the hated Nazi and Nipponese minions caught in our crosshairs, begging for mercy. In the gloriously uncomplicated vision of the preteen soldiers who made up my little circle of allies, it *was* a good war, a very good war indeed.

I had no sense of the economic impact back then, of course, but I realize now that the war was like a huge relief check for my county, a continuation of the New Deal economic recovery plan that had been ongoing since 1933. The signs were all around us: Camp Campbell, with its huge construction force and operational workers, as well as the soldiers themselves; a new Cadiz post office, built by the Federal Works Administration in 1941; a network of concrete streets provided in similar fashion prior to that; a unit of the Civilian Conservation Corps; money for the school system; agricultural assistance agencies with letter names like AAA, FSA, and SCS; a wildlife refuge under the auspices of the Interior Department; a massive TVA dam being built on the nearby Tennessee River, after which a rural electric cooperative would bring power and light to hundreds of previously lantern-lit homes. And an exotic twist: German prisoners of war working in the tobacco fields in our county, so casually guarded as to be almost like trusties, or even regular farmhands.

So much was new and different that there was no way to sort it all out. What it seemed to come down to, though, was this: Practically every program that breathed economic life into rural communities like ours had originated within a ten-year period in the White House or the Congress of the United States in Washington. In the war no less than in the depression, the long arm of the federal government was straining to free the nation from its economic paralysis. Even in a little political jurisdiction like Cadiz and Trigg County, Kentucky, the impact of the New Deal and the Second World War amounted to a one-two punch against hard times. Our community was a microcosm of the revitalization of America, and especially of the rural South.

The military aggression of Germany in Europe and of Japan in Asia in 1939 demanded international attention just as the second Roosevelt administration was floundering in a sea of conservative opposition on the home front. The Southerners who controlled both houses of Congress were in the vanguard of resistance to FDR, joining with the resurgent minority of Northern Republicans to stifle New Deal reforms and set the stage for a conservative return to power after Roosevelt's expected retirement in 1940.

But the threat of war, filled as it was with both peril and promise, compelled all the players to rethink their positions and strategies. For his part, Roosevelt could turn with a certain sense of relief and rekindled vigor to the pleas of France and Britain and other nations for help. Southern senators and congressmen, on the other hand, could proudly lead the call to arms with eloquent orations extolling their region's long heritage of patriotic volunteerism and military valor. And besides, they were tired of fighting each other; the President needed the Southerners' help overseas, and they wanted a diverting issue to foreclose on his domestic reforms—and so they all made a big show of putting aside their differences for the duration.

With each new conquest, the Nazis and the "Japs" grew more menacing to the United States. By the fall of 1940, France was in Hitler's grip and Britain was under daily bombardment; Japan had seized control of China and all of Southeast Asia; and the two aggressors, with Italy, had signed a pact of mutual protection that was widely interpreted as a union of warmongers.

A substantial minority of Americans preferred, for a variety of reasons, to steer clear of these alien troublemakers. The so-called isolationists, a motley assortment of pacifists, anti-Semites, pro-Nazis, and laissez-faire capitalists, included such prominent figures as Charles Lindbergh, Joseph P. Kennedy, and John Foster Dulles. They lobbied for a "fortress America" that would resort to military action only in response to a direct attack.

They got nowhere in the South. Isolationist detachment was denounced as cowardice, if not outright treason; few public figures in the region, aside from "Our Bob" Reynolds, the xenophobic North Carolina senator, dared to associate themselves openly with the movement. Carter Glass of Virginia and Claude Pepper of Florida, poles apart on social issues, stood shoulder to shoulder in the Senate for every military measure FDR proposed—and even thought up a few themselves. The Southern bloc led the way in pushing through a selective-service draft, a major buildup of the national war machine, an offshore defense against German submarines, and a lend-lease plan to supply the British and others with arms. Most of them even went along with Roosevelt's surprise decision to run for a third term in 1940, and he breezed to the nomination over his vice president and chief rival, John Nance Garner of Texas. FDR's choice of Secretary of Agriculture Henry A. Wallace as a new running mate didn't sit well with the party-bound Dixie Democrats, but they held their noses and helped boost the ticket to a five-million-vote victory—another landslide—over New York industrialist Wendell Willkie and the Republicans. As usual, fewer than a fourth of the Southerners old enough to vote actually cast ballots—but of those who did, three-fourths stood by Roosevelt.

For months before the Japanese surprise attack on Hawaii in December 1941, the United States teetered on the brink of war with Germany. In October, German U-boats in the Atlantic torpedoed two U.S. destroyers, killing more than a hundred sailors, but still the President and Congress held back from a formal declaration of war. The December 7 bombing at Pearl Harbor claimed more than 2,400 lives. Within four days, Roosevelt had declared and Congress had affirmed that we were in a state of total war with Japan, Germany, and Italy.

In three years of prelude, the people of the United States and their leaders had cultivated a deep hatred of the Nazis and their puppets, the Mussolini-led Fascists—so deep that when Hitler betrayed his promise to Stalin and invaded Russia, the motherland of communism, the anti-red majority in this country swallowed hard and joined forces with the Soviets. As Nazi atrocities mounted against the Jews, the Poles, the Danes, the Dutch, the Belgians, the French, and others, and as Hitler ranted about the purity and superiority of his Aryan nation against the "mongrelized polyglot of Amerika," this nation took the high road, adding racism and genocide to the moral indictment of its white European enemies.

The Japanese, too, operated from a stance of racial purity and superiority, but unlike the Germans and Italians, they were not white—and so, with a fervor that seems now almost like a parody of the Nazis, we easily matched the Nipponese racism with our own, classifying them as an inferior species of subhumanity barely worthy of our epithets ("yellow midgets," "monkeys," "slant-eyes"). This dismissive bias allowed the United States to round up 110,000 Japanese-American citizens in 1942 and confine them in internment camps for the duration of the war. No such loss of freedom was ever inflicted upon Americans of German or Italian heritage.

Two of the ten internment camps were located in the South, on a marshy floodplain in southeast Arkansas, near the Mississippi River. Inside these barbed-wire-encircled, ten-thousand-acre tracts, tar paper barracks with woodstoves and no running water were thrown up to house a total of seventeen thousand men, women, and children. By day, they worked to clear the mosquito-infested land and raise cotton and other crops; at night, they alternately froze and suffocated in the crowded barracks. They were confined there for two to three years, the last of them not being released until four months after the war ended.

White Americans were virtually unanimous in their ranking of the various enemy nations according to race and skin color. It was not Southern reactionaries but moderate and liberal leaders who were largely responsible for the imprisonment of Japanese-Americans. Journalist Walter Lippmann and California Attorney General Earl Warren repeatedly insisted that it was necessary; President Roosevelt ordered it, and Supreme Court Justice Hugo Black wrote the majority opinion that justified it legally. (At the same time, we were training and sending into European combat a segregated regiment of Japanese-American soldiers whose valor under fire would be unsurpassed.)

What's more, U.S. policy kept Japanese prisoners of war confined in the islands of the Pacific, while nearly a quarter-million captured German and Italian soldiers were brought to this country and treated more humanely. Many were sent to the South, where the conditions of their confinement were generally far less harsh than the daily lives of black citizens in the region.

Official U.S. policy declared in writing that "the Japanese race is an enemy race," and the surprise attack on Pearl Harbor was later included as a justification for the atomic bombing of Hiroshima and Nagasaki. Whether it was the fact of Pearl Harbor or the perception of "an enemy race" of a darker hue that made the Japanese a more despised foe than the Germans was a question that few Americans cared to examine.

When the preliminary hostilities were enveloping Europe and Asia in the late 1930s, the South and the nation were just beginning to climb out of the Great Depression. In the three years it took for the string of explosions to build up to a worldwide conflagration, the people of the United States had plenty of time to discover that war, whatever its horrors, is often good for business—besides being a morale-boosting force for unity and cooperation. What no other energizing power could do—not FDR and the New Deal, not private enterprise, not the prayers of the faithful

millions—World War II did for this nation, and especially for the South:
It ended, once and for all, the economic, social, and psychological woes of
the depression, and set into motion a cultural transformation more sweeping than anything the nation had experienced since the Civil War.

The prewar South was still a peasant society. Barely one out of every
six or seven farms had tractors to plow with or electricity to light their
houses when the forties began. Half the nation's farm population lived
here—and got by on a fourth of the farm income. They still grew mainly
cotton and tobacco, the traditional staples—two inedible crops that required intensive, backbreaking labor and returned a profit to virtually no
one who handled a hoe or walked behind a mule. The region's primary
industry was still textile manufacturing—an enterprise dominated by absentee ownership and characterized by hazardous, small-scale, low-wage
sweatshops in which white women and girls did most of the work. Double-
digit unemployment plagued white men, and the job picture was twice as
dismal for blacks.

Population continued to increase as high birth rates more than matched
the high rates of death and out-migration. In the eleven Old South states,
the 1940 census counted nearly thirty-two million people, more than nine
million of them black. Overwhelmingly, though, Southerners were still
country people; no city in the region had as many as half a million in
population, and only seven had more than a quarter of a million. Florida,
the least populous of the eleven states, could claim fewer than two million
people. Generally speaking, the Southerner in profile had changed but
little in the three generations since the Civil War; compared to Americans
in the East, the Midwest, and the West, Southerners in 1940 were still the
poorest, the sickest, the worst housed and clothed and fed, the most
violent, the least educated, the least skilled, the most lacking in latitude
and power.

Such generalizations are almost an insult to the achieving minority. To
give them their due, it needs to be said that millions of Southerners, white
and black, showed great resourcefulness, courage, and accomplishment
during the depression, and at considerable sacrifice succeeded in making
life better and more secure for themselves and their families. Even in the
depths of poverty, acts of heroism were commonplace; selfless people
everywhere stoically shouldered intolerable burdens for others. Countless
thousands managed, along with their more fortunate neighbors, not only
to survive and endure but to do so with their dignity and pride intact.

Even so, there seemed to be no possible way for the region to catch up
with the rest of the nation. It had been an economic and social ward of the

North since before the Civil War—and along with victory in that tragic clash, the Union had claimed a misguided sense of moral superiority that only made matters worse. Then, through political and social collusion, powerful men in the North had aided and abetted the South in its ever-deepening plunge into inequality by helping the Southern oligarchy to cling to the tattered reins of power. As World War II approached, the decline and fall of the region was complete, its isolation masking such depths of economic deprivation and ignorance as you might expect to find in a lowly Latin American or Asian colony. About half the South's people in 1940 had not the remotest hope of earning as much as $250 a year, and the sheer weight of that rock of poverty threatened to crush the region and leave it permanently crippled.

And then came the war. Its impact was—and still is—incalculable. Between 1940 and 1945, federal investment in war industries and military installations in the South exceeded $10 billion, and that didn't include funding of such related projects as public housing, health-care facilities, TVA dams, and aid to schools in communities where the impact of military buildup was greatest. Open and inexpensive land, cheap and available construction labor, and a favorable year-round climate made the region an especially attractive location for training camps and bases, and more than half of the country's hundred or so such new facilities sprang up here. Camp Blanding, near the little village of Starke, Florida, was a typical example; state officials claimed that it turned Starke virtually overnight into Florida's fourth largest city. Similar stories could be heard in every state.

Southerners did more than their share to populate the camps, too. They volunteered for duty in such numbers that the Dixie bloc in Congress had to push through a draft law to keep their constituents from filling up the armed forces. A proud military tradition had something to do with that rush to volunteer; even in the modern army and navy, many of the top brass—Dwight Eisenhower, Douglas MacArthur, George S. Patton, Chester Nimitz, Omar Bradley, George C. Marshall—had strong personal or professional ties to the Southern and border states. But the perks of service had a lot to do with it too; steady work with a paycheck and assurance of food, clothing, and shelter seemed like a great and beckoning opportunity to the chronically unemployed multitude. Nearly a third of the eleven million white men and more than two-thirds of the one million black men who served in uniform were from the South—and this in spite of the fact that a higher-than-average number of Southern prospects were rejected because of physical or mental deficiencies. There was also a high percentage of Southerners among the quarter-million women in uniform.

The investment of government and corporate funds in war-related manufacturing had as great an economic and social impact on the South as direct military spending. Textile mills were swamped with orders for tents, uniforms, blankets, duffel bags, parachutes; shipyards from Norfolk to Tampa to Galveston operated around the clock; gas and oil fields, coal mines, and steel mills were in full production; wood products, including paper, were in great demand; munitions, tanks, trucks, and airplanes rolled off the assembly lines at massive facilities such as the aircraft plant at Marietta, Georgia, where 28,000 workers were employed. In the sparsely populated Tennessee hill country near Knoxville, the fenced and guarded city of Oak Ridge sprang up on a sixty-thousand-acre tract between 1942 and the end of the war; close to 100,000 workers and their families were there, not knowing that their collective effort would provide processed uranium for the top-secret atomic-energy project that produced the bombs that devastated Hiroshima and Nagasaki.

Altogether, more than a million new civilian jobs propelled the South to a dizzying and unprecedented level of prosperity. Full employment sent wages and per capita income soaring. Union membership shot up. Savings, home-building, and retail sales rose sharply; shortages and rationing were all that kept the consumption of certain foodstuffs and other goods, such as gas and tires, in check. The demand for farm products increased, too, and prices climbed accordingly, giving farmers the greatest percentage boost in income of any category of workers.

Other transforming forces were at work in agriculture. Farm population in the South decreased by a staggering 3.5 million between 1940 and 1945, with almost half of those leaving the region altogether and the rest moving from farms to Southern towns and cities. Mechanization and improvements in fertilizers and insecticides made it possible for fewer farmers working fewer acres to increase crop yields and magnify income as prices rose. No occupation had been as symbolic of the antebellum South as farming—and none was more profoundly affected by what happened in the 1940s.

Take cotton, for example. The brothers John and Mack Rust, cotton growers and cooperative farm advocates in Texas and Mississippi for nearly four decades—and Socialists to boot—devoted much of their energy and resources to the development of a prototype mechanical cotton picker, but they finally ran out of money and motivating energy in 1942. Two years later, a large Northern corporation, International Harvester, in partnership with Howell Hopson, a Mississippi Delta plantation owner, successfully demonstrated a picking machine that could replace fifty hardworking field hands. Here was a social revolution on wheels: Assembly-line production of picking machines and tractors would hasten the end of the feudal reign of King Cotton, displacing mules and people and eventually making tenant farming and sharecropping virtually obsolete. In 1945 the South would produce almost as much cotton on eighteen million acres as it had harvested in 1925 on forty-five million. Still, lost foreign markets and increased competition from synthetic fibers kept a large surplus of cotton in storage, and prices down.

The combination of agricultural technology, industrial growth, and the massive military buildup propelled a new wave of Southern farmworkers and unskilled laborers on a one-way journey to the regional and national urban centers where most new job opportunities were concentrated. (One enterprising New Orleans industrialist, Andrew Jackson Higgins, sent buses into the Louisiana countryside to transport many of the twelve thousand people who worked in his sprawling shipyards.) The great migration had major long-term consequences. Sleepy little Southern cities like Mobile, Charleston, and Norfolk were thrown into chaos, overrun by swarms of workers living in shacks, trailer camps, and tent settlements; public services were inundated, crime and vice reached epidemic proportions, race relations worsened. Cities like Houston, Dallas, and Atlanta experienced runaway growth that would within two decades or so turn them into genuine national metropolises, with all the best and worst consequences that go along with such explosive transformations.

In the North, people from the mountains of southern Appalachia, most of them white, entered the migrant stream with people from the cotton fields of the Deep South, most of them black. Chicago, the only political jurisdiction in America to elect a black congressman in the first four decades of this century, was finally joined in 1944 by New York when Adam Clayton Powell, Jr., was elected from Harlem. The two cities had each had fewer than 100,000 African-American residents in 1900; three-quarters of a century later, they would be the only urban centers in the nation with a million or more blacks.

Racial segregation hindered the American effort to mobilize for war. As before, in World War I, black soldiers were restricted mainly to all-black units commanded by white officers. The marines stayed virtually lily-white. Kitchen duty was the only assignment open to blacks at sea with the navy. (One such sailor, a Texas sharecropper's son named Dorie Miller, was awarded the Navy Cross after he manned a deck gun during the Pearl Harbor attack and shot down four Japanese planes.)

Blacks who managed to become officers in spite of the restrictions stood out as exceptions to the rule. Benjamin O. Davis, Sr., a District of Columbia–born career soldier with more than forty years of up-through-the-ranks service, was promoted to brigadier general in 1940. His son,

Benjamin O. Davis, Jr., was a trailblazer like his father: the first black graduate of West Point in the twentieth century (there had been three in the late 1800s, long before Davis finished in 1936). The junior Davis was also the first black soldier to command a military installation (an airfield in Kentucky in 1945), and he too would rise to the rank of general. Not until 1949 did the Naval Academy at Annapolis produce its first black graduate. Most officer-candidate schools within the service branches were quietly desegregated in 1942, but flight training for black pilots remained restricted to a special school set up at Tuskegee Institute in Alabama. From it came more than six hundred pilots who flew combat missions over Europe.

By far the largest numbers of black servicemen were in the army, often in segregated noncombat units. The prevailing bias within the military hierarchy was that blacks were collectively unsuited for the stress of battle, and it was only after intense political pressure had been generated by indignant black leaders that a few all-black combat units were finally organized. The white officers under whose command they were placed (Southerners, more often than not, the theory being that experience made them skillful at "handling colored men") were reluctant leaders at best; many of them openly expressed bitterness and hostility about their assignments. Sometimes, though, Southern whites did turn out to be well suited for this challenge. The respect they subsequently showed for their black troops was both cause and effect for the generally praiseworthy performance the men delivered, whether behind the lines or in the heat of combat.

Harold C. Fleming, an easygoing young Georgian, was one such officer, a white company commander in charge of black soldiers in the Pacific. The "profound experience" sensitized him to racial injustices that he had previously viewed with detachment and little thought. "It did more to change my life," he said, years later, "than any other experience I've ever had." When he returned to the South in 1947, Fleming went to work in Atlanta at the Southern Regional Council, successor to the Commission on Interracial Cooperation; a few years later he would became executive director of the organization.

Harry S. Ashmore, a newspaper reporter in Greenville, South Carolina, before the war, was a lieutenant in a combat division in Europe; there he saw an all-black tank battalion distinguish itself under fire. Race had nothing to do with valor in combat, Ashmore concluded—except perhaps to make minority soldiers all the more determined to excel. "In the battles they fought under our command," he wrote forty years later, "the black men in those battered old Shermans [tanks] performed as well as any armored troops we saw in action in the bloody campaigns that took us from Normandy to the Ruhr." Later, as editor of the *Arkansas Gazette*, Ashmore would win a Pulitzer Prize for his editorials when the crucible of desegregation came to Little Rock.

Segregation dogged all African-Americans in uniform, wherever they went in the war years—within the ranks of their units, in recreation halls and social clubs, on furlough in the towns around their bases, and even in air-raid shelters. One often-repeated story, incredible but not apocryphal, concerned a group of German prisoners who were being escorted from one camp to another in south Georgia by black GI guards; when they stopped at a café to eat, the Germans were allowed to sit at tables inside, but the blacks had to get their food at the back door. The most insufferable indignity, though, may have been the insistence on segregation as it applied to blood transfusions; because this episode was not Southern in origin, it drove home the reality that racial discrimination was a pervasive national problem, an all-American white character flaw.

William H. Hastie and Charles R. Drew fought and lost the battle to reverse government policy requiring blood segregation in the early 1940s. Scientific knowledge and simple justice were on their side (not to mention the biblical declaration that "God has made of one blood all nations"), but it would be another decade before social behavior advanced that far.

Hastie and Drew had been boyhood friends in Washington, classmates at the all-black and highly regarded Dunbar High School, and 1925 graduates of Amherst College (where another of their classmates was Benjamin J. Davis, Jr., of Georgia, later to gain notoriety as the attorney for Communist organizer Angelo Herndon and then as a member of the American Communist Party himself). After Amherst, Hastie (and Davis) studied at Harvard Law School and Drew went to medical school in Canada. Then, while Hastie was making a name for himself in the New Deal (as an assistant solicitor and member of the Black Cabinet, and as FDR's first black appointee to the federal judiciary in 1937), Drew was breaking new ground at Howard University Medical School in Washington and at New York's Presbyterian Medical Center with his research on classifying, preserving, and storing blood for later transfusion.

Hastie resigned from his judicial appointment in the Virgin Islands in 1939 in order to become dean of Howard's law school; a year later, with war threatening, he took a leave of absence to accept appointment as civilian aide to Secretary of War Henry L. Stimson. Drew also went on leave that year when the government of Great Britain asked him to set up and direct its wartime blood bank and plasma projects. In February 1941, after helping both Britain and the United States establish blood programs in support of military operations, the thirty-seven-year-old Dr. Drew was named medical director of the American Red Cross blood bank program.

William Hastie and Charles Drew found themselves directly in the line of fire in late 1941 when the surgeons-general of the U.S. Army and Navy, with the approval of Secretary Stimson, informed the Red Cross that they would accept blood only from white donors for military use. Scientific studies had proved conclusively that no racial differences existed in the chemical makeup of blood, but the military, under heavy political pressure, yielded to the prevailing social bias. The Red Cross and even the conservative American Medical Association publicly criticized the new policy, although they opted in the end to cooperate "for the sake of the war effort." In January 1942, the War Department modified its stand by agreeing to accept blood from black donors, but rigid segregation of the supply was to be maintained. The Red Cross not only concurred in that decision but declared through its chairman, Norman H. Davis, that the quasi-public agency had no interest in trying to settle racial-social controversies. Later, agency officials suggested that those who persisted in criticizing the policy were unpatriotically attempting to cripple the blood donor service and thus harm the war effort itself.

Angered but not silenced, Charles Drew resigned from the Red Cross and returned to the medical school at Howard early in 1942, declaring publicly that the racial segregation of blood was contrary to scientific fact—and an insult to patriotic black Americans. William Hastie stayed on at the War Department for another year and kept up the fight to change the policy. Finally, in January 1943, he too resigned with a parting shot at Stimson and the military establishment; the secretary quickly accepted Hastie's letter of parting, relieved to see him go.

Resuming the law school deanship at Howard, Hastie continued to speak out against segregation in the military and elsewhere. In 1946, President Harry S. Truman appointed him governor of the Virgin Islands, and in 1949, after campaigning vigorously for Truman, Hastie was named by the President to a seat on the U.S. Third Circuit Court of Appeals, where he would serve until his death in 1976.

Charles Drew's years of public service were to be far fewer in number. He remained on the faculty at Howard through the 1940s, staying out of the limelight but keeping close ties with his old friend Bill Hastie. Then, in the early morning hours of April 1, 1950, as Drew and three of his colleagues were on an all-night driving trip from Washington across the segregated South, en route to a meeting at Tuskegee Institute, the physician fell asleep at the wheel near Burlington, North Carolina, and died when his car left the road and crashed. Though he received prompt medical attention, his injuries were such that his life couldn't be saved.

It was erroneously reported then—and the misinformation has often been repeated since—that Charles Drew, the pioneer of plasma research, died from loss of blood after an all-white hospital refused to admit him. Racial segregation of emergency medical facilities was indeed responsible for the deaths of numerous black accident victims in those years, but not for Drew's. Still, his untimely and bloody death was attributable in part to the fact that segregated public accommodations forced black travelers like him to drive long distances without rest. Whether or not a blood transfusion would have saved him, the cruel fact remains that he died from an unnecessary loss of blood.

Just eight months after Drew's death, the government rescinded its policy on blood segregation. On December 1, 1950, at the direction of President Truman's new secretary of defense, General George C. Marshall—who was also the national chairman of the American Red Cross—officials of both the government department and the volunteer agency agreed unanimously that the time had finally come to do what Charles R. Drew and William H. Hastie had urged upon them a decade earlier. Accordingly, racial distinctions were completely removed from the donor program, and the blood of all Americans at last had only one meaningful color: red.

It might seem peculiar that the outcast black American minority would be clamoring insistently for an active role in World War II before the country had even entered the conflict, but that's exactly what happened. Patriotic fervor no doubt had less to do with it than the infuriating insult—and the economic disadvantage—of being systematically locked out of defense jobs and military combat roles. Whatever their motivations, blacks in general (much the same as Southern whites) accounted for more volunteers and fewer conscientious objectors than the general run of American males, even though segregation and discrimination in all branches of service persisted throughout the war.

In the civilian workforce, blatant racial bias prevailed both in the federal government and in industries with defense contracts, and it mattered little where the jobs were located or what skills they required. Some agencies and departments in Washington were less discriminatory than others, but their extensions around the country strongly favored whites. The aircraft industry was as segregated in Seattle and St. Louis as it was in Atlanta, and the construction industry, even as it begged for workers, turned away 75,000 skilled black craftsmen. Half of all defense industries excluded blacks as a matter of stated policy. The white press seemed inclined to ignore the problem, but it wouldn't go away. Finally, late in 1940, an effort by African-Americans to protest these conditions began to take shape.

It coalesced around the leadership of A. Philip Randolph, the Florida-born, New York City–toughened boss of the Brotherhood of Sleeping Car Porters. In September, he and Walter White of the NAACP and T. Arnold

Hill of the National Urban League were granted an audience with President Roosevelt to discuss the racial-exclusion issue; FDR, affable as always, listened intently but gave them only vague promises that he would look into their complaints. They waited five months for some sign of movement, but none came. In February 1941, Randolph said to one of his union aides, "I think we ought to get ten thousand Negroes and march down Pennsylvania Avenue asking for jobs in defense plants and integration of the armed forces." In the coming weeks, the March on Washington Movement—MOWM—was born.

MOWM turned out to be more effective as a symbolic and temporary threat to the racial status quo than as an ongoing civil rights organization, but Philip Randolph himself had more enduring qualities. With what seemed like perfect timing, he had ridden the late-thirties wave of labor union growth stimulated by the New Deal, and his eventual success with the porters' union assured him of a power base and a degree of visibility that would not diminish for another thirty years.

Randolph was a complex man—a pragmatic Socialist with no patience for Communist ideology, an aggressive activist and radical who was at heart a pacifist, an organizer whose strategies embraced both racial independence and integration. He was a controversial figure, too, having served until 1940 as president of the National Negro Congress, an organization that attracted support from the Communist Party and criticism from such widely separated sources as the House Un-American Activities Committee and the NAACP.

If there was one quality above all that made the streetwise Randolph stand out among the small cadre of agency executives, government aides, intellectuals, ministers, writers, educators, and others who made up the nation's black elite, it was this: He came across forcefully as a wise and confident man of the common people, a straight talker, a social activist who never bent to the weight of someone else's agenda or ideology. A passion for racial justice seemed to burn within him like a pure blue flame, a pilot light that never flickered. Neither the Communists nor anybody white nor even his black contemporaries on the left or right could claim to have him in their pocket. A half-century of survival had left him with a thick skin, a mature sense of mission, and a determination to stay the course.

By March 1941, Randolph had gone public with his plans, and had upped the threatened size of his army of marchers tenfold, to 100,000. Almost all of the nation's black newspapers endorsed the march, and Walter White, with whom Randolph maintained a good professional and personal association in spite of their strategic and ideological differences, was openly supportive of the MOWM initiative. Even when Randolph announced that the protest march would be an all-black affair under the complete control of MOWM, the canny White refrained from criticism. He was in a position to know that FDR was feeling the pressure, and that the administration was looking for ways to make some concessions to its black critics.

Eleanor Roosevelt, clearly conveying her husband's wishes, had made a personal appeal to White to dissuade Randolph, but the NAACP chief replied, in all honesty, that he had no control over his friend. Next, White was invited to a high-level meeting of about thirty New Dealers (Mrs. Roosevelt, Aubrey Williams, Will Alexander, Robert Weaver, Sidney Hillman, and others) to discuss the matter further, and it was there that the idea of an executive order banning discrimination in defense industries was discussed and informally endorsed. White quickly recognized that such an order was obtainable, and he subsequently advised Randolph not to settle for less.

The target date for the march on Washington was July 1. Randolph's forces and the administration were both under intense pressure to yield, but June arrived without any public sign of a compromise. Randolph and White were summoned to the White House again, and the President made a personal promise of fairer treatment for black workers, but Randolph politely held out for a tangible show of improvement. Next, Aubrey Williams and Eleanor Roosevelt met with the two black leaders in the office of New York Mayor Fiorello La Guardia, who had offered to mediate—but again there was no breakthrough. On June 18, one last effort to avert the protest march brought A. Philip Randolph and Franklin D. Roosevelt face-to-face again at the White House, with more than a dozen of the President's top advisers in the room, including Williams.

Roosevelt made it plain that he was not willing, with war imminent, to shake up the armed forces by issuing an order to end segregation, but he showed a willingness to consider some modifications in job discrimination practices if they could be guaranteed not to impede war production. Clearly he wanted to go about it by persuasion, not by executive order. By all accounts, Roosevelt liked and respected Randolph, but he was determined to give him nothing concrete. Looking him directly in the eye, he said, "Philip, what do you think?"

Aubrey Williams remembered Randolph's response as a singular display of quiet courage and determination. In a firm voice, the labor leader told the President that he and his associates had come "to ask you to say to the white workers and to management that we are American citizens and should be treated as equals. We ask no special privileges; all we ask is that we be given equal opportunity with all other Americans for employment in those industries that are doing work for the government. We ask that you make it a requirement of any holder of a government contract that he hire his workers without regard to race, creed, or color." Roosevelt, visibly moved, instructed Williams and two others to draft such a statement.

The next morning they brought in the document for the President's consideration. It barred discrimination by either management or labor in all industries holding defense contracts (the federal bureaucracy itself was later added to the list of those required to pledge fairness), and it called for the appointment of a Fair Employment Practices Committee to handle complaints. No reference was made to segregation in the armed forces.

For almost a week the document lay on Roosevelt's desk. Randolph waited in silence. The march was still on, and tens of thousands of black citizens from all over the country were preparing to descend on the capital. Finally, on June 25, President Roosevelt signed Executive Order 8802. A short time later, Randolph announced that the march on Washington was canceled.

MOWM and its jubilant supporters proclaimed victory, but that view of the outcome was far from unanimous, even among blacks. Roy Wilkins and Charles H. Houston, two men closely associated with the NAACP, criticized Randolph for excluding whites from MOWM; W. E. B. Du Bois was conspicuously quiet, giving no public sign that he supported the organization or its leaders. Some critics saw Randolph as another Marcus Garvey; others objected to his professed commitment to a strategy of nonviolent civil disobedience. (Not among them was James Farmer, a Texas-born, Mississippi-raised Methodist preacher's son who, in 1942, when he was twenty-two years old, started the Congress of Racial Equality in Chicago with Bayard Rustin and others, inspired in part by the strategic and philosophical ideas of A. Philip Randolph.)

Five months later the United States was at war; the people closed ranks and made a show of unity in adversity, but segregation remained the order of the day. The Fair Employment Practices Committee—two blacks and three whites, chaired by Mark Ethridge of the Louisville *Courier-Journal*—began to receive and consider the complaints of people who wanted to work in the war effort but were denied that opportunity because of their race.

The results were hardly impressive. Lacking any enforcement power beyond moral persuasion, the FEPC resolved few disputes and did not recommend cancellation of any defense contracts. At a public hearing in Birmingham in June 1942, Ethridge, who was widely regarded as one of the South's most prominent white liberals, declared that "there is no power in the world—not even in all the mechanized armies of the earth, Allied and Axis—which could now force the Southern white people to the abandonment of the principle of social segregation." If the remark had been made by an avowed white supremacist like Senator Bilbo or Governor Talmadge, no one would have been surprised; coming as it did from the chairman of a government committee responsible for promoting fairness in employment, Ethridge's unfortunate comment was a slap in the face to progressives.

Blasted by Southern whites for doing too much and by blacks for doing too little, the FEPC in reality didn't do much at all. Several of its members, including Ethridge, finally resigned in frustration after three years. The committee was then reorganized, and regional offices were opened in several cities, including Dallas and Atlanta, but the pattern of weak and ineffective performance didn't change. Some Southern railroads, shipyards, and plants openly defied the committee and the government. Finally, after three more years of impotence, Congress would pull the plug in 1946 and leave the FEPC to expire—out of money, out of friends, out of luck and life.

Every step toward equal opportunity had been a challenge, an ordeal, and the road ahead looked no smoother. But in subtle and irrevocable ways, the coming of war marked the gradual beginning of a change in attitudes, beliefs, behavior—for black Americans, for Southern whites, for Americans everywhere. The March on Washington Movement was one sign among many that race, once an ignored topic thought to involve only poor people in the South, was about to become a major public issue in the United States. Scores of Southern politicians, steeped as they were in racist habit and ideology, saw and felt this faint shift in the wind and steeled themselves to resist at all costs the social changes that were coming.

2. *The Locust Confederacy*

In war as in peace, the South was ravaged by the political equivalent of a plague of locusts. Informally bonded by philosophy and temperament—and by the acquired habits of power and privilege—this undemocratic oligarchy of reactionary lawmakers held sway from the city halls and county seats to the state capitols and the halls of Congress. The pattern, established after Reconstruction, had continued virtually unaltered for more than sixty years: A relative handful of economically powerful white people controlled the region by excluding from the political process all except others similar to themselves. With rare exceptions, you had to be white to be in the game at all; in addition, it helped immeasurably if you were a man, and it was also decidedly in your favor to be over forty, wealthy, a property owner, a conspicuously pious Protestant of Anglo-Saxon descent, an outspoken defender of Southern traditions, and a denigrator of Yankees. On top of all that, of course, it went without saying that you had to be a Democrat.

An inventive variety of devices served to limit the franchise. Only since 1920 had the nation's women had legal standing at the polls—and in the South and elsewhere, many people still considered feminine political activity unbecoming if not disreputable. Every Southern state had instituted a poll tax in the 1890s or early 1900s as a transparent means of taking the vote away from blacks and poor whites. The tax of one or two dollars a year was billed as a revenue raiser, but its only effective purpose was to restrict suffrage; in some states, it was retroactive to age twenty-one, cumulative for up to 24 years, and had to be paid months before election time. By 1937, North Carolina, Louisiana, and Florida had repealed their poll taxes, and Georgia, under reform governor Ellis Arnall, did the same in 1945. South Carolina and Tennessee would follow suit in the early 1950s. The other states—Alabama, Arkansas, Mississippi, Texas, and Virginia—would cling to the discredited device until it was finally banned by the Twenty-fourth Amendment to the U.S. Constitution in 1964.

Next to the poll tax, exclusive party membership proved to be the favorite restrictive tool of the political bosses. There were so few Republicans and splinter-party members in the region that the Democrats could control elections simply by excluding certain groups (blacks in particular) from the party, and thus from participation in primary elections. In the 1920s, the Texas legislature passed several laws barring blacks from voting in Democratic Party primaries, but the U.S. Supreme Court overturned them one by one—finally and decisively in a landmark 1944 case, *Smith* v. *Allwright*. Even so, most other Southern states kept up their rearguard attempts to disenfranchise black citizens, and in general to discourage political participation by the poor.

Election returns provided a dramatic picture of the consequences of all these antidemocratic manipulations. In the 1940 general election, populous states such as New York, Illinois, and California counted about half as many votes as they had people (for example, Illinois, with a population of close to eight million, cast more than four million votes). In stark contrast were the Southern states, where an average of only fourteen percent of the population voted. Dead last was South Carolina; not even one in twenty citizens went to the polls there. As for black adults, they almost fell off the charts; less than five percent regionwide were registered to vote, and in the most repressive states, such as South Carolina, fewer than one in a hundred could cast a ballot. (Before the Civil War, no blacks in the region were allowed to vote, but they became a majority of the electorate in five states during Reconstruction, when more than 670,000 blacks from Virginia to Texas were enfranchised; by 1920 their voting strength in the Deep South was almost back to zero.)

Unchallenged one-party segregationist rule kept power in the same hands. Even when there was a changing of the guard (old politicians *did* sometimes die, retire, or lose elections), new ideas seldom accompanied the new faces. At the state level, governors came and went according to the laws of succession, and so there was a predictable turnover. In the U.S. House and Senate, the officeholders, once elected, tended to stay in the Club forever, building up seniority and mastering the art of political manipulation. Either way, though, the quality and character of Southern politicians seldom showed much improvement over the long-established pattern of belligerency, bigotry, and buffoonery. There were always a few exceptions laboring in obscurity, but the rule remained firmly in place.

John Nance Garner, the arch-conservative vice president, retired to Texas in 1941, and that was also the year that W. Lee "Pappy" O'Daniel, a flour salesman and hillbilly bandleader, was elevated from the Texas governor's office to the U.S. Senate in a special election to replace the late Morris Sheppard. O'Daniel defeated Congressman Lyndon B. Johnson in that hotly disputed race by a narrow margin, but Johnson continued climbing up through the House ranks under the tutelage of Speaker Sam Rayburn. Their liberal Texas colleague Maury Maverick had been involuntarily retired to San Antonio in 1938. Another Texan, chairman Martin Dies of the House Un-American Activities Committee, announced his surprise retirement in 1944, although he would return a decade later. Conservative John L. McClellan was elected to the Senate and moderate Brooks Hays to the House from Arkansas in 1942 (the forty-three-year-old Hays had made two unsuccessful runs for governor and one for the House before that). Two years later, Hattie Caraway, the history-making (and able) female senator from that state, lost her reelection bid to Congressman J. William Fulbright.

Tennessee gained a couple of progressive New Deal enthusiasts in the House when Estes Kefauver and Albert Gore were elected in 1938, but Alabama lost one when William Bankhead died in 1940. Alabama's Senator Lister Hill and Representative John Sparkman were also considered dependable New Dealers on most issues, and to a lesser extent so were Congressman Luther Patrick and Senator John H. Bankhead. All in all, some of the Southern states that historically had been rated as inferior frontier regions—Alabama, Tennessee, Arkansas—had managed by the 1940s to send some fairly progressive people to Congress. Far less impressive, by comparison, were the royalist delegations from the Atlantic seaboard states (Virginia, the Carolinas, Georgia), where colonial pride and vanity often bred an altogether unwarranted superior air of self-righteousness and an outright hostility to genuine democratic political participation.

North Carolina, for example, had filled its Senate seats with Josiah Bailey, an unreconstructed Old South Rebel, and Robert R. Reynolds, an early defender and proponent of Hitler—and when the voters decided in 1944 that Reynolds had to go, they replaced him with former governor Clyde R. Hoey, a devotee of the Bailey school of unfettered class privilege. South Carolina also made a big change that year, rejecting Cotton Ed Smith after thirty-six years of dubious service, but in his place elected former governor Olin D. Johnston, a slightly more polished man but one whose social, economic, and racial views were every bit as reactionary as the bombastic Senator Smith's.

Elsewhere in the South, antidemocratic feudal barons so completely dominated the delegations that the token few dissenting moderates were seldom seen or heard. Virginia, the mother of presidents, virtually belonged to its monarchs, Senators Carter Glass and Harry F. Byrd, for life; Georgia was almost as totally ruled by Senators Walter George and Richard B. Russell (though Governor Eugene Talmadge had his own machine in place until Ellis Arnall upset him in 1942). Mississippi Senator Pat Harrison's death in 1942 brought in James O. Eastland, a ranting demagogue who would prove to be as rabid as his unbalanced colleague, Senator Theodore Bilbo. When you added to all these the senatorial excesses of such incumbents as Tom Connally of Texas, Kenneth McKellar of Tennessee, and Allen Ellender of Louisiana, you got a depressingly familiar picture of negative leadership that perpetuated the inferior status of the South. The House of Representatives was equally as devoid of Southern statesmen, the few honest plodders notwithstanding. In this long-suffering region, politics was a game played by older and more privileged white men—sometimes for the entertainment and humor of larger numbers of citizens, but almost never for their benefit.

As unrepresentative of the population as the South's congressional delegations were, however, they were only marginally worse than the North's, in whose ranks all but two members were white and the overwhelming preponderance were males. The state legislatures were not much better: Illinois, Indiana, Ohio, Pennsylvania, and New York had among them only twenty-two black legislators—and in the rest of the states combined, there was a grand total of just six more. More than ninety-nine percent of the nation's elected senators and representatives, state and federal, were white.

It wasn't enough just to be a white man, of course—as President

Roosevelt understood all too well. He entered the war years resigned to a sharp cutback of his domestic reform programs. It pained him to realize that the Southerners, more than any other group, had done him in—and in both houses of Congress, they poured salt on his wounds by dismantling one New Deal program after another. Out went the Works Progress Administration, the Civilian Conservation Corps, and the National Youth Administration in 1943; the Farm Security Administration was decimated, and would be finished off right after the war, along with the Fair Employment Practices Committee. A backlash against the rise of labor unions rumbled through Congress and the state legislatures, and the Senate once again turned back liberal efforts to pass laws against poll taxes and lynching.

Sometimes even the more positive legislative proposals turned sour when Roosevelt's enemies worked their mischief. Congressman John E. Rankin of Mississippi, chairman of the committee handling veterans' affairs in the House, undercut Roosevelt's efforts to simplify voting by soldiers as the 1944 election approached—apparently out of fear that this would open the franchise to blacks. A few months later, the Negrophobic congressman succeeded for a time in blocking passage of the GI Bill of Rights because its education and unemployment compensation provisions would send too many blacks to school and encourage them to refuse low-paying jobs.

Few members of Congress could match Rankin's choleric and abusive diatribes against blacks, Jews, foreigners, Communists, and liberals (although his Mississippi senatorial colleagues, Eastland and Bilbo, were cut from the same bolt of coarse cloth). It is a measure of the House's tolerance—and its staggering insensitivity—that it would allow the malicious congressman to rant and rave against "niggers" and "kikes" without so much as a whisper of protest. (Rankin, admitted one Northern member of the House, "holds the same fascination for me that a big fire does. I hate to think of the waste and destruction, but I simply can't resist the entertainment.") It was not just his words that were harmful, though; the abusive, hot-eyed Mississippian posed a serious threat to the people he hated. As an original sponsor and a staunch defender of the House Un-American Activities Committee, he masterminded a parliamentary maneuver in 1945 that turned the witch-hunting body into a standing committee with almost unlimited investigatory powers, and for the next three years he was its most reckless and feared member.

But not even the Rankins in Congress could slam the door on progress and turn the nation back to its nineteenth-century ways. The soldiers did eventually get to vote (nearly three million cast absentee ballots), and so did more and more civilians, and the GI Bill not only passed into law but revolutionized home-buying and college-going in America; within four years, more than four million ex-GIs would flood onto the nation's campuses, and post-high-school study would never again be thought of as an elite privilege for the fortunate few. Once again, the New Deal had opened opportunity to the "forgotten" folks Roosevelt declared he had come to serve back in 1932.

There were a few other bright lights to cheer the President. The citizenry of the South, white and black, remained steadfastly in his camp, returning to him favorable majorities of seventy-five percent or more at the ballot box and in public-opinion polls. The Tennessee Valley Authority, one of Roosevelt's proudest achievements, was bringing navigation, flood control, and electric power to that vast river basin in the upper South—although the agency had attracted fierce opposition from private power interests and right-wing politicians in and out of the region. (The House sponsor of the TVA Act and an unwavering champion of cheap power for rural areas—including his own home district—was none other than Mississippi's John Rankin.) And in the federal courts, dozens of Roosevelt appointees—including seven to the Supreme Court by 1942— were leading a quiet judicial evolution toward a more responsive and progressive philosophy of government.

Nevertheless, it took grave danger abroad to save FDR and the New Deal from utter defeat at home. The experienced and inspiring President was so firmly established as the people's choice when war threatened in 1940, and again when the Allies invaded Europe in 1944, that his political enemies could not dislodge him. They could and did undercut his attempts to reform America, though, and in Washington they waved the bloody flag of resistance and rebellion in the costly ongoing struggle for democracy. Out in the Southern provinces, the story was pretty much the same.

The political machine was a common substitute for a broad-based and active electorate in many a Southern city and state. In the vacuum created by the assassination of Huey Long in Louisiana, a prolonged power struggle finally put control of the splintered regime in the hands of New Orleans Mayor Robert S. Maestri, a wealthy slum landlord and major financial backer of the Kingfish. Long, a nominal Baptist, had built his political kingdom by forging a union of north Louisiana Protestants and south Louisiana Catholics, bankrolled primarily by immigrant Jews and Italians (Maestri and others) in New Orleans. But the Long legacy made politics and criminality almost indistinguishable, and by 1940, several of the main cogs in the machine, including Governor Robert W. Leche and Louisiana State University President James M. Smith, had been sentenced to prison terms for corruption. Leche's departure elevated the lieutenant governor, Earl K. Long, Huey's younger brother—and thus advanced the checkered career of yet another volatile member of that singularly explosive and unpredictable political family.

Congressman Maury Maverick's combative independence from the political machine that ran San Antonio caused him to lose his reelection bid by 493 votes in the 1938 Democratic primary. Undaunted, he went home and challenged the machine head-on—and, to the surprise of many, won the mayor's office in 1939. Maverick had by then earned a national reputation as a fighting liberal. He was the sole Southern member of Congress to vote for the anti-lynching bill in 1937. A pro-labor, pro-civil-liberties New Dealer, he was a leader in the fight against the poll tax and a strong believer in federal government activism in such fields as housing, health care, and education. FDR supported and encouraged this political gadfly in both his Washington and his San Antonio office; so did Hugo Black, Jonathan Daniels, Walter White, Virginius Dabney, Sherwood Anderson, and John P. Davis—a very mixed bag of left-of-center operatives. His enemies also provided a revealing measure of his liberalism. Among the loudest were a quartet of Texas reactionaries: Governor O'Daniel, Congressman Dies, Senator Connally, and Vice President Garner.

As mayor, Maverick helped the large, poor, and politically quiescent Mexican-American population of San Antonio find its voice. Ever a champion of free thought and expression, he bucked powerful opposition to allow the Communist Party a permit for a political rally in the city auditorium in 1939, and he bore the brunt of criticism when a violent mob broke up the meeting, vandalized the facility, and injured fifteen policemen. And yet, for all his progressivism, the feisty Texan was slow to abandon his traditionally paternalistic views about blacks, who in San Antonio made up a small but potent bloc in the tight grip of the machine. Never able to control them himself, Maverick sometimes went to extremes to keep blacks out of party politics—and thus he presented an embarrassing contradiction as a liberal defender of the Texas white primary until it was ruled unconstitutional in 1944. Indicted himself (and acquitted) on the ironic charge of paying voters' poll taxes in return for their support, Maverick lost his mayoral reelection bid in 1941 and never again enjoyed victory at the polls.

Puzzled and somewhat embittered by the unwillingness of African-Americans to accept his peculiar reasoning on the white primary, Maury Maverick was a long time getting over his hurt (though he did finally come around). "Lord God," he exclaimed to a close confidant in 1945, "I have spent my life fighting for minorities. But what have they done for me? They have shit on me. But I hasten to say, having washed, I am ready to go on defending them. Every now and then, though, I get tired of that stuff."

Race and radicalism hardly figured at all in the Virginia clash of the Byrd machine with a progressive governor just before the war. James H. Price's worst sin was to run for governor—and win—without the permission of Senator Harry Flood Byrd or his lordly Senate colleague Carter Glass, now an octogenarian. Mild though his opposition to the machine truly was, Price became the object of a vendetta aimed at destroying his legislative program and leaving him so damaged personally that he couldn't muster a serious challenge to Byrd in the 1940 senatorial primary.

Both aims were achieved. The moderate Price administration was a tiny blip of anti-Byrd progressivism—one of the few to be seen in Virginia during the Winchester apple baron's forty-year reign as governor and senator (1925–65). Byrd and Glass were a stubbornly old-fashioned team of antidemocratic mules behind whom the Old Dominion meekly and dutifully plowed the same dusty furrows. In years to come, misguided reverence for the reactionary duo would inspire shameful acts of massive resistance to federal authority in Virginia—a century after the Civil War supposedly had settled the sovereignty question once and for all.

The New Orleans and San Antonio examples might suggest that vice and corruption are inevitably the handmaidens of the political machine, but the Byrd organization in Virginia proved otherwise. You could fairly accuse Harry Byrd of being parsimonious, puritanical, dictatorial, vindictive, and reactionary in the extreme, but you'd have a hard time making him out to be a crook. It wasn't what he stole that held Virginia back—it was what he thought, said, believed, and led his subjects to do. Edward H. "Boss" Crump, the longtime political boss of Memphis and most of Tennessee, had a similar reputation for honesty—and yet he was a Byrd of a different feather.

Crump arrived in Memphis as a country boy from Mississippi in 1894, and he was thirty-four when he won his first race for mayor in 1909. In those rough-and-tumble times, Memphis was a reckless river town with an astronomical murder rate nearly seven times the national average. Crump was a progressive reformer with a talent for influencing people; from the start, he concentrated on building organized blocs of voters (including blacks, who made up half the population), and though he left the mayor's job in 1916, he kept on courting voters in the city and surrounding Shelby County, in the west Tennessee congressional districts, and finally in the entire state.

With veteran senator and fellow Memphian Kenneth D. McKellar as his ally, Crump demonstrated his strength by keeping Protestant, Prohibitionist west Tennessee in the column of the Yankee Catholic Al Smith in

1928, and two years later, Crump won a congressional seat for himself. But the feisty, red-haired little battler (the "Red Snapper," some called him) was bored by the stodginess of the Club, and after serving only one term he "retired" to his kingmaker role. FDR could handle things in Washington, he said; Memphis and Tennessee needed progressive leadership back home.

Until the end of World War II, Boss Crump was unassailable. His well-oiled machine ran a clean, efficient, honest city government and a powerful Democratic organization that anointed governors and senators with authority. His ties to Roosevelt got cheap TVA power for Memphis even though the city wasn't located in the Tennessee Valley. Crump managed to keep both the captains of business and industry and the leadership of the AFL (but not the CIO) in his camp; he also kept close ties with an unbeatable combination of Baptists, Catholics, Jews, and blacks, all within the social confines of religious and racial segregation.

Opposition newspapers in Memphis and Nashville railed at him as a dictatorial bully, a ruthless despot, a poll-tax defender (he routinely arranged payment for voters), and a self-appointed guardian of public morals (he kept a bluenose censor of movies and plays on the city payroll). Jennings Perry, an associate editor of the Nashville *Tennessean*, focused an entire book (*Democracy Begins at Home*) on the manifold evils of the Boss Man's poll-tax machinations. But it was all for nought. Crump delivered a huge majority to Roosevelt in 1944 and loyally shored up McKellar's sixth election to the Senate in 1946, even though the arch-conservative senator had long since become a bitterly obstructionist foe of FDR and the New Deal. Not until he was past seventy, and the postwar social revolution was at hand, would E. H. Crump finally lose his magic touch with the Tennessee electorate.

Eugene Talmadge's third occupation of the Georgia governor's mansion in 1941 followed his unsuccessful attempts in 1936 and 1938 to unseat either Walter George or Richard B. Russell from the U.S. Senate. The power of incumbency appeared to make George and Russell unbeatable, so Talmadge resigned himself to a slightly different sort of political machine, one that left national government to others while holding the state capitol in perpetuity. A "county unit" method of tabulating votes kept political power in Georgia weighted heavily in favor of the sparsely populated rural counties. Talmadge calculated that he could thrive by playing the role of a rustic country hell-raiser up against the big-city newspapers and other sophisticated institutions.

But the tyrannical excesses of the hot-tempered governor boiled over when he clumsily attempted a witch-hunt for liberals and other heretics at the University of Georgia, and in the gubernatorial election of 1942—the first in Georgia to award a four-year term to the winner—Talmadge was upset by the state's thirty-five-year-old attorney general, Ellis G. Arnall. (Among those who helped bring about the changing of the guard were the *Constitution*'s editor, Ralph McGill, who wrote some speeches for the young challenger, and the President of the United States, who invited Arnall down to the Little White House at Warm Springs and gave him advice and encouragement.)

Throughout his term of office, Arnall acted and spoke with refreshing candor about Georgia and the South. In the legislature he pushed through prison and parole reforms, a constitutional revision plan, repeal of the poll tax, voting rights for eighteen-year-olds, and reductions in the powers of the governor's office. He called his predecessor a demagogue, a racist, and a bigot, and he faulted the South for self-pity, inertia, evasion of reality, and blaming its woes on "the damyankee." All in all, the young governor did more to rescue his state and region from the defeatist mire of colonial dependency than anyone else had done in decades, if ever.

One clear sign of Arnall's serious intent to change things was his hiring of Daniel Duke, a well-known young Atlanta-area county prosecutor, to be his assistant attorney general for criminal prosecution. Duke had a Jimmy Cagney feistiness about him. He first won notoriety in 1941 at a clemency hearing for some Ku Klux Klansmen he had sent to prison earlier on flogging charges. Knowing that Governor Talmadge had agreed to testify at the hearing as a character witness for the convicts, Atlanta Mayor William B. Hartsfield, a reformed ex-Talmadgeite, told the combative Duke to confront the governor with the leather whip the men had used to flog more than fifty victims. Hartsfield then phoned a tip to Ralph McGill, and Duke told the plan to his father-in-law, Tarleton Collier, editor of the Atlanta *Georgian*. At the hearing, photographers from both papers and the wire services were ready and waiting when Duke brandished the lash in front of the astonished Talmadge and exclaimed, "You could kill a bull elephant with this!" The shock effect momentarily silenced the governor, and his testimony was ineffective.

Duke went on to serve Arnall with the same hard-hitting prosecutorial aggressiveness. For the first time, the Georgia Bureau of Investigation and the attorney general's office actually tried to break up Klan cells, rather than giving them aid and comfort. Arnall even went so far as to hire a young Florida journalist, Stetson Kennedy, as an informer in the Klan to expose its criminal acts. With strong support from the press, the Arnall administration served notice on Georgia's secret societies that terrorist acts would no longer be tolerated. The message certainly helped, but it didn't put a stop to lynching and other atrocities.

Nor did it completely liberate Arnall himself from the old bugaboo of racism. Ambitious for higher fields of service, he spoke and wrote widely about his vision of a progressive new South. But when his liberal message was interpreted as an attack on racial segregation, he felt compelled to "clarify" the remarks with assurances that "we in the South do not believe in social equality . . . we believe that segregation is conducive to the welfare of both the white and colored races." And then, when his term ended and he couldn't succeed himself, Ellis Arnall could only stand aside and watch as Eugene Talmadge once again rode to victory. Georgia was close to breaking out of its ancient Confederate mentality and turning toward genuine reform—but the time was still not at hand.

As the Republican and Democratic conventions approached in 1944, an alliance of thirty black citizens prominent in church, civic, education, and labor organizations signed a widely circulated advertisement warning the two parties that they would have to take affirmative action against discrimination to win the minority vote. The NAACP's top brass headed the roster of signees, but some Southerners were also included: Emory Jackson of Birmingham, Maynard Jackson, Sr., of Atlanta, and Z. Alexander Looby of Nashville.

One more sign of movement against the Democratic Party's entrenched white power structure bobbed quietly to the surface in South Carolina during World War II. There, for the first time in any Southern state, a group of middle-class black citizens organized a political challenge to the exclusively white institutions of privilege and control. They had taken the initial step at a meeting in Columbia in November 1939, when delegates from seven local branches came together to form the South Carolina Conference of the NAACP, and to declare that "All the blessings of life, liberty, and happiness are possible in integration, while in segregation lurk all the forces destructive of these values."

On May 23, 1944, many of the same delegates, meeting again in Columbia, founded the South Carolina Progressive Democratic Party as a vehicle to force open the political process in their state and in the nation. Although V. O. Key, in his classic 1949 study, *Southern Politics*, didn't find this black initiative significant enough to mention, it was an important signal to the Democrats nationally that their party would eventually be forced to live up to its name.

The first chairman of the PDP was thirty-four-year-old John Henry McCray, editor and publisher of the *Lighthouse & Informer*, South Carolina's leading black weekly newspaper. His associate editor and close ally in the political venture, Osceola McKaine, had recently returned to his native state at the age of fifty after a rare odyssey as a merchant seaman out of Boston, a combat soldier in France during World War I, an organizer of veterans in Harlem during the Renaissance era, and a cabaret owner in Belgium for more than a decade. Admitting that he had come home with "at least a splinter on my shoulder," the spirited McKaine nevertheless concluded there was no more Jim Crow segregation in South Carolina's cities than in the North—but it was still far too much to suit him, and he didn't hesitate to say so.

McCray and McKaine, together with state NAACP chairman James M. Hinton and others, launched the PDP after the white South Carolina state legislature converted the Democratic Party into a private club to preserve its racial exclusivity. Among the Carolinians who supported the PDP and helped make it a force to be reckoned with were two black Republicans, physician Robert W. Mance and businesswoman Modjeska Simkins, both longtime critics of racial discrimination. A Jewish couple, Jennie and Jules Seidman, were also actively involved, giving the PDP a biracial image.

Just before the 1944 Democratic National Convention, the PDP came out in support of the reelection of President Roosevelt (a stance the South Carolina "club" of white Democrats had refused to take), and they sent an alternate delegation to Chicago to challenge the regulars. Failing that, they went home and put up a slate of Roosevelt electors after the whites announced that their electors would be uncommitted independents. The PDP also qualified McKaine as its general-election candidate for the U.S. Senate, challenging Governor Olin D. Johnston, who had defeated Cotton Ed Smith in the primary. The tiny percentage of registered black voters and an unknown number of whites mustered an official total of more than three thousand votes for McKaine, but PDP poll-watchers charged that whites had used intimidation and outright fraud to rob him of a legitimate tally of some eight thousand. Even with such a total, Osceola McKaine still would have lost to Johnston by about ten to one—but the very fact that blacks had taken part in the process at all was a symbolic victory, a blinking neon arrow pointing toward the future.

The election of 1944 was Roosevelt's last hurrah. It was also a showcase for renewed hostilities between whites and blacks, liberals and conservatives, the North and the South. Senators and congressmen across the South were in open revolt against the President and his urban/labor/black/Jewish/Catholic/ethnic band of liberals. With each new (or old) progressive idea—anti-poll-tax legislation, the FEPC, desegregation of party primary elections, political action committees in organized labor—the Southerners grew more certain that their power was waning. They lashed out in anger, threatened rebellion, tried to bump the President aside, considered forming a new party. Even the most moderate of them—Pepper of Florida, Hill of Alabama—resorted to public affirmations of white supremacy in order to get themselves reelected. But once again, FDR parlayed his enormous popularity with ordinary people into victory over the Southern political conservatives and their Republican soul mates, whose candidate was New York Governor Thomas E. Dewey, a compulsively neat and cautious politician described by the writer John Gunther as "one of the least seductive personalities in public life."

The triumph—by three million popular votes and a four-to-one margin in the electoral count—was not as easy as it looked. Right-wing governors Frank M. Dixon of Alabama (nephew of the novelist Thomas Dixon) and Sam Houston Jones of Louisiana made a serious attempt in 1943 to corral Southern extremists like themselves into a new regional party, and in 1944 a rebellious Southern faction nominated Virginia's Harry F. Byrd for president at the Democratic Convention (but could muster fewer than a hundred delegates to the cause). Takeovers of the Democratic party apparatus were seriously plotted in at least three states (a rebel ticket of independent presidential electors got 135,000 votes in Texas), and no state in the region remained happily in the bosom of FDR's "solid South" at election time.

It was against this background of ideological and philosophical conflict that one last Rooseveltian political drama was played out in July at the convention in Chicago. The President didn't even put in an appearance; he was away on "war duties," underscoring his leadership role as the tide was turning in our favor in Europe and the Pacific—and besides, he looked every bit the sick man that he was, hollow-eyed and thin, and being seen would only call attention to his obvious incapacities. At the same time they were supporting his nomination almost by acclamation, the Democrats were whispering odds in the corridors that he wouldn't live out the term.

All of which made the vice-presidential nomination a matter of more than casual interest. Just as the national conference of the NAACP was ending in the Windy City, the Democrats arrived. One of the latter—and no friend of the former—was James F. Byrnes of South Carolina, the veteran lawmaker–jurist–presidential counselor who was then serving as director of the Office of War Mobilization. He would, he announced to the press, be a candidate for vice president. Byrnes didn't dwell on the fact that the job was presently held by Henry A. Wallace, who had indicated no desire to step aside and who had broad-based support from many groups, the NAACP among them.

Roosevelt, too, was content to keep Wallace on the ticket, but he was under intense pressure from conservatives in the party—including most of the Southerners in Congress—to dump him and choose someone else. Wallace had moved sharply leftward since leaving the Department of Agriculture, and his liberal views on labor, race, and Russia made him anathema to the right-wingers. Other names were being suggested: Senator Barkley of Kentucky, Justice William O. Douglas of the Supreme Court, Senator Truman of Missouri, Congressman Rayburn of Texas, and

Jimmy Byrnes. The President, still the peerless master of political art, shrewdly accorded each of the named prospects—including Wallace—a measure of hope. Then, quoting a "wise man named Murphy," he smilingly told the press, "The convention will decide."

Truman was the only one on the list who said publicly that he didn't want the job. Byrnes clearly did; in a clever early move of his own, he asked Truman to place his name in nomination before the Missouri senator's own prospects had been aired. Byrnes was gambling boldly. He had drifted out of the Roosevelt inner circle since the late thirties, even though FDR had later appointed him to the Supreme Court and then to important wartime administrative posts. Their differences weren't personal as much as philosophical; Roosevelt's activist approach to government was okay with Byrnes in foreign affairs, but he didn't like it at home—not in the South, at least—and he had openly aligned himself with the anti-labor, anti-black Southern cabal midway through the President's second term. Still, Byrnes had served FDR long and well, and he was hoping for short memories among the liberals. Then the word got out that Walter White of the NAACP, Sidney Hillman of the CIO, and the big-city political bosses of New York and Chicago had all turned thumbs down on his candidacy. Without rejecting Byrnes outright, FDR responded to questions about his candidacy by telling party leaders to "clear it with Sidney." The phrase was widely quoted as a Roosevelt code that meant the dapper little South Carolinian didn't have a prayer.

Byrnes felt betrayed by the President's men, and abandoned by FDR himself. To be told that his hard-line racial views made him a political liability was simply too much for this "Assistant President" who, the press said, had exercised more power than any other appointed White House figure in American history. Later, when Roosevelt spoke to the convention by phone from a cruiser in the Pacific, Jimmy Byrnes was just about the only man in the hall who sat sourly on his hands. After a decent interval, he would resign from the executive staff and return to South Carolina.

In the balloting, Wallace led the first round, with Truman a close second and others (including Barkley and Alabama senator John Bankhead) far back. In the second round Truman inched ahead, and then a sudden flurry of switched ballots threw the nomination to him. Byrnes never had the pleasure of hearing the crusty senator from Missouri tout Byrnes's candidacy to the delegates. (He did, however, come back to the White House later to serve the new President as his Secretary of State.) Considering all the dramatic turns of events that took place in presidential politics and in the South over the next ten years, we can only wonder how different things would have been if, instead of President Harry S. Truman, we had had President James F. Byrnes.

3. Leaders, Followers, Scouts

On his return by rail to Washington after spending the Thanksgiving holiday at Warm Springs in 1938, President Roosevelt stopped to make a speech at the University of North Carolina in Chapel Hill. The Carolina Political Union, a guest lecture series planned and directed by students, had attracted to the campus an impressive lineup of national newsmakers and controversial personalities over the previous two years; they had ranged from bureaucrats and diplomats to Communists and Klansmen, and most had even come at their own expense. In that glittering showcase of big names, the President of the United States was easily the prize catch.

Alexander Heard, a senior political science major, had invested much effort in the long pursuit of FDR during his year as chairman of the Political Union, but by the time the President was finally scheduled to appear, Heard had graduated and gone on to Columbia University for further study. He was present on that rainy December afternoon, though, having caught a train down from New York for the occasion, and he looked on proudly as his successors in the union presented Franklin D. Roosevelt and university president Frank Porter Graham to a turnaway throng at the gymnasium. Viewing the pomp and ceremony as a spectator rather than a participant, Heard could sense the elements of quality and honor and prestige that made President Roosevelt and President Graham and UNC itself such important symbols of hope in the South and the nation.

In the same month that the North Carolina campus basked in the glory of a presidential visit, events elsewhere foreshadowed the continuing struggle for equity and quality that confronted the South and its institutions. The economic and social disparities that had caused the South to precede the nation into the Great Depression were now determining that it would be the last region to escape its punishment. Further discouragement was generated by the seeming inevitability of war, with all its uncertainties.

In Washington, shifting alliances notwithstanding, discord still marred relations within the three branches of government. Congress was gaining momentum in its ongoing tilt to the right; the reactionary Southern bloc, strengthened by heavy liberal-Democratic losses in the November elections, was preparing to resist even more aggressively the President's agenda of domestic reform. Meanwhile, the Supreme Court appeared to be falling in step with the White House as justices elevated to the bench by Roosevelt reached majority status. In *Gaines* v. *Missouri*, announced on December 12, the judges put the states on notice for the first time that they must either attain a meaningful standard of equality under segregation or remove the barriers that denied some citizens complete freedom of opportunity. FDR's six appointees outvoted the two holdover Republican justices in that case. Few in Congress applauded the decision, and most of the Southerners were predictably sour about it.

Out in the precincts, signs of philosophical consensus were likewise hard to find. Even in Chapel Hill, the path ahead looked rocky. As he sat on the platform with Mr. Roosevelt, Frank Graham might well have been preoccupied and troubled with thoughts of the file of correspondence he had left on his desk back at the office. The fallout from the Southern Conference for Human Welfare was hot and heavy—exhortations and admonitions and angry outbursts from a wide range of people, including some who curried his favor and others who longed to see him driven from office. Two of his own UNC colleagues, Howard Odum and W. T. Couch, were anything but happy with the conference's outcome, or with Graham's continuing leadership role in the SCHW.

To add further to his worries, the UNC president was about to be drawn into a racial controversy over Pauli Murray's application for admission to graduate study in the social sciences. No one could question her academic qualifications. Born in Baltimore and raised in Durham, she was a graduate of New York's Hunter College. A young Socialist radical in the early thirties, she had gravitated in time to FDR and the New Deal and, through correspondence, had established a long-distance friendship with Mrs. Roosevelt. Now, at twenty-eight, Pauli Murray epitomized the mature, intelligent, accomplished student around whom Howard Odum had built his reputation. Only one thing stood in the way of her certain admission to his program: She was black—café au lait, actually, with Caucasian features, but black according to the finely calibrated Southern color detector—and therefore ineligible under the law. Even if some of her forebears who were white alumni, trustees, and patrons of the university could have spoken from the grave on her behalf, she would not have been welcome.

Neither Odum nor the dean of the graduate school gave any serious thought to taking a stand in Murray's behalf; her application was quickly and routinely rejected in mid-December. Undaunted, she appealed to President Graham—and his private attention to her file eventually became a matter of intense public interest when news of her application and some of her letters to university officials found their way into the newspapers.

Graham squirmed uncomfortably. He admired Murray's determination, her courage, her perception. Somewhere else she had written, "The testing ground of democracy and Christianity in the United States is in the South," and "it is the duty of Negroes to press for political, economic, and educational equality for themselves and for disinherited whites." Those were Graham's beliefs, words he might have written himself. Furthermore, Murray was keenly aware of the *Gaines* case, and she would come to see her admission to the South's most liberal university as a logical application of that ruling, as well as a powerful sign of Southern liberalism and democracy at their best.

But Frank Graham, as pragmatic as he was liberal, feared an altogether different outcome. State law explicitly mandated segregation; to defy the law would be to court disaster. He watched and listened as debate raged on the campus (graduate students in an opinion poll favored Murray's admission by about two to one, while the student newspaper voiced editorial opposition). Finally, early in 1939, Graham gave his answer. This is not the time for "a popular referendum on the race issue," he wrote to Murray; if she would be patient while he and others worked for genuine equality of educational opportunity, he would, he promised, start searching for "the next possible advance." Not even Eleanor Roosevelt was keen on pushing for that advance just now. "The South is changing," she wrote to Pauli Murray, "but don't press too hard." Later that spring, the North Carolina legislature passed an enabling act to allow graduate and professional courses at the state's black colleges, but no funds were appropriated. And at UNC, it would be another dozen years before a single black student could gain admission.

Such were the realities of segregation and legalized white supremacy as the 1930s wound down. In this Southern citadel of academic liberalism, a serious challenge to Jim Crow segregation could not be advanced past the talking stage. It followed, then, that the issue was effectively closed almost everywhere in the South—and would remain closed, by and large, throughout the war years. Only in a few border-state institutions, some labor unions, parts of the religious community, the military, and a scattering of other arenas would occasional exceptions to this rule come to public notice.

There is no way to measure how much the South's inferior position in the nation was made worse by its mindless devotion to the "separate but equal" myth. In the field of higher education alone, however, you can get some idea of the extent of the problem by looking at a profile of the leading institutions. Virginius Dabney did that in his 1942 book, *Below the Poto-*

mac, and it seems safe to say the numbers he cited would not have changed appreciably until after the war. What he found, overall, was that Southern colleges and universities were woefully underfinanced, overburdened with political and religious intrusion, and seriously deficient in library holdings, Ph. D. programs, and research activities. In other words, they were pretty much where they had been back in the early years of the depression.

Only eight institutions in the region had endowments of $10 million or more, and only three of them—Texas, Duke, and Vanderbilt universities—were in the $25-million-plus range. Texas and Duke were the only schools with more than a half-million library volumes, and Texas alone had a five-figure enrollment (eleven thousand students). None of these totals were in the same ballpark with the country's leading institutions. There was only one Southern university press of national stature (North Carolina's). There were schools of law or medicine or engineering in several of the ex-Confederate states—some even had all three—but Alabama, Arkansas, Mississippi, and South Carolina had no Ph. D. programs at all, and three or four other states were only a thin notch above that rock-bottom level.

Even the best of the universities left a lot to be desired. W. J. Cash, writing in the *American Mercury*, described Duke's student body as "one of the most inert in the country," and went on to explain why old Buck Duke, the tobacco baron, had spent a fortune "to transform an obscure Methodist college in a North Carolina mill-town" into a university that bore his name. "What he wanted was a Babbitt factory," Cash declared, "a mill for grinding out go-get-'em boys in the wholesale and undeviating fashion in which his Chesterfield plant across the way ground out cigarettes."

A few highly regarded colleges for women, public and private, were scattered about the region—places such as Randolph-Macon in Virginia and Agnes Scott in Georgia—and an equally small number of good institutions (Howard, Fisk, Tuskegee, Hampton, Atlanta University, Morehouse) served a black elite. By far most Southern colleges and universities, though, were meant for the primary benefit of a relative handful of high-born white males—and with rare exceptions, those schools, too, tended to be narrow-gauged, orthodox, and mediocre.

With all their manifold shortcomings, most of the institutions had no realistic hope of attaining parity with the average run of colleges and universities elsewhere, much less with the finest. And still, the crippling strictures of racial separation compelled both public and private interests to guard the ramparts against integration and to go through the charade of supporting black schools in the name of separate-but-equal white supremacy, as though there were resources enough to fund two systems.

And on top of all that, some of the state schools were subjected to such outrageous acts of political harassment that their integrity and character were stained for years to come. Much as the Mississippi public colleges had suffered under Governor Theodore Bilbo in the early 1930s, the Georgia public institutions under Governor Eugene Talmadge in 1941 were devastated by a series of political appointments and arbitrary dismissals that caused the institutions to be disaccredited. Then, in 1944, the regents of the University of Texas dismissed the president, Homer P. Rainey, on trumped-up charges that he was an advocate of communism and racial equality—one and the same, in the view of some regents. Congressman Martin Dies was a principal instigator of that purge, but reactionary regents appointed by governors Pappy O'Daniel and Coke Stevenson needed no encouragement from outsiders. Rainey—an ordained Baptist minister, a Mason, and a Rotarian—admitted to being a liberal Democrat and "a friend of the Negroes"; he sealed his fate when he accused the regents of sixteen specific violations of their trust. The richest state university in the country (its coffers stuffed to overflowing by oil-well income) thus entered the postwar era intellectually crippled, politically compromised, and leaderless.

Homer Rainey's courageous and dignified defense of intellectual freedom and the added eloquence of such illustrious Texas faculty members as Walter Prescott Webb and J. Frank Dobie were not enough to save the university from self-inflicted harm. Likewise, in North Carolina, even if Frank Graham could have persuaded every member of the university family to accept Pauli Murray, he would still have had to answer to the state's reigning political-economic-social majority—and that formidable force, Graham instinctively felt, was far more than he and the university could hope to overcome.

These were the two most prestigious state universities in the South, both with progressive leadership at the top administrative level—and yet their limitations and weaknesses and their vulnerability to attack were all too painfully apparent. If UNC and Texas couldn't lead the way to educational and social improvement in the region, how could anyone expect Georgia or Arkansas or South Carolina or any of the other lesser institutions to break free from their political shackles and become forces for regional betterment?

Southern universities, it's true, did occasionally provide a platform and some protection for individual expressions of social criticism by members of the faculty or student body. It was not uncommon in the 1930s for advocates of socialism or communism to speak out on the campuses. At the University of Florida, for example, former student Stetson Kennedy of Jacksonville and a handful of others organized a campus chapter of the leftist American Student Union in 1937, and though it remained small and lasted less than two years, the group did openly identify with the radical "united front" and international peace movements, and even held some meetings with students at black colleges nearby. Similar expressions of student political radicalism surfaced on some other campuses around the region.

Faculty members and administrators from every state had taken part in the Southern Conference for Human Welfare—but some, like C. Vann Woodward of Florida, would be stunned to learn years later that as a result of their participation, they bore a cautionary tag as "security risks." Woodward had finished his Ph.D. at the University of North Carolina in 1937, and his dissertation on Tom Watson, the mercurial Georgia populist, would soon be published as the young historian's first book and as the portent of a new wave of revisionist writing about the Southern past. UNC continued to point to Howard Odum, Rupert Vance, Guy Johnson, Paul Green, W. T. Couch, and numerous others as exemplars of its traditions of freedom and diversity.

Universities of less distinction were by no means devoid of independent thinkers; Alabama, for example, proudly claimed Hudson Strode, a popular and colorful English professor who was a highly regarded travel writer himself but was best known for his classes in creative writing. Two professors at Tuscaloosa in the mid-1930s produced acclaimed volumes of social and cultural criticism: Carl Carmer (*Stars Fell on Alabama*) and Clarence Cason (*90° in the Shade*). Cason, deeply anxious about how people in Alabama would react to his book, committed suicide just before it was published. At Johns Hopkins in Baltimore, economist Broadus Mitchell resigned in 1938 to protest the university's refusal to admit a black applicant to its graduate school.

But these were, for the most part, individual expressions of mild criticism or sharp dissent, against which many opposite examples of intolerance for independent thought could as easily be cited (think of H. C. Nixon's departure from Tulane, and Alva Taylor's from Vanderbilt, and J. William Fulbright's from Arkansas). At best, the picture was mixed and conflicting. As for the institutions themselves, however, no such ambiguity characterized their collective behavior. They were ponderous, impersonal, deeply conservative; they cautiously shied away from controversy of any kind, and rarely addressed themselves to social problems in any activist or partisan way—which meant, of course, that on the volatile issue of segregation and white supremacy, they upheld the status quo.

To the extent that there was any sense of social mission at all in the engine rooms of the South's higher-education institutions, it was most evident in those few schools devoted to serving the least advantaged offspring of racial minorities and the poor. Berea College of Kentucky was one example; it was founded in part on the principle of racial equality, only to be forced by law to abandon it. Some of the private black colleges and universities were similarly committed, among them Fisk, with its activist social science programs headed by Charles S. Johnson; Morehouse, under the forceful presidential leadership of John Hope and Benjamin Mays; and Howard University, during the thirty-four-year reign of President Mordecai Johnson.

Howard was little more than a Negro high school and an instrument of social control in the late nineteenth century, but it blossomed under Johnson's leadership in the 1930s. As a university, it defied classification. It was both public (created and supported with federal appropriations) and private (endowed by philanthropists); it was Southern and Northern, by virtue of its location in the District of Columbia; it was religious and secular, segregated and biracial, a bootstrap institution and an elite community of scholars. Johnson himself seemed a perfect embodiment of all those contrasts; born in Tennessee, descended from black and white forebears, educated in the South, ordained a Baptist preacher, and possessed of urbane sophistication and great oratorical skills, he was passionately devoted to the education and elevation of the African-American minority.

The roster of outstanding faculty members and students at Howard in Johnson's years reads like an honor roll of black distinction. No university in the nation, black or white, could boast a more productive lineup of activist scholars across the board than the likes of Charles H. Houston in law, Charles R. Drew in medicine, Ralph J. Bunche in political science, E. Franklin Frazier in sociology, Rayford W. Logan in history, Sterling A. Brown in English, and Alain Locke in philosophy. It was Mordecai Johnson's genius that he could attract such people, heighten their zeal for social change, and foster a climate of intellectual freedom in which they could stretch themselves to the limit.

The organized church—like the university, like the mainline political parties—was another institutional pillar that shook and trembled as the South tried to find its equilibrium in the tumultuous years of depression and war. On the positive side, religiously motivated individuals worked separately and in groups to improve life in the South, as witness the efforts of the YMCA and YWCA, the Commission on Interracial Cooperation, the Association of Southern Women for the Prevention of Lynching, the Fellowship of Reconciliation, the Fellowship of Southern

Churchmen, and a host of ordained ministers and lay leaders who served in higher education, home missions, charitable service organizations, and even labor unions.

But the influence of the church as an institutional force on such prevalent conditions as unemployment, hunger, homelessness, and racial discrimination was limited and largely ineffectual. In the houses of worship that dominated the architectural landscape of every Southern town and city—and from there right on up to the top of the denominational hierarchies—there was a marked tendency to separate social problems from worship and evangelism. All through those crucial years before the beginning of the postwar era, neither the white nor the black Protestant churches moved to the forefront as advocates of a modern social reformation, and neither did the much smaller Catholic and Jewish bodies. One and all, they seemed more concerned with the past and the future—with venerable traditions and with salvation in the hereafter—than with the urgent physical and social needs of their least fortunate neighbors.

Structurally, the major denominations still reflected the old North-South divisions left over from the Civil War. The Southern Baptist Convention was for whites only, leaving black Baptists to find interchurch fellowship among themselves or in a token few alliances in the North. The mainline Methodist Church in the South had black members, but they were segregated both administratively and congregationally in an all-black "central jurisdiction." Presbyterians, Episcopalians, Catholics, and almost every other branch of Christendom found similar ways of maintaining the color line.

The overwhelming majority of black Protestants belonged to one or another of the independent bodies of Baptists and Methodists that vied with each other and among themselves for whatever power and influence the segregated culture left to them. These all-black denominations, having no latitude to protest discrimination, tended to focus their energies inward and upward rather than outward; not until the mid-1950s would they become the primary moral and institutional force for civil rights in the South.

In *The Negro Church in America*, E. Franklin Frazier delineated the institution's religious and moral influence and its role as "a refuge in a hostile white world"; he also saw it as an economic, political, and educational force among African-Americans. But, he concluded, "on the whole, the Negro's church was not a threat to white domination" before the 1950s; on the contrary, it "aided the Negro to become accommodated to an inferior status." Another student of black social history, C. Eric Lincoln, further noted that although the church had always been "the *symbol* of freedom" for blacks, its leaders seemed unable to agree that it should also be "the *instrument* of freedom." Traditionally, said Lincoln, the churches of black America—until the fifties—had courted a conservative image, and thus were "seldom considered a threat to prevailing social values."

Within the black as well as the white community, religious institutions before midcentury consistently proved to be less courageous and less prophetic than the scattering of selfless individuals in and out of their ranks who kept on trying, at whatever risk or sacrifice, to promote social change. It was preachers and teachers standing alone, not their churches or schools or colleges, who did the most to pass on hope and encouragement to the multitude of besieged citizens at the bottom of the economic heap; it was black shopkeepers, entertainers, skilled craftsmen, undertakers, even bootleggers—people with a modicum of independence—who often showed by word and deed the scriptural spirit of faith and endurance.

The Northern-based and liberally inclined Federal Council of Churches initiated a modest effort to bridge the North-South and white-black chasms in the 1930s, but it found little receptivity in the South. Too many white ministers—even those who were sensitive to racial injustice—found it impossible to buck the tide of white supremacy, and too many black pastors had seen enough terror face-to-face to know that it was dangerous and radical to be a dissenter. An attitude of benevolent paternalism, such as the white Baptist minister M. Ashby Jones of Atlanta exhibited in his longtime involvement with the Commission on Interracial Cooperation, was just about as far as white men of the cloth felt willing or able to go in those years—and cautious ventures outside the walls of the church by Jones and others stopped far short of any semblance of equality.

Benjamin Mays, a black Baptist minister and president of Morehouse College, was elected vice president of the FCC in 1944, and he was influential in guiding the organization to a more activist role in social issues affecting the South. Mays, a South Carolina sharecropper's son who earned a bachelor's degree in New England and a Ph.D. at the University of Chicago, was typical of numerous Southern-born black ministers who seemed to gain effectiveness as critics of segregation with each step they took away from the South or the institutional church—or both. The black colleges, the YMCA, and the NAACP were the most widely traveled routes to non-church-based public service for black ministers from the South. Some left the region; Georgia-born Channing Tobias, to name one prominent example, served as a national leader of both the YMCA and the NAACP. Others chose to stay, among them

Robert E. Jones, who developed a YMCA conference center for blacks in Mississippi, and James M. Hinton, an organizer and leader of the NAACP in South Carolina.

As president of a private college in Atlanta, Benjamin Mays could say and do things that no black church pastor in the Deep South—not even men like Martin Luther King, Sr., of Ebenezer and William Holmes Borders of Wheat Street, Atlanta's foremost black Baptist congregations— would have considered prudent in, say, 1941. (Just two years before that, when the movie version of *Gone With the Wind* premiered in Atlanta, Reverend King had run into a hornet's nest. He drew sharp criticism from many blacks for allowing the Ebenezer choir to put on aprons and Aunt Jemima bandannas and sing for an all-white audience that pointedly excluded, among others, the black actress Hattie McDaniel, who played the role of Mammy in the film). Within the protective circle of the YMCA and other nondenominational groups, Mays and other black leaders could interact with whites in ways that would have been impossible inside the institutional church.

Black ministers who found platforms outside the church for their critical comments on Southern race relations were occasionally echoed by a few whites who left the pulpit for more activist roles. In the late thirties and early forties, Witherspoon Dodge, a wellborn South Carolinian who had held pastorates in two Protestant denominations, found a new calling as a labor organizer and advocate of racial justice. A man of eloquence as well as courage (on more than one occasion, he suffered beatings for his liberal views), Dodge told an audience in 1939 that the South was isolated from the rest of the United States "by mountains of pride and rivers of prejudice and valleys of ignorance and swamps of reactionary stupidity, and every now and then washed out with floods of lawlessness."

It would take a fanciful imagination to think of the South in those dark years just before World War II as a society awakening from decades of social slumber; in fact, you could probably make a stronger case for the argument that a deep-rooted conservative reaction to Roosevelt liberalism had taken hold, and the direction of regional movement had shifted back to the right. But even so, the tiny seeds of American idealism—democracy, freedom, justice, opportunity—that had been scattered across the South for decades were still alive in the dreams of some people, and now and again they sent up little shoots of hope. However faintly the pillar institutions of Southern society seemed to show it, an atmosphere of impending change did nonetheless hover over the region in those lean years of almost imperceptible transition—years dominated by the war, but also marked by a quietly intensifying consciousness of race and class divisions.

To be as isolated as the South was in the early years of the twentieth century was to be handicapped by short rations of economic and cultural nourishment and imprisoned by an ignorance of greater possibilities beyond the magnolia curtain. But the physical separation couldn't last forever; cars and trucks appeared, and after them such marvels as paved roads, radio, talking pictures, phonograph records, washing machines, electric iceboxes, and even airplanes. With each new technological advance, the outside world drew closer. In contrast to the sacred traditions preserved by institutions such as the church and the academy, these profane innovations disrupted the established patterns of a rigidly orthodox society.

Throughout the golden years of radio, from about 1925 to the end of World War II, the South could claim barely more than a tenth of the nation's broadcasting stations (and a similar fraction of the home sets). But among the meager portion were half a dozen or so fifty-thousand-watt clear-channel stations in New Orleans, Atlanta, Nashville, Memphis, San Antonio, Richmond, and Louisville. Others in places like Cincinnati and Chicago also reached into Dixie, and together they brought news, music, entertainment, and offers of commercial products every bit as enticing as the Sears, Roebuck catalog.

The same pop tunes, classical compositions, jazz, and swing that enthralled listeners in New York and Philadelphia now rode the magical airwaves into the South—and for good measure, the folks in Dixie also got homegrown cowboy music, blues, and gospel (to be fused in the midforties into two main channels: country music, mainly for whites, and rhythm and blues, mainly for blacks). Franklin Roosevelt entered by that marvelous new sound-transmitting device, too, and his sonorous voice touched people's minds and hearts as no printed appeal ever could. Broadcasting networks tied local stations to central headquarters in New York, and from these came national news—the same for Pennsylvanians and Californians and Carolinians alike. And, at the New York World's Fair in 1939, citizens stared in wonder and amazement at an exhibit of something called television, a box with a window that showed moving pictures transmitted electronically from another place. Someday, went the spiel, you'll have one of these miracles in your own home. Yeah, sure.

Irresistibly, but ever so slightly and gradually, the South's padlocked doors and shuttered windows were easing open. Bits and pieces of the larger world were filtering in through the cracks. "Your Hit Parade" went on the radio in 1935. By then, big dance bands were touring the country— including the South—and their audiences everywhere seemed to know instinctively that "it don't mean a thing if it ain't got that swing." Racial segregation prevailed—in the North almost as strictly as in the South, or so it sometimes seemed—but the bands and their listeners cared more for the music than for social custom, and gradually they improvised ways to get around the gatekeepers.

The movies, too, brought change. Hollywood proved during the depression and confirmed again during the war how skillfully—and willingly—it could make propaganda films to support government policies. It could also blend myth into history quite effectively, as witness all those Westerns, about cowboys and Indians, and the "Southerns," about plantation colonels and docile slaves. Most movies about the South up to the mid-forties perpetuated these moonlight-and-magnolia stereotypes—but along the way, there were some notable exceptions.

The same silver screen that had presented anti-black provocations like *The Birth of a Nation* and *So Red the Rose* also featured Paul Robeson as a black colossus in *The Emperor Jones*. Claude Rains starred in *They Won't Forget*, a film indicting Deep South racism, and Humphrey Bogart played the lead in *The Black Legion*, an anti–Ku Klux Klan picture. New Orleans–born writer Lillian Hellman's play-turned-movie *The Little Foxes* represented an awakening quest for honesty in new Southern fiction; so did *In This Our Life*, a film drama with a racial theme based on Ellen Glasgow's Pulitzer Prize–winning novel by that name. Depression realism and New Deal propaganda made a potent and sometimes volatile combination, too—not just in the movies but in stage productions, on the radio, in books, and in other forms of artistic expression. The WPA Theater Project's focus on social issues, more than any other single factor, caused enraged Southern members of Congress to lead the attack that finally succeeded in killing the project in 1939.

Classical music in the thirties was barely known to the great mass of Southerners. Even its three leading black artists—tenor Roland Hayes, contralto Marian Anderson, and baritone Paul Robeson—were considered Northern (and therefore superior to Southern blacks) by their admirers. Still, they weren't spared the slights and indignities of white racism. Despite her enormous talent and a quiet dignity befitting her middle-class Philadelphia background, Anderson was barred from singing in Washington's Constitution Hall in 1939 by the Daughters of the American Revolution, who owned the building. Angered and offended, Eleanor Roosevelt resigned her membership in the DAR, and federal officials, taking her cue, promptly arranged an Easter Sunday recital for Anderson at the Lincoln Memorial. A vast and enthralled audience of all races attended the outdoor event. The symbolism of the gathering under the granite gaze of the Great Emancipator was powerfully apparent—and it would be invoked again in years to come.

Roland Hayes had long since left his boyhood in the South and finished his education at Fisk by the time he achieved international fame as a concert singer. In 1926 he went back to Gordon County in north Georgia to buy the farm where his mother had worked as a slave, and he and his family visited the property regularly for over fifteen years. But on a sojourn there in the summer of 1942, he was painfully reminded of the region's abiding hostility to blacks. In the nearby town of Rome one humid afternoon, Hayes's wife sat down to rest and cool off in front of a fan in a store where she had gone to shop. She was promptly insulted by an angry white clerk, who ordered her out. Hayes, a gentle and sweet-tempered man, came rushing in and tried to calm the situation with conciliatory words, but for his trouble he was cursed by the clerk, punched and pummeled by two town policemen, and dragged off with his wife and daughter to jail. They were finally released on bond after calmer heads intervened, and the charges were eventually dropped, but Hayes had had enough. Soon thereafter, he sold the farm and put Georgia and the backward South behind him for good.

Paul Robeson was a native of Princeton, New Jersey, and a two-time all-American in football at Rutgers University, but his father, a Presbyterian minister, had fled slavery in North Carolina as a teenager. A genuine celebrity before he turned thirty in 1928, the younger Robeson attained such stature as a stage and screen actor and concert singer that in his professional life he could usually stand aloof from racism. But the day-to-day indignity of social and economic discrimination against minorities and the poor in the United States enraged him, and he never shrank from attacking it. By the mid-1930s he was an avowed Marxist who supported Communist causes in various parts of the world, and for a time he lived in Russia.

The Soviet Union's wartime alliance with the United States shielded the actor-singer from severe criticism, and his fame grew each time he starred as the Emperor Jones or Othello, or sang "Ol' Man River" (written by Rodgers and Hammerstein with him in mind), or recited the enormously popular "Ballad for Americans," an inspirational "sermon" on brotherhood and unity written by poet John Latouche of Richmond and set to music by composer Earl Robinson. In the postwar years, Robeson would suffer greatly for being red and black and blunt—but before and after, he acted and sang and championed the rights of the disinherited with a booming voice and a biting tongue. White Southerners were aghast; even Northerners who considered themselves liberal sometimes fidgeted uneasily at the sight and sound of black militance coming from a classical and artistic genius—and a fellow Yankee at that.

Meanwhile, back in the South, it was popular music, above all the creative arts, that most expressively and impressively characterized the region at the beginning of the forties. Here was the one positive index in which the South clearly led the nation. It may have been too impoverished to produce much else of genuine excellence, but it did give birth to the three most original forms of American music—the blues, jazz, and the strains of mountain and rural music that came to be called country and Western, or just country. All three now enjoy universal prestige and appeal (having long since overcome the initial resistance of elitists, including many on the home front who at first recoiled from them with disgust and embarrassment). Most of the leading composers and performers of these musical styles in the 1930s were no more than one generation removed from the South, if at all; the fact that so many of them lived and worked outside the region was damning proof that poverty and racial discrimination had forced them to leave.

Country music wasn't exiled from the South, but it was shunned early on by many highbrow purists as crude and primitive "hillbilly" music. But when Mississippi's Jimmie Rodgers played his guitar and sang, and when the A. P. Carter family of Virginia performed, they generated an indigenous blossoming of musicians from the rural hills and valleys of the South whose recordings and radio programs would soon bring them lasting popularity. "The Grand Ole Opry," on the fifty-thousand-watt station WSM in Nashville, was their primary showcase, reaching as it did to most of the states of the union, and phonograph records also added greatly to their success. Country music was a phenomenon with the staying power to become a permanent institution in American culture.

In a parallel vein, black musicians from the Mississippi Delta and other parts of the Deep South—gifted instrumentalists and singers like Bessie Smith, Muddy Waters, Huddie Ledbetter (known as Leadbelly), Ma Rainey, Robert Johnson, Blind Lemon Jefferson (and, a little later, Josh White, B. B. King, and Mahalia Jackson)—were creating and unleashing a basic mix of gutbucket blues and hymns of faith that avid listeners could feel in their bones. W. C. Handy, the cornet-playing composer of "Memphis Blues" (originally a campaign song for E. H. "Boss" Crump) and "St. Louis Woman," earned his title as the "Father of the Blues" by starting early—in the 1890s—and staying active for sixty years.

This was not overt social protest music—that would have been suicidal—but it certainly spoke to the lowly condition of blacks in the social order, and to their endurance in those bleak times. It struck a resonant chord with black listeners—and, as the years passed, with an increasing number of whites. No major radio outlet was available to blues musicians in the early years, but they did make recordings that helped to spread their popularity.

Labor leader A. Philip Randolph

Will W. Alexander (right), receiving the 1940 Thomas Jefferson Award of the Southern Conference for Human Welfare from conference leaders Frank Porter Graham and Louise O. Charlton

When Georgia Governor Eugene Talmadge (seated, left) testified as a character witness at a 1941 clemency hearing for several Ku Klux Klansmen convicted of flogging, prosecutor Daniel Duke brandished the terrorists' lash in front of the startled governor.

Richmond Times-Dispatch *editor Virginius Dabney read part of his 1943 editorial advocating desegregation of the city's public transit system on a segment of the motion picture newsreel,* The March of Time.

Swedish social scientist Gunnar Myrdal directed the six-year study of race in the United States that was published as An American Dilemma *in 1944.*

Before and after he wrote about the South for The New Republic *and* The Nation, *Thomas Sancton was a journalist in his native New Orleans.*

Mississippi-born Richard Wright, author of Native Son *and* Black Boy

Soon after Alfred A. Knopf (left) published The Mind of the South, *he went to North Carolina for a visit with author W. J. Cash.*

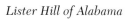
Lister Hill of Alabama

Harry F. Byrd of Virginia and his dog Arno

Some Southern Democrats in the Senate before the end of World War II:
Left: *Hattie Caraway of Arkansas*
Right: *Pat Harrison of Mississippi*
Below: *"Cotton Ed" Smith of South Carolina, voting with his wife at their polling place near Lynchburg, in rural Lee County*

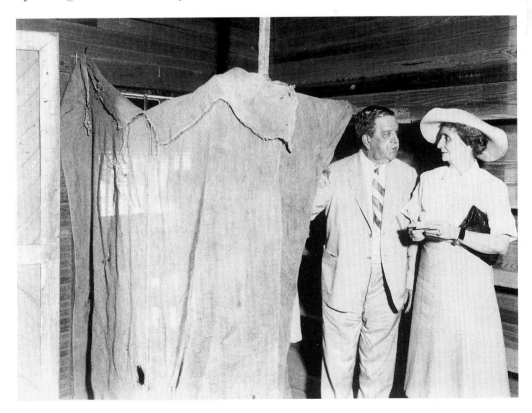

When the Daughters of the American Revolution barred famed contralto
Marian Anderson (right) from singing in their Washington auditorium,
Secretary of the Interior Harold L. Ickes (left) joined Eleanor Roosevelt in
arranging a concert at the Lincoln Memorial. Anderson sang there to a throng
of 75,000 on Easter Sunday, 1939.

With his thumb on a passage in the Bible promising justice to the poor and
afflicted, former Senator James F. Byrnes of South Carolina was sworn in as a
justice of the Supreme Court in July 1941. Witnessing the ceremony were his
wife, Senator Carter Glass of Virginia (left), and President Roosevelt (seated).

After white Democrats barred them from participating in state politics, these men and women, led by Osceola McKaine and John H. McCray (third and fourth from left, front row), formed the South Carolina Progressive Democratic Party in 1944 and sought recognition at the Democratic National Convention in Chicago. McKaine ran for the U.S. Senate that fall.

Atlanta University sociologists Ira De A. Reid (left) and W. E. B. Du Bois on Georgia Tech radio station WGST in Atlanta in 1941

Mary McLeod Bethune (center), president of the National Council of Negro Women, with novelist Lillian Smith (left) and Eleanor Roosevelt, two of sixteen women honored by the council at a February 1945 reception in Washington

President Franklin D. Roosevelt's body arrives by hearse at his funeral train, Warm Springs, Georgia, April 13, 1945.

Right after World War II, another fifty-thousand-watt Nashville station, WLAC, would introduce countless thousands of new listeners to rhythm and blues, gospel, and other variations of the soul music that black Southerners had brought to life. A quartet of white disc jockeys at the station— Gene Nobles, Bill "Hoss" Allen, "John R" (John Richbourg), and Herman Grizzard—were so adept at pitching the music, the commercials, and the jive chatter that few people were aware of their racial identity. One summer night in the early fifties, a young Georgia soul singer, James Brown, showed up at the station with his first recorded song (an old hymn, "His Eye Is on the Sparrow"), hoping to get a boost for his budding career with some airplay from the "Negro deejays."

It was also from the African-American communities of the South that jazz sprang into being, and as the 1940s began, jazz and its derivative, swing, represented the main current of popular American music. Rising on a base established in New Orleans by such early artists as Buddy Bolden, "Jelly Roll" Morton, "King" Oliver, and "Kid" Ory, the music got its modern impetus from Louis Armstrong, a twentieth-century Southern American in the most symbolic and authentic sense: born in New Orleans on the Fourth of July, 1900.

Following the river of migrants to exile in the North, Armstrong added immeasurably to the burgeoning popularity of jazz in the thirties and forties. He got plenty of help from some Northern blacks, including Count Basie, Cab Calloway, "Fats" Waller, Earl "Fatha" Hines, Art Tatum, and Lena Horne. There were whites from the North whose contributions to the music were likewise enormous—people like Artie Shaw, Benny Goodman, Glenn Miller, and the brothers Tommy and Jimmy Dorsey. Even some whites from the South were important to the movement—Harry James, Tex Beneke, Jack Teagarden, Johnny Mercer, Ray McKinley.

But it was the amazing number of black instrumentalists and vocalists from the South who helped carry jazz and swing to the pinnacle of popularity—and if you include such border jurisdictions as Maryland, Kentucky, Missouri, and the District of Columbia in the Southern orbit, the list lengthens considerably. In the same wave with Louis Armstrong came such notable artists as these, all born in the region between 1899 and 1918: Duke Ellington, Lucky Millinder, Fletcher Henderson, Coleman Hawkins, Barnie Bigard, Trummy Young, Jimmie Lunceford, "Hot Lips" Page, Jonah Jones, Jimmie Rushing, Louis Jordan, Milt Hinton, Lionel Hampton, Teddy Wilson, Erskine Hawkins, "Dizzy" Gillespie, Billie Holiday, Ella Fitzgerald, and Pearl Bailey (the last two born within a month of each other in Newport News, Virginia, in 1918).

Consider what a destructive loss this drain of talent was for the South:

scores of black musicians and other creative artists, and a substantial number of whites too, leaving in search of the simplest of pleasures—a chance to sing their songs, to play their music. Add to these the exodus of writers, scholars, and athletes, and you have a diminution of gifted contributors that even the richest of societies could ill afford.

Because the community of jazz artists cut across racial lines, there was within that community a greater effort to remove racial barriers than could be found in any other segment of society, save for a few labor unions and other ventures on the fringes. The musicians were far from solving the segregation problem, but they did at least show signs of trying. It was in 1935 that clarinetist Benny Goodman formed a jazz quartet with drummer Gene Krupa and two black musicians, Texas-born pianist Teddy Wilson and vibraphonist Lionel Hampton, a native of Louisville. And it was a black composer and arranger, Fletcher Henderson—yet another Southerner—who created most of the swinging arrangements for Goodman's big band. Later, Duke Ellington added white drummer Louie Bellson to his band, and Louis Armstrong paired his trumpet with Jack Teagarden's trombone, and Lena Horne sang with Charlie Barnet's orchestra, and Billie Holiday was the vocalist for the Artie Shaw band.

In the entire pantheon of jazz greats, Ellington towers to the sky. Born into the middle-class black culture of Washington, D.C., in 1899, he was well launched in a life of music by the time he was twenty. During most of the turbulent decade of Manhattan ferment highlighted by the Harlem Renaissance, Marcus Garvey's Universal Negro Improvement Association, Prohibition, gangster mobs, and the Wall Street crash, Ellington and his rapidly improving dance band were entertaining whites at two famous night spots: the Kentucky Club at Forty-ninth and Broadway, and the Cotton Club on the fringe of Harlem. For years to come, the Ellington band would remain among America's finest, justly renowned for such classics of swing as "Satin Doll" and "Take the A Train." "Duke plays piano, but his real instrument is that orchestra," his arranger and close friend Billy Strayhorn once said, and the man himself liked to confess that his only mistress was "Madame Jazz."

Music may have been the only thing about which Ellington was unambiguous. By turns charming and manipulative, generous and selfish, fun-loving and moodily withdrawn, he showed little outward interest in politics, religion, or social issues (including race)—and yet his musical compositions revealed how deeply he cared about the heritage of African-Americans and the mysteries of the human spirit. His defense against the racial brutality of the South was to ignore the region and refuse to go there. Finally, in 1933, when his fame had spread across the United States and abroad, Ellington agreed to play a string of engagements at theaters and dance clubs in Dallas, and for the first time in his life he ventured below the Potomac. So wildly successful were the band's segregated appearances in Texas—some for whites, some for blacks—that the suave and confident bandleader began to dream of exerting his considerable influence in behalf of black people in the South and beyond.

While critics hailed the unexcelled quality of the Ellington band but debated whether the music should be called jazz or swing—the new thing—Ellington himself called it "Negro music," and said what he was striving for was "unadulterated Negro melody" that captured "the wealthy heritage of the man of color." He took the band to New Orleans in 1934 (traveling this time in two private railroad cars that served as their hotel), and reveled in the Creole culture so celebrated for its jazz and food. And then, over the next decade, Duke Ellington composed and produced much of the music that stands now as his social statement about racial discrimination in American culture.

In 1939 the last of Thomas Dixon's twenty-two novels, *The Flaming Sword*, was published in Atlanta. He called it, with typical Dixonian hyperbole, "an authoritative record of the Conflict of Color in America." In fact, it was a doomsday screed about an attempted overthrow of the U.S. government by Communist armies of blacks, Mexicans, and other "alien forces." As if to duel Dixon with the rabid white supremacist's own choice of weapons, Ellington promptly answered by composing and recording an instrumental tour de force that he also called "The Flaming Sword" (a phrase that Dixon found, incidentally, in the writing of W. E. B. Du Bois). The book and its author faded into obscurity with the ranting dogma of Old South demagoguery, but the Duke and his music were of a higher dimension. They endured.

Within a few years, Ellington had completed such major compositions as "Black, Brown and Beige" (a fusion of jazz and classical idioms), "New World A-Coming" (borrowing the title of journalist Roi Ottley's "inside black America" book), and "Deep South Suite," a concerto that might be called a complex expression of the composer's deepest fears and hopes about race.

In 1941, while staying on the West Coast, Ellington joined with others to produce an all-black musical revue built around a satirical funeral for Uncle Tom and Jim Crow. *Jump for Joy*, as the production was called, featured Ellington and his band, a big cast headed by Dorothy Dandridge, and a wealth of great tunes and lyrics written by the Duke and more than a dozen others. The fast-paced show seemed to change night by night as new songs and skits bubbled from the minds of the creative staff. It was all hip and humorous, but hard-hitting. "I've got a passport from Georgia," went one tune, "and I'm going to the U.S.A." Another pictured Uncle Tom's cabin as a drive-in eatery at the corner of Hollywood and Vine. Critics and audiences in Los Angeles liked the show—its music, at least, if not its "social significance"—but it closed after three months and never made it to Broadway, let alone to the South. Its backers apparently decided that the theatergoing public wasn't ready for a stage production— even a lighthearted and funny one—that supported the idea of social equality for black Americans.

There are those who say that creative artists, more than philosophers and other intellectuals, are the first to discover the spirit of their age, and the first to define the future. Listen to Ellington's "Deep South Suite," or the pointed lyrics in *"Jump for Joy,"* or Paul Robeson's moving rendition of "Ballad for Americans," or Billie Holiday's haunting vocalization of "Strange Fruit," a song about lynching, and you can believe it. In these and other outpourings and lamentations from that not-too-distant time, you can hear urgent messages to a diverted and unheeding nation, pleas for attention and help.

In every culture, a wise person once observed, there are leaders and followers—and then there are scouts, the ones who go out to the frontier alone and return to warn us of the dangers and opportunities that lie ahead. Duke Ellington and all his musical companions, along with the novelists and other creative artists in this era of transition, played such a role for us. They were our scouts.

4. *Dancing in the Dark*

Newspapers in the United States have always displayed a split personality: servant and master, watchdog and fat cat, defender of the voiceless and voice of the establishment. To understand them at all, you have to take them for what they really are: an oddling hybrid of free expression and free enterprise. In their glory days before the audio-video revolution, they were virtually the sum and substance of that bedrock institution we call The Press. In smoky, ink-smudged newsrooms, as in no other arena, softhearted idealism and cynical, hard-eyed realism met like awkward partners at a nightly dance, and it was hard to watch them straining to stay in step without feeling a surge of admiration.

Southern newspapers in the Roosevelt era seemed at times to stand out in vivid exaggeration of those contrasts. More of their owners and publishers voiced support for FDR over his Republican opponents than did their fellows in the North, but that was an anomaly explainable by the fact that practically all Southerners were yellow-dog Democrats, and had been since the Republican Mr. Lincoln freed the slaves and preserved the Union. By temperament and status and force of habit, Southern publishers were privileged lords of the press as surely as were their counterparts in New York, Chicago, Los Angeles, or London. When they gathered to confer in posh resorts around the region, they talked far more about paper and ink, ad lineage and circulation, unions and profits, than they did about social issues, economic reforms, service to the reading public, or compensation for their editors and reporters (who were, along with schoolteachers, generally the poorest-paid of all professionals; before the war, even the best of them were making do on fifty dollars or so a week). The prevalent tone and substance of Southern news and editorial columns tended to reinforce and confirm, not challenge, the authority of pillar institutions such as the church, the university, the Democratic Party—and, of course, the press itself.

And yet, even among the colonels and majors of Southern journalism (some of whom actually went by those titles), the noble tradition of idealism was vigorous and pervasive. The most reactionary publishers, such as James G. Stahlman of the Nashville *Banner* and Tom Hederman, Sr., owner of two dailies in Jackson, Mississippi, shared a reverent devotion to public service with such moderately progressive owners as J. N. Heiskell of the *Arkansas Gazette* in Little Rock and the Daniels brothers, who succeeded their father, Josephus, at the helm of the Raleigh *News & Observer*. One and all, they aspired to guide and direct what Heiskell once called "a moral and intellectual institution," not just a mindless industry mechanically recording the news. Perhaps inevitably, some found their intellectual and moral duty in a paternalistic defense of social and economic privilege, while others felt their calling was to serve a much larger public. The result was a surprisingly diverse array of styles, philosophies, interests, and emphases among the papers—and workaday journalists—in the post-depression South.

If it were possible to pinpoint the forty or fifty largest papers in the region on a left-center-right spectrum in the mid-forties, chances are they would divide about evenly into three groupings. Several were generally regarded as liberal and progressive for their time and place; Richmond and Norfolk, Raleigh and Greensboro, Atlanta, and Little Rock and Greenville, Mississippi, had such papers. In some other cities—Jackson and Jacksonville, Charleston and Columbia, New Orleans and Houston—the prevailing character of daily journalism was decidedly conservative. But then there were cities such as Nashville, Chattanooga, Macon, and Dallas, where both ends of the spectrum were represented, and still others—

Birmingham, Montgomery, Memphis, Miami, Tampa, Charlotte—where competing dailies gravitated toward the center. Along the border of the South, in St. Louis, Louisville, Washington, and Baltimore, and in Charleston, West Virginia, and Wilmington, Delaware, the papers proudly claimed a progressive tradition.

In virtually all these places, the broad central avenue of moderation was far more visible than were the narrow peripheral paths of radical or reactionary expression. That is to say, the liberal papers were not as far to the left or the conservative ones as far to the right as they were to become subsequently, when the social reformation took root in the generation after the war. No Southern daily paper had spoken out against racial segregation by 1945, and it would be almost another decade before any of them did. Nevertheless, most of them generally made an effort to be fair; even the aggressively right-wing *Banner* in Nashville gave straightforward coverage to the Southern Conference for Human Welfare when it met in the Tennessee city in 1942.

The relatively moderate complexion of the mainstream Southern press remained more or less intact throughout the war years, even though changes in leadership caused some papers to slide to the right and others to slip to the left. George Fort Milton's Chattanooga *News* lost a long and bitter takeover struggle with an extremely conservative rival, the *Free Press*, in 1940, and Milton himself shortly left for a government post in Washington after trying unsuccessfully to start a new paper. He never again lived in the South, but he remained active as a journalist and historian until the early 1950s. As the years passed, his views on social issues became noticeably more conservative. Back in Chattanooga, the reactionary *News–Free Press* (guaranteed to be news-free, said its critics) still had a well-heeled adversary in the *Times* (an older but much smaller relative of *The New York Times*), which was ably edited from 1935 to 1942 by the well-traveled and prizewinning Julian L. Harris, and after that by another liberal Southerner, Alfred Mynders. The guard was changing; both Milton, who had left the region, and Harris, who remained, were out of the picture by war's end, their influence on public opinion appropriated by younger men.

Louis I. Jaffé of the Norfolk *Virginian-Pilot* was in the twilight of his career too, and Lenoir Chambers, his longtime associate and a native North Carolinian, would eventually replace him. In Richmond, Virginius Dabney ran the editorial pages of the *Times-Dispatch* with the authoritative detachment he had come to be noted for (and with an occasional hint of his diminishing liberalism), while his counterpart at the *News Leader*, Douglas Southall Freeman, looked forward to retirement after the war so he could concentrate on his real love, history. At the Montgomery *Ad-*

vertiser, Grover Hall, Sr., died and was succeeded by his son and namesake—after which, complained some of the old man's admirers, the paper
seemed to lose its liberal edge and become duller and more narrowly
provincial.

A similar tone crept into the columns of John Temple Graves II at the
Birmingham *Age-Herald.* An old-school patrician who often came across as
a moralistic and self-righteous elitist, Graves was a classic pre–New Deal
liberal who opposed the Klan, Prohibition, religious fanaticism, and racial
intolerance (all of which he blamed on the lower class of whites), but who
also believed the only way the South would change was glacially and of its
own free will. By 1943, when he wrote a book called *The Fighting South*,
he was so put out with FDR and Eleanor and social reformers and "pushy"
Negroes and Northern leftists that he sounded for all the world like a
latter-day apologist for the Old South.

Two years later, while still insisting that he was a progressive, Graves
drew a racial line in the sand with this declaration: "The will of the
Southern white against racial amalgamation is total. For that he is willing to filibuster, fight, play foul or fair, risk another Civil War. Right or
wrong, the South is not going to have race segregation destroyed."
(Graves's father, as editor of the Atlanta *Georgian*, had contributed to
the outbreak of that city's worst race riot in 1906 by expressing the same
sentiments in a more inflammatory tone.) Such rancor and belligerence
made the *Age-Herald* seem more extreme than its sister paper, the
News, whose widely respected general manager was James E. Chappell.
The rival Birmingham *Post*, of the Scripps-Howard chain, also tried to
avoid an extremist image.

In Louisville, the *Courier-Journal* was rapidly gaining a reputation as
the South's most liberal newspaper—and probably its finest. Owner-
editor Barry Bingham and publisher Mark Ethridge won praise for a
high standard of news reporting and editorial commentary; they were
also deeply involved in a wide range of cooperative ventures for Southern improvement. The Nashville *Tennessean*, under its publisher Silliman Evans, and the St. Petersburg *Times*, with Nelson Poynter in
command, were two more dailies allied with the national (read liberal)
Democrats. Coleman A. Harwell, the *Tennessean*'s executive editor, and
Jennings Perry, who ran its editorial page, were typical of a great many
Southern editors who wielded considerable clout but kept a low public
profile (Perry, however, did take his fight against the poll tax into larger
arenas). Editor William R. "Pop" Smith of the Macon *News* was touted
around the region as a "fighting liberal," and Edgar Ray, editor of the
Tampa *Times*, was active in the highest ranks of the National Urban
League.

The Charlotte *News* had an impressive staff of young editors and reporters and a reputation for scrappiness in the late 1930s—and that was before W. J. Cash gave them all a taste of the limelight with the publication of his celebrated book, *The Mind of the South*. After Cash's early, tragic death in 1941, several alumni of the Charlotte paper went on to prominence. Two of them, Harry S. Ashmore and C. A. "Pete" McKnight, would serve brief stints as editor of the *News* on their way up.

All in all, Southern journalists compared favorably with the nation's best in the years when depression at home and conflict abroad were the main preoccupations of Americans everywhere. It wasn't just the big-city editors who acquitted themselves well, either. Numerous small-town dailies and black newspapers made important contributions; female editors and writers were at least as conspicuous and productive as women journalists in other parts of the country; and Southerners white and black who left the region to write for national publications often did exceedingly well.

Some random examples: In the heart of the Deep South, enlightened and responsible journalism was generated by such editors and publishers as Harry M. Ayers of the Anniston (Alabama) *Star*, O. E. Jones of the Batesville (Arkansas) *Guard*, George McLean of the Tupelo (Mississippi) *Journal*, M. R. Ashworth of the Columbus (Georgia) *Ledger-Enquirer*, and John M. O'Dowd of the Florence (South Carolina) *Morning News*. These and other papers were consistently and courageously bringing hard news and progressive editorials to their small-city readers at a time when the news was often bad and candid comment reflected poorly on state and local leadership.

The region's black papers—all weeklies except for C. A. Scott's Atlanta *Daily World*—generally had a small advertising base and limited circulation, but their readers looked to them as the only substantial source of news and opinion from or for the minority community, and the best of the papers delivered the goods impressively. The Norfolk *Journal & Guide*, published by P. B. Young, was known and respected in Virginia and beyond. Prominent among Young's fellow editors and publishers were Carter Wesley, who put out the Houston *Informer* and other papers; John H. McCray of the *Lighthouse & Informer* in Columbia, South Carolina; Frank L. Stanley of the Louisville *Defender;* Roscoe Dunjee of the *Black Dispatch* in Oklahoma City; and L. C. and Daisy Bates, publishers of the *Arkansas State Press* in Little Rock.

White critics who dismissed the black press as radical and irresponsible or marginal and inferior failed to recognize the extent to which it gave voice to the African-American's unquenchable thirst for the same rights and privileges enjoyed by other citizens. In their newspapers and in numerous national magazine articles, black writers hammered away repeatedly and insistently on the same theme: We want a role—in combat, in the workplace, in the national scheme of things. But too many whites, South and North—even the most well-intentioned—could only counsel polite patience.

Long before the exalted *New York Times* got around to hiring women across the board in news and editorial positions, people like Nell Battle Lewis of the Raleigh *News & Observer*, Margaret Dixon of the Baton Rouge *Morning Advocate*, Willie Snow Ethridge of the *Courier-Journal* in Louisville, Nellie Kenyon of the Nashville *Tennessean*, and Katherine Grantham Rogers of the Charlotte *News* had made names for themselves as true competitors in the male-dominated world of daily journalism. Other women felt they had to leave the South to write. Helen Fuller of Birmingham, having worked as a lawyer in the New Deal and on the staff of the Southern Conference for Human Welfare, opened a Washington bureau for *The New Republic* in the early 1940s and later became the magazine's managing editor.

Many aspiring black journalists departed too. Ted Poston got out of Hopkinsville, Kentucky, in the mid-1920s and put together a career that embraced the Harlem Renaissance, the New Deal, and a pioneering thirty-five-year reportorial tenure with the New York *Post*. Others who later found inspiration in his example and took up journalism in the North included Louis E. Lomax of Georgia, Carl Rowan of Tennessee, and Lerone Bennett, Jr., of Mississippi. Among the numerous young white men to follow similar stars were John Fischer, a Texan who became editor of *Harper's* magazine; William Bradford Huie of Alabama, who for a decade during and after the war was a writer and then editor and publisher of the *American Mercury* (once the barbed spear of H. L. Mencken); and Thomas Sancton of New Orleans, who preceded Helen Fuller as managing editor of *The New Republic*.

Of all the nationally known and respected Southern journalists of the thirties and forties, probably none had more visibility and influence than Richmond editor Virginius Dabney and three others: Ralph McGill of the Atlanta *Constitution*, Hodding Carter of the *Delta Democrat-Times* in Greenville, Mississippi, and Jonathan Daniels of the Raleigh *News & Observer*. These four, all Southern-born between 1898 and 1907, stood symbolically astride the two centuries—and, subsequently, on the bridge between Old South and New, between the painful past and a hopeful future. They approached the prime of their lives and the pinnacle of their profession with a prolific and continuing output of daily columns, national magazine articles, books, speeches, and radio commentaries. Whenever the quartet of editors wrote or spoke about the South, their words were as closely followed and as carefully listened to as those of any other public figures of the time.

Certainly there was a need for perceptive spokesmen. One of the most disturbing consequences of World War II was that it spawned in the South and across the nation the most precipitous deterioration in race relations since the bloody Red Summer of 1919. In some ways, the sudden intensity of the problems seemed worse in the North than in the South, but there was more than enough strife, sorrow, and hostility to go around.

The Southern journalists struggled to understand it all. Before the war started, most white progressives in the region saw themselves as liberals within the context of the prevailing "separate but equal" philosophy. But segregation had consistently failed to bring about any semblance of an equal distribution of resources and opportunities, and in the midst of a global war with heavy racial overtones (even John Temple Graves called Hitler "the greatest race-baiter in history, the Jim Crow of all the ages"), it was harder and harder for blacks to justify risking life and limb in such a fight when Jim Crow and race-baiting were still the daily reality at home. Under the circumstances, it appeared that the old style of Southern liberalism could no longer be sustained; it would be necessary henceforth for thinkers and opinion leaders to begin turning in the direction of greater equality or risk being left behind to hold the old fort with the defenders of white supremacy.

As the center eroded, Virginius Dabney inched cautiously to the right. He had been the first of his generation to extol the virtues of Southern liberalism, enshrining the philosophy in his 1932 book. In those days he was a genteel Menckenite, a mild-mannered iconoclast; now, a decade later, in a new book called *Below the Potomac*, he sounded some of the old themes again but seemed a bit more reserved in his liberalism, a bit more defensive of the South. Thinking about race, Dabney repeated his call for tolerance and fairness, but added what was for him a specific new emphasis: the need to maintain equal but completely separate education for whites and blacks, from preschool to postgraduate study.

John Stewart Bryan had bought the *Times-Dispatch* in 1940, reuniting it and the afternoon *News Leader* under his family's banner, as they had been earlier in the century. Both the previous owner and Bryan had given Dabney complete freedom to shape the editorial policy of the *Times-Dispatch*, but he felt threatened when a new general manager, John D.

Wise, a rigid conservative, was brought in during the war. As John Bryan's health failed and the family awaited a postwar succession to his son, Tennant Bryan, Wise became the de facto publisher and Dabney's cross to bear.

In 1942 the *Times-Dispatch* took the lead in a national campaign for leniency in a racially tinged Virginia murder case. The paper argued editorially that a death sentence against a black sharecropper, Odell Waller, convicted on circumstantial evidence of killing a white man, should be commuted to life. Later that year, Dabney endorsed an effort by a group of highly respected Southern black leaders to address the need for improved race relations in the region, and he then joined with a corresponding group of white moderates to find common cause with the black messengers.

But in between those conciliatory gestures, the Richmond editor took a much more negative and visible stance with an article in the January 1943 *Atlantic Monthly* called "Nearer and Nearer the Precipice." In it he described what he saw as two opposing camps of irresponsible extremists, one Northern and black (A. Philip Randolph, the NAACP, "the radical colored press"), the other Southern and white (Governor Eugene Talmadge, Congressman John Rankin, the specter of the Ku Klux Klan), and blamed them both for "stirring up interracial hate" and "pushing this country closer and closer to . . . the worst internal clashes since Reconstruction."

Dismissing the "white rabble-rousers" as contemptible figures, Dabney concentrated on the "Negro agitators" who were "demanding an overnight revolution in race relations" based on "absolute political and social equality." If blacks made an all-or-nothing assault on legal segregation of the races, he wrote, "the white leaders in the South who have been responsible for so much of the steady progress of the Negro . . . will be driven into the opposition camp." Segregation, he suggested, was a defensible policy, even for liberals; further, the white South couldn't be pressured into giving it up, and federal authorities would not order its abandonment. Reforms in this sphere, Dabney concluded, "cannot be forced by executive fiat but are the fruit of gradual evolutionary development." Separate facilities must be made completely equal, he allowed, "but if an attempt is made forcibly to abolish segregation throughout the South, violence and bloodshed will result."

Dabney thus spelled out his position on segregation in unmistakable terms, and even his most appreciative black acquaintances took exception. P. B. Young, the Norfolk publisher, bluntly compared the message to that of Rankin, Talmadge, and Bilbo, the only difference being that "their language is always coarse and their attitude brutal, while your language is always cultured and your attitude dignified." Stung by such criticism, Dabney made one more public attempt to demonstrate his goodwill. In November 1943, he offered the editorial suggestion—with John Wise's consent—that Richmond and the state of Virginia repeal their laws mandating segregation in public transportation. Jim Crow rules on buses and trains were cumbersome, and totally separate conveyances were an obvious impossibility; here, Dabney felt, was an area where a dramatic act of charity by whites would win the respect and confidence of blacks, and perhaps lead in time to further concessions.

Surprisingly, letters from readers, most of them written by whites, ran about two to one in favor of Dabney's proposal, but local and state officials shunned the idea, and almost no other white newspapers in the South endorsed it (though the NAACP and others did, warmly). The *Times-Dispatch* itself lost enthusiasm for the idea after John Bryan died in 1944 and John Wise solidified his power. Virginius Dabney had tried to stake out a little patch of middle ground from which charitable whites like him could maintain control of the pace and character of social change—but now, he feared, extremists on the right had made it clear that only hostility and conflict would come of any further desegregation initiatives, and radicals on the left had shown that they would not be satisfied with separate-but-equal remedies. With what could only have been an ambivalent feeling of regret and relief, Dabney quietly retreated to safer ground. He had hurled his last lance for the cause of liberalism.

Ralph McGill was less of a patrician than Dabney, and more a man of colorful words and action, but he too showed signs of writhing under the thumb of a more conservative publisher. Clark Howell, Jr., had made him an editorial-page columnist and editor of the *Constitution* in 1938 and then editor-in-chief in 1942, with full authority for the paper's stated positions on issues. From that highly visible perch (his signed column appeared seven days a week on the editorial page), McGill quickly established an emotional bond with the people of the South, and it held through good times and bad for more than twenty-five years. His was not an evangelistic crusade, said his biographer, fellow journalist Harold H. Martin, but "a dialogue . . . directed at the great massed millions of southerners in the middle." Looking back from the perspective of the seventies, Martin described McGill as "a man of good and decent instincts and stubborn courage speaking with the voice of reason in a violent time."

For all his eventual courage, McGill was slow to come to his crucible on the race issue. Even in the late 1940s he was not above citing his publisher's reactionary nature as an excuse for his own lack of enthusiasm for social activism, much as Virginius Dabney was inclined to throw it off on John Wise. Sometimes McGill declared publicly that the South's segregationist policies were a fact of life with which he basically agreed. His racial views were ambiguous, changeable, inconsistent; he showed a genuine affection for and empathy with individuals of the most diverse sort, but he could also lapse into stereotyping rigidity in his comments about amorphous groups—blacks, Communists, Republicans, liberals.

McGill was a self-described moderate, not a liberal; in truth, he held views in the thirties and forties that differed little from those of Dabney and numerous other Southerners of liberal or progressive persuasion (the terms remain frustratingly imprecise and ambiguous). He was an avid New Dealer, a war hawk, a combative anti-Nazi, anti-Communist, anti-Klan adversary. He fought lynching and the poll tax aggressively, but did not favor federal solutions to state and regional problems. He was cool to the Southern labor movement (except for Miss Lucy Mason, whom he greatly admired), hostile to the NAACP and the Southern Conference for Human Welfare, and wary of Northern prescriptions for social reform. He was Gene Talmadge's nemesis and Ellis Arnall's confidant and counselor. He was unabashedly sentimental, even chauvinistic, about the South and its people, white and black, and he was a generous friend and mentor to dozens of idealistic young Southerners of both races.

What set Ralph McGill apart from Virginius Dabney and so many other homegrown white liberals, especially as war turned to peace and racial discrimination moved to the forefront of regional and national consciousness, was simply that McGill somehow managed over time to change his mind, alter his views, and grow into a fuller understanding of what democracy and social justice meant, and what they required of him. A passionate man with a heavy bag of conflicting emotions, he was by turns brooding, humorous, ebullient, angry, engaging, protective, nurturing, pugnacious. He was close to the heart and soul of the common folk, having come up among them, and when he saw his opportunity, as editor of the *Constitution,* to influence them, to help them change and to change with them, he seized it, took it seriously, made the most of it. It didn't happen suddenly, in the twinkling of an eye, but it did finally happen. Somewhere along the way, Ralph McGill took to heart an old adage: If you're not part of the solution, you're part of the problem.

Much the same thing apparently happened to Hodding Carter, Jr. He could have settled quietly into the somnolent Mississippi Delta subculture of Greenville, where he had gone at the invitation of William Alexander Percy and others in 1936 to start a new paper. But at the tender age of twenty-nine, he was already a veteran of the Huey Long wars in Louisiana, and like many others of his generation, he idealized the image of the journalist as crusading public defender. From the first he was an avid FDR enthusiast, and he crossed swords with Theodore Bilbo early and James

Eastland later on. But Greenville and rural Mississippi were by no means as tolerant as urban Atlanta, and Carter, even though he owned his paper, doubtless had no more secure confidence in speaking freely than did Ralph McGill or Virginius Dabney, who so often claimed to see their publishers' shadows falling over them.

In any case, Hodding Carter, always ably assisted by Betty Werlein Carter, his wife and editorial associate, made his way through the late thirties and the war years by being a progressive Democrat, a home-standing publisher concentrating on local and state issues, an advocate of tolerance and fair play for the plain people, white and black, and a silent assenter to the governing social and economic realities of segregation and white supremacy. It was his personal lack of attraction to, or sympathy with, left-wing causes, more than his fear of hometown reprisals, that kept him away from the Southern Conference for Human Welfare. Even so, he wrote early and often for such national publications as *The Nation*, *The New Republic*, *The Saturday Evening Post*, and the magazine of the *New York Times*, not so much defending the South with all its many faults as simply trying to explain the root causes and to prod self-righteous Yankees and self-doubting Rebels alike to move forward. For his pains, the Greenville editor, a careful moderate, was often dismissed by smug Northerners as a phony liberal (as were Dabney, McGill, Daniels, and other editors), while at home he was branded a reckless radical—and by Mississippi standards, he probably was.

While he was away in military service, Carter tried his hand at fiction, and in 1944 a New York publisher brought out his *Winds of Fear*, a novel of racial "hate and suspicion and intolerance" in a mythical but all-too-real town somewhere in the South. In the book's dramatic climax, a young white man faced down a lynch mob. Later, "at the recollection, his spirits rose again; at least he had confronted the Thing, and the Thing had been for the moment beaten. If you stood against the Thing, people would eventually listen."

Hodding Carter was just beginning to define the Thing that loomed in the South's path when he wrote those words midway through the war. Like McGill, it would take him a while to decide when and where to stand—but in due time he would be Mississippi's leading white advocate of social change.

Jonathan Daniels had a longer and more eventful preparation for the postwar drama. Born in Raleigh and brought up for part of his teenage years in Washington, where his father worked with FDR in the Woodrow Wilson administration, young Jonathan earned two degrees at the University of North Carolina, passed the bar, wrote a novel, went to Europe on a Guggenheim fellowship, married twice (his first wife died), wrote for *Fortune* magazine, and was Washington correspondent for the *News &*

Observer before taking over as editor of the paper in 1933, when he was just thirty-one years old.

Having waltzed through the early twenties in a mildly experimental flirtation with the radical left (perhaps in rebellion against his straitlaced and conservative father), he settled into a moderating ten-year editorial stint at the paper with his brothers, Frank and Josephus, Jr., running the news and business departments. (The elder Josephus, meanwhile, had returned to government service as a New Deal diplomat.)

Like so many other Southern editors of his time, Jonathan Daniels was a prolific writer—for his paper, for magazines, for the book trade. In the summer of 1937 he traversed the region to gather material for *A Southerner Discovers the South*, published in New York the following year. In it and all his other writing in the thirties, he spoke with much the same ambivalent voice as did his moderate-to-liberal colleagues in the press, particularly with regard to the constantly nettlesome issue of race. The contradictions of the culture were mirrored in his own vacillating shifts from narrow paternalism to occasional flashes of genuinely democratic and egalitarian conviction.

When the war started, Daniels turned the paper back to his father and went to Washington for three years, part of which he spent serving FDR as an administrative assistant and adviser on race relations; he was the White House press secretary when the President died in April 1945. Standing so close to the center of power, he gained many valuable experiences in those years—with the Roosevelts, with Will Alexander and other Southern whites in the administration, and with black public officials such as Robert C. Weaver and Mary McLeod Bethune, as well as Ted Poston, who worked for a time in his office. Jonathan Daniels was not entirely liberated from the old Southern habits of segregation when he went home to Raleigh in 1945, but he was comfortable with diversity, and he certainly knew that momentous changes were bearing down urgently upon the South. He must have known, too, that when the crunch finally came, the only real choice open to him would be to leave the segs and take a lonely stand on the other side.

In December 1944, thirty-three Southern editors and writers met in Atlanta to open a discussion aimed at increasing participation in the electoral process by simplifying voter registration, opening primary elections to blacks (as the Supreme Court had recently decreed in a case from Texas), and eliminating the poll tax. The objectives were remarkable in themselves, standing as they did in direct opposition to the prevailing dogma of the white political leadership, but the makeup of the group of eventual signees was even more astonishing. Chaired by Mark Ethridge of the *Courier-Journal*, this self-styled Committee of Editors and Writers of the South deliberately included representation from the left, right, and center, among whom were at least ten women and ten blacks. Editors of large and small newspapers, publishers of magazines and journals, independent and academic writers, and even a few expatriate Southerners working in the North made up the list.

Ted Dealey, the conservative publisher of the Dallas *Morning News*, signed on with the likes of Frank Porter Graham, Lillian Smith, Charles S. Johnson, H. C. Nixon, P. B. Young, Clark Foreman, James Dombrowski, and Helen Fuller. The names of Dabney and Daniels headed the big-city editors, along with Louis I. Jaffé, Jennings Perry, Nelson Poynter, and C. A. Scott. The published report, called "Voting Restrictions in the Thirteen Southern States," was signed by a total of sixty-two people—all in all, an impressive representation of the best-known liberals and moderates with Southern ties. (Missing, though, were the names of McGill and Carter, Howard Odum and Francis Pickens Miller, John Temple Graves and George Fort Milton, W. E. B. Du Bois and Walter White.)

Calling themselves "a completely independent committee unaffiliated with any other group" (though the suggestion for such a body had come from the Southern Conference for Human Welfare), the signers declared that "editors and writers have more than the usual obligation to understand and expound correctly the social forces which govern us." Their well-documented report showed that fewer than half as many potential voters in the South as in the other states of the nation had participated in the 1944 presidential election. In the eight states that still required payment of a poll tax, fewer than one in five adults had voted.

There was significance in the fact that a nonpartisan assembly of articulate Southerners had recognized and publicly identified a principal cause of their region's chronic and crippling disadvantage in national life. In essence, this was their declaration: A handful of undemocratically chosen white men control the political machinery, the economic wealth, and the social structure of the South; all the others—the women, the blacks and other minorities, the white men with little or no money or property or education—are thereby deprived, in greater or lesser degree, of their constitutional right to take part in the democratic process.

In calling for these restrictions to be lifted, the editors and writers were not endorsing any particular prescriptions for social improvement—but they were, most emphatically, making a public declaration of opposition to the status quo. As individuals, some of them had spoken out before—but as a diverse and representative group from across the region, they were flying a novel flag in Southern journalism; whether it signaled cooperation or rebellion, hope or desperation, victory or surrender, no one knew for sure.

In any case, though, it was not a banner that stayed aloft for long. Like farmers, writers are difficult to harness—too individualistic and independent and stubborn to sit comfortably in choirs. Still, their valiant attempt to harmonize on a new song of the South is worth recalling, if only because—like the Southern Conference for Human Welfare—it put so many known and respected citizens on record as recognizing the problem, if not the solution. That they were not able to go beyond this initial step toward reform of the electoral system is not so much an indication of their weakness as a measure of the power of political reaction in the South of the mid-forties.

The evolving thoughts and opinions and convictions of the South's leading newspaper editors in those years of transition are still accessible to us, thanks to their books and the books that others have written about them. McGill and Carter, Dabney and Daniels, Graves and Milton, Ethridge, and others who came on the scene in the twenties and thirties have been read and reread for clues to the enduring enigma of recent Southern history. Not so well known—but in some ways more enlightening—were the journalists who wrote for the South's monthly and quarterly periodicals, or for Northern magazines that had a continuing interest in Southern subjects.

Small circulation and avid readership characterized such established journals of the South as the *Virginia Quarterly Review, Social Forces*, the *South Atlantic Quarterly*, and others. (Another of more recent vintage was the *Southern Review*, edited at Louisiana State University by Robert Penn Warren and Cleanth Brooks.) As the depression ended and the war began, some new publications appeared with more of an emphasis on social activism. *Phylon*, a quarterly "journal of race and culture" edited by W. E. B. Du Bois at Atlanta University, was launched in 1940; the *Southern Patriot*, a tabloid published by the Southern Conference for Human Welfare, first appeared in 1942; *South Today* (formerly the *North Georgia Review*), published and edited by Lillian Smith and Paula Snelling from their home base near the mountain village of Clayton, Georgia, began a ten-year run in the mid-1930s. Someone, it seemed, was always launching a new regional publication with a name like *Southern Packet* or *Southern Visions*.

Jim Dombrowski left the Highlander Folk School in 1942 to take over staff leadership of the SCHW (which had by then relocated from Birmingham to Nashville), and one of his principal duties was to serve as editor of the *Southern Patriot*. The periodical attempted to play down its organizational identity, emphasizing instead an all-out effort to win the war against fascism and prepare for postwar justice and equality at home. *Phylon* (Greek for "race") showed early strengths in the guiding hands of Du Bois, with sociologist Ira De A. Reid as managing editor and three Harvard- and Chicago-trained social scientists—Horace Mann Bond, Rayford W. Logan, and Allison Davis—as contributing editors. The first issue featured an excerpt from *Sharecroppers All*, a forthcoming book by Reid and Arthur F. Raper depicting the besieged South as a threadbare tenant hoeing cotton on the nation's back forty. "From race and attendant class demarcations stem the South's economic feudalism, one-party system, white primary, and poll taxes," they wrote. "The result has been the disinheritance and disenfranchisement of nearly all Negroes, a majority of the whites, and of the region itself in national affairs."

Lillian Smith had spent the decade of the thirties experimenting with fiction and learning the hard lessons of small-time magazine publishing— all the while running a mountain camp for affluent white girls—when her views on race began to crystallize following a trip to Brazil and two years of study as a Rosenwald Fellow. A middle-class Florida merchant's daughter, she had trained briefly to be a teacher, then a pianist; for three years in the early 1920s, she had taught in a Methodist mission school in China. Along the way, from a diversity of experiences outside the Southern monolith, she acquired a deep empathy for exploited people.

At the end of 1942, Lillian Smith and Paula Snelling renamed their seven-year-old magazine *South Today*, and Smith marked the occasion with an open letter "Addressed to Intelligent White Southerners," enumerating "things to be done . . . NOW . . . for racial democracy." (Heading the list: "break the taboo of silence . . . the taboo of action . . . take an open stand . . . to bring non-segregation quickly and harmoniously" into being throughout the South.) It was a significant declaration; for the first time, a white Southerner living and working in the South had come out forcefully in public print in favor of abolishing the Jim Crow laws and other racially discriminatory practices.

Northern magazines often were not much further along in their racial views than those in the South. The *American Mercury*, edited by Lawrence E. Spivak, frequently published articles and stories by both whites and blacks from the South, among them Zora Neale Hurston, Saunders Redding, Virginius Dabney, and Gerald W. Johnson—but in the early 1950s the magazine would turn sharply to the right, with William F. Buckley and J. B. Matthews leading a feverish anticommunist attack. *The Saturday Evening Post* generally took a conservative view of Southern life—more so than, say, *Collier's* or *The Atlantic Monthly* or *Harper's*. *Time* and *Life* and *Fortune*, the flashy magazines of Henry Luce, tended to look down upon the South with a mixture of pity and disdain; *Newsweek* did the same.

The most liberal of the Northern magazines were also the smallest: *The Nation*, the *Progressive*, *Survey Graphic* (for which twenty-three-year-old North Carolina native George C. Stoney produced a detailed and critical series of articles on the poll tax and other Southern voting problems in 1940). Another was *Common Ground*, a journal of interracial and international opinion published quarterly in New York beginning in 1940. Pearl Buck, the West Virginia–born novelist and winner of the 1938 Nobel Prize for literature (and a dedicated advocate of racial equality), was one of the principal figures behind the magazine; another was social critic and South-watcher Langston Hughes, the black poet and playwright.

And then there was *The New Republic*. Its reporting and commentary in the forties didn't differ much from that of *The Nation* and other journals, except in this respect: Two Southerners, Thomas Sancton and Helen Fuller, served as managing editor through much of this time—and Sancton in particular was an outspoken integrationist in the same spirit as Lillian Smith.

A native of New Orleans, Sancton had worked for papers there and in New York, as well as for the Associated Press, prior to winning a Nieman fellowship to Harvard in 1941. He joined *The New Republic* as a staff writer the following year, and soon became its managing editor—a job he kept for only a year before returning to live and work in the South. In his brief tenure with the magazine, he wrote with skill and feeling—and uncommon insight—about race relations in America. Sancton had a knack for crafting arrestingly descriptive passages such as this one: "A Harlem tenement is a hundred delta cabins, plus tuberculosis." Once, discussing a novel with a racial theme, he made this observation:

. . . the Negro is going to take a new status in American fiction, as he has in life. Serious white writers in increasing numbers will enter Richard Wright's field of protest. The Negro's own fight for political and social equality is forcing this change in literature. In white men's books he is going to stop being a "nigger" . . . and become a person. . . . Negroes are people. They suffer just as intensely as white people; they get just as hungry. What has happened to them is a vast, cruel story. The South was built by their toil and suffering. So were Northern fortunes. So were English cotton-textile cities like Liverpool and Manchester. The Southerners must start to tell it right.

A war is being fought all around the globe, by many nations and all races, to determine whether people are going to be free to be people, not more, not less. . . . Before this war, our writers, even our artists, could indulge themselves—and the rest of us "ofays"—in the luxury of telling fables about Negroes; but now they must begin to tell it straight.

5. *Speaking Their Minds*

Strange as it seems, the war years were a time of extraordinary ferment in literature. Even as Southerners and other Americans at home and abroad were preoccupied with the global conflict, more than a score of notable nonfiction books about the South and almost as many works of fiction came to public notice. From John Steinbeck's Oklahoma dust bowl drama, *The Grapes of Wrath*, in 1939, to Richard Wright's autobiographical *Black Boy*, in 1945, the books poured forth in rapid succession. Steinbeck's novel and the popular movie that followed captured the universality of the tenant farmer/sharecropper's plight, while the novelistic memoir by Wright was praised by one Northern critic as an "honest, dreadful, heartbreaking story of a Negro childhood and youth" in the South. Like the Mississippi-born author's 1940 novel, *Native Son*, *Black Boy* became a national best-seller.

The fictional torch that had been carried since the 1920s by a handful of resident Southerners (Ellen Glasgow, James Branch Cabell, Julia Peterkin, T. S. Stribling, and others) was gradually being passed to the next generation. In Mississippi, William Faulkner was still turning out novels (*Go Down, Moses* appeared in 1942, and several more would follow, adding to his fame); Erskine Caldwell continued to write Southern fiction (but nothing memorable) from exile in the North; and death brought Thomas Wolfe's career to an early end (though more of his writing would still be published). All the while, new writers kept appearing out of the Southern landscape, and their books—so often developed around themes of spiritual and intellectual isolation, of decadence and loneliness and loss of faith—were further evidence that the new wave of realism had taken hold.

Pale Horse, Pale Rider brought literary acclaim to Katherine Anne Porter, a Texan; Carson McCullers was only twenty-three and a small-town resident of Georgia when she wrote *The Heart Is a Lonely Hunter* in 1940; Allen Tate, the Agrarian *enfant terrible*, won respect for his novel, *The Fathers*, and his friend and colleague Robert Penn Warren was about to burst forth as a major American writer. Two more Kentuckians who had studied writing at Vanderbilt, Jesse Stuart and James Still, displayed contrasting styles—Stuart with *Taps for Private Tussie* and a host of other books of romanticized idealism, and Still with *River of Earth*, foremost in his much smaller but more resonant body of realistic fiction. When Eudora Welty wrote *The Robber Bridegroom* in 1942, she had already found the Mississippi themes and subjects that would dominate her entire career.

Theatrical drama from two writers with strong New Orleans ties also attracted attention. *The Little Foxes*, by Lillian Hellman, was staged in 1941, and Tennessee Williams wrote *The Glass Menagerie* three years later. (Both plays were made into movies.) Like others who passed through before them (Sherwood Anderson, William Faulkner, Katherine Anne Porter), Hellman and Williams eventually found New Orleans inhospitable to the literary spirit, and left for friendlier quarters in the North. William Bradford Huie, the young Alabama writer, made a similar exit soon after *Mud on the Stars*, his novel set at the University of Alabama, was published in 1941. Huie eventually returned to live and write in the South, as did Margaret Walker, a young black writer with Alabama and Louisiana roots. William Attaway, son of a black Mississippi doctor exiled to Chicago, built his 1941 novel, *Blood on the Forge*, around the lives of black and white migrant Southerners working in the Illinois steel mills.

Lillian Smith, an unconventional Southern white woman if ever there was one, published *South Today* until 1944, when her novel, *Strange Fruit*, propelled her into the center of public debate on the race issue in the South and the nation. An explosive drama about a secret love affair between a white man and a black woman in a small south Georgia town, the book leaped to the head of the best-seller list, topping 140,000 copies in two months. It was barred from the U.S. mail, banned in Boston, and panned over most of the South. It knocked over all the traces—race, sex, language, ideology. Some Communists, and even some blacks, including Walter White, took offense at the novel (although White's daughter Jane played the female lead opposite Mel Ferrer when *Strange Fruit* opened on Broadway in November 1945).

At the age of forty-seven, Lillian Smith awoke to the realization that her novel had made her a conspicuous advocate of racial justice and equality. For almost a decade, she and Paula Snelling had been working quietly for those objectives—producing their magazine, writing for other publications, even hosting biracial social gatherings at their north Georgia mountain home. Now, suddenly, she was listened to, quoted, talked about—she was influential—and calmly, without missing a beat, she went on declaring publicly what she had been saying all along to her invited guests, most of them Southern men and women, white and black: Segregation is "cultural schizophrenia," it is "spiritual lynching," it is "unendurable to the human spirit."

Strange Fruit—by which Smith meant all Americans who were products of the culture of segregation—was a phrase used earlier by lyricist Lewis Allan and vocalist Billie Holiday as the chilling symbol of a lynch victim hanging in a tree. The Allan-Holiday image prevailed, not only because of the song but because the dramatic climax of the book also focused on a lynching. *Strange Fruit* was to be Smith's only major work of fiction, but not her only book; later in the forties, in a personal, almost confessional analysis of segregation's crippling effects, she would contribute to the literature of the South one of its most memorable and enduring works, *Killers of the Dream.*

Numerous other imaginative volumes appeared in the war years, adding to the South's luster as a fertile spawning ground of novelists, poets, and playwrights. The reputation would continue to grow into the fifties and beyond, in curious and paradoxical contrast to the continuing scourge of ignorance and illiteracy in the region. Even as Faulkner and his trailing file of compatriot scribes drew widespread praise and admiration from critics, the South continued to languish in the backwaters of intellectual stagnation. It still had the poorest schools, the fewest and least-equipped libraries, the fewest readers of magazines and books, the fewest publishers, the fewest bookstores. Glancing about the South in, say, 1940, you might well have concluded that there would be precious few literary oases anywhere in the region, were it not for the presence of a vital strand of bookstores (many of them owned by Jewish families: Mills and Zibart in Nashville, Gottlieb in Birmingham, Zimmerman and Liebschutz in Louisville). Atlanta's largest outlet for new books was in Rich's Department Store (also Jewish-owned); at the opposite extreme in terms of size and setting was the cluttered and cozy Intimate Bookshop in Chapel Hill. Though they were largely isolated from one another, the enterprises glowed like a string of lanterns in the Southern darkness.

Nonfiction from the South—or about it—was likewise impressively rich and voluminous in the forties. The journalists—Dabney, Daniels, Carter, Graves, Milton—were productive as usual. Joining them was Ben Robertson, a New York *Herald-Tribune* writer and native South Carolinian, who wrote *Red Hills and Cotton* in 1942 (and died soon thereafter in a plane crash over the Atlantic). In New York, James Agee finished his later-to-be-acclaimed *Let Us Now Praise Famous Men,* and Roi Ottley, a reporter for the *Amsterdam News,* wrote perceptively of life inside black America in *New World A-Coming.* A rising generation of historians that included Bell I. Wiley, Thomas D. Clark, C. Vann Woodward, and John Hope Franklin—sons, respectively, of Tennessee, Mississippi, Arkansas, and Oklahoma—took the first tentative steps toward realism and revision in chronicling the Southern past.

From Greenville in the Mississippi Delta came *Lanterns on the Levee*, a nostalgic defense of Old South values by the quintessential planter-aristocrat William Alexander Percy. A shy, gentle, benevolent patrician, the Harvard-educated lawyer-poet showed why his friend Hodding Carter characterized him as "a soft touch for every sharecropper and tenant farmer down on his luck." Percy's prose was all grace and charm; it's hard to imagine anyone putting a kinder face on a planter's noblesse-oblige regard for his dependent workers ("like a man for his dog," said one reviewer). He was no bigot; in 1931 he went to a black church in Greenville to give a gracious introduction to visiting poet Langston Hughes, and over the years the two men stayed in friendly contact. But even in 1941, when *Lanterns on the Levee* appeared, it seemed curiously anachronistic, an old-fashioned brief for upper-class supremacy and privilege. Lillian Smith dismissed it as "a tasteless expression of white arrogance," and even Virginius Dabney regarded Percy as an outmoded paternalist. More significant than his book was the kindly gentleman's personal commitment to raise and nurture three of his young cousins whose father had committed suicide. One of the boys, Walker Percy, would later be acclaimed as a distinguished American novelist.

Howard Odum, Charles S. Johnson, H. C. Nixon, Arthur Raper, and Ira Reid—familiar names to university scholars by this time—kept up their prolific pace. In *Sharecroppers All*, Raper and Reid concluded that the South was "handicapped less by the sharecroppers than by the heritage of the plantation system, less by outside opposition than by inside complacency, less by the presence of the Negro than by the white man's attitude toward him, less by the spectre of class uprisings and Negro domination than by the fear of them. . . . The South's bogeys! What have they made us do to ourselves?" Two years earlier, another white-black team of scholars, economist George S. Mitchell and sociologist Horace Cayton, produced a revealing study of race and organized labor called *Black Workers and the New Unions*.

The war, far from stemming the flow of new books of social inquiry, seemed almost to quicken it. Odum wrote one of his better books, *Race and Rumors of Race*, an up-to-date analysis of heightening wartime tensions between whites and blacks. Georgia-born social scientist Katharine Du Pre Lumpkin produced *The South in Progress* in 1940. Two years later, in *No Day of Triumph*, J. Saunders Redding of Hampton Institute in Virginia vividly reported his impressions from a journey through the Southern states. In 1944, Edwin R. Embree, the Rosenwald Fund executive, profiled some of black America's leading figures in *13 Against the*

Odds. Autobiographies by Langston Hughes (*The Big Sea*) in 1940 and Zora Neale Hurston (*Dust Tracks on a Road*) in 1942 provided further evidence of the productivity of black writers in this period.

The acerbic and irreverent Hurston wrote in a highly original and direct style that made her readers laugh and squirm all at once. She condemned race and class prejudice as "scourges of humanity," and praised "the richer gift of individualism." Earlier, she had poked good-natured fun at the leaders of the Harlem Renaissance (the "Niggerati") and at urbane blacks like James Weldon Johnson, who had tried hard but without success, she said, "to pass for colored." As for those who were considered "race spokesmen," said Hurston, "Anyone who purports to plead for 'what the Negro wants' is a liar and knows it. Negroes want a variety of things, and many of them diametrically opposed." Asserting that "race pride is a luxury I cannot afford," she dismissed racial solidarity as a destructive goal for blacks as well as whites—and impossible besides, in a country with as much ethnic diversity as the United States.

No black writers—and not all that many whites—were more highly regarded in this time between the depression and the war than W. E. B. Du Bois, whose autobiographical *Dusk of Dawn* appeared in 1940, and Richard Wright, who caused a sensation in the literary world with *Native Son* that same year. Du Bois, seventy-two years old and still in his prime, was turning out essays, articles, and books with the acumen and energy of someone half his age; Wright, as it happened, was *less* than half his age— only thirty-two—but his fame after *Native Son* was almost instantaneous, proving once again the dominance of popular fiction over scholarship.

Dusk of Dawn was widely reviewed and praised in the Northern press but virtually ignored in the South, even though Du Bois was by then six years into his second long stint on the faculty of Atlanta University. As always, his egotism illuminated the pages, but some critics thought they detected signs of a mellowing in his assessment of old adversaries. He seemed more objective in his handling of Walter White and the NAACP, more accepting of FDR and the New Deal, more critical of the Communist Party, and more resigned to the inevitability of continuing segregation in the South. In fact, it was his call for a black strategy of "deliberate and purposeful segregation for economic defense" that kept him at odds with the NAACP and gave a controversial tone to his book.

No matter what you might have thought of his pronouncements or his personality, you could not have been a fair-minded person and fail to appreciate and admire W. E. B. Du Bois for his longevity, his assertiveness, his intellect, and his devotion to the cause of equality for disadvantaged minorities. In a career that had spanned almost half a century by 1940 (and would continue, incredibly, for twenty-three years more), he had pounded away relentlessly at the evils of discrimination based on color, caste, and class. He was the preeminent black scholar of the twentieth century—"the founding father of the black intelligentsia," as Arthur Spingarn of the NAACP called him—and on top of it all, he was an incisive and compelling writer, as *Dusk of Dawn* clearly showed. Dozens of younger scholars, as well as some contemporaries (of whom few remained), looked to him for advice and counsel; he was their fountainhead of scholarship and activism.

He was also a prickly burr under many a saddle. His old friend and colleague John Hope had lured him back South in 1934 to head the sociology department at Atlanta University, but Hope died two years later, and Rufus E. Clement, his successor as president, had a much harder time accommodating Du Bois. By 1944, Clement and his board had had all they wanted of the abrasive and cantankerous scholar, and he was retired involuntarily. Turning away offers from Fisk and Howard, Du Bois accepted another call from the NAACP to serve as "director of special research." If they intended to use the old warhorse as window dressing, they miscalculated; he was nobody's mannequin—not then, not ever—and his reunion with Walter White and the association's leadership was destined to be short and stormy.

Richard Wright's education in the hot fields of Mississippi and the mean streets of Chicago and New York gave searing intensity and a ring of truth to *Native Son*, his starkly realistic 1940 novel about the violent life and death of Bigger Thomas, a Mississippi manchild trapped in a Windy City slum. This is what racism and bigotry do to the human spirit, Wright was saying dramatically, and the message resonated throughout the North (though Southern critics, once again, hardly took notice). The enormous success of the book threw new light on Wright's past—his migration from the South, his apprenticeship in the Federal Writers' Project, his former job with the Communist *Daily Worker*, his membership in the American Communist Party. Now, for the first time, he had the attention of a large number of whites, and like no novelist before him, he let them know in blunt language just how devastating racial discrimination was.

Over the next few years, Wright was often in the news. He left the Communist Party, disillusioned by its failure to offer a realistic alternative to American blacks; he was married, divorced, and married again, both times to European women; he gradually became alienated from the black literati and their liberal, elite, upper-class camp followers, black and white. On a few occasions he went again into the South, once to visit his mother and brother in Mississippi (and ride a Jim Crow coach back to Chicago), another time with Orson Welles to the University of North Carolina, where they worked with Paul Green on a stage play of *Native*

Son (eventually to become staged on Broadway). By the time his next book, *Black Boy*, came out in 1945, Wright was widely perceived as an angry, troubled young man, a brooding genius tormented by personal problems. He would shortly move to France and spend most of the remaining fifteen years of his life in exile from America, searching in vain for a harbor of peace and contentment free of racial bias.

If Richard Wright felt alienated from all of America, imagine how profoundly estranged he must have felt from Mississippi and the South. And yet, even as he railed against the evils of white supremacy—an inescapable burden wherever he went—he seemed at times to sense that an unbreakable bond of history encircled all Southerners. "The differences between black folk and white folk are not blood or color, and the ties that bind us are deeper than those that separate us," he wrote in 1941—and in a further word addressed to white listeners he added, "Look at us and you will know yourselves, for *we* are *you*, looking back at you from the dark mirror of our lives." And, in the concluding passage of *Black Boy*, he recalled his thoughts as he left Memphis for Chicago in 1927:

> I was not leaving the South to forget the South, but so that someday I might understand it, might come to know what its rigors had done to me, to its children. . . . So, in leaving, I was taking a part of the South to transplant in alien soil, to see if it could grow differently. . . . And if that miracle ever happened, then I would know that there was yet hope in that southern swamp of despair and violence, that light could emerge even out of the blackest of southern night. I would know that the South too could overcome its fear, its hate, its cowardice, its heritage of guilt and blood, its burden of anxiety and compulsive cruelty.

Even the most well-intentioned Southern whites found it altogether too easy to dismiss Du Bois and Wright as radical extremists. It was bad enough that the two writers were favorably inclined toward the Marxist-Communist philosophy (an acceptable stance for liberals as long as the United States was allied with the Soviet Union against Hitler). But then they had the temerity, the audacity, to lash out at discrimination in words that echoed anger and hostility! To disapproving whites—the vast majority, no doubt—there was something rude and disrespectful, or worse, about such behavior; it was simply too jarring, too unsettling, too unappreciative. They compared it to the boorish extremism of the Bilbos, Rankins, and Talmadges. No solution to racial problems would ever come from the extremes, they said; it would only be found closer to the center, among moderates of goodwill.

The same judgments were applied to numerous other prominent black figures of the forties, from Langston Hughes and Walter White to A. Philip Randolph and Paul Robeson. It was not their race, the white critics insisted; it was their militance, or their ideology, or their Northernness. In point of fact, none of these six black spokesmen—Du Bois and Wright, Hughes and White, Randolph and Robeson—could be called Southern in the present tense (though three of them were born there), and most if not all of them had flirted with or embraced the philosophy of communism at some time, and all were certainly as hostile to the laws and mores of white supremacy as anyone in America. Little wonder that most of the South's white liberals shied away from them.

If they were too extreme, then, who would the liberals find more acceptable? Edwin Embree may have been trying to address that question when he selected his subjects for 13 *Against the Odds*. He included all six of the militants, plus seven more unmistakably moderate to conservative men and women: Mary McLeod Bethune, Charles S. Johnson, George Washington Carver, Marian Anderson, Mordecai Johnson, composer William Grant Still, and boxing champion Joe Louis. (It's hard to see how anyone could have disliked Louis. The humble and benevolent Brown Bomber, a citizen of Chambers County, Alabama, by way of Detroit City, was the pride of all black Americans and many whites, and had been since that magic night at Yankee Stadium in June 1937, when he crunched an Aryan citizen of Nazi Germany, Max Schmeling, to win the world heavyweight crown.)

But the questions remained: Who, if anyone, could speak with authority for the more than thirteen million African-American citizens of the United States, and in particular for the ten million who lived in the South? Who could be their advocate, commanding their respect and that of the whites who claimed that the South would, of its own free will, do right by its citizens of color? And who could say exactly what changes needed to be made?

In the atmosphere of heightened racial tensions that marked the war years in the United States, such questions were heard frequently, and many people attempted to respond to them. Langston Hughes, in a 1941 issue of *Common Ground*, supplied seven explicit answers in an essay titled "What the Negro Wants." (His list: a chance to earn a decent living; equal educational opportunity and an end to segregation in public schools; decent housing; full participation in government; a fair deal before the law; public courtesy; and open access to public accommodations and conveyances.)

Guy B. Johnson, one of Howard Odum's colleagues in sociology at the University of North Carolina, showed the article to William T. Couch, director of the UNC Press, with a suggestion: Why not get a dozen or so prominent blacks of liberal, moderate, and conservative persuasion to write essays on Hughes's theme, and commission Rayford W. Logan, the Howard University historian, to compile them in a book that would sharpen the debate on racial questions? Couch was attracted to the idea. Like numerous other early liberals who held to the belief that segregation was a fixed condition in Southern society, he thought the proper objective of social reform was to make separate truly equal—and, further, that responsible Southern blacks shared that goal. But the foremost black spokesmen were calling for deeper and more far-reaching reforms, and Couch concluded that the best way to counter them was with more restrained and conservative arguments by other blacks. In the spring of 1943 he proposed the book to Logan, who quickly accepted the assignment. They signed a contract for *What the Negro Wants*, and tentatively agreed to aim for publication in the spring of 1944.

The early 1940s had not been kind to W. T. Couch. Tiptoeing past forty, he was no longer the cocky, self-confident boy wonder who had taken the university press by storm back in 1927. Gone was his dashing, daring style of radical activism; he was more cautious and tentative now, more alarmist, more erratic. In 1938 he had plunged into the Southern Conference for Human Welfare with boundless enthusiasm; two years later, Frank Porter Graham had to plead with him to get him to the conference at all. Once there, he lost a shouting match over an irrelevant foreign policy resolution on fascism and communism—and suffered further indignity when a pro-Communist delegate shoved him down in a struggle for the microphone. Shaken and outraged, Couch resigned and went home. Events were not turning out as he had hoped and expected. The radical initiative he had once proudly joined was being torn apart, pulled to the right by Nazi Fascists and to the left by Communists and Socialists—and somehow the race issue seemed hopelessly tangled up in all that. Couch lapsed into self-delusion; he let himself believe that Rayford Logan would somehow steer a course back to a pragmatic accommodation with Jim Crow.

By the end of May 1943, Logan and Couch had reached agreement on a prospective list of thirteen essayists that included Du Bois, Wright, Hughes, Randoph, and White, all identified as being "extreme left" or "left of center," and five academics (F. D. Patterson of Tuskegee, Gordon B. Hancock of Virginia Union, Charles S. Johnson of Fisk, Charles H. Wesley of Wilberforce, and Leslie P. Hill of Cheyney), all classified as "extreme right" or "right of center." Some declined and others were substituted. In the end, fourteen writers ranging from Du Bois and Hughes at one extreme to Patterson and Hancock at the other were formally invited to declare what they thought "the Negro wanted."

When the manuscripts arrived, Couch was almost speechless with shock. One after another, without a single exception, the essayists declared that black Americans wanted the same constitutional guarantees that white Americans took for granted. Like proud soldiers they marched in, counting cadence: "First-Class Citizenship" (Logan); "Full Equality" (Roy Wilkins of the NAACP); "Certain Inalienable Rights" (Mary McLeod Bethune); "Full Participation in the American Democracy" (F. D. Patterson). Du Bois spelled it out as "full economic, political, and social equality with [all other] American citizens, in thought, expression and action, with no discrimination based on race or color." The heart of the matter, declared journalist George S. Schuyler, was "the Caucasian problem." One and all, from the radical left to the conservative right, they called for an end to segregation.

Desperately, Couch looked for an exit. Might Logan want to find another home for these essays? No, thanks, said Logan. The publisher pressed harder, but the editor, citing their contract, hinted that he might sue if it was breached. Finally, Couch opted to write his own "publisher's introduction" for the front of the book, hoping to soften its abolitionist tone.

He would have been wiser to stand back in silence. In fifteen rambling pages of aggressive self-defense laced with rhetorical questions and didactic answers, he managed to lash himself to the mast of segregation and white supremacy, characterizing it not as a social force too powerful to subdue but as a biological fact that ought to be accepted as right and realistic for the foreseeable future. Gratuitously, Couch denounced the recently published and widely acclaimed study of race relations, *An American Dilemma*, as a misguided and harmful distortion of such concepts as equality, freedom, and democracy. Recalling wistfully the subservient acceptance of segregation advocated by Booker T. Washington a half-century earlier, Couch concluded that a rebirth of the Tuskegee founder's ideas was what the South sorely needed now.

It was a sad postscript to the distinguished publishing record of W. T. Couch at the University of North Carolina. Within a year he would be gone to Chicago and another university press directorship. In his wake, Southerners white and black could find, if they cared to look, a singular catalog of social and cultural literature, culminating with *What the Negro Wants*, that vividly chronicled the struggle of black Americans for their constitutional rights and foreshadowed the demise of legalized segregation. Ironically, the man who was most responsible for that catalog now appeared to repudiate it.

And he was not alone. Virginius Dabney, Mark Ethridge, and John Temple Graves were just a few of the many notable Southern whites who applauded Couch's smug assertion of Anglo-Saxon superiority and purity, and the natural inferiority of Africans. Rayford Logan and his essayists and the other black critics who joined the debate were contemptuous of the self-evident contradictions. "They are NOT Southern Liberals," Arna Bontemps said of Couch and the others in a letter to Langston Hughes. "They are old-line Southerners . . . educated men who must somehow justify their way of life if they are to keep their own self-respect." Couch, Bontemps concluded, "is not really a seeker after truth."

Perhaps it was fear or envy, as much as anything else, that drove Couch to attack *An American Dilemma;* ostensibly it was an academic treatise on the state of black-white relations in this country, but its friends and foes alike quickly perceived it as a smoking package of social dynamite. The book was a monumental collaborative work of investigative scholarship organized in the late 1930s by Gunnar Myrdal, a widely respected Swedish social economist, and published in the spring of 1944. The Carnegie Corporation, a New York philanthropy long engaged in programs of social improvement, funded the entire project. The foundation's leaders had wanted "a comprehensive study of the Negro in the United States, to be undertaken in a wholly objective and dispassionate way as a social phenomenon." Myrdal, forty years old at the time, was chosen to direct the effort precisely because of his distance from—and lack of preconceived notions about—America's racial problems.

He got his first look at the South in the fall of 1938 when he and two companions spent two months driving through the region. They attended political rallies (it was the season of FDR's abortive purge attempt), took part in the Southern Conference for Human Welfare in Birmingham, heard firsthand reports of lynchings and other atrocities, stared at the ugly face of racism and poverty and class exploitation. Back in New York, Myrdal told Carnegie officials he was "horrified" by the magnitude of the problems and the enormity of the task he had before him.

The perceptive and engaging Swede made a show of seeking advice from such senior scholars as Du Bois and Odum, but he was careful not to get too close to them. Instead, he hired their protégés as his associates (Ira Reid and Guy Johnson, to name just two). All in all, the research team of more than a hundred scholars, consultants, and assistants was liberally laced with blacks (including Ralph Bunche, Charles S. Johnson, E. Franklin Frazier, Sterling Brown, and Horace Cayton) and Southern whites (Arthur Raper, Thomas Woofter, George Stoney, Guion Johnson—Guy Johnson's wife—Clark Foreman, George Mitchell, and others).

The sheer magnitude and scope of *An American Dilemma,* the pertinence of its subject matter, and the timing of its appearance near the end of the war were more than enough to assure its rapid elevation to the status of a classic. It may have been bought and quoted far more than it was read and studied, but one way or another, its meaning and import worked their way into the nation's consciousness. Four salient features characterized the voluminous work: the torrent of facts documenting the depth and breadth of white racism; the misinformed belief of whites as a race in the innate inferiority of blacks as a race; the existence of an egalitarian American creed that stood in contrast to these facts and beliefs; and finally, consequently, the moral dilemma of how to reconcile the inequitable and discriminatory realities of our behavior with the ideals on which the nation was founded. Pointedly, Myrdal emphasized again and again that the dilemma was not just Southern but American.

This was in no sense a conventional academic research project, and Myrdal was not your garden-variety social scientist (in fact, he criticized members of the fraternity for deceptively concealing their value judgments behind a façade of objectivity). Comfortably set up in that most coveted of roles—the outsider—Myrdal could do whatever his head and his heart suggested, regardless of the consequences. With virtually unlimited support from Carnegie and with his staff and consultants always at hand to help, he was free to look at the evidence, listen to the arguments, form his own opinions, and speak his mind. This he did, with enthusiasm and candor. Half a century later, some of his conclusions were still being debated, but the solid bedrock of fundamental veracity—unlike Couch's rationalized assertions—would be unshaken by time. Myrdal qualified as "a seeker after truth."

He liked the United States—its ideals, its customs, its people, its diversity. He described its creed as an informal mix of hallowed beliefs gleaned from the Declaration of Independence, the Constitution and Bill of Rights, the tenets of Christianity, and the popular culture. This was, people agreed, the land of the free, the home of the brave, the cradle of liberty; here you were entitled to freedom of speech and religion and the press, and words like *justice, equality, tolerance,* and *democracy* had meaning for everyone. The creed, the common body of beliefs, was the glue that bonded the polyglot nation together and made it utterly unique among the nations of the world.

In stark contradiction to these American icons, as Myrdal saw it, were some harsh and sobering truths: A pathological condition of daily desperation marked the lives of most blacks, South and North. Their needs were vast—for jobs, housing, health care, education, the vote, protection of the laws, and an end to Jim Crow segregation and discrimination, a "flagrantly illegal" and disastrous state of affairs. White Southerners deluded them-

selves in thinking that Negroes were more or less content with segregation, happy with their lot; worse, many whites confidently thought that
they, and only they, understood the black mentality and offered to the
darker legions more friendship and protection than anyone else. Myrdal
called such thinking the "convenience of ignorance" that allowed grievous
injustices to flourish.

There was more: Southerners white and black were obsessed with the
race question, Myrdal declared. White preachments about racial purity
belied the fact that seventy percent of all African-Americans had at least
some traces of white ancestry—a consequence of white sexual aggression.
Environment, not heredity, accounted for most differences between
whites and blacks. Whites in the North blamed Southerners for racial
discrimination, but the North was hardly any better, and in time would
face problems just as serious as those that plagued the South. Blacks would
find no salvation in black separatism, in voluntarily segregated institutions
such as churches and schools, or in racial chauvinism. The great hope for
America in the future was not revolution or the status quo but a responsible middle road to change, to integration and equality.

These were breathtaking pronouncements, deserving of far more comment and criticism than they received. Beyond calling *An American Dilemma* "thorough and exhaustive," Virginius Dabney offered little or no
assessment of it. Even at that, he outdid Ralph McGill, Jonathan
Daniels, Mark Ethridge, and most other Southern editors, who greeted
it with silence. Howard Odum, reviewing the book in *Social Forces*,
found fault with Myrdal for his optimism in believing the American
creed would prevail over injustice, and for his failure to offer more concrete recommendations. Rupert B. Vance, an Odum colleague at North
Carolina, acknowledged in the *Virginia Quarterly Review* that "what the
Negro wants is integration in our national culture," and he further declared that "the social myth that dies the hardest death in the mind of
the South is the myth of the Negro as a happy and satisfied race." He
registered surprise, though, that Myrdal had "no course of social action
to present" other than the vague suggestion that "things have to be settled by political means."

Black critics, on the other hand, were highly complimentary of Myrdal's
work. The comments of Du Bois were representative of most others. He
called the book "a monumental and unrivaled study."

The South would take little notice of Gunnar Myrdal and *An American
Dilemma* until a decade later, when the school integration issue he had so
clearly foreseen finally penetrated the national consciousness. Like many
other books before it, from James Weldon Johnson's *Negro Americans,
What Now?* in 1934 to *What the Negro Wants* a decade later, the Myrdal

volume was a long-range forecast of what lay ahead for blacks and whites in the motherland of life, liberty, and the pursuit of happiness.

One more classic book of visions was birthed in the early forties, and no account of Southern social history would be passably complete without some consideration of it. The author was a little-known North Carolina journalist named Wilbur Joseph Cash—"W. J." or "Jack" or "Sleepy" to his family and friends. The book, published in 1941, was *The Mind of the South.*

Whole I opened *The Mind of the South* for the first time, the book was almost two decades old and Jack Cash had been dead for nearly that long. The year was 1960. At the age of twenty-five, I was confined against my will in a hospital room in Tampa, Florida, having landed there for an extended stay after an automobile accident. I had plenty of time to read and reflect, to think about what I was missing outside. On a little black-and-white television set, I watched John F. Kennedy and Lyndon B. Johnson recapture the White House for the Democratic Party; a few weeks later, in his inaugural address, Kennedy would stir inside me (and millions of others) a deep sense of hope and expectation, a desire to *do* for my country. So much cried out to be done. In my homeland, my native South, the black minority was summoning the courage to challenge white supremacy with nonviolence, and the white majority was lashing back violently against adults trying to vote, college students at lunch counters, even little children at school and church.

The impact of Cash's book on me was about the same as if someone had rolled a hand grenade under my bed. In the very first pages, his voice seized my attention: ". . . the South is another land . . . there are many Souths . . . there is also one South . . . far from being modernized, in many ways it has actually always marched away, as to this day it continues to do, from the present toward the past. . . ." *The Mind of the South* echoed in my own mind like Jefferson's proverbial fire bell in the night. As a comatose person might emerge from deep unconsciousness, I slowly began to hear and see and understand. Cash's biographer Bruce Clayton said it well: "No one who reads Wilbur Joseph Cash is ever quite the same again."

Strange that a book of such perception and power should have come from the typewriter of a man like W. J. Cash. A giant in the minds of many who have read his book, he was actually an unimposing fellow who cut an unheroic, unromantic figure. Picture him in about 1938, before his book and his marriage gave him a brief period of happiness: He wore the melancholy expression of a misfit, a shy, withdrawn, moodily petulant bookworm with sad eyes blinking behind owlish, steel-rimmed glasses. Not yet forty, he was a rumpled bachelor lacking in style and social grace; he had lost his youthful slenderness and was losing his hair. He was a neurotic, a hypochondriac, a sickly man given to chronic bouts of depression, a lonely, tortured soul trapped between binding convention and a liberating imagination. One of seven children born to a fundamentalist yeoman couple in a Carolina mill village, he had somehow become an agnostic city dweller who drank and smoked too much, an intellectual without an academic base, an eccentric journalist yearning to write novels. For almost a decade he had been working on a big-idea book of Southern social analysis, but most of the time his friends on the staff of the Charlotte *News*—and he himself—seriously doubted that he would ever finish.

The Mind of the South was recognized early by H. L. Mencken as a potential book buried in Cash's disordered but penetrating thoughts (this after the young Carolina journalist had sold a freelance article by that title to Mencken's *American Mercury* in 1929). The Baltimore editor attracted Alfred and Blanche Knopf to Cash and his idea as a project for their New York publishing house, and for almost twelve years the Knopfs patiently endeavored to coax the book from him. The wait was certainly worth it. What they got was not journalism or scholarship or history, but a many-layered dissection and anatomy of the Southern white male rendered in a brilliantly original, provocative, judgmental, and disarmingly personal narrative to which even its few panning critics (Donald Davidson most conspicuously) conceded certain undeniable virtues.

The book was not perfect. It was more about the Carolina piedmont than about the South writ large; its analyses of women and blacks revealed Cash's lack of close association with both; it could have benefited from a little more documentation—some hard data, some citations, some notes—and at the very least, it needed a bibliography. Sometimes the Cashian flights of rhetorical verbalizing were like Roman candles, a triumph of style over substance.

But forget all that. W. J. Cash evoked the South as few writers before him had done. Drawing from a full bag of literary devices—first- and second- and third-person perspectives, monologue and soliloquy, satire and irony, dialogue and description, detachment and engagement—he could turn a phrase, paint a picture, spin a yarn. He had an organized sense of where he was going with his argument, and he knew how to keep it moving. Above all, he had a point of view; he made independent observations, passed judgment, came to conclusions. Like Myrdal's *Dilemma* and the nonfiction works of Du Bois and other writers, Cash's *Mind* had a moral dimension. Myrdal, with all his credentials and an army of aides, had made his pronouncements from the distant safety of New York and

Stockholm; in contrast, Sleepy Cash was just an ordinary guy standing alone in the heart of darkness, saying things about his beloved and benighted Southland that made his own countrymen wince—and then nod in reluctant agreement and even admiration.

It was the white masses that populated lynch mobs, he said, but it was the upper classes that inspired and protected them, and the failure of this "better sort" was the genesis of the South's undoing, its original sin. The Old South planters, the textile barons, the politicians and bankers and cotton brokers who controlled the region and kept it in feudal backwardness were not really aristocrats but erstwhile dirt farmers just a step or two up from the frontier. The New South was really the Old South in spruced-up garb. The white ruling elite created the illusion of a class-free society by uniting all whites in dominion over the blacks—and the lowly whites, out of a misguided sense of gratitude and superiority, were willing to fight and die for a social system in which they had no real stake. Cash saw through the Rebel-rousing Old South myth perpetuated in literature and history; he saw the hand of the state and the church and the academy in it too, and Yankee acquiescence, if not outright chicanery. In Cash's essentially tragic view of Southern history, the common mindset of the white South conformed to a "savage ideal" that bonded most of its citizens to a narrow interpretation of the past, the present, and the future. And there he left it:

> Proud, brave, honorable by its lights, courteous, personally generous, loyal, swift to act, often too swift, but signally effective, sometimes terrible in its action—such was the South at its best. And such at its best it remains today, despite the great falling away in some of its virtues. Violence, intolerance, aversion and suspicion toward new ideas, an incapacity for analysis, an inclination to act from feeling rather than from thought, an exaggerated individualism and a too narrow concept of social responsibility, attachment to fictions and false values, above all too great attachment to racial values and a tendency to justify cruelty and injustice in the name of those values, sentimentality and a lack of realism—these have been its characteristic vices in the past. And, despite changes for the better, they remain its characteristic vices today.

His friends in Charlotte loved Jack Cash, and out of a sense of loyalty if nothing else, they also loved his book. They were delighted when he married a vivacious divorcee, Mary Northrop, in December 1940, just two months before *The Mind of the South* was published. The friends were proud, too, and even their doleful colleague managed to smile, when strongly positive and favorable reviews of the book began to pour in from

around the South and from the national press. They could not have foreseen, of course, that it would become the best-known and most influential
book of nonfiction ever written about the South, never to be out of print
in the first fifty years of its existence. All they knew was that it was
important and good and true, and that was enough for them.

His friends could not have known, either, that Cash's time was short,
but some of them were aware that he was pursued by his own private
demons, driven at times to hand-wringing depression and anxiety. He
received a Guggenheim fellowship, and in June, he and Mary went to
Mexico, where he hoped to begin work on a novel. Within three weeks he
was an emotional wreck—paranoid, delusional, certain that Nazi agents
were pursuing him. His pleading wife finally got him to see a psychiatrist,
but there was no relief. With everything to live for, with so much to give,
W. J. Cash could only hear the demons. In a Mexico City hotel room on
July 1, 1941, he hanged himself with his own necktie.

There was a certain Southern poignance, a familial quality, to what
happened after that. After Mary phoned Pete McKnight back at the *News*
in Charlotte to get the tragic word to Jack's parents and his other family
and friends, she was left, alone and afraid, in the custody of the Mexico
City police. Hours later, the American embassy sent a driver to police
headquarters to pick her up and bring her to shelter, on orders of the
U.S. ambassador to Mexico. It was more than an impersonal act of courtesy; it was what you would expect from an old Southern gentleman, a
North Carolina patrician: seventy-nine-year-old Ambassador Josephus
Daniels of Raleigh.

In good time, Cash's ashes were given a proper Baptist burial in the
Sunset Cemetery at Shelby, North Carolina, a short walk from the home
of his parents and a stone's throw from the spot where another Carolinian
of note, the novelist Thomas Dixon, the propagandist of romantic racism,
would soon be laid to rest.

Death, like politics, makes strange bedfellows.

6. *The Fire This Time*

The smoldering hostility of white toward black and black toward white
finally burst into deadly flames on the sultry night of June 20, 1943.
Against a backdrop of stifling, overcrowded urban tenements echoing with
the verbal thunder of radio preachers shouting race hatred, white mobs of
Kluxers and other Nazi-like aggressors clashed with street-toughened

black men and boys determined to defend their tenuous escape hatch from the cotton fields. The police force, virtually all white and largely native Southern, gave almost no protection to the migrant blacks; on the contrary, patrolmen were seen and photographed assisting in the racial assault. When order was finally restored several days later, thirty-four people were dead, hundreds injured, thousands arrested; the cost of the riot was estimated in the millions of dollars.

Was this New Orleans, Birmingham, Atlanta? Responsible Southerners had been fearing for years that just such a disaster would eventually befall them. But the dubious distinction was not theirs to endure. Instead, this worst outbreak of urban racial violence in almost a quarter of a century was visited upon Detroit, Michigan, far north of the Mason-Dixon line and deep in the heart of the mythical Promised Land.

Within a matter of a few weeks during that sweltering summer, bands of lawless citizens in a blind rage blew the lid off America's racial powder keg. At army camps from North Carolina and Georgia to Mississippi and Texas, and from New Jersey to Washington State, clashes between whites and blacks left more soldiers dead than either race dared to admit. In places as widely separated as Philadelphia and Beaumont (Texas), Mobile and Newark, Los Angeles and Harlem, deadly rioting spread like a virus. Even as the Allied forces were liberating Italy from the Fascists and driving Japanese soldiers from the islands of the South Pacific, thousands of our own people here at home were escalating racial friction to the level of a domestic catastrophe, a senseless and devastating civil war in the city streets.

Of all the racial clashes in the United States that year (more than 240, by some counts), the most destructive and frightening by far was the murderous rage that swept through Detroit, the nation's fourth largest city. Three years of warnings had fallen on deaf ears. The automobile plants, converted to war production and running round the clock, were hotbeds of competitive racial friction; public and private housing units, symbolized by packed and fetid trailer camps, were a scandal; demagogic evangelists, including Huey Long's old accomplice Gerald L. K. Smith and the fascistic Father Charles Coughlin, fomented violence so skillfully and so relentlessly that some people wondered aloud whose Axis payroll they were on. Reporters and government officials described the riot as "a frenzy of homicidal mania, without rhyme or reason," and predicted that in the future, the nation would "face its biggest crisis all over the North." Wrote Thomas Sancton, the Louisiana-born *New Republic* staffer, "The United States never needed more gravely than it does today a strong and intelligent federal policy on the race issue." It had none.

Almost as disturbing as the riots themselves was the ominous prospect

of still meaner times to come. People who remembered the bloody summer of 1919 as a postwar eruption feared that the same impulses were
raging out of control again, well before World War II was over. The
domestic landscape seemed infinitely more dangerous than before; attitudes of Southern white bigotry had migrated north with the workers (or
emerged from the latent fears of Northern whites), and blacks, for their
part, seemed no longer willing to abide discrimination without resisting.
Vicious rumors of black uprisings and insurrection plots sped through
white communities North and South (the most pervasive and absurd of
these had the President's wife secretly organizing "Eleanor clubs" among
black servants to disrupt the tranquillity of white households). In numerous cases, it was unfounded rumors of some outrage or another, not anything that actually happened, that sparked the 1943 disorders.

But whether their origins were real or imagined, the clashes themselves
were too costly and too lethal to be ignored. In the midst of its prosecution
of a world war on two fronts across the globe, America was compelled to
hear a painful warning that many of its own citizens were on the verge of
war with one another. After Detroit, anyone who was watching and listening could have seen that our social, political, and economic problems
at home were tearing at the national fabric, demanding attention.

From a Southern perspective, the catalog of pressing problems was long
and confusing. So much was changing, and so much needed to change.
The future presented a daunting challenge—and if that suggested a coming time of opportunity to some, it loomed as a time of great uncertainty
and peril for the vast majority. Southerners had never been thrilled by the
prospect of sudden change; they were conditioned to approach it warily,
if at all. But now change was everywhere around them, crackling in the air
and rumbling beneath their feet. The last two years of the war, from the
riotous summer of 1943 to the A-bomb summer of 1945, were filled with
traumatic events, with momentous unions and divisions.

To begin with, there was the war itself, with all its emotional and
conflicting elements of triumph and sacrifice. Among other things, it
ended the worst economic depression in American history—and also set
the stage for massive readjustments in postwar employment. The near-
total eclipse of the New Deal social agenda also came in this period,
simultaneously and paradoxically with the fourth election of Franklin
Roosevelt to the White House. Here began the rise of Harry Truman, too,
and the fall of Henry Wallace—or rather his conversion from Vice President to Secretary of Commerce, after which he would mount a third-party
challenge against Truman in 1948.

The mid-forties were an active time for splinter groups in American
politics—Communists and Socialists on the left, countered by right-wing

sects that got their inspiration from the Nazi and Fascist movements. In the broad mainstream, the Democratic Party revealed a deepening split along North-South lines over civil rights and other social issues, while Republicans had their own liberal-conservative differences to grapple with.

The labor movement tried to concentrate on its age-old conflict with management, but the unions were weakened by warring factions within their own ranks. That same divisive tendency plagued other groups that, like the unions, could ill afford internal strife—African-Americans, for example, and Southern white liberals. The black divisions ran in several directions: between accommodation and self-determination, between conservatives and radicals, between Southern and Northern leadership. To confuse matters further, conservative blacks were aligned with Southern white liberals—until the liberals had to take sides on the race issue. Those who moved away from defending segregation quickly lost their liberal credentials and were branded as radicals, in keeping with the Southern tendency to define almost any proponent of reform, white or black, as an enemy of the people. Gunnar Myrdal's big study (itself a powerful sign of impending change) attempted to sort out some of these distinctions, but the effort was largely wasted in the very region where it was most needed, since few Southerners (and not all that many Northerners) ever made their way through *An American Dilemma*.

What the Southerners felt most acutely—whites in particular, but also blacks—was a continuing sense of inferiority in the national scheme of things, and a chip-on-the-shoulder defensiveness because of it. The Detroit riot showed that America's race and class problems were national, not regional, but that didn't relieve Southern anxieties at all; on the contrary, it almost seemed to make matters worse. The standard Northern slant on that turn of events was that low-life Southerners, Negro and white, had brought their feud to Michigan and spilled it out on everybody. In the eyes of self-righteous Northerners, the South was still the nation's number one problem—and that galling assessment hovered like an accusation, a judgment, a curse. If there was anything that virtually all Southerners shared, whatever their race or class or ideology, it was some degree of dissent from and disgust with the uninformed and insensitive bias of judgmental Yankees. Nobody liked to be forever cast as a whipping boy, an object of scorn and ridicule, the butt of every joke—particularly by smug and arrogant strangers.

It was true: Southerners *were* different. Not necessarily better or worse, just different. Race and sex and other distinctions aside, Southerners were still unlike their upcountry brothers and sisters in many ways. Let Charles S. Johnson stand in illustration of the point.

When he turned fifty in 1943, he had already put in fifteen years as director of social science programs at Fisk University in Nashville, and before that he had worked in New York, studied in Chicago, and spent his boyhood and youth in Virginia. He was a Southerner with Northern refinements of sophistication and urbanity. He would remain at Fisk for the rest of his life, working with single-minded dedication toward the goal that beckoned to the vast majority of African-Americans: to end discrimination by race and caste and class in the South and throughout the nation.

What made Johnson different from his fellow blacks in the North was not the goal but his manner of seeking it. Rayford Logan classified him as "right of center," and by most lights he was undeniably conservative, in his personal and professional deportment as well as in his strategic thinking. He knew instinctively that Southern reformers couldn't get by on aggressiveness and iron will and a clear sense of direction; they also had to have Br'er Rabbit smarts—craftiness, sagacity, a smooth line, an instinct for survival. Johnson was a complex man—shy but ambitious, stiffly formal but persuasive, intense and humorless but always commanding respect. He kept a tight grip on everything under his hand—curriculum, research projects, budgets, faculty and staff in the social sciences, protégés and graduate students. To outsiders, white and black—and, indeed, to those nearest him—he came across as a deeply dedicated scholar and a Victorian gentleman, a man of dignity and quiet strength who seldom let his emotions show. Johnson had many acquaintances, said his biographer, Patrick J. Gilpin, "but few friends and almost no cronies."

Almost from the start of his graduate studies under Robert Park at the University of Chicago, young Charles Johnson had stepped easily into the role of the detached and disinterested social scientist. He established close ties with Edwin Embree at the Julius Rosenwald Fund and Will Alexander at the Commission on Interracial Cooperation. While serving as editor of the National Urban League's magazine in the 1920s, he formed lasting associations with James Weldon Johnson, Langston Hughes, and all the other stars of the Harlem Renaissance. As a sociologist, he worked hard to align himself with others in the discipline, from Howard Odum and the North Carolinians to the emerging network of black scholars across the country. In short, Johnson paid his dues, and earned thereby a wealth of dividends.

Throughout his long career, he raised money with relative ease—from Rosenwald, the American Missionary Association, the John Hay Whitney Foundation, the Field Foundation, and other philanthropies. His mostly white colleagues in the Southern Sociological Society, at the urging of

Odum, threw segregation aside to elect Johnson president of the organization in 1945. His programs of scholarship and research at Fisk were second only to North Carolina's in national prestige, and he had the publications, the faculty, the graduate students, and the outside support to confirm that lofty status. When in 1944 he founded the Race Relations Institute at Fisk—an integrated, three-week summer workshop and seminar for adults—the "conservative" Johnson took a bold but calculated step beyond his time and place. He had the stature to get nationally prominent blacks and whites to participate in the institute, and the courage to withstand local white criticism—even when his own exceedingly cautious president, who was white, nearly caved in to pressure.

More important, perhaps, than any of these accomplishments was the depth of Johnson's involvement in organizations and initiatives to improve the lives of blacks and the poor in the South. He gave expert assistance to several New Deal programs; he served on national panels of education, labor, religion, and race relations; he was a respected leader in the Commission on Interracial Cooperation and its successor, the Southern Regional Council; he drafted the race-relations manifesto of a select group of Southern black leaders in 1943; he was active in the Southern Conference for Human Welfare, the Southern Policy Committee, and various professional associations in the social sciences. Beyond all that, he wrote a dozen books and served as president of Fisk for the last decade of his life. His visibility and influence continued to rise in the postwar years as the South struggled with its social problems. Throughout the thirties and forties and into the fifties, only a small number of black Southerners (and even fewer whites) were able to stay in the region and fight their way to national recognition in the long campaign for racial equality. Charles S. Johnson was one of them.

To be black and Southern in those perilous times, and to stake out a position at variance with the canons of segregation and white supremacy, required a mixture of conservatism and tactful independence that few non-Southerners could understand or appreciate. Patience and diplomacy and flank-covering caution were essential to survival. With rare exceptions, outspoken liberals and leftist radicals, black and white, found the Southern climate too stifling, and few of them lasted very long in it.

Academia provided the base for most Southern black leaders. Along with Johnson, several other presidents figured prominently in the race-relations initiatives of the forties—Benjamin E. Mays of Morehouse College, Rufus Clement of Atlanta University, Horace Mann Bond of Fort Valley (Georgia) State, Frederick D. Patterson of Tuskegee, Mary McLeod Bethune of Bethune-Cookman in Florida, Charlotte Hawkins Brown of Palmer Institute in North Carolina, Albert W. Dent of Dillard

University in New Orleans, and many more. Scholars and ministers were almost as numerous as administrators in these ranks. Charles Johnson's place in the circle derived initially from his stature as a sociologist; the same was true of Gordon B. Hancock of Virginia Union University, Charles G. Gomillion of Tuskegee, and Ira De A. Reid of Atlanta University, and other disciplines were also well-represented.

A few black lawyers were active in Southern race-relations efforts, men like A. T. Walden of Atlanta, Oliver W. Hill of Richmond, Z. Alexander Looby of Nashville, and Arthur D. Shores of Birmingham, who was for a time the only black practicing attorney in the entire state of Alabama. Editors and publishers of black newspapers, notably P. B. Young of Richmond and Carter Wesley of Houston, were sometimes identified with reform efforts, too. Several people who headed local units of national organizations were likewise involved, including Grace Towns Hamilton of the Atlanta Urban League, James E. Jackson of the Southern Negro Youth Congress in Birmingham, Emory Jackson of the Birmingham NAACP, and Ernest Delpit, president of the carpenters' union local in New Orleans.

These tireless advocates and a few others were the ones whose names were always prominent whenever a public effort was made to address the racial and social problems of the South. These were the ones the white moderates and liberals referred to as "responsible Negro leaders" (not a designation they sought, necessarily, but one they kept for just so long as they refrained from direct and pointed attacks on the laws and customs of segregation). They differed among themselves, of course, in their approach to the issues, but by and large they shared certain characteristics that clearly defined them as the Southern black intelligentsia.

By the yardsticks of education, experience, and socioeconomic status, they were middle-class or above. Much of their undergraduate work and virtually all of their graduate training had been done in the North. Decorum, dignity, and good manners defined their relations with others; discipline, order, and personal control characterized their style of leadership and management. They were, for the most part, deeply religious— some were ordained ministers—but their base was the academy, not the church. They avoided confrontational exposure in such organizations as James Farmer's Congress of Racial Equality in Chicago and A. Philip Randolph's March on Washington Movement. They sought and welcomed white allies in all efforts to reform the South. Instead of challenging the insistence of white leaders that there could only be Southern solutions to Southern problems, without interference from outsiders, they quietly pressed for those internal reforms. Using whatever tools they could get their hands on, the black pragmatists chipped away at the mighty rock of segregation.

Consider Charles Gomillion. As a young professor at Tuskegee in the early 1930s, he looked around and saw that even though blacks constituted a majority of the population there in Macon County, Alabama, only thirty-two of them were registered to vote. Gomillion went to work. He spearheaded the formation of a black civic association committed to political equality. In the face of danger and discouragement, they coached new voters over the registration hurdles one and two at a time. It took Gomillion and his allies twenty years to get six hundred blacks on the voter rolls, but they never gave up—and eventually, in the 1960s, they would witness a "one man, one vote" revolution. Only the Southerners seemed to have the patience, the stubborn persistence, to measure out success in teaspoons.

Slightly more aggressive were a few of their collaborators in the North, including Lester Granger of the National Urban League, Mordecai Johnson of Howard University, and Channing Tobias, first a YMCA executive and then director of the Phelps Stokes Fund, a philanthropic organization. All three had Southern roots—but then so did Walter White and A. Philip Randolph and Richard Wright, whose abrasiveness was in sharp contrast to the gentlemanly Southern approach, and who, like Du Bois and Paul Robeson and Langston Hughes, were anything but deferential in their manner. Even Ralph Bunche, later to gain international fame as a United Nations diplomat, often sounded assertively radical in comparison with his more cautious Southern compatriots.

The NAACP had chapters in every Southern state by the early 1940s. In the North, the New York–based organization was often criticized for being too middle-class, too hierarchical, too conservative, even too Southern and too white. In the South, though, hardly anyone shared those assessments; the very notion that the NAACP was somehow a moderate or right-of-center group was simply ludicrous. For decades it had been an uncompromising adversary of the segregationists and had been looked upon by most Southern whites as an alien force—even though numerous members of its staff were exiles from the Southern and border states and the District of Columbia. None of the biracial regional organizations concerned with social issues, including the Southern Conference for Human Welfare, openly sought a close working alliance with the NAACP until after the war.

In the 1940s, most Southern black social reformers channeled their energies into organizations, but a few chose to follow a rockier and lonelier path as independent critics of the established order. J. Saunders Redding was one. Besides teaching English at Hampton Institute near Norfolk, he wrote books and articles that cut to the heart of racism in the South and the nation. John Henry McCray took a similar tack with his small South

Carolina weekly, the *Lighthouse & Informer*. And the inimitable Zora Neale Hurston, back among the common folk of Florida after her years of glory in the Harlem Renaissance, at Barnard College, and in the Guggenheim fellowship program, had a singular gift for colorful invective and unsettling truth. As a folklorist for the Florida Federal Writers' Project and in her own highly original creative work, she put her finger on the essence of blackness and Southernness. "Negroes are just like everybody else," she observed in 1942. "Some soar. Some plod ahead. Some just make a mess and step back in it—like the rest of America and the world."

When Rayford Logan classified the black essayists he was considering as exponents of *What the Negro Wants*, he put F. D. Patterson over on the "extreme right." The Tuskegee president was as Southern and conservative as any of the historian's prospective writers. But as it turned out, his views were not very different from those of Randolph, Du Bois, and Hughes. "Any form of segregation based on race, creed or color is discriminatory and imposes a penalty inconsistent with the guaranties of American democracy," Patterson declared, and he added:

> The more conservative element of Negroes differ from those who hold the most radical views in opposition to segregation only in terms of time and technique of its elimination. In any statement which attempts to speak unequivocally in terms of ultimates, all Negroes must condemn any form of segregation based on race, creed or color anywhere in our nation.

Here was the proof, if any more was needed, that African-Americans everywhere were unified in their opposition to segregation. Nonracist Southern whites, on the other hand, ranged across the spectrum on this fundamental issue. Between Lillian Smith, an outspoken integrationist, and John Temple Graves, an uncompromising segregationist, stretched a chasm too wide for bridging—and yet they had all described themselves as liberals or progressives, and some were considered radicals, and others wore the age-old self-styled mantle of "the Negroes' best friend."

If Northerners had trouble figuring out the thought processes of black Southerners, imagine how puzzled they must have been by the words and actions of Southern white liberals. Graves merely voiced the most radical expression of segregationist sentiment among them; numerous mainstream journalists, academicians, ministers, and other public figures were only slightly more restrained in their articulation of the code. (In fairness to them, it could be noted that they almost always took pains to speak in terms of what "white Southerners will not stand for," rather than what they themselves believed in their hearts to be right and true, but the bottom line was the same: For the foreseeable future, segregation is non-negotiable.)

These were not fire-breathing bigots; these were middle- and upper-class men and women who responded in kind to the decorum, dignity, and good manners of the Southern black leaders, and who spoke from Christian charity or other well-meant motivation in favor of elemental fairness and decency toward blacks, and who lashed out at the violent acts and intolerant attitudes of Klansmen and kooks and demagogic politicians. These were the Virginius Dabneys and Mark Ethridges and Ralph McGills of the South—decent, sensitive, thoughtful, kindly individuals, not hate-mongers or character assassins. The time was coming when they would be compelled to choose whether to cling to segregation or let it go, and most of them would let it go. Whatever Northerners thought of these "conservative liberals," they certainly were not reactionary racists of the Bilbo-Talmadge school.

To the left of them in the peculiar Southern panorama of liberalism was a yeasty collection of New Dealers, laborites, and other activists—including a handful of Socialists and Communists who were as hostile to each other as they were to the sworn enemies of social change. The Socialists included H. L. Mitchell, whose Southern Tenant Farmers Union was losing steam in the post-depression period; Buck Kester, who left the STFU and spent most of the war years in a futile effort to enlarge the little network of radical Christians he called the Fellowship of Southern Churchmen; and Frank McCallister, who worked for the Socialist Party in Atlanta as regional director of the Workers' Defense League. All three of them were completely alienated from everyone they knew or suspected were Communists—the doctrinaire party reps like Donald Burke of Virginia and Rob Hall of Alabama, the Christian radicals like Don West and Claude Williams, and the leaders of such organizations as the Highlander Folk School and the Southern Conference for Human Welfare.

Mitchell and Kester may have been the first white Southerners to act on the principle of racial equality—back in the early 1930s, long before most of their fellow liberals had even begun to think about it—and some people credited McCallister with devising the strategy by which Georgia's reform governor, Ellis Arnall, rescued his state from the grip of anti-black terrorist groups. But race cut one way and ideology another; not until Lillian Smith came along was any white Southerner as committed to openly fighting segregation as Mitchell and Kester, and yet these so-called radicals were just as opposed to Southern blacks with Communist ties (John P. Davis, Benjamin J. Davis, Jr., James Ford, Hosea Hudson) as they were to their white comrades. (Smith, too, turned out to be both pro-black and

anticommunist, but she was likewise skeptical of the ideological motivations of Kester and Mitchell, as well as of Kester's religious aims, and she
never developed a close working relationship with them.)

The militantly anticommunist Southern Socialists were also guilty of
making uninformed and irresponsible charges against some of the men and
women who labored with them in the search for regional reform. They cast
suspicions, if not direct accusations, on Myles Horton, Alva Taylor, James
Dombrowski, Clark Foreman, Claude Williams, and Don West, but none
of these assertions of disloyalty were proven to be true.

Horton continued in place as director of the Highlander Folk School,
working closely with the Congress of Industrial Organizations to broaden
the base of politically liberal and racially mixed labor unions in the South.
The CIO also kept a working relationship with Taylor, the former Vanderbilt University professor who became a labor mediator in the later years of
his career. Dombrowski left Highlander in 1942 to join the Southern
Conference for Human Welfare, and Foreman became that organization's
president soon thereafter. All of these men would be viciously red-baited
by right-wing anticommunist forces in later years—and those attacks
gained a certain ironic reinforcement from the deep-seated enmity of
Southern Socialists like Kester and Mitchell.

Don West and Claude Williams stood apart from all the left-of-center
Southerners of their time. Not only were they never proved to be card-
carrying Communists; in more than a quarter-century of peripatetic activism, they defied characterization in anybody's camp except the one
they found in their reading of the New Testament. To them, Jesus was
the first guerrilla Christian, and they were soldiers in His revolutionary
army. West bounced from one job to another as a preacher, teacher,
laborer, and farmer. In the war years he was superintendent of a small
school system in the mountains of rural north Georgia, his home section;
a little later on, he would make a brief public splash again with a series
of radical poems.

Claude Williams roamed from Commonwealth College and the Arkansas cotton fields to Alabama and elsewhere, preaching an offbeat message
of Marxist-Christian radicalism that kept him constantly in hot water with
his Presbyterian superiors. Finally, in 1942, they shunted him to Detroit
to work as an "industrial chaplain" among displaced Southern whites and
blacks vying for war-production jobs in the industrial plants. There, a year
later, Williams found himself in the unaccustomed role of peacemaker
when the worst race riot in a generation exploded right in front of him.
Later, his dreams of a far-reaching movement called the People's Institute
of Applied Religion would draw him once more into the center of a sensational controversy.

Odd ducks, these Southern liberals and progressives and radicals. Even as Virginius Dabney and Ralph McGill and Hodding Carter were trying to defend—or at least to explain—the peculiarities of the South to national magazine audiences, the dean of Southern liberals, sixty-year-old Will W. Alexander, was going on record against racial bias in the January 1945 issue of *Harper's*. Segregation is a national problem, he declared, not only inconsistent with the American creed (Myrdal's main point) but also doomed to failure when postwar pressures bear down upon it.

In Washington, Southern anomalies were everywhere. While the Bilbos and Rankins raved on through the war years, to the eternal embarrassment of many citizens of Dixie, Alabama native Aubrey Williams was still rattling the cages of the Old South politicians with his egalitarian views, and North Carolina's Jonathan Daniels was loyally serving and supporting FDR in the ailing President's final days.

Still more contrasts: Representative Martin Dies of Texas and his House Un-American Activities Committee associates, including Congressman Joe Starnes of Alabama, had succeeded in bringing J. Edgar Hoover and the FBI into the search for subversives, and in putting the heat on the CIO as a suspected source of Communist infiltration. But the CIO and its Political Action Committee fought back, helped in large measure by Lucy Randolph Mason, its Southern troubleshooter, and George S. Mitchell, director of CIO-PAC in the Southeastern states. Working closely with Highlander and the Southern Conference for Human Welfare, Mason and Mitchell and the rest of the CIO pushed for the labor body's biracial agenda: abolition of the poll tax and other impediments to voting, equitable wage and hour standards, and a permanent Fair Employment Practices Commission with enforcement powers.

For their pains, the CIO incurred the wrath of the mushrooming far right, the militantly anticommunist opposition to the dying Roosevelt and his stagnant New Deal. To George Mitchell and Lucy Mason and the other Southerners in the labor movement, this was old hat. It was routine in the South for those who tried to change the status quo to be criticized and shunned; worse, some were hounded and threatened, branded as radicals, traitors, turncoats, Communists.

The Southern labor activists found some comfort, even vindication, in the 1944 elections when Dies stepped aside to avoid almost certain defeat, and Starnes was unseated by his Alabama constituents. But if such victories made progressive Southerners euphoric, it was only because they savored every inch of progress in a long and painful uphill climb. There were hopeful signs that big changes could come after the war, but that was in the future. For now, the South could count on only a relative handful of reformers, white and black, to answer the postwar call to action. What's more, they were a remnant on the fringes of established power, not a force in the center of it. With them thus far—and only tenuously at that—were the barest minimum of politicians, editors, religious leaders, white academicians, or corporate executives. If the reformers had anything remotely resembling a power base or the nucleus of a movement, it was in two now-familiar organizations: the left-leaning Southern Conference for Human Welfare, and the much older and more conservative—and fading—Commission on Interracial Cooperation.

The progressive response to the first Southern Conference for Human Welfare meeting in Birmingham had been highly favorable. Even some Southern newspapers, including the Birmingham *News*, expressed qualified editorial approval of the gathering and its outcome. Several national magazines also subsequently featured positive critiques by conference participants Lucy Randolph Mason, Charles S. Johnson, Sterling Brown, and George C. Stoney. They observed that police enforcement of the local segregation ordinance had put a damper on the meeting. Johnson noted pointedly that other groups had been allowed to hold biracial meetings in the city without interference; he suggested the possibility that "other interests inimical to the Conference's program found it convenient to use the race issue, in the ancient manner, as the most effective means of confounding or perhaps nullifying the proceedings."

The last of the SCHW delegates were still in town on that Thanksgiving weekend in 1938 when the "inimical interests" fired their first reactionary shot. In a hastily called meeting at the Birmingham City Hall, a group of women and men claiming to represent various Democratic Party organizations in Alabama assailed the local sponsors of the conference, including Judge Louise Charlton and Congressman Luther Patrick, for undermining the poll tax and raising the threat of racial equality. They praised Eugene "Bull" Connor, the police commissioner, for enforcing the city segregation ordinance, and they called on the House Un-American Activities Committee to "ferret out all the facts concerning the so-called Conference for Human Welfare."

Some of the Alabama sponsors quickly ran for shelter. Congressman Patrick, Senators Lister Hill and John Bankhead, and Governor Bibb Graves all pleaded ignorance of what one critic called "the insidious nature" of the SCHW. Birmingham's postmaster, Cooper Green, another of the planners, denied he had been a delegate and swore his allegiance to segregation.

Louise Charlton was not so easily intimidated. Her faithful service to the Democratic Party had secured her appointment as U.S. commissioner in Birmingham—a quasi-judicial position—and her progressive views had made her a natural choice to preside with Frank Porter Graham at the first SCHW meeting. Once the big guns were gone, the reactionaries seemed intent on singling her out for punishment—thinking, perhaps, that as a woman and a middle-level party official, she would offer little opposition.

They were in for a surprise. In a formal statement the next day, Mrs. Charlton stood up to the "little Hitlers" who had met at City Hall, saying these were the same "anti-labor, anti-education, anti-Roosevelt group of do-nothing critics" whose "shopworn smoke screen" hid yet another attack on the much-maligned black minority. "Birmingham has had the honor of being the city where a great and historic liberal American movement had its birth," she said, and the conference was "attended by the greatest Democrats in the South and in America, and financed from their pockets." Someday, she predicted, "Birmingham and the South will count the conference as one of its golden achievements." She expressed personal pride, as chairman of the assembly, in having served with others "to begin a regional program for lifting the level of human life."

Judge Charlton had been present at the City Hall inquisition, and her fellow citizens, women and men alike, had treated her rudely. That was bad enough—but worse was her knowledge that far more extreme reactions lurked throughout Southern white society. The feared Big Mules of Birmingham and the rest of Alabama—the men who controlled politics and business—were not in the habit of tolerating democratic dissent. No one had expected them to roll out a welcome mat for the Southern Conference. Now that the gathering was over, the hunt for its planners was just beginning.

As hostile as the reactionary Birmingham critics were, though, they were not by any means the only group that posed a threat to the SCHW. In fact, considering the kind of "friends" it had on the left, you could easily conclude that the conference had no real need of enemies. The Alabama politicians resigned before the gavel of adjournment fell, and right behind them were other elected officials—Florida Senator Claude Pepper, incoming Governor Burnet Maybank of South Carolina, Democratic National Committee-man Brooks Hays of Arkansas, and Francis Pickens Miller, a member of the Virginia legislature and head of the Southern Policy Committee.

Miller, a Southern liberal of the patrician Virginia gentleman class, had gone to the Birmingham conference with misgivings about its radical temper and a suspicion that it aimed to undercut the SPC and other, more moderate reform efforts. Spying there another Virginian he knew to be a Communist, and hearing calls for racial and social reform that sounded altogether too aggressive to suit him, Miller not only refused an office in the organization but packed up and left two days ahead of adjournment.

Mark Ethridge's verbal account of the meeting to Howard Odum was not quite so alarming, but it was enough to convince Odum that the SCHW might ruin his plans for a regional research council. Within a week, Ethridge had written to Frank Graham—at Odum's private urging—to suggest that "twenty-five or so representative Southerners" meet under Southern Policy Committee auspices during the Christmas holidays and draw up a legislative agenda to present to Congress. While he was at it, Ethridge mildly complimented SCHW as one of several initiatives aimed at Southern problems—but of course, he added, "the ultimate solution is the regional council originally proposed by Dr. Odum."

Graham was too shrewd a politician to align himself against Ethridge and Odum—or with them, for that matter. He had his own agenda, and it was not exactly shrouded in secrecy. In essence, Graham wanted everybody to get into the game—and if some, like Odum, had doubts about the Birmingham gathering, maybe they would find other ways to become active. In the meantime, Graham had agreed to lead the SCHW, and for the next two years he would shelter it from incessant attacks by anticommunists and others. Lucy Randolph Mason was one of many progressive Southerners who stood with him throughout. "After the Red-baiters got in action," she wrote to Graham in early December, "I knew you would feel compelled to accept the chairmanship. . . . You bring to the Conference leadership something that no one else in the South could give."

That something extra was Graham's genuine empathy for the least fortunate, his strength of character and integrity, and his stature as the preeminent spokesman for Southern liberalism. "For years I have known that the South cannot be saved by its middle-class liberals alone," Mason told him. "They must make common cause with labor, the dispossessed on the land, and the Negro. Some liberals may find it too shocking to have the other three groups so articulate about their needs. But this is the basis of progress."

Ethridge and Miller went on to invite about four dozen people to their rump session in Atlanta in January 1939. Two women (Miller's wife, Helen Hill Miller, and Lucy Mason) were on the list, along with one black man (Charles S. Johnson). The rest were all white men, most of them wary critics of the Southern Conference. Graham didn't attend, but Mason and Johnson did, along with Ethridge and Barry Bingham and labor leader William Mitch; those five also remained active in the SCHW for at least another year or two, out of loyalty and respect for Graham. The others in attendance generally sided with Miller and Odum in their criticism of the Birmingham reformers ("irresponsible ideologists and front-page seekers," Odum sneered).

But the Atlanta meeting came to naught. Miller's fadeout Southern Policy Committee and Odum's yet-to-be-born regional think tank couldn't generate much of an alternative to the Southern Conference for Human Welfare. Bitterly, Miller washed his hands of the regional reform movement (an exit that was complete after he lost his Virginia legislative seat in 1941), and turned his attention to international affairs. After the war, he would come back to Virginia for one more dip in the political waters. As for Odum, he had to bide his time and wait for another opening.

To the right and left of Miller and Odum and their followers were other SCHW detractors who eventually came together in a curious duet that made up in fervor for all it lacked in melody and harmony. From Martin Dies and Joe Starnes of the House Un-American Activities Committee and from a bombastic right-wing magazine called *Alabama* came shrill cries that as many as six hundred "dyed-in-the-wool Communists" had attended the conference and were in total control of it. And then, from Buck Kester, H. L. Mitchell, Frank McCallister, and others on the left came whispered charges—just as damaging—that the conference had been conceived, "beyond a shadow of a doubt," by Communists and fellow travelers.

Frank Graham was catching it from all sides. For the multitude of irate strangers who deluged him with anticommunist complaints and demands that he resign, he drafted a generic letter of polite but firm refusal. For all those who had taken part in the conference and might truly know who was what, he posed a challenge: Give me facts—names, proof—or be honest enough to say you have none. To Kester he wrote:

> I had asked that my name not be considered for any administrative position. . . . Nevertheless, I was elected. I would have resigned except for the fact that the special interests in Birmingham set out to smear the Conference in a very ruthless way and concentrated their attacks on Judge Louise Charlton. In the face of pressure and demands that I resign, I then refused to resign. I am glad that I did not resign. I do not object to members of any political party—Democrats, Republicans, Socialists, Communists, or what-not—coming into an open democratic meeting so long as it is open and aboveboard. Nor do I think we should run when we find out that a handful of Communists joined the Conference or would like to manipulate it or claim it as their own. . . . I refuse to run in the face of Communist intrigue on one side or smearing by powerful and privileged groups on the other.

H. C. Nixon, the SCHW executive secretary, acted on Graham's orders to ascertain how many Communists had attended. "Only four," he at first replied, and then amended the count to six. The same names kept popping up: Joe Gelders, Howard Lee, John B. Thompson, John P. Davis, Rob Hall, Donald Burke. The last two of these acknowledged party membership; the first four, when questioned directly, denied it. Graham was satisfied that he had not been deceived, and that in any case the organization was in no danger of becoming a tool of the Communist Party. The critics were after it, he concluded, "not because it is one percent Red but because it is fifty percent Black." (Actually, about one-fourth of those who paid the one-dollar conference registration fee were black.)

In retrospect, the charge that Communists controlled or even seriously influenced the 1938 SCHW meeting seems farfetched. By no criteria could it be fairly pegged as a radical assembly. Almost three-fourths of its delegates and about ninety-five percent of its chosen officers were white, middle-class Southerners, and virtually all of them were New Deal Democrats. Their headquarters in the Tutwiler Hotel was snuggled in the bosom of segregated comfort, and no one, white or black, even hinted that black delegates ought to be allowed to cross that threshold. Aside from their disapproval (hardly unanimous) of the city's enforcement of its segregated-seating ordinance, the conference skirted discreetly around any other word or deed that smacked of "social equality."

The biggest threat to the survival and effectiveness of SCHW was not its enemies inside and out, right and left, but rather its long-term inability to raise membership and money. The CIO labor unions were a major force behind the organization and the top contributor to its first convention budget, but they were not sustaining patrons—nobody was. Membership dues and publications sales produced a little income, but not much. Gifts and donations came to less than two thousand dollars the first year, and annual income from all sources didn't top twenty thousand dollars until after the war. In all that time, the organization was never out of debt, never able to keep up the paltry salaries of two or three staff members, never even sure its utilities and telephone wouldn't be cut off. Labor leaders talked a good game, but put up very little hard cash. Various New Deal units could also be thought of as unofficial founding sponsors, but they offered no material help (although Eleanor Roosevelt was an annual participant and a faithful contributor). The Southern Policy Committee was still another fair-weather friend, as conspicuous in the beginning as it was invisible after Francis Pickens Miller's exit.

H. C. Nixon lasted less than a year as the director, giving up his seldom-paid forty-dollar-a-week salary for a temporary teaching job in Oklahoma and then, in 1940, joining the political science faculty at Vanderbilt (thanks in large part to a supporting salary grant from the ever-helpful Edwin Embree, director of the Rosenwald Fund). Finding himself once again in a conservative academic community—and in an untenured position at that—Nixon seemed to back away from the populist activism that had characterized his earlier involvements. He seldom looked back at the Southern Conference after he left, except to lament its failings. He did put in a brief appearance at one session of the 1942 gathering in Nashville, but showed no enthusiasm for it. Later, when three of the delegates—old friends and former associates—drove out to his home for a visit, they came away convinced that he was no longer sympathetic to their cause.

In its first four years of existence, the Southern Conference for Human Welfare raised the hopes of thousands of progressive citizens in the region, but its concrete accomplishments were few. Its goal of organizing thirteen active state branches and one in Washington fell far short of the mark. A youth group called the Council of Young Southerners was established in Nashville under the direction of Helen Fuller and Howard Lee, but Fuller soon left for Washington, and Lee spent much of his time fending off rumors of his alleged Communist ties. By 1941 the council—or the League of Young Southerners, as it was then called—had all but faded out. Another ongoing SCHW effort, a civil rights committee headed by Joe Gelders, Maury Maverick, and Virginia Durr, focused its efforts on a national campaign to abolish the poll tax in the eight Southern states that still had such a levy. Georgia did repeal its tax in 1945, but the others held out until the fifties or later.

The Southern Conference couldn't come up with enough money to hold a convention in 1939, and after Nixon left, Graham finally named Howard Lee to replace him, other nominees having declined. Lee had support from some respected Southerners, including Brooks Hays and Barry Bingham, and he flatly denied in a formal letter to Graham that he was a Communist. But his political awakening as an Arkansas sharecropper's son had come at the hands of the controversial Claude Williams, and some of his subsequent associations cast further suspicion on him. As soon as the announcement was made that he would be the SCHW's executive secretary, Lee was bombarded with new charges and Graham was pulled deeper into the morass.

Gamely, Graham and Lee and the SCHW executive committee pressed on. They scheduled the second general conference for three days in April of 1940 at the Memorial Auditorium in Chattanooga, and with careful advance planning they managed to bring it off smoothly. Two old journalistic hands, editors Julian Harris of the Chattanooga *Times* and George Fort Milton of the rival *News*, gave sympathetic support. With Frank Graham presiding, close to a thousand delegates, a fourth of them black, came together in the unsegregated auditorium to hear Eleanor Roosevelt and a host of other liberals, white and black, recite the familiar litany of Southern problems and hoped-for solutions. The Thomas Jefferson Award was given to old soldier Will Alexander, who still lived and worked in Washington but also retained nominal leadership of the Commission on Interracial Cooperation in Atlanta.

The only real snag in the proceedings developed at the opening session when W. T. Couch introduced a non-sequitur resolution condemning Communist aggression in Europe. The ensuing debate was emotional and divisive, with Couch finally storming out in anger—but Graham showed once again why so many delegates felt his leadership was indispensable. His draft of a substitute resolution denouncing "the violation of human rights and democratic liberties . . . by all Fascist, Nazi, Communist, and Imperialist powers alike" was overwhelmingly approved by the assembly. Then, with such worldly issues finally put aside, Graham called the delegates' attention to the more relevant concerns of the Southern region. "There are many people in the South who are willing to unite in building a better civilization," he declared. "We must gird ourselves for a struggle that may last two or three generations, and we ourselves must pay the price for keeping this fight alive."

It was largely through the influence of Frank Graham that Lillian Smith came to the Chattanooga meeting and later accepted a seat on the SCHW executive committee. Gordon Clapp, general manager of the Tennessee Valley Authority and thus a prominent New Deal figure, also came aboard. Clark Foreman, another New Dealer, was chosen again as the conference treasurer. Numerous others, from Lucy Mason and Myles Horton and John P. Davis to Louise Charlton and Mark Ethridge and Charles S. Johnson, were there at least in part because Frank Graham was carrying the colors. But Graham, having accepted a draft for a two-year term, was insistent that a new chairman or president must now be picked to replace him. The names of Barry Bingham, Will Alexander, and even Howard Odum were put forth, but no consensus developed, and the decision was put off.

Finally, a month or so after the conference adjourned, the executive committee chose John B. Thompson, a Presbyterian minister and professor at the University of Oklahoma, to take Graham's place. Thompson's Tennessee roots, Union Theological Seminary degree, and Highlander Folk School ties were well known to the SCHW board, but only belatedly did they learn that he was also president of American Peace Mobilization, a pacifist group that some of its critics said was a Communist front. When his name was added to those of Howard Lee and Joe Gelders, Thompson seemed in the eyes of many to tip the scales toward substantial if not dominant red influence in the SCHW. Along with the other two, he explicitly and emphatically denied any Communist affiliation, but the trio's leadership was compromised by the ongoing furor that enveloped them.

Thompson held on to complete his two-year term, but Lee and Gelders were forced to resign their posts in the summer of 1941.

Mark Ethridge and Barry Bingham severed their ties to SCHW out of concern about the communism issue, but Tarleton Collier, their colleague at the Louisville *Courier-Journal*, stayed on—and later even filled in briefly as acting president of the conference. After Lee's departure, the labor movement loaned the services of Alton Lawrence to SCHW to keep its office running, but Lawrence (who once had been bailed out of a North Carolina jail by Frank Graham following a student demonstration in support of striking textile workers) turned out to be yet another suspected Communist. Finally, in a last-gasp effort to keep the conference from self-destructing, the executive committee in January 1942 hired James A. Dombrowski from Highlander to take over as executive director of the SCHW.

As a self-described Christian Socialist with a longtime commitment to radical causes, the forty-five-year-old Dombrowski was hardly a safe choice for the job. He and Myles Horton had kept Highlander in the spotlight as an activist labor school, and not only the Dies Committee and the FBI but the progressive Nashville *Tennessean* and some of Highlander's own staff members described the school unflatteringly. The *Tennessean*, in a six-part series in late 1939, called it "a center, if not the center, for the spreading communist doctrine in thirteen southeastern states." Two departing Highlander staff members, Zilla Hawes and Franz Daniel, also wondered aloud whether Horton and Dombrowski had naively become "dupes" and "stooges" of the Communists.

But those who knew Jim Dombrowski best knew that his dedication to both Christianity and socialism made him a natural enemy of communism. (As for Horton, he was no serious Christian, but no Communist either.) In his nearly ten years as Highlander's general manager, Dombrowski had proved himself to be adept at administration, fund-raising, and organizing. His ongoing commitment to racial equality and to a Southern reformation had won for him the firm support of most SCHW stalwarts, including Frank Graham, Charles Johnson, Lucy Mason, Clark Foreman, and Mary Bethune. In all the institutions from which the organization drew its strength—labor, the church, the university, the New Deal, the press— Dombrowski had friends who knew and respected him, who liked his quiet and steady manner. Their feeling was that if anyone could save the Southern Conference, he could.

From a new headquarters in Nashville, Dombrowski set to work raising funds and recruiting dues-paying members. The third general meeting— now billed as the biennial conference—was scheduled for April 1942 in Nashville, and a monthly publication, the *Southern Patriot*, was launched

later that year. Both John Thompson, the controversial outgoing president, and Clark Foreman, the man elected to replace him, found Dombrowski an easy person to work with, and they and the other officers
pulled together with him to try to repair SCHW's image and keep it alive
as a progressive force for Southern change. Still nearly broke but no longer
leaderless, the organization got its second wind and raced on.

Only about five hundred delegates registered at the 1942 convention,
but five times that many packed the War Memorial Auditorium for the
double-barreled main event: presentation of two Thomas Jefferson Awards
(to Frank Porter Graham and Mary McLeod Bethune) by Eleanor
Roosevelt, and a concert by the famed baritone Paul Robeson—his first
appearance in the South. Amazingly, both of Nashville's fiercely competitive newspapers, political and ideological opposites, put aside their feelings about SCHW, labor, communism, race, and all the other topics they
generally enjoyed chewing on, and gave the conference straightforward
coverage. There were no editorials attacking the unsegregated seating
arrangement, and neither paper made an issue of any of the hot topics that
had enlivened previous conferences.

Robeson's recital was a huge success; his thundering baritone brought
the enthralled audience straight up out of their seats. In brief closing
remarks, he called for patriotism in the war effort (Bataan had just fallen
to the Japanese, and the Allies were chasing General Rommel's German
and Italian armies across North Africa)—but then he added a plea for the
release of Earl Browder, secretary of the American Communist Party, who
was serving time in the federal penitentiary in Atlanta for passport violations. Straight out of left field, Robeson thus made one more unwelcome
link of memory between the Southern Conference and the Communists—
but not even that got a rise out of the newspapers.

The delegates and their leaders leaned over backward to avoid flashing
a radical image to the public. They talked a lot about winning the war,
about youth and industry and agriculture, about citizenship and productivity; they paid homage to President Roosevelt as everyone's commander-
in-chief; and they declined to tackle the segregation issue head-on,
choosing instead to talk about jobs and voting and economic growth—in a
separate-but-equal society, presumably—as the route to racial equality.

Clark Foreman later said the Southern Conference for Human Welfare
was "the peak of the New Deal," the culmination of FDR's efforts to help
the South rise up from feudalism. Historian George B. Tindall more accurately observed that SCHW was not so much the peak as the epilogue,
the aftermath. When the movement was spawned in 1938, the New Deal
was already in decline; Roosevelt's continuation in office for six and a half
more years may have saved the conference from an early grave, but he and

Eleanor didn't have it in their power to make SCHW an effective organization.

Dombrowski and Foreman and their remnant of believers in a Southern reformation carried the effort on their shoulders through the remainder of the war. The budget crisis lifted a little, and membership climbed modestly to about three thousand. The half-dozen charter members who had been singled out and pilloried as Communists in 1938 were all gone within five years; John P. Davis, the last of them, left in 1943 to become a political correspondent for the Pittsburgh *Courier*. The Communists never gained control of the organization—never even came close—but the anticommunists never ceased to see a red hiding behind every bush. The reason was clear. "Integration," one of them said, "is the Southern version of communism." The Cold War was just around the corner.

7. *"We of the South Must Decide"*

Watching the leftward drift of the Southern Conference for Human Welfare, the South's "conservative liberals" saw their initial doubts and fears confirmed. There was something altogether too aggressively radical about it, they felt; right from the start, the Socialists and Communists had come in and muddied the waters with their confrontational tactics, and the delegates had insisted on making an issue of the segregation thing—and now all they had to show for four years of thrashing about was an aroused and suspicious white public on guard against the slightest hint of social change.

But nothing was ever simple. It wasn't enough for the journalists and academics and others who kept their distance from the SCHW merely to dismiss the organization with smug criticism. If they sincerely wanted the South to change—and all of them proclaimed that they did—then they had to acknowledge that nay-saying only begged the question: If the Southern Conference wasn't working, and if the Southern Policy Committee was going nowhere, and if the New Deal was for all practical purposes finished, and if the Commission on Interracial Cooperation was petrifying from inactivity, what in heaven's name would it take to break the stalemate? What could be done to start the ball rolling toward moderate reform?

Howard Odum had felt for years that he knew the answer. Throughout his long and productive career as a social scientist, he had tried to deal in a disciplined, rational, scholarly way with problems that ordinary people tended to approach politically or emotionally, even physically. He was a teacher, a professor; he had little use for the grimy give-and-take of politics, and none at all for raw conflict, whether verbal or physical. His style was to study problems, to make them more palatable through patient discussion, and finally to resolve them by indirection. For several years, Odum had been promoting the creation of a regional research and development council that would defuse the volatile race issue by incorporating it with other public concerns, such as economics and labor relations, agriculture, and planning. By 1938 he was on the verge of consolidating these social science initiatives with the remaining programs and resources of the Commission on Interracial Cooperation, of which he was then president, when a succession of events beyond his control upset the strategy.

Odum was beside himself. Suddenly, it seemed, everyone had cock-eyed notions about what should be done with his South. The Tennessee Valley Authority and other New Deal busybodies were brazenly co-opting his regional planning ideas. President Roosevelt had launched that quixotic and ill-fated campaign attack on the Dixie demagogues. The Southern Policy Committee was drawing off the cream of the region's intelligentsia. Odum's own university president, Frank Graham, was leading the charge toward Birmingham and the big conference there. And if all that weren't enough, we were about to get caught up in another world war. "Between the Right Honorable FDR, the Southern Conference for Human Welfare, and twenty other groups that are literally taking the lead," he wrote to a colleague, "I think I'll go heat-wave haywire."

His grand design was in limbo. He made a slight adjustment in 1939, working through Mark Ethridge to join forces with Francis Pickens Miller's Southern Policy Committee right after the SCHW meeting, but nothing came of that. Then the war started, and the South receded from view as a public concern, and Odum was compelled to wait for events to present him with a new opening. As luck would have it, the opportunity came when Jessie Daniel Ames decided to pursue her own agenda at the CIC.

For a decade or more, Mrs. Ames had carried two imposing titles in her Atlanta professional life: Director of Women's Work for the Interracial Commission, and Executive Director of the Association of Southern Women for the Prevention of Lynching. By the beginning of the forties, the ASWPL held the signatures of more than forty thousand Southerners—mostly white women—who were openly committed to the abolition of lynching. They took some credit for the fact that this once-flagrant and near epidemic atrocity was diminishing (from an average of thirty a year in the 1920s to about six a year in the last half of the thirties), and that community sanction of it had been destroyed. Ames and her organization had shunned the very idea of help from Washington—even lobbying against a federal anti-lynching statute—and now, she proudly asserted, the South had almost eliminated this stain on its soul, and the ASWPL could soon bow out with its mission accomplished.

Business was slow at the CIC, too—not because the South had solved its racial problems, but because the organization was about to wither on the vine from a drought of ideas, a lack of energy, and an absence of leadership. Its director, Will Alexander, had been in Washington since 1935, and though he was still the CIC's nominal leader, he gave almost all of his time to the Farm Security Administration and the Rosenwald Fund in Chicago, of which he was a key board member. Arthur Raper, the CIC's research director, had also moved to a job in the Department of Agriculture in Washington after his increasingly critical attacks on Southern feudalism and racism cost him his teaching post at Agnes Scott College in Georgia. The CIC's information director, Robert B. Eleazer, was about to retire after twenty years on the job, and the president, Howard Odum, seldom came to the office in Atlanta anymore because there was simply nothing left for him to do there.

Jessie Daniel Ames and the office manager, Emily Clay, did their best to give the organization some vitality, but it was a losing battle. Mrs. Ames was a complex person; a committed social activist and reformer, she was also a states' rights true believer and a disaffected ex–New Dealer, an adversary of Walter White and the NAACP, a lukewarm supporter at best of the CIO labor organizing drive, and a strident critic of the SCHW. Like Virginius Dabney and W. T. Couch and other old-school liberals, she was for racial equity within the bounds of a separate-but-equal society; segregation was more of a nuisance, in her estimation, than it was a cancer on the South. Most of all, she wanted the CIC to regain its authority as the region's leading voice for gradual but steady social change—and yet there it was, losing membership and foundation support, becoming more and more isolated from the progressive currents of Southern life. In frustration and anger, Mrs. Ames concluded that the men who controlled the CIC were ready and willing to let it die.

In December 1941, a newspaper column distributed by the Associated Negro Press and written by Gordon Blaine Hancock, a sociologist at Virginia Union University in Richmond, caught Jessie Ames's eye. It was called "Interracial Hypertension," and the gist of it was that American society, with its growing racial tensions, was like a man suffering from high blood pressure—risking disaster unless prompt and judicious treatment was administered. Hancock was critical of both blacks and whites who took what he considered to be extremist positions on racial issues;

far from helping to cure the disease, he said, they actually made it worse.

Ames liked the tone and spirit of the article, and wrote Hancock to tell him so. She picked up on his assertion that "the better-class whites and Negroes" could resolve the American dilemma, and would bear a heavy responsibility if they failed to make the effort. "Now is the time of all times," she asserted, for this "better class" of Southern whites and blacks to get the jump on Northern radicals and Southern reactionaries by agreeing on an agenda for social reform. After they had exchanged several letters, Ames went to Richmond in February 1942 for a meeting with Hancock, and there they agreed that he would organize a committee of black leaders from the region to draft a statement of "minimum advances" that needed to be made, and she in turn would convene a similar group of whites who would take the statement seriously and make a conciliatory response. Soon thereafter, at Ames's invitation, Hancock wrote a longer piece for *Southern Frontier*, a CIC periodical, on the "leadership" approach to social change, and Ames gave it an explicit title: "Needed: A Southern Charter for Race Relations."

Ames and Hancock had much in common. Both were effective speakers and good writers, outspoken activists but moderates, and both were caught in the crossfire between radicalism and reaction. Hancock in particular was a favorite target of black critics, who considered him an insufferably pompous arch-conservative (and he did at times give them cause). The Baltimore *Afro-American* blasted him as a stooge of Virginius Dabney and Mark Ethridge; the historian Rayford Logan, a bitter foe, also accused him of being a lackey of certain pseudo-liberal whites. They said he was cautious and timid, but Hancock's blasts at black firebrands were anything but that, and he minced no words when he attacked whites, either; he said Lillian Smith's *Strange Fruit* "disparages the Negro race and blasphemes Negro womanhood," and "the author's pronounced literary powers are sacrificed on the altars of this country's moral and intellectual depravity."

He relished such verbal combat. In his view, radicals really weren't concerned about people who had been "bushwhacked, lynched and ku-kluxed into submission." It's always "the lowly Negro who will do the suffering and dying," he charged, "while the stall-fed Negro with his head in some jim-crow trough withdraws to his swivel-chaired retreat until the fires of persecution burn themselves out." Hancock could dish it out, but he could also take it; he told Ames that the race issue would not be lifted from the realm of extremist rhetoric and put onto the table for substantive discussion until there emerged some whites who were not afraid of being called "Nigger Lovers" and blacks who could stand up to being called "Uncle Toms." Certain in his own mind that neither whites nor blacks had him in their pocket, he seldom let the critics' barbs penetrate his thick skin.

During the first few months when they were in close contact, Ames made it clear to Hancock that she, too, was acting on her own, not at the direction of Will Alexander or Howard Odum, and she asked him to keep their conversations in confidence, ostensibly because she didn't want it to appear that the initial gathering of blacks was being manipulated by whites. Her unexpressed objective, though, was to save the Commission on Interracial Cooperation, to resuscitate it even as Odum and Alexander were about to administer last rites. In one dramatic stroke, she might be able to restore black confidence in the CIC, silence the organization's radical critics, and put white Southerners in a position of having to respond affirmatively to a reasonable overture from responsible blacks.

By the time she had published Hancock's essay in *Southern Frontier* and he had sent out a letter to a select group of well-known Southern black leaders, asking them if they would meet in response to the challenge of a "concerned white Southerner," their plan was no longer a secret. Odum and Alexander may have first learned of it from black friends like Charles S. Johnson and other recipients of Hancock's letter. In any case, when they did finally get all the details, they were hardly in a position to criticize Ames for putting forth an idea that the blacks so heartily endorsed. By that time, she and Hancock had a six-month start on their joint venture; there wasn't much left for Odum and Alexander to do except stand back and watch.

Working closely with publisher P. B. Young of the Norfolk *Journal & Guide* and Luther P. Jackson, a historian at Virginia State College in Petersburg, Hancock first convened a group of black Virginians to plan the drafting conference. They secured a place and date for the meeting— Durham, North Carolina, on October 20, 1942—and then got into a bitter wrangle over who should be invited. Hancock and Young prevailed with the view that only Southern blacks should participate, lest the whole effort be dismissed by whites as the work of Northern agitators.

More than seventy-five prominent black professionals (all but seven of them men) from throughout the South were invited to the Durham meeting at North Carolina College for Negroes, and fifty-seven of them attended, with the remainder sending letters or telegrams of support. Many Northern black activists heaped criticism on the gathering as a weak conclave of Hancock conservatives, and his credibility was not helped when W. E. B. Du Bois, the only bona fide radical among resident black Southerners, declined to attend.

But Hancock didn't buckle under pressure. He opened with a challenge to the delegates to act, "absolutely unfettered and unintimidated," for the

good of the South and the nation—and with that, they organized themselves into the Southern Conference on Race Relations and elected Hancock as their director. Seven committees were formed to take up issues
topically (political and civil rights, industry and labor, education, agriculture, and so forth). A drafting committee headed by Charles S. Johnson
took the task-group reports and fashioned them into a final conference
statement.

The one-day gathering ended before the work was finished, but the
Johnson committee (including Hancock, Young, F. D. Patterson, Benjamin Mays, Rufus Clement, Horace Mann Bond, and three others) continued to work on the document. Johnson was the principal drafter, and it
was he who finally released it to the press on December 15, 1942. It was
called "A Basis for Interracial Cooperation and Development in the South:
A Statement by Southern Negroes," but it would soon come to be known
as the Durham Manifesto, and it opened the way for "responsible white
leaders" to reciprocate in good faith. Moderate in tone and balanced in its
specific calls for action, the statement covered the now-familiar range of
issues affecting the lives of Southern blacks (the vote, criminal justice,
jobs, military service, equal educational opportunity, access to health
care, and the like).

The thorny question of segregation was broached in a carefully worded
preamble. In diplomatic language that bore Charles Johnson's imprint,
the signers declared themselves "fundamentally opposed to the principle
and practice of compulsory segregation in our American society," but went
on to say that, for the present, it seemed "both sensible and timely" to
concentrate on "the current problems of racial discrimination and neglect," rather than to insist on the immediate abolition of segregation
itself. "We have the courage and faith to believe," the statement continued, "that it is possible to evolve in the South a way of life, consistent with
the principles for which we as a nation are fighting throughout the world,
that will free us all, white and Negro alike, from want, and from throttling
fears."

Benjamin Mays and one or two other members of the drafting committee had argued for a forthright and unequivocal call for the abolition of
segregation, but Johnson, Hancock, and the rest were convinced that the
South's white liberals, whose support they considered essential, would be
frightened away by such a declaration. Johnson's careful wording of the
final draft was aimed at giving the Durham conferees a statement they
could endorse unanimously—and it worked.

It also succeeded rather well with a larger audience. Reaction to the
document in the Southern press was generally favorable, and the black
response was mixed, with Northern newspapers predictably critical but

Du Bois and Walter White and numerous others supportive. Ralph McGill set the tone for the white South with a column praising the black leaders for their moderate statement, and especially for its acknowledgment that segregation would, in McGill's words, "be retained for a long time." With that endorsement, Jessie Daniel Ames was able, after a couple of nerve-racking delays, to keep her side of the bargain with Gordon Hancock by attracting more than a hundred Southern white moderates and liberals to an Atlanta hotel on April 8, 1943, for a meeting of response and affirmation.

With an abundance of caution, that group excluded virtually everyone who was active in the Southern Conference for Human Welfare (Lucy Mason, William Mitch, and Mark Ethridge were exceptions), all fringe-party political activists except the Socialist Frank McCallister, and even New Deal operatives like Will Alexander. Of the 553 people who were invited, 115 attended and 292 eventually signed the conference statement. Educators, religious officials, journalists, businessmen, and civic leaders made up the bulk of the delegates. With McGill presiding, they managed after a few hours of discussion to agree on the wording of their response.

The Southern Negro leaders in Durham had been "so frank and courageous," they declared, and so "free from any suggestion of threat and ultimatum, and at the same time [showed] such good will, that we gladly agree to cooperate." Discrimination based on race is indeed unfair, they went on; "primary justice and a simple sense of fair play demand" that we do better by all our citizens. The laws and customs of segregation and the "separate but equal" doctrine were not specifically mentioned; the emphasis was on cultivating an atmosphere of cooperation, goodwill, and mutual understanding. It was, all in all, a tepid endorsement of the black leaders, who had crawled carefully but courageously out on a very high limb.

There were those, of course, who wanted less from the whites, and some who wanted more, but Ames and Hancock were relieved and elated that the delicate process of step-by-step maneuvering was still on track. The next move would be to bring together a collaboration committee from the Durham and Atlanta meetings, and to keep the forward motion going.

Thirty-seven whites and an equal number of blacks were named to the joint committee that met at historic old St. Paul's Episcopal Church in Richmond on June 16, 1943, and thirty-three representatives of each race showed up on that hazy and humid Wednesday morning. By mutual consent of the planners—including the journalists Virginius Dabney and

Ralph McGill—the meeting was cloaked in secrecy, for fear that enemies right and left might be tempted to spoil the effort.

Among the few appointees who couldn't be present in Richmond were McGill, away on "war business" overseas, and Methodist Bishop Arthur J. Moore. The two influential Atlantans had played pivotal roles in bringing the committee of whites into cautious alignment with the Durham statement. In general, the blacks were represented by their acknowledged leaders—Johnson and Mays, Hancock and Young, Rufus Clement, Luther P. Jackson, Horace Mann Bond, and Charlotte Hawkins Brown, among others; the whites who took part, except for Dabney, Jessie Daniel Ames, and Howard Odum, were generally not people of regional stature. Dabney declined to serve as chairman. Most of the advance preparation, including a last-minute rush to prepare the agenda, fell to Ames, Hancock, and Young. They were discouraged, tense; this was not the smooth beginning they had wanted. When the appointed hour came, Young stood up to preside and called on Hancock for an opening statement.

St. Paul's was a fitting stage for this dramatic interracial gathering. Since the 1840s, the Greek Revival structure had maintained an imposing presence at the corner of Ninth and Grace Streets. It had architectural compatibility with another marble-columned edifice, the Classic Revival–style Virginia State Capitol, standing majestically on a shady lawn just across Ninth Street; Thomas Jefferson had designed the legislative forum in the 1780s, modeling it after a Roman temple.

The opulent interior of St. Paul's had sheltered many a famous son of the South. Jefferson Davis, president of the Confederacy, was sitting in his center-aisle pew there on April 2, 1865, when a messenger brought him the somber advice of his military leader, Robert E. Lee, to flee the city and avoid capture by Yankee invaders. Three years later, so one eyewitness account claimed, the gracious General Lee, defeated but not diminished, thereby "arose in his usual dignified and self-possessed manner" from his own St. Paul's pew and walked to the chancel rail to kneel beside a tall, well-dressed black man and partake of the communion sacraments with him, while others in the hushed sanctuary stared in shocked amazement. Who, sitting there in 1943, could not hear those echoes of history? Gordon B. Hancock certainly heard; when he stood to address his black and white fellow delegates, he was inspired by what he called "a now or never feeling," and his deep voice was filled with emotion.

"We have come upon one of those rare occasions of history when the clock of Destiny is striking a mighty hour," he said. Here is an unparalleled opportunity for the white South and the black South to save themselves and their nation. Negroes have been patient and loyal, and also super-patriotic; they have "borne their burdens with poise and courage."

The general absence "of open conflict between the races is due far more to the wisdom of Negro leadership than to the might of the white man." That leadership "can be strangled or strengthened," depending on how serious the white leadership is about making changes. The South "must cease waiting for outside sources to extort from it in the courts concessions that should be made without a fight"—equalized teachers' salaries, to cite one example. "It makes a world of difference to the cause of race relations whether the capitol of the Negro race is in New York City or Atlanta," Hancock declared.

Brick by brick, the Richmond social scientist built to his climax: "The South must save the Negro or itself be lost. . . . Men must be brotherized or they will be brutalized. . . . When it becomes dangerous to do right and when it is risky to be just, we are headed for social and economic damnation. . . . Negroes and whites who sit about today's counsel table are verily the saviors of our Nation. . . . The time is at hand when we of the South must . . . decide what we are going to do . . . if we have the moral courage to follow through."

The air inside St. Paul's was charged with emotional energy. Pride, fear, and anger were evident. It was the anger that first found its voice. M. Ashby Jones, the venerable Baptist minister from Atlanta who had served on the interracial commission since its inception, jumped up to denounce Hancock for "going too far," and went on to lecture "the colored people" in his patented paternalistic manner. In a rush of feeling, several people began to speak at once, and then to shout. The fragile coalition was about to blow apart.

It was precisely here that Howard W. Odum saw his long-awaited chance, and seized it. Stepping to the podium, he delivered a mild put-down of Jones for his outdated views, and supported the spirit and substance of Hancock's remarks. Not only that, but Odum also just happened to have in his pocket a modified new version of his old blueprint for a regional research and development council. As he talked on, it became apparent that the mood was shifting once again. Here was a compromise the delegates could all endorse with gratitude and relief—all except Jessie Daniel Ames and a few others.

Within a matter of hours, a committee headed by Odum had drawn up, and the group had approved, a statement of consensus (to be published later, when the fact of the meeting itself was revealed). In it they urged "the general adoption of the Durham statement" and pledged to "recognize now the importance of affirmative action, without which we shall fall far short of our hopes and possibilities." Then they chose from within their ranks about twenty whites and twenty blacks to meet in Atlanta, "working out methods and practical means of approach" for what would become a new biracial organization in the South, a council very much like Howard Odum's dream—or as near to it as he seemed likely to get. Virginius Dabney and Charles Johnson were chosen to lead the way in Atlanta.

Hancock's gratitude to Odum for saving the day would be eternal. He heaped praise on the sociologist (and saved a little for Jessie Ames, too), calling him "a moral and intellectual giant." Odum modestly accepted the plaudits. "Early that morning we realized that the Negroes had their top-flight leaders present and that most of the southern white leaders had defaulted," he told Hancock later, "and when your magnificent address on the crisis of Negro leadership had been rebuked by Dr. Jones . . . it became clear that there was a crisis."

As they looked ahead to the next phase, the principals in this long and subtle ritual maintained their formality and decorum, even when signs of strain and exasperation showed through. Still addressing one another as "Mrs. Ames" and "Mr. Dabney," "Dr. Hancock" and "Dr. Odum," they showed a determination to keep their composure that was in marked contrast to their more volatile counterparts in the Southern Conference for Human Welfare.

It is difficult to find descriptive terms for people like Hancock and Ames. Unlike Dabney and Odum, they were aggressive—more than willing to become personally involved in pressure-group politics, to plunge into the midst of controversy, to act instead of talk. Those who knew them best called them independent, moderate, conservative—anything but leftist or radical or revolutionary. They were very much alike in many ways— and yet they thought differently about the issue of race, and misunderstood each other on that subject. Hancock, like almost all black Southerners across the spectrum, wanted segregation to go away, to wither up and die; Ames, like many a white Southern liberal, didn't. She thought she could live with it, in part because it placed no shackles on her; he knew he couldn't, because the yoke was too heavy. In their moment of truth, Hancock was an open book, but Jessie Ames was still a puzzle. I can't help wondering what she really believed, and what she was after.

Hancock told Ames he was greatly distressed by "the difficulty of finding strong Southern white men who dare to assume the responsibility [for] the leadership of your group." The black leaders, he said, "risked everything" to make their statement at Durham; "unless white leaders are willing to risk something . . . to 'live dangerously' for noble ends, then we are hopelessly lost." For his part, he declared, "I am willing to go all out and risk my moral life if by so doing I can save the South from something that might happen to it."

Mrs. Ames seemed not to be listening; her mind was racing, trying to fathom the quickness of Odum's coup. What a twist of fate! There she was, about to rescue the CIC from its executioners, when all of a sudden one of the axmen prevented an ambush—and now, her own co-conspirators were about to help the executioners administer the coup de grâce. There were enough organizations already, she told Hancock testily, and no need for another. "I would not have you think that I personally am opposed," she quickly added. "If the group meeting in Atlanta decides that the times call for a new organization . . . I am the last person who would raise my finger to block it." But, she went on, although "Dr. Odum did prepare a masterly statement . . . it was prepared before he got there. It was what the white man thought should come out of that meeting and it was what came out of that meeting."

To Dabney, Ames confided that Odum, in all his years as president of the interracial commission, had given only "casual attention to our work. . . . He is a man of ideas . . . but unless he has a large staff of people to carry out his ideas, they seem to circulate in a vacuum." And Hancock, she said, wanted to have a new organization that "will immortalize the Negroes who met at Durham." Her last reed of hope was that the upcoming Atlanta meeting would choose William E. Cole, a University of Tennessee sociologist and the acting director, on a part-time basis, of the CIC, as permanent director of the new organization.

Forty delegates (including Ralph McGill and Bishop Arthur Moore) convened at Atlanta University on August 4 and 5 to take the next step. Dabney had sent last-minute regrets that he couldn't be there, but Charles Johnson presided, and with Odum looking on and the blacks in enthusiastic accord, he got through a resolution to create "a strong, unified Southern Regional Council." Unlike the old CIC (which would promptly be laid to rest) or any other group before it, including the Southern Conference for Human Welfare, the new organization would bend every effort to be equitably biracial—but like the others, it would not confront the burdensome question of segregation.

Odum and Johnson were named temporary co-chairmen of the new entity, and white-black parity was also reflected in the choice of William Cole and Ira De A. Reid as co-directors and the appointment of sixteen white and fourteen black board members. Preparations were made to set up the board and staff in the old CIC offices in Atlanta. Through the fall and early winter of 1943, those plans went forward. Finally, in an Atlanta courtroom on January 6, 1944, the Southern Regional Council was granted its charter, with five of its leaders—Odum, Johnson, McGill, Moore, and Clement—signing the incorporation papers. A charter meeting at Atlanta University on February 16 and 17 drew more than two hundred participants. They elected Odum to be president (after Bishop Moore declined) and Charles Johnson to be chairman of the executive committee, but William Cole was passed over in favor of Guy B. Johnson, a colleague of Odum's in the University of North Carolina sociology department.

Johnson, charitably endorsed by Cole, was made executive director, with Atlanta University sociologist Ira Reid as the associate director.

The Commission on Interracial Cooperation was officially dissolved, and Jessie Daniel Ames made her exit emotionally but gracefully with a stirring exhortation to black and white Southern women to lead the march for change after the war. (Though she left the staff, Ames did retain a seat on the SRC board of directors.)

Another page had been turned in the long saga of Southern liberalism. One more homegrown campaign for social reform was about to begin. The founding members of the Southern Regional Council, using words taken from their charter, closed their first official meeting with a pledge "to attain, through research and action, the ideals and practices of equal opportunity for all the peoples of the South."

When the executive committee met a month later, on March 22, the SRC was already under fire from the left. The Spring 1944 issue of *Common Ground* contained articles by J. Saunders Redding and Lillian Smith taking the white and black Southern liberals to task for ducking the segregation issue. Guy Johnson, speaking as executive director, was indignant; he vowed to have a strong rebuttal in the magazine's next issue. (*Common Ground* had asked Virginius Dabney and Howard Odum to give their views in the same issue with Redding and Smith, but they had declined.)

Redding, a Hampton Institute professor and one of the few regularly published black social critics in the region, faulted the SRC for "three basic contradictions": replacing a failed organization (the CIC) with a duplication of it, pursuing racial equality without opposing segregation, and trying to find a regional solution to a national problem. "The very conception of the Negro problem as one to be solved by the South alone is part of the old conceit that has kept the problem so long stalemated," said Redding. "It is the South's old cherished conceit that it *knows* the Negro and knows what to do about him."

Lillian Smith, facing toward Atlanta from her mountaintop in north Georgia, tried to be understanding. "I, too, am a Southerner," she wrote. "I know all the temptations not to speak out, all the fears . . . of losing jobs, losing prestige, losing friends." The "color conditioning" of white children in the South has required that "they learned from the people they loved most . . . that segregation is right. . . . And when one breaks the taboo of segregation . . . one feels a profound sense of guilt." But it was time to cast off those "infantile learnings and fears." The leaders of the SRC were not hypocrites, not evil people; they were sincere and able—

but confused. Said Smith, "Not much is going to be done to bring about racial democracy by this group until its leaders accept and *acknowledge publicly* the basic truth that segregation is injuring us on every level of our life and is so intolerable to the human spirit that we, all of us, white and black, must bend every effort to rid our minds and hearts and culture of it."

Smith had been nominated for a seat on the SRC board of directors at the February meeting, but no invitation had been sent to her. The executive committee agreed unanimously at its April meeting that she should promptly be asked in, but when she declined in June—and sent copies of her letter to the press—some members of the committee considered it good riddance. "We are not going to strengthen our position by inviting our hecklers to come in," Gordon Hancock wrote to Guy Johnson; such critics "do not belong with us." (The feeling was mutual, as far as Smith was concerned. She never did go in much for big-group relations. The Southern Conference for Human Welfare couldn't hold her, either; she resigned in 1945, after three years on its board, in part because it, like the SRC, was not forthright enough to suit her in its stance on segregation.)

Guy Johnson, when his turn came, wrote in *Common Ground* that Smith and Redding and the magazine's editors were "talking nonsense" if they believed the only way to "solve the race problem" was to "come clean and acknowledge publicly" that segregation is wrong and has to be abolished forthwith. "Our goal is democracy and equality of opportunity," he declared. "We are striving to improve the social, civic, and economic life of our region in spite of a deep-seated and undemocratic pattern of segregation. This pattern, we think, will be with us for a long, long time regardless of what any of us might think or say or do, and we believe that someone has to do the very things that we are doing before the dissolution of this pattern can even enter the realm of possibility."

Johnson's frustration ran deep. He was out of patience with sideline critics who couldn't see that it was "more realistic to base a movement on the support of thousands who are willing to do something than on a few lonely souls who denounce injustice but are powerless to do anything about it." Coming out of rural Texas in the early twenties to study under Robert Park at the University of Chicago, Johnson had developed an early and sincere empathy with the besieged black minority. With his wife, Guion Griffis Johnson, a historian, he had gone on to serve on the UNC faculty for twenty years. His interest as a sociologist was in minority and folk cultures, and from early in his career he had consistently argued that the South "owes the Negro a new deal," as he put it in a 1934 magazine article—by which he meant full and equal justice, opportunity, and encouragement. Johnson was highly regarded in the black academic world, not only as a good scholar but also as a decent fellow, fair-minded and sympathetic—but the sound and fury of public forums like the Southern Regional Council caused him almost nothing but grief and worry, and it only took a little while for him to tire of it and long for the soothing tranquillity of Chapel Hill.

Throughout its first year, the officers and members of the SRC debated the segregation question whenever and wherever they met. At one session of the executive committee, Francis R. Bridges, Jr., a state government official in Florida and one of the few council members who was a bureaucrat or a politician, argued that the organization ought to acknowledge and accept segregation as the law in the South, or else they would soon "alienate certain people" in power. Odum replied that he could never sign "any statement that says segregation forever is right." Black publisher Carter Wesley of Houston wanted to "by-pass" the question for the time being; he couldn't endorse the philosophy, he said, but "an open attack" on it would surely alienate the white establishment. In the end, the committee punted to the general membership.

Close to a hundred members attended the first annual meeting of the council at Atlanta University on December 6, 1944, and another hundred and fifty sent proxies. They passed a number of resolutions having to do with returning veterans that showed the general sentiment of the group: to guarantee voting rights, job opportunities, low-cost housing, equal education, access to transportation, and a fair justice system. Then they got around to the old sticking point: segregation.

At the risk of being accused of fostering racial separation, Carter Wesley said, "We must be realistic if we are going to accomplish anything in the South." He introduced a resolution acknowledging that legal segregation existed and saying the SRC would "center our efforts on gaining equal facilities as provided by law and equal opportunities for all the people of the South." Virginius Dabney supported that view; segregation meant discrimination, he conceded, but for the time being, they had to reassure people that it was far from the SRC's purpose to do away with it.

Then it was Gordon Hancock's turn to say the question shouldn't be addressed. "I'm more interested in getting something done than in getting something said," he declared. Frank McCallister seconded that view.

Benjamin Mays and Forrester Washington took a third position. Mays cast it in the form of a substitute resolution putting the council on record as opposing "the principle and practice of segregation" (the same language used in the Durham Manifesto), but adding that as long as it existed legally, the SRC would "work within the law to equalize all opportunities for Negroes."

Howard Odum spoke in opposition to both resolutions. Either way, we run the risk of being shot down, he said. A motion was made to table the two formal proposals. It passed easily. The council had cautiously stepped back to an ante-Durham position.

Will Alexander was allowed the last word on the insoluble problem. Sooner or later, he said, this council "must do something about segregation, but I'm not sure that we know anything effective to do about it at this moment." Whatever he thought about the council's options, Alexander had finally decided what his personal position must be; he had already written for the following month's issue of *Harper's* his critical article on "Our Conflicting Racial Policies," in which he concluded that "unless the problem of segregation can be solved, there is no hope of any alleviation of the race problem in America."

Alexander and Clark Foreman, who was by then the president of the Southern Conference for Human Welfare—and also a member of the SRC board—briefly discussed the possibility of merging SCHW and SRC, but few on either side were interested, and the idea died aborning. The organizations were at once too different (radical versus moderate) and too much alike (biracial, all-Southern, essentially middle-class) to be anything but wary rivals—or more accurately, small boats passing in the dark.

The Southern Regional Council had quickly run aground on the same treacherous rock that had disabled all the social-reform movements before it, liberal or progressive or moderate or what have you. Snared in the binding net between radicalism and reaction, it was already in the process of dividing into three factions: the anti-segregationists, the pro-segregationists, and those who wanted, if at all possible, to avoid the subject and follow other avenues to reform. Guy Johnson had been in the third group, but by January 1945 he recognized that the stalemate had to be broken by a turn in one direction or the other.

"We can't go on this way," he wrote to Dabney, who was solidly in the pro-segregation camp. "We either have to take [an anti-segregation] stand such as Mays proposed, lose most of our white support and see the Council become more and more an agitation agency, or we have to take the alternative course as embodied in Wesley's resolution, sacrifice some of our Negro members, and go out for the support of influential Southerners who are not now willing to come into the Council. Personally, I am now ready to support the latter course. In fact, if we don't do something of this sort pretty soon, I don't see much point in my being here. We might as well turn it over to somebody like Lillian Smith."

Even with Johnson on his side, Dabney was unwilling to accept the nomination to succeed Odum as the SRC's president. "The whole thing is fraught with explosive issues," he said, and he questioned whether "I can afford to be connected with the organization at all." Johnson turned next to Mark Ethridge, but he too declined. Finally, in February 1945, a disheartened Odum reluctantly agreed to stay in office one more year.

By mid-1945, fewer than a thousand people had paid their dollar-a-year membership dues, the executive committee was having trouble getting a quorum for its monthly meetings, and people like Ralph McGill and Frank Graham were on the outside, beyond the SRC's beckoning—where, like Lillian Smith, they would remain. The staff was planning to undertake a two-year study of segregation problems in the region, to be directed by Ira Reid, and a grant was obtained from the Rosenwald Fund to set up a support-service program for returning GIs, under the direction of George S. Mitchell. Regardless of its manifold problems, the Southern Regional Council was trying to go forward.

Meanwhile, a lot was happening in the outside world. The nation had a new President—Harry Truman—and the war would soon be over, and the entire South was teetering on the rim of the new world, wondering, like the Southern Regional Council, which way to lean.

8. *Farewell to the Chief*

At about five o'clock on Thursday afternoon, April 12, 1945, sixty-year-old Vice President Harry S. (his middle name, not an initial) Truman stopped by the private office of House Speaker Sam Rayburn in the Capitol for an end-of-the-day sip of bourbon with a few of his friends. "Call Steve Early," someone told him when he walked in. The message from FDR's top aide turned out to be a cryptic but urgent call to come to the White House. There, a short time later, Truman was escorted into Eleanor Roosevelt's sitting room, where a solemn First Lady rose to meet him. Gently she touched his shoulder and said, "Harry, the President is dead."

Truman was dazed, speechless; he felt tears welling up. Finally he managed to respond. His voice had a peculiar twang—Midwestern, nasal, scratchy, a little on the high side. Soon it would be familiar to millions of people around the world. "Is there anything I can do for you?" he asked.

Mrs. Roosevelt's answer was swift but sympathetic. "Is there anything *we* can do for *you*? *You're* the one in trouble now."

Just eighty-two days into his mission of joint service with a man he hardly knew, with whom he had conferred privately less than a half-dozen times, Harry Truman struggled with the realization that the ship's pilot was gone, and he was alone at the wheel.

Press Secretary Jonathan Daniels was among those present in the cabinet room an hour later when Chief Justice Harlan F. Stone administered the oath of office to the thirty-third President of the United States. Daniels would carry with him for a long time a vivid image of Harry Truman on that occasion: "He looked to me like a very little man as he sat waiting in a huge leather chair." More like a man on the way to his execution.

The Southerners who ran the Senate saw him as a little man too—the little man from Missouri—and they thought they had an understanding with him. He had been their colleague for ten years before being elected Vice President in 1944, and though he seldom voted with them on filibusters and states' rights issues, they believed he would pass a litmus test on white supremacy. After all, they reasoned, his grandparents were Kentuckians and Confederates, and Truman himself had that unmistakably Southern habit of cracking jokes about colored people in private conversation. "Everything's gonna be all right," said South Carolina Senator Burnet Maybank to a friend on the way back from Roosevelt's funeral. "The new President knows how to handle the niggers."

The Southern feudal lords had long been ready and eager for Franklin D. Roosevelt to fade from the scene. Ever since the mid-1930s (remember the court-packing scheme, the reforms that smacked of socialism, the attempted purge of his congressional enemies?), they had wanted him gone, but the war had saved him. Now, at last, the New Deal and the man who made it were out of the way, and the war seemed headed for a favorable conclusion, and the Southerners were still in the saddle on Capitol Hill. Confidently, they thought they could pour Truman a drink, butter him up a little, call him Mr. President instead of Harry but still make him feel like one of the boys—and get him to nip this civil rights nonsense in the bud.

Roosevelt had won their enmity—and the eternal praise of millions of Americans—not so much by what he actually did as by what he thought and felt and said. Beneath his friendliness and good cheer, the politicians were convinced, FDR really cared more for the unwashed masses than for the elite class of privileged movers and shakers to which they themselves—and he—belonged. The Southerners had witnessed in silent frustration the crippled President's strong bond with ordinary people; it was as if his handicap made him one of them, and gave them a feeling of kinship through shared vulnerability. To watch the man in action was to sense a feeling of personal courage, of fearlessness in the midst of every crisis. (Congressman Lyndon B. Johnson of Texas, weeping for the man he said was "just like a daddy to me," described the deceased FDR as "the one person I ever knew, anywhere, who was never afraid.") The vast multitude of Americans were touched by his compassion and convinced of his sincerity, but the Southern barons were much more cynical; they read his concern for the weak as a sign of his own weakness, and concluded that he was soft—on blacks, on reds, on radicals.

His grip on Congress had grown weaker with each succeeding election since 1936. Back then, the Republicans had been reduced to twenty senators and eighty-nine representatives; by the 1942 and 1944 elections, the GOP was threatening to recapture both houses—and, in league with the President's Southern enemies in his own party, they had effectively seized control. It was really the Southerners who held the reins, for they were not only in the majority party but claimed through seniority the chairmanships of most congressional committees. For a little while in the thirties, Roosevelt had felt that he no longer needed them; their revenge was to see to it that he couldn't get along without them—and in his helplessness, they delighted in frustrating his every move on the domestic front.

If FDR was reduced to such impotence, then, why did they still fear him and hate him? Part of the answer is that he managed to do a lot in spite of them; the rest of it is that his aspirations for the "forgotten" Americans, such as the South's peasants, white and black, were almost as important as his achievements in their behalf.

Roosevelt broke new ground. His cabinet substantially increased the desegregation of the federal bureaucracy, and FDR himself appointed more than a hundred African-Americans to upper-level administrative positions, including the first black citizen to be a federal judge and the first to be an army general. The black American minority as a whole had not made a significant economic or social advance by 1945; all but the exceptional few still had no integral role in the society other than subordinate labor, no secure prospect of adequate education or housing or health care, no promise of the equal protection of the law. But a start had been made, and the Roosevelt administration did at least seem to acknowledge the need for such changes.

Under FDR's leadership, the Democratic Party had seated black delegates for the first time at its 1936 convention, and four years later it put into the party platform a pledge "to strive for complete legislative safeguards against discrimination" in employment and military service. The President attracted some liberal white Southerners into the New Deal, and his eight appointees to the Supreme Court—including even James F. Byrnes, during his brief stay—set in motion a judicial reformation that would gradually but steadily eliminate the segregationist bias that had subverted the language and spirit of the U.S. Constitution over the previous half-century.

And not least, there was the President's wife. Eleanor Roosevelt was a new kind of First Lady, an activist who deliberately used her visibility and status to achieve social aims. To many, her words and actions were truly radical—scandalously so to some, gloriously so to others. Actually, there was very little in her manner or her thinking that fit the radical mold; she was a gracious patrician lady—an evolutionary, not a revolutionary. Like her husband and most other New Deal liberals, she believed that simple fairness and steady economic growth would be enough to make race and class discrimination disappear—and so believing, she was reluctant to confront the laws and customs of segregation and white supremacy.

But Mrs. Roosevelt was a shining symbol of justice and hope for the least fortunate of America's millions, and their affection for her, no less than for her husband, was boundless and constant. Together, Eleanor and Franklin gave downtrodden Southerners of both races (and others too, of course) reason to believe, for the first time in their lives, that things were better for them than they used to be, and would be better still tomorrow.

B etween April and August of 1945, the world was jolted by a rapid succession of epochal events. Less than three weeks after FDR died—so we were eventually told—Adolph Hitler committed suicide to avoid capture by the Allies. Germany surrendered on May 8. The charter of the new United Nations organization was completed and signed in late June, and the U.S. Senate ratified it by a vote of eighty-nine to two on July 28. (Secretary of State Cordell Hull, an old statesman from the Tennessee hills, was awarded the Nobel Peace Prize for his central role in birthing the world body.)

On August 6, a B-29 Superfortress dropped the first atomic bomb, a horrific new weapon with the explosive equivalent of forty million pounds of TNT, on the Japanese city of Hiroshima, killing or injuring more than 130,000 people. (The patriot South played a big part in this, as in so many other military missions: The plane had come off the assembly line of the Bell Bomber Plant, at Marietta, Georgia; the pilot was Colonel Paul W. Tibbets, Jr., of Miami and the bombardier was Major Thomas W. Ferebee of Mocksville, North Carolina; their devastating cargo, as powerful as the payload of two thousand conventional bombers, got its destructive force from an atomic substance, U-235, produced in the top-secret laboratories at Oak Ridge, Tennessee.) Three days later, another of the big bombs was dropped on the city of Nagasaki, with similar results. On August 14 the Japanese surrendered, and World War II was finally over.

So many earth-shattering developments in such a short time were too much to assimilate. Americans reeled from the pit of grief to the pinnacle of exhilaration; finally, in a euphoric frenzy, they put aside their doubts and worries and partied in the streets. Even before Japan's surrender, there was a tendency for people to shrug off the hard questions: What would be our role in the postwar world? What were we going to do with a menacing ally like the Soviet Union? How were we going to manage reconversion, the complex process of turning the war machine back to the service of a peacetime economy? What would life after Roosevelt be like?

The South had questions of its own. Nobody knew if the men and women in uniform or in war production would come back to the farms and small towns and take up where they had left off. Probably nobody imagined—not many, anyway—that King Cotton was permanently dethroned, that tenant farming and sharecropping would be replaced by corporate farming, or that the South in one short generation would be transformed from an overwhelmingly rural and agricultural society to a predominantly urban-industrial one. And only the dreamers gave much thought at all to what the white and black citizens of the region would do, if anything, to reduce discrimination and raise the living conditions and expectations of the vast multitudes of poor and needy people who lived among them.

The time for dreamers to become doers was almost at hand. Liberals and conservatives alike could see the new world a-coming; they had to know that, one way or another, the mighty wave of reformation that was sweeping across the world would not skip over them. Southern progressives, white and black, dreamed not only of the liberation of Europe and Asia but also of the liberation of their homeland from the feudal barons. There would be a fight for control of the South, a fight to redefine it and say what it stood for, as there would be virtually everywhere. Old Dixie was firmly in the grasp of the oligarchy now, as it had been for nearly three-quarters of a century—as it had been, you could almost say, forever—but in the postwar emergence of a victorious and renewed society, the South's liberals would have the best chance since the days of Thomas Jefferson and Andrew Jackson to take their case to the people.

Claude Pepper and Mark Ethridge and Ellis Arnall were prominent among those who were saying things like that in speeches and magazine articles and books. "There is no section of the country that needs liberalism so much as the South," Pepper told an Atlanta audience shortly before Roosevelt died. Ethridge, speaking in the same city a month later, declared that nothing but "aggressive liberalism" could save the region from further decline in the fast-moving and competitive postwar world. Arnall, the young Georgia governor whose term of office would end after the 1946 election, got national attention with his predictions of a dawning liberalism in the South. When the war ended, he was putting the finishing touches on a book, *The Shore Dimly Seen*, to convey his progressive ideas to a larger audience.

Most of the Southerners who had helped to invigorate the New Deal with liberal ideas had left the government by the time FDR died. Ethridge was long since out of the Fair Employment Practices Committee and back at the *Courier-Journal* in Louisville. Clark Foreman had moved to Nashville as president of the Southern Conference for Human Welfare. George Mitchell and Ira Reid were on the Southern Regional Council staff in Atlanta. Will W. Alexander had shifted his primary work station to Chicago, where he would remain as a principal figure in the Rosenwald Fund until it gave away all its assets and voluntarily dissolved in 1948. Aubrey Williams, perhaps the most liberal of them all, moved back to Alabama to publish the *Southern Farmer* in 1945 after the Senate, with its Dixie reactionaries in the lead, refused to confirm Roosevelt's appointment of him to head the Rural Electrification Administration.

Will Alexander, in league with Edwin Embree and Charles S. Johnson, took the Rosenwald Fund out in a blaze of glory. Over a twenty-year period, they had awarded fellowships to more than a thousand blacks and five hundred whites, most of them young Southerners whose potential for productive service had caught their eye. The three men, honoring their own strong Southern ties, had turned the largesse of Julius Rosenwald to the service of many a Southern school and social reform initiative. Toward the end, they addressed larger issues of segregation—in the nation's capital, in the Federal Council of Churches, in the U.S. armed forces. In all of those arenas, Rosenwald funds and ideas were instrumental in bringing about change.

As he neared retirement age, Alexander prepared to go home to the South. While he was away from his family all those years, Mabelle Kinkead Alexander, his wife, had raised their two sons in Atlanta and then, with her husband's blessing, had moved to Chapel Hill. There, Howard Odum helped her find a little farm to buy, and she supervised the building of a house that she and Dr. Will would share after he retired. Her project and his career would wind up at about the same time, and they would be there together, enjoying the simple pleasures of country life, just as the South and the nation entered the heated election season of 1948.

It may have been more than coincidental that the New Deal agencies most committed to assisting minorities and the poor and to being fair and nondiscriminatory in their employment practices were headed by Southern liberals: Alexander at the Farm Security Administration, Clark Foreman (under Harold Ickes) in the Public Works Administration, Mark Ethridge as chairman of the Fair Employment Practices Committee, Aubrey Williams and Mary McLeod Bethune at the National Youth Administration. Certainly it was no coincidence, either, that those agencies were among the primary targets of the Southern reactionaries in Congress. Almost from the start, they had exhibited an undisguised hostility toward all do-good programs and the bleeding hearts who ran them, but they reserved a special disgust and hatred for any and all "traitors to the South" whose egalitarian ideas deviated from the code of white supremacy.

In his gentle and affable manner, Alexander had given a humanitarian dimension to his tenure in the labyrinth of government. While many others were struck dumb and blind by a vast and impersonal bureaucracy, his eye was always on the sparrow; he saw more virtue in putting a roof over the heads of one struggling sharecropper family than in codifying all the arcane laws and regulations and directives of the U.S. Department of Agriculture. Having fought the evils of sharecropping and tenant farming for most of his years in Washington, he found himself at the end of his FSA days defending small family farm operations against the crushing juggernaut of corporate agribusiness.

In a sense, nothing had really changed. The South had gone from plantation slavery to planter-controlled tenant farming to what would eventually become high-tech corporate farming. Tractors and cotton-picking machines and other modern implements had given planters an excuse to evict tenants; when they needed seasonal cheap labor, they turned more and more to prisoners of war, to migrant workers recruited from Mexico and the Caribbean, to prison contract labor, or to former tenants held against their will for nonpayment of debts. All the evils the Vanderbilt Agrarians should have attacked but didn't in their 1930 manifesto on rural life were now beginning to crowd the yeoman farmers off the land. When Alexander looked around and saw that the American Farm Bureau, the federal land-grant colleges of agriculture, and even some branches of the USDA (such as the Extension Service) were often arrayed with the planters and other big-time commercial operators against the small-scale tillers of the soil, he knew that he had lost the battle if not the war. He resigned from the Farm Security Administration in 1940, but filled other emergency posts in the government on a temporary basis through much of the war before moving on to Chicago.

If Alexander's exit from Washington was quiet and undramatic, Aubrey Williams's was more like a theatrical display of thunder and lightning. His enemies in the Senate, led by Kenneth McKellar of Tennessee, thought they had disposed of him in 1943 when they abolished the National Youth Administration, of which he was the director. Williams left the government briefly to work for the National Farmers Union, but FDR wanted him back, and in January 1945 the President nominated him to head the Rural Electrification Administration, an agency in constant hot water with the nation's private power and utility interests. Roosevelt's "forgotten man," out there holding back the dark with a kerosene lantern, could not have wished for a more willing and able advocate—or a better man—than Aubrey Williams.

But McKellar and his allies were determined to stop him. They had just fought a losing battle to prevent former Vice President Henry Wallace from becoming Secretary of Commerce, and they were in no mood to swallow another bitter pill. At hearings before the Senate Agriculture Committee, the McKellar forces went after the nominee with a vengeance. They alleged that he had criminally misused public funds, and fumed that he advocated equal employment even when it meant "whites are forced to use toilets with the blacks"; further, they charged that as a teenager, he had "denied the divinity of Christ." Then they brought out the "communism file," ever the favorite weapon of antidemocratic adversaries; Williams was accused of "being a member of either four or five of the Communist-front organizations."

He was a combative witness, never yielding ground. He challenged the committee "to produce one single iota of evidence" that he had ever been connected in any way with the Communists. He flatly denied ever having misspent public money. He refused on principle to discuss his religious beliefs, saying they were "a matter between myself and my God." He said the ability to perform a job ought to be the only requirement for getting it, even if that meant toilet-sharing. "I am a Southerner," Williams declared, in his best Alabama voice. "I was born in the South, and I have been proud of the fact . . . but I have been saddened that the South has not progressed as the other sections of the country have." One of the main reasons, he asserted, was that the bosses pitted working-class whites and blacks against each other and kept both groups from advancing or getting fair treatment.

The fight spilled over onto the Senate floor. Williams was not entirely without Southern support; Claude Pepper, Lister Hill, and Alben Barkley were for him, and so too, surprisingly, were Allen Ellender of Louisiana and Clyde Hoey of North Carolina. Broad-based approval came from labor and from a national "Friends of Aubrey Williams Committee" that included Mark Ethridge and Jonathan Daniels. But McKellar, Bilbo, and company had all the rest of the Southern votes, and they brought more than enough others along with them. When the count was finally recorded after weeks of jockeying, it came out fifty-two to thirty-six against Williams. The New Deal liberals had taken another heavy hit.

Bitterly discouraged—and soon to be shocked and depressed by the death of the President he so revered—Aubrey Williams packed his bags and left Washington. In his eyes, and in those of many of his supporters, it was the race issue that had done him in. His home-state senators—Hill, who braved the wrath of the Big Mules to vote for him, and John Bankhead, who went the other way—both indicated that a little less candor on his part would have brought him at least half of the nay-saying Southerners, enough for a narrow victory.

But nobody really expected less candor from Williams; no doubt all of them, friends and enemies alike, would have lost their respect for him—or their fear of him—if he had equivocated. He would go on speaking out against race and class discrimination and for his all-souls vision of democracy. And besides, he said, it was not his racial views but those of McKellar and Bilbo and all the others of their ilk that contradicted the ideals and principles of American democracy—the very principles for which our troops had been fighting and dying around the world.

As America and its allies gradually gained the upper hand in Europe and the Pacific, discrimination against black citizens on the home front had the double-barreled effect of escalating both black protest and white reaction. On the one side, there was a spreading sense of outrage that discrimination based solely on skin color was locking people out of jobs, housing, hospitals, schools, and even most combat units fighting fascism and imperialism abroad; on the other, retaliation and repression seemed to be the motivating instincts of whites who blocked the routes of upward black mobility.

For all the differences that separated Southern from Northern blacks and Southern from Northern whites, the deeper meaning of these conflicts was that America was dividing more along racial than regional lines. Urban riots and other manifestations of violence in the war years were as likely to surface above the Mason-Dixon line as below it. Job discrimination was a problem in all industries, regardless of their location. It was the U.S. armed forces that segregated blacks or excluded them altogether, and it was the Red Cross—American, not Southern—that segregated blood. In the upper echelons of the New Deal, there were some Yankees whose pronouncements on white supremacy sounded every bit as bigoted as any run-of-the-mill Southern politician's; Secretary of War Henry L. Stimson, a New Yorker with degrees from Harvard and Yale, blamed racial tensions on "the deliberate effort . . . of certain radical leaders of the colored race to use the war for obtaining . . . race equality and interracial marriages."

White residents in every section of the country were at best deluded about the extent of racial bias, and at worst actively engaged in aggressive stimulation of it. Three out of every five whites, according to opinion polls, thought Negroes already had all the rights and opportunities they deserved, and were satisfied with what they had. Even in the North and West, a clear majority of whites expressed a preference for segregation, considered the lowly position of blacks to be a direct consequence of their own inadequacies, and anticipated no significant improvement in their status after the war.

But for depth and breadth of hostility, the white South still easily swept the field. Notwithstanding the emergence of such groups as the Southern Conference for Human Welfare and the Southern Regional Council, the vast majority of white citizens in the old Confederate states and those bordering them had no positive urge to join in any expression of interracial solidarity, no matter how conservative its aims. The lion's share of them may simply have been too timid to risk the disapproval of their neighbors, but it was the rest—the demagogues and ideologues of right-wing extremism—who stole their courage.

The U.S. Congress was stymied and silenced by its rebel faction of Southern Democrats and their reactionary (mostly Republican) cohorts. The states were operated in blatantly undemocratic fashion by governors and legislators whose allegiance was not to the people at large and least of all to the blacks, but to the planter-banker-businessman oligarchy whose feudal domain the South truly was; local governments were almost as unresponsive. The scattered few individual exceptions—a Claude Pepper here, an Ellis Arnall there, a white liberal or even a black minor official yonder—only proved the rigid rule: Segregation reigned supreme. A tiny handful of journalists and ministers, college presidents and professors, civic and charitable group leaders, did sometimes speak out against violence and injustice, but only a minuscule fraction of them openly challenged segregation itself—and they were vilified and ostracized for doing so. The Ku Klux Klan, the German-American Bund, and the shirted factions of fascism had more standing in the average Southern community than any outspoken integrationist. In the South, almost anything could be done in the name of white supremacy.

The black press, organizations such as the NAACP and the National Urban League, and a host of individual African-Americans grew increasingly bold in their demands for simple justice, and their "Double-V" slogan—victory in the fight for democracy both here at home and overseas—became the proud watchword of virtually all Americans of color. The NAACP nearly tripled the number of its local chapters and increased its membership ninefold between 1940 and 1946. With growing confidence, the *Crisis* and other black publications spoke for these rising numbers with ringing declarations: "We want democracy in Alabama and Arkansas, in Mississippi and Michigan, in the District of Columbia—*in the Senate of the United States.*"

What may have angered black men the most—and at the same time underscored their patriotism and courage—was being rebuffed in their demand for a full and equal combat role in the war. It took a storm of protest to bring about the reactivation of two segregated infantry divisions, spiritual descendants of the celebrated "buffalo soldiers" of the nineteenth century and World War I. By mid-1944 the army had close to three-quarters of a million blacks in uniform, more than half of them posted overseas—but only a handful of the thousand-plus black officers were assigned to combat units. In Europe and Africa and in the Pacific, the black soldiers stood tall; in the Ninety-second Division alone, more than six hundred men won combat medals in North Africa and Italy, and General Mark Clark, under whose command they fought, described their service as "glorious." Generals Patton, Eisenhower, and MacArthur had similar praise for their units of black soldiers. Said MacArthur in 1945, "Their patience, their fortitude, their courage, and their complete devotion to their country mark them as belonging to the nation's noblest citizens."

I said *almost* anything could be done in the South in the name of white supremacy. But not absolutely anything. There was a limit, and Mississippi's outrageous senators, Theodore Bilbo and James O. Eastland, finally reached it in June 1945, just before the war was over, with a broad-brush fusillade of slanderous and defamatory blasts at black soldiers and various others not blessed with white Anglo-Saxon Protestant purity. In the slow heat of a Southern filibuster (ultimately successful) to prevent a vote on the creation of a permanent Fair Employment Practices Commission, the Mississippians and their allies indulged in their usual excesses of oratory. It was Eastland, though, who plumbed new depths.

He had been told, he said, by "numerous high-ranking generals" what he already knew to be true: that "nigra soldiers" in the U.S. Army had been "an utter and abysmal failure" in the war—deserters, cowards, quitters, rapers of white women. They had "no initiative, no sense of responsibility, and very low intelligence." They had "disgraced the flag of their country." In just four years as a senator, James Eastland had proved himself to be every bit as rabid a racist as Bilbo and their House colleague John Rankin—even though that took some doing. (When an Italian-American woman from Brooklyn "with four brothers fighting the Nazis" wrote him a critical letter, Bilbo shot back a snide and abusive reply that began "Dear Dago"; to another critic, he wrote that his mission was to stop the 13 million blacks and 5 million Jews in America from "running roughshod over the rights and freedoms of the 120 million white American citizens.")

Never mind what the generals had really said about black heroism and valor—Eastland and Bilbo considered such praise to be nothing but propaganda, lies. It was harder, though, for them to dismiss the words of a white Mississippi hero, Lieutenant Van T. Barfoot of Carthage. Awarded bronze and silver stars and a Medal of Honor for his numerous acts of bravery, Barfoot seemed shyly ill at ease when he met with the Mississippi congressional delegation in Washington. But he stiffened when Bilbo asked him, "Did you have much trouble with nigras over there?"

"I found out after I did some fighting in this war that the colored boys fight just as good as the white boys," the lieutenant drawled. "I've changed my ideas a lot about colored people since I got into this war, and so have a lot of other boys from the South." Barfoot went on to relate a story about having dinner in the diner with a black captain on the train trip up to Washington. "I've fought with colored men—why shouldn't I eat with them?" he asked. Bilbo and Eastland fumed in silence.

The daily newspapers of the South were almost unanimous in their condemnation of the Mississippi senators; fewer than five percent saw any truth in their slanders against the black soldiers. It was one thing to oppose the integration of juries or police departments or political parties, but it was something else altogether to say that men who had fought a common enemy heroically, who had risked and sometimes given their lives for others, were nothing but cowards and traitors. That was simply too much.

It was a genuine novelty for white newspaper editors in the South to rise in unison to defend black Americans—Southerners and others—from attacks by Southern politicians. The war did that; it had a profound effect on the social consciousness of the American people. Keep in mind that this was not a military action against faceless aggressors; this war was billed as a crusade to save democracy from fascism and imperialism and racism, as a life-or-death battle pitting liberty against totalitarianism, freedom against dictatorship. At a cost of a million casualties and tens of billions of dollars, the United States came to the aid of its allies and saved "the free world" from an "outlaw world" personified by Hitler and Mussolini and Tojo. And then, having done that, we had to face the question of whether all those things we were fighting for would be the birthright of whites only, or of all Americans.

It was World War II, more than the Great Depression or the New Deal, that ushered in the modern age. The war turned hard times into hopeful times, it moved people up and out, it changed our ways of thinking and working and living. It ended in a cataclysmic flash of blinding light and searing heat, a paradoxical mushroom symbol of death and birth; it heralded the realignment of nations, the coming of new technology, the beginning of the cold war. Practically everything about this war, from the way we got into it to the way we got out of it, suggested transformation.

After this, the times and the experience seemed to tell us, nothing will ever be the same again; this is an end and a beginning.

Southern blacks shared the hopeful view of many others that great and positive changes would come from winning the war, and they were willing, even eager, to fight the battles in order to enjoy the spoils of victory. Charles S. Johnson said in a radio address late in 1944 that time and history were on the side of the colored populations around the globe, for they far outnumbered the Caucasians. Seen in that light, Jim Crow segregation was a ridiculously outmoded relic. Harold Preece, a columnist for several black newspapers, said in "an open letter to the Southern boys, white and Negro," that if they would stick together after the war, they could prevent "the riding boss and the mill owner" from returning to the divide-and-conquer strategy of old. "If we black folk perish, America will perish," Richard Wright had warned the white majority in 1940, and he had held up a lantern on "the common road of hope which we all have traveled."

Realistically, though, black Southerners in particular and all Southerners in general faced massive opposition in their struggle for racial and regional equality. The defining pillars of society—political parties, the church, the academy, the press, the commercial-industrial complex, the moneylenders, the military—still functioned confidently according to the laws and habits of segregation and inequality. A few labor unions had broken out of those restraints, and there were scattered signs of change elsewhere—in the music world, for example, and in some reformist organizations, and even in certain factions of the Democratic Party in the North. But by and large, the white South still followed the lead of men who would not hear of any lessening of white supremacy, even if the status quo also meant a perpetuation of the South's inferior ranking in the nation—and without a doubt, it did.

Even for those who traveled on the road of hope—soldiers bonded by the shared dangers of war, for example—homecoming usually meant a return to old ways of thinking and acting. The new American Veterans Committee, a liberal and interracial organization of ex-GIs, was forming chapters around the country (Atlanta, Nashville, and Chapel Hill were among the first in the South), but it was dwarfed by the American Legion and the Veterans of Foreign Wars, both of which were conservative and—in the South, at least—segregated. In most of the Southern states, the American Legion not only maintained all-white posts; it even prohibited the formation of all-black units. In the District of Columbia, an effort by two hundred veterans of both races to establish an integrated post was vetoed by the organization's national leadership.

Racial friction broke out repeatedly on public buses and trains. The

Southern Railroad routinely sided with whites in these disputes—but so did the Louisville & Nashville, the Illinois Central, the Chesapeake & Ohio, and other lines running through the South. A lawsuit filed by black riders ejected from a Southern Railroad train in Virginia in 1943 would eventually result in a 1946 ruling of the U.S. Supreme Court outlawing forced segregation on interstate routes. In 1944, Benjamin Mays, the president of Morehouse College, also sued the Southern for forcing him out of a dining car (this after one of his faculty members, English professor Hugh Gloster, was pulled off a crowded train in Tupelo, Mississippi, severely beaten, and jailed for asking the conductor to make more seating available to black passengers). Reports of such mistreatment were heard repeatedly from every state in the South. Every time someone gained an inch, it seemed, the yardstick got longer.

The catalog of imposed and self-inflicted problems was distressingly old and lengthy. Southerners seldom had the pleasure of coming out on top in anything they did. For most of them, the view had always been from the bottom looking up, from the outside looking in. "Been down so long, looks like up to me," they sang through the hard times. How could they not be hopeful now that the war had ended? Their problems were still before them, still weighing them down—but glowing on the horizon was that breathtaking sense of possibility which blossomed out of military victory. Things *would* be different, they had to be—and if they were different, surely they would be better, not worse.

Tens of thousands of Southerners would remember years later—and some of them remember yet—the mournful sight of the train taking Franklin Delano Roosevelt's body back to Washington. On his widow's instructions, the Southern Railroad steam locomotive took twenty-five hours to crawl the more than eight hundred miles from Warm Springs to the Union Station terminal, across the way from the Capitol. The route through Georgia and the Carolinas and Virginia was a watercolor canvas of redbuds and dogwoods and azaleas, a landscape awash with the floral brilliance of spring. It was as if the South had come in its coat of many colors to pay its heartfelt respects, and to say farewell to an old friend.

Throughout the day and night, people stood all along the route to watch and cry, to sing hymns, to pray. In cities and towns, at whistlestop crossings, in newly plowed and planted fields, they were there in twos and dozens, hundreds and thousands. The numbers were astonishing; some guessed two million, the newscaster David Brinkley later wrote. They were the South's own best image of itself—men and women and children of all ages, races, and classes whose deeply held beliefs and aspirations came not from the feudal barons who kept them in check, but from this crippled yet towering, irrepressible, and invincible Yankee who had given them hope and courage. They may have feared the demagogues of Dixieland, but this was the leader they respected and admired, the one who had brought out the best in them, the one they would have followed to the ends of the earth—and now they watched sadly as he left the South for the last time, rolling away to his grave.

In the last car, the curtains were kept open and the lights on for the entire trip, so that people along the way could see the flag-draped coffin, the military honor guard—and, some of the time, Eleanor Roosevelt herself, sitting there alone. When the train had moved past them and disappeared from sight, the Southerners went back to their hoeing and other labors, wondering what in God's name would happen next.

FDR's last journey out of Warm Springs was not the only indelible image the South would have as a keepsake of 1945, of course. There would be the first impressions of the crusty new President, his Missouri ways so different—and yet somehow familiar, like distant kin. There would be the bombs of August, the mushroom clouds, the formal acceptance of Japanese surrender by General Douglas MacArthur (who, proud citizens of Little Rock were quick to tell you, was born there in 1880). And there would be the joyful and rambunctious victory celebration, a unifying act of thanksgiving that stitched the frayed fabric of America together, however briefly.

And these scenes of stark contrast, like old snapshots browned with age: the mules of yesterday and the tractors of tomorrow, turning the good earth side by side; cotton-picking people in a losing race with cotton-picking machines; TVA power lines strung like spiderwebs over lantern-lit shacks; the black engine of the South—nurses, cooks, housekeepers, field hands—holding body and soul together in a society that denied them the vote, the law, even a sip of fountain water or a place to relieve themselves.

Penny postcards and three-cent stamps, a nickel cup of coffee, Lucky Strikes and Camels for a dime a pack, dinner at Antoine's for three or four bucks, a good pair of leather shoes for ten, a wool suit for twenty—and before long, a new Ford or Chevy for five or six hundred. It was a portentous time, ominous and glorious, threatening and promising. One door closing, another opening.

The South was alive with anticipation, expectation, foreboding. Eighty years after Appomattox, here was another chance to start again on a clean slate. Who could not be tempted? Who wouldn't want to stick around to see what happened next?

Interlogue:
Yesterday and Tomorrow

Ralph Emerson McGill leaned out the window of his fourth-floor office at the Atlanta *Constitution* and beamed happily at the swelling throng of revelers down on Forsyth Street. Late on that Tuesday afternoon, August 14, 1945, confirmation of Japan's long-awaited surrender had finally come, and World War II was officially over. The street scene filling McGill's field of vision had a dreamlike quality, an air of unreality. In that euphoric moment of triumph, words seemed pitifully inadequate, even to a voluble Southerner with the eyes and ears of a reporter and the heart of a poet. Like so many others, McGill had waited anxiously for the long night of deadly warfare to end, for dawn to break. It was time, past time, for a new day—and surely, he thought, no one yearned for it more earnestly than did the long-suffering people of the South.

McGill had his own very personal reasons to celebrate. At the age of forty-seven, he was the best-known newspaperman in Georgia, if not the entire South. Having supported the political and social goals of Franklin Delano Roosevelt and the New Deal from 1932 onward, he had found himself in a position, as editor of the *Constitution* in 1939, to give influential backing to the President's military policies, and he had stuck to those editorial guns with unflagging zeal for six long years. Now the fruits of victory were America's and the South's to savor—made less sweet only by the death of FDR four months earlier—and McGill, a relentless newshound, was eager to get out on the road and take the pulse of his readers, to talk with and listen to the salt-of-the-earth country folks of Georgia.

He had been overseas in April when Roosevelt died, and he was still away later that month when his wife gave birth to their only son and named him Ralph Junior. After the death in infancy of a daughter in 1936 and the subsequent death at age five of an adopted daughter, Mary Elizabeth and Ralph McGill had not expected, in the seventeenth year of their marriage, to get another chance at parenting. They received the blessing with grateful hearts. Fatherhood seemed to mellow the middle-aged editor, to elevate his spirits and give him a newfound sense of hopefulness and optimism. The outbreak of peace added further to his mood of well-being. By the time he got home on that exhilarating night of victory,

McGill had hatched a plan to take a little trip through the Georgia countryside with his wife the next day, leaving the baby in capable hands at
home.

McGill never learned to drive an automobile; it was a chore he gladly
left to his wife and friends. Mary Elizabeth piloted the family car, and on
this occasion she had the rare pleasure of launching the journey with a
tankful of just-unrationed gasoline at twelve cents a gallon. Heading south
on U.S. 41, with the windows rolled down and the heat rising in shim-
mering waves off the pavement that stretched in front of them, the McGills
seemed not to mind poking along at the thirty-five-mile-an-hour speed
limit. Gradually they relaxed and surrendered to the slow country rhythm,
absorbing the healing warmth of a Georgia summer day in a world at
peace.

As the morning wore on, McGill used a yellow legal pad to jot down
quotes from some of the people they encountered, as well as some of his
own thoughts and impressions. Later he drew from the notes to compose
his next day's column. Away from the city it seemed like Sunday, he
wrote—quiet and tranquil, with lots of businesses closed and people
lounging in the shade, relaxed but happy, talking and laughing, celebrating. It could have been the Fourth of July.

They made a pilgrimage to Warm Springs, seventy-five miles from
Atlanta. At the Little White House, McGill removed his hat and stood for
a reflective moment of silent tribute to his fallen leader. At the military
hospital nearby, he and his wife attended a service of remembrance and
thanksgiving conducted by war-wounded patients, and McGill was deeply
moved by their heartfelt prayers and by the gentle dignity and simplicity
of the occasion. Here was the strength and glory of America, he clearly
saw, embodied in such heroic young people as these. When he got on the
phone in Columbus that night to call in his column to the paper, McGill's
spirits were soaring. "All I can see for this country is the green light," he
concluded.

There were plenty of problems lurking out there, no question about
it—management versus labor, capitalism versus communism, Democrats
against Republicans, whites against blacks, the North over the South—but
McGill the conciliator looked with hope to an era of genuine progress. He
had recently been to Russia, and though the Soviet system of government
repelled him, he expressed great admiration and respect for the "brave,
enduring" Russian people. (In the *Constitution* on August 8, it was bigger
news that Russia had declared war on Japan than that the United States
had dropped an atomic bomb on a Japanese city.) The Russians were our
allies, McGill argued. The American Communist Party was too puny to
worry a great nation like ours. Instead of finding a red conspiracy in every

act of friendship—such as General Dwight Eisenhower's just-concluded visit with Joseph Stalin in Moscow—we ought to be celebrating the defeat of fascism and imperialism, the signing of the new United Nations charter, and the coming conversion of swords into plowshares. Ralph McGill wanted desperately to believe that people were basically decent and that, given a chance, they would do the right thing.

All around him in Atlanta and elsewhere in Georgia and the South, he saw people who reinforced his sense of hope, his belief in the future. Mayor William B. Hartsfield, a Eugene Talmadge conservative when he took office in 1937, was turning out to be a progressive leader (his service to the city would eventually extend for almost a quarter of a century). Governor Ellis Arnall was in the third year of a highly successful four-year term, and there was talk of a constitutional amendment to allow him to seek reelection. The state's two senators in Washington, Richard B. Russell and Walter George, were more conservative—but they were statesmen, not yahoos, McGill believed. They had joined the Southern revolt against President Roosevelt, but now they had Harry Truman in the White House—a former member of their club and a border-state Southerner besides—and that augured well for the future.

The Southern Regional Council, created in 1944 with the help of McGill and others to succeed the Commission on Interracial Cooperation, was poised to bring improvement in race relations to the city and the region. Leaders of the higher-education community, men like Rufus Clement, Goodrich White, and Benjamin Mays—presidents, respectively, of Atlanta University, Emory University, and Morehouse College—were joining with other professionals to point the way to cooperation among the many elements of political and social thought in the city. Others besides Clement and Mays who represented the growing black middle class— people like attorney A. T. Walden, editor C. A. Scott, Urban League director Grace T. Hamilton, ministers William Holmes Borders and Martin Luther King, Sr.—were showing their determined intention to become active participants in Atlanta's postwar civic dialogue.

Even the forces of business and labor, perennially at war with each other, displayed a promise of better things to come in the cooperative spirit of such McGill allies as Robert W. Woodruff of the Coca-Cola Company and Lucy Randolph Mason of the Congress of Industrial Organizations. Conversion of the big aircraft and automotive plants in the Atlanta area to nonmilitary production was imminent, and that was more good economic news for the city. Governor Arnall's antitrust suit against twenty-three railroads was on appeal to the U.S. Supreme Court, and the Interstate Commerce Commission in Washington, anticipating the probable outcome of the case, was finally bestirring itself to equalize freight rates.

The arbitrary advantage of cheaper shipping costs long enjoyed by Northern business and industry was a galling bias that symbolized to many Southerners the intolerable perpetuation of Yankee dominion; now, at last, there was good reason to believe that the discrimination and inequality would soon end.

Atlanta had grown big enough to have a significant impact on postwar life in the region; with a half-million people in its metropolitan area, it would soon rank (along with New Orleans, Houston, and Dallas) among the South's first real cities on a national scale. Moreover, it was acquiring a progressive image as a prosperous and enlightened place, or so its leaders liked to think. A turn-of-the-century historian had credited Atlanta with "a spirit of pluck and push," and that tag still seemed apt. (You may recall that it was Henry Grady, a forerunner of McGill at the *Constitution*, who popularized New South boosterism in the 1880s.) As its visionaries and dreamers saw it, postwar Atlanta was an oasis, a beachhead, a base camp for building the competitive, productive, tolerant New South that generations had heralded in vain.

Ralph McGill was a vital factor in the realization of such hopes and expectations as these—indeed, it was he who regularly put the idealism of Tomorrow's South into words for his readers. Encountering his column day in and day out, all sorts of people were drawn to a sober but positive consideration of what the future promised. McGill himself could not have imagined just how transforming and revolutionary some changes would be: air-conditioning in stores, buses, churches, factories, homes, cars; jet engines that would bring Atlanta hours closer by air to the rest of the country, and freeways that would shrink driving time; television as a fact of daily life in practically every home; the miracle of penicillin; the virtual eradication of tuberculosis, polio, and other once-dreaded diseases; the massive influx of veterans to colleges and universities under the GI Bill, giving birth to the notion of universal higher education; a consumer-driven economy that would put more cash in people's pockets and more conveniences in their homes than any other society had ever come close to having.

And those marvels would only be a beginning, the first fruits of a long and bountiful harvest. McGill also recognized the obstacles, of course, and wrote about them honestly—but on the eve of Tomorrow he saw only the green light, and he told his readers, and they saw it too.

A boy of ten doesn't think much about such things, especially in a town without any traffic lights. In those golden days of postwar glory, Cadiz, Kentucky (population 1,228), had all the markings—as I saw it then, and as I look back on it now—of a great place to be a kid. Small and isolated though it was, Cadiz left little to be wished for by prepubescent boys like me. It was safe. Summer mornings, you could leave home on your bike after breakfast and stay gone all day without alarming your mother. Everybody seemed to keep up with everybody else; a familiar query I still remember was "Does your mama know where you're at?" No one thought anything at all of young boys hitchhiking to Hopkinsville, twenty miles away, or swimming in the murky depths of Little River, or spending long hours in the poolroom up on Main Street—the nearest thing Cadiz had to a YMCA or a community center.

In those days, when television was still a pipe dream, porch talk was a favorite medium of exchange on warm evenings. Children grew up around adults for whom talk was one of the few available forms of entertainment, and youngsters soaked up stories and gossip and debates as if by osmosis. Talk was something you just took without thinking, like sweet milk and Sunday school and the Pledge of Allegiance. The richly varied voices of Southerners still resonate deep within me—languid, lyrical, melodious voices, soft and slow, with inflections and intonations that shift subtly from place to place, person to person, story to story. Little did I realize then how much I gained from all those Southern voices, and from the many other benevolent manifestations of local, rural, regional culture—family, food, music, religion, history. It had its negative and destructive aspects too, of course, but somehow the good side of Southern life in the forties is what I remember best. It was a culture on the threshold of rapid modernization, and it is now so transformed from that simpler time a half-century ago as to be almost beyond recognition.

I went into the fifth grade that fall after the war ended. Some of my friends and classmates were hard up, to use a then-familiar term, but I don't recall that poverty, by itself, was a dividing force among us, and almost no one that I knew of, regardless of need, grew up with a debilitating sense of being poor. Nobody called attention to the fact that we all lived in a poor town of a poor county of one of the poorest states of the impoverished and disadvantaged South, and that our education, our health, our employment opportunities, and the general state of our lives suffered in comparison with more affluent Americans elsewhere. What mattered most to us was none of the above; it was how good a ballplayer you were, whether or not you shot a decent game of pool, what you thought of girls, and how you handled yourself in a fight.

I didn't know much about what was going on in the world—only that the war was over, Roosevelt was dead, and Truman was the new President. But closer to home, I was beginning to notice a few things. With the return of our fighting men from the war came some strangers, like the wonderfully exotic Johnny DeName, an Italian-American Catholic from Brooklyn who married a local girl and dazzled us all with his accent, his jitterbugging, and the authentic zoot suit he wore to the Methodist church every Sunday. Camp Campbell, the army base that had taken a twenty-thousand-acre chunk out of Trigg County, brought many more newcomers to us, and some of them stayed, and together they enriched the local population. The base became a permanent fort, and thus a major employer of civilians in our county.

In the opposite direction, forty miles northwest of Cadiz, the Tennessee Valley Authority's huge hydroelectric dam at Gilbertsville was completed after the war (President Truman himself came to dedicate it in October 1945), and more commuter jobs were created around that facility. Federal projects would eventually take more than a third of our county's land area and become, at least indirectly, the primary source of its non-agricultural income. Historically Democratic Trigg County showed its appreciation by handing Roosevelt four straight landslide victories, and it would do even better for Truman and his running mate, Kentucky Senator Alben Barkley, in 1948, giving them three times as many votes as the Republican Thomas Dewey, the Progressive Henry Wallace, and the Dixiecrat Strom Thurmond combined.

In those uncomplicated days of my budding adolescence, I lived in blissful ignorance of all but the most immediate concerns—family, school, church. Wide-eyed, I saw and heard for the first time such new-age wonders as television sets, gas-powered lawnmowers, window air-conditioning units, clothes dryers, food blenders, and car radios. I read the sports pages of the Louisville *Courier-Journal*, listened to radio broadcasts of St. Louis Cardinals baseball games, played Ernest Tubb and Hank Williams honky-tonk songs on the poolroom jukebox, and discovered the sublime enigma of the opposite sex. In my innocence, cigarettes and beer were just about the only habit-forming substances I ever heard of, let alone tried, and my introduction to both was blessedly harmless and untraumatic.

One more sign of ignorance stands out starkly in retrospect. Kentucky was a border state with a black population of well under ten percent, and it was in most ways less obsessed with white supremacy than were its Deep South neighbors. Its politicians didn't talk much about race, and blacks were not locked out of the voting booth or the jury box. But segregation was ingrained in the culture, and everybody, white and black, abided by its laws and customs unquestioningly, and their obedience gave a false presumption of logic to the inequitable rules. About one-fifth of Trigg County's total of nine thousand or so residents were black. They held no political offices, owned few businesses, and had no professional class other than teachers and preachers. They were not welcome in the Main Street churches, the public swimming pool (built with New Deal dollars), the movie theater (except in a tiny balcony area), or the pool-room. The county school system offered them only marginal instruction through the eighth grade; parents who wanted more than that had to send their children to board with family or friends in Hopkinsville so they could attend Crispus Attucks High School (an institution with such noted alumni as New York journalist Ted Poston).

I knew a good many black people by name and personal association. In my remembrance of them and of the times, I can recall nothing but friendliness and warmth between us. But if that was so, it stood against the fact that segregation and discrimination and inequality held us all, regardless of race, in a social and cultural straitjacket from which escape seemed not only impossible but unthinkable. My mother taught me, on threat of painful punishment, not to say "nigger" or to assume superiority over others less advantaged than I, but I never heard anyone—at home, at church, in school—utter a straightforward declaration that colored people, as they were then commonly called in polite company, deserved the same privileges and freedoms that all whites claimed as a birthright. It would be a long time before I ever thought about that at all, and even longer before I accepted it as a fundamental truth.

My adolescent hiatus in Cadiz lasted from the war-ending summer of 1945 until the fall of 1953, when I went away to college. The nation was then caught up in a mood of near-hysteria over communism, and we were once again at war, this time in Korea. Eight months later the U.S. Supreme Court would issue its historic school desegregation decision. By then I would be three months away from the beginning of my own bittersweet experience as a soldier, and from my first real introduction to multicultural diversity and equality.

The same traffic signal that showed the green light to Ralph McGill and hid itself completely from my view was blinking yellow for most Southerners in the summer of 1945—and for the ruling oligarchy, it not only glowed red but flashed a U-turn arrow pointing back to the past. Those who saw the green were not in perfect political and philosophical harmony by any means, but in general they subscribed to a progressive line of reasoning: The New Deal had brought relief to the South, and the war had generated an economic boom that furthered the region's recovery; the next logical step should be to effect reforms that would give the South full and equal status in the nation. Those who saw the red—a more numerous and powerful group—were first in favor of relief, then wary of the Rooseveltian methods of recovery, and finally downright hostile to what they characterized as radical notions of reform. The majority of Southerners followed neither the green nor the red; they waited at the caution light for more guidance and leadership.

This silent majority was enormous and pervasive. There is no way to tote up its numbers, obviously, but I'll risk a distorting oversimplification and guess that about seventy-five or eighty percent of the South's population fell into this broad category. Though they were people of wide-ranging doubts, fears, beliefs, and convictions, they were, by inclination and temperament, followers—not leaders, not scouts—and they looked to more vocal and articulate others to speak for them and lead them in one direction or another. By race, sex, religion, occupation, and economic status, they more or less matched the regional profile; what they had in common was nothing so much as the fact of their silence, whatever the reasons for it.

Here were the masses of Southern poor, black and white—tenant farmers and sharecroppers, migrant workers, transients, the unemployed, urban slum dwellers. Here were Mexican immigrants in Texas, refugees from Latin America and the West Indies in Florida, and a number of isolated and impoverished American Indian communities—the Cherokees in North Carolina, the Seminoles in Florida, the Choctaws in Mississippi.

There was silence above the poverty line, too: Here were Protestants and Catholics and Jews who deferred to their generally cautious ministers, priests, and rabbis; here were inarticulate young people just awakening to questions of social choice, and upwardly mobile strivers eager for a taste of middle-class life, and elders for whom big changes, even beneficial ones, were unsettling. Having survived the long ordeal of depression and war, the silent majority's needs and hopes were not grandiose but simple, basic, primary. There is some evidence in the record to indicate that race, by itself, was not always a matter of overriding concern to them. I am led to wonder, in fact, if the multitude of white, black, brown, and red Southerners would have chosen to fight among themselves over a matter as irrelevant as skin color if their conservative leaders had not been so obsessed with perpetuating Jim Crow segregation and discrimination and white supremacy.

Above and to the right of this huge segment of the South's population were the established political and economic leaders who looked to the distant past for their model of an ideal society. What the South had—in 1945 almost as solidly as in 1845—was a ruling class, a powerful elite defined by money or property or position, or all of these, plus rock-ribbed conservatism. They were all white, of course, and overwhelmingly male, and middle-aged or older. They completely controlled politics and business, and exercised great influence in the church, the press, the university. They disdained democracy, opting instead for one-party rule, handpicked candidates, and the smallest possible electorate (for example, less than ten percent of South Carolina's voting-age population and fifteen percent of Mississippi's and Alabama's took part in the presidential election of 1944).

The planters, bankers, lawyers, mill owners, and others who sat atop the feudal empires of the South saw themselves as the deserving rich, and they ruled as if by divine right. Unchallenged for over half a century (since the Republicans and Yankees capitulated, the Populists were subdued, and the African-Americans were disenfranchised), this ruling elite had come to dominate Congress and the Southern statehouses and court-houses by a simple combination of longevity and solidarity. With few exceptions in the first half of the twentieth century, the states of the Old Confederacy had anointed leaders who stood shoulder to shoulder for men over women, whites over blacks, old over young, business over labor, conservatives over liberals, rural areas over cities, and politicians over everybody. Ever faithful to the tiny cliques that kept them in power, the lawmakers vigilantly defended low taxes, low wages, high profits, and balanced budgets; states' rights, limited government, and selective federal aid without interference from Washington; a cheap, plentiful labor force without unions; and always, unfailingly, an abiding devotion to segrega-tion and white supremacy.

To lump all of the South's senators and congressmen and governors together in this sweeping indictment would be patently unfair; several of them were New Deal stalwarts in the first and second Roosevelt admin-istrations, and a few remained loyal to the President and the party through thick and thin. But if you pay close attention to the postwar rhetoric of Southern Democrats, you will hear the same tone of militant defiance that prevailed when FDR and the Southerners came to loggerheads in the late 1930s—a tone borrowed then from generations past. The dominant, guid-ing voices in the Dixie pantheon of twentieth-century rulers defended a way of life based on nineteenth-century principles: hierarchical control, Victorian order and rigidity, conformity of thought, massive denial of faults, hostility to all criticism, avoidance of reality, and a patriotic nation-alism more Southern than American. At bottom, it was a way of life that required legions of underlings to do the scut work. Once slavery had supplied the drones; now drones were plentiful because of the segregated and inferior status of all blacks and a steeply vertical informal class struc-ture among whites.

Opposite the small but powerful and dominant bloc of Southern barons stood the even smaller liberal remnant. This sprinkling of white progres-sives and black antisegregationists tried to point the South to the future, but no individual among them could reach far enough to embrace their collective views on social change; no one had arms that wide. It would be impossible to say in a few words what set them apart from the reactionary rulers of the South in 1945 (though a decade later, the dividing line would be sharp and clear: for or against desegregation). Here were left-of-center radicals, liberals, moderates, and conservatives; avowed integrationists and separate-but-equal segregationists; activists motivated by religious beliefs, economic theory, political considerations, and enlightened self-interest. Here were some—but not necessarily all—of the leaders of the Southern Conference for Human Welfare, the National Association for the Advancement of Colored People, the Southern Regional Council, the National Urban League, the Truman administration, the National Democratic Party, the American Veterans Committee, the labor movement, the church, the universities, the press, and numerous other alliances, great and small.

For a little more than five years after the war, these two minority factions of Southerners—those who saw the red light, and those who saw the green—struggled for the heart and soul of their region, and for the allegiance (or subjugation) of the majority, who waited at the yellow caution light for someone to tell them which way to turn. Looking back on those years from a vantage point in the 1990s, it seems to me that a combination of favorable circumstances had opened a narrow window of opportunity through which the South might have reached both internal social reform and external parity with the rest of the nation.

At times it appeared that the underdog advocates of reform were gaining ground. Many ex-GIs wanted to clean out corrupt courthouses and statehouses; black critics of Jim Crow segregation grew ever more numerous and vocal; some young political activists managed to get themselves elected; President Truman proved to be more liberal on the race issue than FDR had been; a lengthening string of federal court decisions forecast a more inclusive application of democratic principles and ideals. When the renegade States' Rights Party—the Dixiecrats—failed to seize the South from the Democrats in 1948, some liberals and moderates thought for a moment that their idealistic "renaissance of good intentions" might succeed.

But the reactionary politicians in power used every weapon at their disposal to subdue the reformers. By 1950, just as racial injustice was beginning to press to the forefront of public consciousness throughout the South, the "Old Guard" was poised to mount a strong counterattack. In the frenzied atmosphere of cold war anticommunism—just then reaching its peak nationally—the cabal of Southern demagogues succeeded in linking racial equality to "the red menace" in the eyes of their constituents. Using this potent tool as a blunt instrument in the Democratic primaries that summer, they whipped the South's two leading liberals in the U.S. Senate, Frank Porter Graham of North Carolina and Claude Pepper of Florida.

These right-wing strikes—"public muggings," as one liberal called them—had a chilling effect on those who had enlisted in the postwar movement for a Southern social reformation. In time, all the white liberals who had tried to straddle the fence on the race issue would be forced to declare themselves on one side or the other, and virtually all blacks were automatically relegated to the left flank. These and other signs of continuing reactionary rule brought to an end, for all practical purposes, whatever hope remained that either whites and blacks or the South and the nation would voluntarily reach an equitable accommodation with each other. With that estrangement, a deepening silence settled over the region in the early 1950s, giving Southern reformers cause to wonder if the tomorrow they longed for would ever come.

Tomorrow would dawn, finally, on May 17, 1954. The principal figures in its deliverance would be an unlikely combination of dedicated NAACP attorneys, courageous black plaintiffs, and conservative white judges. Together they would put the South and the nation on course toward the fulfillment of American democratic and constitutional ideals. The pattern was set: Instead of voluntary acts of enlightened self-interest, it would take lawsuits, court decisions, protest demonstrations, needless casualties, and long years of struggle to establish this new direction and realize a more equitable result.

III

1945–1950:
Breaking the Mold

Shocked to the bone, we began to perceive that the white race was now on the defensive. The mirrors of the world were turned on us, and we did not like what we saw there. . . . But the more thoughtful were searching for insight, and questioning their own souls, and struggling to find a way out of trouble for our people. Ministers, church women, little magazines, fact-finding groups, more and more books, more and more decisions from the U.S. Supreme Court glowing with human justice stirred the Southern conscience as never before in history. Almost by the sheer weight of words the old Southern mold had cracked open and we were looking at ourselves inside it.

—LILLIAN SMITH,
Killers of the Dream

1. *Postwar Opportunity*

"This is the place," said Carl Sandburg, a Yankee emigrant from the windy shores of Lake Michigan. Standing for the first time on the porch of Connemara, the farmhouse he had come to buy in the Blue Ridge Mountains of western North Carolina, the famed poet and Lincoln biographer felt a strong sense of belonging, and the vista of forested slopes before him brought a smile to his face. It was the summer of 1945. In serene disjunction with the times (whether behind or ahead, he had no way of knowing), Sandburg, at the age of sixty-seven, was about to plunge into the northward-flowing American population stream and swim south against the current.

You could read a lot of symbolism into his choice. In a period when millions of people, white and black, were leaving the South in search of the elusive Promised Land, Sandburg was moving into the region. Someone of his national stature taking such an affirmative step could not fail to boost the spirits and the pride of people all over the much-maligned South. Not even the bigots among them were boorish enough to dismiss him as a Jew, a Socialist, a Swede, or a Chicagoan (all elements of his heritage); on the contrary, Sandburg and his wife were washed by waves of Southern hospitality. Until his death there, more than twenty years later, the poet would proudly remain an adopted Southerner, delighting in the porch talk at Connemara with such frequent visitors as his friend and biographer, Charlotte writer Harry Golden (also a Northern emigrant), and a well-known native of the up-country South, Ralph McGill.

This is the place, Sandburg said—and, he might have added, now is the time: time for the South to turn its gaze from the past to the future, to secure the blessings of liberty and equality for all its citizens, to cast off the stigma of inferiority and take its rightful place as a full and equal partner in the family of states. It was time for the South to decide whether it was going to be a backward-looking feudal society or a modern and progressive democracy. Idealism certainly pointed the South toward a democratic future—but realism and tradition stood in the way.

At war's end, the eleven states of the old Confederacy still lagged far behind the other thirty-seven by almost every measure of collective strength, from education, employment, and income to health, housing, population growth, and political participation. (It is an arbitrary convenience to define the modern South as comprising the eleven Confederate states; Kentucky, Maryland, and other border jurisdictions could justifiably be counted as well, and I do include them from time to time in this narrative, but for obvious reasons, the historically rebellious states make a suitable unit for statistical comparison.) And not only did the South trail the North; in much the same way, blacks in the region were shortchanged compared with whites. A few numbers from the field of education drive home the point.

The Southern states averaged spending only about $50 per pupil in their public schools in 1944–45 (compared with over $100 in the other states)—and of that meager sum, roughly eighty percent went to schools serving whites and twenty percent to the black schools. Expenditures for teacher salaries, books, buildings, and equipment were likewise imbalanced, both North to South and white to black. While teachers in, say, Michigan or Colorado were earning above the national average of $1,500 a year, white teachers in Mississippi or South Carolina were drawing less than $800, and their black counterparts got only about $500.

Schooling in the South remained a privilege, not a right. Almost a million people over the age of twenty-five had not completed a single year of school, and one of every four (compared with one in eight nationally) hadn't even made it through the fifth grade. In Atlanta—vaunted oasis, fount of opportunity—the more than 100,000 black citizens could avail themselves of only one public high school. Fewer than one in every twenty-five adult white Southerners had a college degree, and an even smaller fraction of blacks had finished the twelfth grade. The proportion of college-age young people in the region who were enrolled in degree-granting institutions in the late thirties and early forties was extremely low too—about one in twelve whites and one in twenty-five blacks. Southern schools awarded fewer than two hundred doctoral degrees a year—a scant five percent of the national total.

Inseparably linked with the dismal state of education were numerous other measures of inadequacy. The South had 27 percent of the nation's population and 40 percent of its natural resources, but only 12 percent of its money and its manufacturing capacity. Housing for a huge segment of the population could be described fairly as primitive, devoid of the basic comforts and conveniences that mainstream Americans considered standard. Poor health was manifest in the low number of doctors and hospital beds, the high number of mothers and babies who died in birthing, the high homicide rate (but, curiously, a below-average suicide rate), and lower life expectancy overall for every racial and sexual category of Southerners. And perhaps most telling of all was the chronic poverty of millions of people in a society historically structured to favor an elite leisure class. As late as the start of the 1940s, some ten million people in the region— one of every three—had cash incomes of less than $250 a year. Even as the South was about to enter the modern age, its leaders clung to the slavery- inspired notion that the many should sweat for the comfort of the few. And, in so believing, they perpetuated a distorted Southern concept of work—its methods and traditions, its outcomes and rewards, its status, its very nature.

Much non-farm employment in the South amounted to little more than low-skill, low-wage drudgery, not only unsatisfying but often mind- numbing (textile work, for example) or hazardous (coal mining). Unem- ployment had fallen sharply and family income risen for this segment of the population during the wartime boom, but wages hadn't gained much relative to those paid in other parts of the country—and wouldn't, with- out more labor unions and collective bargaining. Furthermore, with the manufacture of the tools of warfare now ending, it was unclear how suc- cessfully the factories would be able to convert to the making of con- sumer goods. Regardless of the products they turned out, Southerners on hourly wages typically earned only half to two-thirds as much as Northern workers. And once again there was an added racial disparity: The median income of Southern blacks was only about half that of Southern whites.

It was still true in 1945 that more Southerners were engaged in farm- related work than in all other occupations, but that was changing rapidly. Farmers worked longer hours for less pay than anyone else—and South- erners, not surprisingly, were the poorest of the nation's farmworkers. As in earlier times, big planters dominated the region's agricultural economy, and it took tens of thousands of laboring men, women, and children to keep the old-fashioned system in operation. It would be well into the 1950s before the rural-urban balance in the South shifted decisively to the cities, largely as a consequence of the mechanical revolution that escalated on the region's farms after the war. In 1945 the typical Southern farm still ran on mule power; more than three million of the beasts of burden were in the fields, compared with fewer than 150,000 tractors. A substantial majority of the region's farms had no electricity, no telephones, and no indoor plumbing.

Still, the most profound change in Southern agriculture in the forties may have been more demographic than technological: the mass exodus of tenant farmers and sharecroppers and field hands, black and white alike, from the cotton and tobacco patches to the towns and cities. Two million more blacks moved out of the South than into it during the 1940s; the net loss of whites owing to emigration was much smaller but still substantial.

These declines were masked by high birth rates in both races, resulting in an overall population increase of about four million whites and 200,000 blacks.

By 1950 there would be more than thirty-six million people living in the eleven-state region; over nine million of them—one of every four— were African-Americans. (The South had been thirty-five percent black in 1910 and thirty percent black in 1930; now the percentage was twenty-five, and that pattern—a five-percent decline every twenty years—would be repeated once again in 1970, when the black-to-white ratio would slip to about 20–80.) Other races (mainly American Indians) accounted for fewer than sixty thousand of the South's people in 1950—a seemingly understated number, until you consider the fact that the Census Bureau at that time had no category for Hispanics; it simply counted them as whites. The South at midcentury was still classified as rural, but only by a margin of fifty-three to forty-seven percent—meaning that about eighteen million people lived in towns and cities, more than twice as many as in 1930.

In spite of the absolute gains realized during the transition from a state of depression to a wartime economy, Southerners in the mid-1940s still presented an image of pervasive disadvantage and need. So much had changed for the better in the dozen years since the coming of the New Deal—and yet so many problems were still there, unresolved, and new ones were riding on the wings of postwar reconstruction. Far from ushering in paradise, this "peace era" would be turbulent and unsettling. Inflation, layoffs, strikes, labor-management violence, a shortage of consumer goods, political conflict, racial antagonism, cold war anticommunism, the atomic threat—there would be no end to the concerns, and they would be deeply troubling to all Americans. To Southerners caught up in the long and frustrating search for equal opportunity in the national arena, the obstacles would be especially dispiriting.

The region had been at rock bottom when the Great Depression struck, but the whole nation and much of the world was spiraling downward then; Southerners could rationalize their lowly status—cold comfort though it was—in the knowledge that at least they weren't the only people who were hurting. But now, with the war at an end and the South's condition still poor relative to the rest of the country, an altogether different impetus—a forward thrust—was propelling the ship of state. America seemed on the verge of a great renewal, a reinvention of itself. With an air of invincibility, it was facing the future in an expansive, opportunistic, idealistic mood. Implicit in that positive spirit was the admonition that the time to move was at hand, and those who didn't get on board would be left on the dock when the ship sailed.

The South could not have skipped the postwar revolution of new technology and rising expectations no matter how hard it might have tried. The Roosevelt New Deal and the war itself had already opened up too many possibilities, too many visions of a better life for the taking; Southerners, like all Americans, had to be included in that bright and promising picture.

Innovation seemed to have a multiplier effect. Consider the impact of the Tennessee Valley Authority: From its inception in 1933, the agency generated cheap and accessible electric power in the upper South by building hydroelectric plants next to its dams. Soon, town and country people alike had electricity, and they bolted out of the dark ages in a rush. When rationing and austerity ended after the war, a pent-up demand was loosed for appliances, radios, record players, motor vehicles, and a host of time- and labor-saving tools and gadgets. This was also the time when mass advertising came into its own as a consumer stimulus (not that people really needed stimulating to snap up the new cars, refrigerators, boats, clothes, and other goods as soon as they came off the assembly line).

Novelty begat novelty in private enterprise and government programs alike—in fact, they fed off each other. The postwar boom in automobile sales led directly to massive roadbuilding programs and eventually to the interstate highway network, begun in the 1950s. Cars allowed people to drive longer distances to work, shop, and play, and that mobility greatly reduced the South's isolation. (One unwelcome consequence of the increased traffic, though, was a soaring highway death toll.) Motels, fast-food chains, expanded parks and recreational facilities, supermarkets, and drive-in theaters would head the long list of developments spawned by the car culture. A nation on the go, America roared out of the war years with practically everyone behind the wheel; cars (and, especially in the South, trucks) quickly ceased to be thought of as luxuries and were looked upon as necessities.

Air-conditioning likewise modified social behavior, particularly in the subtropical Gulf Coast states. The tobacco and textile industries had begun to use cooling systems to maintain quality control of their products even before the First World War, and by the end of the thirties, most of the railroads and movie theaters operating in the region had put in temperature-regulating devices for the comfort of their customers. Soon after World War II, technological advances made air-conditioning commonplace throughout the society; in less than a quarter of a century, the South would be converted from a muggy, oppressive, sweat-drenched summer place to a labyrinth of air-cooled cocoons—cars, homes, schools, churches, even shopping malls and sports stadiums. Air-conditioning spurred industrial growth in the region, and stimulated trade at restaurants and hotels, and even influenced architecture. So quickly did we become accustomed to refrigerated air that the inescapable heat we once tolerated with hardly a passing comment became an agitating and intolerable discomfort whenever we were forced to stay in it.

It was the blessed relief of air-conditioning that eventually lured people away from long-winded conversation on the porch and into the cool, enclosed parlor or "family room," there to watch in enthralled silence as yet another major postwar technological force—television—cast its magic spell. Within a few years, TV would be acknowledged as the most powerful tool of education and culture available (proving, its critics said, that not every novelty is an unmixed blessing). In the final analysis, television probably has done more to transform American culture than all other technological innovations of the twentieth century, including air-conditioning and automobiles.

Richmond, Atlanta, Fort Worth, Louisville, Memphis, and New Orleans were in the first wave of Southern cities to inaugurate commercial television stations in 1948—the same year CBS and ABC began operating as networks in competition with NBC, the 1946 TV pathfinder. The video screen profoundly altered the way all Americans thought and acted about virtually every aspect of their lives. The South would be especially affected. Think, for example, of the rise of professional sports, the desegregation of pro teams, and their entry into Southern urban markets in the 1960s—all spurred by the pervasive power of television. And think of the impact on journalism brought about when visual renditions of the news could be delivered instantaneously to virtually every home. In a sense, the civil rights movement was a made-for-television drama. Not surprisingly, Georgia Governor Herman Talmadge (son of Gene) and other segregationist Southern politicians would complain publicly in the early 1950s that television was undermining segregation. In point of fact, it was.

By midcentury, a substantial majority of Southerners would be totally dependent on their cars and trucks, and soon thereafter they would embrace television and air-conditioning as essential to their workaday lives. Those who still lived on farms would be mastering mechanical cottonpickers and other harvesting machines, and assembly-line workers would be learning to use ever more sophisticated equipment (with computers soon to come), and homemakers would be cleaning, cooking, and freezing with the latest electric or gas appliances. Their health would be further protected by miracle drugs like penicillin and the polio vaccine; still another revolutionary medical marvel, birth-control pills, would be introduced in the early 1960s. All in all, these irreversibly Americanizing influences served to push the people of the Southern states ever closer to the national fold.

For nearly a century the United States had lived with the destructive consequences of regional hostility and estrangement. Now the cumulative effects of the depression, the New Deal, and the war were breaking down those sectional barriers and compelling all Americans to think in national rather than regional terms. The United States in 1945 was vastly different from what it had been in 1929. The federal government's role as a provider of services (health, housing, jobs, education, welfare, highways) and as a regulator of activity in such fields as agriculture, banking, broadcasting, and interstate travel had expanded enormously, and that trend would not be reversed as the nation grew ever larger and more complex.

The national economy, having tripled in size during the war years, was severely tested in the mid-1940s by two daunting challenges: the absorption of ten million military men and women into civilian life, and the conversion of industry to the production of consumer goods. Some of the pressure would be relieved by federal investments in education, job training, and housing under the GI Bill of Rights—yet another example of a national response to what had once been thought of as state or local or even private concerns. As a practical matter, however, no force except the federal government was powerful enough to remove price controls, lift wages, and try to keep a lid on inflation and unemployment—just as, by the same token, only the nation had had the resources to overcome the depression and win the war.

Now, for a brief moment in history, the United States stood proudly as a victorious and unified country—a single people under one flag, one army, one political system, one currency, one language (albeit diversely accented). The same basic institutions—religious, academic, economic, informational—undergirded the national structure. Ever since the Southern war of rebellion in the 1860s, the issue of federal sovereignty had been sticking in the South's craw. Now, eighty years later, the answer finally seemed abundantly clear: Like it or not (and many old Rebs didn't), this was one nation, indivisible.

National authority was unquestionably secured as the United States took up its domestic agenda in the late summer of 1945. More decisively than ever before in American history, federal solutions were widely seen as the primary response to an expanding array of problems. Government was no panacea, but it was the essential engine of a progressive society, and most people adjusted to that fact. (It would remain for the next generation to discover the flip side of big government: the arrogance of power, the paralyzing crush of bureaucracy, the susceptibility of politicians and parties to corruption, and all the rest.)

The cry of states' rights would still be raised, but it would never again prevail against higher authority exercised in the national interest. Even so, the certainty of failure had not been enough to deter the breakaway South in the 1860s, and it would not be enough in the 1950s and beyond. Though they would stop short of war this time, the region's leaders would foment yet another rebellion in the name of states' rights and Southern sovereignty—with the same disastrous results as before.

No matter how passionately the guardians of Old South culture yearned to live by antiquated social rules, there was no realistic possibility that the region could go on following its traditional course indefinitely. Isolated, undemocratic, backward in many ways, beset with contradictory feelings of superiority and inadequacy, determined at all costs to maintain a rearguard defense of its race and class divisions, the South was hopelessly stranded in the trailing ranks of the national parade—and all for the comfort and glory of a handful of its citizens. The end of the war brought with it a pervasive sense that a new age was beginning, and nothing would be quite the same as it had been. Change would not come to the Land of Cotton swiftly or precipitously—but it would come.

What was it that set the South apart from the rest of America in the middle of the twentieth century? Was it history, tradition, geography, isolation, ruralism, violence? Was it culture, class, religion, mythology, language, music, food, families? There were many elements, some positive, some negative, but one was paramount. What divided the South from the nation—and Southerners from one another—was race.

The wall had loomed since European explorers first encountered the native inhabitants of the Americas in the late fifteenth century, and since the first Africans were brought to this continent against their will in 1619. Periodic epidemics of religious and ethnic discrimination and xenophobia down through the years have underscored the pervasiveness of intolerance. It was never just Southern whites but whites in general who separated the races and assured the one of perpetual advantage over the others; as Gunnar Myrdal so convincingly showed in *An American Dilemma* in 1944, white supremacy was a product of national, not regional, failure.

Even so, the vast majority of blacks in the population of America had always been in the South—first as slaves, then as freedmen, and finally as the lowest segment in the regional labor pool. In spite of massive migration to Northern cities, three-fourths of the country's thirteen million black citizens still lived in the states of the Old Confederacy after World War II (as did much smaller numbers of Hispanics, Indians, and Asians). It was primarily here that segregation and discrimination and inequality were so blatantly practiced and so intricately woven into the fabric of everyday life.

The white South had never spoken with one unified and unwavering voice against the humanity of the African-American population. To be sure, most politicians and lesser numbers of journalists, scholars, and religious leaders did often perpetuate the myth of a solid white South, but there were always dissenters who spoke and worked for some degree of justice and fair play for people of color. Most of them voiced a kindly and well-intentioned paternalism; others stressed the need for equal protection of the laws; still others felt that blacks were entitled, on an equal but segregated basis, to all the programs and services available to whites. But it was one thing to favor nonviolence and common decency, and quite another to stand up and speak out for complete racial equality. When it came to outright criticism of segregation itself, only a handful of Southern whites with any public stature or following at all had found their voices by 1945—and all of them were on the outer margins of power, not at its center.

The writer and editor Lillian Smith was getting national attention as an outspoken integrationist. H. L. Mitchell, Lucy Randolph Mason, and other regional leaders of organized labor were firmly in favor of full equality for blacks, and so were James Dombrowski of the Southern Conference for Human Welfare and Myles Horton of the Highlander Folk School. A few religious radicals—Howard Kester, Alva Taylor, Claude Williams, Don West—stirred controversy by living out their belief in the brotherhood of man. (Some denominational bodies passed resolutions on racial tolerance, but virtually none gave up segregation.) Ex–New Dealers Will Alexander, Aubrey Williams, and Clark Foreman had all declared their opposition to Jim Crow laws by the end of the war. Broadus, George, and Morris Mitchell, the three sons of Samuel Chiles Mitchell, the aging liberal scholar, were all activists like their father. Social scientists Howard Odum, Guy Johnson, Rupert Vance, and Arthur Raper headed the list of academics linked to progressive causes.

Georgia Governor Ellis Arnall and Florida Senator Claude Pepper stood out among a handful of practicing politicians who called themselves liberals, though they didn't feel free enough to take advanced positions on racial issues. Perhaps the most noted Southern liberal in a role of real authority (unless you count Supreme Court Justice Hugo Black) was the longtime president of the University of North Carolina, Frank Porter Graham, soon to be appointed to fill a vacant seat in the U.S. Senate; he too felt compelled at times to equivocate a bit on matters of race, but he and Dorothy Rogers Tilly of Atlanta, the only Southern members of the U.S. Committee on Civil Rights appointed by President Truman in 1946, would distinguish themselves as forthright advocates of a new national course in race relations.

A number of the South's leading newspaper editors leaned modestly in the direction of liberal progressivism, but not on all issues; race continued to hold them back. Even in the late forties, most of them shied away from federal solutions to what they saw as state or local or private problems— lynching, job discrimination, poll taxes and other impediments to voting. Early liberals, including Virginius Dabney in Richmond and John Temple Graves in Birmingham, were drifting further to the right, while Atlanta's Ralph McGill, Raleigh's Jonathan Daniels, Mark Ethridge of Louisville, and Hodding Carter of Greenville, Mississippi, were searching for a middle course between what they saw as radical and reactionary extremes. Younger men just back from the war would soon offer progressive editorial leadership, among them Harry S. Ashmore in Little Rock, William C. Baggs in Miami, and C. A. "Pete" McKnight in Charlotte; John N. Popham, a native Virginian, would play an influential role as the first Southern correspondent of the *New York Times*. But not one newspaper in the region editorialized against Jim Crow segregation laws until after the U.S. Supreme Court's 1954 *Brown* decision mandating desegregation of the public schools. Only a scattered few independent journalists, like Thomas Sancton in Louisiana and Stetson Kennedy in Florida, were on the leading edge of this approaching wave.

More than a few black Southerners had seen clearly for a long time the urgent need to end legalized segregation and extend the privileges of full citizenship to their race, but their power to effect such changes was severely limited. Often they were caught between oppressive whites close at hand and militant blacks voicing criticism from the relative safety of the North. Some black newspapers in the region tried to fly the flag of racial liberation, but they were essentially conservative enterprises with small circulation and limited influence—and in any case, only a few had writers of the caliber of someone like John H. McCray, editor of the *Lighthouse & Informer* in Columbia, South Carolina. The Southern black church was conservative, too, and without much latitude in the struggle for equal opportunity; a postwar decade would pass before it joined the battle against white supremacy.

In the thirties and forties, independent educators headed the list of progressive black leaders in the South. Prominent among them were Charles S. Johnson, Mary McLeod Bethune, Charlotte Hawkins Brown, Benjamin Mays, Rufus Clement, F. D. Patterson, and Gordon Hancock. Numerous others, inside and outside the region, showed a prophetic understanding of social issues in those years. Among the most eloquent in their advocacy of racial equality were writers James Weldon Johnson, Richard Wright, Langston Hughes, Zora Neale Hurston, Arna Bontemps,

Saunders Redding, and Sterling Brown; attorneys Thurgood Marshall and Charles Houston; activists W. E. B. Du Bois, Walter White, Paul Robeson, and A. Philip Randolph. The list of black reformers was longer than that of whites, even though it was defined by one restraining reality: Only those who were not dependent on whites for their livelihood could afford the risk of speaking their minds candidly.

These are some of the now-familiar figures, black and white, whom we have encountered in this chronicle of the early struggle for racial and regional equality—and most of them would still be there on the liberal side in the postwar battle for human rights in the South and the nation. If their numbers were small, it only proved how hard it was to speak out with logic or even pragmatism on an emotional issue like race. More than three centuries of white dominance had developed and reinforced traditions that defied logic and ignored self-interest. Segregation gripped the minds of many Southerners like a chronic disease, an incurable addiction; in their fervor for it, some whites would prove themselves to be ready to ride it down to defeat, just as their forebears had ridden slavery.

If the liberal-progressive remnant had been able to agree on goals and methods, ends and means, they might have won a substantial following among the South's silent majority. With united leadership and a little luck, both the black minority and the region as a whole might have managed in the late forties to break free from their long-standing positions of enforced disadvantage. But human nature had the last word as the liberals fell into conflict among themselves.

The Southern Conference for Human Welfare and the Southern Regional Council, the two leading social-action organizations of the 1940s, eyed each other more like suspicious rivals than collaborative allies. The SCHW spun off a new organization in 1946—the Southern Conference Educational Fund—ostensibly to receive tax-exempt contributions and leave the SCHW free to engage in political action. But in truth, the decision cloaked a personal and philosophical split within the group and marked the beginning of the end for the SCHW. For its part, the Southern Regional Council would be locked in internal debate about segregation for several years after the war. Even at that, the SCHW and the SRC fared better than the Southern Policy Committee, an earlier conclave of liberals that by 1940 had all but dissolved in frustration and anger.

Blacks in the region who courted either Southern whites or Northern blacks in the campaign for social reform had critics aplenty, no matter which way they turned. More-militant blacks in the North often branded them as Uncle Toms, while white liberals sought to exploit them as buffers against the more conservative whites—who in turn regarded even the most diplomatic black reformers as disruptive troublemakers. Whites who showed even the most modest inclination toward racial accommodation were likewise squeezed between reactionary white politicians on the right and radical activists, black and white, on the left.

Internal squabbling, petty jealousies, and personal hostility sometimes brought almost as much grief to the liberal-progressive cause as did ideological opposition from the right. (Conservatives had to face internal dissension too, but they had the advantages of incumbency, vested power, and majority-white privilege on their side.) Ralph McGill and Lillian Smith had never liked each other, and they were too proud to meet and iron out their differences. McGill also had little use for Don West, Claude Pepper, the SCHW, or the labor movement—but he greatly admired labor's Lucy Randolph Mason, who was a friend of Pepper and West and a member of the SCHW. Smith was a harsh and disdainful critic of the Southern Regional Council, and though she eventually joined the rival Southern Conference, she didn't stay long in its ranks. Frank Graham never was active in the SRC. Howard Kester, a Christian Socialist, and H. L. Mitchell, an agnostic Socialist, shared an abiding distrust of all activists they suspected of being Communists—including fellow agnostic Myles Horton and fellow Christian Jim Dombrowski. Blacks were equally as hard on one another; the conference of black Southerners out of which the Southern Regional Council grew was soundly criticized by black leaders in the North even before it began.

And so it went, as the thin ranks of reform-minded Southerners and their outside allies struggled against tradition, inertia, ignorance, silence, the old guard of ruling reactionaries—and themselves. For all their differences, the progressives seemed to have enough interests in common to lay the foundation for a coalition. By and large, they were Roosevelt-Truman Democrats. Consistently through the years, they had opposed the Ku Klux Klan and other right-wing terrorist organizations. They were for better race relations, expanded civil rights for blacks, full and fair application of the rule of law. Most of them had more positive than negative opinions of labor unions and the federal government, and they enthusiastically welcomed the postwar emergence of nontraditional young politicians in the aging ranks of demagogic officeholders. And still they fought among themselves.

Their real adversaries were those very demagogues, and the people on the right who kept them in power. Here were the most strident critics of Roosevelt and Truman, the sworn enemies of federal authority, the defenders of states' rights; here were anti-union, anti-black partisans who slapped the red label on all who strayed from conservative orthodoxy on race, religion, and politics; here were people who not only tolerated the Klan but supported it, even belonged to it; here were the beneficiaries of democratic exclusion and apathy.

And yet, as clear-cut as the left-right ideological split was, the liberals could never muster more than a thin shadow of the unity that kept the conservatives in harness throughout. Always outnumbered and constantly working against the grain of the culture that had evolved over generations, the progressives couldn't overcome emotion with logic. Once again, the reason was race: When all was said and done, white Southerners were more willing to stand against racial justice than for it.

In the nine years that separated the coming of world peace and the historic *Brown* decision, the white South tried in vain to deal with race by avoidance and indirection, hoping all the while that somehow the issue would resolve itself and simply fade away. Conservatives and liberals alike knew how crucial the matter was to the future of their region, but they could see no way to settle it, and so they resisted it as an unthinkable thought, an issue only to be approached defensively, in reaction to initiatives taken by others. Conservatives saw disturbing trends coming out of the war—trends toward urbanization, industrialization, a broader franchise, diversification of the Democratic Party, the re-emancipation of blacks. Liberals were not so much alarmed as encouraged by those trends, but they saw and dreaded the hardening of reactionary resistance, the rise of violence against blacks, the signs of hostility to organized labor, the national outbreak of red hysteria, and the stain of the Communist taint on all progressives.

Throughout the Roosevelt years and right on into the first postwar months of adjustment, race was a low-priority agenda item for virtually all whites, North and South, left and right; most seemed inclined simply to let things rock along until a crisis of some sort forced the public to pay attention. But black Americans—the targets of discrimination—were not so indifferent. By war's end, they seemed more universally determined than ever to gain the basic freedoms for which they had fought overseas. Their first order of business in the summer and fall of 1945 was to make rapid progress in two areas: employment (access to jobs, union membership, equal pay for equal work) and political-civic standing (voting rights, political party participation, fair treatment at the hands of the police, the law, and the courts). There were other pressing needs, of course—in education, housing, health care, transportation—but working and voting came first.

Much had happened in the previous decade or more to forewarn all Americans that the whole range of racial issues would eventually have to be opened up and examined. A small library of novels and nonfiction books about race had been written—illuminating volumes by such noted authors as James Weldon Johnson, Richard Wright, Gunnar Myrdal, Rayford Logan, W. J. Cash, Lillian Smith, and numerous others. Many more stirring portents of change echoed through popular music, art, movies, and theatrical productions. Blacks who had been locked out of combat roles and defense-industry jobs had won concessions by threatening a massive march on Washington. In the armed forces and in labor unions, blacks had fought successfully for certain basic rights, and more victories were coming. Here and there in the church, the university, and the press, individual voices raised calls to conscience. The Democratic Party, once the fiefdom of conservative Southern politicians, was becoming more diversified, more responsive, more liberal. Hundreds of thousands of African-Americans now lived in cities such as New York and Detroit, and white intolerance there was fueling deep hostility, even deadly riots. Federal courts had issued several pathfinding decisions against racial discrimination. Presidents Roosevelt and Truman had gradually shifted the moral weight of the White House toward a more inclusive democracy.

Only those who weren't paying attention could fail to notice that the United States was moving ever closer to a formal acknowledgment of its 325-year-old racial dilemma, its crisis in black and white. The lines were being drawn for a classic ideological face-off between the conservative right and the liberal left—tradition versus change, old opposed to new, the past standing with arms folded against the future. Many people knew the odds, and the stakes; even though the vast majority of uncommitted citizens remained on the sidelines awaiting instructions, the factional leaders on the right and left knew that a crucial test was at hand.

The South would have a few months, at most a couple of years or so —only a little time, as time is measured—in which to determine its future course, and to establish the pace and tone and tenor of its response to the pressures for change. Realistically, the odds still favored the continuation of white supremacy. It was decreed and enforced by the politicians, reinforced by the social institutions, chiseled into the hard stone of Southern history; it permeated the culture. The South had virtues and graces that were not minor or insignificant, but they were largely obscured by the deep-rooted heritage of exploitation, violence, and demagoguery. The seemingly immovable object, white supremacy, stood across the field of battle from some elements of opposing energy that held out the threat, the promise, of becoming an irresistible force. According to the laws of physics, the meeting of such powers invariably produces a violent explosion. The laws of history and humanity that came to be applied in the postwar South would eventually bring a similar consequence.

On October 11, 1945, a mob of white men went to the county jail in Madison, Florida, a small town near the Georgia border, and removed a prisoner, Jesse James Payne, from his unguarded cell. The thirty-year-old black laborer had been awaiting trial for the alleged rape of a little girl. The mob took Payne out into the countryside and tortured him to death. Sheriff Lonnie Davis later said the prisoner had been removed by someone who had a key to the cell. Further questioning revealed that the only known key was the one belonging to the sheriff himself.

The semiofficial statistics on lynching in the United States compiled annually by Tuskegee Institute in Alabama recorded Payne's death as the only such incident in the country that year. But Payne was by no means the only victim of Southern mob law in 1945. Within three months of V-J Day, published reports told of at least five other black men summarily slain by whites without due process of law in small Southern communities—one in Union Springs, Alabama, two in the southwest Mississippi towns of Liberty and Woodville, and two others in north Florida, at Branford and St. Augustine.

Atop Stone Mountain, just east of Atlanta, an October rally of the Ku Klux Klan came off as both a celebration of these acts of terror and a warning to blacks of more violence to come. Dr. Samuel Green, Grand Dragon of the Georgia Klan, claimed that there were more than twenty thousand members of the secret society in his state alone. The huge cross that the Atlanta obstetrician and his hooded followers torched that night could be seen glowing on the horizon from sixty miles away.

One war had ended. Another was heating up again.

2. *Epidemic of Violence*

The volatile subject of racial equality never had much potency as a twentieth-century political issue until the 1940s, for one simple reason: Before that, no one in power could see much likelihood at all that Southern blacks might regain the democratic standing they had enjoyed briefly after the Civil War. But the wind shifted ever so slightly in the late 1930s, and then, even as the nation was swept up in global conflict, one color-related incident after another broke to the surface of public consciousness.

For a long time before that, though, the South had been whistling "Dixie" to an acquiescent nation. Southern politicians who rose to power and stayed there between, say, 1880 and 1930 almost invariably espoused a party line that decreed segregation and white supremacy, and their edicts were carried out by whatever means necessary, including repression and terrorism. If any Northern politicians took serious exception to such behavior, they uttered their complaints in discreet whispers. In the first thirty years of this century, race was not a compelling national or regional issue; it had been taken beyond the pale of discussion and debate. Notwithstanding those who condemned violence, hardly any white person of prominence went so far as to condemn the laws and customs and routine practices that systematically deprived black American citizens in the Southern states of virtually all the rights and liberties of citizenship.

The most extreme of those "routine practices" was lynching, the ever-present symbol of the white South's tolerance for terrorism. As a socially sanctioned criminal act, lynching was epidemic in the South from the last quarter of the nineteenth century through the first quarter of the twentieth, after which it diminished but by no means disappeared. The Tuskegee Institute statistics placed the number of such incidents nationally at more than 4,700 between 1882 and 1950—and if the truth could be known, the total was surely much higher. More than eighty-five percent of the atrocities took place in the Southern and border states, and the overwhelming majority of victims were black. All fourteen of the states with a hundred or more lynchings during that period were either in the South or on its border. Between 1900 and 1930, more than 1,500 blacks and about 150 whites were lynched in the South—but it was exceedingly rare for anyone to be punished for taking part in a lynch mob. (Coincidentally or not, the eleven Southern states have also carried out more than half of the approximately 18,500 legal executions of convicted criminals in the nation's history.)

Opposition to lynching did increase noticeably during the New Deal years. In the early 1930s, the Atlanta-based Commission on Interracial Cooperation published a major study condemning the practice, and the Association of Southern Women for the Prevention of Lynching brought moral pressure to bear upon the problem in a grassroots campaign that lasted for the better part of two decades. The NAACP and other organizations fought hard to eradicate the scourge, and Congress tried repeatedly to pass stiff federal laws against it. But it was all to no avail. Nobody wiped out lynching; it gradually diminished because it became too outrageous, too widely condemned, and too socially unacceptable for the perpetrators to keep it up.

The criteria for defining a lynching, drawn up at a Tuskegee conference in 1940, were narrowly construed; they required, among other things, legal evidence of an illegal death at the hands of a group acting under the pretext of serving justice. Untold dozens and scores of additional deaths—people in custody or suspects "resisting arrest," prisoners alleged to be attempting to escape, fugitives pursued and "brought to justice" at the end of a rope by unofficial posses—all these would have doubled or even tripled the numbers of unjustified and extralegal killings that Southern society tolerated in the long reign of vigilante terror that stretched from the end of Reconstruction to the aftermath of World War II. The sheer number of atrocities committed with impunity against blacks by mobs of white men, or by individuals—often with the knowledge or assistance of law-enforcement officials—was self-evident proof of the South's chronic and unrelieved racial pathology.

The recorded annual total of lynchings fell steadily as time passed—from an average of 150 a year in the last two decades of the nineteenth century, to an average of thirteen a year in the 1930s, to a total of eight in the decade of the 1950s—but the terrorist act remained a shocking tool of intimidation and inhumanity inflicted by a tiny handful of whites and tolerated by a multitude of others. This shameful aspect of the Southern heritage commanded such visibility for so long that the names of the politicians who reigned in the South during the worst of those mean times—men like "Pitchfork Ben" Tillman of South Carolina and James K. Vardaman, the notorious "White Chief" of Mississippi—live in infamy to this day.

When you consider how many men the South sent to the U.S. Senate in the first half of this century who encouraged or at least condoned lynching (two dozen would be a conservative guess, and that's giving the benefit of the doubt to many a filibusterer), it's hard to escape the conclusion that promises of continued segregation, white supremacy, and violent repression of the black minority were usually helpful, if not essential, to a winning election strategy. The names and faces of politicians did change from time to time, but the dominant character of social and racial conservatism continued to hold liberalism and reformation at bay. Neither the church, the press, nor the intelligentsia presented much of a challenge to the reactionary leadership of Southern politicians.

The Dixie denizens of the U.S. Senate wielded extraordinary power in that body and in their home states throughout the late nineteenth century and the first half of the twentieth, as did their companions in the House of Representatives and in the governors' offices of every state. When World War II ended, almost all of them were eager to resume control under the old rules of race and class privilege. While a spirit of liberalism and restoration was catching on with many veterans and with some institutional leaders, the hard-line white supremacists seemed determined at any cost to stop racial reform cold, even if it took violence to do it.

In the early months of 1946, the all-white Birmingham city police department under Commissioner Eugene "Bull" Connor solidified its reputation as a repressive force hostile to the resident minority population. As many as five black men, all military veterans, were reportedly killed by uniformed officers in the first six weeks of the year (the exact number was in dispute, owing to Connor's control of the flow of information from inside the city government). For months and years to come, so many racially motivated beatings and killings would be laid to the police, and so many unsolved home bombings would occur there, that a local black newspaper editor, Emory O. Jackson of the Birmingham *World,* charged Connor and his crowd with "creating the climate for outrages to breed and break out."

As a festering hotbed of police brutality, Klan terrorism, racial hostility, and commonplace violence, Birmingham had few peers—but it wasn't alone in its extremism. Reports out of Gretna, Louisiana, and El Campo, Texas, that February told of black ex-servicemen dying at the hands of white officers of the law, and in the same month, two other incidents made front-page news all across the country. Neither fit the narrow definition of a lynching, but both—the maiming of a soldier in South Carolina and an outburst of racial violence that took two lives in Tennessee—signaled an ominous turning of the racial screw by Southern whites.

As soon as Isaac Woodard got his discharge papers at an army base in Georgia on February 12, he gathered up his belongings and hurried to catch a bus for home. Just back from fifteen months in the South Pacific, he was eager to return to civilian life. His wife was waiting in North Carolina, and they were going on to visit his parents in New York. After the bus had left Augusta and crossed the Savannah River into South Carolina, Woodard and the driver exchanged words over some minor point of racial etiquette. When the bus reached Aiken, the young soldier got off to go to the restroom. In the meantime, the driver called ahead to the police station in Batesburg, the next stop, to ask for help in dealing with a drunk and disorderly passenger.

Woodard later conceded he had taken "a drink or two," but insisted that he wasn't drunk. Apparently he didn't need alcohol to bolster his courage. The driver resumed his verbal harangue when they were on the road again, and Woodard responded in kind; soon the angry words were flying between the front and back of the bus. At the Batesburg depot, Woodard was ordered off, and as soon as he stepped out the door he was grabbed by the local police chief, Linwood Shull, and a deputy, who struck him before he could speak. They took him around a corner and beat him severely. The bus pulled away, and Woodard was dragged off to jail.

When the bloodied veteran was brought into court the next morning, he was unable to see. Because of the obvious seriousness of his injuries, the judge had Woodard taken to an army hospital for examination. There, doctors finally determined that a blunt instrument (a billy club, as it turned out) had been jammed into his eye sockets so violently that both of his eyes were mutilated beyond repair. The soldier was hospitalized, and the charges against him were dropped.

Isaac Woodard's plight didn't come to public attention until mid-July, when Walter White of the National Association for the Advancement of Colored People released a sworn affidavit signed by the victim. White got others, including the actor Orson Welles, to take up the call for justice. Their insistent pleas spurred the Federal Bureau of Investigation to look into the case. Finally, in the fall of 1946, Linwood Shull was indicted in Columbia, South Carolina, and brought to trial in federal court. The jury acquitted him, said White later, "to the cheers of a crowded courtroom." Woodard had moved to New York by then, having spent two months in the veterans' hospital without recovering his sight. He was permanently blind.

The Tennessee incident, which would be described in the national press as a race riot, took place in another Columbia, a county-seat town of about five thousand whites and three thousand blacks some forty-five miles south of Nashville. Three lynchings there since 1925 had left scars, but the postwar months had been placid, and business was brisk in the stores, including those in a row of black-owned shops and residences known as Mink Slide, just a block from the courthouse square.

On the morning of February 25, Gladys Stephenson and her son James, a navy veteran just back from the Pacific, went to the appliance section of a department store on the square to pick up a small radio she had left to be repaired. A dispute arose (accounts differed on the substance of it) between the black woman and the clerk, a young white man who, witnesses said, abused her verbally and then struck her. James Stephenson stepped in. He and the clerk got into a scuffle, and soon the white fellow was lying on his back, with cuts and other injuries, after crashing through a plate-glass window.

The Stephensons were arrested and swiftly charged with breach of the peace. They entered a guilty plea and paid a fifty-dollar fine, but the young ex-sailor was promptly rearrested when the injured store clerk's father swore out a warrant accusing him of assault with intent to commit murder. A prominent black businessman, Julius Blair, posted bond, and all the parties in the dispute went their separate ways, pondering the events of a very traumatic day.

But the episode wasn't over. As dark approached, a milling throng of white men on the square was passing rumors, whiskey bottles, weapons. The old lynchings were brought up, and some said it was time for another.

Along the Mink Slide row, black veterans sensed the danger; they got weapons too, and set up lookout posts, and put out all the lights. The throng of whites was growing louder and angrier. Hoping to keep control of the situation, the chief of police drove to the edge of the black section with a carload of officers and told four of them—half of his entire force—to patrol on foot through the darkened area. The men had not gone far when they heard shouted orders to halt—and when they didn't comply, shots rang out. All four were wounded, one seriously, and they retreated.

An eerie quiet followed. By ten o'clock that night, the state safety commissioner and a unit of highway patrolmen had arrived, and together with some of the local white men they surrounded the area; soon thereafter, a National Guard brigade was deployed. Just before dawn, the police and soldiers swept through Mink Slide, shooting into businesses, destroying property, cleaning out cash drawers and taking other valuables, ransacking scores of homes, and seizing about three hundred weapons. More than a hundred people were arrested; all of them were denied bail and counsel. Only blacks were targeted in the sweep. Miraculously, no one was killed.

Walter White and Thurgood Marshall of the NAACP flew into Nashville later that day. White went to see the governor and then started calling newspaper reporters and organizing a national defense committee (Eleanor Roosevelt agreed to serve as one of its leaders). Marshall, by now a battle-toughened civil rights lawyer, enlisted two Tennessee attorneys, Z. Alexander Looby of Nashville and Maurice Weaver of Chattanooga—one black, the other white—to help him plan the defense.

Three days after the outbreak, when a measure of calm had returned to Columbia and the troopers and guardsmen had been pulled out, another crisis erupted as local law-enforcement officials were questioning three of the black men in custody. According to the official police account given later, two of the prisoners suddenly grabbed guns from the patrolmen and started shooting. Both men were quickly struck down dead, and a third was seriously injured. The other prisoners firmly believed the men had been murdered in retaliation for the wounding of the white officers.

The papers were full of all this, not just in Columbia and Nashville (where the blame was put on "outside agitators" and "Communists"), but in New York, Washington, and elsewhere. The U.S. Attorney General called a federal grand jury to investigate, but the all-white panel of Tennesseans concluded that the law-enforcement officials had not violated anyone's civil rights. The legal maneuvering that followed over the next seven months produced several strange twists: Twenty-five blacks were tried for attempted murder of the Columbia policemen, but an all-white jury in another town where the trial had been moved found twenty-three of them not guilty, and the other two were later freed while seeking a new trial; most of the other defendants, including the Stephensons and a few whites, were never tried; and only one person—a black man accused of shooting at a state trooper—actually served a sentence. Perhaps the most significant message to come out of the Columbia incident was this: Besieged black citizens had stood up and fought back, and lived to tell about it.

As the long and emotional conflict drew to a close in November 1946, Thurgood Marshall and his fellow attorneys, Looby and Weaver, had one more close call. Driving out of Columbia for the last time, they were trailed by eight policemen in three cars. Twice the lawyers were stopped for alleged violations and then allowed to continue; when they were pulled over a third time, Marshall was accused of drunken driving and arrested. The cops drove away with him—not back toward town, but down a side road. Looby and Weaver followed, fearing the worst. The convoy took a long and circuitous route through the countryside, eventually ending up at a magistrate's office back in Columbia, where the charges were dropped. The three lawyers then sought help from their friends in Columbia and were escorted safely back to Nashville. Marshall would never know whether his abductors had intended to harass and terrorize the trio—or whether they had lost their nerve and finally decided not to kill him.

As murderous as the first two months of 1946 were, they would seem almost tame in comparison with a four-week stretch in July and August, when no less than a dozen black men met with violent death in the Deep South. A gang of whites lynched Leon McTatie near Lexington, Mississippi, for stealing a saddle—and then found out after he was dead that someone else had taken it. Maceo Snipes, a veteran, was murdered in Butler, Georgia, soon after he became the first black registered voter in Taylor County. In Eatonton and Gordon, Georgia, in Hattiesburg, Mississippi, in Bailey, North Carolina, and Elko, South Carolina, white men driven by rage or fear or some other base emotion committed homicide with the slightest provocation, or none at all.

An epidemic of random murder and mayhem was sweeping like a fever through the region, fueled by white fears that black veterans might become a revolutionary force, and that blacks in general would no longer stay "in their place." It would be too much to suggest that a massive conspiracy to drive out or eliminate the African-American minority was lurking in the postwar South. No such master plan was necessary; fear and ignorance were enough to loose the vigilante mobs.

According to the Tuskegee statistics, six lynchings occurred in the South in 1946—but more than four times that many unlawful deaths with racial overtones were widely reported in the newspapers. To these could be added the many unconfirmed racial homicides, the narrowly averted lynchings, the mysterious deaths of men in jails and prisons, and the riot situations where death was somehow dodged (as when forty black draftees were arrested and beaten in Columbus, Georgia, in April, or when a racial fight between a few veterans in Athens, Alabama, in August escalated into an assault on several dozen blacks by a mob of more than two thousand whites). Even some reportedly accidental deaths were of sinister origin: A Ku Klux Klan cell in Atlanta boasted of kidnapping and running over a black cabdriver "to punish him" for picking up a white fare; the man's death had been reported as a hit-and-run accident.

Georgia and Alabama were the principal killing fields, each with seven of the confirmed racial murders in 1946. It was no coincidence that they led the nation in the overall number of homicides per 100,000 of population that year—Georgia with 25.3, Alabama with 24.4 (New York, by contrast, had 3.6). Georgia was also the scene of the most shocking racial crime of the summer—the ambush and execution in broad daylight of two young men (one an army veteran) and their common-law wives (one of them pregnant) by a band of about two dozen unmasked white men.

The two couples, in their twenties, were tenant farmers in the Cotton Belt of Walton County, east of Atlanta. Roger and Dorothy Malcom lived and worked on a farm owned by Bob Hester southeast of Monroe, the county seat; George and Mae Dorsey lived northeast of town and worked for Loy Harrison, one of the largest cotton growers in the area. George Dorsey was Dorothy Malcom's brother. On Sunday, July 14, an altercation on the Hester property ended badly for Roger Malcom and the farm owner's son, Barney Hester. Some said Barney was trying to break up a fight between Roger and Dorothy; others claimed Barney had a sexual interest in the young woman, who was expecting a baby in the fall. Whatever the case, Roger and Barney ended up in a scuffle, Barney was stabbed with a pocketknife, and the two men were subsequently taken away, one to the hospital, the other to jail.

It happened that Georgia Democrats were choosing a candidate for governor the next week, and old warrior Eugene Talmadge was trying to regain the office after losing it to Ellis Arnall four years earlier. Talmadge campaigned in Monroe on the eve of the primary, just two days after the incident. He told a courthouse crowd that even though a federal judge was allowing some colored people to vote, "if I'm your governor, they won't vote in our white primary the next four years." Whispers of a lynching party for Roger Malcom were in the air, but Talmadge took no public note of them; before he left town, though, he had a talk with Barney Hester's father and others upset about the stabbing. (In Walton County the next day, Talmadge squeezed past the Arnall candidate, James Carmichael, by 2,201 to 2,123 votes, and thus claimed total victory there under the notoriously inequitable Georgia "county unit" system; Carmichael won the popular vote statewide, but lost the election—and immediately, political power began to shift away from the reformers and back to the reactionary Talmadge faction.)

A week passed. Barney Hester was recovering but still in the hospital; Roger Malcom, fearing a lynch mob, was still in jail, unable to make bond. Loy Harrison had been asked by Dorothy Malcom and her parents, who also worked for the planter, to help get Roger out of trouble. On Thursday, July 25, Harrison picked up George and Mae Dorsey and Dorothy Malcom and drove to the jail in Monroe. After talking with the prisoner, he said he was going to put up the bond and get him out. Telling the three tenants he had some business to attend to, Harrison left them outside the jail. As soon as he returned, Roger Malcom was released; the two black couples climbed into Harrison's car with him, and they started for his farm, twelve miles out the Athens highway, across the Apalachee River in Oconee County.

It was then five-thirty in the afternoon, and the sun was still high in the summer sky. Near the river, Harrison turned off the highway onto a winding dirt road that went past the Dorseys' house, across an old wooden bridge at a spot called Moore's Ford, and eventually on to the Harrison plantation. But he didn't stop to let the Dorseys out at home; he drove on to the bridge. There on the other side, the men were gathered, waiting.

In his account to the authorities later on, Harrison spoke as a helpless witness. He said the way was blocked and the men, none of whom he recognized, held him at gunpoint. They took the two black men out of the car and started for the woods. One of the women, said Harrison, called out to a man she recognized and pleaded for her husband's life—whereupon the leader of the mob told the others to bring the women too. With awful suddenness, he said, the four young people were lined up and shot—and then the men got back in their cars and drove away. Harrison told how he "got a hold of myself" and went to call the sheriff and report the crime.

News of the massacre at Moore's Ford swept like a fire across the state and the nation. Governor Arnall expressed his humiliation and offered a $10,000 reward for information leading to arrests. An outraged President Truman and his attorney general, Tom Clark, promised the full cooperation of the Department of Justice. The NAACP sent its own investigators to Monroe, and so did other groups. "The mark of the beast, the curse of Cain, is upon those men [the killers]," declared Ralph McGill in his column. "And it is on the State as well." The Walton County sheriff called for help from the Georgia Bureau of Investigation, and the FBI was also asked to assist in the case.

Local ministers, expressing shock and shame, called the crime "an outrage against humanity." Even Eugene Talmadge, during whose six years as governor fourteen lynchings had been committed, told the press that "such incidents are to be regretted"—but he added a gratuitous remark about the unfitness of black people for equal rights in Southern society. (Those very rights were demanded in one of the many letters of protest carried by the Atlanta *Constitution* in the weeks following the lynching; it was signed by a rising junior at Morehouse College, seventeen-year-old Martin Luther King, Jr.)

All through the remainder of 1946, the story stayed in the news. FBI agents swarmed over the county; more than a dozen of them worked out of a hotel in Monroe for six months. A federal grand jury hearing was ordered, and more than a hundred witnesses were called. (One of them, a young black man, was brutally beaten after giving testimony.) At one point, Governor Arnall told the press that investigators had identified fifteen to seventeen members of the lynch mob, but were having difficulty "getting evidence to convict them." Walter White said the NAACP gave the FBI and the GBI "evidence naming seven ringleaders of the lynching party."

Finally, though, no one was ever charged with the crime, and no case was brought against any suspects. "The best people in town won't talk about this," complained the head of the GBI. A reign of terror had silenced everyone, white and black; not even rewards that eventually totaled close to $100,000 were enough to bring any witness forward.

But one person who did see what happened on that terrible day at Moore's Ford could never shake the memory of it—and in the fullness of time, he would speak up. Clinton Adams was a ten-year-old white boy whose family also farmed for Harrison and lived near George and Mae Dorsey. The boy liked Dorsey, and the ex-GI proved to be a good friend and neighbor to the Adamses, often helping with chores and such. Clinton Adams had a chore of his own that day—to take a cow out to pasture—and he was crossing a field near Moore's Ford when he heard screams and shouts coming from over near the bridge. He ran to the edge of the woods and then crouched low, crawling closer, to within about a hundred feet of the cars and the shouting, screaming people.

In hushed fright, the youngster saw the men subdue his friend George Dorsey, tying his hands and hitting him with their guns. Dorsey's wife and sister were screaming hysterically—Clinton could see them clearly, and recognized both of them. The white men roughly pushed and dragged the four blacks along a path beside the river—and then, Clinton Adams remembered, "these guys just walked up behind them and shot them. There were four shooters initially." When the victims fell to the ground, most of the men in the mob "just stood over them, shooting into the bodies." And when it was over, Adams recalled, "they just walked back up to the road, talking and laughing."

The traumatized youngster ran home in a fearful trance. A few days later, he confided to a deputy sheriff that he knew who did the killing, but the officer warned him never to speak of it again to anyone. Adams tried to forget, but he couldn't—and neither could others who knew he had seen the crime. Finally, when he was twenty-one, he moved away from Walton County after being threatened and told that he "made people nervous."

Thirty-five more years would pass before the once-youthful witness could bring himself to break his silence. In 1992, Clinton Adams, fifty-six years old and in failing health, would come forward voluntarily to tell his awful secret to the FBI and the Atlanta *Constitution,* so he could "get it off my conscience." One of the five automobiles at the murder scene, he said, was a state police car. He named four of the men (all since dead) who took part in the massacre; one of them was Loy Harrison: "Lord knows, I saw him shoot."

In 1981, on a return visit to Walton County, Adams had gone to see Loy Harrison and found him willing to talk freely about the crime. The subject of the Dorsey family came up. "I told him I didn't understand why they had killed George and Dorothy," Clinton Adams remembered. "They always worked hard. They were good people. And he said, 'Let me tell you something about them you don't know. Up until George went in the army, he was a good nigger. But when he came out, they thought they were as good as any white people.' That's what Loy told me. It was civil rights that got them killed."

The inability of prosecutors—local, state, or federal—to bring racist criminals to justice was a problem that would frustrate reformers and plague the South for many years to come. Two more sensational atrocities—one in Louisiana less than two weeks after the Walton massacre, and the other in South Carolina the following February—increased the pressure on Congress and the states to protect the basic civil liberties of ordinary citizens.

At Minden, Louisiana, in Webster Parish, thirty miles east of Shreveport, army veteran John C. Jones, twenty-eight, and his seventeen-year-old cousin, Albert Harris, were accused of prowling in the backyard of a white woman. Though the woman would not press charges, the police jailed the two black men anyway. Jones had been tagged as "an uppity nigger" by some local whites after he suggested that unfair advantage was being taken of his grandfather in a land-rental deal. The ex-soldier also had rebuffed a man who coveted a war souvenir Jones had brought back from overseas.

Jones and Harris were held without charges for several days. Then, on the night of August 8, a jailer unlocked their cell and said they were free to go. Suspicious of an ambush, they refused to leave, whereupon several law officers threw them out. As soon as they landed on the street outside the jail, a band of armed white men grabbed the two prisoners and shoved them into waiting cars. On a seldom-traveled country road a short time later, the mob pistol-whipped Albert Harris and tossed him in a ditch, apparently thinking he was dead. Harris was the lucky one; John Jones was tortured to the point of death, viciously mutilated with a meat cleaver and a blowtorch, and left to die in horrible pain.

Harris, regaining consciousness after the assailants had gone, heard his cousin's agonized moans and crawled to him, but Jones was soon dead. The terrified teenager somehow found his way home. His father, on hearing what had happened, drove the boy that same night to medical attention and safety at a relative's house in Arkansas. Later, after taking a beating for not revealing where his son was, the father went into hiding with the boy. Back home in Webster Parish, meanwhile, the remains of John C. Jones, too badly butchered for his wife and child to gaze upon, were dressed in his corporal's khakis and placed in a closed, flag-draped casket for burial.

The federal district attorney for north Louisiana, Malcolm Lafargue, asked the FBI to investigate the incident. In September the Webster Parish grand jury met in Minden, but refused to return any indictments. Nothing more might have been said or done about the torture-lynching of John Jones and the flight of Albert Harris, had not Walter White of the NAACP finally tracked Harris down and persuaded him to tell his story to U.S. Department of Justice investigators. An aide of White's escorted Harris and his father to New York from Michigan, where they had been hiding, and White continued with them to Washington. "Never before had we been able to locate an eyewitness who could and would give firsthand evidence of what had taken place during a lynching," said Walter White later.

Editor Paul C. Corwin of the Minden *Herald* complained editorially of "false accusations by outside interests that cries were heard in the rear of the jail and a gathering of men seized the two negroes directly after they were released." He expressed "complete faith in the ability of the local officers" to see that justice was done without help from Washington. But soon thereafter, Albert Harris positively identified five men, including two deputy sheriffs, Charles M. Edwards and Oscar H. Haynes, Jr., as participants in the lynch mob. Lafargue was then able to get a federal grand jury to indict the five men, and in February 1947 he brought them to trial in Shreveport.

The Minden paper didn't report on the proceedings, but the Shreveport *Times* gave extensive coverage. Lafargue, a veteran prosecutor and son of a Louisiana judge, skillfully laid out what he felt was a foolproof case against the defendants, but as the week wore on, he knew instinctively that the jury of twelve white men was not going to return a guilty verdict. Before he left home on Saturday, March 1, Lafargue told his wife that he wanted her and their son to be in the courtroom for the closing arguments later that day.

A dynamic man in his late thirties, Malcolm Lafargue was a highly respected prosecutor, fair-minded and fearless; in his son's remembrance years later, he was "an honest, straitlaced, aboveboard man who was not afraid to tangle with anybody." When he made his presentation to the jury that afternoon, the short, stocky attorney cut to the heart of the matter. The case was in federal court, he said, "because free government and good government were not available in Webster Parish." The defendants "knew they couldn't convict the Negroes of a crime—they wanted to beat somebody. . . . They never intended to give those Negroes a fair trial. Their trial was by ordeal." The local grand jury had considered the case in September, he declared, "but it didn't do a cockeyed thing, because it was whitewashed." Searching the faces of the jurors, Malcolm Lafargue finished:

> I come from this state. My grandfather had slaves. But to me, civil liberties mean human rights, God-given rights for all Americans. This is not a social question. This is not an economic question. It is a question of God-given rights. If you want a feudal society with over-lords, or a Hitler or Mussolini government, then this country is no place for you. We can have as much danger from within this country, from groups of intolerant men who would destroy the rights our forefathers gave us, as from any outside enemies.

After less than two hours of deliberation, the jury found all five of the defendants not guilty.

At about the time the Minden lynching case was coming to trial, a self-appointed deputation of taxi drivers in and around Greenville, South Carolina, took a black prisoner out of jail and pulverized him with knives, clubs, and shotgun blasts at close range.

The victim, twenty-four-year-old Willie Earle, an epileptic ex-convict, was in the county jail at Pickens, twenty miles west of Greenville, charged with the February 15, 1947, stabbing of a white cabdriver (who would later die of his wounds). In the predawn hours of February 17, a convoy of about fifteen cars, most of them taxis, pulled up at the jail; the drivers and others with them—some forty or fifty men in all—told the jailer to turn Earle over to them. They took him to the vicinity of a livestock slaughter-pen between Greenville and Pickens. His mutilated body was found there a short while later, after a black funeral home director received a call about "a dead nigger in need of his offices."

Within thirty-six hours, U.S. Attorney General Tom Clark had sent FBI agents to Greenville, and they quickly obtained statements from twenty-six men who freely admitted to being members of the mob and witnesses to the lynching. South Carolina's newly elected governor, forty-four-year-old J. Strom Thurmond, a highly decorated army officer in World War II, decried the lawless act and subsequently backed up his words with the appointment of a well-respected special prosecutor, Sam R. Watt of Spartanburg. (The line on Thurmond, a Carolina editorial writer noted with approval, is that he "tends to be liberal without being radical.") Thirty-one men were indicted for conspiring to murder Willie Earle; one of them, R. C. Hurd, Sr., was named in several of the confessions as the trigger man.

The following May, the case went to trial before Judge J. Robert Martin, Jr., and a jury of twelve men in Greenville. White sentiment in the class-conscious community seemed curiously divided, with working people generally vocal in their support of the defendants but some in the middle and upper classes whispering disdain of the "poor whites" and "millhand lintheads" who had taken the law into their own hands. Similar slurs were directed at the jury, which was made up entirely of working-class whites. (The opinions and feelings of blacks were more or less ignored, as if they had no stake in the matter.)

But interest was high, and it reached far beyond South Carolina. The escalation of racial violence since the war and extensive publicity about this particular crime attracted press coverage by *Time* and *Life* magazines; *The New Yorker* sent English novelist and critic Rebecca West (whose father had once lived in the South), and the *New York Times* was represented by its recently named Southern correspondent, John N. Popham.

Defense attorneys attacked the signed but unsworn confessions as forced statements obtained under extreme duress, but none of the defendants were called to testify, so they couldn't disavow their words directly. (One cabdriver who did take the stand said he had been asked to join the mob, but had refused; before the trial was over, the witness received a severe beating, and he left town for his own safety.) To the surprise of many, the team of lawyers for the defense included one of South Carolina's most outspoken liberals, John Bolt Culbertson of Greenville, a labor lawyer and former FBI agent who often outraged other whites by addressing blacks as Mr. or Mrs., shaking hands and socializing with them, and generally treating them as equals. But in a perplexing display of Southern chauvinism, he attacked the FBI, the federal government, the Northern press, and Willie Earle—who, he drawled, "is dead, and I wish more like him was dead." Before the judge indignantly gaveled him to order, Culbertson smiled at the defendants and said, "There's a law against shooting a dog, but if a mad dog were loose in my community, I would shoot the dog and let them prosecute me."

The *Life* reporter would praise prosecutor Watt for his skill and declare that Judge Martin had "conducted the trial from start to finish with admirable fairness." (Martin would sustain a reputation for judicial integrity throughout his later tenure as a federal district judge.) It had all taken eight days, including five hours of deliberation by the jury. When the end finally came, a spring thunderstorm was hammering against the courtroom windows. The judge looked with a grim expression at the slips on which the jurors had recorded their verdicts. He rose and left the courtroom without speaking after the clerk announced the not-guilty decision. The roar of the victors was louder than the storm outside.

Rebecca West, in her account of the trial in *The New Yorker*, saw the South's wall of caste and class and color in historic and universal terms. "Here was a curtain cut of the same stuff as hangs between England and Ireland," she wrote. From behind that magnolia curtain stepped two white Greenvillians, a man and a woman, to speak quietly to West as they left the courtroom. "This is only the beginning," the man said. The woman was more descriptive. "It is like a fever," she whispered, with tears in her eyes. "It spreads, it's an infection, it's just like a fever."

The fever kept popping out all over the South, fed by the inability or unwillingness of local, state, and federal prosecutors to bring terrorists to justice. Time after time in the wake of some outrageous crime, the police made no arrests, the district attorney brought no charges, the grand jury refused to indict, or the trial jury could not convict. More serious by far was the fact that many of these cases involved acts of violence, even killing, by officers of the law—jailers, prison guards, policemen, sheriffs, state troopers.

Whether all of the racially motivated killings and maimings of 1946 and 1947 were simply episodic coincidences erupting at random across the unstable South, or whether they added up to a predictable, even calculated, surge of reactionary power, they came in the end to the same chilling result: scores of dead, hundreds of injured, thousands of terrorized citizens for whom the protection of the law was at best a meaningless ideal, and at worst a threatening reality.

Inexplicably, Georgia seemed in 1947, as in the preceding year, to have a worse case of racial bloodlust than most of the other Southern states. In May, a black farmer arrested on suspicion of aiding a fleeing murder suspect was lynched in the Harris County jail at Hamilton. In July, at a prison camp near Brunswick, eight black convicts were killed and five others critically wounded in a hail of bullets fired by Warden H. G. Worthy and several guards. (Even some local white officials scoffed at the warden's claim that the prisoners were trying to escape, but a grand jury took his word for it.) And at Ellaville in Schley County that November, a forty-nine-year-old widowed black sharecropper, Rosa Lee Ingram, and two of her twelve children—sons in their early teens—were sentenced to die in the electric chair for killing a white sharecropper who had held the woman at gunpoint and viciously whipped her when she resisted his sexual advances. (The sentences were later reduced to life in prison.)

The resurgent Ku Klux Klan and other ragtag units of political and cultural extremism were often in the news—and these, too, showed a more imposing presence in Georgia than elsewhere. Hiram W. Evans, the Imperial Wizard of the national KKK, operated out of Atlanta for several years in the late thirties and early forties. After the war, the newly menacing statewide Klan in Georgia had as its Grand Dragon a fire-breathing Atlanta physician, Dr. Samuel Green, and the local Klan Klavern in the Georgia capital was led by Sam Roper, a onetime city cop who had headed the state highway patrol under Governor Talmadge. Roy V. Harris, speaker of the Georgia House of Representatives, was a key figure in the formation of the Cracker Party, an Augusta-based right-wing movement hostile to black political participation. Still another white supremacist outfit, the Columbians, emerged in Atlanta in 1946 as a Nazi-like cadre of brown-shirted bullies preaching hatred of blacks, Jews, and Communists.

From so much hostile intent and violent behavior, so much pervasive meanness, you could easily draw the conclusion that the white South was effectively stifling dissent and enforcing conformity, uniting behind a banner of racial discrimination, reactionary politics, and religious intolerance. But the opposition to right-wing extremism had not dissolved; on the contrary, some Southern whites and almost all blacks were more determined than ever to usher in an era of postwar social change. Clearly, the ancient Southern animosities between right and left, white and black, ruler and subject, had reached a new and more ominous stage. The old expectations and fears no longer applied; a meaner game, a cutthroat game, was in the offing, and all that seemed consonant with the past was the Southern habit—recently honed by the war—of settling things violently, with knives and fists and guns.

Even in Atlanta, supposedly the beacon light of urban progressivism in the region, signs of ultraconservative narrowness and resistance to change were visible at every turn. And yet it was precisely here, in the flagship city of New South idealism, that the black and white opposition to political and racial and cultural extremism was strongest. If Talmadge and the Klan and the Columbians and segregation and religious fanaticism and violence were here, so too were Arnall and McGill and visionary black leaders and the CIO and the Southern Regional Council and the American Veterans Committee.

No matter how the South might eventually resolve its postwar conflicts, they would first have to be fought out in hundreds of local and state arenas; not until that happened could the legislative, executive, and judicial wings of the federal government be compelled to pay attention to those problems, and eventually to help resolve them. And of all these regional battlefields where the struggle for the South's future would be waged, none was larger, more central, or more vital than Atlanta, and none was more impressively arrayed with formidable combatants of the right and left.

With absolute certainty, the reactionaries knew that if they could stop change here, they could stop it anywhere in the South—and with just as much conviction, the progressives knew that if reform failed here, it would fail everywhere. In that sense, Atlanta was the ultimate testing ground, the crux of it all.

3. *Spotlight on Georgia*

Between 1937 and 1969, Mayors William B. Hartsfield and Ivan Allen, Jr., would preside almost continuously over Atlanta's transformation from the Old South to the New World. Unabashed hucksters that they were, the two men never tired of extolling the manifold virtues of their beloved phoenix, rising since 1864 from the cold ashes of history. In time, both of them would be associated with the phrase "the city too busy to hate." But that would be later, in the 1960s and beyond; in 1945, Atlanta was not yet a city at all, in the fullest sense, but a sleepy, suddenly overgrown Southern country town that had been jarred awake by a depression-ending war and singled out by geography and economics, by chance and circumstance, to be the model metropolis of the postwar South.

To any objective witness, it must have seemed a poor candidate for such prominence. As it swelled with refugees from the poverty-plagued countryside, Atlanta was skirting unsteadily on the edge of disaster, barely staying one step ahead of the rest of the South, a long stride behind the rest of the nation, and a short arm's length away from a violent explosion. If the South were likened to a third-world country—an Argentina, an Indonesia—then Atlanta was its Buenos Aires, its Jakarta, a teeming hub of extreme wealth and deprivation, of sophistication and naiveté, of grand visions and petty intrigues and run-of-the-mill corruption. When the residents of Georgia's capital city looked away at last from the preoccupations of war, they could see displayed before them in their own community all the multiple fragments of the split personality that was the South.

At Georgia Tech and Emory and Atlanta universities, at Morehouse and Spelman and Agnes Scott colleges, young men and women, white and black, went quietly about their separate pursuits of learning. A swift and sustained burst of industrial growth was creating thousands of new jobs in the city—so many that the value of manufactured goods would double in just five years. An average of fifty flights a day winged in and out of Atlanta, ranking it among the half-dozen busiest airports in the country (but ground transportation still dominated, with twice that many daily trains and four times as many buses rolling through the downtown depots). Preening in the dogwood and azalea-banked beauty of spring and the gold and crimson glow of autumn, Atlanta tiptoed toward the future, led by a team of elected or informally chosen players who seemed casually inclined toward a calm and cautious, moderately progressive approach to change.

Their outwardly reasonable demeanor hid the fact that Atlanta was as deeply mired in race and class divisions and inequality as almost any other city in the South. Virtually all of its institutions acceded to the reality of Jim Crow segregation in an insular society that presupposed the superiority of all Caucasians over other races; what's more, there was a pecking order among whites that robbed the poor of practically every privilege except racial bigotry. Few people of any race dared to question the maze of contradictions and inconsistencies that propped up the system. Atlanta had no black policemen or other officers of the law, no black judges or elected officials, few black voters (and thus virtually none as jurors), and only a handful of black professionals other than teachers and preachers. Medical care for the city's 100,000 black residents, measured by the presence of only twenty-five physicians and fifty hospital beds to serve them, was still languishing in the "kitchen surgery" era. Though they made up fully one-third of the population inside the city and one-fourth in the metropolitan area, African-Americans were largely hemmed inside a central district that comprised about one-eighth of the city's land area.

Segregation prevailed in all the libraries, parks and playgrounds, community centers, public housing projects, buses and streetcars, taxicabs, hospitals, churches, schools, jails and prisons, restaurants, theaters, bars, bowling alleys, elevators, swimming pools, and cemeteries. Only the thinnest pretense of a fair-share division of resources was offered. The all-white board of public education divided its 1946 capital budget for new school construction seventeen to one in favor of whites. In Atlanta and throughout the South, just about the only institutions that permitted any biracial involvement at all were the military services, YWCA and YMCA groups, some labor unions, jazz bands, bootleg joints, and whorehouses.

Mayor Hartsfield, who was recognized by whites and blacks alike for his moderate leadership, frequently expressed confidence that "the better element of white and colored people" in the city would work together to solve the problems of slum housing, poor health care, job discrimination, lack of police protection, and inadequacy of public programs and services for blacks. The Atlanta *Journal* gave editorial support to such cooperation, but added a caveat that white-black initiatives such as these must "rest on the major premise that segregation shall continue. Segregation is not discrimination, if accompanied as it should be by a just apportionment of community benefits." Ralph McGill's sustained opposition to Eugene Talmadge and the Ku Klux Klan and his insistence that the *Constitution* capitalize the word *Negro* and use standard courtesy titles without regard to race enhanced his reputation as a progressive, but he still didn't endorse the abolition of legalized segregation.

As limited as their liberalism was, the Atlanta newspapers and Mayor Hartsfield and Governor Ellis Arnall gave high visibility to the promise of a progressive awakening in postwar Georgia and the South. They had begun to hear prodding voices of exhortation from several quarters on the left: from Atlanta's black leadership, with its growing fervor for voting rights and other liberties; from returning veterans attuned to reform, particularly those in the American Veterans Committee; from the Congress of Industrial Organizations and its locally based "Operation Dixie" drive to organize labor unions; from the Southern Regional Council, a potentially powerful force for change in the city and throughout the South; from various factions of Protestants, Catholics, and Jews with newly formed agendas for social betterment. Lillian Smith, along with other outspoken intellectuals—people in religious or academic institutions and the Northern press—pushed even harder for a Southern renaissance, with Atlanta as its generating station.

From the far right came the reactionary drumbeat of the Klan, the Columbians, the Cracker Party, the Talmadge forces, members of the Georgia congressional delegation, most of the legislature, and a variety of religious groups, monied interests, American Legionnaires, and others. Facing their liberal adversaries at close range in the streets of Atlanta, the right-wing groups were spoiling for a fight, confident of victory. Before 1945 was over, Atlantans on the right and left and in the middle were on edge, waiting nervously for the ideological and psychological battle to begin.

Ellis Gibbs Arnall had begun his tenure as governor of Georgia in 1943 with all the right credentials. His forebears had been stalwarts of the rural middle class—lawyers, judges, merchants, teachers. He himself had graduated first in his law school class at the University of Georgia, had served in the legislature, and had been the state's attorney general. Bright and ambitious, he yearned to break the grip that Eugene Talmadge had held on Georgia politics for the better part of a decade. When Talmadge met with embarrassing criticism for political meddling in the state's higher education system, Arnall seized the issue and rode it to an upset victory over the incumbent in 1942.

Barely thirty-five years old, he took up his chosen role as a progressive reformer with eager enthusiasm. He had close ties to Ralph McGill, who had written some campaign speeches for him, and to William Hartsfield, with whom he had collaborated on some novel state and local government initiatives. With admirable skill and a flair for publicity, Arnall coaxed the legislature or acted on his own to rack up one success after another— paying off the state's debt, restoring academic freedom to the university, reforming the penal system, lowering the voting age to eighteen, abolishing the poll tax, rewriting the state constitution, suing the railroads for their discriminatory freight rates, revoking the Ku Klux Klan's charter. Most impressive of all, wrote Gerald W. Johnson in 1946, "he has done it without ever using the word 'nigger' and without denouncing the Pope, the Elders of Zion, Stalin, or the reptile press."

When he was pushing to get the vote for eighteen-year-olds, Arnall packed the legislative galleries with wounded young soldiers. As part of his prison-reform effort, he stunned a joint session of the legislature by introducing to them an escaped convict, Robert E. Burns, whose exposé of medieval brutality against Georgia convicts had been made into a sensational film, *I Am a Fugitive from a Chain Gang*. At the 1944 Democratic

National Convention, Arnall even managed to hold the Georgia delegation solidly in line behind Henry Wallace in the bitterly fought vice-presidential contest. So completely had he captured the state political machinery from the Talmadge forces that he was able to persuade a substantial majority of statehouse members in January 1946 to amend the new constitution's rule against gubernatorial succession and make way for him to run for another four-year term.

But that crucial vote, 126 to 74, was just eight shy of the two-thirds majority he had to have, and Ellis Arnall, instead of being a shoo-in for reelection, was suddenly a lame duck in troubled waters. Seeing his career in jeopardy, the governor made known his interest in being Harry Truman's running mate in 1948. (Gerald Johnson, writing in the *American Mercury,* strongly touted him for that post.) His hope of retaining a political base in Georgia was gone, though, and Arnall, an outsider while still in his thirties, would never return to power. His final departure from the state capitol in 1947 would stand out in the minds of those who witnessed it as perhaps the most bizarre and spectacular episode in Georgia's political history.

One clear sign of Arnall's determination to break the shackles of the past was his aggressive pursuit of right-wing terrorists. As attorney general under Talmadge, he had sued Hiram Evans, Imperial Wizard of the Klan and owner of an asphalt company, for manipulating prices in his dealings with the state. Then, as governor, Arnall chose Daniel Duke, the Klan-bashing former prosecutor for Atlanta Mayor Hartsfield, to serve as an assistant attorney general with the primary mission of putting terrorists out of business. The governor and his attorney general, Eugene Cook, gave Duke wide latitude to accomplish that task—and for the first time in memory, Klan leaders found Georgia's government harassing them instead of giving them protection.

"When you're trying to break open a conspiracy," said Duke, recalling his role years later, "you have to play rough. We used some dirty tricks, including planted evidence and fake confessions, to smoke some of those guys out." In 1945, Duke hired Stetson Kennedy, a twenty-nine-year-old Florida journalist who had infiltrated the Klan in Atlanta, to work for him as an undercover agent. (Calling himself John S. Perkins, Kennedy had used a deceased uncle's Klan membership in a daring ploy to gain an audience with Eugene Talmadge, and that had opened the way for him to join a local Klavern.)

Duke had other informers in the Klan, and so did William Hartsfield and Ralph McGill. One occasional supplier of inside information during the war was James R. Venable, a lawyer whose family owned Stone Mountain near Atlanta and staged Klan cross-burnings there for years. Venable was later to be the Imperial Wizard of a national KKK organization. But no other secret agent would ever make a public splash like Kennedy, Duke's man in the sheets.

Raised in middle-class comfort in a conservative Jacksonville family, Stetson Kennedy had found himself at odds with the tenets of race and class discrimination during his college years, and because of that he was ostracized by his closest relatives. His dissenting views were further shaped during a stint with the Florida unit of the Federal Writers' Project just before the war. While still in his mid-twenties he wrote *Palmetto Country*, a volume in the American Folkways Series edited by Erskine Caldwell. By the time he got to Atlanta in 1944, he was freelancing for several magazines and had developed close ties with Washington political columnist Drew Pearson and the Southern leadership of the CIO—to both of whom, in addition to Daniel Duke, he was soon supplying inside information on the Klan. The Fellowship of Southern Churchmen, the Southern Conference for Human Welfare, and the Southern Regional Council also came to rely on Kennedy's insider reports.

Hounded and bedeviled by the leaks inside their rickety gunboat, the Atlanta Klan and other cells of the terrorist organization in Georgia would lash out with deadly force in 1946. But before that happened, alarm bells were sounded in every stronghold of white supremacy after federal court rulings in Texas and Georgia cracked open the ballot box for Southern blacks. A coalition of respected black leaders in Georgia used those decisions to test both the conservative will of the reactionaries and the liberal mettle of the progressives.

The U.S. Supreme Court had opened the way for electoral reform with its ruling in the Texas case, *Smith* v. *Allwright*, in April 1944. To get around the constitutional directive that no citizen shall be denied the right to vote because of race, Texas Democrats had claimed their all-white primary was not a state function but a private organization's mechanism for choosing candidates. Dr. Lonnie Smith, a Houston dentist, sued for damages in 1941 after he was turned away from the polls because of his race. The lower courts upheld his exclusion, but Thurgood Marshall and William H. Hastie of the NAACP finally prevailed in the U.S. Supreme Court. In an eight-to-one decision written by Justice Stanley F. Reed of Kentucky, the court said in effect that the preliminary round of voting was an essential prerequisite of the general election, and had to be conducted under the same rules. Thus, "the right to vote in such a primary . . . is a right secured by the Constitution." Years later, Marshall would call this his most significant victory—not excepting the *Brown* v. *Board of Education* decision.

The day after the court handed down its ruling in the Texas case, an

Atlanta NAACP official urged Georgia blacks who were already registered to go to the polls and vote in the state's July primary. Some tried, but they were turned away. One of them, a Columbus minister named Primus E. King, subsequently sued in federal court, asking monetary damages for the denial of his right to vote. Governor Arnall decided that he was not yet ready to add the voting rights of African-Americans to his list of reforms; he instructed his attorney general to defend the white-primary law. The legislature, when it convened in early 1945, omitted all references to primaries in the new state constitution and left in place several provisions designed to restrict the access of blacks to the ballot. Arnall went along with them. In speeches and comments to reporters, he said he was opposed to an open primary that put no limits on the right of Negroes to vote.

Federal judge T. Hoyt Davis of Macon heard the Primus King case, and the NAACP provided counsel for the plaintiff. In Atlanta, a delegation of black leaders called on Arnall to disavow the white primary, but the governor avoided a direct response.

When the judge decided the case in October 1945, he followed the precedent of *Smith* v. *Allwright*. The primary was an integral part of the election process, he ruled, and withholding the right to vote was a violation of the Constitution. The decision was upheld on appeal in March 1946. After the Supreme Court declined to consider it further, Arnall finally spoke out in support of an unrestricted ballot. Whether he liked it or not, he said, this was the law of the land, and Georgia would abide by it. He rejected the demands of many politicians that he call a special session of the legislature to circumvent the ruling.

The leaders of right-wing extremism in Georgia turned on the governor with a vengeance. House Speaker Roy Harris and Agriculture Commissioner Tom Linder, two outspoken racists in his administration, publicly denounced and deserted him. Gene Talmadge, his old adversary, quickly declared that he would be a candidate for governor in the July primary, and vowed that no blacks would vote in primary elections after he resumed control of state government. The Klan promised to punish blacks who dared to vote.

For the time being, though, the federal court decision opened the 1946 primaries to blacks—to those already registered for the general election, at least, and any others who could sign up—and they quickly showed the power of their numbers. (In one-third of the state's counties, there were more blacks of voting age than whites.) In Augusta and Richmond County, Roy Harris's home district, more than seven thousand blacks went to the polls and helped an independent candidate defeat Harris by almost two to one. Later in the summer, more than fifty thousand blacks voted in the statewide primary for the first time, causing Talmadge to lose the popular vote to his main challenger, James V. Carmichael—but the former governor squeaked through with enough county-unit-system points to claim the office once again.

That spring and summer of 1946 was a pivotal season in Georgia's postwar history, a seesaw time of highs and lows. It was then that the CIO launched its million-dollar "Operation Dixie" drive to bring a million Southern workers, white and black, into the labor movement. The federation also hired George S. Mitchell to head a political action committee aimed at making voters out of those new union members. The American Veterans Committee chapter in Atlanta (one of about twenty in the Southeast), took an activist stance on a wide range of public issues, including desegregation of the city police department and the libraries.

The significance of the open primary ruling was underscored by Roy Harris's defeat in Augusta and the collapse of his budding Cracker Party, a militantly anti-black political group that never really got off the ground. Mayor Hartsfield, viewing the potential of the black vote with a realistic politician's steely eye, told the minority leadership of Atlanta that if they could register ten thousand new voters before the July primary, he would listen carefully to any concerns they had about public programs and services. In fifty-one days they put eighteen thousand new names on the rolls, and Hartsfield responded promptly by initiating a series of administrative moves designed to lower the Jim Crow barriers.

The newly empowered black voters of Atlanta were instrumental in former legislator Helen Douglas Mankin's win over several conservative opponents in a special election to fill a vacant seat in Congress early in 1946. (She again won a popular plurality in the regular election that fall, but the notorious county unit system tabbed her an eight-to-six loser, and she was turned out of office.) In spite of their gains, though, the statewide total of adult blacks who actually registered and voted still amounted to only a small fraction of the whole. Nevertheless, white politicians alarmed by the increases bent to the task of planning new ways to prevent the masses, black or white, from entering freely into the political process. With the return of Eugene Talmadge, they fully expected to succeed.

Governor Arnall, his state power almost used up but his national hopes still alive, continued to walk a liberal tightrope, balancing his reformist aims with a racial view that affirmed legal rights but also the principle of social segregation. During his last months in office, he put the finishing touches on a book, *The Shore Dimly Seen*, that would be published in New York late in 1946 as both a summation of his experiences and beliefs and a platform for his future candidacy. (Most of the spadework on the book and on numerous magazine articles published under his byline was done by DeWitt Roberts, a former south Georgia journalist and trusted Arnall cadreman.)

The return of Eugene Talmadge to political power that summer was at least coincidental, if not somehow correlated, with the surge of extremist posturing and violence that swept across the state. The quadruple lynching in Walton County happened just before his campaign visit there and his subsequent primary victory; the Klan was marching and burning crosses in almost every section of the state, even as Arnall's informants and prosecutors nipped at their heels; and in Atlanta, the Nazi-style group that called itself the Columbians had suddenly burst upon the scene just in time to climb aboard the Talmadge bandwagon.

Two young toughs—Emory Burke, up from a life of poverty in Alabama, and Homer L. Loomis, Jr., down from the patrician comforts of Princeton University and his father's Wall Street law firm—were the spotlighted bosses of the Columbian cult. They and their followers, dressed like Hitler's brown-shirted youth gangs, could be seen goose-stepping in formation on the city streets. They sounded like Nazis too, glorifying "Anglo-Saxon purity" and heaping vilification on Negroes, Jews, Communists, and the rich. Undercover agents for Daniel Duke (including an attractive blonde named Renée Forrest, a young Jewish woman from New York, who posed as a secretary) soon provoked the leaders into clashes that landed them in jail on charges of assault and incitement to riot.

Duke was closing out his tenure in the attorney general's office with a flourish, pursuing several lines of legal attack against terrorist groups. "The Klan and the Columbians are one and the same thing and ought to be tarred with the same brush," he said. Focusing specifically on the Columbians, he added, "The Klan and Gene Talmadge are the hens that hatched this biddy." At a court hearing on Duke's petition to revoke the Columbians' charter, Emory Burke so angered the prosecutor with interruptions and insults that Duke suddenly hauled off and floored him with one punch. He apologized to the court for his "inappropriate behavior," but the judge professed not to have seen the offense. "I must have looked away for a moment," he said with a straight face. A short time later, Burke and Loomis were found guilty and sent to prison, and the Columbians joined the Crackers in quiet oblivion.

Stetson Kennedy also climaxed his undercover work in spectacular fashion, publishing *Southern Exposure* early in 1947 and shedding his "John S. Perkins" alias when he appeared as a witness at the trial of the Columbians. Some of the terrorists whose secret sanctums he had infiltrated were present when he was called to the stand, but they could only watch in shocked and silent rage as the mole calmly surfaced. It took a special escort to get Kennedy past his betrayed Klan "brothers" when he left the courtroom.

In February 1947, Kennedy and Ellis Arnall met in person for the first time while promoting their books in Manhattan. Arnall subsequently wrote a favorable review of *Southern Exposure* for the *New York Times*. Both men, and Dan Duke too, had shaken Georgia's reactionary establishment to its heels, but now the old guard was coming back to power. In later years, Duke would become a judge and Arnall would run again for governor (without success); as for Kennedy, two later books of his, *I Rode with the Klan* and *Jim Crow Guide*, would be published overseas in the 1950s. None of the three reformers would have as much of an impact later as they had had during and after the war.

Kennedy's *Southern Exposure* was the first nonfiction volume by a white Southerner to confront what he called "the Squalid South" in all its white-supremacist disarray. In tone and focus, the book was cast in the mold of a muckraking exposé. Kennedy hammered especially hard at the forces that denied black Southerners their constitutionally guaranteed right to full and fair treatment in the workplace and the political arena.

In a chapter called "Total Equality, and How to Get It," Kennedy noted that all but the most rabidly anti-black reactionaries were at least giving lip service to equal opportunity, while still holding firm against what they called "social equality"—that is, any hint of lowering the barriers of segregation. In stating his own opposition to Jim Crow laws and his belief in full equality, Kennedy conceded that "the means for the forcible overthrow of segregation are not at hand," but he went on to lay out a strategy for "the real Southern liberals, white and black," to follow. "So long as white supremacy remains an economic and political reality," he said, "no amount of education or agitation can bring about the abolition of segregation in the South by the South." He added:

> Short of another civil war, *the Southern Negro must be emancipated economically and politically before he can be emancipated socially*. This means that he must first join democratic labor unions and beat a democratic path to the polls. Once these two things have been accomplished . . . the abolition of Jim Crow will be as inevitable as was the abolition of chattel slavery after Civil War broke out. . . . If this strategy is not followed, there may be no progress in any direction, but reaction in all directions. Hence this is not at all a strategy of appeasement, but the most radical of practical programs for achieving total equality without abortive violence.

Kennedy went on to reiterate his belief that blacks were "entitled to total equality now," but that "by suffering segregation another decade (no more)," they would do much to ensure that equality, once it came, was more than an empty gesture. In any case, he warned, social change would never come easily: "White supremacy is going to die a hard death—almost as hard as slavery's. It will take the South approximately as long to get over the death of Jim Crow as it is taking to get over the passing of Old Black Joe, the slave."

Drew Pearson, the liberal columnist, was yet another nemesis of the right wing in 1946. He spoke from the steps of the state capitol in Atlanta that summer. Governor Arnall introduced him to a huge throng and a national radio audience, and Pearson, sensing the tensions that divided the region, tempered his critical remarks with some words of praise for the South. But his main topic was the curse of terrorism. He drew catcalls and boos from some in the audience—and cheers from others—for his blunt denunciation of Talmadge and his characterization of Klansmen as latter-day carpetbaggers. Later in the fall, when the state's Democrats convened in Macon and turned the party machinery back to Talmadge, Pearson published the names of seventeen Klansmen among the governor-elect's delegates—a list, he said, that reads "like a roll call of the nightshirt brigade at Stone Mountain."

The list of Georgia organizations and individuals speaking out for racial tolerance and against hate groups in 1946 continued to expand. Governor Arnall and Mayor Hartsfield and much of the press led the way, along with the CIO, the American Veterans Committee, the Southern Regional Council, the NAACP, the Urban League, organizations of churchwomen and university professors, Baptists and Methodists and Catholics in their annual state meetings—and each new voice emboldened others. Many small daily and weekly newspapers across the state expressed strong editorial opposition to the reactionary racism of the Talmadge machine. Gradually, people stood up to be identified with the forward-looking philosophy of renewal and reform that Arnall had espoused, and that scattered groups of liberal and progressive Southerners had struggled to give birth to since the early 1930s. Among all of them there stirred the barest glimmer of hope that white and black Southerners would somehow come to a fair and just accommodation with one another as mutually entitled and interdependent residents of the same region, the same country.

But those who were realistic also knew that racial accommodation was an emotional issue for most Southerners in that violent summer of 1946; they knew from the fierceness of the opposition that every step toward equality would be a struggle. Even if a majority of whites could have been persuaded that simple justice for blacks was both a moral and an ethical imperative and a matter of enlightened self-interest, relatively few of them seemed eager to become activists for the cause—and even fewer were clamoring for the hides of terrorists and other reactionary wrongdoers. The surest proof of that was on display to the world in Walton County, Georgia, just then: four young people executed in broad daylight by two dozen men, and no one—not the governor, the state attorney general, the Georgia Bureau of Investigation, undercover agents, local prosecutors and grand juries, the U.S. Attorney General, the FBI, or the President of the United States—could get enough hard evidence to charge a single soul with the crime. The conservative elite, the Klan, the terrorists, and the Talmadgeites still held the upper hand.

The charade of final balloting had to be observed, but Eugene Talmadge's primary victory was essentially his election, there being no Republican Party candidate to oppose him in November. The recording of his automatic victory that fall coincided with some surprising election outcomes elsewhere in the South; altogether they added up to the emergence of a mixed bag of new progressives and old reactionaries in state and local offices. Nationally, the Democratic Party of Harry S. Truman took an unmerciful drubbing, so shattering that when the ballots were counted, the Republicans controlled both houses of Congress for the first time in almost twenty years. From the perspective of Southern liberals and moderates, it was a terrible time for the country to turn right; the reactionary South was extreme enough without more encouragement in that direction.

In all the drama and excitement of Arnall's fall and Talmadge's revival, few except those closest to him realized that old Gene was a sick man. It thus came as a final shock to emotionally drained Georgians in that topsy-turvy year of 1946 when the governor-elect died of cancer in an Atlanta hospital on December 21—and before the body was cold, a battle royal was raging for the right to fill his shoes. (As if to symbolize the blazing excesses of that year, a fire swept through the Winecoff Hotel on Atlanta's Peachtree Street one December night, killing 119 people. It was the worst hotel fire in American history—one more outrage in a time and place already burdened with far too much violence and death.)

Among those who did know that the governor-elect was in failing health were his chief political adviser, Roy Harris, the deposed former House speaker from Augusta, and the Talmadge heir-apparent, his thirty-three-year-old son, Herman E. Talmadge, a lawyer and ex-navy officer who had returned to Georgia from the South Pacific in the fall of 1945. Under the provisions of the new state constitution, a lieutenant governor was to be chosen for the first time. Ellis Arnall's candidate for the post, Melvin E. Thompson, had won in the primary, and like Gene Talmadge, he was unopposed in the general election. If something happened to Gene later on, Thompson would succeed him. But what if something happened to him sooner, before the November election or before his inauguration in January? In that case, the Talmadge advisers concluded, putting their spin on the ambiguous language of the constitution, the state legislature would choose between "the two persons having the highest number of votes" for the office—not the dead governor, obviously, and not the new lieutenant governor either, but whoever had a legitimate majority of write-in votes for governor. Say, for instance, Herman E. Talmadge.

Quietly they put out the word to get Herman's name written in on a few ballots. "You might call it an insurance policy," the son explained years later. "If I couldn't keep Papa from dying, at least I could keep him from dying in vain." But the secret strategy didn't remain a secret; others got into the act. All told, thirty-two people received write-in votes, including Gene's primary foe, James Carmichael, and one D. Talmadge Bowers, a north Georgia tombstone salesman—both of whom, along with Herman, garnered close to seven hundred. To the vast relief of the Talmadge forces, Carmichael said he wanted no part in a subterfuge. Then, as if on cue, Gene died a few weeks later, and "Hummon," the choice of a few hundred of the state's three million people, took his case to the friendly court of the Georgia General Assembly.

The lawmakers convened at the capitol in Atlanta on January 13 in an atmosphere of chaos and high tension. Ellis Arnall would be governor until his successor was sworn in—presumably on January 18—and he vowed to hold office until a proper transfer of power had taken place. M. E. Thompson claimed that as lieutenant governor he should be the legitimate successor; the younger Talmadge, of course, was supremely confident that the assembly would give the job to him. Georgia, it seemed, was about to have not one but three governors.

The two houses met in joint session on the fourteenth to settle the matter. Milling about freely among the legislators and jamming the corridors and galleries were hundreds of lobbyists and state employees reinforced by a motley legion of clamorous partisans from around the state—some of them armed, most of them drinking, all of them rowdily disruptive. "Those were right squalid times," Herman Talmadge later recalled. The session dragged on for hours with hardly a pretense of order. A count of the general election votes showed the deceased Talmadge with 143,279, Carmichael with 699, Talmadge Bowers the tombstone drummer with 637, and "Hummon" with 617, later amended to 675 when an envelope of uncounted ballots happened to turn up at the last minute. Arnall's forces tried to get Carmichael declared the winner and, failing that, retreated to their former position that Thompson was the only legitimate choice. But a clear majority of the legislature knew from the first how the session had to end. Finally, they sent the chamber into convulsions by designating Herman Eugene Talmadge to be their governor.

It was now two o'clock in the morning of January 15. With a grinning Herman in tow, a delegation of the solons marched downstairs to literally install their man in the governor's office. Arnall and his lieutenants were holed up there, waiting nervously for the inevitable invasion. Accounts differ on whether the aggressors banged the door in with a battering ram, took it down from the hinges, opened it with a key, or simply turned the knob and walked in. In any case, Herman made a dramatic entrance, flanked on one side by his mother, Mattie Talmadge—"Miss Mitt" to her friends—and on the other by Roy Harris. Standing before the embattled Arnall, Herman said, "I presume you have been informed that I've been elected governor by the General Assembly."

"Herman, you have no claim to the office of governor," Arnall replied. "I refuse to yield the office to you. I consider you a pretender."

A scuffle broke out between the teams of seconds; one of Arnall's men suffered a broken jaw. Herman, fearing a destructive melee that might harm his cause, regrouped his forces in the corridor and told Arnall he'd be back. Finally, an uneasy calm returned to the capitol.

Later, in the last hour before dawn, a Talmadge hit squad that included a locksmith and an escort of state troopers crept through the darkened halls, broke into the governor's office, and changed the lock on the door. Another team took over the empty governor's mansion (Arnall and his family having vacated it earlier) on The Prado, a fashionable north Atlanta residential street. Arnall made an attempt to enter his office later that morning, but he was unceremoniously shunted aside; briefly, he set up a makeshift workstation in the capitol rotunda, but that too was soon denied him. Meanwhile, M. E. Thompson and "Tombstone" Talmadge Bowers, the other claimants, put up only a token protest to the Talmadge takeover.

As bizarre and incredible as it was, this disorderly changing of the Georgia guard—a virtual overthrow by force—stirred more amusement than alarm in the Atlanta press. Ralph McGill "showed a strangely detached, nonpartisan attitude" about the whole affair, his friend and biographer Harold H. Martin later wrote. Inexplicably, McGill seemed almost to favor Talmadge in the affair, much to the chagrin of his friend Arnall, who likened the experience to being ousted "by a military coup d'état." On the scheduled inauguration date, the ex-governor finally yielded, saying he would step aside "until the courts remove the pretender who by force and storm troopers" had seized Georgia's highest office.

For sixty-seven days, while the state supreme court pondered the mess, Herman Talmadge ran Georgia. During that time he got the legislature to repeal all laws regarding primary elections, and told the state Democratic Party it was free to make its own rules off the books, like a private club. At hearings on these proposed changes, legislative committees allowed testimony from a surprising number of critical citizens. "Don't sink back to the period of 1865," pleaded one of them, R. W. Hayes, a young ex-GI. "Free Georgia from its Reconstruction complex. If the Negro was good enough to carry a gun in the war, and pay taxes, he should vote." By far the most impressive witness was Helen Dortch Longstreet, the octogenarian widow of Confederate General James Longstreet. In a quavering voice, she came in answer to "the call of duty within my soul," and then summoned the courage to invite "the scorn of honest men against this monstrous measure," which she warned would "set up a dictatorship under the lying guise of white supremacy." Unmoved, the lawmakers voted overwhelmingly to stand fast against the dike and keep democracy out.

By a vote of five to two, the supreme court ruled in March 1947 that the legislature had exceeded its authority, and that M. E. Thompson should serve as acting governor pending a special election in 1948 for the remaining two years of the term. Ellis Arnall would still be ineligible to run under the no-succession clause, but Herman Talmadge would not—and he announced his candidacy even as he vacated the capitol and the mansion to make way for Thompson. Before the smoke finally lifted from Atlanta's "War of the Governors," it was already becoming clear that a new Talmadge dynasty would soon begin.

Georgia was a roiling pit of political intrigue in the postwar South, but it was hardly unique in that respect. Almost every state in the region—and many a city, too—found itself whipsawed by the ideological and pragmatic scheming and the undisguised chicanery that characterized the clashing factions vying for power. Every Southern state held at least one gubernatorial election between 1944 and 1947, and the collective outcome of those races seemed to presage a little more of the spirit of reform than reaction. Some of the winners managed to sound downright progressive and forward-looking—compared, at least, with their predecessors.

James E. Folsom, the folksy populist chosen in 1946 to lead Alabama, made the best copy of these newcomers, but Jimmie Davis of Louisiana ran a close second. A sharecropper's son who became a teacher, Davis also wrote and sang country-and-Western songs. One of his depression-era tunes, "You Are My Sunshine," became a huge hit in 1940 (Gene Autry, Bing Crosby, and Ella Fitzgerald were among the many vocalists who recorded it), and Davis rode the wave of popularity into the governor's mansion near the end of the war. He was regarded as a member of the faction that had been trying to wrest Louisiana from the clutches of the Long machine ever since the godfather, Senator Huey Long, was assassinated in 1935. Another postwar reformer, thirty-four-year-old De-Lesseps S. Morrison, an ex–combat officer and a lawyer, was elected mayor of New Orleans in 1946 on a promise to throw out the machine crowd and clean up the city.

Earle C. Clements, Kentucky's postwar governor, was a dependable New Dealer in the Alben Barkley mold. As he had done previously in the House of Representatives and as he would do subsequently in the Senate, Clements almost always stood with the liberal wing of the Democratic Party on the issues his Southern conservative colleagues filibustered to defeat. Wilson W. Wyatt, the wartime mayor of Louisville and President Truman's housing czar after that, was another conspicuously liberal Southerner of the time, a cofounder of the left-wing, anticommunist pressure group called Americans for Democratic Action. (Kentucky politicians in general were seldom drawn into Southern displays of reactionary bigotry; other, more pressing economic and social problems kept them busy.)

Governors Millard Caldwell of Florida, Jim Nance McCord of Tennessee, R. Gregg Cherry of North Carolina, and J. Strom Thurmond of South Carolina all appeared to stick somewhere in the middle between Arnallian reformism and Talmadgeite reaction. Thurmond was billed as a liberal in his 1946 race for governor, even though he denounced the labor movement and the push for racial equality as "communistic" (and two years later he would lead the Dixiecrat mutiny in the Democratic Party).

The other Southern states either stayed in ultraconservative hands or made a turn to the right. Mississippi was one of the former, first under Thomas L. Bailey and then under Fielding L. Wright (Thurmond's Dixiecrat running mate in 1948). Texas, too, camped out on the far right throughout the forties, with Coke R. Stevenson and Beauford H. Jester tending the fire; Jester defeated Homer Rainey in 1946, two years after Rainey was ousted from the presidency of the University of Texas by its reactionary trustees. Arkansas replaced a middling governor, Homer M. Adkins, with a militant right-winger, Benjamin T. Laney, in 1945. The following year, Virginia gentleman Colgate W. Darden, Jr., a soft-spoken moderate, was replaced by William R. Tuck, a throwback reactionary handpicked by the minions of Senator Harry F. Byrd.

The Byrd machine still kept Virginia in its hip pocket, as it had for nearly two decades. E. H. "Boss" Crump ran Tennessee in pretty much the same fashion from his kingdom in Memphis. From the Carolinas to Texas, white politicians scurried right and left to cover their flanks as federal courts opened the way for black Southerners to vote. Calculating governors such as Thurmond of South Carolina, Wright of Mississippi, and

Laney of Arkansas looked to the 1948 election as a looming crucible for right-wing Southern Democrats; at the same time, pragmatic mayors like Hartsfield of Atlanta and Morrison of New Orleans, and even Governor Folsom of Alabama, showed themselves willing and able to broaden the base of their constituency.

Political pundit Stewart Alsop, eyeing the South from a lofty perch in Washington, could hardly make heads or tails of all this. If a political revolution is in progress in the South, Alsop wrote in late 1946, "it is surely an odd and confusing revolution, proceeding rapidly in several different directions at the same time." How could it be, he wondered, that Alabama ("the liberal oasis") could elect a progressive senator like John Sparkman and a governor like Jim Folsom—and keep sending Lister Hill to the Senate, too—while its neighbors, Mississippi and Georgia, remained in the grip of raving reactionaries?

It was a fair question—and Alsop didn't grasp the half of it. Even to those who knew the state intimately, Alabama was inscrutable, precisely as Russia was to Winston Churchill—a riddle wrapped in a mystery inside an enigma. It had those fairly liberal senators, yes, and that flamboyant new governor, true enough, and a few pretty decent House members to boot. It could claim the liberal Justice Hugo Black of the Supreme Court, and loyal New Dealer Aubrey Williams (back in Montgomery now, publishing a newspaper for farmers), and highly respected labor leaders like William Mitch of the CIO. It had produced journalists and writers, activists and scholars, teachers and preachers—some white, some black—who believed in and tried their best to live by liberal and progressive humanitarian principles. On the far left, it had had active factions of Communists and Socialists in the thirties and early forties—more of them, perhaps, than any other Southern state.

And yet, as surely as Alabama coal fired the steel mills of Birmingham, Alabama racism and reactionary extremism fueled the political and economic and social machinery of the state. On the same summer day in 1946 that Alabama's voters chose Jim Folsom to lead them, they also approved the Boswell Amendment, a new provision in the state constitution giving voter registrars broad latitude to judge applicants on the basis of "good character and good citizenship" and on their ability to "understand and explain" any part of the U. S. Constitution. Retiring Governor Chauncey Sparks campaigned hard for the amendment, which he said was needed to prevent "a flood of Negroes" from registering to vote in the wake of recent rulings by the federal courts. Sparks took his stand for "absolute segregation" and admonished Democrats to do everything necessary to maintain an all-white party.

Lined up with Sparks and sounding the racial alarm with him were such prominent Alabamians as former Governor Frank Dixon, former Senator Tom Heflin, state Democratic Party Chairman Gessner T. McCorvey, and Horace C. Wilkinson, a Birmingham lawyer long active in the fight to preserve white supremacy and segregation. The Big Mules of the industrial belt, the big planters of the Black Belt, and the Ku Klux Klan also joined the anvil chorus.

Folsom, Senator Hill, Senator-elect Sparkman, the labor movement, and the Birmingham and Montgomery newspapers all called for defeat of the Boswell Amendment, but the voters, particularly in upper-class and working-class white precincts, sided with the racists; it was ratified by a margin of about twelve thousand votes. If that outcome sobered and quieted most of the amendment's opponents, it had little effect at all on Jim Folsom; with a wink and a wave, he went about his daily rounds delivering his populist message as if nothing had happened. Big Jim Folsom cast a long shadow across the length and breadth of the state.

He was an overgrown country boy with roots in the Pea River valley of southeast Alabama and later ties to Cullman in the north. In 1946 he was thirty-eight years old, a strapping six feet eight and well over two hundred pounds, a veteran, a former insurance salesman, a perennial candidate (having lost two races for Congress and one for governor). The voters had never seen or heard anyone quite like "Kissing Jim" Folsom. He was a handsome, mischievous widower who charmed the ladies; a gentle, garrulous giant who liked the common people (and made sure they knew it); a good-humored and easygoing fellow with a taste for liquor, an expansive instinct for camaraderie, and no apparent hangups about race or class. For the first time in Alabama politics, here was a leader who talked about making life better for everybody. What's more, he went about his business as a public figure in a humorous and entertaining way, sometimes leading a hillbilly band and brandishing a suds bucket and a corn-shuck mop which he promised to use in Montgomery to scrub out the capitol and wash away "the political ring that is strangling Alabama."

For all his shortcomings as an organizer and a manager, Folsom had a message that resonated with the rank-and-file citizens of the state: better schools for the young, paved roads for the isolated, jobs and unions and the ballot for working people (white and black), and pensions for the elderly. There was "no such thing as too much democracy," Big Jim assured the people. The message was nothing short of alarming to the industrialists, planters, bankers, lawyers, publishers, and others who made up Alabama's privileged establishment. They nearly panicked when he led a field of five candidates in the first primary. Then, on June 4, they were stunned and shocked when James Elisha Folsom, populist prophet of a new Alabama, posted a sixty-thousand-vote victory in his final hurdle to the governor's office.

From his first day there in January 1947, he faced a wall of opposition—much of it from the reactionary right-wingers who hated his reformist ideas, some of it from honest critics who faulted his inexperience, and some, too, from liberal supporters who despaired of his fragmented and undisciplined attempts to turn laudable ideals into sound and effective programs. Folsom's performance never matched his promise, but the people were starved for democracy, and they never lost hope in him; when he was again eligible to run for the office in 1954, they gave him their votes once more.

Who, indeed, could understand Alabama, or know what to make of a character like Folsom? And who could ever explain how a state with two progressive senators and Big Jim in the governor's mansion could have its Democratic Party so vanquished by renegades in 1948 that the Harry Truman–Alben Barkley ticket would not even be allowed a spot on the ballot?

Not all the theatrics and controversy of postwar politics in the South took place in the cities and the statehouses; sometimes, tense scenes of high drama were played out in small towns, between the forces of entrenched power and groups of reformers who dared to challenge their tight control of public affairs. Athens, Tennessee, was one such stage. The McMinn County seat, a hilly town of about seven thousand people midway between Knoxville and Chattanooga, echoed with explosions and gunfire in the early evening of August 1, 1946, as a band of ex-GIs declared war on a corrupt courthouse gang that ran the county.

The racial clash in Columbia, Tennessee, was still a fresh memory—in fact, the trials of people arrested in that incident were just then coming to court—when the remarkable chain of events surrounding a heated election campaign boiled to the surface in Athens and attracted nationwide attention. Though the affair was not at all typical of Southern confrontations in that volatile season of postwar adjustment, the intensity of it did emphatically underscore the pervasive yearning of common folks for democratic reforms—and the inclination of veterans in particular to act impulsively, decisively, even violently, on their instincts and convictions.

McMinn was one of the predominantly white east Tennessee counties that opposed secession in 1860 and voted Republican for seventy-five years after that. Finally, in 1936, Democrat Paul Cantrell was elected sheriff, and over the next ten years, he and a handful of men displaced the Republican "royal families" that had built a political oligarchy there over the years. For all their surface differences, the two factions were remarkably similar in their use of machine power to sustain corruption and subvert the democratic process. By 1946, Cantrell, having moved up to county judge and then to a state senate seat, was the unchallenged boss of a courthouse gang that ruled by fraud and force; the Republicans offered little more than token resistance, and the majority of citizens had no voice or standing in either party.

As more and more veterans came home from the war, they met with increasing harassment from local law-enforcement officers, particularly a strong-arm cadre of about fifteen deputy sheriffs who had a "fee system" incentive for making arrests. The deputies, reinforced on election day by special officers imported from surrounding counties, kept a tight rein on voting and then took the boxes of paper ballots to the jail, where no prying eyes could watch the machine count them and announce its reanointment.

In the spring of 1946, a small number of Athens veterans led by James Buttram and Ralph Duggan met quietly to form the GI Non-Partisan League. In May they drew four hundred ex-servicemen, including a few blacks, to a mass meeting at which a slate of five candidates was chosen to run in the August county election. Two of the five were Democrats and the other three Republicans, among them the challenger for sheriff, thirty-year-old Knox Henry, an ex-sergeant in the air force. The local Republican Party, having no other candidates, endorsed this slate. After a tense and torrid summer campaign, the Cantrell machine and the aggregation of GI rebels came to the showdown on Thursday, August 1.

Close to two hundred deputized lawmen patrolled the precincts, and soon they clashed with poll-watchers deployed by the veterans. By early afternoon, reports of assaults and arrests were circulating. At one polling place, two veterans being held at gunpoint jumped through a plate-glass window and escaped; at another, several deputies were disarmed and beaten by GIs who took them far out into the country, relieved them of most of their clothes, and left them stranded. An hour or so before the polls closed, an elderly black man, Tom Gillespie, was assaulted by deputies after casting his vote, and when he tried to run away from them, one of the officers shot him in the back. At least three veterans were in custody when the balloting ended at 4:00 p.m. Promptly at closing time, the ballot boxes were picked up and rushed to the jail.

Hours before that, though, some of the GIs had gone home to put on their battle fatigues and pick up weapons; others managed to get arms and ammunition from the nearby National Guard armory. Buttram and Duggan, the GI organizers, talked on the phone to Governor Jim Nance McCord in Nashville—himself a "Boss" Crump machine candidate for reelection that same day—but the governor, who had rushed troopers and guardsmen to Columbia the previous February, declined this time to intervene.

The events of the afternoon were a call to combat. For three hours after the polls closed, the men milling restlessly around the GI Non-Partisan League headquarters seemed to be waiting only for someone to lead them. At about seven o'clock, twenty-one-year-old Bill White, wearing a navy uniform, got up and told the others he had "faced a thousand bullets for democracy" and he was ready to face some more "to get those ballot boxes back." When he started toward the jail, two blocks down the street, the men fell in behind him with pistols, rifles and bayonets, submachine guns, hand grenades, tear gas, dynamite, and one .50-caliber machine gun.

Nobody knew exactly how many veterans and other combatants were in the streets of Athens that night, but the most-repeated estimate was two thousand, with another thousand or so spectators gathered out of range to watch the battle. The disciplined ex-servicemen deployed a company of about sixty men to the front line. They surrounded the jail. Shouted demands for the ballot boxes were answered from inside by shouted refusals. The commandos waited for darkness, some of them remembering, with a mixture of anxiety and exhilaration, how they had felt before the invasion of Normandy or the Philippines. At ten after nine, they opened fire.

Fifty-five deputies were barricaded in the jail with three GI hostages. The sheriff and the rest of the deputies had escaped and fled, along with Paul Cantrell and his courthouse followers. The shooting continued until well past midnight. Finally, an ex-army demolition expert planted four dynamite sticks on the front porch and blew away the door to the jail. Within minutes the besieged deputies came out with their hands on their heads. Twenty of them were wounded badly enough to need hospitalization, but no one was dead. The veterans suffered no casualties.

To the cheers of the spectators, the victorious servicemen marched their prisoners around the town square and then took them back into the jail and locked them up. C. M. Wise, the deputy who had shot Tom Gillespie in the back, was handled roughly by his captors, as were some of the others. A lynch-mob mood was in the air, but Ralph Duggan, in a stirring speech to the troops, reminded them that their mission was to recover the ballot boxes, and they had accomplished that. The boxes were promptly broken open, and enough of a count was made to ascertain that the reform slate had won an overwhelming victory. The winners were declared on the spot. Then, three respected local citizens were named to a committee to run the county government until the new officials could be sworn in.

Out in the streets, meanwhile, a jubilant mob using axes and firebombs destroyed fourteen automobiles belonging to the deputies. The rampage was halted when, at three in the morning, the GIs announced that the jailed deputies would be released and guaranteed safe conduct to their homes. Only C. M. Wise was kept in custody. (Later, Wise would be the lone combatant in the Athens hostilities against whom criminal charges would be brought. He pleaded guilty and was given a one-to-three-year sentence in the state penitentiary. Gillespie recovered from his wound.)

When daybreak came, Athenians, in a mood of relief and optimism, started cleaning up their battered buildings and streets. The Reverend Bernie Hampton, chairman of the three-member interim government committee, spoke for many others when he said, "I am prouder of my community today than I have been at any time since I came here." George Goodwin, a reporter for the Atlanta *Journal*, captured the same spirit. "What happened here," he wrote from Athens two days after the battle, "was more than mob violence. It was a revolution—a revolution in which the better element of this community threw off a ten-year-old yoke of armed intimidation and corruption." (Two years later, Goodwin would receive a Pulitzer Prize for his reporting on the postwar South.)

It would be immensely satisfying to report that the revolution in Athens, Tennessee, in August 1946, sent the torch of democracy out to every community in the South, there to burn forever with a clear blue flame— but nothing as dramatic as that ever came to pass. Some dividends did accrue to Athens and McMinn County: There was a greater level of citizen participation in government, elections were obviously cleaner, the sheriff's office was reformed, and the courthouse was purged of machine-style politics. But the GI Non-Partisan League didn't become a permanent new organization of grassroots democracy in action. Within a year or so, the Democrats and Republicans had politics all to themselves again, and eventually the Republicans regained their pre-1936 dominance.

Even as the Athens insurrection was reaching its climax, Governor Jim McCord and Senator Kenneth D. McKellar were riding the Crumpmobile to another predictable Tennessee reelection victory party. Broad-based democratic participation as direct and dramatic as McMinn County citizens enjoyed that summer was utterly foreign to the experience of voters in Nashville and Memphis. Still, city sophisticates there found the Athens incident humorous; many of them dismissed it as a hillbilly coup, a zany drama much like the overthrow of some remote South American dictatorship.

They missed the point. There was an imperishable message buried in that east Tennessee uprising, and though it would lay smoldering for almost two decades, it would not be extinguished. The essence of it was simple and straightforward: The ballot is the birthright of every citizen, and no force, however powerful, can forever separate any person who has not forfeited that right from the full and free exercise of it.

The emergence of a few reform-minded governors and mayors, the court-ordered opening of primary elections to black voters, and the return of veterans to challenge the status quo in local and state politics were all signs of the postwar awakening, the stirring to consciousness, that was being seen and heard and felt across the South. The Athens episode notwithstanding, this was not a revolution, not by any realistic yardstick of regional change. It was nothing more than a turning, a modest realignment—and even that was susceptible to reactionary opposition. Still, the signs of movement were there to raise hopes—or fears—that the old patterns of power and control would never again be the same.

"This time the Negro is in Southern politics for keeps," wrote University of Florida political scientist William G. Carleton in the St. Louis *Post-Dispatch* in the spring of 1946. Court decisions and simple arithmetic were his assurance of that. There would be no sudden, sweeping transformation to democracy, he said; "the Bilbo type" would not disappear all at once, "but their number will be whittled down little by little." Southern liberals "will not, like Hugo Black, need to be elevated to the Supreme Court in order to speak their real views on race prejudices."

Part of Carleton's optimism was traceable to voter registration numbers. In 1860, no blacks had voted in the South. Eight years later, after the Civil War, more than 700,000 cast ballots—a total that exceeded the vote of Southern whites. By 1900 the black vote was back to near zero again. In 1932, at the dawning of the Roosevelt era, only about 50,000 Southern blacks were registered—less than one percent of the voting-age population. Gradually over the next twelve years, the number rose to approximately 250,000—five percent of the potential. In 1946, as Carleton and others clearly saw, there was a sudden surge of new registrations, and two years later, an estimated fifteen percent of adult black Southerners—some 750,000 people—would be included on the voter registration rolls.

It was the warning siren set off by numbers like these that caused white supremacists in the Deep South to purge voter lists, raise court challenges, adopt new laws and constitutional amendments—do anything, in short, to prevent the large African-American minority from regaining the power of the franchise. The success of these tactics would be borne out by one overriding fact: In spite of the increases in minority voter registration, fewer than half a million black Southerners—not even one of every ten of voting age—actually managed to cast ballots in the crucial 1948 elections.

It was no coincidence, either, that in the same year you could count the number of elected black officials in the region on the fingers of one hand.

No single issue, no reform, was more important to all sides than the ballot. To blacks and white liberals, the right to vote was the prerequisite to every other reform the South so desperately needed. To white conservatives everywhere, from the county courthouses to the halls of Congress, the specter of a full and free franchise for five million African-American adults in the Southern states was terrifying to contemplate.

4. *Old-Guard Politics*

The peculiar set of historical circumstances that created the Southern bloc in Congress in the late nineteenth and early twentieth centuries still worked to maintain that tight little circle throughout the Roosevelt-Truman era, and for a dozen years or more beyond that. Repeatedly in these pages, the pillars of that construction have stood out in sharp relief: the poll tax, the white primary, one-party politics, race-class ideology, the seniority system in Congress. An elaborate mythology sustained the motley assortment of ensconced Southerners in Washington, and provided their faithful followers with a stone tablet of sacrosanct beliefs: the Lost Cause, the common Yankee enemy, Jim Crow segregation, states' rights, the solid South, and the undefiled purity of the white female.

What appealed to the political mind of the Southern officeholder in that century-long winter of the soul was not democracy but its opposite: the concentration of power in as few hands as possible. The way to get power and keep it, so the wise men said, was to control the size of the electorate by excluding blacks, discouraging low-income whites, and maintaining the subordinate status of women—and then to rule with enough force and fear to stifle dissent. The incumbent Southern politicians talked a lot about state sovereignty, but what they practiced was the sovereignty of kings and lords and masters, the reign of a chosen few over the many.

All the veneer of solidarity and the rhetoric that propped it up could easily lead you to the belief that the Southerners in Congress were true lodge brothers, if not blood kin, and that they thought and acted as one on all the important issues of the day. Occasionally a stray sheep—a Claude Pepper, a Lister Hill—might get past the fence and mingle with the wolves on an issue like health care or federal aid to education, or on a confirmation vote for a liberal nominee like Aubrey Williams. But the emergence of civil rights as a public policy issue in the 1940s caused the

Southerners to tighten their grip on the strays. Thereafter, whenever a subject was directly and unavoidably racial and unanimity was deemed to be vital to a successful defense against it, even the most liberal of Southern senators found it almost impossible to break ranks. Not one of them endorsed the Supreme Court's 1944 *Smith* v. *Allwright* decision affirming the voting rights of African-Americans, or the recommendations of President Truman's special panel on civil rights in 1947, or the President's civil rights legislative package the following year.

Behind that façade of unanimity, however, the Southern senators were a jumble of contradictions: statesmen and party hacks, prudes and lechers, teetotalers and sots, courtly gentlemen and court jesters, cavaliers and rogues, the pious and the profligate. Striking differences in demeanor separated a fire-breathing racist demagogue like Mississippi's Theodore Bilbo from a tight-collared reactionary like Virginia's Carter Glass or Walter George of Georgia. Bombastic Texan Tom Connally, an internationalist, and his clownish colleague Pappy O'Daniel, an isolationist, had precious little in common but their arch-conservatism. Just as reactionary, and as dissimilar, were North Carolina's senators, Josiah Bailey and Robert R. Reynolds. Alabama's John H. Bankhead, Jr., was a diplomat and a scholar, a benevolent Saint Francis sowing seeds of peace and brotherhood, in comparison with a tempestuous rabble-rouser and buffoon like his Senate Agriculture Committee colleague Cotton Ed Smith of South Carolina. Next to all of these, Florida's Pepper and Alabama's Hill could not help but seem like a couple of left-wing radicals on every subject except race, and even on that they were considered soft—and suspect.

You might wonder why the Dixie senators remained Democrats when the big-city bosses and labor chieftains and Northern blacks were gaining a foothold in the party during Roosevelt's last years. The answer is simple: Seniority and one-party rule back home assured them of a permanent power base in Congress, and they were loathe to give that up. The Democrats sank to a twenty-year low in the midterm elections of 1946, losing fifty-five House seats and twelve in the Senate. But while relinquishing control of both houses for the first time since the Herbert Hoover years, the party saw its Dixie members grow in relative strength, retaining virtually all their seats while the Northerners and Midwesterners were being routed. When the Democrats rode Harry Truman's coattails to a surprise victory in 1948, the Southerners—most of whom hated Truman for his civil rights initiatives—would find themselves back in the catbird seat.

The more things changed, the more they stayed the same. Between 1944 and 1947, five Southern senators with 108 years of collective tenure—Glass, Bailey, Bankhead, Bilbo, and Smith—were removed from the Club by death or defeat. But five others with exactly the same number of cumulative years in office—Connally, George, Richard Russell of Georgia, Kenneth McKellar of Tennessee, and Harry F. Byrd of Virginia—would still be there into the fifties or beyond, piling up more than forty additional years of service while maintaining their rigid opposition to social change.

What's more, the old right-wingers who departed as the postwar period was beginning didn't exactly open the gates to a horde of liberals (the few exceptions notwithstanding). Among the new reactionaries of the forties who would last about as long, on the average, as their spiritual forebears were James O. Eastland and John C. Stennis of Mississippi, Olin D. Johnston of South Carolina, Spessard Holland of Florida, and John L. McClellan of Arkansas. (Joining them early in the fifties would be more soulmates, including Herman Talmadge of Georgia and Strom Thurmond of South Carolina.) On balance, the Senate in, say, 1955 would be less progressive and more reactionary than it had been in 1937.

The departure of Pepper and short-termer Frank P. Graham in 1950 would mark a low ebb for liberals in the Senate, even though a few men had risen to join them with something more than a racist screed as their calling card. Alabama voters chose John Sparkman to succeed the respected John Bankhead, and he complemented Lister Hill rather well. Lyndon Johnson, an opportunistic Texas New Dealer, moved up from the House in the wake of Pappy O'Daniel's merciful departure. Estes Kefauver of Tennessee advanced from the House with Johnson in 1948, and four years later, Kefauver's fellow Tennessean and former House colleague Albert Gore finally and thankfully sent Kenneth McKellar home from the Senate.

The performance of Congress in this period of gradual transition from depression and war to domestic renewal was not etched in glory, particularly with respect to the South and its social and economic needs. Fair employment guarantees, anti-lynching legislation, the demise of the poll tax, and new programs in education, housing, health care, and veterans' affairs were all introduced and debated, but the Southern oligarchs saw to it that no transforming changes were embraced by the South, especially if they benefited the black minority. In the House, John Rankin of Mississippi celebrated twenty-five years on the job with a pledge to hold fast against any hint of creeping equality for those unfortunate enough to stand outside the protective tent of white Anglo-Saxon Protestantism. And in the Senate, if there was any one person who symbolized the rigid and enduring intransigence of white racism, it was Rankin's sulfuric brother in bigotry, Theodore G. Bilbo.

No word or deed from "The Man" was outrageous enough to weaken his hold on the voters of Mississippi, and no scandal could dislodge him from his perch. Short, jug-eared, potbellied—a "runt" by his own description—

Bilbo dressed like a country undertaker, swore like a drunken sailor, ranted and raved like a sidewalk preacher. His rural audiences, sick and tired of being a national laughingstock (an image derived in large measure, paradoxically, from the senator's antics), lapped it up as he viciously picked his enemies apart in a hoarse, raspy voice dripping with Southern syrup and smoking with Bilbonic acid. He was an orator, a comedian, a skillful entertainer—all talents highly prized throughout the rural South—and thousands of people, including some blacks, turned out to watch the spectacle, if only to find out what bellicose extremes he would resort to next.

Since 1934 he had honed his act as a lonely martyr who stood toe-to-toe with Yankee politicians, the urban press, and even Delta planters without giving an inch. No one mistook the depths of his bigotry, but that was only half of what accounted for his seemingly invincible strength. The other half was his crafty and calculated identification with the struggling white farmers of Mississippi's hill country and piney woods against the aristocratic planters of the Delta. The two factions had no serious quarrel about race; blacks made up over half of the state's population, and neither the "peckerwoods" nor the planters showed any inclination to free them from the bonds of white supremacy. But, as V. O. Key, Jr., observed in *Southern Politics,* Bilbo "went down the line for the New Deal," while its social programs were anathema to the landed gentry who ruled the Delta (a vast territory, wrote Key, where "no great middle class . . . dulls the abruptness of the line between lord and serf"). Playing his anti-black, anti-planter tune to perfection, Bilbo masqueraded as a progressive. To William Alexander Percy, fuming in helpless frustration on his Delta plantation, the senator was "a little monster, glib and shameless, with that sort of cunning common to criminals which passes for intelligence."

Not until Roosevelt was on his deathbed and the Democratic Party was veering to the right did Bilbo abandon all pretense of populist progressivism and vent his spleen on a reactionary crusade to preserve white supremacy. On a national radio broadcast in 1946, he said he was still a Klansman ("once a Kluxer, always a Kluxer"), and he threatened repeatedly during his reelection campaign that summer to punish "any nigger" who tried to vote. By his count, only about two thousand of the more than one million blacks in Mississippi were registered, but even that tiny number galled him.

His bigotry bedeviled more than just Mississippi; as chairman of the Senate committee on the District of Columbia, Bilbo was the ex officio mayor of Washington, and he did everything he could to keep the city segregated. His own long-term solution to America's race problem was embodied in a bill he introduced in the Senate: the "Greater Liberia Act." It called for the purchase of colonial lands in Africa and the mass deportation of millions of African-Americans to those lands.

As he and four opponents (none of whom challenged his racial views) roamed the dusty back roads of Mississippi seeking white votes in 1946, Bilbo concentrated his fiercest attacks on white Southerners who deviated in any degree from the segregationist party line. Georgia Governor Ellis Arnall was "the South's public enemy No. 1." Lillian Smith and her novel about an interracial love affair "sickened and disgusted" him. President Truman, "a Southerner by ancestry," was "a traitor to his heritage." And as for Hodding Carter, the Greenville editor who had long been his adversary, Bilbo wrote him off as nothing but "a miserable little Quisling . . . as bitter an enemy to our customs, ideals and way of life as any Russian." (That must have come as quite a shock to Carter's readers and his peers in the press; he was awarded the Pulitzer Prize that year for his editorials against racial intolerance.)

"I could have taken the easier road, but I'd have been a traitor to the South, to my people, to my white blood," said Bilbo, clad in his well-tailored martyr's cape. He breezed to victory in the first primary, carrying all but six counties and polling more votes than all his opponents combined. Before the general election, an intrepid handful of Mississippi's eighty thousand black ex-GIs who had been systematically denied the right to vote sought in federal court to have the primary results invalidated, but the challenge was shunted aside. In Washington, members of both parties who were fed up with Bilbo said they would investigate charges that he had helped war contractors win bids and then had taken kickbacks from them. He was denounced publicly as "a disgrace to the Senate," and in an unprecedented move, his colleagues refused to administer the oath of office to him in January 1947, pending the outcome of the investigation. (They did, however, approve continued payment of salaries to him and his staff.)

Discouraged, tired, and too sick to serve (he was suffering from cancer), the sixty-nine-year-old firebrand packed his bags and headed south to Mississippi, vowing to return and demand his seat as soon as he was well. From "Dream House," his mansion on the Pearl River near Poplarville, he wrote and self-published a book that year that summarized his views on race, the fundamental obsession of his life. *Take Your Choice: Separation or Mongrelization* was "an S.O.S. call to every white man and white woman in the United States of America for immediate action" to save their race. Bilbo, with the most serious intent, concluded that annihilation would be preferable to "intermingling"; better to see civilization "blotted out with the atomic bomb," he wrote, "than to see it slowly but surely destroyed in the maelstrom of miscegenation, interbreeding, intermarriage, and mongrelization."

As he lay dying from cancer of the mouth and throat in August 1947, Bilbo sent word for Leon Lewis, a black journalist with the Associated Negro Press, to call on him in his New Orleans hospital room. Their conversation, as reported by Lewis, was a model of Southern manners and civility—and evasion. "I don't hate your people, nor do I deliberately fight their progress," Bilbo told his visitor. "In fact, I feel I've done more for their progress in Mississippi than any other individual." While acknowledging that he was "honestly against the social intermingling of Negroes and whites," Bilbo expressed a belief that interracial unity and progress were possible in the South—where, he said, "there is room for all of us." Was this a deathbed confession, a bid for absolution? If so, it was totally out of character—and as weak as it was tardy.

Congressman John Rankin was one of six ardent segregationists who ran in a special election that fall to fill Bilbo's seat, but he finished far back in the pack with only twelve percent of the vote. The winner was a rather quiet and colorless country judge named John C. Stennis. Even Mississippi, it seemed, needed a respite from the racial wars.

I t was abundantly clear by the summer of 1947, two years after World War II ended, that the South would never be led on a progressive march into the modern era by its politicians. From Capitol Hill to the far-flung county seats and town councils, Southern lawmakers seemed more inclined to march back to the days of feudalism. Of all the region's senators, congressmen, governors, legislators, mayors, and councilmen, only a tiny handful had shown themselves ready and eager to step out front with reformist ideas and initiatives. Plans that might benefit minorities or women or the have-nots were especially controversial, and thus avoided.

More often than not, law schools, bar associations, and the legal profession itself—from whence most lawmakers came—seemed to line up on the side of resistance. The American Bar Association, historically and traditionally a lily-white group, resisted integration long after its national governing board finally relented in the late forties and let a token few black attorneys become members. There were exceptions to such rigidity, of course. Black attorneys working through the NAACP were consistently in the forefront of social reform, pressing to make the revolutionary tenets of the Constitution and the Bill of Rights instruments of that renewal. From New York and Washington, the bar association's leading attorneys, Thurgood Marshall and Charles Houston, directed a twenty-year attack on segregation prior to the Supreme Court's *Brown* decision in 1954. Only a persistent few resident black lawyers had managed to take up practice in the South, but from their thin ranks came several who acted with skill and courage to give the NAACP team the vital help it needed in rooting out Jim Crow discrimination. Equally as courageous and as helpful to the cause were the few white attorneys, scattered here and there, whose understanding of the law compelled them to cut against the grain of white opinion in those lonely years before *Brown*.

But the overwhelming majority of lawyers had no enthusiasm for the philosophy of social action rooted in law—in fact, it seems that most of them were resistant, even hostile, to such a notion. If the South was going to free itself from the dead hand of conservative tradition, it would have to find its standard-bearers elsewhere—in the White House, perhaps, or in the federal courts, or among the intellectuals in the university and the church, or in the black minority, or among left-wing activists. Help had been sought from these sources before, with results that were far short of spectacular, but signs of ferment could be found in many places, and so there was a sense of hope and anticipation, even in the face of discouragement.

The reactionary character of the lawmakers and much of the legal fraternity stood in negative contrast to one small but lofty segment of the profession—namely, federal judges. Not that all of them were liberals by any means, but think of this: From the mid-1930s on, the impetus for dismantling Jim Crow laws and expanding legal and constitutional protections against discrimination in the South came repeatedly from the studied opinions of jurists on the federal bench; even more remarkably, most of them were conservative white men of comfortable means and mature years, men born and raised and educated in the region—Democrats in the main, but some Republicans as well—and all of them, every one, having risen to the bench from service in the mainstream of political and social orthodoxy that many whites reverently worshiped as "the Southern way of life."

A historical antecedent of this phenomenon was the career of Supreme Court Justice John Marshall Harlan. Born into a Kentucky pioneer family in 1833 and named for the most notable chief justice of the Supreme Court, he was appointed to that tribunal by Republican President Rutherford B. Hayes in 1877, and for thirty-five years his was an eloquent voice of conscience against the erosion of civil liberties. It was Harlan's heroic, lonely dissent in *Plessy* v. *Ferguson,* the 1896 case that established "separate but equal" segregation as the law of the land, that would still be seen a century later as a beacon illuminating the most fundamental of constitutional principles. "The common government of all shall not permit the seeds of race hate to be planted under the sanction of law," he wrote. "Our Constitution is color-blind, and neither knows nor tolerates classes among

Atlanta Constitution *editor Ralph McGill (left) visiting with Carl Sandburg on the poet's porch at Connemara, near Flat Rock, North Carolina*

Paul Christopher and Lucy Randolph Mason, two of the South's most effective figures in the labor movement, worked closely with such homegrown progressive enterprises as Highlander Folk School near Monteagle, Tennessee.

Mass arrests of black residents by Tennessee national guardsmen and state highway patrol officers followed the February 1946 outbreak of racial violence in Columbia.

After a day and night of election-related violence in the McMinn County seat of Athens, Tennessee, in August 1946, ex-GIs bent on ousting the corrupt local government captured the jail, locked up some of the county's public officials there, and overturned their cars in the street.

About twenty men deputized by the McMinn County sheriff ended up in jail after they failed in their attempt to prevent local citizens from observing the vote count. The deputies barricaded themselves in the jail with the ballot boxes, but surrendered after a six-hour gun battle with reform-minded ex-GIs.

Using his full name, interim governor Herman Eugene Talmadge signed a Georgia white-primary bill into law on February 20, 1947, hoping thereby to circumvent federal court decisions affirming the right of blacks to vote. Among the watching legislators were Senator Iris F. Blitch (seated), later elected to Congress, and House Speaker Roy V. Harris (hand on document).

Combat veteran Isaac Woodard was permanently blinded when he was viciously beaten by South Carolina policemen shortly after his military discharge in 1946.

Walter White of the NAACP examining a cut on the head of Albert Harris after the young Louisiana mob victim and his father (left) arrived in New York in August 1946. Harris was beaten and left for dead near Minden, Louisiana; ex-GI John C. Jones, who was with him, was killed with a blowtorch and a meat cleaver by the lynch mob.

Stetson Kennedy, author of Southern Exposure *and an undercover agent in the Ku Klux Klan, posed in Klan regalia for this late 1946 photo promoting his book.*

Former Georgia Governor Ellis Arnall (left), in New York in early 1947 for the publication of his book, The Shore Dimly Seen, *met Stetson Kennedy face to face for the first time. Kennedy had worked as a state undercover agent in the Klan during Arnall's administration.*

When Paul Robeson came to Columbia, South Carolina, in October 1946 to take part in the Southern Negro Youth Congress, local black leaders were as much in awe of his outspoken racial and political criticism as of his legendary singing and acting skills.

Bandleader and composer Duke Ellington, in Louisville for a public performance, greeted shop owner Horace Roth (left) and an appreciative crowd at Variety Record Shop, February 5, 1948.

About a hundred Southerners, black and white, made a pilgrimage to Charleston on November 26, 1950, to honor Judge J. Waties Waring and his wife Elizabeth for their contributions to the cause of racial equality. In the courtyard outside the Warings' Meeting Street home, the group gathered for this picture. Kneeling in front of the judge is his court bailiff, John Fleming.

These men, all admitted members of a mob that lynched a black man charged in the murder of a Greenville, South Carolina, cab driver in 1946, were tried and acquitted by an all-white, all-male jury.

Before his campaign for the presidency, Henry Wallace (second from left) sought support from Southern liberals. On a visit to Austin, Texas, in 1947, he was photographed with Clark Foreman (left), humorist John Henry Faulk, and James Dombrowski of the Southern Conference Educational Fund (right).

"Lend a Hand for Dixieland," a Southern Conference for Human Welfare fund-raising drive, was kicked off in New York in September 1946 with actor Orson Welles and boxer Joe Louis as honorary co-chairmen. Louis (right) was the star attraction at a dinner attended by (from left) SCHW leader Clark Foreman, entertainers Frank Sinatra and Carole Landis, and others.

Several board members of the Southern Conference for Human Welfare were photographed at a January 1946 meeting in Durham, North Carolina. Seated are James Dombrowski and Clark Foreman (holding newspaper); standing (from left) are Lucy Randolph Mason, Virginia Foster Durr, George S. Mitchell, Charlotte Hawkins Brown, Alva W. Taylor, and Tarleton Collier.

Southern Conference for Human Welfare and Southern Conference Educational Fund representatives convened this assembly of regional progressives at Thomas Jefferson's Monticello estate in Virginia on November 20, 1948. SCEF president Aubrey Williams is center-right in photo, wearing hat. The group signed a Declaration of Civil Rights rejecting all forms of racial segregation.

Senator J. William Fulbright, Democrat of Arkansas, was serving his first term when the Republicans won a majority in both houses of Congress in 1946.

A tired but happy Lyndon B. Johnson, having won a seat in the U.S. Senate with an eighty-four-vote victory over Coke Stevenson in the Texas primary, posed with his friend Tom Clark, the U.S. Attorney General, outside President Truman's campaign train in San Antonio on September 27, 1948.

Senator Estes Kefauver, Democrat of Tennessee, wearing the coonskin cap that became his victory symbol in the 1948 election

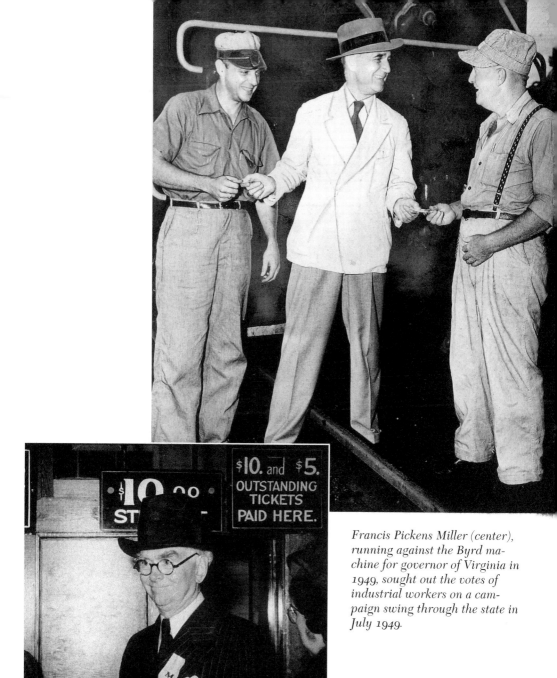

Francis Pickens Miller (center), running against the Byrd machine for governor of Virginia in 1949, sought out the votes of industrial workers on a campaign swing through the state in July 1949.

Longtime Memphis political boss E. H. Crump was a frequent visitor and bettor at the racetrack in Hot Springs, Arkansas, throughout his political life.

President Truman's Committee on Civil Rights, appointed in 1946, stood for a White House picture when it issued its report, "To Secure these Rights," in late 1947. Only two Southerners were on the fifteen-member commission—Dorothy Rogers Tilly of Atlanta and Frank Porter Graham of the University of North Carolina. They are standing side by side on Truman's left in the picture.

On a stop in North Carolina during the 1948 campaign, President Truman and his vice-presidential running mate, Senator Alben Barkley of Kentucky, smiled for the cameras and a friendly crowd. With them were the President's daughter, Margaret Truman, and his former press secretary, Jonathan Daniels (left), editor of the Raleigh News & Observer.

More than ten thousand delegates to the national convention of the NAACP heard an address by President Truman from the steps of the Lincoln Memorial in June 1947. No previous president had ever spoken to the group.

Before Claude Pepper (seated, right) lost his U.S. Senate seat to Congressman George Smathers (back row, center) in 1950, the two Florida Democrats and others were congenial guests of President Truman (seated, center) at his "little White House" in Key West. This November 1948 occasion was a celebration of Truman's upset victory over his Republican, Dixiecrat, and Progressive challengers.

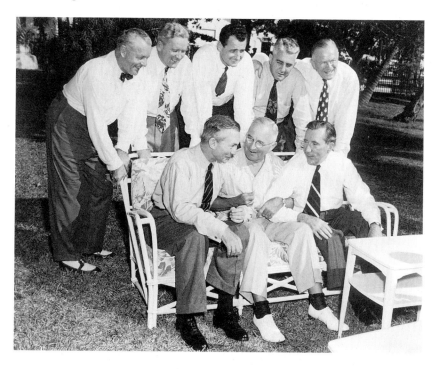

Black voters stood in line for hours to cast ballots in the August 1948 Democratic primary in South Carolina—the first statewide election to follow Judge J. Waties Waring's ruling against the white primary. About thirty thousand blacks voted.

On a tumultuous campaign swing through the South in the late summer of 1948, Progressive Party candidate Henry Wallace was often heckled and threatened. In Memphis on September 3, he was assigned a plainclothes police bodyguard (wearing hat). Also with Wallace was his campaign manager, Clark Foreman (far left).

Senator Theodore G. Bilbo went home to Mississippi in January 1947 after his colleagues refused to seat him pending an investigation of alleged irregularities in his reelection campaign. The sixty-nine-year-old senator died of cancer a few months later.

A floor demonstration at the States' Rights Party (Dixiecrat) Convention in Birmingham, July 17, 1948

Governors Strom Thurmond of South Carolina (center) and Fielding Wright of Mississippi (and Thurmond's wife Jean) were at the beginning of their quixotic Dixiecrat campaign for the White House when this photo was made at the Jackson airport in the summer of 1948.

North Carolina Governor Kerr Scott (left) announced the appointment of Frank Porter Graham to the U.S. Senate at the climax of a campus luncheon honoring the University of North Carolina president in March 1949.

Senator Frank Graham, running in the spring of 1950 for election to a full term, tried to get his message directly to the people—as in this campaign speech from the back of a pickup truck in Wake County, June 17, 1950.

citizens. . . . The law regards man as man, and takes no account of his surroundings or of his color when his civil rights as guaranteed by the supreme law of the land are involved."

After the mid-1930s, with Harlan's words as a background echo, the Supreme Court came more and more to the aid of individual citizens who had been denied their civil rights. Appointees of Franklin Roosevelt would make up a majority of the nine justices by the end of the thirties. Over the next three decades, the judicial branch of the federal government, through its careful interpretation of the laws of the land, gradually moved the nation's public policies and social practices into closer alignment with its constitutional principles. With Southerners Hugo Black of Alabama and Stanley Reed of Kentucky prominent among them, the justices took on some cases that dealt directly with the racial dilemma: exclusion of blacks from juries, segregation in colleges and universities, limitations on the right to vote. Later, when Harry Truman was in the White House and his appointees had joined the court (among them Tom C. Clark of Texas and Fred M. Vinson of Kentucky), decisions were handed down against restrictive covenants in housing, segregation on interstate buses and trains and in railway dining cars, and further efforts by the states to restrict voting rights.

But this was the U.S. Supreme Court speaking, a high and mighty tribunal in the most literal sense. Its members deliberated in monklike isolation, above the sound and fury; seldom were they exposed to the raw emotions of contending parties whose conflicts they were adjudicating. The sort of trench warfare that took place in the courts below was a lot messier and more abrasive, and the judges, ruling alone rather than collectively, were much more vulnerable to criticism. It was there, in the federal district courts of Shreveport and Austin, Nashville and Richmond, Tampa and Macon and Columbia, that the real drama of judicial give-and-take was played out. It was there, too, that a chosen few conservative white men sworn to uphold the Constitution of the United States were compelled by conscience and professionalism (and, to be sure, by a dislike of reversals on appeal) to extend the fruits of democracy to all citizens. Some were galled by the necessity, others liberated by it. All were prodded by that instigating band of roving lawyers who lived in the bracing faith that the Constitution was on their side: Thurgood Marshall and the NAACP.

Thomas Hoyt Davis, the judge who decided the Georgia white-primary case, was one of those home-guard jurists in the trenches. Born and raised in a small town near Atlanta, he had gone to college at Mercer, a venerable Baptist institution in Macon, and then had "read for the law" (an acceptable route into the profession in his day) in the office of Walter F. George of Vienna, fifty miles south of Macon. Davis settled there, eventually becoming a partner in the firm and filling coveted legal posts in the state and federal governments after George became a U.S. senator in 1922. Throughout the New Deal years, Davis was U.S. Attorney for the middle district of Georgia, headquartered in Macon. One of President Roosevelt's last acts in the spring of 1945 was to name him to the bench in that district.

Hardly had Judge Davis donned his black robe when the Reverend Primus E. King of Columbus, supported by the NAACP, sued local election officials for depriving him of the right to vote in the 1944 Democratic primary—the only meaningful election in a state like Georgia, there being no effective opposition party. King sought damages of $5,000 and a judgment against the practice of exclusion. The case was scheduled for hearing in the federal courthouse in Macon in September 1945.

Both sides showed an acute understanding of the significance of this legal skirmish. A pressing home-front issue was being raised just as the world war ended. The black petitioners, armed with the entitling language of *Smith* v. *Allwright*, were determined to win the ballot; the white defenders, alarmed by this threat to their continued political control, were desperate to keep the large black minority subordinate. Judge Davis, at fifty-three a lifetime member of the ruling class, was being called upon to listen and interpret and finally to resolve the conflict with the wisdom of Solomon.

For three sweltering days, his courtroom was jammed with a racially mixed—and segregated—audience of interested Georgians from around the state. A young white attorney from Macon, Harry S. Strozier, gave the main argument on behalf of Reverend King and the NAACP, contending that the right of any citizen to vote in a primary, no less than a general election, was "a right secured by the Constitution." Defense attorneys claimed that it was not the state but the Democratic Party, as a private organization, that had control of the process.

"What alternative do the Negroes have?" Judge Davis asked, and he pressed the point until (said one newspaper account) "counsel for the defense was forced to admit that under the present interpretation of the state primary, Negroes have no other alternative than to organize a party of their own or join some white group who may wish to fuse with them."

A month later, T. Hoyt Davis delivered a twenty-nine-page decision in favor of Primus King, awarding him only a token $100 in damages but citing *Smith* v. *Allwright* to declare that the denial of his right to vote in any state-sanctioned election on account of his race was a violation of the Constitution. It was a signal victory for black citizens in the South, and for all Southerners—one small foothold at the start of a long and difficult climb to political equality. It isn't clear from the record how costly the decision was to Judge Davis personally, but his friends and associates (including his mentor, Senator George) could hardly have seen it as other than a breach of trust at best, and at worst an act of treason. Unfortunately for the judge, he would not be remembered by scholars for this quiet act of valor, but for a later and less worthy decision declaring a 1957 federal voting rights act unconstitutional.

Still, the price of courage was not nearly so great for the Georgia jurist as it was for another federal judge, J. Waties Waring of Charleston. Raised in refined if somewhat threadbare gentility among the bluebloods of South Carolina's queen city, Waring had all the right credentials for a patrician son of the Old South. His Episcopalian lineage reached back to seventeenth-century Charleston. His paternal forebears were slaveowners, aristocrats, Confederates, noblesse-oblige paternalists. Julius Waties Waring, proudly bearing a venerable family name, went through private school and the College of Charleston, read the law and then practiced it in a prestigious firm on Broad Street, joined all the right clubs and fraternities and exclusive societies, married and worshiped and voted as was expected of him—and did it all within the splendid isolation of the warm cocoon that enveloped historic old Charleston. Everything he wanted was there, and most of it within walking distance of his comfortable home on Meeting Street. He was sixty-one years old when South Carolina's senators, Cotton Ed Smith and Burnet Maybank, both of whom he had supported and served, gave their blessing to his selection as a federal district judge. The courtroom he presided over, beginning in January 1942, was a five-minute walk from his front door.

For three years, Judge Waring gave his conservative neighbors little cause for concern. He did support black teachers in a couple of equal-pay cases, the first in 1944, but in the main he stayed safely within the tradition of his surroundings, building a solid reputation as a careful and efficient jurist. Then two of his actions shocked and outraged Charleston society. The first was his divorce and remarriage in June 1945; the second was his ringing declaration in July 1947 that South Carolina's frantic efforts to bar blacks from the Democratic primary were unconstitutional.

Waties Waring was feeling trapped in a lifeless marriage in the early forties when he met and fell in love with a Northern society matron who wintered in Charleston with her husband. After a time, the judge told his wife he wanted a divorce, and she sorrowfully but dutifully went to Florida and severed the marriage. (So unheard-of was divorce in South Carolina at the time that the state didn't even have laws on the subject.) His lover did likewise, and so, in a period of less than two weeks, Charleston was consumed with gossip about the judge who had ditched his old wife of thirty-two years and taken a new one, a twice-divorced Yankee fifteen years his junior.

Whether the Warings subsequently resigned from the Charleston social register or were expelled from it depended on whom you asked. Elizabeth Avery Waring, smart and attractive and supremely self-confident, gave no sign of wanting to be an inoffensive Southern lady; as the walls of rejection and isolation went up around her, she was abrasive and aggressive in the best Yankee tradition, and that confirmed the low opinion that others had formed about her. For his part, the judge was equally defensive and disdainful. He turned inward, working harder than ever at his job and spending all his free time with his new wife.

In 1946 he was on the bench in Columbia—and Elizabeth Waring was in the courtroom—when the white policeman who had blinded Isaac Woodard with a billy club was tried for violating the black ex-GI's civil rights. The acquittal of Linwood Shull and the cheers of the white spectators sent Mrs. Waring to her hotel room in tears and nudged her husband closer to a break with his racist heritage. Over the next year or so, he did a number of small things that revealed changes in his thinking. He desegregated the seating and the jury roster in his courtroom, made the use of courtesy titles standard procedure, and hired a black bailiff, John Fleming, to call sessions to order. Several of his rulings indicated his growing concern about segregation and white supremacy. At home, he and his wife began to read some books that took on a new importance for them—Gunnar Myrdal's *An American Dilemma* and *The Mind of the South* by W. J. Cash.

In June 1947, Waring presided at the trial of George Elmore, a black merchant who had sued election officials for denying him the right to vote in the 1946 Democratic primary; the Columbia businessman was represented by Thurgood Marshall. Barely two weeks after the Supreme Court struck down the white primary in Texas in 1944, South Carolina's Democratic hierarchy, called to arms by Governor Olin D. Johnston, had systematically stripped all references to primaries from the state's legal documents, in keeping with Johnston's vow to maintain white supremacy at all costs. (That was also the year that John H. McCray, Osceola McKaine, and other South Carolina blacks organized the Progressive Democratic Party, tried to seat a delegation at the Democratic National Convention in Chicago, and offered McKaine as a general-election opponent to Johnston in the fight for Cotton Ed Smith's vacant seat in the Senate.) The white Carolina Democrats succeeded in keeping blacks out of the primary in 1944 and again in 1946. It was this blatant lockout that Elmore and the NAACP challenged in the spring of 1947, and that Judge Waring focused his wrath upon when he ruled in the case.

On July 12, the judge cut the last slender cord that tied him to the ruling elders of Charleston and South Carolina. "Negroes are voting in Texas and even in Georgia," he wrote. "I cannot see where the skies will fall if South Carolina is put in the same class with these and other states." He called it "pure sophistry" to say the state Democratic Party was not operating under statutory control. Racial distinctions had no place in the election process, he declared, and added, "It is time for South Carolina to rejoin the Union. It is time to fall in step with the other states and to adopt the American way of conducting elections."

For good measure, Waring issued another ruling the same day in a higher-education discrimination case initiated by a black plaintiff. If the state didn't open a law school at its public college for Negroes, he said, it would either have to admit qualified black applicants to the University of South Carolina law school—or stop providing legal education to anyone.

White Charlestonians reeled from the double blow. The Charleston *News & Courier*, whose editorial page editor was the judge's nephew, Thomas R. Waring, Jr., heaped scorn on the decisions and the man who had written them. The judge and his Yankee wife were already pariahs in the clubs, the newspapers, the church, the neighborhood; now they were persona non grata in the state Democratic Party and the University of South Carolina as well. It mattered not at all that several South Carolina papers—the *Morning News* in Florence, the *Record* in Columbia, the *News* in Greenville—agreed with the voting decision and called on the Democratic Party to obey it. Nor would it matter that the ruling would be upheld on review by the appellate court in December and allowed to stand by the U.S. Supreme Court in the spring of 1948. All that really counted to the ruling elite of Charleston and South Carolina was that one of their own, a native son, had sold them down the river.

J. Waties Waring had come late to his epiphany, but once he saw the light of racial justice, he focused on it with all the energy and fervor of a new convert. There would be much in the months ahead to test his faith, for the worst—and the best—was yet to come.

Nothing takes place in a vacuum; every unfolding development has a context, and eventually, it all connects. Some things may simply happen willy-nilly, but what makes them meaningful or insignificant is the chain of circumstances to which they are linked in time and space. Like the Congress and the courts, the President of the United States was at least as much a passenger as he was an engineer on the train of postwar events. That fact shaped and colored what Harry S. Truman thought and said and did about the South in those years of turbulence and realignment.

He had not wanted to be President in the first place, and having the job didn't do much to change his mind. Harry Truman was as plain and old-fashioned and uncomplicated as a Missouri mule—and as set in his ways, to the point of being rigid at times. His critics saw him as a petty, hot-tempered little tyrant whose combative demeanor hid deep feelings of insecurity. Even those who liked him saw his flaws; one said he was a modest man with a lot to be modest about. He had the misfortune to be an ordinary fellow from the heart of middle America whose soft-shoe dance with hat and cane happened to follow the classic theatrical performance of a renowned Yankee patrician who exuded charm and charisma. Two decades later, Lyndon Johnson, with a similar tough act to follow, would sing the same lament.

Truman had no patience with fakery and pretense. His understanding of original sin freed him to be a Baptist who swore and drank whiskey—but never condoned cheating or lying or infidelity. He was as scornful of liberals with soft hands and clean fingernails as he was of reactionaries who wrapped themselves in the flag or a white sheet. Liberalism to him was no scholarly abstraction, no romantic indulgence; it was a practical philosophy of fairness for all, a populist notion that rewarded honest effort instead of bootlicking or buck-passing. His Fair Deal domestic agenda was more than just a me-too imitation of the Roosevelt master plan—it was the unadorned essence of what the new President truly wanted to deliver: a fair deal for everyone. The difficulty he encountered in doing that was less a reflection on him than on those who blocked his way.

In the first three years of his presidency, Truman made some historic and highly controversial decisions that sparked intense criticism from all sides. He ordered the atomic bomb dropped, not once but twice, taking the lives of almost a quarter of a million people; he steered the United States into full support of the new United Nations; he championed the Marshall Plan for European recovery and the American occupation of Japan; he supported the UN partitioning of Palestine into Jewish and Arab states; he articulated the Truman Doctrine of Soviet containment; he rapidly dismantled the mighty American war machine. On the home front, he outraged the left wing by requiring government workers to sign a loyalty oath renouncing any ties to communism—and infuriated the right wing by desegregating the armed forces and endorsing his civil rights committee's broad condemnation of racial segregation in American life. He may have agonized over these decisions before he made them, but he was not consumed by nagging doubts or recriminations or pangs of guilt about them afterward. That was his way, like the mule's: Keep plowing a straight furrow, and don't look back.

It was inevitable that someone so resolute, so blunt-spoken and hard-headed, would clash with many of the movers and shakers who vied for power in the public arena. The nation's postwar economy was reeling from a wage-price squeeze and soaring inflation, from shortages, strikes, and high unemployment. In his efforts to address these problems, the President fell into serious conflicts with labor leaders and corporate bosses, with members of Congress, and even with some of his own cabinet officers (including Secretary of Commerce Henry A. Wallace, whom he dismissed in September 1946). The right-wing press, from Henry Luce's *Time* magazine in New York to Colonel Robert McCormick's Chicago *Tribune* to the William Randolph Hearst empire on the West Coast (but not many Southern papers), regularly gave Truman unshirted hell; his enemies on the left, from the Americans for Democratic Action to the Communist Party, were hardly more charitable.

All this turmoil left the President feeling betrayed and abandoned by his friends no less than his enemies. He clearly didn't like his job, and plenty of people didn't like the way he was handling it; the ever-expanding public-opinion polls showed that his support had eroded to less than one-third of the electorate, and those results were emphatically confirmed when the Democrats suffered massive losses in the 1946 midterm elections. And with all he had on his plate, he still had to come to terms with his Southern colleagues in the administration, in Congress, in the courts, and in the states of the region. Their agendas and his had to be reconciled. The process would be wrenching, and the outcome would forever separate him from the diehard defenders of white supremacy.

The Southerners in Congress had gone into the postwar period with a sense of confident assurance that Truman would help them keep a tight rein on the region. They were counting on him as an ally, and no wonder: He was a borderline Southerner with a slaveholding heritage, and a descendant of Confederates with long memories; the word "nigger" rolled off his lips as easily as it did those of his Southern poker-playing cronies on Capitol Hill. But somehow, they failed to heed his commitment to fair play, and misread his expressions of moral outrage at the epidemic of racial violence that gripped the region in 1946. They thought he was just playing to the minority crowd, the nagging liberals, as politicians occasionally had to do. They thought wrong.

He did get off on the right foot with them, though, by calling James F. Byrnes back from South Carolina to be his Secretary of State. Byrnes's long and varied experience in the federal government made him a logical choice for the post, even though he had left the White House staff in Roosevelt's waning months embittered by the President's choice of Truman, and not him, as a running mate to replace the deposed Henry Wallace. The fact that there was no spillover of bad blood between Truman and Byrnes made it possible for the new President to reach out to the former presidential adviser. Byrnes, in league with his Southern friends, had long since shown his stripes as a narrow reactionary on domestic issues, but he was highly experienced in foreign affairs, having been at Roosevelt's side in all his dealings with the European allies, and Truman desperately needed such a practiced hand.

Jimmy Byrnes leaped at the chance to get back to the fount of power (first in line of succession to the presidency, actually, because there was then no vice president; the law was changed in 1947 to move leaders of the House and Senate ahead of cabinet officers in this hierarchy). Privately, Byrnes had little respect for Truman—or so the President's daughter, Margaret, would declare in a later book, in which she also noted Byrnes's "extravagantly high opinion of himself." The President was not unaware of his Secretary of State's feelings, or of his ego, but he was able to keep things in perspective. Byrnes was "able and conniving"—but Truman needed him.

Other appointments won favor with the Southern bloc, among them Fred M. Vinson of Kentucky to be Secretary of the Treasury and Tom C. Clark of Texas to be Attorney General; both men would later be elevated to the Supreme Court, Vinson as Chief Justice. At the same time, Truman upset the Southerners by naming William H. Hastie to be governor of the Virgin Islands, a U.S. territorial possession in the Caribbean. It was one more first for the black attorney who had held several administrative and judicial posts under FDR, and who would move up to the federal appellate court in 1949. Ralph Bunche was another black official whose public service Truman continued, at the State Department; from there he went on to the United Nations, where he would win the Nobel Peace Prize in 1950 for his mediation of the Arab-Jewish conflict in Palestine.

No one Truman appointed was more fiercely attacked, however, than David Lilienthal, a liberal Midwesterner who had been a director of the Tennessee Valley Authority since 1933. The President wanted him to head the new Atomic Energy Commission, and thereby to control the secrets of the atom bomb. Tennessee Senator Kenneth McKellar, calling the TVA "a hotbed of communism" and Lilienthal the ringleader of the nest, tried every trick in his obstructionist bag to stop him, but Truman got his way.

A subtle but significant shift away from right-wing reaction could be detected in Harry Truman's pattern of appointments, and in the more general tone and character of Southern newcomers to national prominence. Kentucky, for example, seemed to blossom with bright young men of political promise. Senator Alben Barkley, a close friend of Truman's, was a stimulus to this surge of moderation, and so were Fred Vinson and Stanley Reed when they served together on the Supreme Court. But the younger Kentuckians were equally as impressive: Paul A. Porter, chairman of the Federal Communications Commission; Wilson W. Wyatt, chairman of the National Housing Agency; Edward F. Prichard, Jr., chief counsel of the Democratic National Committee; and A. B. "Happy" Chandler, the ex-governor and senator from Kentucky who in 1945 became commissioner of baseball—where he would help to open the way for Jackie Robinson and other black athletes to play in the major leagues.

By no act of subterfuge did Harry Truman pursue his liberal agenda; with characteristic directness he simply spelled it out, bit by bit, and the Southerners kept waiting, in a state of puzzled confusion, for the man to come to his senses. In the fall of 1945 he sent a domestic policy message to Capitol Hill calling for an expanded federal housing program, a universal health plan, a strengthening of federal wage and hour legislation, and a permanent Fair Employment Practices Commission—the last like a red flag waving before the enraged Southern bulls. Practically every Southerner in Congress except the maverick Floridian, Claude Pepper, detested the very idea of the FEPC; strict equality in the job market was to them a surrender of a fundamental white advantage that they were determined to fight for to the bloody finish. Truman never gave up the effort to achieve permanence and power for a federal antidiscrimination agency overseeing employment, but the goal would not be achieved for many years to come.

What could the bemused Southerners possibly make of their President? He expressed disgust for "professional liberals," calling them "intellectually dishonest . . . fakers . . . phonies," and he didn't like it at all when someone called him a liberal or a progressive—but that's what he was. He revered the memory of Franklin Roosevelt, but included him at times—and Eleanor, and Claude Pepper—on his critical roster of phony liberals. Even more perplexing was Truman's mixture of racist stereotyping and egalitarian thought, both exemplified in a single statement he once made in reference to Jimmy Byrnes and his colleagues: "Why does a South Carolinian hate to eat at a table with a nigger? It's a prejudice, it doesn't make any sense, but it's there."

The white supremacists would never understand Truman—and many blacks and white liberals would not get a much clearer fix on him, either. In the fall of 1946, with the election returns showing huge gains for the Republicans and a sharp tilt to the right in his own party, with mounting problems of labor unrest at home and Communist aggression abroad, with his fortunes fleeing and his critics right and left raking him over the coals, the President did a most remarkable thing. On December 5 he announced the formation of a fifteen-member Committee on Civil Rights to study and recommend new legislation aimed at protecting all segments of the population from discrimination and intolerance. (Edwin Embree and his Rosenwald Fund colleagues Charles S. Johnson and Will Alexander had suggested such a study in 1943, but no one at the White House was receptive to the idea then.) Walter White of the NAACP wrote later that Truman's advisers warned him that this initiative "was nothing short of political suicide"—whereupon the Missouri mule gripped the bit firmly between his teeth and plowed on.

He had not acted impetuously or desperately, but deliberately, with anger building in him like steam in a kettle. One after another, the Southern racial atrocities of 1946 came and went in newspaper stories until the very frequency of them dulled the sense of shock and outrage they provoked. The blinding of Isaac Woodard in South Carolina, the "race riot" in Columbia, Tennessee, the quadruple lynching in Walton County, Georgia, the torching and dismemberment of John C. Jones in Minden, Louisiana—these and other lethal assaults, most of which targeted black men who had served their country in uniform, were finally more than Truman could take. "We've got to do something!" he told Walter White and others in a biracial delegation that called on him in mid-September.

A few days later he met with another delegation that included the fiery Paul Robeson, and the two men took an instant dislike to each other. Robeson had just electrified a New York rally with this challenge: "Are we going to give our America over to the Eastlands, Rankins, and Bilbos? If not, then stop the lynchers! What about it, President Truman? Why have you failed to speak out against this evil?" When they met at the White House, the question hovered over them, though Robeson didn't repeat it directly and Truman didn't acknowledge that he had heard it. That abrasive encounter shook the President, but he must have realized that White and Robeson—one using honey, the other vinegar—had served up to him the same indicting question: Why hadn't he spoken out? The answer he decided to give was to appoint the new civil rights committee, with Charles E. Wilson, president of the General Electric Company, as its chairman. When they met with him to get their marching orders, Truman told them to deliberate without fear or favor, and then to bring him back a written report with recommendations for new laws and procedures to protect civil rights.

The committee included only two blacks—Sadie T. M. Alexander, a city attorney in Philadelphia, and Channing Tobias, a New York foundation officer and former YMCA executive. Two white Southerners were on the panel: Frank Porter Graham, president of the University of North Carolina, and Dorothy Rogers Tilly, a race-relations activist in the Methodist Church and the Southern Regional Council. The other ten members, like Charles Wilson, were prominent non-Southern white men. Throughout most of 1947, as the committee and its supporting staff worked on the study, President Truman's time and energy were drawn elsewhere—to wrangles with the rebellious new Congress, and to rising concerns about Communist aggression in various parts of the world. In January, James F. Byrnes resigned as Secretary of State, citing poor health, and went home to South Carolina—not to retire but to position himself for a new role in domestic politics. On the national scene, communism loomed ever larger as a threat to peace and security. As Americans reacted with heightened alarm to what commentators had come to call "the red menace," the President was under heavy pressure to take some sort of direct action.

Responding to the advice of Attorney General Tom Clark, FBI Director J. Edgar Hoover, and others, Truman signed an executive order in March 1947 requiring all federal employees to swear an oath of loyalty to the United States and a vow of enmity to the doctrine of communism. In the hope of mollifying his political foes, the President had agreed to hand them this seemingly innocent tool. They would soon give him, in return, ample cause to wish he had never tried to soothe them.

Three months later, on the steps of the Lincoln Memorial, Truman addressed ten thousand people assembled for the annual conference of the NAACP—the first such appearance a U.S. president had ever made—and said forthrightly that full civil rights and freedom must be guaranteed to all Americans. This nation could no longer tolerate the continued existence of insult, intimidation, violence, prejudice, and intolerance, he declared: "We cannot wait another decade or another generation to remedy these evils. We must work, as never before, to cure them now." The historian David McCullough, writing almost fifty years later, said the speech was "the strongest statement on civil rights heard in Washington since the time of Lincoln."

In late October, the President's Committee on Civil Rights issued its long-awaited report: *To Secure These Rights*, a 178-page document dissecting the manifold scourges of segregation and offering detailed recommendations to "cure the disease as well as treat its symptoms." The policy of "separate but equal" development was a failure, the committee said. Citing Justice John M. Harlan's dissent in *Plessy v. Ferguson* ("Our Constitution is color-blind"), the committee said the achievement of real equality in a segregated society "is one of the outstanding myths of American history." To dispel the myth, the panel flatly recommended "the elimination of segregation, based on race, color, creed, or national origin, from American life." It then followed with a number of specific proposals, including a federal anti-lynching law, abolition of the poll tax and other impediments to voting, creation of a permanent commission on fair employment, an end to all forms of segregation in the armed forces and in the

District of Columbia, an end to segregation in public housing and public accommodations, and a cutoff of federal funds to all recipient bodies that continue to practice segregation.

Never before had an official agency of the United States government uttered an explicit rejection of racial segregation and its philosophical and legal foundations. President Truman, in his acceptance of the report, strongly endorsed its findings—and thus placed the executive branch in formal and official opposition to segregation for the first time. Six and a half more years would pass before the judicial branch crossed that great divide; the legislative branch would follow in fits and starts a decade after that. *To Secure These Rights*—its title lifted from the language of the Declaration of Independence—should have marked Wednesday, October 29, 1947, as a day to remember in the nation's long pursuit of its venerable and elusive ideals, but the nation hardly took notice of it at all.

The South, too, would little note nor long remember the day. Its liberal remnant of black and white activists would take heart from the document and the President's endorsement of it, but many moderates would consider it too radical. The newspapers found fault, the scholars counseled caution, the churches were silent. The Southern Regional Council commended the men and women who made the study and the President for commissioning it, but added its voice to the mild dissent appended to the report by Frank Graham and Dorothy Tilly, its two Southern members; they favored "the elimination of segregation as an ultimate goal," but opposed the imposition of it by means of federal laws and sanctions.

Still, a corner had been turned. As 1948 drew nearer—a crucial election year, a fateful year in many respects for the future of American democracy—the tattered factions of liberalism, almost as much at war with one another as with their true adversaries on the far right, faced the coming fight with faint hope and a deepening sense of dread. They had won some allies, gained some ground, established a solid base of support for their progressive ideas—but the ultraconservative minority, in the vanguard of which was the South's radical leadership, still dominated political and social thought and action in the region. The liberals simply didn't have the numbers to overcome their opponents. But they had sufficient resources to make a fight of it.

5. New Signs of Reform

If a team of assessors had gone through the South taking stock of the resources of liberalism in the first two years or so after the war, they might have been surprised by what they found. In politics, in the community of war veterans, in the church, in the university, in the labor movement, in organizations such as the Southern Conference for Human Welfare and the Southern Regional Council, in the various factions of socially active blacks and white liberals, in the press, in literature and the arts—in all these arenas of social and cultural ferment, there were modest signs of a renewal in the making, indications of another New South rising. Old South conservatism still prevailed in the mainstream—but these little currents, these creative freshets, were bubbling up all over the place, and in number and variety they were a genuine source of encouragement and optimism.

The venerable literary journals, such as the *Virginia Quarterly Review*, featured essays and criticism by many of the South's most noted scholars and journalists, and foremost in their minds were the burning postwar questions of Southern social policy. Political scientist William G. Carleton set the tone in 1946 with a revisionist dissection of "the myth of the conservative South." Soon thereafter, Rupert Vance, Guy B. Johnson, Tarleton Collier, and numerous others wrote provocatively on regionalism, race, class, and the South's place in the nation. Even more pointed were soundings on the South in such national magazines as *Survey Graphic* and *Common Ground*. *Survey Graphic* devoted an entire issue to the segregation problem in 1947; New Orleans journalist Thomas Sancton served as special editor for the project.

The *Southern Packet*, a sprightly new journal calling itself "a monthly miscellany of Southern books and ideas," emerged from Asheville, North Carolina, in the summer of 1945. Its publisher, George Myers Stephens, managed to keep it alive for almost a decade, though it was frail and skeletal in its last years. Clearly more liberal than the *Virginia Quarterly* and others of that older and somewhat stuffier class, the *Packet* gave voice to white and black activists who had a youthful sense of urgency about Southern problems.

By far the most ambitious regional magazine venture of those years was Philip G. Hammer's effort to launch *Pace*, "a weekly review of Southern affairs," modeled in unabashed imitation of *Time*. Hammer, an ex–New

Dealer in his early thirties and a product of the University of North Carolina, saw the postwar period as a rare occasion for bridging the liberal-conservative chasm in the region. He hired a former classmate, Calvin Kytle, to put together a dummy issue, dated June 19, 1946, and used it to attract subscribers and investors. But the volatile and erratic postwar economy after the removal of price supports kept Hammer from finding the necessary backers, and finally, after a year and a half of striving, he had to abandon the project.

Far more successful was a monthly magazine published in Chicago but having enormous appeal to black readers in the South: *Ebony,* made to look and read like a black version of *Life,* was started in 1946 by twenty-eight-year-old John H. Johnson. Having been born among hardscrabble migrants in rural Arkansas and "jerked up" in the urban jungle, Johnson nursed an abiding ambition to live out his own Horatio Alger fantasy. He would go on to become the nation's foremost black publisher.

Early postwar fiction from Southern writers was neither voluminous nor memorable, except for one classic and acclaimed novel: *All the King's Men,* Robert Penn Warren's Pulitzer Prize–winning 1946 portrayal of a Louisiana politician strikingly reminiscent of Huey Long. Warren, one of the Vanderbilt Fugitive-Agrarians, had taught at Louisiana State University during the last sensational years of Long's despotic rule. The native Kentuckian's fame as a novelist and poet came after he left the South in 1942, but all his novels were set in the region. He alone among the Vanderbilt writers would attain fame and a degree of permanent stature as a national literary figure. But social consciousness was not a hallmark of white writers from the South in those years; in fact, you could make a case that the thirties were a more fertile decade for "social message" literature than the forties—for black writers no less than whites.

From a commercial standpoint, practically every novelist, regardless of race, was overshadowed by the phenomenal Frank Yerby, a black Georgian who earned a master's degree at Fisk University and then, after several searching years of exploration, started writing Southern historical romance novels in the mid-forties. With his first best-seller, *The Foxes of Harrow,* he hit upon a formula for book-to-movie adventure stories that would serve him handsomely for years to come. Downplaying his own race, Yerby amassed a fortune by turning out more than two dozen Old South sagas for primarily white audiences. When he moved to Europe in 1952, it was not to bitter exile but to the comfortable life of an affluent working writer, as far removed from contemporary social issues and black self-consciousness as were his books.

One book of poetry stands out in fascinating contrast to the general tone of regional fiction right after the war. *Clods of Southern Earth*, published in New York in 1946, was written in rural Georgia by Don West—another fugitive, but of the lowercase kind. The self-styled "mountaineer agitator" had been in hot water ever since he and Myles Horton opened the Highlander Folk School in Tennessee back in 1932. Temporarily living again in his native north Georgia hills, West wrote emotional verses celebrating tenants, miners, millhands, and others with whom he identified—the poor, white and black. He also singled out for praise a wide range of activists, from his radical friend Claude Williams to the paternalistic old Atlanta Baptist minister M. Ashby Jones—plus Ellis Arnall, Langston Hughes, and Lucy Randolph Mason. One of his poems, "They Take Their Stand," was a slashing attack penned "for some professional Agrarians." West dedicated the collection to his friend and mentor at Vanderbilt, Alva Taylor.

The nonfiction written by Southerners in those postwar years was another matter; unlike the novels, these books were mainly works of social commentary, with race as the major theme. The first and most talked-about was *Black Boy*, Richard Wright's bare-knuckle autobiography, which had enough sharp edges in it to cut just about everyone, blacks included. A seven-page spread in *Life* magazine in June 1945 capped the sensational reception of the book, which had shot to the top of the best-seller list even as most Southern reviewers panned it or ignored it (some papers would not even accept advertisements for it). At thirty-seven, the ex-Mississippian was already famous for his 1940 novel, *Native Son*—and notorious for his earlier membership in the Communist Party and his marriages to two white women. As his fame soared, Wright was intently planning a move to Paris to escape the pervasive racism in America. He and his second wife, Ellen Poplar, and their daughter sailed for France in May 1946. For all intents and purposes, he would remain an exile for the rest of his life.

Buell Gallagher, a white educator who had been president of Talladega, a black college in Alabama, was another angry exile of sorts. He had left the region when he wrote *Color and Conscience: The Irrepressible Conflict* in 1946, spelling out many of the contradictions of racial inequality that he said were keeping the South in a state of permanent disadvantage.

Still more volumes of nonfiction came from native Southerners whose life experiences, submerged in scholarly detachment, gave their work an authoritative ring of truth. Young historian John Hope Franklin's chronicle of the black experience in America, *From Slavery to Freedom*, was well received from the time it first appeared in 1947. Katharine Du Pre

Lumpkin's memoir, *The Making of a Southerner*, was another of these knowing and notable books with a certain inner light; so, in a more scholarly way, were Howard Odum's *The Way of the South* and Charles S. Johnson's *Into the Main Stream.*

Race preoccupied many nonfiction writers who sensed how pivotal the postwar years were. Gunnar Myrdal declared in a 1946 essay that "American Negroes can be satisfactorily integrated into [the country's] democracy," but he warned that the time for such an equality-based union "is rapidly running out." If it should "follow its own deepest convictions," he said, "America can show that justice, equality and cooperation are possible between white and colored people."

It was in 1947 that three already-noted volumes from the left, center, and right (in that order) first appeared: Stetson Kennedy's *Southern Exposure*, Ellis Arnall's *The Shore Dimly Seen*, and Theodore Bilbo's *Take Your Choice*. A conservative scholar, Charles W. Collins, brought out *Whither Solid South?* that same year. A studious attempt to "prove" the innate inferiority of blacks, it became a virtual bible for segregationists. Acknowledging that slavery was "a great crime against Africa," Collins went on to say, in effect, that white supremacy is a reality that cannot and must not be compromised. "The South will never submit to manhood suffrage for the Negro," he declared, "nor to the abolition of segregation." His conclusion dovetailed with Bilbo's; a last-resort alternative might be "a forty-ninth state in Africa."

Race was far more of an open topic of discussion all over the United States in the postwar years than it had ever been before. Bobby-sox crooner Frank Sinatra received a special Academy Award in 1945 for his work in a movie short called "The House I Live In," which accentuated positive efforts to promote racial tolerance. Still among the biggest stars of popular music were black artists Louis Armstrong, Duke Ellington, Count Basie, Ella Fitzgerald, and Billie Holiday, and coming along fast was a young jazz pianist and singer, Nat "King" Cole of Montgomery, Alabama, by way of Chicago. Joe Louis, another Alabama expatriate, continued his decade-long reign as heavyweight boxing champion of the world; he was an exalted figure among descendants of Africa everywhere, but he also had a large and appreciative following among whites.

A purely Southern creation, country music, started its climb to national and international popularity after the war, thanks in large measure to the "honky-tonk" sounds of Hank Williams and other celebrated picker-singer-songwriters. Rufus "Tee-Tot" Payne, a black street musician in Greenville, Alabama, is generally credited with the discovery and early nurturing of Williams's considerable talents when the brooding, footloose teenager was drifting away from home and school. In a brief span of just fifteen years, Hank Williams went on to create a body of music that drew deeply from the white and black reservoirs of Southern poverty. His fame soared before and after his death at the age of twenty-nine from a variety of chemical excesses; he was called "a hillbilly Shakespeare," and his songs had a universal quality that transcended their origins. More than twenty thousand people attended his funeral at the city auditorium in Montgomery in 1953.

For millions of Americans, the most noteworthy postwar development in race relations was the debut on April 11, 1947, of twenty-eight-year-old Jackie Robinson as a major-league baseball player with the Brooklyn Dodgers. Because of racial discrimination, he was years late getting his chance as a rookie—but once he was out there, nothing and nobody could hold him back. An outstanding hitter, fielder, and base-stealer, he would remain the Dodgers' second baseman for thirteen years. Three months after Robinson made his debut in the National League, the Cleveland Indians brought up a twenty-two-year-old outfielder, Larry Doby, to be the first black player in the American League. Leroy "Satchel" Paige, a forty-four-year-old "rookie" with a quarter-century of experience as a pitcher on all-black teams, followed Doby to Cleveland in 1948. Twelve more years would pass before the last all-white major-league team, the Boston Red Sox, finally desegregated; soon after that, the first big-league franchises would be established in the South—in Houston in 1962 and Atlanta in 1966. With the barriers removed at last, scores of black players came on to raise the level of the big-league game—and a substantial majority of them, like Robinson (Cairo, Georgia), Doby (Camden, South Carolina), and Paige (Mobile, Alabama), were natives of the South.

Robinson's real confrontation with the Jim Crow character of baseball had actually begun earlier, in March 1946, after he and his wife, Rachel, had made they way across the segregated South to spring training in Daytona Beach, Florida. The Dodgers' owner, Branch Rickey, had recruited the versatile athlete, a Californian since his childhood days, and assigned him to the minor-league Montreal Royals. At training camp, Robinson won his spikes with outstanding play and a steely knack for fending off racists. Helped by another black player, John Wright of New Orleans, who withstood the slings and arrows of bigotry alongside him, and by Montreal manager Clay Hopper, a white Mississippian, Robinson blazed a trail that brought the Dodgers organization—and the city of Daytona Beach—into the modern era well ahead of their competitors. Play-by-play announcer Red Barber, another Southerner, also helped, as did the baseball commissioner, former (and future) Kentucky politician "Happy" Chandler, who ignored the negative reaction of almost all the other major-league club owners and approved Rickey's plan to transfer Robinson's contract from Montreal to Brooklyn in early 1947.

Baseball mirrored a larger evolution in race relations that gained momentum after the war. The tiny hairline cracks that had been spreading across the surface of segregation and white supremacy for the past dozen years were becoming larger and more noticeable. Politicians still generated the laws and customs that kept the nonwhite minority in an inferior—often invisible—status, and the caretakers of the churches and schools and civic institutions still tended to reinforce those social patterns. But increasingly, there were other sources of information and guidance besides the decrees of traditional authority figures: books, magazines and newspapers, popular music, movies and the theater, spectator events, radio, and now this mind-boggling thing called television. In myriad ways, often subtle and almost imperceptible, they whispered a message that contradicted the official wisdom: Segregation can't be sustained in a democratic society.

In baseball—an institution of much greater importance to many Americans than politics—the message of April 11, 1947, was not a whisper but a shout. More than the complexion of the players began to change when Jackie Robinson became a Dodger. Fans of every race, sex, age, and home address, people who loved the game and made heroes of its luminaries, had a new star to follow—a dark, handsome, dashing combatant who was in every way as good as the best. The game, the big-league cities—and the South—would never be the same again.

The pillar institutions, for all their conservatism, did not blindly follow the politicians, nor were they without the capacity or the will to chart their own future direction. Religious and educational institutions in particular showed occasional flashes of independence, and some individual leaders among them raised spirited dissenting voices questioning the status quo.

In Chapel Hill, the stately Presbyterian church across the street from the University of North Carolina campus, which counted UNC President Frank Porter Graham as one of its officers, formally declared in 1945 that "We do not close our doors or discriminate against . . . any sincere worshipper who may present himself"—and thereafter, blacks occasionally attended and were welcomed. The liberal-minded pastor, the Reverend Charles M. Jones, was sometimes in conflict with the local community and with denominational higher authority during the decade or so of his tenure at the Chapel Hill church, but his congregation, Graham included, was solidly behind him.

In April 1947, Jones performed an act of charity that was somewhat shocking even to the university community when he hosted a biracial group of travelers testing the desegregation of interstate buses in the wake of a Supreme Court ruling on the subject. After Bayard Rustin and three others were roughed up and arrested at the Chapel Hill bus station and then released on bail, Jones took them back home with him, trailed by menacing carloads of angry white men. The four "freedom riders" were soon escorted out of town by a supportive convoy of Carolinians. They returned more than a year later to be tried, convicted, and sentenced to thirty days' labor on a road gang.

Of all the white denominations in the South, the Methodist Church may have been the most interested in improving race relations. Methodists in the region—women more conspicuously than men—had shown an interest in social issues for decades. Individuals seemed to stand out more admirably than groups or congregations. One whose contributions were felt in several areas was Dorothy R. Tilly. She was a genteel lady who took her identity from her husband (she always signed as "Mrs. M. E. Tilly") but got her conscience and her courage from deep within. In her church, in various ecumenical organizations, in the Southern Regional Council, and in President Truman's Committee on Civil Rights, the diminutive Mrs. Tilly was a towering figure.

Another Methodist, former minister Will W. Alexander, neared the end of his long career with the Commission on Interracial Cooperation, the Farm Security Administration, and the Rosenwald Fund with decided views on the race issue. As chairman of a commission on race relations for the Federal Council of Churches in 1946, Alexander guided the drafting of a report that formally aligned the ecumenical association—and, by implication, its member denominations—with the principle of racial equality. Renouncing segregation as "unnecessary and undesirable and a violation of the gospel of love and human brotherhood," the commission called on the federal council to "work for a non-segregated church and a non-segregated society."

Postwar ferment in the state convention of the all-white Southern Baptist denomination in Georgia, and in some other Southern states as well, pointed to the possibility of a breach in the wall of segregation there. White and black Baptists, meeting separately but simultaneously in Savannah in 1946, first agreed to hold a precedent-breaking joint worship service. Then, at the urging of Joseph A. Rabun, a young minister from a small town in south Georgia, the white Baptists "put some teeth" in a social service committee report, approving a declaration that "no man shall be discriminated against because of race, creed or color." The delegates stood up and denounced the quadruple lynching in Walton County four months earlier, and the recent spread of hate groups in the state. As noteworthy as the resolutions themselves was the fact that Rabun, a thirty-eight-year-old ex-marine chaplain in the Pacific, was pastor of the First Baptist Church of McRae, where Eugene Talmadge, Georgia's white supremacist governor-elect, kept his letter of baptism.

Something invisible but palpable was tugging on the coattails of the Southern Baptists. In North Carolina the following week, white Baptists in convention first passed a resolution authored by the Reverend Das Kelley Barnett of Chapel Hill condemning racial segregation in the church—and then rescinded it by a narrow margin after Barnett and other liberal delegates had left for home. Similar rumblings were felt in Kentucky, Tennessee, Texas, and other states.

Joseph Rabun went back to face the wrath of his McRae congregation with his message of Christian brotherhood undiluted. Talmadge was too sick to attend church by then—he died a month later—and the controversy might have been laid to rest too, if Rabun had said no more. But in February 1947, with Herman Talmadge having emerged as his father's stand-in for governor, Rabun showed up at legislative hearings on the segregationist white-primary bill and testified in support of "my Negro neighbors . . . politically beaten, robbed, and left for dead" by the proposed legislation. "My stand might place my position in the community where I live in jeopardy," he declared, "but cost me what it will, I cannot consent to silence against a threat to the welfare of my state. The real issue is not a white primary, it is democracy." (Another Georgia Baptist, former Governor Ellis Arnall, recalling that testimony years later, would describe Rabun as "a very courageous and sincere man.")

Members of Rabun's McRae congregation hurriedly telegraphed the younger Talmadge to assure him that their minister didn't speak for them. Rabun offered to resign, but his deeply divided flock was, for its own unreported reasons, not ready to endorse a divorce. Finally, after six months of agonizing, they decided by a vote of sixty-seven to thirty-five to accept his resignation. Soon, labor organizations and other liberal groups in the state were touting Rabun as an attractive Democratic contender in the 1948 Georgia governor's race. There was already one announced candidate: Herman E. Talmadge.

Nobody criticized Rabun for blurring the lines of separation between church and state; it was his lowering of the barriers between black and white that got his fellow Baptists upset. At a time when denominations North and South were issuing pious pronouncements on brotherhood and equality, local congregations were marching to a different and more conservative drummer. All but a tiny fraction of Protestant congregations, in or out of the South, were "composed exclusively" of a single racial group, wrote Liston Pope in *Survey Graphic* magazine in 1947. There was, he said, "very little difference between southern and non-southern white churches" in their racial makeup.

Catholics did a little better, even in the South. The church's presence in the region was slight, and its percentage of black parishioners was low, but the hierarchy had acknowledged the need "to improve social conditions" by creating the Catholic Committee of the South in 1940. Gerald P. O'Hara, the Bishop of Savannah, and Paul D. Williams, a lay leader in Richmond, put their weight behind the effort. Milwaukee Archbishop Samuel Stritch, a native of Nashville and an activist on social issues in the church, was their instigator.

With Williams as its first executive secretary, the Catholic Committee of the South became a liberal voice for social justice within the church, and a collaborative partner with Protestants and Jews of like mind—often to the dismay and irritation of conservative bishops in the region. In fact, it was the bishops' tight control of funds that kept the committee from having a significant regional impact, though it continued—in name, at least—for more than fifteen years. Paul Williams, whose early awakening to Southern social problems had come from reading Howard Odum, was elected to succeed Odum as president of the Southern Regional Council in 1946, and he would hold that post for six years.

Black churches in the South, the vast majority of which were Baptist or Methodist congregations, had emerged from the nineteenth century not as segregated institutions of their own invention but as products of two external and inconsistent developments: emancipation from slavery and exclusion from the white churches. Over the years, the black churches came to be the strongest institutions in African-American life; unlike political parties, libraries, hospitals, and even schools, churches appeared to find broader fields of service in a segregated society than they might expect in a more equitable and integrated one. Sociologist E. Franklin Frazier, a longtime student of black culture, predicted in 1947 that "vested interests" among denominational leaders in the black church would have the ironic effect of making those institutions, like their white counterparts, resistant to racial and social reform. Desegregation of churches, he predicted, probably "will follow rather than precede the breakdown of the secular color line."

More often than not, the institutional church, white and black, did prove to be an obstruction to the prophetic voices that arose within it, rather than a stage for them. Many a Southern activist was led by his or her religious faith and teachings into a deepening personal commitment to social reform, only to find that the church was more interested in preserving its traditions and privileges than in reforming itself or the larger society. The church, like the university, may have been a wellspring for the intellectual and philosophical stimulation out of which some reform movements came—but when the institutions themselves shrank from joining the fray, it was often their sons and daughters, acting in new alliances or as individuals, who moved the dialogue and the action to a higher plane.

Thus it was not the Methodist Church but the Association of Southern Women for the Prevention of Lynching that dared to challenge a social evil; not the Presbyterians but the Fellowship of Southern Churchmen; not the Baptists or the Episcopalians or the Congregationalists but the Young Men's (or Women's) Christian Association; not the black church but its leaders speaking through the NAACP. And finally, in 1955, it would not be the black Methodist and Baptist denominations but the Southern Christian Leadership Conference that would originate the plan of nonviolent resistance to racial oppression.

The YMCA and YWCA were among the first church-related agencies to address social concerns. Many of the Southerners who yearned to do something about race relations in the twentieth century—and almost all of the ones who had strong religious ties—could trace their awakening in some degree to the exposure they got at the Y. Student associations for men and women, white and black, were opened across the South by W. D. Weatherford and others in the first quarter of the century; in the second quarter, these young people became the leaders who moved the associations forward. Among other things, they did away with the racial barriers that the culture imposed and that paternalistic leaders like Weatherford enforced.

The women were the first to hold local biracial meetings, beginning in the 1930s, and those led to the first interracial regional conference for YM and YW delegates at the YMCA conference center for black students at Kings Mountain, North Carolina, in 1938. But the Blue Ridge Assembly across the state continued to resist such equity, even after Weatherford, its founding father, resigned from his commanding position at the center in 1944. Many of those who had worked there under his reign felt it was past time for a changing of the guard. "Dr. Weatherford was a sweet man, good and well intentioned, beloved and respected," said one of them, "but he was an obstacle to change, not an inspiration for it." His influence on racial policy would linger for eight more years; not until 1952 would Blue Ridge host its first racially integrated regional conference of student YMCA and YWCA leaders.

The policy of exclusion almost spawned a tragedy in 1946. Leaders of the biracial YWCA, having been turned away from Blue Ridge, leased a private campground near Hendersonville, North Carolina, that summer and convened a series of meetings there, some of them involving male students, white and black. Word of the gatherings found its way into the nearby town; rumor spread quickly that the Ku Klux Klan would raid the camp and punish the participants. Rosalie Oakes, a member of the regional YWCA staff in Atlanta, and Jean Fairfax, dean of women at Tuskegee, remembered years later the fear that swept through the camp. "We asked every clergyman in town, white and black, to help us," Oakes recalled, "but none of them would." State and local police were likewise uncooperative. (A possible expression of moral support might have come from Carl Sandburg, had the women known that his new mountain home was only minutes from them.)

"We sat up all night, singing and praying, waiting for the assault," said Fairfax. "It was a terrifying experience." The night passed uneventfully, and the conference ended the next day. Later that evening, a caravan of cars brought more than a hundred Klansmen with guns and torches to the empty campground. Apparently the hooded men had targeted the wrong date for their invasion.

The National Association for the Advancement of Colored People was also heavily influenced by religious institutions—but driven by ideological, political, and social interests that the denominations considered too radical or too advanced.

In spite of the horrendous racial murders of 1946, the NAACP had reasons to be optimistic. By the end of the year, the civil rights organization had more than a thousand branches throughout the nation and a total membership of nearly half a million people. Walter White still served as its executive secretary, heading a strong staff that included his longtime assistant, Missouri-born Roy Wilkins; field secretary Ella Jo Baker, who came from the Virginia–North Carolina region; and youth secretary Ruby Hurley, a native of the District of Columbia. In the association's Legal Defense Fund, Thurgood Marshall was orchestrating a two-phase strategy that had begun as a challenge to the inequality of separate-but-equal segregation—and later would question the constitutionality of segregation itself. The venerable and irascible but still-brilliant W. E. B. Du Bois, involuntarily retired from the Atlanta University faculty, was back in the New York office, having agreed in 1944 to end his old feud with Walter White and take a position as director of a program of special research. The truce between the two strong-willed men would be predictably short-lived.

The Southern chapters of the NAACP were in most instances the only open and organized resistance to Jim Crow segregation and discrimination existing in their communities. A few cities, such as Atlanta, had strong National Urban League chapters, but the NAACP was in every major city, and even in many smaller ones, providing direct cooperation and support to the handful of black attorneys in the region and backing the local and state chapter secretaries in their ongoing battles with white authority.

From the perspective of some Northern liberal critics, the national organization was too hierarchical, too elitist, and too much in the grip of the smooth and resourceful White, who enjoyed his ties to establishment power and didn't mind flaunting them. But whatever else he was, White was a forceful and courageous foe of segregation, and he never backed away from his mission to eradicate it. What's more, the association's fieldwork in the South grew steadily more effective under Ella Baker and Ruby Hurley, and the legal work directed by Marshall was simply indispensable, and local leaders were often uncommonly inspired and productive. To their Southern critics on the right, the NAACP was not a high-society club of punch-bowl moderates at all, but a disruptive aggregation of black radicals. No matter which side the detractors fired from, though, they all had to acknowledge that throughout most of the South, the "N-Double-A" was the only antisegregationist game in town—and a pretty tough game at that.

In Richmond, for example, attorneys Oliver W. Hill and Spottswood W. Robinson III had several lawsuits in progress in the fields of voting rights, education, and public transit when the war ended. It was their groundwork that enabled Thurgood Marshall to win a major Supreme Court victory in 1946, arguing successfully against state-imposed segregation in interstate travel. Hill would be elected to a city council post in Richmond two years later—becoming the first black ever to serve on that body—and he and Robinson, NAACP stalwarts in Virginia, would render timely and effective service again when the school desegregation issue came to court.

And in Columbia, black activists in the NAACP and several other groups made South Carolina stand out among the Southern states for the high level of its grassroots involvement in public affairs. Black Republicans had organized the Lincoln Emancipation Clubs to push voter participation; black Democrats, told that they couldn't belong to the state party, had formed their own Progressive Democratic Party; a statewide organization of black teachers won court cases on the issue of equal pay for equal work—and in all of these, the NAACP was the prime mover and shaker. James M. Hinton, the state president, and Modjeska M. Simkins, the state secretary, together with the other black leaders of South Carolina, were in the thick of every issue that enlivened the social agenda in that state in the mid-forties, from local hassles over the hiring of black policemen to federal cases that ended up in Judge Waties Waring's courtroom in Charleston.

Osceola McKaine was easily the most intriguing figure of them all, with his rare combination of experiences as a World War I lieutenant, a cabaret owner in Belgium, a cofounder of the Progressive Democratic Party, and the party's 1944 candidate for one of South Carolina's seats in the U.S. Senate. After that campaign, he tried unsuccessfully to unite the state's black Democrats and Republicans, and served on a national advisory board for the Southern Negro Youth Congress, and demonstrated his commitment to an interracial reform movement in the South by working (with white South Carolinian Witherspoon Dodge) as an organizer for the Southern Conference for Human Welfare. But in mid-1946, McKaine was diverted by urgent calls from Ghent, Belgium, where his supper club, Mac's Place, was in need of his attention. He left the South, never again to see his Carolina homeland; in 1955 he died in Brussels at the age of sixty-three, and his body was returned to Sumter for burial.

People like McKaine and his South Carolina companions were the life-blood of the NAACP. They gave it legitimacy as a grassroots organization, and proved its effectiveness as a creative, responsive, aggressive advocate of democracy for all Americans. There were other black organizations, and groups of well-intentioned whites, and even a few biracial coalitions that tried to nurture a more progressive and equitable climate in the region, but none had the single-minded commitment of the NAACP. Without the association at work in the South, there would have been no broad-based pressure to end Jim Crow segregation, and no effective push for racial justice, during the first half of the twentieth century.

The public schools of the South had more money to spend in the mid-1940s than a decade earlier, but they still lagged far behind the rest of the nation. Teachers in New York averaged three times more in salary than teachers in Mississippi—and white teachers in Mississippi drew about twice as much as blacks. The gap in expenditures per pupil was proportionally as wide, North to South and white to black. Instead of being a force for progressive growth and improvement in the region, the schools were little more than pawns in the perpetual struggle for political and economic power that preoccupied local and state governments; for years to come, they would contribute little to the rescue of the South from its isolation and stagnation.

At the higher levels of education there was considerably more ferment, but most of it was generated by such outside stimuli as the GI Bill of Rights and other manifestations of federal aid. Segregation was virtually complete in both public and private colleges and universities, although some of the states bordering the South—West Virginia, Delaware, Maryland, Missouri—had moved on their own or under court orders to admit a few blacks to graduate and professional schools. In the states farther south, black veterans seeking admission were turned away; some, like Heman M. Sweatt of Houston, excluded from the law school at the University of Texas, enlisted the aid of the NAACP to sue the university and the state. Texas responded by opening a makeshift law school for blacks in Austin and a new institution, Texas State University for Negroes, in Houston, hoping to hold back the march of reform. Sweatt's petition was rejected by a federal district court, but his case was appealed, and more would be heard from it. Ten campus organizations at the University of Texas, meanwhile, took up his cause and that of other black applicants, announcing their support for a race-free admissions policy and offering to raise funds for Heman Sweatt's appeal.

The university, like the church, was not disposed to take advanced positions on social questions, but it often did provide a sanctuary of sorts for individuals of a more activist bent. A large majority of the black Southerners who spearheaded reform movements were either academicians or ministers—and some, like Benjamin E. Mays, were both. As for whites, people like Frank Porter Graham and Howard Odum of the University of North Carolina were still actively involved in a variety of academic and social projects aimed at regional betterment. On the explosive issue of race, however, not much had changed from previous years: Separate was still separate, and equal was still a myth, and the impetus for change, such as it was, came from outside—from the NAACP, from veterans, from lawsuits—and not from within.

Segregation was simply one more costly burden for the overextended Southern states and their public and private colleges. Burgeoning postwar enrollments, outmoded facilities, underpaid faculties, poorly qualified new students and poorly financed older ones—these would have been handicaps enough. Dual facilities and programs to serve the separate-but-equal charade were the last intolerable straw. Since the late 1930s—long before they started talking about ways to maintain postwar segregation—the states and their academic leaders had been casting about for ways to hold down costs by encouraging interstate cooperation. When black veterans started applying to schools of medicine and law in the white universities, a new urgency crept into the search for regional solutions.

As early as 1944, Governor Colgate W. Darden of Virginia had proposed that black students seeking specialized instruction in programs not available to them be given scholarships to schools in other states. In a frequently cited example, it was suggested that Meharry Medical College in Nashville, the only school in the South training black physicians, would expand to accommodate students from other states in the region, with those states providing the necessary funds through scholarships. One consequence, of course, would be that segregation of white medical schools could be maintained. At four consecutive annual conferences of the Southern governors, beginning in 1944, plans for an interstate compact on educational cooperation were discussed and refined, and Governor Millard Caldwell of Florida emerged as the movement's leader. There was even talk of vesting ownership of some institutions in a regional body— this being one proposed alternative to the demise of Meharry, which entered the 1947–48 academic year skirting unsteadily on the edge of financial collapse.

In the fall of 1947, the governors of sixteen Southern and border states unanimously approved the concept of an interstate educational compact. The following spring they incorporated the new entity, committed their states to annual budget appropriations, formally requested additional funding from foundations, established a headquarters in Atlanta, and appointed John E. Ivey, Jr., a protégé of Howard Odum's, as its director. Over the next three or four years, the compact would become permanently established as the Southern Regional Education Board. Both those who had eyed it hopefully as an instrument for perpetuating segregation and those who had opposed it in fear of that outcome would have reason to be surprised by what the interstate agency eventually was able to accomplish.

American higher education had one more opportunity to provide social leadership in 1947. The previous year, Harry Truman had appointed the President's Commission on Higher Education, a twenty-seven-member panel of scholars, administrators, and others, and charged them with making a comprehensive study of the nation's colleges and universities. In their voluminous report, *Higher Education for American Democracy,* issued in December 1947, the commission offered a mountain of statistics to document the strengths and weaknesses of higher learning, and urged greater efforts by the federal and state governments and the private sector to finance a wide range of improvements.

The report condemned both the doctrine and the underlying principle of separate-but-equal education, not only showing the failure of the policy but declaring that "it contravenes the equalitarian spirit of the American heritage." The "tragic paradox" of discrimination, said the commission, was its costliness to those least able to afford a dual system: all blacks, Southern whites, Southern colleges and universities, and the states of the South. "There will be no fundamental correction of the total condition," the report concluded, "until segregation legislation is repealed."

Two of the Southerners on the commission—O. C. Carmichael, the recently retired chancellor of Vanderbilt University, and F. D. Patterson, president of Tuskegee Institute—stood with the majority in support of that conclusion, but three others issued a sharply worded dissent. Lewis W. Jones, president of the University of Arkansas; Goodrich C. White, president of Emory University; and Douglas Southall Freeman, editor of the Richmond *News Leader,* signed the disclaimer (as did Arthur H. Compton, president of Washington University in St. Louis), and their action quickly attracted supporting statements from a host of other Southern and border-state educators, including the presidents of Virginia, Mississippi, Texas, Tulane, and Johns Hopkins universities, and B. Harvie Branscomb, Carmichael's replacement as chancellor of Vanderbilt.

While acknowledging that "gross inequality of opportunity" was a fact of life for black citizens that should be corrected "as rapidly as possible," the dissenters went on to assert their belief "that efforts toward these ends must, in the South, be made within the established patterns of social relationships, which require separate educational institutions for whites and Negroes." The commission may have spoken with "high purpose and theoretical idealism," they said, but it had taken "a doctrinaire position which ignores the facts of history and the realities of the present." Such pronouncements, they asserted, would only jeopardize the existing social arrangement, impede progress, "and threaten tragedy to the people of the South, both white and Negro."

Once again, Southern leaders could not muster the vision and courage to direct their region onto a new path. Day by day, the options born of postwar euphoria were diminishing, and those that remained would be further eroded in the stormy tumult of 1948. For all its hopes and its promise, the South was still spooked by goblins of its own creation.

6. *Homegrown Progressives*

Of all the South's homegrown efforts to tackle regional social problems arising from the depression and the war, none were more extensive and substantial than those of the Southern Conference for Human Welfare and the Southern Regional Council. When they were created—the former in 1938, the latter in 1944—they constituted the primary internal responses to Old South conservatism and white supremacy. Throughout the forties, they provided the truest measure of liberal-progressive thinking in the region.

They were rivals in some respects, the more intensely so because of their similarities. Back and forth across the fence, they whispered criticisms of each other: too much reckless radicalism, too much conservative caution, too much activism, too much empty talk. Many people, including a few key individuals who served in both organizations, wanted them to work together toward mutually shared goals; some hoped they would merge into a single, broad-based movement, an activist army for social reform. They never did unite, and neither grew to the size of a battalion, let alone an army, but both had a significant impact on the postwar South. If you want to know what was being said and done by white and black Southerners before 1954 to place the explosive issue of race relations on the public agenda, you have to look closely at the Southern Regional Council and the Southern Conference for Human Welfare.

The Council (as SRC was known by its regulars) emerged from the locust shell of its twenty-five-year-old predecessor, the Atlanta-based Commission on Interracial Cooperation. The Conference (as SCHW and its subsidiary group, the Southern Conference Educational Fund, were both referred to) was founded in Birmingham and later based in Nashville and New Orleans. The two organizations entered the postwar era in the summer of 1945 full of hope that the South was on the cusp of a great advance. By the end of 1947, that breakthrough was still within their long-range vision but not within their grasp, and the continuing struggles of both groups were a telling measure of the chronic division and instability within the South itself.

Academicians predominated on the SRC staff and board. Both Guy B. Johnson, the executive director, and his part-time associate, Ira De A. Reid, were sociologists, Johnson at the University of North Carolina and Reid at Atlanta University. (Reid was also the only black staff member.) Howard W. Odum of UNC was the council's president, and Charles S. Johnson, the soon-to-be president of Fisk University, was chairman of the executive committee—and both of them were sociologists too. George S. Mitchell, an economist, would soon join them, and there would be others from academia.

The SRC described itself as a leadership body, not a mass-membership organization; it had a large board of directors (seventy-five to a hundred members), and it hoped to develop branch councils in each Southern state, but its regional roster of rank-and-file recruits was never large. The staff and board were broadly representative of the region in terms of race and geography, but they were solidly, almost exclusively, middle class, and only about a dozen women (all but two or three of them white) were members of the charter board and staff. Nothing about the organization could fairly be called radical. If any NAACP leaders, Communists, Socialists, or right-wingers were present—or even any elected or appointed public officials—they kept a very low profile.

Most of the prominent Southern black leaders of the postwar era were central figures in the SRC, including all those who had started the dialogue in Durham and had held up their end of the discussion in subsequent meetings—Charles Johnson, Gordon Hancock, Benjamin Mays, P. B. Young, Rufus Clement, and others. Many of the best-known white liberals and progressives in the region also gave their names if not their energy to the council (but, for reasons both various and complex, there were some notable exceptions, including Ralph McGill, Frank Porter Graham, Lillian Smith, and Jonathan Daniels). It had taken nearly two years of delicate maneuvering by dozens of active Southern men and women of both races to bring the council to life in 1944. But even though the organization was finally on its feet, it was still a long way from being unified. Not only did those who kept their distance accentuate the disunity; internal factions also clashed over purposes and priorities. Usually the underlying cause was that same old bone of contention that Southerners had been gnawing on for ages: segregation.

The most conservative faction of SRC members came together around the notion that any overt attempt to eradicate segregation would be too antagonistic to the ruling elite in the South, and thus counterproductive. Their strategy was to acknowledge segregation as the existing law, and to pledge SRC to work within it. This group was predominantly white, but included a few blacks as well. Some were pragmatists who reasoned that no progress was possible without support from the white establishment; others believed that the separate-but-equal philosophy could be made to work, and would be best for both races in the long run.

The liberal faction—a balanced biracial mix—was convinced that the South was shackled by the ball and chain of segregation, and that both the black minority and the white majority would be permanently crippled if they didn't cut themselves free. Here, too, pragmatism and ideology were at work, with some advocating desegregation as a more efficient and fair use of human resources, and others saying it was a constitutional or religious or moral imperative. In general, the antisegregationists wanted the SRC to support the budding sentiment for an integrated society, and thus to be positioned on the breaking wave of history.

In between were the moderates—perhaps the largest faction of all. They wanted to avoid at all costs an up-or-down vote on segregation. Personal views aside, they were convinced that neither the separate-but-equal group nor the integrationists could win the larger society over to its philosophy. Fearful of a resurgent backlash that would cast the South down into its nightmarish past, they preferred to see the council concentrate on programs and research that would deal with Jim Crow laws only obliquely, if at all. In general they were philosophically opposed to segregation, but they expected it to prevail in the South for decades, even generations.

With Howard Odum presiding and Guy Johnson as executive director, SRC seldom wandered far off that middle road. So many problems cried out for attention; there was more than enough to be done, they said, without getting hung up in ideological debate. The council spread its thin resources as far as it could, trying to bring help and hope to Southerners in need without unduly alarming the guardians of vested power. A modest annual budget of less than $50,000 was raised, with the Rosenwald Fund and other foundations providing most of it. In no sense was SRC an extreme group; everything about it bespoke caution, diplomacy, moderation.

The staff had its hands full. Ira Reid was assigned to direct a two-year study of racial discrimination in the South (soon narrowed to Atlanta, and then further to public transit in the city). George Mitchell, former director of a political action committee in the labor movement (and, like Reid, an ex–New Dealer), was hired to set up a program for returning veterans. Dorothy Tilly took over Jessie Daniel Ames's old assignment as head of what had once been called "women's work"; she soon developed it into an outreach program that opened SRC branches in several states and enlisted church groups in various social-concern programs. A monthly magazine, *New South*, was launched in 1946 to replace *Southern Frontier*, the old CIC journal. A year later the council started a radio series called "Southern Roundtable," modeled after a popular discussion and debate program from Chicago. The moderator was a new SRC staffer, Harold C. Fleming, a native Georgian and an army veteran just out of Harvard.

Women were influential members of the council, out of all proportion to their small number. Among them were three whites and two blacks who filled important offices or argued persuasively from within the ranks for a progressive agenda. Josephine M. Wilkins, a longtime leader of the Georgia League of Women Voters and founder of a social-action group called the Georgia Citizens Fact-Finding Movement, became a council vice president. Jane Havens of Florida and Alice Spearman of South Carolina shared Wilkins's progressive vision. The two leading minority women were Grace T. Hamilton, executive director of the Atlanta chapter of the National Urban League, and Charlotte Hawkins Brown, a veteran North Carolina educator whose involvement in Southern social reform reached back to the 1920s.

Teetering on the highwire between liberal activism and conservative caution, the Southern Regional Council inched along. Virtually every proposed program of staff action, every resolution praising or condemning the acts of others, every utterance of organizational policy or philosophy, was subjected to the most intense scrutiny. Drafted statements in support of a permanent Fair Employment Practices Commission and federal anti-lynching legislation, or in opposition to the poll tax and the white primary, were often watered down by fears of "what this will cost us"—meaning white friends in high places, money from foundations and other donors, perhaps even the council's tax exemption as a nonprofit organization. Ira

Reid's study of discrimination suffered the same cautionary fate; so did George Mitchell's investigative report on the 1946 racial disturbance in Columbia, Tennessee. Council resolutions assailing mob violence were passed in response to the rash of lynchings that summer, but they only highlighted the obvious impotence of law-abiding citizens besieged by an epidemic of lawlessness.

The council was constantly worried about lack of support, both financial and popular. All the way through 1947, its revenues were insufficient to support a budget of $5,000 a month for all expenditures, including salaries. Dues-paying members to that point numbered fewer than two thousand. Guy Johnson resigned that summer and returned to Chapel Hill; George Mitchell took his place as executive director and set a goal of five thousand members, with a commensurate increase in the budget. Ira Reid was also gone by then, having taken a teaching post in New York (Harold Trigg, a black educator from North Carolina, became the new associate director). In the winter of 1946, Howard Odum retired as SRC president, and Paul D. Williams of Richmond replaced him. Only sixty-five people were in the audience when Williams spoke at the council's annual membership meeting in November 1947.

In his remarks that day, Williams cited the council's thoroughly biracial makeup as a model of cooperation and equity for others in the region to emulate, but not everyone was comfortable with such a self-conscious focus on race—or on SRC's presumed virtues. Virginius Dabney, an influential figure of long standing, was one council member who believed that calling attention to integration was an enormous tactical mistake.

"I can think of nothing more disastrous to the SRC's future than its identification in the public mind with an effort to abolish the segregation system," Dabney told Guy Johnson and others. "If SRC spends not only a good bit of its funds but a large portion of its energies in fighting segregation, we will lose both the battle and the war." Responding to increasing national criticism of the South as violence spread across the region in 1946, Dabney had written a defensive piece for the *Saturday Review of Literature* titled "Is the South That Bad?" Said Ira Reid in emphatic response: "Yes!"

A single question and a one-word answer thus captured the essence of SRC's—and the South's—perpetual dilemma. Capable, earnest, well-intentioned people, different from one another in many ways but having in common a lifelong bond to the South, were trying to work together to build a framework for the region's future. But some wanted to follow the Old South model, others thought it had to be replaced, and those in between were stymied, not knowing which planks to use and which to discard.

Howard W. Odum and Charles S. Johnson, ultimate symbols of the dilemma, were foremost among those who gravitated to the center. They had been primary leaders of the Southern Regional Council experiment from the very beginning. Johnson had drafted in 1942 the vital document at Durham that led to the founding of the SRC, and Odum had spoken up at the right moment in Richmond in 1943 and saved the embryo council from self-destruction. The two men were philosophical and tactical moderates who tried to persuade those on either side to join them in the middle and work cooperatively for the good of all. On most issues, Odum and Johnson could find common ground. But for all their wisdom and experience—as sociologists, as policy-makers, as sensitive human beings—they couldn't see eye to eye on what to do about the burden of segregation.

Odum's retirement from SRC leadership effectively signaled the end of his durable dream: to create a powerful regional institution of research and development that would define the South of the future. Grand designs had always danced in his head, but he lacked the heart for conflict—without which no grand design could be realized. For all his temporizing and his abundant caution, Odum clearly understood the biracial nature of Southern culture. He knew it was race above all else that had set the South apart from other regions for centuries. He knew, furthermore, that the South would ultimately have to attain integration and equality within itself if it was ever to achieve those standards within the nation. He understood those verities intellectually; it was their practical realization that stymied him.

Odum was advancing into the twilight years of his long and productive career when he quietly gathered up his papers and left SRC in 1946. It was a parting more significant than it appeared: The man with the regional plan was stepping down, his dream unfulfilled. He wrote *The Way of the South* that year, and published it the next. In it he summarized and restated his concept of regionalism more succinctly than ever before. He saw the United States divided into six regions, of which the Southeast was one. These, he said, should be balanced and complementary—equal but not identical, different but not inferior or superior, integrated into a national whole but not homogenized. Through planning and cooperation, "the regional equality and balance of America" could be achieved. He viewed the ongoing dispersal of the South's large black minority throughout the country as a promising development, and favored incentives to support this long-term process of "voluntary migration."

The sociologist acknowledged that regional equality presupposed citizen equality irrespective of race—but this, too, would have to be achieved voluntarily, and over an indefinite period of time. He rejected out of hand any "coercive enforcement by the nation of a non-segregation economy advocated by many agitators." Was he, in his heart of hearts, still unable at that time to see thoroughgoing equality as a positive good? The record is fuzzy on that crucial point. His readers, though, were left to draw a virtually inescapable conclusion: In Odum's eyes, the segregated and inequitable and divisive "Southern way of life" was not yet a subject open for debate and negotiation; for the foreseeable future, it would remain the prevailing reality.

In his private reverie, Charles Johnson must have read Odum's words with deepening discouragement. The two men had known each other for more than twenty-five years; they were professional associates, collaborators, personal friends. But Johnson had written in the Durham Manifesto that he and his fellow black petitioners were "fundamentally opposed to the principle and practice of compulsory segregation in American society." Quietly but firmly, he had always made clear his conviction that "separate but equal" was a flawed and failed principle of law and social custom. He obviously wanted the United States and its constituent assemblies to abolish segregation and discrimination based on race. By those lights, he came dangerously close to belonging to the band of rivals dismissed by Odum as "agitators."

Johnson had spent his entire career trying to build bridges—from the past to the future, from a closed South to an open nation, from a prevailing attitude of white supremacy to a new belief in multiracial democracy. As a young man, he came to see that race relations—the interplay between the white majority and the colored minorities—would be America's glory or its doom, and he devoted himself wholeheartedly to a pursuit of the glory. For his pains, he had been called just about everything in the book: a reformer, an accommodationist, a liberal, a conservative, an integrationist, an Uncle Tom, a diplomatic gentleman—and now, an agitator. If he and Howard Odum, the quintessential centrists, couldn't stand together on the rock of race, the prospects for the Southern Regional Council were bleak.

Simultaneously with Odum's *The Way of the South* in 1947 came Johnson's *Into the Main Stream,* published by the University of North Carolina Press. It was a book of "promising signs in the South's development toward better human relations," and a search for the one main stream by which all Americans could be transported to full citizenship. No doubt thinking of his white friends, Johnson wrote with empathy and insight:

The fear of disturbing the controls of the racial system frequently places restraints upon progressive action in racial matters of any sort. Always there are in every locality a few well-meaning humanitarians willing to do something, but action carries a responsibility that only the stoutest hearts can sustain for long. . . . That is undoubtedly why it so often happens that the intellectual liberals who know what should be done are torn between their private convictions and their public caution, and the most forthright declarations of the need for change are made by persons who are estimated by the community to have so little weight as to be innocuous.

As a board member of both the Southern Regional Council and the Southern Conference for Human Welfare, Charles S. Johnson no doubt saw clearly how much alike the two organizations were, and yet how different. The leaders of SRC were—to use Johnson's descriptive phrase— "intellectual liberals . . . torn between their private convictions and their public caution." Those who directed the SCHW were more action-oriented and more candidly expressive of an equalitarian point of view. It was precisely because of those "forthright declarations" that they were widely regarded as radicals and extremists with little influence on the majority of Southerners.

It would be hard to make a solid case, though, that they were really radicals. Middle-class white Southern males accounted for almost all of the officers and staff of the SCHW, as they did at the SRC, and the conference's board of directors was roughly three-fourths white and eighty-five percent male—again, much the same as SRC's. Even by Southern standards, they weren't all that far out, either; it would have been more accurate to call them liberal Christian Democrats—and that, too, was an apt description of the SRC. (Cross-fertilization was heavy between the two organizations. SCHW President Clark Foreman was a member of the SRC board, and SRC staff members George Mitchell and Ira Reid were on the board at SCHW. At least a half-dozen others, including Will Alexander, Charlotte Hawkins Brown, Lucy Randolph Mason, Aubrey Williams— and, of course, Charles Johnson—served on both boards.)

The accusations of Communist sympathy that shadowed half a dozen or so conference stalwarts between 1938 and 1942 had driven off almost all of the suspects; only John Preston Davis's name was still on the list of SCHW officers and directors—and Davis, former head of the National Negro Congress, had moved to Pittsburgh and was no longer active in the organization. If Communist influence had ever truly penetrated the SCHW, it had long since been filtered out. But right-wing opponents never tired of hurling the charges—and the conference gave them a larger target by refusing to exclude any potential members solely because of their political beliefs.

The conference was generally more liberal than the SRC—in its activism (protesting, circulating petitions, lobbying), in its associations (with Northern liberals, the labor movement, the NAACP), and in its pronouncements on the issues of the day. It went on record in 1946 against "discrimination on the grounds of race, creed, color, or national origin," calling it "fundamentally undemocratic, un-American, and un-Christian." Even so, the leaders chose not to attack Jim Crow laws explicitly at that time, taking instead the New Deal tack that the way to relieve blacks of the yoke of discrimination was to give them political and economic power. That might have been considered radical when members of the Roosevelt administration advocated it in the 1930s, but it was the standard position of the Democratic Party's liberal wing now. If there was anything revolutionary about the SCHW's goals in the mid-forties, it was its announced intention to bring about genuine majority rule in the oligarchic South, where roughly three of every four adults didn't vote, and most of the ones who did were in some incumbent politician's hip pocket.

Conference President Foreman and James A. Dombrowski, the executive secretary, were more advanced in their views on race than were most of the other whites in the organization—or, for that matter, those in the Southern Regional Council. Both men had shown by word and deed years earlier that they recognized segregation as a white problem that was crippling the South. Still, it was one thing to hold that view personally, and quite another to espouse it as organizational philosophy; not even the SCHW was quite ready for that. Instead the conference concentrated on labor and voting-rights issues (the National Committee to Abolish the Poll Tax was one of its major projects)—and unlike the SRC, it was aggressive enough to draw a visceral response from the likes of Mississippi's bombastic Senator Theodore Bilbo. This "mongrel conference," this "un-American, communistic outfit of white Quislings" that caters to "negroes, Jews, politicians and racketeers," was demanding repeal of poll taxes and other measures the senator held dear. "If I were called upon to name the Number One Enemy of the South today," he thundered, "it would be the Southern Conference for Human Welfare." Cleverly, Foreman and Dombrowski used the quote as an endorsement in reverse.

During the first year or so after the war, the SCHW far outpaced SRC in size and scope. Its membership was close to three thousand by the end of 1945, and fiscal receipts for the year totaled almost $85,000 (one-third of it from labor unions). Membership was concentrated in the Southern and border states, and branch chapters were organized in some of them, with Georgia and Alabama having the strongest. To boost its lobbying and fund-raising capabilities, the conference also developed large and active membership groups in Washington and New York. On any given issue,

SCHW had both the resources and the activist inclination to make a bigger impact than SRC.

It was in 1946, an ominous year of instability and crisis for the South and the nation, that the Southern Conference for Human Welfare reached the pinnacle of its strength—and, almost simultaneously, found itself caught up in a train of events that led to its own unraveling.

From headquarters in Nashville, Foreman and Dombrowski had wide latitude and authority to act for a compliant board of directors, and they concentrated on laying the foundation for a mass-membership organization. Two South Carolinians were hired as traveling recruiters: Osceola McKaine, the black political organizer, and Witherspoon Dodge, the white former minister whose organizing skills had recently been utilized by the CIO unions. Mary McLeod Bethune, back at her school in Florida after more than a decade of service in Washington, also made a speaking tour on behalf of the SCHW. As a result of these and other outreach programs, Conference membership quickly doubled, and, by the end of the year, was said to have reached ten thousand.

A series of successful fund-raising events outside the South (starring such famous personalities as Joe Louis, Orson Welles, and Frank Sinatra) led to heady SCHW predictions of a $200,000 income for 1946 (the actual total turned out to be more like $120,000). Judging by the national exposure and the rising numbers, any casual observer might well have been impressed; the Southern Conference was starting to look like a force to be heeded. In a reorganization aimed at achieving greater flexibility and clout (and to prevent the SCHW from losing its tax exemption because of political activity), the officers and directors decided in January 1946 to create a new entity, the Southern Conference Educational Fund. Under the plan, SCEF would be a tax-exempt body engaged in teaching, publication, and other forms of nonpolitical persuasion, leaving the SCHW free to pursue activist goals in the political arena. Both would answer to the same administrative and governing hierarchy.

All these new developments were full of promise. But even as they raised the hopes of Southern progressives, negative currents radiated out of the conference. Since the first assembly in Birmingham in 1938, a steady falling away of erstwhile supporters had continued year in and year out, until the number and quality of losses gave pause even to the most loyal defenders. In war and peace, these defections continued.

Forget for a moment the ones who never darkened the door: McGill, Dabney, Daniels, Carter, and other journalists; Odum, Guy Johnson, Paul Green, the Vanderbilt Agrarians, and other academics; Gordon Hancock, P. B. Young, Grace Hamilton, Jessie Daniel Ames, and other blacks; and women. Look past the quickly disillusioned, too—Francis Pickens

Miller, John Temple Graves, W. T. Couch, Howard Kester, H. L. Mitchell. These were not the hard-to-lose; the Southern Conference never really had them in the first place. But it could ill afford to do without the services of those who had quickly seen in SCHW the possibilities of genuine reform, and had worked together for that goal. Frank Porter Graham, Louise Charlton, H. C. Nixon, Eleanor Roosevelt, Maury Maverick, Mollie Dowd, Benjamin Mays, Mark Ethridge, F. D. Patterson, Rufus Clement, and Tarleton Collier were among them; their absence left a void. Another was Joseph Gelders, the controversial Birmingham radical and suspected Communist who had been a key figure in the founding of SCHW; he settled in California after serving in the army in World War II.

And one more important name: Lillian Smith. She had stayed away from the first meeting in 1938—citing, among other things, her suspicion that Communists were playing too much of a behind-the-scenes role in the organization. But so many people she admired and respected kept imploring her to join, that finally she agreed to attend the 1940 session in Chattanooga; then, in 1942, Smith accepted a seat on the board at the urging of Foreman and Dombrowski, both of whom she liked and trusted. After *Strange Fruit* catapulted her to fame in 1944, she had less time to be involved with the SCHW, and in May 1945 she resigned from the board. But in her characteristically blunt and direct way, she skipped the polite excuses and told Foreman and Dombrowski exactly why she was quitting.

"You see, my dreams of the Conference were so different," she wrote. "I saw it as a great coming-together of Southerners" in an assembly free of segregation "by color or religion or bank account or sex or the kind of job we work at or the political beliefs we hold. . . . I wanted us to prove to our country that *democracy works.*" But for all its talk of majority rule, she said, SCHW was actually being run in a grossly undemocratic fashion— "like a labor union"—by a little clique of officers and board members. She wasn't one of those insiders, and didn't want to be. And so with that, the independent lady from Old Screamer Mountain took up her lonely post outside the Southern Conference for Human Welfare, as she had a year earlier outside the Southern Regional Council.

Not only was the loss of old allies hurting SCHW; from the perspective of wary Southerners, so was its choice of new ones. When racial tension flared in February 1946 at Columbia, Tennessee—right in the backyard of the conference, so to speak—Jim Dombrowski worked with Walter White and the NAACP to investigate, and together they set up a national defense committee for those arrested in the disturbance. It was the first time a Southern-based biracial organization dared to work openly with the activist civil rights group from New York. For that, and for his open criticism

of local and state officials, Dombrowski was denounced by the Nashville
Banner and other Tennessee papers, called before a grand jury, and characterized by the American Legion as "a seasoned, well-trained agitator for
the Communist Party."

Such charges were old hat, of course; the right wing had fired them at
SCHW since 1938, and at Southern liberals in general for a lot longer than
that. But something profoundly different was at work in 1946. In the wake
of World War II, the surviving political-economic systems of capitalism
and communism were fighting for world dominance. The United States, in
league with its traditional allies in Western Europe, was trying to hold the
line against communism in Eastern Europe and the Pacific rim. The Soviet Union under Joseph Stalin was pressing its advantage all along the
postwar border with the West (a dividing line that Britain's Sir Winston
Churchill, in a March 1946 speech in Missouri, would call an "iron curtain"). Communist regimes in China and elsewhere were also putting
pressure on the possessions of the crumbling colonial empires. Soon,
Russia would have the atomic bomb, and the arms race would escalate
ominously. A little later on, onetime South Carolinian Bernard Baruch
would coin a phrase that gave the unofficial but deadly serious East-West
conflict a name: the Cold War.

On the domestic scene, the United States was drifting to the right in
reaction to world events. The Soviet Union, never esteemed by American
conservatives, was quickly relegated from World War II ally to Cold War
adversary. The Federal Bureau of Investigation, the Central Intelligence
Agency, and other forces within the federal government stepped up their
activities as spy chasers, and countered the espionage work of the Communist world with secret ventures of their own. Tensions between management and labor over jobs and wages deteriorated into verbal and
sometimes violent battles punctuated by slanderous assertions of treason;
the American labor movement was under heavy pressure to disavow communism and take a patriotic turn to the right. Suddenly, anticommunism
was not just a rumbling bass note, like distant, rolling thunder; it was a
howling crescendo in American political life.

For many a left-wing organization like the Southern Conference for
Human Welfare, the consequences were enormous. It was not that they
changed their ways of thinking and acting, and took up a more radical and
adversarial and unpopular stance; what really changed were the rules of
the game. The pressure for political and social conformity increased, and
dissent was equated with disloyalty. In the South, anticommunism raced
through the culture like an electrical current. Its power to shock and stun
was demonstrated in dramatic fashion by the example of SCHW and its
relationship to organized labor.

The most intimate ties had always bound the SCHW to the labor movement, and particularly to the Congress of Industrial Organizations. Many Southern CIO leaders, including William Mitch, Paul Christopher, and Lucy Randolph Mason, were influential figures in the Conference. The SCHW also tried to stay on good terms with the rival American Federation of Labor, and even saw itself as a potential bridge for the eventual reconnection of the two confederations. In April 1946, the more liberal CIO announced the beginning of its second "Operation Dixie" organizing drive (it had conducted another such campaign four years earlier), and the following month, the AFL started a Southern drive of its own. But labor was already feeling the pinch of anticommunism, and when Van A. Bittner, director of the CIO's Southern initiative, announced the plan to the press, he went out of his way to say they wanted no help from Communists or Socialists—and added, "That goes for the Southern Conference for Human Welfare and any other organization living off the CIO." AFL leaders, guarding the right flank, quickly upped the ante by characterizing the CIO itself as a hotbed of communism.

Those two blows—one from the CIO's Bittner, and the other delivered by George Googe of the AFL, a former vice president of SCHW—were devastating to Clark Foreman, Jim Dombrowski, and others who thought their relationship with the unions was unbreakable. Helplessly they saw Mitch and Christopher and Mason lose influence in the CIO as Bittner climbed. The unions not only cut off most of their financial aid to the SCHW; they also fell away from their prior commitments, nurtured by the conference, to embrace integration and racial equality. As Foreman put it later, "the leaders of 'Operation Dixie' resorted to opportunism in the hope of making the CIO respectable in the South." Needing even less prodding from the right, the AFL did the same.

The loss of union money and members had many repercussions for the conference. The field organizing work of Osceola McKaine and Witherspoon Dodge, so successful in the beginning, was now at a standstill. The two men had been recruiting members not only for the SCHW but for the unions as well—and pushing voter registration for good measure. The labor movement had funded these efforts. But McKaine and Dodge struggled through the summer without receiving salary checks or expense money; finally they had to resign.

The Southern Conference had suffered a crippling reversal of fortune, swift and unexpected, but the full effect wouldn't set in until later. In the fall of 1946, the leadership decided to move the organization's headquarters from Nashville to New Orleans (thinking, mistakenly, that the cosmopolitan old city might provide a less hostile environment). The fourth South-wide convention of the SCHW—and the first since the 1942 meeting in Nashville—was booked into the city auditorium of New Orleans for three days, beginning November 28.

More problems arose. City officials, giving in to local protests, canceled the auditorium lease to prevent a racially integrated assembly, and only a last-minute move to the hall of the local carpenters' union saved the day. Fewer than three hundred official delegates registered, though upwards of twelve hundred people attended the opening session. The speakers included Senator Claude Pepper, Walter White of the NAACP, Mary McLeod Bethune, Aubrey Williams, and Georgia's lame-duck Governor Ellis Arnall, recipient of the Conference's Thomas Jefferson Award. For the first time, Frank Porter Graham and Eleanor Roosevelt were absent; there was no telegram of support from the White House, as in past years, and the CIO delegation was greatly diminished. But the most troubling development arose after the convention adjourned, at a meeting of SCHW's officers and executive committee.

To Jim Dombrowski's complete surprise, Clark Foreman proposed— and the committee affirmed—a plan to widen the distinction between SCHW and the Southern Conference Educational Fund, which had been established earlier in 1946. In effect, Foreman wanted SCHW, under his leadership, to become a national political action committee for left-wing causes (including Henry Wallace's bid for the White House); the Washington and New York chapters would serve as its principal bases. Dombrowski didn't figure in those plans; his role would be to direct SCEF and its narrower regional agenda. The way he and many others saw it, he was being offered a sop, a consolation prize.

In their five years of close association, Foreman and Dombrowski had not grown closer. They were quite different in temperament and personality, with Foreman more of a political schemer (even his friends acknowledged that he was sometimes aggressive, ruthless, devious, manipulative), and Dombrowski more inclined to the quiet, persistent, stubborn pursuit of an idea or a principle. In the months that followed, the reorganization was delayed, and a compromise preserved the status quo while each man rallied support from within the organization. More people departed, including Mrs. Bethune, Lucy Mason, and Margaret Fisher, director of the conference's strongest state chapter, in Georgia. Thus stalemated, the SCHW limped through the first half of 1947 with its loyalties divided and its resources drained.

By late spring, Foreman was poised to refocus the energies of the SCHW into the Wallace campaign, which was by then a virtual certainty. Dombrowski was still resistant to reorganization, but at length he did agree to leave SCHW in favor of SCEF. Before either of them had made a move, however, one more problem landed in their laps. In an apparent effort to embarrass both Henry Wallace and the SCHW, the House Un-American Activities Committee in June published a lengthy report, allegedly based on nine years of undercover work, condemning the Southern Conference for Human Welfare as a "most deviously camouflaged Communist-front organization."

Condemnation of the report was widespread, from the Southern press to the *Harvard Law Review*, but great harm was done nonetheless. Among the many people smeared by innuendos, half-truths, and unsupported assertions of fellow-traveling and disloyalty were Foreman and Dombrowski, Frank Porter Graham, and Herman Clarence Nixon, one of the original organizers of the conference. Nixon's untenured faculty position at Vanderbilt University was jeopardized when publisher James Stahlman of the Nashville *Banner*, a university trustee, tried—but failed—to get him fired. Ralph McGill, who had a weakness for the soft soap of the red-hunters, also took up the attack on the SCHW, suggesting in his column that the organization was Communist-infiltrated. He later printed a partial and narrowly technical retraction of his assertions after being threatened with a lawsuit.

A long season of anticommunist reaction had begun in the United States. That probably would have been enough, by itself, to destroy a small and vulnerable organization like the Southern Conference for Human Welfare, but its demise was hastened by self-inflicted wounds. Still and all, SCHW would hang on until the end of 1948. Ironically, the Southern Conference Educational Fund, the orphaned "weak sister" in Clark Foreman's scenario, would last for a lot longer than that.

The new rules of the Cold War game were especially penalizing to the Southern Conference, but they were also hard on the more moderate Southern Regional Council, and on others interested in reformist ideas and progressive change. SRC had a fairly strong and diverse base in Atlanta, primary support from academic and religious circles, and good connections with the press; moving cautiously, it played for time and a change in the political climate. Elsewhere in the region, few if any organizations made much headway in advancing a liberal agenda in the overheated months of 1947 and 1948.

The Southern Tenant Farmers Union had entered the 1940s in a state of impotence and disarray, buffeted by internal conflict over socialism and communism and external hostility to unions of any kind, let alone one that practiced racial equality. Thanks largely to the sympathetic help of Aubrey Williams, the National Youth Administration director, Mitchell worked for a couple of years with the NYA in Washington before resuming leadership of the shell-shocked STFU. In 1948 the tiny union was saved from oblivion by its eleventh-hour conversion into the National Farm Labor Union, an affiliate of the AFL; Mitchell would run it on a shoestring from a slum-area office in Washington for twelve years before returning to the South. Though the irrepressible Mitchell was active in the labor movement for almost two more decades, neither he nor the Southern Tenant Farmers Union would be instrumental in the region's postwar struggle for reform.

Howard Kester, one of Mitchell's closest allies in the STFU and another of the old-school radicals of the 1930s, went through a similar eclipse after the war. Throughout the forties and early fifties he held a variety of jobs, mostly in the South, all the while keeping an active hand in the tiny Fellowship of Southern Churchmen, which he and a handful of others had founded back in 1934 as a liberal expression of their religious faith. Kester was a pioneer among white Southerners working openly for racial integration, starting as a student YMCA leader in the 1920s. His low profile in the postwar years may have resulted in part from a loss of stamina after more than twenty years of activist involvement. No doubt it was also a consequence of the growing hostility to social progressivism in the South.

And then there was the Highlander Folk School. Others, like Don West and Jim Dombrowski, had come and gone from the Tennessee training center for adults, but cofounder Myles Horton remained. By war's end, Highlander was serving mainly as an instructional component for organized labor. Lucy Mason and Paul Christopher of the CIO were members of its board, and so was George Mitchell of the Southern Regional Council, a former CIO official. The AFL also made use of the school's facilities, and both groups accepted (though at times without much enthusiasm) Highlander's commitment to racial inclusion and equality in its operations.

When the Cold War blew its frosty breath on labor, Highlander got the same stiff-arm treatment from both the AFL and the CIO that the Southern Conference for Human Welfare received. When the going got tough, labor turned out to be disappointingly similar to other institutions (the church, the university, the press): strong on ideals in the abstract, but weak on their actual defense. And there was another similarity: Many Southern labor officials who worked for change in the region in the thirties and forties—Mason, Christopher, William Mitch, Ernest Delpit, H. L. Mitchell, and others who followed their liberal example, including Steve Nance, John Ramsey, and William Dorsey—proved to be more committed to the ideals of racial and social equality than were the institutions for which they worked. Most of these men and women continued as individuals to support and serve Highlander, the SRC, the SCHW, and other liberal initiatives in the region long after the CIO and the AFL had abandoned ship.

In all of the organizations that struggled to extend and expand the liberal-progressive initiatives of the thirties into the post–World War II period, a familiar litany of common failings could be heard. Whether radical or moderate, aggressive or low-key, they were plagued by a chronic shortage of money and members. None of them managed to raise funds in the South as successfully as they did among liberals in the North, and none could have survived for long without those Yankee dollars. What's more, they couldn't put together anything that approached the dimensions of a mass movement in the South—and without the numbers, they couldn't get the press or the populace to take them seriously as an influential force for change.

Failing these two crucial tests, the Southerners then reduced their prospects for success still further by fighting among themselves almost as tenaciously as they battled their common enemies. From one small and resource-poor group to the next—and even within the ranks of some, like the Southern Regional Council and the two wings of the Southern Conference—people who desperately needed to join forces often spent their energy drawing swords against one another. For the right-wing reactionaries who were starting to play their anticommunism card, this competitive and divisive behavior of their enemies was a welcome windfall.

7. Anticommunism, Southern-Style

On Monday, March 4, 1946, President Harry S. Truman and Sir Winston Churchill left Washington's Union Station on a special train bound for Fulton, Missouri, where Churchill, the wartime prime minister of Great Britain, was to deliver a major address the following day. The event had been in the planning stages for weeks. Westminster College in Fulton, a tiny Presbyterian school for men, had enlisted Truman, Missouri's favorite son, to write a note of encouragement on the formal invitation. To their surprise and delight, Sir Winston promptly accepted.

His ruling Conservative Party had suffered a stunning election loss to the Labourites in mid-1945, demoting him unceremoniously from prime minister to leader of the opposition. But the Churchill name and face and voice were still virtually synonymous with Great Britain itself, and his personal popularity and influence had hardly diminished at all. As he followed postwar developments around the world, Churchill had grown increasingly worried about Communist ambitions and intentions. For months he had wanted a high-visibility forum in the United States to say what was on his mind about East-West relations; Truman's presence on the Missouri platform with him would ensure maximum exposure.

With a dozen White House staffers and more than forty members of the press in the traveling party, Truman and Churchill settled into the *Ferdinand Magellan,* the late President Roosevelt's armor-plated private coach, for the overnight journey. An ample store of supplies had been laid on: liquor, food, playing cards, Churchillian cigars. Before the train had crossed northern Virginia, the two luminaries had shed their coats and their formality; it was "Harry" and "Winston" the rest of the way. They and some of their aides kept a friendly game of poker going until about three o'clock in the morning.

The spirited socializing masked Churchill's seriousness of purpose. His speech had been carefully prepared and thoroughly discussed in advance by both British and American officials, including Truman. They all knew this was to be no windy, platitudinous little talk, but a serious exploration of what should be the U.S.-British response to world communism. Churchill would later call the Westminster speech the most important of his career—a remarkable assessment, considering his fame as an orator.

Standing before the assembled crowd in his scarlet Oxford robe, he entered into the substance of his remarks with praise for his wartime ally Joseph Stalin and the people of Russia. But then, speaking in that universally familiar tone and cadence that were his trademark, Churchill proceeded to lay out his principal theme: An "iron curtain" had descended across the continent of Europe; behind it, to the east, was the "Soviet sphere," largely controlled by the Communist Party from the Kremlin in Moscow; the "expansion of their power and doctrine" was a threatening development that called for a strong, vigilant union of the democratic states in the West as a bulwark against Communist aggression.

Thus, in a little college gymnasium out in the heartland of America, the Cold War was acknowledged and joined, more or less officially, by the most famous spokesman in the Western world, and by his guide and host, the President of the United States. The speech was criticized in the press and in Congress for its harsh, somber tone. Up to that point, public opinion in the United States still favored an accommodation with the Soviets, our allies in the war. But right-wing reaction against communism had blossomed in this country almost simultaneously with the Bolshevik Revolution of 1917, and now it was stronger and more virulent than ever. Churchill's pronouncements gave the anticommunist movement a measure of hope and respectability; from that day on, Stalinist Russia would be held up to the American people as an outlaw state, and the stigma of communism would become a national obsession.

We know far more now than we did then about Joseph Stalin and his dictatorship. Oppression, forced labor, denial of basic human rights, mass extermination of "enemies of the people"—all these and more were brutal elements of the terror that reigned in the secret world of international communism. From a post–Cold War perspective—and especially from the vantage point of the winners—the evils of Stalinist butchery and Communist imperialism are a stain on human history; they cry out for condemnation.

The Soviet strategy for expansion in the wake of World War II was no mirage; what alarmed Churchill (even more, apparently, than it did Truman and his Secretary of State, James F. Byrnes) was a pattern of aggression that would soon be apparent all around the globe. The Communists seemed to be everywhere, grabbing for power—in Czechoslovakia, in Korea, in Iran, in Greece and Turkey, in France and Italy. Within a few years, the Communist Mao Tse-tung would finish pushing the Nationalist Chiang Kai-shek out of China, and one-fourth of mankind would be added to the swelling red sea. Even in the United States there were Soviet spies and espionage agents at work, sent here to steal secrets, to probe the weaknesses of the established government, and to look for vulnerable pressure points where internal disruption might be fomented.

But for all its overpowering force in world affairs, communism couldn't establish an influential presence in this country, either underground or in the public arena. The Communist Party in the United States was never outlawed in those years of deep anxiety (not that its enemies didn't yearn to do it in, had they been able to get past the U.S. Constitution's protection of political expression). Various legal shackles were applied to hobble it, though, such as requiring party members to register as agents of a foreign power. In part because of those restrictions, the party was unable to offer a presidential candidate after 1940, when it garnered only 46,000 votes. It never elected anyone to Congress or to any significant state office.

By 1944, Communists in the United States were in such turmoil and disarray that they finally dissolved the party and tried to reorganize as a new entity. One faction was allied with former presidential candidate Earl Browder; it was so near to the political mainstream that Browder himself publicly endorsed FDR. A rival wing headed by William Z. Foster, the aging former party chief and three-time candidate for the White House, stuck to its more radical guns and to its international party allegiance.

The American Socialist Party limped along under the leadership of Norman Thomas, meanwhile, as another left-wing presence in American politics but an implacable foe of the Communists—a basic reality that most Democrats and Republicans seemed unable to grasp. Thomas ran for president three times in the 1940s and six straight times in all, going back to 1928, but like the Communist candidates, he never received as many as a million votes.

The things Thomas dreamed of and fought for in his heyday—a minimum wage, unemployment insurance, a five-day workweek, reform of child labor, old-age pensions—were destined to become essential elements of American democracy, eventually to be institutionalized by the progressive wings of both major political parties, but the Socialist Party itself remained a splinter group. The entire left-of-center alternative to two-party politics in the United States thus showed itself to be microscopic, fragmented to the point of open dissension, and largely impotent against the prevailing political might of a more conservative nation.

As for subversive activity, the hard evidence and end results support the conclusion that it, too, was largely ineffectual. Communism never became a serious threat to the ruling parties or to the social order. No alien menace emerged as a clear and present danger on American soil; there were no sophisticated conspiracies to seize government power, no attempted coups d'état, no elaborate terrorist plots, no major acts of sabotage. There was, in sum, a minimum of action—but a maximum of reaction.

Right-wing organizations in the private sector generated much of the postwar hysteria that surged through the society, but that energy would have been dispersed and spent with little effect had it not been for the focusing power of the reactionary wing in Congress. Together, these public and private forces were potent enough to drive the Truman executive branch and the courts further to the right. Looking back on those frenetic times, it is clear that disruptive or criminal acts by Communists inside this country were less frequent and less harmful than the paranoid and reactionary behavior of rabid anticommunists driven by fear or hatred or insecurity.

President Truman's performance in office in 1946 made him look like both a victim and an instigator of the red scare—and neither image was becoming. The lift he got from his trip to Missouri with Churchill was quickly erased by the controversy that enveloped the "iron curtain" speech. Liberals had been poor-mouthing the President, and he had answered with sour notes of his own—and when the right wing joined the fray, and he returned their fire too. The economy was reeling, management and labor were at each other's throats, and the South was staggering into a violent summer of civil rights abuses. It was a season of discontent, and Truman was as unhappy as everyone else. He had fallen out of favor with the American people, and out of enthusiasm for his job.

And that was only the beginning. The tide of anticommunist passion was running strong. The U.S. Chamber of Commerce weighed in, charging that the federal government was infested with reds and fellow travelers. The Catholic Church flailed away at the godless Communists. The Republican Party, smelling blood, declared that the 1946 elections would be a national referendum on Communist versus Republican values. Truman got rid of his left-wing Secretary of Commerce, Henry Wallace, in September, but that appeased no one; then he appointed his civil rights committee in October, and that didn't help either.

Meanwhile, from his unassailable fortress, FBI Director J. Edgar Hoover—entrenched there for nearly twenty-five years already, and with that many more still ahead of him—had declared war on the Communists. Claiming that 100,000 undercover reds were already running loose in the country, he kept a steady stream of messages and secret reports flowing to the President, warning him that it was time to clamp down hard on radicals, subversives, and all other disloyal persons.

The Republicans won big in November and took control of both houses of Congress. (Two of the GOP newcomers who rode red-baiting campaigns to victory, incidentally, were a Wisconsin senatorial candidate named Joseph R. McCarthy and a young California congressional campaigner, Richard M. Nixon.) Organized labor, on reading the election returns, virtually capitulated to the right wing; both the American Federation of Labor (with Truman-hater John L. Lewis and his United Mine Workers union back in its good graces) and the Congress of Industrial Organizations loudly proclaimed their loyal and patriotic Americanism and their newfound hostility to left-wing causes.

From all sides, Truman was beset by demands that he stand up to the red menace. His White House team showed signs of internal stress. As 1947 began, Jimmy Byrnes left the State Department and returned to his native South Carolina, publicly giving ill health as his reason, but privately citing policy differences with the President. General George C. Marshall, one of the heroes of World War II, became the new Secretary of State (he was soon to be celebrated as the architect of the Marshall Plan for European postwar recovery), but that popular appointment was offset by deepening alarm over Communist incursions on the global stage and at home.

In a desperate effort to reassert his administration's authority, Truman went before a joint session of Congress on March 12 to spell out the details of a new foreign policy. Its principal features were two: "containment" of

Soviet expansion in Europe, and an open-ended pledge to defend our "free world" allies from threatened aggression by the Communist powers.

This so-called Truman Doctrine was a hard-line strategy advocated by the President's more conservative advisers, but it still didn't satisfy his harshest critics in the reactionary new Congress. The Republican majority and its supporting cast of rebellious Southern Democrats, embittered and enraged by Truman's civil rights pronouncements, were making a mockery of his leadership and threatening to shove his administration into oblivion. As the liberal remnant on Capitol Hill grew smaller and quieter, a chorus of angry voices both in and out of the government demanded action against the threat of Communist infiltration at home.

A clever parliamentary maneuver by Mississippi Congressman John Rankin in 1945 had given the House Un-American Activities Committee permanent status and greater power; now it was moving recklessly under its rabid new chairman, Republican J. Parnell Thomas of New Jersey, to throw a red blanket of suspicion over thousands of government employees. Only slightly less alarmist in their counsel to the President were J. Edgar Hoover and the Attorney General, Tom Clark of Texas.

In his heart of hearts, Harry Truman thought people were too wrought up over what he called "the Communist bugaboo," but he finally concluded that firm action on his part had become a political necessity. And so, on March 21, 1947, he signed Executive Order 9835, calling for a comprehensive loyalty and security review program for all federal employees. Hoover and Clark were its principal drafters, and would be its chief enforcers. Armed with a list of groups declared by Clark to be subversive organizations, Hoover commanded an investigative task force that included units of the Civil Service Commission as well as his own agents. They were free to question the loyalty of any and all government workers and to take action against those deemed to be suspect. Loyalty boards were set up in every government department to legitimize the FBI probes; there was no provision for judicial review.

Definitions and rules of procedure were vague at best, and abuses were inevitable. Truman himself would admit in his memoirs years later that the investigations were "not in the tradition of fair play and justice." But at the time he testily defended his own action in tones of righteous indignation. Henry Wallace once remarked that the President had a way of feeling and acting "completely sincere and earnest at all times," even when he had abruptly changed his position on an issue. The loyalty order was a perfect example of that unblinking certitude.

In a climate of extreme secrecy and suspicion and fear, the federal government, in the words of Truman biographer Robert J. Donovan, "placed a perceived need for national security ahead of the traditional rights of individuals." At the same time, it also gave license to right-wing zealots who concentrated their fiercest attacks on enemies other than Communist subversives. The interrogation of some government employees included such questions as these: "Do you ever entertain Negroes in your home?" "Did you ever write a letter to the Red Cross about the segregation of blood?" "How do you explain the fact that you have an album of Paul Robeson records in your home?"

The loyalty review program and other reactionary moves on Truman's part were acts of political expediency calculated to improve his standing with the general public. Sure enough, as the year wore on, he inched upward in the polls. On the liberal side, he also won praise from many blacks and some whites for appointing the civil rights study committee, and for the tough antidiscrimination speech he delivered to the NAACP at the Lincoln Memorial in June. The President was still at odds with right-wing Republicrats, and with much of the left—especially those who backed Henry Wallace and his new third party, the Progressive Citizens of America, in their open challenge to Truman's candidacy in 1948. Seeing himself as a sane moderate between two extremes, Truman didn't object when his top political advisers began to chart a campaign strategy rooted in the broad center of the American electorate.

Congress passed a tough anti-labor law, the Taft-Hartley Act, in June 1947, and then rammed it through over the President's veto. His willingness to go to the mat on that issue, knowing that he would lose, won back for him a few friends in organized labor. In a similar way, he was praised by some once-friendly liberals after his civil rights panel issued its report in October calling for an end to segregation. Here and there, signs of his rehabilitation peeked out like spring crocuses. These little bouquets, together with his rise in the polls, told the President that he might at last be regaining a little momentum. In just over a year, he had made enough of a comeback to feel a new energy for his job, and to start his political adrenaline flowing again. To the surprise of many in his administration—and even some members of his family—the scrappy Missourian decided before the year ended that he was ready to make an underdog fight for a full term in the White House.

But even as Truman dreamed of redemption, the increasingly frantic hunt for Communist demons went on, unaffected by presidential politics. Having taken on a life of its own, the purge would lurch clumsily into the late forties and early fifties. The concerted efforts of the Attorney General, the FBI, the loyalty boards, the military, various congressional committees, and other divisions of the federal government to expose, prosecute, convict, and punish disloyal Americans eventually touched virtually everyone who drew a check from the U.S. Treasury—millions of people. After four years and more than three million FBI and Civil Service investigations, the massive dragnet would cause about three thousand employees to resign "without prejudice"; another two hundred or so were dismissed from their jobs for "reasonable doubt" about their loyalty. Not one person exposed by this penetrating and invasive scrutiny was hauled into court and found guilty of high crimes against the government and people of the United States.

Over the course of the first postwar decade, a tiny handful of citizens— perhaps two dozen in all—were indicted following investigations incidental or totally unrelated to the presidential loyalty order. These individuals were charged with serious crimes—spying, conspiracy, treason, selling government secrets, or plotting to overthrow the government. Some of them had to face sensational trials that dominated the news for weeks on end. Finally, in an atmosphere of extreme divisiveness and controversy, a few convictions were obtained—in one trial against eleven top leaders of the U.S. Communist Party (including Benjamin J. Davis, Jr., far removed in time and thought from his Atlanta Republican upbringing), and in separate proceedings against about a dozen others. Two of them, Julius and Ethel Rosenberg, were convicted of espionage and paid the supreme penalty of death by electrocution in 1953.

At a cost far greater than it could possibly measure, the United States government thus made a presentment of having cleansed itself. Historians of the period have found otherwise; most have come to share the assessment of William Manchester that "the anti-Communist terror was pathological," a hysterical overreaction that couldn't be calmed by evidence or reason. Like a fever, it had to run its course.

It was probably inevitable that the campaign against communism in the nation would be joined in common cause with the campaign against social change in the South. Racial equality had always struck the Southern ruling elite as an insanely radical notion, probably Communist in origin. Anxiously, they stayed on the lookout for subversive outsiders—agitators sent to stir unrest among the black masses. Whites who harped on racial issues, and those who tiptoed into the social arena by talking about class inequality or the scourge of poverty and ignorance, were maligned as troublemakers—and Southern whites of that ilk were singled out as the most dangerous of all. From the narrow perspective of the rulers, anyone who believed that the existing social contract needed revision was already a fellow traveler and an enemy of the public good.

"Communism has chosen the Southern Negro as the American group most likely to respond to its revolutionary appeal," wrote U.S. Army Major R. M. Howell in an intelligence report in 1932. Eight years later, Congressman Martin Dies expanded the assertion: "Moscow has long considered the Negroes of the United States as excellent potential recruits for the Communist Party." In his militantly anticommunist book, *The Trojan Horse in America*, Dies said the House Un-American Activities Committee had uncovered evidence of a massive attempt by the Soviets to win black support—mounted, he said, because "Moscow realizes that it can never revolutionize the United States unless the Negro can be won over to the Communist cause." But even the Texas congressman, fulminating reactionary that he was, conceded that the strategy wasn't working. Its failure, he concluded, was "a tribute to the patriotism, loyalty, and religion of the Negro."

African-Americans never had much use for communism. According to the most widely quoted estimates, the number of blacks who belonged to the Communist Party in the United States probably never exceeded eight thousand—a tiny fraction of one percent in a population of over thirteen million. Aside from a few highly visible converts, blacks kept their sights on the long-standing promise of democracy. You could almost count on the fingers of one hand all of the prominent Americans of African descent who became entangled with the Communist Party in the thirties and forties— and several of them were out of the picture by the time the war was over.

Richard Wright gave up on the party in the early 1940s—and then, a few years later, more or less gave up on his country. James W. Ford, thrice the Communist Party's vice-presidential candidate, was seldom heard from after his last appearance on the ticket in 1940. John Preston Davis, linked to communism through the National Negro Congress, an organization he sparked in the thirties, went on to write for the Pittsburgh *Courier*, to publish his own journal, *Our World*, and finally to gravitate to the political mainstream as a paid employee of the Democratic Party. The few who continued to stand on the firing line as left-wing activists in the fight against discrimination eventually paid a heavy price: Paul Robeson, W. E. B. Du Bois, and Benjamin J. Davis, Jr., all of whom had butted heads with white authority throughout their careers, were to find in the Cold War deep freeze that their political troubles as "dissidents" were just beginning.

But the near-universal rejection of communism by Southern blacks did nothing to convince the spy-chasers of their loyalty. As far back as the 1920s, secret U.S. police and military units were closely monitoring suspected Communist efforts to recruit black Americans; they kept up the surveillance without interruption for fully half a century, stealthily invading the privacy of thousands of individuals but uncovering virtually no enemy agents. The black minority was not the only target, of course. Throughout most of that period, spying by government operatives on all kinds of left-wing organizations suspected of having the remotest interest in communism—including virtually every group seeking social reform in the South—was a routine practice and an open secret.

Despite all the dire warnings about Communist infiltration in the South, the fact was that only two or three states—Alabama and North Carolina, and possibly Louisiana—registered enough of a red presence during and after the war to leave even a trace fifty years later. The labor movement in Louisiana was said by some to be deeply tinted with a red hue, but in all the charges and countercharges of patriotism and disloyalty that swirled around the CIO and the AFL, it was hard to separate fact from fiction. In any event, the militantly anticommunist Catholic Church, an unsleeping watchdog and a dominant public force in the state, was always far more influential with the working-class population of New Orleans and south Louisiana than any other religious or political body.

In North Carolina, the Food, Tobacco, Agricultural and Allied Workers union local in Winston-Salem had close ties to the Communist Party in the 1940s, and was directly responsible for the rapid growth of the NAACP there. Both the union and the party encouraged active participation in local politics, and those who did get involved were soon able to see positive results: A local black candidate, Kenneth Williams, won a seat on the city board of aldermen in 1947. His backers said he was the first African-American public official in the twentieth-century South to win an election against white opposition.

Another Carolina locale where there was Communist activity after the war was Chapel Hill. Junius Irving Scales, a native of Greensboro and an ex-GI, returned to the University of North Carolina in 1946 to find a loosely united coalition of students and faculty members active in local chapters of the American Veterans Committee, the Southern Conference for Human Welfare, and the Communist Party. Scales became an officer in all three groups, which shared many of the same social goals: avoiding World War III, combating racism, promoting organized labor, and raising the South's standard of living.

In the fall of 1946, the U.S. Communist Party sent thirty-six-year-old Sam J. Hall into the Carolinas as its district chairman. A native of Alabama, he had worked as a reporter for the Anniston *Star* and a Birmingham labor newspaper before joining the navy the day after Pearl Harbor. Already a Communist by that time, he served honorably in the military for four years, two of them on combat duty. In North Carolina, the short, chubby, amiable, soft-spoken Hall acted and sounded more like a Rotary Club regular than a scheming radical. He didn't conceal his purposes; he trumpeted them. In February 1947 he ran advertisements in several North Carolina newspapers announcing a Communist recruitment drive, and in a long interview with the Raleigh *News & Observer* he stated his and his party's aims in terms that could have served as the credo of a devoted liberal Democrat: to help the working class, to defend democracy, to prevent fascism, to erase poverty. Only one aim sounded a little strange: to bring about "the establishment of Socialism by the free choice of a majority of the American people."

The *News & Observer* story, quoting unnamed sources, reported that "there are not more than 200 to 250 Party card holders in both North and South Carolina, and approximately one-fourth of these are affiliated with the Communist Club in Winston-Salem." Whether or not those numbers were accurate, the fact was that the party never grew to any strength in the region; by the end of 1947 it had peaked and fallen, its various factions chased in all directions by the deepening anticommunist hostility of the larger society.

Alabama probably had more Communists in the 1930s than any other Southern state, and Birmingham, the hub of party activity, was a busy left-wing political arena in spite of regular harassment from Eugene "Bull" Connor and his police department. A weekly tabloid, the *Southern News Almanac,* began there in January 1940 with under-the-table help from the party; among its principal staffers were Joseph Gelders, the Southern Conference for Human Welfare organizer, and Sam Hall. The lively little journal had its own distinctive character. One of its most curious features, rich with the flavor of religious radicalism, was a regular column contributed by two white preachers: the well-traveled radical Don West, a native Georgian, and Fred Maxey of Leeds, Alabama.

Two other Birmingham-based organizations of the early 1940s kept strong ties to the Communist Party: the League of Young Southerners, a mostly white group of youthful radicals spun off from SCHW, and the Southern Negro Youth Congress, an offshoot of the National Negro Congress. The LYS was first called the Council of Young Southerners when it was organized at the founding assembly of SCHW in Birmingham in 1938. Helen Fuller of Alabama and Howard Lee of Arkansas headed it in the beginning, and Lee continued his close association with it.

The Southern Negro Youth Congress was larger than LYS, and it lasted longer. Beginning in 1937 with a two-day conference in Richmond, the SNYC met once a year until the war started—each time in a different city—and then erratically after that, until it folded a year after its eighth conference in Birmingham in 1948. In a little over a decade, SNYC nurtured leadership qualities in dozens of young black Southerners, including Ed Strong, James E. Jackson, Jr., and Esther Cooper, all Virginians, and

Alabamians Ethel Lee Goodman, Herman Long, and Sallye Davis. (Two decades later, notoriety would follow Davis's daughter, militant Communist Angela Davis.)

For as long as they existed, LYS and SNYC tried hard to work together across racial lines, and they succeeded to a degree, even though the laws and customs of segregation made that exceedingly difficult. Not all of their members were Communists, and in many ways the two organizations showed refreshing flashes of independence from orthodoxy of any stripe— but still, the party connections were there, as Robin D. G. Kelley showed in *Hammer and Hoe,* his revealing history of communism in Alabama. (Kelley asserted, incidentally, that Gelders, Lee, and Don West were Communists, though all three of them steadfastly denied the affiliation throughout their careers.)

Many of the young Southern activists of this period, white and black, found the primary outlet for their idealism in either the League of Young Southerners or the Southern Negro Youth Congress. However much they may have had in common with some of the aims and purposes of communism, most of them were something other than deep-dyed, ideologically devoted Communist Party loyalists. They were interracialists, democratic Socialists, progressive reformers—and, in their own way, devoted Southerners too. More than they wanted to destroy the South or turn it over to outsiders, they wanted to make it a place that met the needs of all its native people.

Of course, most mainstream Southerners didn't see them in that way at all; they saw them as dangerous troublemakers, and treated them as such. The young activists were red-baited with increasing vehemence during and after World War II. The League of Young Southerners folded before the war was over. The Southern Negro Youth Congress held on until 1949, by which time even its former allies in the labor movement, the university, the church, and the NAACP had distanced themselves from the organization.

The "invisible army" of Alabama Communists—including several labor union locals—could never have called itself large or powerful or even united. Its ranks thinned rapidly after 1945. By the time the reactionary forces of anticommunism were ready to smoke out all of Alabama's subversives in the late forties and early fifties, there was no one left for them to attack.

The South—out of step, as usual, with the national march of events— generally experienced less Communist subversive activity than the other regions of the country. As for anticommunist reaction, it found a warm and inviting climate when it swept in like a winter wind out of the North. Southern politicians were adept at damning Yankees and the feds with one breath, and demanding government support (for agriculture, military bases, protective tariffs) with the next. In the name of Americanism, these same right-wing lawmakers now insisted that the national government they loved to hate should go to any extreme, including suspension of civil liberties, in order to subdue and vanquish the encroaching red enemy.

Significantly, for the first time on a major issue, the Southerners were joined in their anticommunist extremism by a large and growing reactionary force of arch-conservative Republicans from all over the country. In fact, it would be more accurate to say that the Rebels joined the Yankees. The national epidemic of postwar anticommunism was essentially a made-in-the-North pathology engineered by right-wing Republicans; whether or not they also shared the anti-integrationist feelings of their Dixie brethren, they certainly gave them a conveniently sheltered platform from which to mount their attacks. Thus protected by outside interests, the segregationist Southern Democrats proceeded to dine freely on red herring for the next generation.

8. *Striving for Equilibrium*

"When I went to North Carolina to become editorial-page editor of the Charlotte *News* in September 1945," said Harry Ashmore, remembering back almost fifty years, "there was a little hint of change in the wind. Nothing powerful—just a feeling, really, that it might be a good time for some fresh thinking. North Carolina wasn't the most backward Southern state by any means; it had abolished the poll tax years before, and it had one of the best state universities in the country. The *News* was a fairly progressive paper—W. J. Cash was on the editorial staff there before the war. I felt I could get establishment support on any plea for fair treatment of blacks—if it stopped short of what they called the social question. In other words, *equal* was negotiable, or at least open for discussion—but *separate* was not."

Two years later, when Ashmore moved out to Little Rock to edit the *Arkansas Gazette*, that faint stirring of liberalism was beginning to die down. The report of President Truman's civil rights committee came out that fall, and a few months later the Dixiecrats bolted out of the Democratic Party over the civil rights issue. The Cold War had started, too, and communism was getting the blame for almost every deviation from the political or social status quo. From then on, social reform of any kind was a hard sell. The time for quietly making little changes was past—if there ever really had been such a time.

The experiences of war had given Harry Ashmore a new perspective on his country and his native region, and in that he was not unlike thousands of others returning to take up their lives "down home." But most Southerners—young ex-GIs in particular—weren't temperamentally inclined toward passive introspection and soul-searching. They didn't spend a lot of time worrying about the South's readiness and capacity for social or economic or spiritual renewal; the region's problems didn't yield to such reflective analysis. Instead, a twenty-nine-year-old journalist like Ashmore, having a daily page to fill and an audience waiting, was much more likely to focus on the issues of the moment from a middle-ground perspective. In the postwar South, that meant moderate progressivism: not harking back to the romantic myths of the Old Confederacy, but also studiously avoiding, as much as possible, the sacrosanct totems of segregation and white supremacy.

To anyone then active in the field of daily journalism, it must have felt like a great time to be living and working in the South. Newspapers had a virtual lock on the communications business, and local papers enjoyed an influence that far exceeded their size. The chains had not yet penetrated to all corners of the region; except for a couple or three Hearst and Scripps-Howard papers, almost every operation was locally owned. The television networks were just then forming in New York, and they wouldn't break into the Southern city markets until the end of the decade. Radio was doing a little news and information programming, but not much. Some papers, like the *Courier-Journal* in Louisville and the *Arkansas Gazette,* to which Ashmore gravitated, blanketed their states with both news coverage and circulation; they were indispensable to anyone who tried to keep up with what was going on.

Personalities dominated the papers. Owners, publishers, editors, and even some lower-echelon writers were widely recognized as influential and important people. Readers all over Georgia and even beyond the state knew who Ralph McGill was and what he was saying in the *Constitution;* likewise, Virginians followed Virginius Dabney, and North Carolinians knew Jonathan Daniels. The Birmingham columnist John Temple Graves had a following that extended well beyond the circulation area of his paper. And, quiet little man that he was, even publisher J. N. Heiskell of the *Gazette* was no stranger to his Arkansas subscribers.

When conservative and liberal owners locked horns, as did Jimmy Stahlman of the Nashville *Banner* and Silliman Evans of the *Tennessean,* readers in their area followed the fight avidly. When reactionary rivals competed daily, as Thomas M. Hederman of the *Clarion-Ledger* and

Frederick Sullens of the *Daily News* did in Jackson (even though Heder-man owned both papers), an entire state could be affected. Against that dominating influence, Hodding Carter and his smaller, more isolated *Delta Democrat-Times* in Greenville gave Mississippians an offsetting moderate voice, magnified by Carter's 1946 Pulitzer Prize and by the regional and national recognition his magazine articles and books received. (In *The New Republic* that fall, fellow Southerner Thomas Sancton called Carter "a new and extremely articulate 'Southern liberal'—with more genuine claim to the label than a number of others who have borne it.")

Young Turks like Harry Ashmore represented at once a continuation of certain Southern traditions and a departure from them. The papers he worked for in both Charlotte and Little Rock were family-owned compa-nies that regarded racial issues with a certain benevolent inattention. Theirs was not a philosophy of dehumanization; they were intellectually but passively accepting of the basic rights undeniably due to black citi-zens. They wanted to be tolerant, enlightened, and fair on the subject—but not crusading. They were not fight-to-the-death defenders of a rigid and inflexible segregationist orthodoxy, but they weren't destroyers of it either; more accurately, they were resigned to it as a reality that they felt would not soon change.

"You couldn't have stayed at home and had any influence at all if you openly opposed segregation," Ashmore observed. Looking around at his contemporaries back then, he concluded that a majority of editors in the region tended to see things in more or less that way. There was a broad mainstream of acceptable opinion—moderate, reasonable, informed, but carefully circumscribed—and he fit comfortably within it.

The seasoned old hands of Southern newspapering were the dominant figures—McGill, Dabney, and Carter, still restrained by a defensive al-legiance to the South's traditions, and Daniels, whose loyalty to the Dem-ocratic Party, by virtue of his White House service to Roosevelt and Truman, was perhaps stronger than his faithfulness to the South.

Beyond them, Ashmore could look up to a variety of experienced and talented editors and publishers, including the *Courier-Journal*'s progres-sive team headed by Barry Bingham, Mark Ethridge, and Tarleton Col-lier; Louis I. Jaffé and Lenoir Chambers of the Norfolk *Virginian-Pilot;* Coleman Harwell of the *Tennessean,* Alfred Mynders of the Chattanooga *Times,* and others. With McGill and his fellow deans and mentors in the craft, these men represented a tradition of political moderation and public-spirited service that had long been a part of the Southern press.

Nearer to Ashmore in age were Pete McKnight, who would succeed him as editor of the Charlotte *News;* Reed Sarratt, another *News* staffer who would later become editor of the Winston-Salem *Journal;* Don Shoemaker, a University of North Carolina graduate who edited the Asheville *Citizen* for publisher Hiden Ramsey; Nelson Poynter, successor to his father as editor of the St. Petersburg *Times;* George Chaplin, editor of the New Orleans *Item;* and William C. Baggs, a Georgian and McGill protégé who would become editor of the Miami *News*—and, like McGill, write a daily column. In Ashmore's native South Carolina, a few forthright moderates led by George Buchanan of the Columbia *Record* and John M. O'Dowd of the Florence *Morning News* sometimes wrote in vigorous dissent against the dominant voices of reaction.

At a number of the smaller dailies throughout the region, there were editors and publishers whose moderation and tolerance were an inseparable part of their sense of duty as public servants. Buford Boone in Tuscaloosa, Alabama, Earl B. Braswell in Athens, Georgia, and George McLean in Tupelo, Mississippi, were representative of many others in every Southern state.

There were weekly editors with a nontraditional perspective, too. Neil O. Davis, a Nieman Fellow with Harry Ashmore and Thomas Sancton at Harvard in 1941, returned from the service to edit the Lee County *Bulletin* in Alabama, and throughout his long career there, his paper was a model of professional responsibility. J. W. Norwood, publisher-editor of the Lowndes County *News* in Georgia, fought fearlessly when he got mad—as, for example, when he squared off with the Talmadge "white primary" advocates in 1947. In a scorching editorial, he condemned the behavior of the state Democratic Party leadership: "Given a choice between crooked, scheming politicians and voting with the Negroes, I choose the latter, and to paraphrase those famous words of Patrick Henry, 'If that be treason then make the most of it.' "

These, collectively, were representative echoes of the majority voice of the Southern press in the first two or three years after World War II. Though they weren't exactly editorializing in close harmony, they did tend to follow the middle path of pragmatic progressivism, on which there was a high degree of consensus. They were Southerners bonded by choice to a region with which they closely identified; they were editors who seemed ready to face realistically the South's problems and needs; they were white men (and a very few women) who thought they were as well qualified as anyone, and better than most, to offer enlightened leadership in the eternal Southern challenge of race. *Time* magazine, writing in 1947 about the "realistic and readable" Harry Ashmore ("neither a Yankee-lover nor a deep-dyed Southerner"), described him as an editor who "tempers his enthusiasm for reform with consideration of the facts of Southern life." No one had to be told that foremost among those facts was segregation.

The editors were no anvil chorus of Jim Crow–busting reformers; no one in daily journalism in the South was on that mission in the forties—and, for that matter, neither were very many Northerners. Only the black papers and a handful of regional writers outside the mainstream press dared to confront segregation in print from within the region. Lillian Smith's articles exhorting the South to reform its racist ways were widely published in other journals, but her own *South Today*, which she and Paula Snelling had edited in north Georgia, was discontinued in 1945. Alabamians Aubrey Williams and Gould Beech enjoyed a period of success in Montgomery with the *Southern Farmer*, their populist and racially inclusive monthly tabloid for families who worked the land, and they got in some good licks against segregation—but again, it was not daily journalism, and it lasted for barely a decade.

The black papers often published news and commentary on racial issues that couldn't be found in any white publication, but few outside the black neighborhoods paid much attention. Black publishers and editors in the South got little except grief from a mixed bag of critics—liberal and conservative, black and white, North and South. (They were spurned by the white press, too; in 1946 the association of newspaper correspondents in Washington voted to bar the Atlanta *Daily World*'s representative from the congressional press galleries.) If the papers were at all conciliatory on social issues, they were viewed as timid and Uncle Tom-ish; if they were combative, they were called recklessly radical; if they tried to entertain or amuse or titillate as well as inform, they were dismissed as sensationalist rags. But in their denunciation of segregation and its crippling effects on all Southerners, the black papers were not only first and right but prophetic; the problem was not with them but with the whites who ignored their warnings.

It was also in the 1940s that the *New York Times* and *Time* magazine sent reporters to open bureaus in the region. John N. Popham of the *Times* established a base in Chattanooga and started roaming the South by car in 1947, and before that, William S. Howland set up an office in Atlanta for *Time* and its sister publication, *Life*. Meanwhile, transplanted Southerners were making their mark at publications in the North, sometimes writing critical and hard-hitting stories about the South and its problems. Included in that group were Henry Lesesne of Charleston, who wrote for the New York *Herald-Tribune* and the *Christian Science Monitor;* Birmingham native Helen Fuller, managing editor of *The New Republic;* Thomas L. Stokes of Savannah, a nationally syndicated columnist; and Kentuckian Ted Poston, a pioneering black reporter for the New York *Post* beginning in the late 1930s. George Streator, a Nashvillian and a Fisk alumnus, was the *New York Times*'s first black general-assignment reporter, beginning in 1945. Rarest of all were the expatriate journalists who returned to the South to write; Thomas Sancton in New Orleans and William Bradford Huie in the little north Alabama town of Hartselle were two of the few.

There were, to be sure, some urban papers in the South, and numerous smaller dailies too, that controlled public opinion on the conservative flank of the mainstream journals. Stahlman's Nashville *Banner*, the Hederman papers in Jackson, and the Charleston *News & Courier* were usually in a reactionary class by themselves. E. M. "Ted" Dealey's Dallas *Morning News*, George Healy's New Orleans *Times-Picayune*, the Houston *Post* owned by William and Oveta Culp Hobby, and Jesse Jones's Houston *Chronicle* were also staunchly conservative on most economic, political, and social issues. So, too, were the Memphis and Knoxville papers, the Chattanooga *News–Free Press*, the *Florida Times-Union* in Jacksonville, and the *State* in Columbia, South Carolina.

D. Tennant Bryan, who owned the Richmond papers and the Tampa *Tribune*, moved them ever closer to the camp of the conservative resistance. Virginius Dabney, in his long tenure as editor of the Richmond *Times-Dispatch* for the Bryan family, had endorsed FDR four times— "with diminishing enthusiasm," he later explained, adding, "I held my nose and stayed with Truman in 1948." But the tide was turning fast; soon after that, Bryan named a twenty-nine-year-old conservative reporter and editor, James J. Kilpatrick, a native of Oklahoma, to replace the retiring Douglas Southall Freeman as editor of the *News Leader*, and in the next five years, Kilpatrick would pull both his paper and Dabney's *Times-Dispatch* sharply to the right. (Harry Ashmore had interviewed for Freeman's job before Kilpatrick; he came away convinced that Bryan and his general manager, John Wise, would fill the job with someone to the right of Dabney.)

Similar signs of change were evident in other states. In Alabama, a moderate-to-liberal tradition had put Hugo Black and then Lister Hill and John Sparkman in the U.S. Senate, and had sent Jim Folsom, a genuine populist, to the governor's office—all more or less with the blessing of newspapers in Birmingham and Montgomery, papers that fancied themselves as progressive or even liberal. And yet it was to be Alabama, almost as much as Mississippi or South Carolina, that fueled the Dixiecrat revolt, with party bosses and an aroused force of reactionary whites riding roughshod over the senators and governor. They also pressured and punished any newspapers that didn't swear the new oath of allegiance. By 1950, John Temple Graves would be a defiant ex-Democrat, and the leading daily papers in Alabama would all be tilting sharply to the right.

But such wrenching reactionary changes as these were not particularly noticeable right after the war; the extremist mood came into its own with the Dixiecrats in 1948, and gained momentum after that. The Richmond papers and their management didn't trumpet a belligerently hostile editorial tune before 1954. In keeping with their carefully tended self-image as Virginia gentlemen and Southern patricians, they were restrained and dignified in their opposition to social change, and they made a weak pass at remaining nominal big-*D* Democrats. Only the handful of arch-conservatives in Jackson, Charleston, Nashville, and a few other places went to verbal extremes in venting their postwar displeasure with political and economic and social liberalism. The bellicose, saber-rattling posture of defiance that all but a dozen or so Southern papers would eventually strike to one degree or another was the trademark of only a few in the years before 1948. Even the messy Dixiecrat separation and estrangement didn't cause a majority of the press to start clamoring for a divorce.

What was most surprising about the postwar positioning of Southern publishers, editors, and writers on the liberal-to-conservative spectrum was that the balance continued to weigh in favor of the more moderate and progressive papers all the way to the end of the 1940s, as it had for most of the previous decade or more. Thus a curious and inexplicable anomaly continued: a press more forward-looking, more open-minded and liberal, than its political representatives, its pillar institutions, or the generality of its readers. It bears repeating that the journalists were not integrationists, not left-wing radicals, not revolutionary reformers. But except for a few, they were not right-wing reactionaries either.

"We were saying that the South should live up to the promise of the 'separate but equal' doctrine," said Harry Ashmore. "That was as far as we felt we could push. But at the same time, I think most of us knew that there was no way to make separate equal—and so in a sense, we were really forcing the integration issue."

Newspaper publishers and editors and reporters—the principal dispensers of adult education in the pre-television South—might well have led the region to a quicker, more direct, and more equitable resolution of its racial conflicts had the choice been left to them. Before the Cold War cranked up in 1946, before the President's Committee on Civil Rights called for the abolition of segregation in 1947, before the Dixiecrats seceded from the Democratic Party in 1948—in other words, before race became a pressing issue on the public agenda of the South and the nation—all but a few of the region's newspapers fell somewhere on the modern side of the dividing line between Old South white supremacy and whatever the newest New South was going to be.

But then the Dixiecrats forced the issue, and the dividing line became an unbridgeable canyon. "We had to stick with the Democratic Party or take up with the Dixiecrats," said Ashmore. "The other third party—the

Progressives, with Henry Wallace—was not a realistic alternative in the South. They were as far out on the left wing as Strom Thurmond and the Dixiecrats were out on the right. The way we saw it, the traditional Democratic Party occupied the middle ground. The only real choice the Southern liberals had at that point was to stand and fight as yellow-dog Democrats. Party loyalty was all that saved us."

I like to look at newspapers as diaries or ledger books, as vast repositories for the daily accumulation of raw material from which history is shaped and made permanent. From that perspective, the ratio of waste to essence is very high—about like gold mining or pearl harvesting. All those pages, all that ink, all that effort, and so much of it expendable, come and gone and forgotten in a matter of hours. But pause and look carefully at everything—the news and editorials, the photos, the display ads, the classifieds—and a pattern begins to emerge. You learn what people said and did, what they ate, what they wore, what they drove; deeper still, you learn what they thought, what they believed, what they valued.

Reading Southern newspapers from the postwar forties now, you can get an acute sense of a region and a people striving for equilibrium in a time of great uncertainty. After the exhilaration of victory in the summer of 1945, consensus quickly eroded and then evaporated into the magnolia-scented atmosphere. The South was still confused, ambivalent, defensive, still a place divided—against outsiders and against itself. There had to be some sorting out of feelings, attitudes, beliefs, some settling of the air. By the end of 1947 the preliminaries were over, and the real struggle for the future of the South was about to begin.

For two and a half years the newspapers had been full of signs:

They told of PFC Jack Thomas of Albany, Georgia—a black orphan raised by his grandmother—being awarded the Distinguished Service Cross for battlefield heroism in Germany. But he heard little cheering when he came home. The outpouring of public adulation that awaited most war heroes returning to the South died to a whisper when the heroes weren't white. There were other African-Americans like Jones, including Eugene Jackson of Fayetteville, North Carolina, and Frank Steger of Tuscumbia, Alabama—decorated combat veterans who had risked their lives for liberties they weren't allowed at home. There was George Watson of Birmingham, posthumously awarded the Distinguished Service Cross for valor in the South Pacific; his life and death served as a telling indictment of a social system that accepted the courage and sacrifice of blacks who defended freedom—even as it judged them inferior, and thus undeserving of freedom themselves.

The newspapers reported on the efforts of the American Veterans Committee to become an activist organization with a biracial membership and a liberal agenda. In contrast to the more conservative and segregated groups—the American Legion, the Veterans of Foreign Wars, and others—the AVC was determined to right social wrongs at home. Its motto was "Citizens first, veterans second." Upwards of two dozen chapters were started in the South, primarily in university communities or in big cities like Atlanta. Their appeal was to former officers and enlisted men, to male and female veterans, to whites and blacks—to any veteran who was ready "to work for change in the community," said Lester Persells, one of the Atlanta organizers. He and a handful of others, including Johnny Glustrum, Robert A. Thompson, Harold Fleming, Odum Fanning, Sylvan Meyer, and Calvin Kytle, formed the nucleus of an activist group that grew to more than 250 members.

Newspaper reports also described each new addition to the lengthening file of civil rights decisions by the U.S. Supreme Court and the lower federal courts. With increasing frequency, plaintiffs were mounting challenges against the exclusion of blacks and other minorities from jobs, from juries, from primary elections, from certain kinds of housing and hospitals and schools, from the full services of interstate buses and trains. In response, a clear pattern was emerging: The courts were chipping away at the elaborate legal framework of racial segregation and discrimination, slowly but surely extending and reapplying the equal protection of the law to all citizens.

Newspapers in practically every Southern state were casting a critical eye on the woefully inadequate schools, hospitals, housing projects, and other public facilities to which black citizens were confined under the "separate but equal" doctrine. The papers minced no words: "Indifference bordering on criminal neglect" plagued the schools, said one; another reported that health facilities had not advanced beyond "the kitchen surgery era," and a third said slum housing "resembled something from a grim chapter of Dickens." Most Southern dailies supported teacher pay equalization and the hiring of black policemen, and roundly condemned the poll tax and the white primary. Nor did they shrink from showing the South's disadvantages vis-à-vis the nation after the war: fewer of its citizens in school, more in prison, more rejected by the military for mental or physical disorders, more living in substandard housing, more diseased or illiterate, more unskilled, unemployed, unfulfilled.

In Mississippi, the papers reported, an organization of blacks headed by A. W. Wells of Jackson was telling the governor and legislature that the cost of continued segregation could be measured by whatever it took to bring about complete equality: a nine-month school term for black children, a "free and untrammeled ballot," an end to the poll tax and the white primary, equal justice in the courts, equal pay for equal work, a redistribution of education funds from nine-to-one in favor of whites to fifty-fifty (matching the racial makeup of the population), and "a full-fledged state university for Negroes equal in all respects to the University of Mississippi."

The press presented daily evidence that inadequate delivery of medical care was a region-wide social problem made infinitely worse by segregation. The crisis went beyond underdeveloped or nonexistent hospital facilities for African-Americans and a chronic shortage of doctors to serve them. A public-health specialist in Florida concluded that the basic concept of "separate but equal" health services was wasteful and self-defeating; it not only left blacks at a great disadvantage compared to whites, but the South lagging far behind other regions. There was, he said, no such thing as a segregated solution to health problems. "It is impossible to wipe out diseases like tuberculosis and whooping cough and scarlet fever in one race without taking measures to wipe them out in the other." Calls for a single, unified public-health initiative and a system of national health insurance were being raised in some quarters.

Press reports of lawsuits seeking desegregation of higher education in several states were frequently published. Cases in Texas and Oklahoma were wending their way through the federal courts. In virtually every Southern state, debate was spreading on the issue of black admission to graduate and professional schools—for which hardly any "separate but equal" alternatives existed. In the states bordering the South, a handful of black students had managed to scale the walls of segregation in medicine, law, and other upper-level fields of study, but the ex-Confederate states were utterly unyielding. The political and academic leadership of Southern universities and colleges wouldn't bend, even though student editorials and opinion polls there showed substantial support for the notion of desegregation and equal educational opportunity.

The newspapers reported on the deliberations of biracial community groups in such widely scattered cities as Chattanooga, Winston-Salem, and Tampa. White and black ministers meeting together also got favorable press treatment, whether in rural Hertford County in eastern North Carolina or in the Georgia-Alabama state-line cities of Columbus and Phenix City. Southern state and local chapters of the YMCA and YWCA, the National Conference of Christians and Jews, the American Civil Liberties Union, and the National Urban League worked openly and actively for tolerance and fairness in race relations. Edgar Ray, editor of the Tampa *Times,* was president of his city's Urban League chapter and a frequent speaker at regional and national conferences of the league and other interracial organizations. He was also one of more than a dozen editors on the board of the Southern Regional Council.

Repeatedly in the newspapers of the South after World War II, the voices of individual advocates of social reform were recorded and amplified. In those pages appeared Kentucky attorney Ed Prichard, telling a Charleston civic club audience that the day of all-white elections in the South was over. And North Carolina educator Charlotte Hawkins Brown, saying in a speech to a gathering of New Yorkers that they, too, were being tested, because "the pursuit of justice in America—for blacks, for women, for Southerners—is everyone's responsibility." And Glenn W. Rainey, a white English professor at Georgia Tech, declaring that many whites in the South were "on the side of the Negro in the struggle to end segregation and inequality." And Arthur Shores of Birmingham, taking on the white power structure single-handedly in a class-action lawsuit to open the polls to black citizens in Tuskegee.

And Jonathan Daniels, who said in a public forum in Richmond that Virginia, a diehard defender of the poll tax, was "both the cradle and the graveyard of democracy." And Aubrey Williams, telling an audience of North Carolina educators that the South "brings up the tail end of everything in this country because we are deep in conflict with ourselves." Before the region could "move out of bondage," he said, "we must eliminate segregation—hook, line and sinker."

And finally, against the hope and promise of progressive change, the Southern press also recorded and magnified the strident voices of political demagogues and Klan terrorists and a host of other reactionary extremists. Their views on race and class and democracy were diametrically opposed to those of the progressives. As these forces of reform and resistance came ever closer to open conflict, the narrow demilitarized zone between them was diminishing rapidly, its occupants crossing over to one side or the other, or abandoning the field altogether. Among them were some troubled men and women who believed in fairness and justice, but whose deference to Southern traditions restrained them from advocating the sudden demise of Jim Crow.

Even the most prominent Southern journalists—McGill, Dabney, Carter, Daniels—reacted negatively to the report of President Truman's civil rights committee, and their consternation underscored the deep and conflicting feelings that divided the South's progressives and liberals and moderates almost as much from one another as from the majority on the right. (Jonathan Daniels was only mildly disturbed by the report, and he soon came around to its defense, but he stood aside while his eighty-five-year-old father, Josephus, still writing just two months before his death, composed the *News & Observer* editorial lambasting the committee for prescribing "radical" remedies that "would prove worse than the disease.")

Of them all, McGill seemed the most troubled—not so much by the contents of the committee's report as by its broader implications and its probable long-term consequences. The committee, he wrote, had "tried to cut the cloth to fit many patterns." The result was "a report with Christian aims . . . but it can't be enforced, even with troops. It still has to be accomplished by improving the human heart." This coercive effort, he said, would only "harden resistance and widen the gulf." Containing his own anticommunist impulses, McGill scoffed at the reckless charges of communism being thrown at the committee. Lurking behind the harsh resistance, he declared, was a mean-spirited determination on the part of many whites to deny blacks "a chance at being good Americans." That was simply wrong, he said, and he added, in an apocalyptic closing line, that "some day the Lord's going to set this world on fire."

The Atlanta *Constitution* editor was still several years away from joining the fight against segregation and discrimination, but he was beginning to see the unavoidable struggle that lay ahead. "I cannot be a good crusader," he wrote in that portentous fall of 1947, "because I have been cursed all my life with the ability to see both sides of things." For a long time he had seen and felt the white South's troubles most acutely; now, with each passing month and year, the black side of the case for simple justice was weighing ever more heavily in his troubled mind. Seeing both sides in the South's undeclared civil war as 1948 was dawning, Ralph McGill surrendered to the melancholy muse within him and waited in fatalistic resignation for the lines to be drawn and the battle to begin.

9. *Democrats and Dixiecrats*

The summer I turned thirteen, Senator Alben Barkley came to Cadiz on a campaign swing through western Kentucky. A native of Paducah, sixty miles away, he had been our congressman or senator for thirty-six years, and now he was running for the vice presidency on the Democratic ticket with Harry Truman. Barkley was strictly home folks to the proud people of Trigg County, and when he mounted a platform in front of the courthouse on that warm, sunny day, a big crowd was there to welcome him. The applause was lusty, the cheers were loud. I was right there in the middle of all that, caught up in the excitement of the occasion and feeling very grown-up to be a part of it.

This must have been in late August or early September—somewhere near the midway point between the nominating conventions and the election. Barkley was in his seventies, but he was a smooth and effortless campaigner with a folksy manner, and the rigorous demands of stump politics seemed not to tire him at all. He was totally in command of the podium. His performance (and that's exactly what it was) displayed his considerable talents as a skillful entertainer—actor, storyteller, humorist, preacher, all appealingly blended in a grandfatherly character wearing a rumpled seersucker suit.

"Don't change horses in the middle of the stream!" he pleaded, using a familiar country metaphor to convey his central message. The audience responded knowingly, and with their encouragement, Barkley went on to parade before them a barnyard menagerie: braying Republican donkeys (Thomas Dewey and friends), maverick scrub cattle (Henry Wallace and Strom Thurmond), crowing roosters (scrappy Democrats in general), and finally a stubborn, courageous, fighting Missouri mule, Harry S. Truman.

I knew next to nothing about Republicans, let alone Progressives and Dixiecrats. (My grandfather may have been a closet Republican, but I never heard him talk politics even in private conversation, and there was no party organization in the county for anyone except mainline Democrats.) Truth to tell, I really didn't know all that much about Truman and Barkley—just that they were underdogs in a free-for-all that had everybody pretty heated up. I saw the *Courier-Journal* every day (the sports pages, mainly), and that was practically the only source of outside news and information available on a daily basis to anyone in Cadiz, as far as I knew. The *Courier's* advice was the same as Barkley's: Give this Democratic team of thoroughbreds a chance to finish pulling our national wagon to safety. Standing there in the courthouse yard with people who strongly affirmed and supported that point of view—people I knew and liked—left me with no unanswered questions, no doubts, no misgivings. I was wild about Harry. "Give 'em hell, Alben!" I shouted.

All the rest of that volatile and dramatic political season of 1948 passed right over my head: the rebellion of the "states' rights" Southerners inside the Democratic Party, their walkout at the nominating convention in Philadelphia and their subsequent rump convention in Birmingham, the equally alarming defection of left-wing Democrats to the Progressive camp, the outcry over Truman's actions on civil rights and desegregation of the armed forces, and the pulsing currents of emotionalism that subjected almost every public act—and even some private thoughts—to an anticommunist litmus test.

But what would a rising teenager in a country town of the upper South know about things like that? I could have told you plenty about Citation winning the Triple Crown with Eddie Arcaro in the saddle (Kentuckians were supposed to be conversant on racehorses). I could have given you a blow-by-blow account of Joe Louis's knockout of Jersey Joe Walcott in the twenty-fifth successful defense of his heavyweight boxing title. And, though I was a St. Louis Cardinals fan, I could have recounted the exploits of Jackie Robinson with a certain grudging admiration, and told you that, for the second year in a row, his Dodgers and not my Cardinals were going to the World Series.

Even more memorable to me in that eventful summer of '48 was a big double wedding in the church next door to our house—and on my birthday, of all days. With my brother and me serving as nervously inexperienced but prankish ushers, our sisters married a couple of nice guys from out of town—ex-GIs they had met at college. My brother had a Band-Aid above his left eye. On a dare, he had shaved off his eyebrow, to see if anyone would notice that it was missing. (They did.) I think back on those leafy days of innocent boyhood with the sobering realization that ignorance really is bliss—or can be, as long as it isn't hurting anyone.

And yet there were signs of a gradual awakening and subtle heralds of inevitable change even in the little that I knew. For the life of me, I couldn't square the common white assumption of black inferiority with the lightning and thunder of Louis's left jab and right hook, or with Robinson's explosive speed on the base paths. I heard Arcaro called a "wop," but I also noticed that this grown man, no bigger than I was, had an uncanny knack for riding beautiful horses to fame and fortune, while his critics were trudging behind mule-drawn plows. My new brothers-in-law, a Kentuckian and a Virginian, had served in Europe and the Pacific, where they had experienced their own awakening to a wider world. When the GI Bill opened college doors for them and eventually brought them to Cadiz, I noticed how mature and sophisticated they were. And now they were part of my family.

Just about everything else I know about 1948 I learned years later. Had I been reading the front page of the *Courier-Journal*, I might have been curious enough about the feverish hunt for Communists in Hollywood and New York and Washington to wonder what a Communist was, and how I'd know it if one came strolling through the streets of Cadiz. If I had been paying attention, I might have noticed that President Truman issued an order requiring white and black soldiers to train and serve and, if necessary, fight together. Maybe the reason that didn't make an impression on me was that I didn't hear anyone grousing about it. I knew some avid baseball fans who had quickly grown accustomed to the dazzling play of Robinson and other black stars who followed him to the majors. Could it be that wearing an army uniform would turn out to be about the same as wearing a baseball uniform?

But those were sideline issues. The main event, the big story of 1948, was politics. Everyone, it seemed, was laying it all on the line—not just the Democrats and the Republicans, but the Progressives, the Dixiecrats, the Socialists, the Communists, you name it. You didn't have to be a voter or a campaign worker to realize that this was no ordinary contest. For one thing, it was the first time in sixteen years that Franklin D. Roosevelt's name wasn't on the ballot; when that had happened previously, I hadn't even been born.

No one knew it then, of course, but 1948 was to be the last presidential contest in which the candidates traveled primarily by train, and campaigned only on the stump or in the newspapers or on the radio. Four years later they would be flying around in airplanes from city to city, and the television cameras would be there, and the very essence of the political process would be profoundly changed.

And, in a sense, this was the year when political parties and candidates first began to look away from the past—from depression and war, from the heavy hand of tradition—and to focus on the world of the future. Certainly the South, a past-haunted society throughout its years, was being compelled to consider some new ideas. I didn't have any inkling of that then, but I see it clearly now: The dominant question in people's minds, if not on their lips, was how we might become something different and better, rather than how we must remain what we had always been.

I don't think it's an overstatement at all to say that the 1948 campaign was this country's twentieth-century turning point between the past and the future. Except for Lincoln's election in 1860 and Franklin Roosevelt's in 1932, there has never been a more crucial contest than this in the history of U.S. politics. For the South most especially, 1948 was an end and a beginning.

From the minute he decided in his own mind that he was going to run, Harry Truman had convinced himself that he would win, and to all outward appearances he never lost that assurance, even when all the signs pointed to a certain and crushing defeat. Many a self-deluded politician has calmly and confidently floated over the falls with far more reason to believe in miracles than this President had in the waning days of 1947. But he was a proud man and a fighter, driven by instinct and ego to hate the thought of quitting almost as much as losing—and, as anyone in his position would naturally do, he had to be wondering how he would come out in the history books.

His closest advisers wanted him to run (they had a lot at stake too). One of them, Clark Clifford, had given him a long memo—called "The Politics of 1948"—that laid out a strategy for snatching victory from his overconfident enemies. A new book by Henry Lee Moon of the NAACP underscored what political operatives like Clifford knew to be true: that in several key industrial states of the North and Midwest, black voters could hold the balance of power in a close election. Proceeding from the premise that Truman had to get those votes in order to win, Clifford urged him to go all out for them—rhetorically speaking. No civil rights bill was going to pass Congress now, he conceded, but a strong proposal would certainly pass muster with the minorities. And what about the Southerners? Clifford said the President could ignore them: "As always, the South can be considered safely Democratic."

This was Clifford's logic: Tom Dewey and the Republicans will talk a little civil rights, but they're not serious about it, and they won't go very far. Henry Wallace and the Progressives will try harder, but they're a fringe element with no chance of winning—and besides, they're vulnerable on the communism issue. To outbid both of them for the black vote, the things you've got to say and do will enrage the Southern Democrats. But you've already lost the most rabid racists anyway, and the more reasonable ones won't surrender tradition and habit and desert the party just to spite you. They're smart enough to know that if you lose, they lose. Once you've locked up the nomination—and it's almost impossible to deny that to an incumbent—you can go on from there to win.

Truman was not resistant to this reasoning. He could see himself using the report of his Committee on Civil Rights as a text for preaching the gospel according to the Constitution and the Bill of Rights. He had done that for the NAACP at the Lincoln Memorial, and it was very effective. His own record on civil rights was certainly defensible, and he had already praised the committee's report as "an American charter of human freedom." He had faithfully carried on FDR's programs and policies, but now that era was ending; it was time for him, Harry Truman—the President, the Boss—to step forth with his own agenda. And what better chapter and verse could he proclaim than racial equality, an ideal embedded in the nation's spirit—and one that Roosevelt, for all his liberalism, never quite got around to endorsing?

Truman's State of the Union address to Congress—an unapologetic exposition of his traditionally liberal philosophy—got a cool reception from the Republicans and Southern Democrats who predominated in the chamber. Almost as an aside, he told the lawmakers that he would soon be sending them a special message on civil rights. "Our first goal is to secure fully the essential human rights of our citizens," he stated simply, before moving on to other matters.

Three weeks later, without prior consultation on Capitol Hill, Truman did as he had promised. In a carefully crafted message, he went beyond the Republicans and the Roosevelt liberals—but not quite as far as his own civil rights committee had gone. He called for full protection of the right to vote, including an end to poll taxes in the seven states that still required them; a severe federal penalty for the crime of lynching; a permanent commission on fair employment, with enforcement powers to stop discrimination; an end to segregation on interstate buses and trains; and a civil rights enforcement division in the Department of Justice and a joint congressional committee on civil rights. The President asked for statehood for Alaska and Hawaii, home rule for the District of Columbia, and compensation for the Japanese-Americans incarcerated during the war "solely because of their racial origin." And he told his listeners that he had asked the Secretary of Defense to start planning for the imminent end of racial discrimination in the armed forces.

The President didn't get into the specifics of his committee's proposals concerning desegregation in education and in accommodations that served the general public. He also avoided mentioning the committee recommendation that federal funds be withheld from any program or service that did not comply with the nondiscrimination standards. But what he did say was more than enough to draw effusive praise from black leaders (one called it "the greatest freedom document since the Emancipation Proclamation")—and screams of outrage from the Southern reactionaries.

Those screams had been loud but brief when the committee released its report back in October. As far-reaching as it was, it nevertheless represented only the thinking of an ad-hoc group of lay citizens. But now, in February of an election year, the President of the United States—who happened to be an unannounced but certain candidate for a full term in that office—was making by far the strongest pitch for racial equality under the law that any chief executive of the Republic had ever made. Almost to a man, the Southerners in Congress took it as a declaration of war.

Senators and congressmen and governors outdid one another in their vilification and slander of the President. Truman was a vicious and immoral man, they said, a back-stabber, a traitor, a crook, a coward, a Communist. His civil rights program, said Senator Tom Connally of Texas, was "a lynching of the Constitution." Mississippi Senator James Eastland growled with disgust at a President who would "turn over the government to mongrelized minorities" that were trying to "Harlemize" the nation. Senator Richard Russell of Georgia accused him of planning a Gestapo putsch to eradicate segregation in the South. Governors Thurmond of

South Carolina, Wright of Mississippi, and Laney of Arkansas, joined by their colleague William M. Tuck of Virginia, echoed the charges and threats of defiance.

In the House of Representatives, Mississippi's chief fire-eater, John Rankin, was rendered momentarily speechless with rage by the Truman program (remarkable for a man who earlier had advocated that African-Americans be deported to Arizona or New Mexico and not allowed to leave without a passport). Then, recovering his voice, he attacked the President for trying to "ram the platform of the Communist Party down the throats of the people of the United States." Every member of the Mississippi delegation in the House joined in the verbal mugging. "We are not going to stand idly by and watch the South be mongrelized," thundered Congressman John Bell Williams. The repeated references to sex—mongrelization, amalgamation, miscegenation, rape—prompted this angry response from W. E. B. Du Bois: "The rape which your gentlemen have done against helpless black women in defiance of your own laws is written on the foreheads of millions of mulattoes, and written in ineffaceable blood."

One after another of Dixie's congressmen and senators rose to excoriate the President, and not one spoke a conciliatory word. Frank Porter Graham also came in for abuse as a Southern member of the civil rights committee (this just a year before the University of North Carolina president would take a seat in the Senate himself). Finally, after Senator "Pappy" O'Daniel of Texas said Graham had a long record of "connections with Communist fronts," North Carolina's Senator Clyde Hoey came to the liberal academician's defense.

All through the spring and early summer, in meeting after meeting, white Southerners led by their elected officials rallied around Confederate flags to condemn the President and plot rebellion and secession as their forebears had done. Finally, at a huge conclave in Jackson on May 10, the States' Rights Party met in formal convocation, with some fifteen hundred delegates from a dozen states. Strom Thurmond told them in a rousing keynote speech that "all the laws of Washington and all the bayonets of the army cannot force the Negro into our homes, our schools, our churches, and our places of recreation." The rebel-yelling Dixiecrats then vowed to walk out of the Democratic Convention in Philadelphia if Truman was nominated, and to reconvene in Birmingham and choose a States' Rights Party ticket to run in the November election.

All this extreme and extended reaction must have come as a profound shock to Truman—and to Clark Clifford, who had seemed so confident that the party regulars in the South wouldn't break away. (He was, as it turned out, partly right; the rebellion took hold in four states—South

Carolina, Alabama, Mississippi, and Louisiana—but leaders elsewhere in the region confined their protest to verbal harangues and held on to their Democratic Party privileges.) The President took the heat without flinching, but he avoided the subject of civil rights for a time, and it was clear that the punch he had thrown and the blows he had taken in return had not whetted his appetite for more. Still projecting a confident air, he formally announced his candidacy on March 8.

Trouble seemed to await him at every turn. Ominous rumors of war echoed around the increasingly hostile relationship between the United States and the Soviet Union. In April, Congress passed the Marshall Plan, a multibillion-dollar economic assistance and recovery program for war-torn Europe, but conservative Republicans moaned that it was too costly, and Henry Wallace Progressives complained that it was too militantly anticommunist. In May, Truman went against the advice of Marshall and gave U.S. approval to the partition of Palestine and the emergence there of a new Jewish nation, Israel. And in June, just as the Republicans were about to nominate Thomas Dewey and Governor Earl Warren of California—two highly regarded progressives in the liberal wing of their party— the Soviets raised the Cold War stakes by blocking the United States and its allies from land access to Berlin. The President's response was to order an airlift of supplies to the cut-off city—a daily lifeline that would be maintained for almost a year. In foreign affairs no less than at home, it was a tense time of conflict for the accidental President.

Not all the news was bad. Labor-management conflicts were declining; a strike of coal miners ended quickly, and a walkout of railroad workers was averted altogether. The American economy had rebounded from the postwar period of adjustment, and a booming phase of productivity and growth was bringing prosperity to farmers, industrial workers, stockholders, and consumers. Eerily, the euphoria occasioned by an expanding economy floated above the nervous concern, bordering on paranoia, that more and more people felt about communism and the threat of another war. With so much trouble and danger lurking everywhere, the times looked and felt almost too good to be true—so much so that not much credit for the strong economy rubbed off on the President. As summer began, he looked like the lamest of ducks, with his left wing amputated by the Wallaceites, his right one cut off by the Dixiecrats—and some of his so-called friends about to roast the carcass.

Virtually all of the Southerners who remained in the middle with Truman made no attempt to conceal the fact that they would like to see him head for Missouri as soon as a new President was inaugurated. Some were every bit as vitriolic as the most hostile defectors, but lacked their willingness to resign and take up arms with the mutineers; Senators Russell and George of Georgia, McKellar of Tennessee, Connally of Texas, and Byrd of Virginia were the most conspicuous of these in-house rebels. Alabama's moderate senators, Hill and Sparkman, didn't take public delight in carving Truman up, but they paid him a personal visit to tell him they wouldn't support him, and they urged him to step down.

Claude Pepper may have delivered the unkindest cut of all. The liberal Floridian had stayed with Truman when the Wallaceites pulled out— hoping, apparently, that a Truman-Pepper ticket might materialize. But when that seemed unlikely, Pepper and other members of the liberal Americans for Democratic Action tried to spark a movement to draft General Dwight D. Eisenhower, the war hero, as the man to push the President aside. Pepper even suggested dropping party labels and more or less anointing Eisenhower by acclamation. But the general refused, firmly and emphatically. (The act was not as altruistic as it seemed; Truman, as commander-in-chief, had given Ike an order to stay out of the 1948 political picture. The general's statement of refusal to be a candidate was written for him by Truman aide Clark Clifford.)

Pepper then tried to run up a trial balloon touting his own candidacy—a gesture more futile by far than Wallace's, or even Thurmond's. Eventually, Pepper and the ADA came around to Truman in the November showdown, but the President never forgave the liberals for their fair-weather friendship—or the Florida senator for his transparent ambition.

These were just some of the machinations and intrigues to be revealed in that most uncommon of political campaigns. Truman spent half the month of June on a "nonpolitical" trip to California and back by train— partly to get in some caboose campaigning, and partly to get away from his critics (and this was *before* the Eisenhower-Pepper-ADA adventure). The Republicans met in Philadelphia while he was gone, and their choice of Dewey over Senator Robert A. Taft of Ohio, a classic conservative, was another bit of bad news for the President. Instead of conceding the votes of urban blacks in the North, the GOP had apparently decided to fight for them—and most black newspapers in the country, historically Republican as they were, would endorse Dewey. By the time 1948 was half over, Harry Truman and the Democrats were being buffeted on all sides by their enemies—and the nomination, the campaign, and the election still lay ahead.

Some things are hard to figure. Why would the President's strategists counsel him to move out front on civil rights? The Progressives were already out there, and the Republicans were sure to play their old "party of Lincoln" tune—and the reactionary Southerners could be counted on for knee-jerk opposition to just about anything short of a return to slavery. On the face of it, you have to wonder how Truman thought he could outpoint all three of his adversaries on this issue. And why would the Republicans put up a moderate-to-liberal ticket instead of a more conservative one when they knew that Truman, an announced candidate and probable nominee, had already bet the farm on the most far-reaching civil rights program ever?

People who probe for deeper meaning in politics—planners, advisers, pollsters, pundits—are generally more inclined toward making educated guesses about the future than they are to offering informed explanations about the past. Politics, like economics and weather forecasting, is a very inexact science. But if you look upon the jockeying of candidates and political parties (those seriously intent on winning, anyway) as a search for the center, and if you think of civil rights as a middle-of-the-road issue in a democratic society, then the moves of the strategists and candidates and parties in 1948 begin to seem more logical.

Both major parties, anticipating a close election, saw the heavily populated states of New York, New Jersey, Pennsylvania, Ohio, Michigan, and Illinois as the crucial contests—and in all of them, the newly emergent black vote was vital, perhaps decisive. Furthermore, they saw Henry Wallace on the left and the rebellious Southern Democrats on the right as the boundary poles that defined the playing field, and their instinct was to stay inside the lines and close to the center.

Truman had alienated his liberal wing by adopting a hawkish and aggressive foreign policy, and also by ordering a loyalty oath in response to the anticommunist hysteria; instinctively, he wanted to refurbish his image and restore some balance by giving a more liberal tone to the rest of his domestic program. As for the Republicans, their natural inclination was always to slide to the right, but they had to have some moderate and liberal votes in order to put together a majority, so they too were inching back toward the center.

And there the two parties met—backed into each other, you might say—somewhere near the middle of the field. Contrary to the preachments of the Southern reactionary leaders, that was the natural location of the civil rights issue as a question of public policy in America. The nation's founding documents contained all of the resonant words: liberty, justice, equality, freedom. Since the Civil War, it was understood—written into the law, in fact—that the rights and privileges of citizenship belonged to every American. When the Supreme Court narrowly construed equality so as to permit its guarantee in separate facilities and services for whites and blacks, only the Southerners and some of their border neighbors wrote that arrangement into their laws—and then withheld the right of equality from the black minority.

Through all these twists and turns, the ideal of civil rights and civil liberties remained a fundamental principle of national life. Whether or not they abided by it, the Democratic and Republican parties dutifully gave it lip service. Not even in this overheated postwar season of presumed and alleged disloyalty did they repudiate the principle. Neither the Truman Democrats nor the Republicans ever seriously claimed that the effort to improve the civil rights of minorities in the United States was a wicked plot hatched by the Communist Party and carried out by its secret agents; on the contrary, they often felt a need to say and do more to ensure people's rights, in order to negate the effect of Cold War propaganda exposing segregation and white supremacy.

Only in the South were people called subversives and conspirators for demanding the right to vote or the equal protection of the law. Elsewhere in the country, those suspected of communism were left-wing activists: writers, intellectuals, moviemakers, labor leaders. Almost all of them were white. They were accused of spying, lying, stealing government secrets, aiding and abetting foreign powers. Only in Dixie did the alleged sins of aggrieved blacks and their white allies read more like a recitation from the Constitution and the Bill of Rights than an actual bill of criminal particulars.

Throughout the presidential campaign of 1948, events in the South revealed that reactionary extremism was spreading faster than the drive for political and social reform. It was the emergence of the latter, in fact—and particularly the issue of racial equality—that lit the fuse of the former. A classic illustration of this activist imbalance was provided in February at a conference on civil rights convened by the Southern Regional Council, and the sudden and extreme response it drew from right-wing elements in Georgia.

The council's continuing struggle to have a secure financial structure, a broad-based constituency, and a clear consensus on objectives grew no easier as the end of the forties approached. The organization was operating on an annual budget of less than $50,000—and half of that came from the Julius Rosenwald Fund, which was about to terminate its philanthropic services. George S. Mitchell, the SRC's executive director, was supposed to be getting a salary of $7,500 a year, but he was instead lending money to the council to cover its debts. Acknowledging that it had to have "the broad support of the people" to generate a movement that could bring about "a more prosperous and more democratic South," the SRC was now appealing openly for rank-and-file members, but the response was disappointing. By the end of 1948, only about 2,700 people were on the rolls, and many of them were there in name only.

To make matters worse, the council was no nearer to agreement on what its official position should be on the question of segregation. In general, its black members wanted the organization to take a public stance against Jim Crow laws, while most of its whites, doubting the effectiveness of government coercion, were still hopeful that a combination of forces would eventually bring about that result voluntarily. Those two positions were exemplified by charter members P. B. Young of Norfolk and Virginius Dabney of Richmond, both of whom had more or less dropped out of the organization—Young because he concluded that the council would never speak out against segregation, and Dabney because he feared that it would.

It was in this atmosphere of stalemated inertia that the SRC convened a regional meeting in Atlanta in late February of 1948 to review the civil rights issue. (At about the same time, the council also published a booklet called "The Condition of Our Rights," a state-of-the-South report on race relations that gave documentary proof of pervasive discrimination against blacks in the "separate but equal" society.) About four hundred people from eleven states attended the conference. Dorothy Tilly, whose identification with the SRC and the Methodist Church was now broadened by her membership in the Truman Committee on Civil Rights, was one of the speakers. (She spent much of 1948 traveling in the South, urging support for the committee's report.)

In reviewing the work of the civil rights committee and the current state of Southern race relations, most of the speakers at the Atlanta meeting called for a comprehensive program of change—though not for the general eradication of segregation laws. Resolutions were passed urging an end to lynching, employment discrimination, and all barriers to the ballot, including poll taxes—by federal legislation, if necessary. A majority of the delegates also asked President Truman to revoke his executive order on loyalty probes of federal employees. And, in the day's only direct reference to Jim Crow laws, they passed a resolution recommending that segregation in graduate and professional schools, public and private, be eliminated. The plan of the Southern governors to support regional higher education programs in certain fields through the newly formed Southern Regional Education Board was "designed to perpetuate the present pattern of segregation," they declared, and should be opposed.

At an evening session of the conference, Ralph McGill appeared on a panel with several of the delegates and expressed what had become a virtual litany of liberal white editors across the South: A rising tide will lift all boats; growth and expansion and modernization of schools, housing, and health care are our first needs; industrialization and unionization will open employment opportunities; fairness and justice in law enforcement, the courts, and the jails and prisons must be guaranteed; inequality is an unacceptable condition and must be eliminated, but segregation is not and won't be.

(A few days earlier, McGill had asserted on a national radio program that the Southern Regional Council, "including its Negro members," was officially on record in opposition to federal legislation against lynching, poll taxes, and job discrimination. Walter White of the NAACP, listening in New York, expressed his outrage at the claim, and drew denials from George Mitchell and several black council members. The SRC had never opposed federal laws in the area of civil rights, Mitchell said; it had, however, urged the South to assume responsibility itself for guaranteeing the rights of its citizens.)

The booming voice of right-wing reaction in Georgia was raised six days after the SRC conference in an issue of the *Statesman*, a weekly paper published in the Atlanta suburb of Hapeville. (Its editor was listed as "The People" and its associate editor as Herman E. Talmadge.) The paper devoted its entire four-page news section to the SRC event; it was essentially one long diatribe, with pictures, against the "white and negro political agitators from over the South" whose "battle cry is EQUALITY NOW!" Several other right-wing papers, politicians, and pressure groups echoed these attacks on the "subversive" council.

Having been ousted from the governor's office by the state supreme court in 1947, Herman Talmadge was primed and waiting for the upcoming special election in which he was challenging the incumbent, M. E. Thompson. At stake were the last two years of the term that Herman's father, Gene Talmadge, had won before he died in 1946. Herman himself referred to this as "the restoration," as if he were a king being returned to the throne—and in the 1948 balloting, he did give Thompson a royal licking. (Also in the race as a protest candidate was the Reverend Joseph A. Rabun, the ousted pastor of Eugene Talmadge's Baptist church in south Georgia; he finished far behind.)

Though he had been thwarted in his attempts to lock black voters out of primary elections in the state, Talmadge vowed to use voting-list purges, literacy tests, and any other means at his disposal to hold the black vote to a minimum. "There are many good white people in our counties who can't read or write," he said, "but they own farms and they do their own thinking," and therefore should be granted the right to vote. But no more than "ten or fifteen percent of our Negroes" should have the same right, he added. Blacks made up about one-third of the Georgia population at that time.

The restoration of Herman Talmadge was just one of many signs that the

South was nowhere near establishing a favorable climate for political and social reform. Instead, what seemed imminent as the spring and summer primaries approached was a nightmarish breakaway gallop by the Southern Democrats. When the political leaders of tiny Jasper County in rural South Carolina resigned en masse from the national Democratic Party as a protest against racial liberalism, *Newsweek* magazine took the occasion to assert that the South's rebellious governors and senators "were not stirring up a popular revolt. They were reflecting it."

That may have been true—but the leaders were vigorously fanning the flames. Governor Wright of Mississippi sounded an ominous note in May, just as the Dixiecrat radicals were getting organized. In a statewide radio speech, he said white Mississippians would never tolerate desegregation, no matter what the federal government said or did. Then, specifically addressing the state's blacks, who made up more than forty-five percent of the population, he said, "If any of you have become so deluded as to want to enter our white schools, patronize our hotels and cafés, enjoy social equality with the whites, then kindness and true sympathy requires me to advise you to make your home in some state other than Mississippi." Wright didn't spell out what the consequences would be for those who stayed.

John A. Griffin, a thirty-six-year-old member of the Emory University faculty and administration in Atlanta, was awarded a Rosenwald Fellowship in 1948 to complete his doctorate at the University of Wisconsin. One of the highlights of that year for him was a convocation and ceremony in Chicago to mark the formal closing of the Julius Rosenwald Fund. Thirty years after the late president of Sears, Roebuck and Company endowed it, the fund had spent its principal, as specified in the philanthropist's will, and was preparing to suspend operations. Griffin, a native Georgian and a lifetime Southerner, was one of a relative handful of the fund's beneficiaries fortunate enough to be present for the finale. His recollection of it was still vivid and particular more than forty years later.

Rosenwald's generosity had been especially salutary for the South. Over the years, this son of Russian Jewish immigrants had poured more than $20 million into programs to build hundreds of rural schools for the poor, black and white; to pay for textbooks and teacher training; and to provide fellowships for more than fifteen hundred creative people of promise, two-thirds of them black and by far the most of them Southern.

The list of fellowship recipients included dozens of people who went on to make notable contributions to education, journalism, scholarship, the arts, and public service in the South: Ralph McGill, Arna Bontemps, Clark

Foreman, Sterling Brown, James Dombrowski, Horace Mann Bond, Lillian Smith, James Weldon Johnson, H. C. Nixon, Zora Neale Hurston, John Henry Faulk, John Hope Franklin, C. Vann Woodward, Pauli Murray, Josephine Wilkins, Rayford W. Logan, Tarleton Collier, Ira De A. Reid, Thomas Sancton, Margaret Walker, and on and on—a hundred times this many.

"It was a coveted prize," John Griffin recalled. "The stipend was about $2,500—a lot of money at that time. I was very proud to have been chosen as a recipient. Then, because I happened to be nearby at the time, I got to go to that very special event in Chicago. The program that day included speeches, panel discussions, poetry readings, and performances of music and dance. It was an impressive lineup, to say the least—W. E. B. Du Bois, Gunnar Myrdal, Langston Hughes, and many others. Also, I remember that there was a real outpouring of appreciation and affection from the audience for the three men who had been so instrumental in putting the Rosenwald fortune to work in the South—Edwin Embree, Charles Johnson, and Will Alexander."

They had been addressing Southern issues as a team for two decades, and as individuals for a lot longer than that; together they had posted almost a hundred years of public service. The Rosenwald endowment had given Embree, as president of the fund, enough resources to make a real impact in the public arena, particularly in an impoverished region like the South. He met Alexander and Johnson in the mid-1920s, and the three men went on to turn the potent combination of money and good ideas into a long list of impressive achievements. In 1948, Embree and Alexander, in their mid-sixties, were about to retire; Johnson, who was a decade younger, had just been inaugurated as the first black president in the eighty-year history of Fisk University.

The loss of this major source of funding for programs of social and cultural uplift in the South would be felt acutely in a variety of institutions that had come to depend upon that support—such as the Southern Regional Council. As a member of its board, John Griffin knew how hard it was to marshal people and resources even for the most moderate and cautious attempts at social betterment. Three years after the end of the war, the spirit of unity and optimism that had momentarily flickered throughout the country was now dissipating rapidly in the South. In its place, an old and familiar mood was rising, a conservative, backward-looking, tradition-bound mood of defensiveness and defiance. Once more, the South was falling back into the same old problem, the same dilemma, the same trap: the bugaboo of race—white against black, segregation and discrimination and white supremacy against the ideal and promise of liberty, justice, and equality for all.

Whenever he ventured outside the South, Griffin could see and feel this rock of judgment weighing upon his homeland, and upon him as a person. He was aware of it in Chicago, as he listened to the telling and incisive poetic lines of Langston Hughes, and to the commentary of eighty-year-old W. E. B. Du Bois. A few years earlier, when Griffin was teaching at Georgia Tech and hosting a public-affairs discussion program on a local radio station, he had invited Du Bois from Atlanta University to take part. Now, such an invitation would be much harder—perhaps impossible—to extend. The aged scholar was embroiled in controversy—pursued by red-baiting investigators, and soon to be separated yet again from the NAACP and its temperamental director, Walter White, whose tolerance for Du Bois's blunt and stinging criticism was by then almost completely exhausted.

Earlier, on a trip to New York, Griffin had gone to a fund-raising rally for Henry Wallace and the Progressive Party at Madison Square Garden. The continuing scourge of racial violence in the South was brought up by Wallace, who blasted in particular the brazen murders of four young blacks in Walton County, Georgia. When the money buckets were passed around, Griffin put in a ten-dollar bill folded with a note of support from "a white native of Walton County"—not so much because he was wild about Wallace, but because he was angered by the willingness of far too many Southern whites to tolerate and excuse criminal atrocities in their midst.

It was when he got back home from these Northern forays that John Griffin realized how long and difficult the road to reform would be. Henry Wallace clearly didn't have a ghost of a chance to win, and Harry Truman was in serious trouble too. The Dixiecrat movement was in full cry, and anticommunism was blending and merging with the militant philosophy of states' rights. The mood of the white South was changing in 1948, growing more fixed and intransigent—but among black Southerners and elsewhere in the country, nothing seemed likely to extinguish the determination to secure the rights of citizenship. No matter who won the election, big changes were probably coming to the South and the nation—whether for better or worse, no one could say. In the interim, a feeling of uncertainty prevailed. The watchword was caution.

In times past, Griffin had felt at liberty to take a modest stand with others against racial and social injustice in Atlanta and across the South. He and a colleague who taught at Georgia Tech, Glenn Rainey, were active in the Committee for Georgia, the state-based affiliate of the Southern Conference for Human Welfare. They had taken part in protest demonstrations against the poll tax, and written letters to the local papers criticizing the reactionary behavior of Senator George and Governor Talmadge. They had worked for Governor Arnall's reform agenda, and made friends with social critics like Lillian Smith, and joined with others in urging Ralph McGill to favor more of the racial and social adjustments that the South so desperately needed. In the Southern Regional Council's ongoing internal debate over segregation, they sided with the anti–Jim Crow faction of blacks and white liberals.

But Griffin's boss at Emory, President Goodrich White—himself a former Rosenwald Fellow—had joined with other dissenting members of the Truman Commission on Higher Education in the fall of 1947 to record his opposition to desegregation of Southern colleges and universities. Griffin didn't have to be told to be less critical, less visible, less liberal; the danger in not doing so was all too obvious. "White didn't warn me," he recalled, "but others did. In spite of some positive signs here and there, I knew—everybody knew—that the side favoring segregation was getting stronger."

All across the South before the election of 1948, events pointed to the unmistakable rise of race relations as a primary and continuing social issue. Before that, going all the way back to the early thirties and beyond, it was a subject more often treated by indirection, if not outright denial. But from this point on, it was to become the single most urgent and unyielding public issue—certainly for the South, and eventually for the nation. Before 1948, it was possible for Southerners, white and black, to operate on both sides of the question, or to avoid it altogether; after 1948, people were compelled more and more to take a stand on one side or the other, or else to abdicate their duty as citizens. Before, the South had looked backward, all the way to the antebellum era, for its moorings and its sense of direction; hereafter, it would have to look forward, toward a new and different future.

From a most unlikely source came a positive account of the progress that had been made in the previous three decades. "There can be no question but that the relations between American Negroes and the balance of the population in the United States have improved during the last generation," wrote W. E. B. Du Bois in *Phylon*, Atlanta University's social science journal. He went on to catalog some of the evidence, with particular reference to the South: the emergence of biracial groups such as the SRC and SCHW; the help of national foundations, religious bodies, labor unions, and organizations like the NAACP; the decline of lynching; the hiring of blacks as police officers in more than fifty Southern cities (Atlanta finally joined that list in 1948); a sharp increase in black voter participation following court rulings against white primaries; an increase in the number of black elected officials (including an NAACP lawyer, Oliver W. Hill, to the city council of Richmond from a majority-white district); and some improvement in schooling, health, housing, and employment.

"All this gives us hope and courage," Du Bois wrote. "Yet we know quite well that the race problem in the United States is not settled." Indeed it was not. After Judge J. Waties Waring's decision outlawing the white primary in South Carolina had been upheld by the appeals court and allowed to stand without further review by the U.S. Supreme Court in 1948, two of that state's congressmen, L. Mendel Rivers and William Jennings Bryan Dorn, introduced a resolution calling for Waring's impeachment. In a speech on the House floor, Rivers reached a level of unbalanced and uncontrolled hatred that had become all too common among Southern members of Congress. The judge, he shouted, was "as cold as a dead Eskimo in an abandoned igloo. . . . He should be removed by the force of a boot . . . he is a disgrace to the Federal judiciary of South Carolina. . . . Every lawyer in South Carolina lives in mortal fear of this monster. . . . Unless he is removed there will be bloodshed."

Slanderous abuse in this same extreme style was also being heaped upon Frank Porter Graham. Back in the president's chair at the University of North Carolina after the issuance of the civil rights committee report, he faced a barrage of mail for months concerning his service on the committee. Some of the letters expressed "heartfelt appreciation" or "abiding thanks" for his contribution, but the vast majority were critical, and many were mean. A few newspapers, including the Winston-Salem *Journal & Sentinel* and the Norfolk *Virginian-Pilot*, were supportive of him; others were more in line with the Wilmington *News*, which advised Graham to "stop playing God." He dutifully and patiently responded to almost all of his mail, including a letter that said, "You are not worthy to live in the South. You have precipitated and agitated more assault, more rape and more bloodshed than the South has ever seen."

When his old friend Gerald W. Johnson of the Baltimore *Sun* wrote to complain that "the advocates of social equality are using political means to deal with an ethical problem" when they should be appealing to conscience rather than the courts, Graham gave him a thoughtful and incisive two-page reply. He found himself "in the midst of a crossfire" between "dogmatists on each side." He expressed admiration and support for President Truman for his stand on civil rights, federal aid to schools, and other issues. And, to the point of the racial issue itself, Frank Graham wrote:

> Our Negro fellow citizens are taking seriously the propaganda and preachments of two world wars: self-determination of peoples to make the world safe for democracy, and the war against Nazism and the preconceptions of a master race. With advancing education, the ideas

of the Declaration of Independence, the Bill of Rights, Lincoln's Gettysburg address . . . and the four freedoms of Franklin D. Roosevelt are bearing fruit in the minds and aspirations of the present generation, white and colored. The young people in the churches are asking direct questions about the teachings of Jesus concerning all men as brothers and sons of God. The majority of students in a large number of Southern colleges and universities are quite ready for the admission of Negroes in the colleges, especially in the graduate and professional schools in those fields for which no provision is made by the State for Negro students. However, boards of trustees [including his own] are just now more adamant in their resistance to such attitudes. This more stubborn resistance was precipitated by the storm and fury of the civil rights discussions and misrepresentations.

Some think that when the present furor subsides that the old ways will continue to prevail. This is a mistaken view. There is, of course, always an ebb and flow in human movements, but the democratic currents . . . move eventually onward to the larger sea.

Frank Graham saw the whole canvas—the spirit of liberty and the spirit of defiance. Both his heart and his head told him what few other Southern white leaders were ready to acknowledge: that nothing could keep the black minority from rising with the flow of the democratic current.

The opening of state university graduate and professional schools to black applicants was proceeding slowly across the Southern and border states as a direct consequence of federal court orders. A U.S. Supreme Court ruling in 1948 compelled the state of Oklahoma to provide Ada Sipuel, a black plaintiff, with a chance to get a law education, and other cases were pending in Texas, Oklahoma, and Delaware. Then, in Arkansas, the first step toward voluntary change was taken with surprising ease.

President Lewis W. Jones of the University of Arkansas, reading the legal handwriting on the wall, persuaded his board of trustees to admit three black applicants in 1948—Silas Hunt and Jack Shropshire to the law school and Edith Mae Irby to the medical school. (The previous year, Jones had defended segregation when he signed the minority report of the Truman higher education commission.) Irby, a recent graduate of Knoxville College, decided on her own to apply for medical school in her home state. The school's dean, H. Clay Chenault, noted that she was from Hot Springs (that was his hometown too), and he convinced Jones that it would be better to lower the barriers for her than to wait for a court order. Governor Ben Laney bitterly resented the university decision—"They pushed a white boy aside for this Negro," he fumed—but Jones and Chenault had anticipated his complaint and increased the size of the entering class from ninety to ninety-one students. Segregation laws compelled Irby to find lodging and meals apart from her classmates (Little Rock black-newspaper publisher Daisy Bates helped her in that), but her classroom and laboratory experiences were free of discrimination, and she graduated in 1952 in the upper half of her class.

Harry Ashmore had been in Little Rock only a few months when the university-desegregation vote was taken. The decision was duly noted on the front page of the *Arkansas Gazette,* and Ashmore expressed approval in a low-key editorial. "I was convinced that desegregation was inevitable," he wrote later, "and I saw the *Gazette's* mission as alerting the community" to prepare for what was certain to be a difficult adjustment.

In North Carolina, Jonathan Daniels was coming to the same conclusion. Back from Washington to run the Raleigh *News & Observer* after the death of his father, he was a Harry Truman partisan, as would be expected of the President's former press secretary. Daniels was also serving on a United Nations subcommission on human rights, and that experience added further to his growing belief that white prejudice, not any real or imagined condition of black inferiority, was the root cause of discrimination. He backed into a qualified defense of the civil rights committee report and Truman's proposals based on it. He attacked the Dixiecrats as "bush league secessionists," and warned the South that the nation "cannot wait forever for local action to end violence, inequality and disenfranchisement." Even so, Daniels stopped short of calling for the dismemberment or death of Jim Crow, insisting instead that simple justice and fair play were the objectives. Like most other Southern white liberals of the time, he separated political and economic rights from social rights. The latter were not defined or specified; he simply dismissed them as an irrelevant false alarm in the present debate.

Across the line in South Carolina, the most compelling journalistic voice would have been John Henry McCray's, had there been enough people to hear him. The few thousand subscribers to his *Lighthouse & Informer* were treated to a weekly education in the nefarious ways of white politicians. The paper was also a primer for blacks who wanted to take the political (as opposed to religious or litigious or conciliatory or revolutionary) route to equality. With his fellow instigator Osceola McKaine no longer on the scene, McCray threw himself into the newspaper, the NAACP, and the Progressive Democratic Party of South Carolina with obsessive abandon. Those three causes were so closely intertwined as to be one and the same to McCray. After the white primary was outlawed once and for all, he and the NAACP and the PDP got 30,000 of the 35,000 registered black voters in the state to go to the polls in the August primary in 1948.

Predictably, the Virginians were more restrained and dispassionate. But even as Virginius Dabney was receiving a Pulitzer Prize for his editorials in 1948, he had grown so disenchanted with all four major presidential candidates that it was hard to tell whether he would mark his own ballot for any of them. Truman, Dewey, and Wallace had all moved so far to Dabney's left—or he to their right—that he and the *Times-Dispatch* could offer little except negative commentary. And, since Thurmond had not succeeded in luring Harry Byrd out of the Democratic tent, the Richmond papers weren't about to venture out either. The *News Leader*, in the twilight of Douglas Southall Freeman's long tenure, gave over most of its editorial columns to the subject of civil rights as the fall election campaign was drawing to a close. The paper's conclusion: Segregation will continue in most dimensions of Southern life, whether it's fair or not; that may be too bad, but that's how it is. And in the campaign, no endorsement: "The choice is between evils, known and unknown."

Over in Norfolk, Louis I. Jaffé of the *Virginian-Pilot* seemed much less bothered by Truman and the civil rights issue, but found little to attract him to the President overall—and anyway, he wrote, Dewey was "certain to be elected President by a large popular majority," with Truman and Thurmond dividing the scraps. (As it turned out, Truman carried the state by a comfortable margin, with Thurmond a distant third.)

The white liberals in Georgia, and their black allies as well, were strung out along a continuum that stretched from Lillian Smith on the left to Ralph McGill on the right. Smith's views were expressed in a long letter published in the *New York Times* early in April of 1948. "I cannot be heard in Georgia," she complained, "even in the letter columns"—to which the *Constitution* replied in a snippy note on its letters page, "We have no record or recollection of ever having received a letter from her."

In tone and content, Smith's message in the *Times* was at least as hard on liberals as on reactionaries. "Georgia, U.S.A., still has a lot in common with Georgia, USSR," she wrote, citing one-party totalitarian rule as an indicator. But that didn't explain why Southern liberalism "maintains its old grim silence" while the demagogues, with "the same tricks Stalin uses," give their docile masses "an external enemy to hate (the damyankee), an internal enemy to fear (the Negro)," and an iron curtain to hide the mess from public view. "It is only the liberal who can win against the demagogue, whether Fascist or Communist," she declared. But, she continued, while the demagogues are "fanning hate, giving the green light to violence by their almost traitorous incitements against their own national government [the liberals], stand by silently," leaving the way open for the

Communists to exploit the situation. "It is our caution, our lack of energy, our moral impotence and our awful if unconscious snobbery, that make demagoguery unafraid of liberalism," she concluded. "We just don't love human freedom enough to take real risks for it."

Ralph McGill hated communism too, but that didn't bring him any closer to Lillian Smith, whom he ignored in public and dismissed in private as a shrill, meddlesome radical. Though he ridiculed the Dixiecrats, McGill also kept up his attacks on the NAACP and Walter White, the Southern Conference for Human Welfare, Henry Wallace, and the civil rights program of President Truman—particularly the call for a permanent federal agency to ensure and enforce fair employment practices.

More revealing, though, were the Atlanta editor's articles in national magazines such as *The Saturday Evening Post*. There, he sounded much more like a regular liberal Democrat. "Examination reveals the Truman recommendations, aside from the FEPC, to be relatively mild," he wrote in the *Post* in May of 1948. "It is highly probable that had not the South reacted so immediately and with such violence, Negro leaders and organizations would have protested the proposals as weak and mealymouthed." Few Southerners seemed to realize, McGill said, that with the opening up of the ballot to blacks, "the Supreme Court has already smashed the old political pattern. No amount of feudal party loyalty will put it back together again."

Between McGill and Smith, Georgians who longed for the South to face up to its caste and class and color problems tried to find some program to follow that they could think of as neither a suicidal sellout to the left nor a reactionary cop-out to the right. The only such program around, and the one that almost all the liberals finally embraced (including, ironically, both McGill and Smith), was the national Democratic Party that Harry Truman would lead into battle in November. That's also where most of the Southerners writing for national publications came out, including Henry Lesesne in the New York *Herald-Tribune*, Thomas Stokes in his syndicated column from Washington, and Helen Fuller and Thomas Sancton in *The New Republic*. Sancton said the Dixiecrats, in mounting "a challenge as serious as the Populist movement" of the 1890s, were intent upon "making a cruel amalgam of the Russian question and the race question."

Alabama's traditional liberals were so fragmented that they made their Georgia neighbors seem like one big happy family. At one end stood the backsliding John Temple Graves, the Birmingham columnist who had introduced Hugo Black at the first Southern Conference for Human Welfare meeting; his pitch now was a reactionary call for Southern politicians to "seize the balance of national power" by bolting from the Democratic Party and holding out for concessions to preserve and protect white supremacy. "This is the witching hour," he wrote. "Not since the War Between the States has there been such an opportunity" for the Southern ruling class to prevail.

And at the other end was Aubrey Williams, the New Deal Populist turned publisher. In Montgomery, he and another native Alabamian, editor Gould Beech, bankrolled by a couple of wealthy Northerners, Marshall Field and James P. Warburg, had given the sagging *Southern Farmer* a new lease on life. The monthly tabloid was now an entertaining farm-family magazine and a liberal political journal rolled into one, and its paid circulation soared to more than a million copies. At first critical of Truman for his anti-Soviet foreign policy and his domestic surveillance of federal employees, the paper came around to support the President in the 1948 election. (The fifty-fifty partnership of Williams and Beech had broken up, in the meantime, because of financial and personal differences.)

It was Truman's stand on civil rights, more than any other single factor, that kept Williams in the Democratic camp, much to the consternation of friends like Virginia Foster Durr, who was a protest candidate for the U.S. Senate on the Progressive ticket in Virginia that fall. Even Williams's collegiate sons, Aubrey Junior and Morrison, were actively working for Wallace. But the elder Williams had long considered race relations the South's paramount problem, and because of that he wouldn't desert Truman. "The central evil in the South is segregation," he editorialized in the *Farmer*. "Until decent Southerners face this fact, little progress will be made toward solving any other problem in the South." The same deep concern had also drawn him back into an active role in the Southern Conference for Human Welfare in 1946, and when the SCHW folded in 1948, Williams ended up as president of its surviving subsidiary, the Southern Conference Educational Fund.

To Hodding Carter in Mississippi, the abolition of segregation was still unthinkable. Sounding on almost every point like his friend Ralph McGill, he criticized the secessionist talk of the Dixiecrats, opposed the Klan and other white extremist groups, prodded the states to invest heavily in a good-faith effort to make separate truly equal, and insisted that the South was making progress in race relations and would correct its problems without federal coercion. Mississippi politicians ganged up on the hot-tempered Carter more viciously than the Georgians attacked McGill, and he answered their fire with hot lead of his own. Unlike McGill, the Greenville editor said he would "likely turn Republican" if the GOP chose Dwight Eisenhower as its nominee. After Ike said no, Carter hoped the

Democrats would draft the general in place of Truman, and when that failed, he said Dewey—"the best of the candidates"—would win easily.

In Oxford, Mississippi, far from the sound and fury of the 1948 political campaign, the reclusive and enigmatic William Faulkner finished his latest novel just as the dogwoods and azaleas brought a blaze of color to the woods around Rowan Oak, his home. *Intruder in the Dust*, his first book in six years ("a blazing novel about murder and violence in a small Southern town," the dust jacket proclaimed), would soon prove to be his most commercially successful effort to date. His Hollywood connections had secured the sale of movie rights before publication. Was this Faulkner for a mass audience? Not quite. Was it Faulkner in a studied attempt to be current and contemporary? Perhaps. Was it Faulkner in a struggle with his own conscience and the conscience of the South? Undoubtedly. Others before him had been driven by the urge to decipher the South, to plumb its depths and explain them to whoever would listen. The Vanderbilt Agrarians Richard Wright, William Alexander Percy, W. J. Cash, Lillian Smith, and others had all tried, in vastly different ways, to say what it was, what it meant. Faulkner, too, had tried, but never this directly.

Intruder in the Dust is a tightly strung murder mystery about an elderly black farmer accused of murdering a lower-class white man, about the efforts of certain others to unravel the crime and prevent a lynching, and about a garrulous, paternalistic old white lawyer whose instinct is to defend the accused. Interspersed with the action are lengthy conversations, mainly between the lawyer and his sixteen-year-old nephew, whose role in the climax of the case is pivotal. In these rambling exchanges, the lawyer—and, we are tempted to assume, Faulkner himself—clearly shows his own mixed emotions about the South's racial crucible.

"I'm writing about people, not trying to express my own opinion," the author told an interviewer in Japan after the book was out—but he added that *Intruder* would be a good place for someone reading his works to begin, because it "deals with the problem which is important not only in my country, but, I think, important to all people."

As in all of Faulkner's complex prose, there are many twists and turns. At one point, the lawyer, Gavin Stevens, ruminates about his client, Lucas Beauchamp, in such a way that the two men come to represent not just themselves but the whole South, white and black. Finally, Stevens says:

> We—he and us—should confederate: swap him the rest of the economic and political and cultural privileges which are his right, for the reversion of his capacity to wait and endure and survive. Then we

would prevail; together we would dominate the United States; we would present a front not only impregnable but not even to be threatened by a mass of people who no longer have anything in common save a frantic greed for money and a basic fear of a failure of national character which they hide from one another behind a loud lip service to a flag.

And then, near the end of the drama, as Stevens and his nephew try to puzzle out what has happened, the lawyer delivers this impassioned homily:

> Some things you must always be unable to bear. Injustice and outrage and dishonor and shame. No matter how young you are or how old you have got. Not for kudos and not for cash: your picture in the paper nor money in the bank either. Just refuse to bear them.

It was Faulkner the scout, the explorer, formulating his report to the advancing South, telling us in lines too cryptic for our understanding—or his—what was waiting just over the mountain.

10. *Truman's Triumph*

For Harry S. Truman, the big fight was almost at hand, and though he came to it gamely, bravely, there was no denying that the pugnacious little bantamweight from Missouri was facing overwhelming odds. The clash was shaping up less like a championship match in the ring than a mugging in the street. Henry Wallace and the leftists had broken off in one direction, Strom Thurmond and the rightists in another. A. Philip Randolph was threatening massive civil disobedience by blacks against continued segregation in the armed forces, even as Russia's blockade of Berlin raised the specter of a military conflict. First the Republicans and then the Democrats had tried to draft General Eisenhower for a tour of duty in the White House, and the GOP had gone on to pick Thomas Dewey and Earl Warren from its progressive wing to deliver the knockout blow to an already staggered and bleeding stand-in president, the candidate nobody wanted.

The weather was appropriately stormy and steamy when the Democrats arrived in Philadelphia on July 12, and there was no air-conditioning in the convention hall to soothe their frayed nerves and hot tempers. The liberal Americans for Democratic Action, led by brash young Hubert H. Humphrey, the mayor of Minneapolis, promised to beef up the platform committee's civil rights plank—partly to counter a mild statement by the Republicans on that subject, and partly to tighten the screws on Truman, whom the ADA had wanted to throw overboard for Ike.

From a lackluster beginning, enlivened only by Senator Alben Barkley's rousing keynote address, the convention stumbled into a dreaded Wednesday-afternoon showdown on civil rights, with the battle lines drawn in three or four directions. Finally, after a bitter floor fight, the liberals prevailed—and in the end it was Humphrey, borrowing specifics from the pages of Truman's own civil rights committee report, who carried the day with a ringing exhortation "for the Democratic Party to get out of the shadow of states' rights and walk forthrightly in the bright sunshine of human rights."

Three attempts to soften the plank with amendments failed, and then the convention voted by a narrow margin to adopt the ADA version and put the party on record with the strongest pledge of racial equality it had ever made. With that, all of the Mississippi delegation and half of Alabama's stalked out into a drenching rainstorm on the hard sidewalks of Philadelphia.

The carefully orchestrated walkout would be remembered years later by one of those who departed, Mississippi newspaper publisher J. Oliver Emmerich, as an ill-advised acting out of the late Senator Bilbo's "cotton-field philosophy" of aggressive and obsessive racism. It was not just lower-class whites—"the rednecks, the coonasses, and the hillbillies"—who were fueling the Dixiecrat revolt, said Emmerich; it was "the political elite as well," and they deserved much of the blame. Without the money and power of "the most prestigious and responsible leaders of the Deep South," this second futile attempt at secession from the national consensus probably wouldn't have happened at all—and if it hadn't, perhaps the rebellion of the ensuing quarter-century might also have been resolved more constructively.

Strom Thurmond stayed in the hall to second the nomination of Senator Richard Russell of Georgia, the only remaining challenger to a Truman victory (and a hopeless one at that). Except for thirteen North Carolina delegates who voted for the President—and a lone maverick from Florida—all of the remaining Southerners threw in with Russell, but they were alone in their protest. It was past midnight when the formal balloting confirmed, by better than three to one, what the party had known when the long day started: that Harry S. Truman would carry the flag in November.

Thurmond had emerged as one of the States' Rights Party's probable nominees in the autumn free-for-all, and as he left the hostile North for Birmingham and the promised Saturday convention of the new rebel party, he was still seething over the disagreeable turn of events. First, John H. McCray and his Progressive Democratic Party of South Carolina had embarrassed the governor by showing up in Philadelphia with an all-black delegation and raising a credentials challenge against the white party regulars. Then, back home, federal judge J. Waties Waring had refused once and for all to let those same South Carolina white Democrats lock black voters out of the upcoming primary election. And to top it all off, there was Harry Truman, a "half-breed" Southerner and a traitor to the cause of white supremacy, crowing in proud satisfaction over his deliverance of the Dixie delegates into exile. (But Franklin Roosevelt had made many of the same promises of justice and equal opportunity to the blacks, a reporter reminded Thurmond; what was now so different and disturbing about Truman's civil rights rhetoric? The governor shot back quickly and angrily: "Truman really means it.")

With the old Kentucky warhorse Alben Barkley at his side, the once and future President finally emerged from a smoky, stuffy back room at the Philadelphia convention hall shortly before two o'clock in the morning to accept his party's reluctantly proffered nomination.

They should replay the scene time and time again for today's media specialists and public-relations experts and campaign consultants, just to show them what hell is really like. Picture this: The far right has decamped to Birmingham, and the left hasn't shown up at all; the most primitive television facilities imaginable have done almost nothing but heat up the hall with blazing lights; the interminable process of nominating and seconding and voting creeps in its petty pace from tedium to apathy; most Americans and even a great many of the delegates have long since given up and gone to bed; the remaining friends and enemies of an unpopular President wait in marginally sober judgment of the man, for whom they lack both confidence and enthusiasm.

As the band goes "Wild About Harry" and placards bob lackadaisically in the exhausted crowd, floodlights focus on a floral Liberty Bell display suspended high above the floor. At the climactic moment, forty-eight white pigeons—low-budget substitutes for doves of peace, one for each state in the Union—fly free from a cage inside the bell. Having been cooped up in the stifling pen for hours, the liberated birds are disoriented and delirious; they come bursting like crazed bats into the cavernous hall, careening and crying, fluttering and defecating, in frenzied confusion. Some of them fly into the huge fans that stir the stale, humid air; others swoop close to presiding officer Sam Rayburn, and he swings his gavel to ward them off. (One of the birds was later said to have left its calling card on Rayburn's bald pate; the stone-faced Texan never saw anything funny in the apocryphal tale.)

And just then, onto this surrealistic stage of comic madness steps a smiling Harry Truman, dapperly dressed in a white linen suit and white shoes, as cool and confident as a Broadway hoofer, lacking only the hat and cane to fit the part. And here begins what one clever wag would call "the greatest comeback since Lazarus."

His acceptance speech was pithy, pungent, stinging, and blessedly short, delivered off the cuff, without text or notes. He blasted the Republicans, ignored the Progressives and Dixiecrats, extolled the virtues of the Democrats, and vowed that he and Barkley would win the fight against "the common enemy." Then, in the first of many surprise maneuvers he would pull out of his hat during the campaign, Truman announced that he was calling the Republican-controlled Congress into special session ten days hence (that would be Turnip Day in agrarian Missouri, a time to sow, wet or dry) to deal with inflation, the housing crisis, aid to education, and civil rights—all issues the Republicans "are saying they are for in their platform."

The crowd went wild. Just when he seemed to be finished, their little fighter was up off the canvas, bobbing and weaving around the ring, throwing fresh punches. Miraculously, he had found his second wind.

Not since the Southern Conference for Human Welfare's first meeting there, ten years earlier, had so many people jammed and wedged themselves into Birmingham's Municipal Auditorium. It was Saturday morning, July 17, 1948, and the overflow crowd of more than six thousand white Southerners had come to carry out their threat of rebellion against Harry Truman and the Democratic Party's national hierarchy. The States' Rights Democrats, as the rebels liked to call themselves (or Dixiecrats, as the press had taken to calling them), had come steaming down from Philadelphia filled with righteous indignation and hostile intent. Their party had been stolen from them, their leaders bitterly complained; now it was time to strike back.

They were a curious hybrid of somebodies and nobodies, bosses and "hands," the powerful and the impotent. Those who wheeled and dealed and tossed out quotable quotes to the press were mostly politicians, lawyers, planters, bankers, mill owners, oilmen; those who shouted the rebel yells of approval were laboring-class wage-earners and middle-level managers whose deepest anxieties were more economic—and perhaps more racial—than political. All eleven of the Southern states plus Kentucky, Oklahoma, and Maryland had delegations in the hall, and a scattered few others were there from Pennsylvania, Illinois, California, and elsewhere. There were no blacks at all, of course, and very few women. One of the

Birmingham papers described the convention as having "all the pent-up fever of a giant, boisterous revival meeting."

The governors of Alabama, Mississippi, Arkansas, South Carolina, and Virginia were all on hand. Mississippi was also represented by both of its senators, James Eastland and John Stennis, and by most of its members of the House of Representatives; no other state—not even Alabama, the host—had a delegation of its congressional members in the hall. (Jim Folsom did deliver a greeting and some vague words of encouragement, but the Alabama governor, who had briefly touted his own candidacy against Truman, was considered too unpredictable for any faction to embrace.) Among the Birmingham notables present were two men who had figured prominently in that first Southern Conference gathering ten years earlier: newspaper columnist John Temple Graves, now a born-again Dixiecrat, and "Bull" Connor, the arch-segregationist police commissioner (and a leader of the delegate walkout in Philadelphia). Also in on the Philadelphia and Birmingham proceedings was a young country lawyer and member of the Alabama legislature named George Corley Wallace.

Three men who played central roles in this meeting and the subsequent activities of the States' Rights Party were Walter Sillers, speaker of the house of representatives in Mississippi; Horace Wilkinson, a right-wing Birmingham lawyer; and Gessner T. McCorvey, state chairman of the Democratic Party in Alabama. Sillers headed a solid phalanx of Mississippi public officials who had cast their lot with the rebels. Wilkinson and McCorvey had no such consensus in Alabama, but their control of the Democratic Party was virtually absolute. In defiance of party loyalists, including Governor Folsom and Senators Lister Hill and John Sparkman, they conspired to put before the Alabama voters a November election ballot that listed the States' Rights Party ticket under the traditional Democratic rooster emblem—and excluded the Truman-Barkley slate altogether.

Former Alabama Governor Frank M. Dixon opened the convention with a saber-rattling keynote address that set the tone for what followed. Truman's civil rights offensive was a blatant attempt to destroy the South, he cried, "to reduce us to the status of a mongrel, inferior race." When he vowed to fight this new wave of Yankee invaders, the crowd erupted in a frenzied roar of approval, and the tumult grew louder and more uncontrolled as the day went on. The morning line favored Dixon or Arkansas Governor Ben Laney or Mississippi Governor Fielding Wright as the presidential candidate, with Strom Thurmond for vice president, but by afternoon the Dixon and Laney fortunes had fallen. A consensus materialized around a ticket led by Thurmond, with Wright as his running mate.

The delegates roared their approval on the first ballot. Senator Eastland predicted a two-man race between Thurmond and Thomas Dewey. And what about Truman? Why, he "won't carry a single state," the Mississippian predicted.

For all their unity in mounting this opposition drive, the Southern anti-Truman Democrats were seriously divided on a key point of strategy. All of the Mississippians, some of the Alabamians, and a few others were driven by philosophical and ideological extremism to declare their undying hostility to the Democratic Party for its overtures to blacks and other "undesirables." Many others, while sharing those racial views, doubted that a secessionist third-party movement could be successful, and preferred instead to simply lock their states' electoral college votes in a "ransom" account—available, if needed, as bargaining chips to break a Democrat-Republican deadlock. All of Georgia's political leaders, including Senators Richard Russell and Walter George and the gubernatorial front-runner, Herman Talmadge, steered clear of the Dixiecrat rebellion for just such doubts and fears as these, and so did Virginia's Senator Harry Byrd. The same thinking may have led Ben Laney to withdraw from consideration as a party candidate. Governors William Tuck of Virginia and Beauford Jester of Texas, two of the early cheerleaders for a rebellious third party, also backed away from the movement.

Strom Thurmond, exceedingly ambitious and opportunistic, was prepared to go either way. In considering the possible consequences of third-party leadership, he had to weigh whether it would help or hurt him if he decided to challenge South Carolina's Olin D. Johnston for his U.S. Senate seat in 1950. Concluding that he would in all likelihood gain favor with white voters in South Carolina no matter how the 1948 race turned out, Thurmond readily accepted the Dixiecrat nomination.

His strategy was, first, to raise the specter of a black invasion of the South's lily-white temples of segregation—churches, schools, theaters, swimming pools, bedrooms—and then, denying racial motivation, to "defend as a matter of principle" what he described as a federal assault on states' rights. In his acceptance speech, Thurmond repeated his crowd-pleasing line that there were "not enough troops in the army" to force desegregation down the throats of the white South. To reporters, he would say over and over that he wasn't preoccupied with white supremacy—what really worried him were the dangers of "police state tactics . . . a federal gestapo . . . a totalitarian state and . . . the threat of Communist infiltration." Meanwhile, Fielding Wright, a true believer in white supremacy, would be free to carry heavier weapons, and to fire them at will.

The throng of Dixiecrat partisans quickly finished their work inside the

Birmingham auditorium, and they were in boisterous high spirits when they came pouring out onto the Eighth Avenue sidewalk in the late afternoon sunshine. Soon they were heading for home or for the party's headquarters at the Tutwiler Hotel, a few blocks away. There the rump-session festivities were kicked off with as much lighthearted camaraderie as a football crowd might generate, and the parties went on far into the night.

It remained for a strike force of anonymous individuals, acting under a cloak of secrecy in behalf of all Dixiecrat partisans, to climax the evening with a chillingly familiar ritual of symbolic terror. Sometime after dark, a dummy wearing a Harry Truman name tag was lowered from the hotel balcony above Twentieth Street, suspended by a noose around its neck. TRUMAN KILLED BY CIVIL-RIGHT read a crudely lettered sign pinned to the dummy's coat. The mock lynching of the President of the United States was a visible reminder to the South, and to all who watched from afar, that this was no game; this was war. The spirit of white supremacy—to some an inspiration, to uncounted others a shame and a curse— was alive and well in Birmingham.

A few more pieces had to slip into place before the fall lineup would be complete. In the last week of July, the Progressive Citizens of America met in Philadelphia and formally nominated Henry A. Wallace for president and Idaho Senator Glen H. Taylor for vice president. Clark Foreman, head of the then-moribund Southern Conference for Human Welfare, served as the party treasurer and a chief strategist; C. B. "Beanie" Baldwin of Virginia, a former director of the Farm Security Administration, was the campaign manager. Wallace received with mixed emotions his subsequent endorsement by the Communist Party, U.S.A. Then, when the labor movement cut its ties to the Progressives and both the CIO and the AFL refused to give him their support, the maverick Midwesterner must have known that his liberal revolt was not going to get very far. But that would not keep him from running hard.

Norman Thomas, onetime boy wonder and now the grand old man of the Socialist Party, signed on for his sixth and last symbolic try for the White House, and a scattering of tiny splinter parties came in too. Finally, in the dog days of a blistering late summer and fall, the presidential sweepstakes began in earnest.

When the Turnip Congress was called to order by its Republican leaders on July 26, Harry Truman was out sowing his victory garden, and it promised to yield a bushel of surprises. To begin, he chose that same Monday as the day to sign two executive orders, one declaring a policy of nondiscrimination in federal employment and the other requiring "equality of treatment and opportunity for all persons in the armed services."

Almost everyone was caught off guard. Thomas Dewey, sitting on a huge lead in the polls, said little, having decided to follow a cautious, hands-off strategy on civil rights issues. Henry Wallace, whose party had explicitly condemned "segregation and discrimination in all of its forms and in all places," denounced the Truman move as "an empty gesture," but it clearly stole the Progressives' thunder. As for Strom Thurmond and the Dixiecrats, they were left to thrash about in helpless rage, outfoxed and outflanked once again by their adversary in the White House. Even A. Philip Randolph was unprepared for the announcement, and though he wasn't convinced that the President was sincere, he did announce in mid-August that his threatened civil disobedience campaign had been called off.

On the second day of the special session, Truman appeared before both houses to tell the lawmakers what he hoped they would accomplish in the two weeks set aside for their deliberations. Housing and inflation topped the President's list, but he also mentioned civil rights high up on a longer slate of concerns. Before him as he spoke sat a sullen audience dominated by the controlling Republicans and the small but powerful bloc of Southern Democrats, both of whom would have gone to any lengths to deprive him of a victory—as Truman knew all too well.

Neither he nor the minority of liberals who supported his proposals had any illusions of solid accomplishment coming from this brief assembly. It was politics, pure and simple—an elaborate charade, a parlor game called "Democracy at Work." The trick was done with smoke and mirrors, and all the players knew the secret, the hidden answer; only the audience was in the dark. As in a game of chess, a certain protocol was observed, an obligatory order of act and response. First the President moved; then the Republicans countered with a foredoomed piece of legislation (in this instance, a bill to abolish the poll tax); then the Southerners filibustered, and all efforts to limit debate were futile. Quick as a wink, the two weeks were up and it was time to adjourn. Thereafter, at every stop on the campaign trail, each candidate blamed the others for the predictable stalemate that all but Henry Wallace had helped to bring about.

Even though Dewey remained comfortably ahead in the polls, neither he nor the other two major challengers ever seemed able to knock Truman off his game. He played the advantage of incumbency to perfection. When his opponents accused him of being too aggressively hawkish in his posture toward the Soviets, his supporters countered by pointing to the Berlin airlift as a humanitarian peacekeeping mission. Domestic alarm over Communist infiltration—an epidemic of hysteria that the President himself had fed with his order mandating employee loyalty investigations—focused more critically on Henry Wallace and the House Un-American Activities Committee than it did on Truman.

Just three days before the Progressives opened their nominating convention, twelve members of the Communist Party, U.S.A. were indicted in New York under the Smith Act, a broad 1940 statute that made it unlawful for any person to advocate or teach the overthrow of the government by force or violence. The timing of the arrests was said by more than one critic to have been orchestrated by the President, but he heatedly denied it. Both Attorney General Tom Clark and FBI Director J. Edgar Hoover were clearly to the right of Truman on the issue of communism, and so were Thomas Dewey and Strom Thurmond; Wallace's alignment on the opposite flank conveniently made the President appear, once again, to be safely anchored in the center.

He was accused of playing politics on the military desegregation order, too—and as far as his timing was concerned, there can be little doubt that he acted with one eye on the campaign. But who saw any political advantage in taking the initiative on such a controversial issue? A 1946 national opinion survey had found that two-thirds of all white Americans believed blacks were already being treated fairly in the society at large. Congress passed a new Selective Service Act in June 1948 that left segregation in place, and Truman signed it into law. Southerners in both houses were fighting tooth and nail against any modification in the racial rules of the armed forces, and most of the military top brass were also dragging their feet on the issue. Just about the only person pressing Truman to take action was A. Philip Randolph—a forceful and persuasive man, to be sure, but not one who wielded great power. Some of the President's advisers did see political capital to be made from a liberal stance on race, but prudence might have led them to suggest waiting until after the election to take Jim Crow out of uniform.

But on the substance of the issue, Truman was completely in accord with several convincing points of fact and logic: Racial discrimination was America's Achilles' heel in the struggle against communism; segregation was tremendously wasteful and inefficient, and nowhere was that more apparent than in the armed forces; the civil rights committee had recommended a year earlier that the government "end immediately all discrimination and segregation based on race" in the military; and, having triumphed in a war with foes who lived by a master-race ideology, there was no way the United States could go on practicing such a philosophy itself. Whether or not these arguments made for smart politics or effective public policy in 1948, the commander-in-chief decided that he was ready to act on them. For a man who was looking like a double-digit loser in the polls, it was a bold decision.

The front-runner, ex-Governor Dewey of New York, was considered a progressive Republican—which was to say, well to the left of the Robert Taft wing of the party but still to the right of Truman. Dewey was a stiff, cool, polished little man with a self-important air that didn't endear him to the common folks. As far as the South was concerned in this election, he more or less wrote it off, concluding that Truman would get what Thurmond didn't. Nevertheless, the GOP had measurable support in Virginia, Florida, North Carolina, Kentucky, and Texas, and Dewey got some press endorsements in those states. The Houston and Dallas newspapers saw at least as much to like in Dewey as in Truman; the Richmond and Norfolk papers favored the Republican with compliments, if not with their formal blessing; Hodding Carter in Mississippi, after his pleas to Eisenhower were unavailing, eventually gave Dewey and the Republican Party a "soft" nod of approval. (Joe Louis, who earlier had lent his name to the cause of the Southern Conference for Human Welfare, also gave Dewey a celebrity endorsement.)

Henry Wallace's campaign attracted substantial support from the left flank of American politics, from liberal activists (including some Southerners) who felt that Truman had not been faithful to the Roosevelt legacy. In many ways, Wallace foreshadowed the effort of Eugene McCarthy twenty years later: a liberal Midwesterner trying against great odds to revive the spirit and promise of a fallen hero's unfinished dream. Racial equality was just one of Wallace's idealistic goals (and a latter-day one at that, since he had not had much to say on the subject until the last year or so of his vice presidency), but when he rode into the South on a campaign swing in late August, race was just about the only subject that he or anyone else seemed to have in mind.

For the first time, a candidate for president of the United States was going around the Deep South attacking segregation, one-party politics, and the denial of civil rights. Wallace wouldn't address segregated audiences or patronize segregated hotels and restaurants. His seven-state Southern tour was like a crusade in enemy territory, and he and his biracial campaign crew of young and dedicated associates got a taste of regional hostility that they would long remember. Southerners associated with the campaign—Palmer Weber of the CIO Political Action Committee, Louis Burnham of the Southern Negro Youth Congress, Virginia Durr of the National Committee to Abolish the Poll Tax, Clark Foreman of the Southern Conference for Human Welfare, Beanie Baldwin, and others— had seen it all before. Unseasoned Northerners, though, wondered if they had stumbled into a war zone.

"They were terrified," Weber told an interviewer forty years later. "They knew they had been to the edge of hell." In North Carolina on the first day, Wallace was pummeled with eggs and tomatoes. After witnessing a stabbing and several near-riots, some campaign strategists counseled retreat, but the candidate said no. On they went to Birmingham, where a welcoming party of club-toting whites jeered and heckled the motorcade; police stood by as the mob rocked the candidate's car and chanted, "Kill Wallace!" Still, when he finally stood before his audience, he told them that "greedy men, the Big Mules . . . have ruled the South for generations and kept millions of common people in economic poverty and political bondage." And the worst of it, he said flat-out, was race, "the major obstacle" to Southern progress: Segregation was not only an economic and political and social travesty—it was a sin, a violation of "the fundamental Christian and democratic principles in our civilization."

This courageous foray was an inspiration to black voters, Palmer Weber told Thurgood Marshall when the trip was over. The "Negro communities were electrified and tremendously heartened to see one white man with guts willing to take it standing up." A few Southern liberals and leftists, inspired by Wallace's willingness to face the lions, qualified as protest candidates in the Democratic primaries or on the Progressive Party ticket in the fall, among them Virginia Durr and Howard Carwile in Virginia and Joseph Rabun and James L. Barfoot in Georgia. (For his daring act, Barfoot, a University of Georgia professor, was promptly notified of his dismissal from the faculty.) In the end, though, the Progressive Party's campaign in the South had more to do with symbolism than substance; in November, Henry Wallace could muster fewer than four thousand votes in any Southern state except Florida, where he got about twelve thousand.

Strom Thurmond and his Dixiecrat ramblers had much bigger dreams in the South, and to some extent they were realized. Only in Alabama did they shove the President off the ballot, but in Mississippi, Louisiana, and South Carolina they got the States' Rights Democrats listed under the traditional sign of the Democratic Party, with the Truman-Barkley slate treated as a fringe tandem of interlopers. (It was thus no mere coincidence that those same four states all went to the Dixiecrats.) At the start of the campaign, every Southern senator except Claude Pepper was an ostensible ally of the third-party rebels, all twenty-one of them having gone on record in defense of states' rights and in unyielding opposition to the Truman civil rights program; every governor except the quicksilvery Jim Folsom was likewise committed—and even he had poked his head in at the Dixiecrat convention.

But getting them to denounce civil rights and proclaim states' rights was one thing; getting them to leave the comfort and safety of the Democratic

Party for a philosophically and geographically confined band of renegades on a suicide mission was something else altogether. Some of the more cynical "friends" of the movement, while applauding Strom Thurmond and Fielding Wright, were busy planning their own path to the exits. A few papers in the region supported the Dixiecrats, but many more were critical; even the Montgomery *Advertiser* could find no groundswell of support for the rebels, and predicted that the ticket would capture no more than sixty electoral votes—not enough to make a difference unless the contest was extremely close.

Doggedly, sometimes wildly, Thurmond pressed on. "I did not risk my life on the beaches of Normandy," he fulminated from the stump, "to come back to this country and sit idly by while a bunch of black politicians whittle away your heritage and mine." He and Wright grew ever more shrill and slanderous as the days dwindled down. They warned darkly that the Truman programs were communistic edicts to be enforced by "Gestapo-like agents," and characterized all of their opponents as totalitarians and subversives. When the end was near, practically all of the Southern politicians except the Mississippi diehards had tiptoed out, quietly covering their tracks as they left.

While he continued to insist that it was not race but states' rights that got his dander up, Thurmond's actions frequently proved otherwise. In midsummer he wrote to Governor William H. Hastie of the Virgin Islands, inviting him and his family to pay a visit to South Carolina and "be our guests at the Mansion." (Hastie, a prominent African-American official in the federal government since the early days of the New Deal, had been appointed to the Virgin Islands post in 1946, and was widely noted in the press as "the first and only Negro governor," but the news had somehow escaped Thurmond's notice.) Hastie replied with appreciation and reciprocated, inviting Thurmond and his family to the island territory. Inevitably, the letters got into the papers. "I would not have written him if I knew he was a Negro," Thurmond huffed tactlessly. "Of course, it would have been ridiculous to invite him."

President Truman suffered few such lapses. As the weeks slipped by, he seemed to be enjoying himself more and more. He didn't bang the drum for civil rights—in fact, he seldom brought it up at all, and except for brief stops in Oklahoma, Texas, Florida, North Carolina, and Kentucky, he stayed out of the South altogether. Thurmond and Wallace might as well not have existed, as far as Truman was concerned; he never so much as acknowledged their presence in the race. To hear him tell it, it was just him and "the other fellow," Dewey, whom he never called by name.

Crisscrossing the rest of the country by train, the President whistle-stopped like a man possessed. Some days he made fifteen or twenty speeches, relentlessly attacking "the other fellow" and the "do-nothing Congress" with such give-'em-hell gusto that his large and growing audiences shouted for more, loving nothing so much as an entertaining aggressor—or to hear the truth, as Truman liked to say. Alben Barkley did most of his traveling by airplane—he called it the first "prop-hop" campaign—and his great skill as a storyteller blended smoothly with Truman's folksy manner. The ticket picked up vocal support from Eleanor Roosevelt, Mary McLeod Bethune, Will Alexander, Aubrey Williams, and other New Deal stalwarts—and quiet but solid backing from Walter White of the ostensibly nonpartisan NAACP (providing the last straw of estrangement between him and W. E. B. Du Bois, a Henry Wallace backer).

Still, the Eastern establishment looked condescendingly upon the Democratic heartlanders as a couple of backcountry rubes, and the pollsters and the press said their quest was doomed. Professional gamblers offered odds of 15 and 30 to 1 against them. In Hollywood, Truman got a boost from such stars as Frank Sinatra (another former Southern Conference backer) and Ronald Reagan, but a much larger group of celebrities stood up with the Republicans. Most of the big newspapers in the East and Midwest and West endorsed Dewey. The Washington *Post* was for Truman, but said in a front-page story on Election Day that Dewey was "a sure winner," and editorialized that "it would be a miracle" if the President pulled out a victory. In the South, Truman got the nod of leading papers in Louisville, Atlanta, Nashville, Chattanooga, Raleigh, Little Rock, St. Petersburg, Miami, and a few other places, but they weren't exactly wild about Harry—and many others were downright hostile.

In his own mind and heart, Truman was completely convinced that he would win, or so he led everyone to believe. He stuck to his guns: Attack the Republicans and Congress, ignore the other candidates, campaign close to the people, defend your own liberal record and liberal program, and leave the South to take care of itself (which, incidentally, he believed to the end that it would do in his favor). And, in the firm conviction that the urban black vote in the North would provide the decisive margin in several key states, Truman shrewdly played that trump card late in the game. William Hastie came up from the Virgin Islands to help, putting together a strategy that effectively halted Wallace's efforts to lure away black votes. John Preston Davis, the veteran founder of the United Negro Congress and formerly an activist in the Southern Conference for Human Welfare (for both of which he was accused of being a Communist), was hired by the Democratic National Committee as an assistant director of publicity for the Truman-Barkley campaign, and his work in the Northern cities was especially beneficial. J. Edgar Hoover was prosecuting men with tidier credentials than Davis's, but the Democrats took a much more pragmatic and unbiased reading of his loyalty, and they didn't hesitate to recruit him when they needed his help.

Finally, in the last week of the campaign, Truman went to Boston to appeal for the Catholic vote, to Lower Manhattan to seek Jewish and ethnic-American backing, and to Harlem, on the first anniversary of his civil rights committee's report, telling a throng of 65,000 that he would work for the full realization of equality and justice in America "with every ounce of strength and determination that I have."

On Election Day—Tuesday, November 2, 1948—the President was at home in Missouri. With his wife and daughter, he went early in the morning to the polling place to cast his vote. Late that afternoon he sneaked out of the house, rode to a little resort town not far from Independence, and checked into the Elms Hotel, where he got a steam bath and a rubdown, had himself a sandwich and a glass of buttermilk, listened to the radio until about nine o'clock, and then turned off the light and went to sleep. He woke up around midnight, just long enough to get a radio update. NBC commentator H. V. Kaltenborn was saying that even though the President was ahead by more than a million votes, he was still "undoubtedly beaten."

Harry Truman was sleeping peacefully at 4:00 a.m. when one of the Secret Service agents protecting him at the Excelsior Springs, Missouri, hotel came into the room to tell him his lead had climbed to two million. The radio networks were still expecting a late surge of rural votes in the Midwest to pull Dewey to victory, but Truman knew better. "We've got 'em beat," he said, and about an hour later, he was headed for Kansas City.

The outcome was still in doubt for three more hours, but the President kept a remarkably serene composure. He listened with no show of emotion as the radio reported at eight-thirty that Ohio had slipped into his column by just seven thousand votes—and that appeared to give him enough for a victory in the all-important electoral count. An hour later, California and Illinois also went Democratic, erasing any remaining doubt about the outcome. Forty-five minutes after that, Dewey conceded defeat. The miracle had happened. Just about everybody had been wrong—except Harry Truman.

In the end, he beat Dewey by 24 million to 22 million in popular votes, 303 to 189 in electoral votes, and 28 to 16 in states. Henry Wallace got about 1.1 million popular votes (700,000 of them in New York and California, and only 30,000 in the South) but he carried no states. Strom Thurmond's total was also about 1.1 million (fewer than 5,000 of them outside the Old Confederacy and Kentucky); he carried Alabama, Mississippi, Louisiana, and his native South Carolina, finishing with 39 electoral votes.

The results were much closer than they seemed. A switch of fewer than fifty thousand votes in Ohio, Illinois, and California could have given Dewey a slim victory in the electoral count; had he won any two of those three, the election would have been thrown into the House of Representatives for a final decision. (But which House? The old one, with a Republican majority of fifty-eight seats, or the newly elected "Truman coattail" assembly, with its Democratic majority of ninety-two seats? Either way, it would have been a messy can of worms.)

The Senate also turned over, going from a Republican advantage of six seats to a Democratic margin of twelve. Truman got close to seventy percent of the black vote, and in such key non-Southern cities as Chicago, Cleveland, and Los Angeles, his winning margin among African-Americans was greater than the total of his plurality statewide. Without those crucial ballots, he could have ended up winning the popular vote but losing the election.

In all the celebrating and second-guessing that went on in the wake of Truman's stunning upset, the losers quickly faded from public view. On his return to Washington, the President found close to a million people lining the streets to welcome him, foul- and fair-weather friends alike. He was amused by an invitation from the *Post* to attend a "Crow Banquet," at which he would be served turkey while all the pollsters and press wore sackcloth and choked down the symbolic bird of humility. Truman replied magnanimously that he wouldn't enjoy watching such a spectacle—but he would like to see all Americans "get together now and make a country in which everybody can eat turkey whenever he pleases."

For all his graceful good humor, however, the President did allow himself privately to gloat a bit over his conquest of the Republicans, the liberal Northern Democrats who had deserted him—and most of all, the Dixiecrats. Close analysis of the numbers gave him good reason to be pleased with his showing in the South. When he was nominated, Truman had the public backing of not one single sitting member of the U.S. Senate from the eleven Southern states, and very few Southerners in the House of Representatives; furthermore, no incumbent Southern governor was firmly in his camp at that time. His most vocal support in the region came from the least powerful of its constituent groups—blacks and white liberals. His press endorsements, though numerous, tended to be soft and tentative.

And yet he polled more than 2.5 million votes in ten Southern states, and that was more than all the other candidates combined could count in eleven. Not only did he beat Dewey by two to one in the South, he beat

Thurmond by more than that. If you were to credit blacks in the region with 750,000 registered voters, and speculate that eighty percent of them voted, and ninety percent of those voted for Truman—generous estimates all— that would account for nearly twenty percent of the President's total in the South. But even if you set that number aside and counted just his white votes, he still won easily. The President spotted Strom Thurmond an un- contested 171,000 votes in Alabama and yet routed the South Carolinian in Dixie, white on white, by 2 million votes to 1.1 million. And, if more than the paltry twenty-two percent of adult Southerners had been able to vote, no doubt the President's margin would have been even greater.

The Dixiecrat leaders had shouted to the white people of the South and the nation that Truman had sold them out, that he was imposing commu- nistic programs of racial amalgamation that would reduce the South to a police state and its white people to a mongrelized breed of second-class citizens. And those same Southern whites, by a margin of almost two to one, rejected Thurmond's mean-spirited attack and returned their verdict in favor of Harry Truman. Even the Southern black minority, no more than fifteen percent of whom were registered to vote, garnered almost half as many ballots for the President as their white denigrators could amass for Thurmond.

Virtually all of the South's political leaders—both those who eagerly joined the Dixiecrat movement and those who stayed in the Democratic Party but refused to support the President—were shown by their pro- nouncements and their actions to be far behind their people rather than in front of them. It was not the multiplicity of Southern common folks who failed; rather it was their leaders, utterly and completely. They were the ones who defied Truman with so much vehemence, and stirred such a spirit of rebellion in the general population, and gave people outside the South evidence to reinforce their uninformed and stereotypical views about Southerners in general.

While most of the attention the South received was focused on the Truman Democrats and the Thurmond Dixiecrats, the election also gave a few old names and new faces a chance to shine on the political stage, and they added further to the tiny wave of Southern progressivism that had surfaced earlier with Ellis Arnall and Jim Folsom.

In Louisiana, Huey Long's son Russell and his brother Earl were both elected in 1948, Russell to the U.S. Senate and Earl to the governor's office. Earl Long had been lieutenant governor and acting governor be- fore. When he won the top office in his own right, he was intent on continuing the Long legacy—but in his own zanily original style. He threw an inauguration party in the Louisiana State University football stadium, serving hot dogs and soft drinks and buttermilk to the masses, white and black. "Meet each other," he instructed the assembled throng. "Shake hands. Exchange ideas. Make up your minds that we are going forward . . . and work together unselfishly. . . . I hope to see this state where every man is a king and every lady a queen but no one wearing a crown." Long wasn't enamored of the Dixiecrats, and, eccentric though he was, he demonstrated early and often his untraditional approach to Southern politics.

In Texas, Truman's old friend, former Vice President John Nance Garner, joined with Speaker of the House Sam Rayburn and incoming Senator Lyndon B. Johnson to lasso the governor, Beauford Jester, and get him out of the Dixiecrat corral. Together they led Texans to give Truman a half-million-vote margin over Dewey, and hold Thurmond to just nine percent of the vote. The aggressively ambitious Johnson, moving up from the House to take Pappy O'Daniel's seat, had outlasted former Governor Coke Stevenson by just eighty-seven votes in a sensational primary punctuated by a crossfire of charges covering just about every imaginable impropriety. One pivotal box of "late returns" gave Johnson 202 votes—all executed in alphabetical order by the same pen and the same penman. It was Texas politics at its theatrical best. Johnson was a conservative New Deal Democrat but a political animal to the marrow of his bones. When the times changed, he would change with them.

Arkansas elected a new governor in 1948 to replace the conservative Ben Laney, and he was a breath of fresh air. Sid McMath had come out of the war fired with ambition to be a populist reformer. He first joined a slate of ex-GIs in ousting a corrupt political machine that ran the city of Hot Springs. Then, at the age of thirty-six, he was elected to a two-year term as governor. McMath was critical of the Truman civil rights program at first, but he was also hostile to the Dixiecrats. In the years to come he would prove to be one of Truman's closest allies in the South.

Florida's new governor, Fuller Warren, was at least as moderate as Millard Caldwell, the man he succeeded (neither was a Dixiecrat), and North Carolina replaced R. Gregg Cherry with W. Kerr Scott, a man of some liberal inclinations. Earle Clements was Kentucky's most progressive governor in recent memory. In Tennessee, the aging E. H. "Boss" Crump, who supported Thurmond, suffered deeper humiliation when the state's voters spurned his candidates and chose Gordon Browning for governor and former Congressman Estes Kefauver for the Senate. (Browning edged out a Crump candidate in the primary and breezed to victory in November against his Republican opponent, country music star Roy Acuff.) When Crump branded Kefauver a "Communist sympathizer" and a "pet coon" of the reds, the candidate took to wearing a fur cap "made from a genuine Tennessee coon" on his campaign trips around the state, and the trademark hat boosted him to public attention and to victory.

Not all the winners were moderates or forward-looking reformers. Mississippi voters gave Bilboesque Senator James O. Eastland a resounding vote of confidence; Arkansans did the same for reactionary Senator John L. McClellan, and the voters of Georgia easily reelected mossback Senator Richard Russell.

What's more, Georgians also gave a clear majority to their governor-in-waiting, Herman Talmadge, for the last two years of the term his late father had won in 1946. "Hummon" bored in so hard on the white supremacy issue that his opponent, incumbent M. E. Thompson, took up the same cry—causing the crafty Talmadge to tag him "M. E. Too." Even Ralph McGill took a "neutral" stance in the race, much to the consternation of former Governor Ellis Arnall, who was backing Thompson. McGill, sounding downright hopeful, expressed the belief that Talmadge would forestall federal imposition of forced social changes from the top down by initiating voluntary reforms from the bottom up. He did nothing so progressive as that, reverting instead to the racial posture that had always worked for his father. In 1950, with Arnall sitting inexplicably on the sidelines, Talmadge subdued Thompson again in a close race for a full four-year term.

On balance, the 1948 election appeared to settle the bitter warfare between the liberal-leaning, forward-facing national Democratic Party, with its borning consciousness of inequality, and the reactionary, backward-looking Southern right wing of the party, with its obsessive devotion to white supremacy. The Truman regulars had won a tremendous victory nationally, and even in the South—especially in the South. Harry Ashmore wrote in the aftermath of the election that the Dixiecrat movement "was one of the most conspicuous failures in American political history." The naked appeal to racial prejudice and fear was no longer effective, he said; "white supremacy, in its classic form at least, is a dead issue." With more and more blacks voting, the practical result would be "the passing of the one-party system"—but also the demise of Dixiecrat racism under the guise of states' rights.

Without a doubt, the Dixiecrats were indeed a one-issue party with a narrow sectional base; they were a defensive army of white supremacists motivated by bigotry and dedicated to the proposition that some men and women—nonwhites, that is—are created unequal. But far from being decimated by their 1948 defeat, they looked ahead hopefully to a merger of conservative Southern Democrats and right-wing Republicans, united (in the South, at least) around the philosophy of states' rights and white supremacy. Southern Republicrats, Helen Fuller called them in *The New*

Republic; their goal was "to take over the existing Democratic Party organization. They are already campaigning for 1952."

The initial impression that the Truman Democrats had won a huge victory in the South, thereby silencing the conservative threat, would prove to be premature. The States' Rights Party and the Republicans were soundly defeated separately, but together they were a force representing fifty percent of the existing Southern electorate—and together they would surely be in the years to come.

11. *One Last Chance for Change*

Just at the moment of Harry Truman's triumph, the South got one more golden opportunity—in retrospect, its last best chance—to take control of its own social reformation. In the same year that the ruling white Nationalist Party of South Africa succeeded in imposing a policy of racial domination known as apartheid, the ruling white nationalists of the American South had failed to win voter approval, in the region as well as the nation, for policies of a similarly racist nature. Truman's victory may have been something less than a mandate for integration, but Strom Thurmond's defeat was certainly a clear sign that the Southern white majority was not willing to proclaim its second rebellion in a century for the lost cause of white supremacy.

The Dixiecrat defeat was only one sign among many that transforming changes were sweeping through the postwar world, and no country, however remote—certainly no region of the United States—would be sheltered from the cleansing winds. The United Nations was soon to adopt a pathfinding Declaration on Human Rights that was fundamentally incompatible with the practice of racial segregation. The armed forces of the United States were already launched on a desegregation course that in just five years would be declared a mission accomplished. African-Americans were emerging from invisibility in the professions, in labor unions, in the academy, in the church, and in the pages of newspapers and magazines. (On August 8, 1950, Jackie Robinson became the first African-American to appear on the cover of *Life*—fourteen years and more than seven hundred issues after the magazine was founded.) Federal court rulings were consistently opening the way for blacks to enjoy the same rights and liberties that most whites took for granted. In the practice of law, in the rules of courtroom procedure, and in the ranks of police officers—even Southern police officers—there were hopeful signs that some movement toward racial equality was beginning.

All these portents of accelerating change, highlighted by the Democratic political successes of Truman and the little band of "New South" moderates who rode into office with him, pointed to 1949 and the soon-to-begin second half of the twentieth century as a fruitful season of significant development in the South, much as 1933 and the early Roosevelt years had been. It was this prospect that Harry Ashmore, now emerging as a progressive young New South spokesman, alluded to when he wrote that the Dixiecrat defeat had exposed white supremacy as an ineffective and fading political issue. Just before Lillian Smith's incisive new book, *Killers of the Dream,* was published in 1949, she predicted in a newspaper column that "in five years there will be little legal segregation left in the South."

Aubrey Williams, writing from Alabama, came to a similar conclusion in a post-election article citing numerous signs of the South's receptivity to racial reform. All of the states bordering the region were acting on court orders or on their own to desegregate their colleges and universities, he noted, and four Southern governors (Folsom of Alabama, Scott of North Carolina, McMath of Arkansas, and Warren of Florida) had spoken out clearly in favor of several features of President Truman's civil rights program. In Alabama, three federal judges—lifelong residents, not outsiders—had found the state's notorious Boswell Amendment to be an unconstitutional device aimed at denying the vote to black citizens. In the South at large, the voters themselves, white and black, had "flatly refused to snap up the Dixiecrat bait."

With characteristic optimism, Williams professed to see a bright new Southern dawn on the horizon. "The Dixiecrats are on the run," he declared. "Despite the yapping of the politicians and the hysterical echo of the press, despite even the failure of many liberals to do anything but shout 'Leave us alone!' there is a break in the South. And one is justified in concluding that this break is a sign that the infamous structure of discrimination and segregation is beginning to crumble."

Even so cautious a strategist as Howard W. Odum, the venerable University of North Carolina sociologist, seemed convinced at the beginning of 1949 that the time had come for the South to move forward. Writing in the *Southern Packet,* the monthly journal of intellectual thought published in Asheville, he put forth an agenda "for the creative South to work out its own positive, practical adjustment" to the problems of segregation, and to make the region "a more useful part" of the nation. He called on the South to abide by the decisions of the federal courts; to adjust to national civil rights legislation; to stop "prevailing lawlessness by violence and by evasion"; to extend greater opportunity to all Southerners in the workplace; to equalize educational facilities; to provide graduate and professional instruction in the same institutions for qualified individuals of both races; to eliminate segregation in transportation "and other public services"; to guarantee the vote to all citizens without hindrance; to support federal laws against lynching and poll taxes; to "help all southerners see the justice" of these reforms; to "help the whole nation understand the problems—human, political, and economic—in changing a biracial civilization rooted in two centuries" of white privilege; and finally, to "stop being afraid of democracy."

New circumstances had led him to a revised assessment, Odum wrote. The presidential election, the clear civil liberties trend in the courts, social pressure from the rest of America and the world, and the South's own manifest desire "to find ways out of its multiplying dilemmas" were all compelling reasons for a comprehensive program of change. The new mood of the black minority was also a factor: "It is as if some universal message had reached the great mass of Negroes, urging them to dream new dreams and to protest against the old order."

In his own awakened conviction, the aging dean of Southern social scientists saw the region and the nation "facing their greatest domestic dilemma of the century . . . failure to meet which might very well destroy the soul of the South and cripple a great nation." His agenda for "the second half of an epochal century" was a call for reappraisal and action that went far beyond anything Odum had ever spelled out before, but the magnitude and urgency of the problem—and the fleeting availability of the opportunity—demanded such a response. "God helping us," he wrote, "we can do no other."

It would be easy to read too much into these post-election expressions of "now is the time" optimism and reformist energy. In point of fact, a small minority of powerful white men still controlled the political and economic machinery of the South, from the backcountry courthouses to Capitol Hill, and they were not about to share their power, much less surrender it, simply because others told them they should. Their hold on the national Democratic Party had been substantially weakened, but their grip on the party reins in their states and in the region was almost as tight as ever. Seven of the states still relied on the poll tax to limit voting by blacks and low-income whites, and almost all Southern election officials used a variety of devices to screen out potential voters whose color or class or gender made them unwelcome to the oligarchy. In spite of court-ordered increases in voter registration, only about one-tenth of black adults in the region were actually allowed to cast ballots in 1948.

Even in defeat, the Dixiecrats managed to retain their bases of local and regional strength, and no serious breach developed between them and their colleagues who chose for a variety of reasons not to declare themselves in open rebellion against the party of Roosevelt and Truman. The only real difference between Strom Thurmond and someone like Herman Talmadge or Olin D. Johnston (whom Thurmond would challenge, incidentally, in the 1950 South Carolina Senate race) was that Thurmond was more willing than the others to declare war against an incumbent president. Still, he was not the most extreme of the Dixiecrats; Thurmond tried harder to disguise his white supremacy behind the constitutional rationale of states' rights than did some of his more rabid allies, such as Fielding Wright of Mississippi and Gessner McCorvey of Alabama. But whatever differences they had, one from another, the South's political and economic rulers could still come together themselves—and bring a majority of their white followers along with them—to chant an ancient mantra, a virtual pledge of allegiance. It played as strongly with the Dixiecrats as it had a century earlier with the Confederate rebels. It was a hostile, hateful boast, a battle cry: "This is white man's country."

When he was back in his office in the South Carolina capitol, Governor Thurmond was not treated by the white citizenry as a failed and discredited bolter; in the eyes of most whites, he was a returning hero, the stronger and more admirable for having shaken his fist at the President, the Yankees, the liberals, and the black minority. What he exhibited and his constituents applauded was a prideful arrogance, at once defensive and belligerent, and it would plague the benighted South for years to come.

Tallulah Bankhead, daughter of the late Congressman William B. Bankhead of Alabama, had lent her celebrity to the campaign for Harry Truman's election, and the actress was on center stage, reveling in the sweet taste of victory, at the inauguration festivities in January 1949. From the presidential box in the reviewing stand at the inaugural parade, she glared at Governor Herman Talmadge as he rode by in his official car; Truman had his back turned at the time. Then, when Governor Thurmond passed in review and doffed his hat to the President, the stone-faced Truman responded with an icy stare. That would have been embarrassing enough for the subdued rebel—but the uninhibited Tallulah, never one to hold back her feelings, put sound effects on the silent snub with a conspicuously loud and lusty boo.

Harry Truman had earned the right to savor that moment. All the dire threats and derisive outbursts of his adversaries—Eastern liberals in his own party, Republican conservatives, Southern reactionaries—had ended in public humiliation for the detractors and a satisfying last laugh for the

President. Now, with a Democratic majority in both houses of Congress, he was ready to move forward with his own liberal agenda. His legislative program called for increases in social security and the minimum wage, federal aid to education, repeal of the anti-labor Taft-Hartley Act, national health insurance, low-cost public housing, and enactment of the civil rights measures he had first put forth a year earlier. "I stand squarely behind those proposals," he declared in his State of the Union address on January 5.

In those first days and weeks of the new administration, there were numerous indications that the momentum for civil rights reform generated in the campaign and the election was still a driving force. For the first time in history, all of the inauguration events were unsegregated. Walter White of the NAACP and most of the black press were effusive in their praise of Truman and full of great expectations for the future. In speeches to labor and civil rights groups and in meetings with his national committee investigating racial discrimination in the District of Columbia, the President emphasized again and again his determination to implement reforms. To Thurmond and the other defectors, he offered an olive branch of reconciliation if they would pledge to support the party platform—and when most of them declined, Truman and the Democratic leaders in Congress quietly concluded that the spoils of victory ought not to be lavished on unrepentant Dixiecrats. Some of the rebels lost their committee seniority; others, including Thurmond, were removed from the Democratic National Committee.

But the liberals' hopeful and promising prospects in January would gradually fade to dust, finally ending in fruitless and frustrating defeat for a bitterly disappointed President Truman, for black Americans in general, and for Southern progressives of both races. From the day Congress convened in January 1949, the coalition of Southerners and right-wing Republicans was busily working its will against the legislative agenda.

Through a series of complex parliamentary moves, they made it harder than ever for sponsors of legislation to get their bills through committee and onto the floor for a vote. The House Rules Committee, after being stripped of its power to bottle up legislation indefinitely, soon managed to recapture that leverage. In the Senate, the not-so-loyal opposition cleverly engineered a change in the cloture rule that made it more difficult to limit debate and force the members to vote. Liberal efforts to undo that damage were stymied by the very thing they sought to control: a filibuster. It consumed most of the first two weeks of March. As usual, the Southerners were the backbone of it, with all except Claude Pepper of Florida and freshman senator Frank Porter Graham of North Carolina taking part (Graham was absent, sick with pneumonia). The twenty obstructionist

Southerners, joined by a minimum of fourteen Republicans, could thus block virtually anything Truman proposed—and they didn't hesitate to do exactly that.

One after another, the President's civil rights bills and other measures were finessed into oblivion: the plan to create a permanent Fair Employment Practices Commission, anti-lynching and anti-poll-tax legislation, federal aid to education, national health insurance, reform of labor laws. Only the public housing act was passed—and at that, fewer than half of the units it called for would actually be built.

All through 1949 and 1950, Congress fiddled while Truman burned in a helpless rage, knowing that the Southerners and their Republican soulmates were extracting their pound of flesh for his disloyalty to their club. At one point, House Speaker Sam Rayburn of Texas, no civil rights enthusiast himself, pointedly evaded a rare opportunity to bypass the rules committee and let a bill get to the floor for a vote. Others, thought to be a shade more moderate than their colleagues—Senators Hill and Sparkman of Alabama, Senators Johnson of Texas and Kefauver of Tennessee, Senator Fulbright of Arkansas and his colleague in the House Brooks Hays—were all parties to the obstruction. Finally, on July 12, 1950, the last attempt to pass a fair employment practices bill succumbed to yet another filibuster (even Frank Graham was with the Dixie diehards this time), and the curtain fell ingloriously on a dismal scene of stalemate and impotence.

To make matters worse as these unproductive months were slipping away, Harry Truman found himself increasingly drawn to foreign affairs. The yearlong airlift finally broke the Soviet blockade of Berlin in May 1949, but after that one success the administration would have few others. In October, the bad news broke that the Russians had developed an atomic bomb. China was, for all practical purposes, a new red star in the Communist orbit. Former State Department official Alger Hiss was tried twice on charges of passing government documents to the Soviets; first left in limbo by a hung jury, he was convicted in January 1950 and sent to prison. Congressman Richard M. Nixon of California, a vigilant member of the House Un-American Activities Committee, accused Truman and his Secretary of State, Dean Acheson, of a softness and tolerance for Communist infiltrators in the government. In February, Senator Joseph McCarthy of Wisconsin bulled his way to instant notoriety during a West Virginia speech by making the sensational and unsubstantiated claim that he had "here in my hand" a list of 205 policy-level employees of the U.S. Department of State who were known to be "members of the Communist Party and members of a spy ring." The paper McCarthy waved before his audience that night turned out to be his laundry list, and he never produced the names to back up his charge, but he had loosed the red genie, and not for years would it be lured back into the bottle.

For every diligent public servant from the President on down, Joseph McCarthy was the embodiment of a terrifying nightmare brought to life. He was a demagogue running amok, feeding on his own paranoia and that of the already alarmed general public. Like a spider, he spun from the menacing threat of Russia and China an ominous web of suspicion and intrigue that entangled and immobilized the entire federal government and all private groups and individuals who gave any resistance to the frenzied offensive.

An obsession with communism seized the troubled consciousness of the nation and derailed the Truman administration's legislative agenda so completely that it was hard to imagine what more could happen—until it happened: In June, Communist forces from North Korea invaded South Korea, where the United States and the United Nations had "vital interests." After just five years of a troubled peace (during which the U.S. defense budget had been slashed to allow funding of domestic programs and to reduce the federal debt), American GIs were back on the battlefield again, and the beleaguered government had another war to finance. If ever there had been a chance for Truman's legislative program to be seriously considered and acted upon, it was gone now, swept away by the fierce winds of suspicion at home and armed conflict abroad.

Most congressional Republicans were egging McCarthy on in his witch-hunt. Defiant Dixiecrat John Rankin of Mississippi had been relieved of his duties on the House Un-American Activities Committee, but his non-Southern colleagues were managing quite well without him. In September, the Internal Security Act, a measure that stopped just short of outlawing membership in the Communist Party altogether, breezed through both houses and weathered a Truman veto. The new law required registration of Communists and "Communist-front" organizations, detention of suspected reds during national emergencies, and closer scrutiny of immigrants.

Gearing up for his 1950 run for the Senate, Strom Thurmond told the South Carolina electorate that he and his fellow Dixiecrats wanted to give them a choice "between the candidates who are following the President and those who are willing to stand up and be counted in opposition to his un-American, Communistic and anti-Southern programs." With such rhetoric as this, Southern politicians had been blasting all and sundry advocates of social change since Franklin Roosevelt's first day in office. But now the attack was taking on a new and different complexion. For the first time, non-Southern politicians were stirring up the American people with a frenzied assault on "subversives" and "fellow travelers" from New York and Washington to Hollywood, and virtually no one was strong enough to stand the heat. Here was a potent weapon being used in the North to enforce political conformity; if it was effective against sophisticated Yankees, why wouldn't it work against the racial liberals who had established a foothold in the South?

The Southerners in Congress and in the statehouses knew perfectly well that communism had failed miserably in its efforts to win support from blacks and liberal whites in the region; the few visible exceptions scattered about in Alabama, North Carolina, and elsewhere emphatically proved the rule. On any given day, you could have held a Communist Party convention in the South in a boxcar or a school bus, if not a phone booth. But the very idea of racial equality was so alien to the ruling elite that they could easily imagine its proponents to be reds. In any case, if calling them Communists would stop them, that was all that mattered. When other measures were losing their effectiveness, the reactionaries found that Joe McCarthy and the Republican right had handed them a new club, a blunt instrument to force the dissidents into line. From 1950 on, they would swing it with ever-increasing frequency.

On the home front, governors and legislators and local elected officials ruled with every bit as much manipulative skill as their counterparts showed in controlling the legislative process in Congress. The very structure of state and local governments in the South assured a high level of inefficiency, waste, misrepresentation, neglect, and corruption. A half-century of one-party rule by little cliques of handpicked white men, often without so much as a hint of periodic reapportionment, had produced encrusted oligarchies of rural barons who reigned as if by some divine right. As different as they were from each to the next, all of the states in the region suffered to some degree from gross imbalances such as these. In general, legislatures had more power to obstruct democracy than did governors—but more often than not, the two branches either checked each other into stalemate or collaborated to protect their mutual interest in the status quo.

Given the circumstances, the wonder is not that so few moderate or liberal or progressive men (and, rarely, women) were able to win and retain office, but rather that any at all could do it. For Governors Arnall, Folsom, McMath, and Scott to win statewide races, or for Pepper, Hill, Sparkman, and Kefauver to capture and keep seats in the Senate, was a tribute to the better judgment of the voters. What's more, Arkansas chose Sid McMath for a second two-year term in 1950 over the former governor, Dixiecrat Ben Laney, and in Alabama that same year, Birmingham arch-segregationist Bull Connor finished sixth in the primary race for governor, while Lister Hill was being returned to the Senate.

It was in 1949 that North Carolina's new governor, Kerr Scott, appointed Frank Porter Graham to fill a vacant Senate seat. In Virginia that same year, Francis Pickens Miller, a moderate patrician who had organized the Southern Policy Committee in the late 1930s, challenged the Byrd machine's candidate, John S. Battle, for the governor's office. Promising to "set Virginia free" from the iron grip of Harry Byrd, Miller came close to winning, even though the Richmond newspapers withheld their support and the Byrd forces smeared the challenger as a captive of labor, blacks, and Communists. In comparison to Byrd, Miller seemed more liberal than he truly was—but he was a choice, at least, and not an echo.

In spite of these thrusts against the conservative grain of Southern politics, the rebellious and reactionary segregationist mind-set was still the rule, not the exception. Herman Talmadge's capture of the Georgia governor's office in 1948 and his reelection in 1950 put the state back onto the race-baiting course his father had followed before the Ellis Arnall upset of 1942. Arnall had been the hope of liberal reformers, but he declined to run again in 1950, and years later he acknowledged that "Herman had pulled everybody so far to the right that there was no way I could have won." During his six-year tenure, Talmadge took every opportunity he could find to segregate and restrict black Georgians in the schools, the courts, the workplace, and the voting booth. He also led a majority of Southern governors in expressing a formal resolve to fight President Truman and his "unconstitutional civil rights legislation by every means at our command."

The Dixiecrat leaders were, if anything, madder than ever after their 1948 defeat, and even though their grassroots support was eroding, they showed no signs of giving up. Horace Wilkinson of Alabama, one of the rebel stalwarts, swore that he would "rather die fighting for states' rights than live on Truman Boulevard in a nigger heaven." Leander Perez, a hard-bitten parish political boss from Louisiana, went to Washington in 1949 to open a liaison office for the party, and quickly joined with Ben Laney of Arkansas and Birmingham columnist John Temple Graves in a concerted effort to build an alliance with right-wing Republicans.

Strom Thurmond's unsuccessful attempt to unseat Senator Olin Johnston in 1950 was read by some as an indication that the Dixiecrat revolt was over, but that didn't necessarily mean that the aims of the rebels were no longer attractive to white voters. On the contrary, the repeated successes of a dozen or more old-guard defenders of white supremacy and the return to public life of James F. Byrnes as governor of

South Carolina in 1950 were unmistakable signs of the continued vitality of arch-conservative reaction in the South.

These were the dominant and prevailing sentiments of the Southern political oligarchy at the turn of the half-century. The fire-eaters of the Bilbo-Eastland school and the urbane sophisticates like Byrnes had only one sure thing in common: They could put aside their differences and sign a blood oath to "keep the Negro in his place." They had seen and heard more than enough to convince them that the old order they cherished was threatened as never before—and it was that perceived peril, more than anything else, which accounted for their unity, their extremism, and their obsessive preoccupation with race.

It is no great feat to recognize these characteristics from the distant perspective of nearly fifty years; what is truly remarkable, however, is that Valdimer Orlando Key, Jr. (who went, understandably, by the initials V.O.), saw them at the time they were taking shape, and wrote about them with great clarity in his classic 1949 study, *Southern Politics in State and Nation.* The book came about after a University of Alabama political scientist, Roscoe C. Martin, secured a grant from the Rockefeller Foundation to finance a three-year study of the electoral process in the South. Martin then persuaded Key, a forty-year-old fellow Texan with a Ph.D. from the University of Chicago, to assemble a staff and direct the project. Key was on the faculty at Johns Hopkins University in Baltimore at the time, and soon would move to Yale.

In microscopic detail, Key and his team of research assistants dissected and analyzed the Southern body politic from Virginia to Texas, amassing mountains of data and interviewing an average of fifty people in each of the eleven states. University of North Carolina alumnus Alexander Heard, just out of the navy and bound for Columbia University to finish his Ph.D., spent three years on the project as Key's principal field worker, interviewer, and draft writer. Though its seven hundred pages were heavily salted with statistical analysis, *Southern Politics* was a refreshingly candid, informative, readable volume—even, at times, entertaining. The study carefully compared the differences and similarities among the states and concluded that their common denominator was the solidarity and power of wealthy and conservative whites in the 180 majority-black counties of the region—the so-called Black Belt.

"The South may not be the nation's number one political problem," Key wrote, "but politics is the South's number one problem"—and "if the politics of the South revolves around any single theme, it is that of the role of the black belts." The one-party system, the factionalism, the machine bosses of state and city, congressional solidarity, malapportioned legislatures, the Dixiecrats, the minuscule electorate, the poll tax, and other

impediments to voting—all these and more were traceable to one fundamental fact: "that the black-belt whites succeeded in imposing their will
on their states and thereby presented a solid regional front in national
politics on the race issue."

The appearance of white unity for the sake of preserving the racial
status quo gave rise to the myth of the solid South, Key suggested, but
in fact there was much diversity of thought within the region. In the
cities and the "rim" states surrounding the Deep South, in the hill regions with their populist traditions, in the labor unions and other institutions, and in the black population, he wrote, "an underlying liberal
drive permeates southern politics," and it "will undoubtedly be mightily
strengthened" as the principles of democracy take root. "The Dixiecrats
beat the drums of racial reaction in 1948 without impressive results; the
Dixiecrat movement may turn out to have been the dying gasp of the
Old South."

The unflattering frankness of *Southern Politics* was made all the more
remarkable by the fact that Southern scholars at a Southern institution had
produced it. It was, however, apparently too hot for a Southern university
press to publish, and so it was issued at a safe distance, from a commercial
house in New York. The result, ironically, was that many more people saw
the book or read reviews of it than would have otherwise—reviews that
characterized the political South as a sick patient in need of a psychiatrist,
or a threadbare emperor in need of a suit of clothes.

It was almost time to call the roll and close the book on the forties, and
on the first half of the twentieth century. V. O. Key had taken the measure
of the South's political institutions, and various of his fellows in other fields
were also leaving benchmarks of summary and conclusion. From the Deep
South to the District of Columbia and beyond, the march of time and
events had jolted an awakening land out of its colonial lethargy. Here was
the South in search of itself, trying to discover and come to terms with its
own identity and purpose—and displaying in the process all of its traits of
character and personality, the best and the worst.

Some were distressingly familiar echoes of the inescapable past: racism, demagoguery, violence. The reappearance of an intemperate Talmadge in the Georgia governor's office was soon followed by an upsurge
of the Ku Klux Klan. One young country editor, twenty-four-year-old
Amelia Knoedler of the Unadilla *Observer*, outraged by blatant acts of
terrorism in her town, blamed the governor personally for creating a
climate that allowed race hatred and lawlessness to breed. There were
lynchings yet again in two rural Georgia counties, and for the twenty-

sixth time in less than two decades, according to the Atlanta *Journal's* count, the murderers went unpunished. "Georgia is sabotaging its own sovereignty," the paper declared. Terrorist acts were also reported in several Southern cities, including Miami, Chattanooga, Birmingham, and Knoxville.

Protestant and Catholic church bodies in most Southern states debated and sometimes passed resolutions condemning racial discrimination and injustice. The association of Southern Baptists in Virginia, following the lead of their sisters and brothers in North Carolina, Georgia, and Tennessee, narrowly approved a committee report candidly confessing "that we are prejudiced on this question . . . that we are fearful, that we are afraid—for political, or ecclesiastical, or social reasons—to follow the way of Christ . . . in our relation to all races." For local congregations and individual ministers, it was much harder to stand alone against the extreme hostility that often sprang up close around them.

For many Southerners of both races, the matters of color and caste and class—the problems and the solutions—were essentially religious questions, moral and ethical in nature. Others preferred to think of racism as a political or economic problem, or an educational one. To Lillian Smith, "the terrible curse of segregation" was at root a psychiatric disease, mentally and psychologically crippling to whites and blacks alike. In *Killers of the Dream,* her fervent and intense book of autobiography and analysis published in 1949, she described and defined the illness at length and exhorted her readers to overcome it. Few of the South's white liberals, including Ralph McGill, could find much to like in the book, leading Smith to retort that "75 per cent of the 'liberals' in the South seem to favor segregation." McGill and some others dismissed her as a strident, preachy, pedantic, sanctimonious woman. Perhaps she was—but rare was the Southerner of either race or sex who could give her credit in those years of the forties simply for being right.

One who did—and who was himself a besieged "prophet without honor"—was federal judge J. Waties Waring of Charleston. He and his second wife lived in a virtual state of internal exile from all except a few black friends and occasional visitors from outside the city. In large measure because of his rulings against the South Carolina white primary, the judge's national reputation for courage soared even as his local stock plummeted.

Elizabeth Avery Waring was, if anything, more combative than her husband. In 1950 she drew screams of outrage for a speech she made at the black YWCA in Charleston—touted in advance to the press—in which she declared that Southern whites were "a sick, confused and decadent people . . . full of pride and complacency, introverted, morally weak, and low." Her bristling words opened new and deeper wounds. From as far away as Mississippi came a hot retort from Hodding Carter that Mrs. Waring was "as guilty of bigotry and deliberate inflammation of racial feeling as ever Bilbo was."

There followed a cross-burning on the lawn, pistol shots in the garden, and rocks smashing through the windows of the fashionable Waring home on Meeting Street. A delegation of black South Carolinians and liberal whites from other states, including left-wing stalwarts Aubrey Williams, Clark Foreman, and James Dombrowski, came to call on the Warings and to honor the judge for his "great and good works." It was also in that same month of November 1950 that the NAACP's legal director, Thurgood Marshall, came before Judge Waring for a pretrial hearing in a school discrimination case from rural Clarendon County, South Carolina. It was to become one of the most significant civil rights cases in the long history of the federal judiciary.

The U.S. Supreme Court had rendered two opinions earlier in 1950 that stopped just short of declaring the old *Plessy* doctrine of "separate but equal" to be an outmoded and unworkable relic. The court implied in the case of Oklahoma plaintiff G. W. McLaurin—and declared explicitly in the case of Texas plaintiff Heman Sweatt—that *Plessy* v. *Ferguson* "can never provide the equality required by the Fourteenth Amendment." In Virginia, a federal district judge ordered a county to equalize funding of its separate white and black public schools or be prepared to see them merged. In Atlanta, a suit was brought by black plaintiffs asking the district court to declare the city's segregated schools unconstitutional. According to one informed estimate, it would take more than a billion dollars to bring the South's black schools to parity with its white ones. Some states scrambled to address the problem, but its solution by appropriation in the poverty-ridden region was demonstrably impossible. Gradually, inexorably, the wall of segregation was cracking apart.

In all but five Southern states—Mississippi, Alabama, Georgia, Florida, and South Carolina—there was either token desegregation of graduate and professional schools or serious talk of it by the end of 1950. The quasi-independent Southern Regional Education Board, formed by the several states after the war to facilitate interstate cooperation in higher education, was dogged in its formative years by suspicions that the unofficial aim of the governors in creating it was to perpetuate segregation. The SREB staff, headed by John E. Ivey, Jr. (and made up almost entirely of graduate school alumni of the University of North Carolina), was at first on the receiving end of some of that criticism, but in a 1949 desegregation lawsuit in Maryland, the staff advised the board to intervene on behalf of the plaintiff. It did, declaring that it was "not the purpose of the Board that the regional compact . . . shall serve any state as a legal defense for avoiding responsibilities" regarding desegregation. Thereafter, the SREB gradually distanced itself from the segregationist label, even though charges of obstruction would still be raised against it, and another fifteen years would pass before the last racial barriers fell in the universities of the Deep South states.

The Southern Regional Council was also moving gradually—as it had since its beginning in 1944—to weave a safe path to equality through the tortured thickets of Never, Later, and Now. From 1948 on, as the larger society was inching closer to desegregation reforms, the factions within SRC seemed to be drifting ever further apart. Gordon B. Hancock, the convenor of the Durham conference that led to the council's founding, finally lost patience with the ever-cautious Virginius Dabney, accusing the editor of foot-dragging and of making "a strategic retreat" from his earlier liberal positions—and that was before Dabney chose to resign from SRC rather than move along with it toward an eventual resolution of the segregation question. Old New Dealer Aubrey Williams resigned for the opposite reason in 1949, saying the council simply hadn't moved far enough fast enough against discrimination.

The blacks most active in the organization—Hancock, Benjamin Mays, Rufus Clement, Forrester Washington, Grace Towns Hamilton, A. W. Dent, Charles S. Johnson, and others—continued to push for a forthright policy of desegregation and full equality. Realistically speaking, though, the Southern Regional Council was in debt, losing members, and barely holding body and soul together; it simply lacked the energy, the means, or the will to forge ahead. Its executive director, George S. Mitchell, was borrowing money on his life insurance policy to pay some of the council's operating expenses. At the annual meeting in November 1950, only a few dozen members were present.

One positive highlight in an otherwise discouraging period for the SRC came in the fall of 1949, when it co-sponsored, with an interdenominational panel of churchwomen, an Atlanta conference at which Eleanor Roosevelt appeared, making her first visit to Georgia since the death of her husband. She spoke warmly of the South, the churchwomen, the SRC, and the cause of social reform, all to the delight of the sponsors, central among whom was Dorothy R. Tilly—field secretary of the council, a leader of the churchwomen, and a member in 1947 of President Truman's Committee on Civil Rights.

Press coverage of the church conference was extensive. One reporter who attended was John N. Popham, then two years into his assignment as the regional correspondent of the *New York Times.* His frequent trips to Atlanta had brought him into close association with Ralph McGill, and over time he would also develop a bond with others there, including the council's director of information, Harold Fleming, and SRC board members John A. Griffin and Benjamin Mays. Thereafter, reports on the council appeared often in the pages of the *Times.*

Popham gave new meaning to the term "roving reporter." A tireless extrovert, he covered great distances by car, showing up at so many church, farm, university, and political party gatherings that he rivaled the legendary Kilroy. While covering the Dixiecrats in 1948, he went to a meeting at a black church in Jackson, Mississippi, and was picked up and taken to jail by white plainclothes officers on a stakeout there. A black newspaperman phoned word of the arrest to a white reporter, who called Governor Fielding Wright, who called the police chief and forcefully suggested Popham's release. From such exploits were the tales of Johnny Popham spun—stories that originated in all manner of Southern locales and situations, from dormitory bull sessions at Fisk University's summer Race Relations Institute to political shoptalk in the smoky back rooms at Brennan's Restaurant in New Orleans.

A sense of humor was a saving grace in those increasingly intemperate times. Popham was so blessed, and he gravitated to others who shared the gift, among them Harold Fleming, Harry Ashmore of the *Arkansas Gazette,* and Bill Baggs of the Miami *News.* McGill and Hodding Carter were also prized friends and trusted companions, but more serious or tormented or combative. Carter was a "liberal spokesman" in Mississippi, the most reactionary state in the Union—which made him a conservative in New York or Chicago. But the Greenville editor never ducked a fight, whether with demagogic Southern Dixiecrats or self-righteous Yankee liberals.

One of the latter, a white Pittsburgh reporter named Ray Sprigle, had written an exposé of the South after spending four weeks there "disguised as a Negro." A popular ABC network radio series called "Town Meeting"—given added exposure by the new medium of television—invited Carter and Ashmore to debate the segregation issue with Sprigle and the NAACP's Walter White. Ashmore would long remember with high humor what happened before the broadcast: The pink-cheeked, white-haired White, who was black, "seemed the most conspicuous Aryan among us, while the swarthy Carter's skin was dark enough to prompt a Mississippi theater usher to direct him to the balcony. The makeup man was instructed to darken down Walter and lighten up Hodding." Both sides held their ground in the inconclusive debate, but afterward, White put to Ashmore and Carter the one question they couldn't answer: "You know that segregation is morally indefensible and has to go. Why don't you admit it? What are you afraid of?" Said Ashmore years later, "He knew that I knew that he had earned the right to ask the question."

By 1950, when he wrote *Southern Legacy*, Hodding Carter had come to feel that the primary responsibility for the South's racial problems rested on the shoulders of racist whites. Discrimination, he wrote, "has infected the white South with a moral sickness." He would never refer to himself as an integrationist, or like others to call him that, but by Mississippi standards he clearly was a liberal—and he grew more so as the South's crisis worsened.

Ralph McGill didn't like those labels, either; he thought of himself as a moderate, but he was without a doubt the number-one house liberal of the Atlanta newspapers, and like Carter, he kept moving left. All through his tenure at the *Constitution*, he had worked for Clark Howell, the owner, but in 1949 the conservative Howell sold most of his holdings to former Democratic presidential candidate James M. Cox of Ohio, who had owned the Atlanta *Journal* for a decade, and Cox gave McGill full authority to say whatever he wanted in the paper—and in a front-page column at that. A new general manager, George C. Biggers, was sent in by Cox to oversee operations of both papers. Biggers and McGill developed a mutual dislike and fear of each other, but each had his own turf to protect, and for the most part they avoided direct conflict.

By the late forties, McGill had taken up rather consistently the theme that the South's continued refusal to obey its own laws (for separate-but-equal schools, against lynching, and so forth) would eventually cause the states to face hard new realities imposed by judicial command. He wasn't yet ready to declare for federal legislation himself, but he was coming closer.

Another of McGill and Carter's shared opinions was a hard-nosed anti-communism; both of them were prone to shoot from the hip at radical white Southerners who stepped outside the traditional conventions of politics or race or religion. Don West and Myles Horton had suffered McGill's wrath in the 1930s, when they were organizing the Highlander Folk School and aiding the labor movement; the Southern Conference for Human Welfare and most (but not all) of its principals had been similarly criticized, and Senator Claude Pepper of Florida would take a heavy hit from McGill when he was running for reelection in 1950.

The national paranoia over communism had reached epidemic proportions by the summer of 1950. In the South, the manifestations of that pathology bordered on the absurd, and would have been laughable had they not been so dangerously destructive. No honest critic could name a time when there had ever been a Communist threat to the peace and safety of the South—and yet, as the tiny cell shrank to microscopic proportions, the hue and cry against it grew louder, and the emboldened witch-hunters, sensing how utterly safe they were, imagined themselves slaying red dragons at every turn. When the last little handful of radicals in the Southern Negro Youth Congress convened one final time in Birmingham in 1948, the red-hunting police force under Bull Connor arrested the whites in attendance (James Dombrowski and Progressive Party vice-presidential candidate Glen Taylor among them) for violating the segregation ordinance. Another local law, called the Communist Control Act, gave Connor a license to harass "subversives"—the ones responsible, he asserted, for the Klan-like bombings and other terrorist acts that plagued blacks in the city.

Not just the South was caught up in this madness. An outburst of violence against "niggers, kikes, and commies" marred two consecutive weekends at a Peekskill mountain resort in upstate New York in the summer of 1949, with Paul Robeson the primary object of hostility. Since the war, Robeson had been cast down from the pinnacle of celebrity to the pit of scorn for his criticism of American racism and his support of Russia. Black and red proved to be a deadly color combination for him and W. E. B. Du Bois and Benjamin J. Davis, Jr., the three most prominent African-Americans associated with communism. Davis went to prison for his beliefs, and both Robeson and Du Bois were hounded by the government and driven into exile. Of the three, only Davis was a true party loyalist; the other two showed themselves to be more committed to liberty and equality than to party—or to race.

Their troubles in this country had little if anything to do with the South, though—a fact that underscores both the "Northern" tenor of anticommunism and the national sweep of racism. The South's red-hunters showed repeatedly that their primary target was not Marxist ideology but race-mixing. It was the presence of black students at the Highlander Folk School, more than any sign of doctrinaire communism, that brought press attacks, FBI surveillance, and congressional committee investigators down on the Tennessee institution. The same was true of the Southern Conference for Human Welfare and its spin-off group, the Southern Conference Educational Fund.

Highlander had been closely associated with the labor movement since its founding in the early thirties, but the Congress of Industrial Organizations, having troubles of its own with red-hunting government investigators, was trying to back off to a safe distance from the school. Even though several Southerners with close ties to labor, including Lucy Randolph Mason, Paul Christopher, George S. Mitchell, and Aubrey Williams, would maintain an intimate relationship with Highlander, the formal link between the school and the CIO was about to be broken, and it wouldn't be repaired.

The two Southern Conference factions, already weakened to the point of exhaustion by assaults from the outside, were seriously divided internally by 1948, with the Clark Foreman–Human Welfare faction putting all its energies into the Henry Wallace campaign and the Jim Dombrowski–Educational Fund wing shifting its focus to a reformist push against racial segregation and discrimination. Wallace's crushing defeat signaled the final collapse of SCHW. On November 21, 1948—exactly ten years after the first conference in Birmingham—a remnant of the charter delegates, including Dombrowski, Foreman, Aubrey Williams, Virginia Durr, Myles Horton, and Alva Taylor, met in Richmond to pull the plug and draw a sheet over the corpse. They left a few belongings to the surviving Southern Conference Educational Fund.

This "death and transfiguration," as historian Thomas A. Krueger called it, had been preceded a day earlier by a symbolic gathering at Monticello, the Virginia home of everybody's favorite civil libertarian, Thomas Jefferson. There the SCEF leaders, principally Dombrowski and Williams, and about fifty more Southern progressives of both races, acting "as Americans deeply committed to our form of government and our way of life," gathered to read aloud and sign a pledge—"A Declaration of Civil Rights"—calling for the total abolition of segregation. With its ranks now thinned to a faithful few, the SCEF turned its eyes toward the fifties.

But the climb to the mountaintop at Monticello was far easier than the uphill marches that lay ahead. The soaring hopes of Southern reformers in the wake of Harry Truman's 1948 upset had turned to despair as Congress gridlocked, the red panic spread, and Korea exploded. The home front was almost as dangerous a battleground as the war zone. An ominous sign of the vicious infighting ahead was posted in early May of 1950 when a suave and handsome young Florida congressman, George A. Smathers, turned on his benefactor, Senator Claude Pepper, in a slashing, smearing, McCarthyesque attack aimed at unseating the liberal senator. "Red Pepper" was pictured with Paul Robeson and Joseph Stalin; he was anonymously branded a "nigger lover" and a subversive. (Even Ralph McGill called him a "spell-binding pinko.") Character assassination worked: Smathers won by 64,000 votes. The smear tactic worked again in November for California senatorial candidate Richard M. Nixon against his opponent, Helen Gahagan Douglas. And, most devastatingly of all, it claimed another Southern victim in North Carolina: the best-known and most widely respected liberal in the region, Frank Porter Graham.

Only three months after W. Kerr Scott became North Carolina's governor in 1949, he surprised just about everyone except his wife and his friend Jonathan Daniels, editor of the Raleigh *News & Observer*, by appointing Frank Graham to an interim vacancy in the U.S. Senate. Scott, a dairy farmer of moderately liberal leanings, and Daniels, back home from his White House service to Presidents Roosevelt and Truman, both saw the longtime University of North Carolina president as the ideal choice for the Senate seat, but it took them more than a week of intensive effort to persuade Graham that he had to accept the appointment. The sixty-two-year-old educator had spent all of his adult life at the university in an ever-expanding mission of service to the state, the South, and the nation. Along the way, he had built an enormous reservoir of goodwill. He had enemies on the right, but not all conservatives opposed him by any means; friend and foe alike acknowledged that he was an exceedingly popular public figure and a good and decent man.

A year after his appointment, Graham had to run for the remaining years of his predecessor's unfinished term. He drew early opposition in the Democratic primary from an involuntarily retired former senator and booster of fascism, Fascist-leaning Robert R. Reynolds, but serious Graham foes wanted a more stable candidate, and they got blue-chip Raleigh attorney Willis Smith, a former president of the American Bar Association, to enter the race. With the help of several arch-conservative advisers and staff assistants—including a twenty-eight-year-old radio newsman, Jesse Helms, who wrote press releases and advertising copy—Smith went after Graham bare-fisted, hammering on the theme that he was soft on communism.

In the May 27 primary, Graham got more than 300,000 votes to Smith's 250,000, with another 58,000 going to Reynolds. By a whisker—some 5,000 votes—the incumbent fell short of a majority. Smith then waited until the last minute before exercising his perogative to ask for a runoff.

The second round of campaigning was marked by a shift in the challenger's attack; the "Communist fellow traveler" charge became a scurrilous racial offensive. A doctored photograph showing Graham's wife dancing with a black man was passed around with whispered innuendoes. UNC was labeled, in a phrase credited to Helms, as the "University of Negroes and Communists." Fliers and newspaper ads warned whites to WAKE UP BEFORE IT'S TOO LATE, asking, "Do you want Negroes working beside you and your wife and daughters . . . eating beside you . . . sleeping in the same hotels . . . teaching and disciplining your children in school . . . occupying the same hospital rooms . . . using your toilet facilities?"

Here was the raw nub of Southern demagoguery, the essence of its deceit and venality, summed up in a few words. The message: "Race-mixing, with all the worst sexual and social and economic consequences, is a Communist plot masterminded in Moscow and carried out through the seemingly innocent offices of sympathizers and dupes and traitors like Frank Porter Graham; for the sake of the sovereign South and its traditional way of life, these demons must be cast out and destroyed."

Frank Graham was too soft-spoken and self-effacing, too gentlemanly, too repelled by the coarse tactics of hand-to-hand combat in the political trenches; he couldn't bring himself to get down in the mud and slug it out. He turned the other cheek, and went on trying to appeal to the better judgment of North Carolina's voters.

In the runoff on June 24, Graham fell almost twenty thousand votes short. At 9:45 p.m., he left his sixth-floor suite at the Sir Walter Hotel in Raleigh and went downstairs to the ballroom to congratulate Willis Smith on his victory. A little while later, one of the senator's assistants, Bill Friday, drove Frank and Marian Graham home. They rode in silence. There was nothing left to say. Not with self-pity or bitterness or tears but with a certain innocence, a bewilderment, a painful disbelief, Frank Porter Graham held his wife's hand and stared out the window into the summer darkness. The first major defeat of his life would also be the worst. It would be a long time—if ever—before he got over it.

IV

1950–1954:
Days of Grace

So the governors went forth to help pull down their own temple—refusing to face the problem they themselves counted as paramount, and worse still, trying to convince the world that it didn't exist. . . . And the great irony is that [the positions of both national political parties on civil rights] were irrevocably shaped by the South—by inaction in the days of grace, and by blind defiance when time began to run out.

—HARRY S. ASHMORE,
An Epitaph for Dixie

1. *Coming to a Choice*

It's hard for me to think of the fifties as a fearful time of silence. My own coming of age (I turned fifteen in the summer of 1950) still plays back in my memory as a carefree time, unclouded by strife or deprivation. The fact that there was a war going on, and that a paranoid search for Communists had the nation's adult population in an uproar, made no deep and indelible impression on me. My native South's impending racial crucible was still an indistinct shadow in the public consciousness, and I was only vaguely and superficially aware of it.

But my circle of exposure was gradually enlarging, and while I was passing through high school I had a succession of experiences that introduced me to the world beyond the confines of Cadiz and Trigg County, Kentucky. By car, truck, bus, and train, I ventured out into the first ring of cities around us—Nashville, Chattanooga, Knoxville, Louisville, Evansville, Memphis—and even got a fleeting glimpse at others more distant, from St. Louis and Chicago to Atlanta and New Orleans. There was a thrilling sense of great expectations that went along with climbing aboard a passenger train and starting off on a long journey. I never grew tired of watching the passing landscape slip away into the evening shadows at sunset, or listening to the mournful notes the engineer played intermittently on his horn. Even now, the plaintive sound of a train whistle fills me with wistfulness and wanderlust.

Having two aunts and an uncle who worked for the federal government in Washington, I was privileged on summer trips there to see the big house on Pennsylvania Avenue where President Truman lived, to dine at the famed Willard Hotel (my grandfather had been there, at a Gridiron Club dinner in the early 1920s, when a disastrous fire struck), and to ride a bus up the broad "Main Street of America" to the Capitol, where my old neighbor from Paducah, Vice President Alben Barkley, presided over sessions of the United States Senate. Five or ten minutes of droning speeches there was enough for me, though; the *real* Senators, in my book, were the guys who played baseball out at Griffith Stadium, and that's where my cousin Jack and I preferred to be.

It didn't take me long to figure out that there was a lot more action and excitement to be found in the cities than in little country towns like mine.

Not that there weren't plenty of things for teenage boys to do out there in the heartland. Sports and girls were the two principal interests, with school, church, home chores, and even odd jobs for pay ranking far down the list. My first regular job was as a delivery boy for the Louisville *Courier-Journal*. At times, the responsibility of it weighed as heavily on my skinny shoulders as a bag full of Sunday papers. We still depended on the *C-J*, reliable old gray lady that she was, to keep us informed—as well as on *Life* and *Look, The Saturday Evening Post,* and the *Reader's Digest.* All in all, we were not devoid of cultural assets, far from it; even in Cadiz you could get some sense of what the larger possibilities were.

Fantasy as well as reality filtered in to us via the radio, the movies, phonograph records, books and magazines, and the mesmerizing novelty of television. I actually knew a kid whose father had bought a TV set—the first in our town. We watched the Cleveland Browns on winter Sunday afternoons. Sometimes we couldn't tell whether the snow on the screen was a storm blowing in over Lake Erie or just poor reception in that primitive dawn of video transmission.

By the time I graduated from high school, in 1953, I felt that I had seen and done more than most youngsters coming up in the rural South—or the rural North and West, for that matter. Along the way, I had developed a taste for adventure, a love of travel, and a fascination with the endless variety of life in the greater U.S.A. But still I was oblivious to the political, social, and economic issues that gave off a low rumble like summer thunder all across the South as the U.S. Supreme Court deliberated at length on the school desegregation question.

My first job out of high school was a three-month stint as a lowly file clerk in the fingerprint archives of the Federal Bureau of Investigation. One day as I was waiting for an elevator, I saw J. Edgar Hoover himself—a man known to me in legend as the crime-busting king of the G-men. Through my supervisor I learned that I could have a personally autographed photo of "the big Boss," free for the asking. It turned out to be the only memento I took back to Kentucky with me when I returned in the fall to enter college. The FBI director's aggressive pursuit of Communists and other radicals was no secret in that anti-red decade. It would be years, however, before the public learned about his clandestine surveillance of black leaders, his "black is red" logic in harmony with Southern reactionaries and others of the radical right, or his cozy relationship with some of the same organized-crime figures to come under the scrutiny of a Senate subcommittee headed by Tennessee's Estes Kefauver in the early fifties. Hoover was above criticism in those days; to impressionable kids like me (not to mention most adults), he was as clean and pure as Dick Tracy, a straight-arrow cop who could do no wrong.

The summer I went to work in Washington, Dwight D. Eisenhower was just settling in at the White House, and Harry Truman had retired to his home in Missouri. The Republican Party controlled both houses of Congress. The Korean War had claimed two million lives, of whom more than thirty thousand were American servicemen, and hostilities continued despite a tenuous negotiated truce. While the United States and the Soviet Union solemnly debated a proposed United Nations ban on nuclear weapons, both major powers were secretly testing hydrogen bombs, some with up to twenty-five hundred times more explosive power than the atomic blast that had destroyed Hiroshima. Julius and Ethel Rosenberg, convicted of passing atomic secrets to the Russians, were executed at Sing Sing prison in New York; I read about that in the Washington *Post* one morning on my way to work.

Republican Senator Joseph R. McCarthy of Wisconsin, after winning election to a second term in 1952, soon reached the height of his powers (but not the depth of his disgrace) as a public official. In his capacity as chairman of a permanent investigations subcommittee, he went about irresponsibly hurling sensational charges of subversion and disloyalty at a wide assortment of Americans in and out of government. Millions of angry, frustrated citizens, from Presidents Truman and Eisenhower to the lowest level of Civil Service employees, found it almost impossible to counter the demagogic senator's broad-brush smear tactics. As time passed, his adversaries grew hesitant, cautious, fearful, silent—not because they were convinced, as McCarthy and J. Edgar Hoover asserted, that the nation was infested with hundreds of thousands of closet Communists and other traitors, but rather because they longed to placate and tame and finally to subdue the fanatical witch-hunters.

The McCarthy virus would not soon be arrested; it was keeping the FBI busy, and giving new life to the discredited House Un-American Activities Committee, with its heritage of invasive snooping passed down from Southern reactionaries like Martin Dies of Texas and John Rankin of Mississippi. And, beginning in 1951, there was yet another team of spy-seekers in the game: the Internal Security Subcommittee of the Senate Judiciary Committee, whose chief flamethrower was James O. Eastland, the spiritual heir to Mississippi's racist godfather, the late Theodore Bilbo.

Whistling and singing, the Class of '53 marched blithely right into the midst of all these tumultuous happenings. It wasn't the sound of silence that got our attention; what my generation heard were the swelling heralds of a new age reverberating all around us. In spiritual company with most American teenagers of the post–World War II era, we were, as the talk had it, grooving on the popular music of our day. We may have given dutiful tribute to the authority figures closest to us—parents, teachers, preachers—and even shown some fleeting attentiveness to the politicians and others who spoke from a higher platform. But in my recollection, the musicians and their music elicited far more respect and admiration from us than did anyone in an adult leadership role. In truth, we marched to a different drummer—or guitar, or brass horn—and the beat was its own reward.

The music of the fifties foretold a time of turbulent change. It was a rich and yeasty mixture of traditional and modern sounds—jazz and swing, bop and pop, country and Western, rhythm and blues, rock and roll—and a great deal of it had Southern roots. The first decade after the war was an especially fertile time of musical creativity. I still think reverently of such artists as Louis Armstrong and Duke Ellington, Dizzy Gillespie and Peggy Lee, Nat "King" Cole and Ella Fitzgerald, Hank Williams and Patsy Cline, Mahalia Jackson and "Leadbelly" (Huddie Ledbetter). All but a couple of those were native Southerners, either black or white, but in those days I didn't think about where they were from or what color they were—only that I liked the music they made.

Late at night I tuned in to WLAC in Nashville and listened to "Hoss" Allen and Gene Nobles spinning rhythm-and-blues platters from Randy's Record Shop in Gallatin, Tennessee. I never would have believed that they were white guys who just sounded black (not many blacks believed it, either). In the mainstream of pop music, the incredibly sensuous and exotic voice of Eartha Kitt singing "C'est Ci Bon" had me convinced that she was French, and I assumed that she was white; in fact, though, she was young and black and Southern—not long out of her teens, but a far piece from her origin in the tiny cotton-field hamlet of North, South Carolina.

A diverse variety of Southern musical traditions began to merge and cross-fertilize in the fifties. The folk music of the mountains and the fields, black blues and white honky-tonk, jazz and its derivatives, and church music in its many forms met in an ongoing instrumental and vocal exploration that would always produce a tension between traditionalists and innovators—and some very creative new music in the bargain. One consequence of the fusion would be the rock-and-roll revolution, which was then almost upon us. Among my favorite performers in that musical explosion of the mid-fifties were three young Southerners—two white, one black—whose artistry both blended and transcended race and color: Elvis Presley, "Little Richard" Penniman, and Jerry Lee Lewis. (One reason I identified with them, I'm sure, is that they were among the first of my generation—depression babies—to make it in the big time.) Ray Charles was coming on strong, too—black, blind, and brilliant. A teenage refugee out of south Georgia and north Florida, he could play and sing anybody's music—his own best of all. I marveled at his genius.

To think of all those performers in racial or regional terms made no sense at all; the music they created was simply beyond such classification, and though it had Southern roots, it was rapidly being nationalized by means of radio, television, records, and live performances on the road. The music was becoming integrated, in the fullest and truest sense of that word: united in its diversity, enriched and strengthened by a process that combined separate parts into an expanding whole, yet not robbing those individual elements of their distinctiveness and their integrity.

If music spoke to the possibilities of union, literature brought a more troubling message—or so, at least, did the premier novel of the mid-passage years: Ralph Ellison's *Invisible Man*, published in 1952. Deeply symbolic and metaphorical, Ellison's narrative traced the odyssey of an anonymous and nameless young black Southerner out of his oppressive motherland and into the forbidding, white-dominated world of the urban North. It was more, much more, than the author's thinly disguised autobiography; it was a universal tale of alienation and the search for identity, and it won critical praise, capped by the National Book Award.

Growing up on the black side of Oklahoma City, Ellison developed a boyhood appreciation of music and literature, and when he went to Alabama in 1933 to enroll at Tuskegee Institute, he aspired to a career in music. But three years later, seeking a respite from the dehumanizing racism of the Deep South, he took a summer job in New York and never returned. In the offices of the Federal Writers' Project, Ellison came under the influence of Richard Wright and Langston Hughes; it was with their encouragement (and with the help of a Rosenwald Fellowship and other kinds of support) that he was able to spend seven years writing the novel that would not only define his career but also the essence of the African-American experience after 330 years on this continent. The title alone spoke volumes: To be black in contemporary America was to be unseen and unvalued—ignored—by the white majority.

Once again, as they had in the thirties and forties, creative artists were preparing what amounted to a scouting report, an early forecast of the social climate. Out of the depths of their exploration and creativity, they were giving us a portent of variegated and interdependent but still inequitable things to come. And as before, few people heard and heeded these inner voices of admonition.

The turn of the midcentury provided a timely occasion for individual and collective stock-taking, the sort of backward and forward gazing that newspapers and magazines are wont to do. In the pages of the Southern press, the picture that came across in this largely numerical accounting was a mixture of positive and negative elements, heavily weighted to the former.

The population of the eleven-state region had increased by almost 5 million during the 1940s, to a total of more than 36.5 million. Virtually all of the growth was among whites; blacks had a net gain of only 196,000 people for the ten-year period, and now numbered slightly more than 9 million, or one-fourth of the South's census—down a full five percentage points in just twenty years. An estimated 2 million blacks left the rural South during the decade. By far the most of them had "gone up North," as it was commonly explained, but a substantial number, along with a great many whites, had moved into the urban South. Consequently, by 1950 there were thirty cities in the region with 100,000 or more people, ten of them with at least a quarter of a million. Just a half-century earlier, in the vast sweep of land south of the Ohio River, from the Atlantic Coast to the Southwestern desert, only New Orleans, Louisville, and Memphis could boast of a six-figure population.

Along with urban growth had come an industrial boom that would have made Henry Grady and the New South advocates of the 1880s swell with pride. World War II was responsible for much of it, bringing munitions plants and other war-production facilities that remained in peacetime (as did many military installations). Petrochemicals, textiles, wood-pulp and tobacco products, furniture, and soft drinks (led by the Atlanta-based Coca-Cola empire) were among the industries that helped to lift the South out of cotton serfdom. New nonfarm jobs and the higher wages they paid caused personal income in the region to increase by 225 percent in the 1940s, and for blacks the gains were even more dramatic—close to 400 percent. Life was at least relatively better for the generality of Southerners. Unemployment stayed consistently below five percent for whites in the midcentury years (but for blacks it was higher).

Still, the numbers concealed a chronic and pervasive pattern of inequity. For every ten dollars received by the average wage-earner elsewhere in the United States, the Southern worker got about seven. Black males employed in the South typically made only about half as much as their white counterparts. Unemployment was high and headed higher among the multitude of unskilled workers, particularly blacks. Job discrimination blocked many women and virtually all nonwhites from a vast array of attractive career opportunities. Efforts to correct these problems by guaranteeing fair employment practices through federal legislation were completely stymied by the ad-hoc coalition of Southern Democrats and Northern Republicans in Congress.

The on-again, off-again efforts of the national government to keep prices and wages from flying out of control were only marginally successful; while strike-plagued industries and labor unions blamed each other for the scourge of inflation, the value of a dollar fell to half of what it had been in the late 1930s. Inevitably, impoverished areas like the South were hardest hit—yet their political bosses in Washington and their economic bosses at home steadfastly opposed governmental economic planning, not to mention federal solutions to the problems of employment, education, health, and poverty.

The resistance of Dixie senators and representatives to Washington's intervention wasn't necessarily philosophical; when the primary beneficiaries were people like themselves—white, male, upper-class, conservative, and by their lights patriotic—the lawmakers could be exceedingly generous. They saw to it that their South got more than its share of military and agricultural largesse, but outside of those two pipelines there was precious little infusion of federal funds into the region. One notable exception was the Tennessee Valley Authority, by far the largest single government program of economic and social uplift below the Mason-Dixon line. It had the appealing virtue of earning a large portion of its budget from the sale of electricity. Even so, the agency stayed in hot water with the power lobby and with right-wing critics who opposed its "socialistic" policies and longed to do it in—or, better yet, convert it into a "free enterprise" utility. TVA had almost as many Southern detractors in Congress as it had defenders.

On the surface, the South showed signs of growth and progress similar to those in other parts of the country. The affluent new suburbs of Dallas and Houston and Atlanta were not unlike New York's and Chicago's. Consumer goods were the same for everyone who could afford them, whether they lived in California or the Carolinas. In 1951 alone, the number of American homes with television sets quadrupled, from three million to twelve million, and the South was in on that revolutionary development, too—not only as a "consumer" of the appliance, but also as a recipient of the homogenizing and culture-shaping content of TV programs.

This was not a time of intense regional or national preoccupation with the chronic problems of the South. The Truman administration and both houses of Congress had too many other pressing concerns, the war in Korea and the threat of Communist infiltration at home being foremost among them. What's more, Americans from every race, class, and region faced real or imagined worries—the Bomb, communism, unemployment, debt, divorce, social upheaval—and they were tired of war and postwar strife. And then, all too soon, there we were again, mired in another overseas military operation—this one euphemistically called a "police action."

The people had had enough conflict to last them a lifetime; they longed for rest, for peace and quiet—but Joe McCarthy was telling them they had to be watchful and suspicious, for even their most trusted associates might be spies. Almost no one wanted to stir up any more trouble. As long as the South was tagging along with the rest of the country, no elected officials and few others in public life seemed at all inclined to raise such troubling issues as the continuing denial of basic rights and opportunities to blacks, or the ongoing disadvantage of the South in the nation. That, they reminded one another, was the very sort of disruptive talk the Communists were using so deceitfully to undermine our confidence.

Yet it was precisely these problems of racial and regional inequity—the one sustaining the other—that festered beneath the surface of midcentury life in the region. In no remote sense could these be thought of as new problems. For nearly seventy-five years—since the end of Reconstruction—the political and economic rulers in the states of the Old Confederacy had gradually tightened their oligarchic grip until their control was more secure than it had ever been, even in the days of slavery. With the indulgence and complicity of their Yankee conquerors, they had locked the black minority in a straitjacket of segregation and built a self-perpetuating hierarchy based on political, economic, religious, and racial monopoly.

To sustain this "Southern way of life," the barons managed for decades to make voting not a right but a privilege reserved almost exclusively for educated, property-owning, middle- and upper-class white males. Inevitably, the same candidates got elected repeatedly to Congress, where seniority and parliamentary skill gave them power and influence far greater than their numbers. And so, over the years, an undemocratic pattern of vested privilege evolved. It was based in large measure upon an informal bargain: In the name of "states' rights," political control was restored to white Southerners, economic dominion remained with the North, and the troublesome race problem was controlled by a legal principle called "separate but equal."

That was the South that emerged around the turn of the century, and it was essentially the same South that remained in place through two world wars sandwiched around the Great Depression. Since the Civil War, the South had stood apart from the rest of the nation more by choice than compulsion. If it had ever intended to step forward as a full and equal national partner, rather than the separate nation it had tried to be, the right time would have been in 1945, when an energetic spirit of reform and renewal was sweeping across America and the world. White colonialism was in eclipse almost everywhere; the United Nations Declaration on

Human Rights was a formal affirmation of an idea whose time had come; and the U.S. Supreme Court, in case after case, was telling us that the separate-but-equal doctrine was a legal idea whose time had almost expired. And not only was white supremacy in doubt; the South's one-party, one-crop, one-church pillars were shaking too.

But Dixie couldn't bring itself to face the future; it kept looking to the past for its guiding light. Not even the prospect of genuine equality within and among the other states was enticement enough to make the region extend that guarantee to its own citizens, or to stop blaming its failures and shortcomings on "outside agitators"—whether Yankees, Communists, black militants, or the federal government. There's plenty of discrimination up North, they said; who are they to tell us how to run our states?

There *was* pervasive racial discrimination outside the South, of course, and complacent Northerners were no more prepared to confront it than were their neighbors below. They took reassurance from the exceptions they saw to the "invisible man" message of Ralph Ellison. Joe Louis had just ended a long and glorious reign as heavyweight boxing champion of the world; William Hastie, appointed by President Truman in 1949 to the federal appeals court bench in Washington, held the highest judicial post ever occupied by a black American; Jackie Robinson of the Dodgers was a dashing, handsome, and highly visible major-league baseball star, and others were already following him to that pinnacle; in 1950, Gwendolyn Brooks became the first black poet to win a Pulitzer Prize, and Ralph Bunche, winner of the Nobel Peace Prize that year, also desegregated the faculty at Harvard University, his alma mater.

Still, the exceptions only proved the rule. Harvard was more than three centuries old when it finally found a chair for Ralph Bunche, and in all of the nation's colleges and universities that weren't historically intended for blacks only, the presence of African-American students, let alone teachers, was still highly exceptional. For almost a decade, Judge Hastie would be the only black jurist on the federal bench. When the Supreme Court outlawed segregation in 1954, the American press was about as segregated as the church or the university; only twenty or so black general-assignment reporters worked at white-owned papers (none in the South, except for a few who wrote "colored news"). The election of a black congressman from Detroit in 1954 would bring to just 3 the number of members of his race then included among the 535 men and women serving in Congress. Worse than that, the number of black elected officials at all levels of government, from Washington down to the tiniest American municipality, was probably under a hundred.

It helped not at all for self-righteous white Northerners to turn away with eye-rolling condescension from the poor, struggling, benighted South—or for white Southerners to assume a judgmental air of moral superiority over Yankees. Behind both attitudes loomed large and discouraging realities: The nation, in its social blindness, was not yet ready to address its own racial prejudices, whether in the North or in the South— and the South was still far from coming to grips with the racial problems it had been bringing upon itself since the day the first slave ship docked at Jamestown in 1619.

Old habits die hard. Many Northerners persisted in thinking of all Southerners as their inferiors—or worse, as racists living in an other-worldly land of snakes and alligators. In the South, conservative whites held to their belief in the inferiority of blacks and the evil nature of Yankees, while liberals continued to struggle with their conflicting notions of political and social equality—as if the two could be defined and dealt with separately.

As it moved into the fifties, the South was still deeply divided within itself, unable to reconcile its conflicting identities. Was it to be an agricultural region or an industrial one, or both? Would it be hobbled forever with memories of its Lost Cause? Could it overcome its inferiority complex as a vanquished province, a colonial dependency, and become an equal partner in nationhood? Could it find a way to bring all of its sons and daughters into the Southern family—or would tens of thousands of the best and brightest continue the yearly exodus in search of a better chance in another social climate, leaving millions more to languish in a bleak state of deprivation and disadvantage?

The South was a land blessed with natural abundance—with rich, deep mineral deposits and bottomless fountains of fresh water, with soil so fertile that almost no amount of abuse could keep it from fecund productivity. It had enough heat and light and moisture to grow just about anything you planted, from a corn patch to a pine forest. The wooded mountains and hills teemed with wildlife. Even the sea that lapped at the eastern and southern shores of the region yielded a boundless harvest of nourishment, free for the taking. And yet, in the midst of this embarrassment of riches lived the poorest people in America, a biracial majority kept in line by violence, racism, isolation, and ignorance—all for the benefit of a small ruling class of politicians and their "invitation only" electorate.

The resources of the South stood in telling contrast to its vulnerability— one more contradiction in a land of eternal paradox. And for all its natural wealth, nothing it had was worth more than what it valued least: its treasure of human resources, the men and women of talent and character and courage who, down through the years, had given so much to it and for it—and who generally had gotten far less than they deserved from their leaders. The South at its best was quite simply the sum of its people. Many of them were generations deep, others more recently arrived. Some were going or gone; the rest, by fate or by choice, had stayed behind.

Some who left became famous. William Warfield of West Helena, Arkansas, and Leontyne Price of Laurel, Mississippi, had in common their African-American and small-town Southern roots and their careers as concert singers. They also shared two memorable experiences in 1952: co-starring roles in a revival of George Gershwin's *Porgy and Bess* that would play to packed houses on Broadway for two years—and their marriage, an event of some note even in blasé Manhattan, far from the cotton fields back home.

Much more avidly celebrated in the big city and around the country the year before that was a hot new baseball star, a twenty-year-old black kid from Fairfield, Alabama, by the name of Willie Mays, center fielder for the New York Giants; he led his team past the Dodgers and into the World Series in 1951, and was the National League's Rookie of the Year.

The exodus of black Southerners through the thirties and forties was a landmark in the history of human migration. To see it in personal terms, consider the story of William Gordon, born into a family of black Mississippi sharecroppers in 1919. Seventy years later, describing his childhood, Gordon still remembered the instability, the deprivation, the fear in which his family lived—two steps from slavery, one from peonage. They moved a lot; he and the other children seldom saw the inside of a school. But he was smart, and a teacher convinced his parents that they ought to send him away to a city, where he might get a good education. So, on a sweltering summer afternoon in 1933, fourteen-year-old Bill Gordon hopped on a cotton truck in Marked Tree, Arkansas, and rode away into another world across the Mississippi River in Memphis; he spent his first night in the city sleeping under a bridge.

Less than a year later, the Southern Tenant Farmers Union brought a little hope to sharecroppers around Marked Tree, but the youngster had a job and a school by then, and he never considered going back. Gordon finished high school and college in Memphis, worked for a black newspaper, spent two years in the army, got more education and newspaper experience in New York, and finally, in 1948, returned to the South as associate editor of the Atlanta *Daily World.* For the next ten years (after which he would have another career with the U.S. Information Agency), Bill Gordon tried, in his words, "to give back to my people and the South some of the hope and encouragement and support I had received." In

1952, with a recommendation from Ralph McGill of the *Constitution*, he won a Nieman fellowship to Harvard.

Margaret Walker was another black expatriate of the thirties who returned to the South. Her parents, both schoolteachers, were alumni of Northwestern University, and her father was also a Methodist minister in New Orleans. Those connections eased the way for their seventeen-year-old daughter to enter Northwestern in 1932. She returned eight years later with two degrees, three years of experience in the Federal Writers' Project, and a book of poetry, *For My People*, that would capture a young-poets' prize at Yale University after its publication in 1942. Richard Wright and others with whom she worked in the Chicago-based literary project sometimes dismissed Walker as "a little Southern bourgeois girl," but the spirited young woman showed tenacious determination and a confident sense of self-worth. She wrote *For My People* in lieu of a master's thesis at the University of Iowa in 1940, and then, for the better part of forty years, she taught at black colleges in the South, last and longest at Jackson State in Mississippi. Along the way she also married, raised three children, and returned to Iowa for her doctorate in the 1960s. That time, instead of a dissertation, she wrote a Civil War novel, *Jubilee*. Some critics called it another *Gone With the Wind*—only better—from a black Southern woman's perspective.

Not all of the migration was by blacks, and not all of it was out of the South; sometimes people moved *in*. A few, like Carl Sandburg, were famous before they came south, while others gained a certain celebrity after they arrived. Harry Golden was one of the latter. A Jewish immigrant from Eastern Europe, he had been raised on New York's Lower East Side. Upon moving to Charlotte, North Carolina, in the early 1940s, he managed by the force of his wit and personality to make a local place for himself—and eventually a national splash—with his highly personal journal, the *Carolina Israelite*. Golden was outspokenly critical of segregation; his most effective weapons were a keen knowledge of history, a storyteller's gift for gab, and an irrepressible sense of humor. Once he reported seeing three thermometers in a Southern hospital emergency room—one marked "white," one marked "colored," and one labeled "rectal." That, said Golden, "is what I call gradual integration."

Occasionally, the bright light of international fame fell upon a deep-rooted native Southerner. In October 1949, the resident novelist of Oxford, Mississippi, William Faulkner, wearing a tattered tweed jacket over a T-shirt, stayed unobtrusively in the background as the movie version of his latest book, *Intruder in the Dust*, had its world premiere in his hometown. A little over a year later, the author was formally dressed in black tie and tails when he stepped into the limelight at ceremonies in Stockholm, Sweden, to receive the Nobel Prize for Literature.

Next to the fame of Faulkner or that of his cross-state contemporary, Greenville's Hodding Carter, P. D. East of Petal, Mississippi, near Hattiesburg, was an absolute nobody—but he had a knack for getting people's attention. A self-made journalist like Harry Golden, East had Golden's satirical turn of mind, but with a more aggressive twist—and he picked a much more volatile place to give it expression. Born and raised in orphaned white poverty, he was thirty-two when he founded the *Petal Paper* in 1953, just as the race issue was about to explode across the South. For the remainder of the decade and on into the 1960s, he would keep up a lonely and risky monologue of taunting ridicule and cutting wit against the outraged sensibilities of white segregationists. No integrationist himself—at least not when he started the paper—East couldn't resist skewering racist politicians and their political-action committees, the Ku Klux Klan and the all-white Citizens' Council. Typical of his gallows humor were the "classified ads" he ran for cross-burning kits and summer-weight sheets of "Cotton Eyelet Embroidery" for Klansmen. ("Klanettes may enlarge the holes for arms, but your head will fit nicely through the eyelets as they are.")

And then there was William Bradford Huie, an enigmatic Alabamian who had practiced a sort of lone-wolf journalism for twenty years, generally on the right-wing side of politics, but who often managed to confound his critics by popping up in the most unexpected roles. A self-described "yellow-dog Democrat," he nevertheless admitted voting for Eisenhower in 1952, and he made no claim to racial liberalism. But in 1954, at the urging of novelist Zora Neale Hurston, he went to Live Oak, Florida, to "help establish the truth" in a sensational murder case involving a jailed black woman, Ruby McCollum, and her slain lover, a white doctor named C. LeRoy Adams, who was also the acknowledged father of her child. Huie, well known by then as the author of several books, including *The Execution of Private Slovik,* was a relentless investigator; before his inquiry was over, he had been convicted of contempt of court and ordered to jail in Live Oak. Whatever his racial or political views, he was never afraid to go where the facts led him.

People like East and Huie—white Southerners who wouldn't conform to the rigid racial mores of their neighbors—stood up and rocked the boat from time to time in the late forties and early fifties. They appeared to have little in common except this gadfly instinct, and the courage it took to exercise it. Most of them didn't start out with any deeply felt sense of moral outrage against segregation; they were, after all, products of a society that had always taken white supremacy for granted. But a higher motive eventually claimed their allegiance: a compelling need to tell the truth. It's hard to say what sparked it—religious conscience, professional ethics, economic practicality, or simply an unwillingness to pretend that the myths and self-delusions of racial privilege had to be accepted in a democratic society. As Gavin Stevens said in Faulkner's *Intruder in the Dust,* some things you must refuse to bear.

Such refusal might have been tolerated in the Roosevelt-Truman years, but it was becoming unacceptable to most Southern whites by the political season of 1950, and downright dangerous by the time Dwight Eisenhower was elected two years later. No one seemed more vulnerable in this regard than journalists who ran daily or weekly newspapers—and the smaller their papers, the greater their risk. They and only they (with the possible exception of preachers) were compelled by their professional calling to report and comment upon those who made the law, those who broke it, and those who needed its protection. When civil rights rulings by the federal courts brought all these players into focus, a common reaction to the unwelcome news thus generated was to stone the messengers.

The Southern press had always had a stubborn streak of independence, if not liberalism, and it could be argued persuasively that in the thirties and early forties, editors and writers from the region were at least as progressive in their social views as were their counterparts elsewhere. (The case is strengthened considerably if you count the expatriate writers, white and black, who were products of the South.) Even in the fifties, no less than ten newspapers and editorial writers from eight Southern states would receive Pulitzer Prizes—among the writers being Harry Ashmore and Ralph McGill.

Newspapering in some parts of the region was becoming a hazardous trade as the fifties unfolded. Every editor who survived at it must have felt that he or she was risking life and limb to perform an unprofitable public service that pleased almost no one. At Greenville in the Mississippi Delta, Hodding Carter caught hell for attacking the Citizens' Councils, the Klan, and the NAACP; for exposing lynching and opposing federal imposition of civil rights protections; for defending the South and blasting Bilbo and Eastland; for backing Roosevelt in 1944, Dewey in 1948, and Eisenhower in 1952. Some Northern critics called him a phony liberal, and even some beleaguered Southern activists, like Lillian Smith, had no kind words for him.

But only those who were on the firing line daily, like Carter and his wife and colleague, Betty Werlein Carter, could fully appreciate what it was like to meet deadlines and payrolls in an environment of extreme hostility—to turn a profit so you could come back tomorrow and tell your readers something else they didn't want to hear. And no state was tougher than Mississippi, where a simple call for obedience to the law came to be considered a radical act, and a strong defense of due process or respect for the courts and the Constitution was tantamount to betrayal. The handful of such "treasonous radicals" around the state—Ira B. Harkey in Pascagoula, J. Oliver Emmerich in McComb, Hazel Brannon Smith in Lexington, George McLean in Tupelo, and the quixotic P. D. East in Petal—all looked up to Carter as a model and an inspiration. "What it came down to," said Ashmore, "was courage, sheer guts. Hodding faced a lot more danger than I did in Little Rock, or McGill did in Atlanta." Covering the explosive race issue from Greenville in the fifties and sixties was akin to covering the Civil War from a little newspaper office in, say, Vicksburg or Bull Run or Shiloh—and finding daily fault with the Confederates as well as the Yankees.

Until the end of World War II, the term "liberal segregationist" was not an oxymoron in the South, but after the war it gradually became uncommon for anyone to be accorded the luxury of such a contradiction. By 1955, when the middle rock had eroded to a razor's edge, people had to choose to be one or the other, a liberal or a segregationist. A few, like Carter, kept hoping for some sort of compromise to emerge that would allow whites and blacks to live in tolerance and fairness and simple decency as equals in a society that still permitted and protected some racial separation. Ralph McGill's thinking closely paralleled Carter's on this, and neither of them was as pragmatically and philosophically accepting of complete integration as Harry Ashmore came to be. Both of them were also more inclined than the Little Rock editor to see the sinister forces of communism lurking behind the drive for racial equality.

But no one who was white, and thus spared the daily hazard (not to mention the indignity) of segregation and discrimination, could possibly see how absurd and obscene and insane this entire drama was becoming. To get that picture fully, you had to be on the receiving end; you had to be black and brave, visible and outspoken, a lightning rod.

John Henry McCray was such a man. Like Ashmore and the others, he was a journalist—writer, editor, publisher. His weekly *Lighthouse & Informer* in Columbia was called "the political bible of the new Negro voter in South Carolina." It was McCray, with Osceola McKaine and others, who had led the fight for black participation in the political process, and he was also a mainstay of the South Carolina NAACP, helping it to enroll the largest membership of any state in the South. McCray's popularity among black voters had made him a force to be reckoned with in and around Columbia. Every week in his paper, he had a bone to pick with his adversaries, white and black. "What has the South done for the Negro?" he asked rhetorically, and then answered, "Nothing. Nothing they didn't have to do. Everything that has been done has been done by the Negro, or by the threat of Federal court action."

In 1950, as a record number of black voters waited to pass judgment on the senatorial candidacy of Strom Thurmond and the gubernatorial bid of old-guard segregationist and ex–New Dealer James F. Byrnes, McCray got hit with a charge of criminal libel. He and a white reporter, working independently of each other, were indicted after writing stories about a convicted black rapist and his alleged victim, a white woman. Neither writer had named the victim, but under state law they could be prosecuted for defaming her in the eyes of those who knew her. McCray entered a plea of guilty at a hearing and was given a sixty-day suspended sentence and probation. The white reporter was not prosecuted.

In a surprise action in 1951, McCray's sentencing judge ordered him to serve sixty days on the chain gang, saying he had violated his parole by going out of the state to make two speeches. McCray appealed the ruling, but in 1952, the day after then-Governor Byrnes had tried to nudge South Carolina into the Republican column for Eisenhower (only to be thwarted by a massive turnout of blacks voting Democratic), the state supreme court—coincidentally or not—upheld the sentence. McCray's followers were outraged, but the editor himself reacted calmly. "Somewhere along the way I was bound to catch it," he wrote philosophically. "I accept it as nothing more than another step in our battle to obtain respect, and our rights as Americans. Remember: It costs to try to push forward the cause of our people. Let no man unwilling to be spent, if this befalls him, enter into the affray. So be of good cheer. I'll be back here soon, and when I return, I'll try to make up for lost time."

So John McCray went off to the chain gang, not knowing what the South Carolina penal system had in store for him. And in a little while he came back uncomplaining, having "no regrets" for anything he had done to end up in leg irons ("I'd do it again," he wrote). Thus restored, he took up with renewed enthusiasm the battle he had joined with the white oligarchy.

The white dissenters against injustice faced trials and tests of courage too, but nothing like this. Whatever else they had to endure, none of them ever came close to a stretch on the chain gang.

South Carolina was a study. It had produced a remarkable string of white-chauvinist politicians, from John C. Calhoun and Ben Tillman and Cole Blease to Cotton Ed Smith and Strom Thurmond—and on the other side an equally remarkable line of black and white believers in democratic parity: Osceola McKaine, John McCray, Modjeska Simkins, Witherspoon

Dodge, J. Waties Waring, and others not so well remembered—like Jack O'Dowd, editor of the Florence *Morning News.*

His father, publisher John M. O'Dowd, was for years a moderate and fair-minded defender of the rights of black citizens in the courts and at the polls. In 1952 he began grooming his son, a graduate of the Citadel and a veteran of the Korean War, to take over the paper. For a couple of years the young editor tried to steer a middle course on the volatile race question. But when the U.S. Supreme Court outlawed school segregation in May 1954, O'Dowd urged his readers to accept it in good grace. In his editorials and in speeches in the community, he was earnest, forthright, candid, realistic. He was also harassed and threatened, and the paper suffered heavy losses in advertising and circulation. Finally, in July 1956, twenty-nine-year-old Jack O'Dowd would bow to extremist pressure and the silence of what he believed was a moderate majority. His father, facing the loss of the paper he had been publishing since 1912, asked his son to resign, and he did. Jack O'Dowd took another newspaper job in Chicago, and never again lived in the South.

South Carolina and the other states of deepest Dixie (Georgia, Alabama, Mississippi, Louisiana) were to become the molten core of volcanic reaction to desegregation, the hardest places for honesty and courage to survive. And yet, in those very places there were people of vision, whites and blacks alike, who saw the trouble that was coming and dared to describe it. One more example from South Carolina underscores the point.

James McBride Dabbs, the resident farmer-philosopher of Rip Raps Plantation near Mayesville, had about him an image of Old South gentility. He had been born near there in 1895, and had moved into the big house, his grandfather's place, in 1937. Dabbs was an English professor, a gentleman planter, a softhearted patrician somewhat reminiscent of Mississippi's William Alexander Percy. But when the issue of race confronted him in the forties, his intellect and his sense of practicality and his Presbyterian probity brought him to an unshakable conviction that segregation had to go.

He joined the Southern Regional Council in the 1940s, and later, in 1957, he would be elected its president. Dabbs was a thinker and a writer—a quiet man, not a crusader. He and his wife lived alone in the old plantation house that was a mere shadow of its long-gone glory. What he thought about there, and said eloquently with soft-spoken courage in his books and articles, came down to this: As different as Southerners are in many ways from one another, they all belong ultimately to one culture, and the time had come to recognize that. "We're first cousins talking about one another, don't you see, cultural first cousins." Whatever Southern whites and blacks claim to think about each other doesn't matter in the end: "I really don't bother much about their *liking* one another," Dabbs said. "The more fundamental fact is that they are *alike* one another"—and eventually, so his faith told him, they will evolve a diverse but united society better than any the South has ever known.

Integration was not simply our best choice, wrote Dabbs in the first of his several books, *The Southern Heritage;* it was our only choice: "It is too late now to live by the past. The wall of segregation is crumbling," and the South has suffered ever since it "enthroned a god upon the wall and made of segregation a sacred thing" and made Southerners "the people of the wall." In another realm of its history, the patrician scholar reminded his readers, the South looked to a worthier deity, one whose guidance was credited with saving many a beleaguered and oppressed society, including the people of Israel. Now it was Southerners, the modern-day Israelites, who waited for leadership and liberation. And now, once again,

> there looms against the sky the ancient Southern god, the pillar of fire
> by night and cloud by day, forever leading us out of the wilderness
> into the Promised Land. For we are not simply being pushed into the
> future; we are also going by our own free will.

It was not just to the choir and the converts that James M. Dabbs addressed himself. His faith was that the rank and file of decent Southerners were the real majority, and his aim was to touch them gently, to appeal to their innate sense of fair play.

His spiritual and philosophical brother in black in this pivotal time of Southern history was J. Saunders Redding. He too was a professor of English (at Hampton Institute in Virginia, one of the foremost black colleges of the region); he too was a writer, a philosopher, a cultural critic— and, as time would tell, a prophet. And, again like Dabbs, Redding wanted to challenge a larger audience of Americans.

His experiences in academia had taken him to various Southern campuses, to New York and New England, and finally in 1943 to Hampton, where he would remain for more than twenty years. Redding wrote fiction and history with admirable style, but his first strength was in personal essays of social observation and opinion. In the spirit of his intellectual and cultural hero, W. E. B. Du Bois, he stripped away all scholarly pretense to objectivity and detachment and spoke his mind about the myth of race, "a barrier to nearly everyone, white and black, in America," he wrote,

> a burden on the conscience and on the soul! This is what the books by
> both Southern apologists and liberals mean. This is what Lillian Smith
> and Hodding Carter and Howard Odum mean. I can even believe
> that John Rankin and Richard Russell and James Byrnes and Strom
> Thurmond signify this in their acts and in their words, and that

Theodore Bilbo signified this too. Whiteness does not mitigate the relentless warping by the race situation in America. White men are half-men too—sick men, and perhaps some of them the more to be pitied because they do not know they are sick. Some of them—the good, lucky ones, like Lillian Smith—have succeeded somewhat in objectifying it; but neither for them nor for me is there a neutral ground on which to stand. Neither they nor I can resign from the human race. The best I can hope to do is to externalize the struggle and set it in the unconfined context of the universal struggle for human dignity and wholeness and unity.

The looming racial crisis of the 1950s led Saunders Redding to declare, "It is time that the scholars' conscience spoke out in the world." But the cost of speaking out was escalating rapidly for all who harbored doubts about the direction in which the South was moving. Since long before the 1930s, black Southerners of all classes and callings had been the ones whose words and deeds were the most compelling, for it was they who bore, in mind and body, the brunt of painful blows from segregation and white supremacy.

Now, for many whites in all parts of the South, a time of agonizing decision was at hand, a time to stand up and speak out for the principles of equality—or else be counted in the ranks of the reactionaries. To choose the former would not be easy, because virtually no white leaders were actively and openly pledged to the democratic and constitutional ideal. By appealing to the basest emotions of greed and hatred and fear, they had built a majority in favor of—or at least acquiescent in—the wrong choice, a majority willing to be led to march backward.

Southern blacks, though, had a much different perspective. For the vast majority of them, a return to the old patterns of unchallenged white supremacy was out of the question. For them, the choice of equality had long since been made.

2. *Anticommunist White Supremacy*

Chapel Hill was a different place, and the University of North Carolina a diminished institution, without Frank Porter Graham. The picture-perfect little village and the shady campus facing it across Franklin Street still had an idyllic, movie-set appearance—but Mister Chips was gone, and so was an era. The university he had shepherded to greatness entered a new phase in its long history on the spring day in 1949 when he resigned as president and accepted an appointment to the U.S. Senate. Not all of the changes that followed were immediately evident, and not all were for the worse—and some may have had little if anything to do with Frank Graham—but his departure after a tenure of nearly twenty years was unquestionably a great loss, not only for the university but for the state and the South.

The worst of it was not his resignation, though; it was his defeat in the special election of 1950. For well over a decade, Graham had been the most visible and influential liberal spokesman in the South, the one to whom every would-be reformer and even some conservatives looked with great respect. His figurative mugging in a bitter and vicious campaign not only toppled him from the pinnacle of regional leadership; it also signaled the end of a season of modest social reforms and opened the floodgates of right-wing extremism.

Deeply wounded by the meanness of his undoing, Graham was an enigma to his friends and enemies alike when he returned briefly to the Senate after the primary. Inexplicably, he sided with his obstructionist Southern colleagues in blocking creation of a permanent Fair Employment Practices Commission. Then he inserted a lengthy "farewell statement" in the *Congressional Record*, a minutely detailed and somewhat defensive explanation of his liberal involvements down through the years; it dismayed his admiring defenders, and struck his enemies as a weak apology.

At sixty-four, Graham was a selfless public servant whose defeat had left him with no resources to fall back on—no house, no job, no estate. After turning down several posts offered him by President Truman, he worked briefly at the Department of Labor and then, moving with his wife to New York City, took up a new career at the United Nations. Sixteen years later he would return to Chapel Hill to live out his last years alone, a widower with no children. He was charming and gracious as always, but his sunny demeanor hid an ineffable sadness. He died in 1972.

The Frank Graham era is still remembered by those who were part of it as the golden age of the University of North Carolina. His friend and fellow alumnus Jonathan Daniels characterized it in 1941 as "the freest university in the South—as free as any in America." It had been a place of no particular distinction early on, Daniels wrote, describing it as "starved and sleepy, set-upon from without and also at times eruditely complacent within the superior indolence of cultivated minds." Graham, continuing a reformation started by his predecessor, Harry Woodburn Chase, had skillfully turned the scholarship of the institution from esoteric detachment to utilitarian engagement; in a word, he made the place useful, to the end that it might enhance "the human qualities of the State and the South."

Against the opposition of religious and political extremists who accused him of protecting radical crackpots and leading innocent youths into atheism and communism (how could such a faithful Presbyterian be a Communist?), Graham had depended on such progressive activists as Howard Odum and the social scientists, Paul Green and his theater, W. T. Couch and the university press, to lift UNC into the front rank of American universities. They succeeded far beyond anyone's expansive dreams— making Graham, in the estimation of Jonathan Daniels, "the single most important human force for enlightenment" in North Carolina—or, for that matter, in the entire South.

Will Alexander certainly agreed. Having left the federal government before Roosevelt died, left the Commission on Interracial Cooperation when it became the Southern Regional Council, and left the Rosenwald Fund when it folded, Alexander retired with his wife to their farm outside Chapel Hill, there to raise cattle, receive visitors, and reminisce about his thirty years as a Southern activist. His many friends, white and black, came from around the country to visit, and he kept his hand in as an adviser and consultant to some of them.

Alexander declined to support his former boss, Henry Wallace, in the 1948 election, favoring Harry Truman instead, and he raised funds for his old friend Frank Graham in 1950. But by that time the retired administrator and his wife were feeling the chill of Cold War conservatism creeping up around their ankles. Rumors circulated that the Alexanders were "buying up land for Eleanor Roosevelt and the Jews to give away to niggers." A suggestion that "Dr. Will" be awarded an honorary degree by the university died aborning. He was thought by several members of the UNC board of trustees to be trying to engineer the desegregation of the school, and some of those critics joined in an organized effort to force Alexander out of the community.

Some of his former friends on the campus seemed to be shying away from him, so much so that he decided to distance himself from the academic environment, lest he bring Graham and others under suspicion of guilt by association. After Graham was defeated, a deeper sense of isolation set in, and while some of Alexander's campus friends still drove out to the farm to visit and others continued to come from out of town, the dean of Southern liberals sensed a permanent change for the worse in his relationship with the liberal community in Chapel Hill.

The telling signs were not just figments of the old warrior's imagination: UNC in 1951 was not "as free as any university in America," as Jonathan Daniels had characterized it a decade earlier. The institution's trustees chose a wealthy and conservative Winston-Salem businessman, Gordon Gray (then Secretary of the Army under President Truman), to replace Graham, but he was poorly suited for the post, and left it in less than five years. The annual list of new books from the UNC Press after the war clearly showed a declining interest in Southern social problems, in progressive and liberal topics, and in black writers. The social science empire that Howard Odum had built up over a thirty-year period was losing its primacy in applied research and service. Many of the luminaries whose contributions had brought distinction to the campus—Odum, Green, Couch, and others—were either nearing retirement or already gone. But worst of all for Will Alexander was the atmosphere of cautious silence that seemed to permeate liberal circles around Chapel Hill after Frank Graham's departure. Feeling at times like a stranger and an outsider, Dr. Will was saddened and puzzled by this unexpected turn. The estrangement would linger until his death in 1956.

UNC's legacy of tolerance and progressivism was tarnished further in 1951. Desegregation of the university—one of the few things Frank Graham had failed to accomplish—was mandated by a federal appeals court that fall, and while no physical violence accompanied the historic event, neither was there a display of charity or hospitality or sportsmanship such as one might expect of a truly great institution. Many individual members of the faculty and student body did welcome the change, but the university administration, having fought it in court for over a decade, put up an official front much like that usually presented by losers in protracted legal battles, with unrepentant, tight-lipped attorneys delegated to rationalize the defeat.

Four of the entering black students had been attending the makeshift law school thrown up by the state at North Carolina College for Negroes in Durham after Pauli Murray's application to UNC was sidetracked back in 1939. They had sued for equal treatment as citizens and taxpayers—and twelve years after Murray blazed the trail, they finally won the right of admission to the Chapel Hill campus. One of the students, Floyd B. McKissick, a World War II veteran, practiced law in Durham after graduating from UNC, and later would become national director of the Congress of Racial Equality.

In 1952, the liberal minister of Chapel Hill's First Presbyterian Church on Franklin Street, the Reverend Charles M. Jones, was accused of heresy by the governing body of North Carolina church leaders to whom he and his local members answered. Ostensibly the conflict was about liturgy and creeds, but beneath the surface was a festering hostility toward Jones and his supportive congregation, which was made up largely of free-thinking university people, including Frank Graham. Jones had guided his flock to a collective expression of social consciousness that included de-segregation of all church functions, and he was well known in the community for his progressive leadership. But the ruling elders forced him out, and though he remained in Chapel Hill as the pastor of a popular new nondenominational church, his resignation from the top Presbyterian pastorate thereabouts was widely viewed as yet another chilling sign of the right-wing ascendency.

Almost within arm's reach of the First Presbyterian Church, the celebrated little Intimate Bookshop, founded in the 1920s by Milton Abernethy, had recently changed hands, but Abernethy was still an inspiration to the loose network of avant-garde intellectuals around the campus—and he became their hero in 1953 after he was hauled before a congressional committee and accused of being a Communist. In his student days, the enterprising Abernethy had not only run the bookshop but had also published a literary paper, *Contempo*, that boasted of original manuscripts from the likes of William Faulkner, T. S. Eliot, and Langston Hughes. The Senate Internal Security Subcommittee, with Frank Graham's political executioner Willis Smith playing a prominent role, aggressively probed Abernethy's past, alleging that he had run an underground press for the Communist Party from the back room of his shop in the 1930s. The inquisition was an empty charade that came to naught, but its intimidating effect was immeasurable.

The mention of Langston Hughes in connection with Abernethy brought to mind the black poet's visit to UNC in the early 1930s. Though his reading before a packed house in the university theater had stirred some controversy, Hughes had been invited to the campus by Paul Green and Guy B. Johnson, and had gone to dinner at a local restaurant with Abernethy and some of his friends. James Weldon Johnson had been even more warmly received at UNC earlier, and Richard Wright was also welcomed before the war—but now, in the forbidding fifties, the very thought of a distinguished black guest was out of the question. What's more, the hostile pursuit of Milton Abernethy by an official committee of the U.S. Senate underscored a fundamental new reality in Chapel Hill: Intellectual freedom and personal liberty were no longer the guiding principles that distinguished the town and the university.

Junius Irving Scales learned that lesson the hard way. He had moved to Chapel Hill with his family from Greensboro in 1935, when he was fifteen years old, and thus was immersed from an early age in the liberal spirit of the town and the campus. Scales had impeccable credentials as a Southerner—his father was a wealthy lawyer, his late grandfather had been a colonel in the Confederate Army, and the family was comfortably ensconced in all the right social and political and church circles.

Between the time of his enrollment at UNC in 1937 and his induction into the army in 1942, Junius Scales experienced a personal transformation of great magnitude. From an early age he had been sympathetic with people who were quite unlike his family and friends—the ones his Sunday school lessons identified as "the least of these"—and in those idealistic years he came to see the lowly black minority and the laboring class of both races as fitting that description. Dabbling in radical politics, Scales eventually became an active and committed member of the American Communist Party, dropping out of school once to undergo training as a labor and party organizer.

When he came back to Chapel Hill after four years in the military, the university was bursting at the seams with ex-GIs (enrollment soared to eight thousand, triple its prewar level) and the political scene was more volatile than ever. Quickly, Scales became a leader in the student chapters of the American Veterans Committee, the Southern Conference for Human Welfare, and the Communist Party; in the fall of 1946 he was elected a vice president of the Southern Negro Youth Congress—the only white officer ever to serve in that organization. The personable and well-connected young radical was soon acknowledged as the leading left-wing spokesman in Chapel Hill.

But events elsewhere were about to signal open season on radicals, and no Southerner would be more profoundly affected than Junius Scales. In the fall of 1947, just as the anticommunist campaign was kicking into gear and the Truman civil rights committee was condemning segregation and the anti-Truman Democrats were joining the Henry Wallace revolt, Scales announced his allegiance to the Communist Party. Instead of winning him a larger following, however, the "coming out" caused many veterans, union loyalists, church and university activists, and liberals in general to run for cover, leaving Scales and a handful of others to drift ever deeper into a deadly cat-and-mouse game with intelligence agents of the federal government.

Benevolent motivations had made him a strident critic of inequality. In formalizing his outrage by pledging loyalty to an international political ideology, he had naively become a walking contradiction: a true believer in peace and brotherhood and democracy who was giving himself in blind obedience to a violent and oppressive foreign hierarchy. Junius Scales was about as serious a threat to the peace and liberty of North Carolina and the South as you might expect almost any upper-class, college-educated, Presbyterian idealist from Greensboro or Chapel Hill to be—which is to say, not much of a threat at all. But in the harrowing Cold War struggle that had evolved, he fit the strict definition of a "Soviet agent," and that made him a prime target of the spy-hunters.

For seven years the game of chase dragged on. When it started, Scales was passing out press releases while agents lurked in the shadows; when it ended, in November 1954, FBI and Justice Department officials would be telling reporters how they had tracked Scales to Memphis, lured him out of hiding, and arrested him. Almost everything changed in that seven-year period. The Soviet Union was first celebrated as our wartime ally and then denounced as a terrorist regime; the U.S. Communist Party was first pictured as a potent force and then exposed as a house of cards; surveillance was maintained by a relatively small cadre of government spies in the beginning, and an army of counter-subversive agents in the end. Scales was a small fish when he dived out of sight—but when they reeled him to the surface, he was a prize catch.

Another seven years of legal skirmishing would drag by before Scales, charged with joining an organization in the knowledge that it "advocated the overthrow of the U.S. Government by force and violence," would finally be convicted in a federal courtroom in his native Greensboro and sent to serve six years in prison. (No more severe penalty would ever be meted out under the notorious Smith Act, and the law itself would eventually be declared unconstitutional.) The liberal community of UNC and Chapel Hill was made profoundly uncomfortable by this native son whom most of them knew and many had encouraged in his radicalism. Three of them—Charles Jones, the ex-Presbyterian minister; Raymond Adams, a Thoreau scholar in the English department; and Fletcher M. Green, chairman of the history department—testified to his good character, as did Mary Leigh Pell Scales, the defendant's mother. Numerous others could have followed them to the witness stand, but they decided for their own reasons to let that cup pass.

When he went to prison in 1961 (by which time he had repudiated the Communist Party in disillusionment), Junius Scales would have the dubious distinction of being the only Southerner ever tried and convicted in a Southern court on any charge having to do with communism. After years of surveillance and detection, the red-hunters had finally nabbed "a nigger-loving commie," as some of them delighted in calling him. It hardly seemed to matter that Scales was their only official captive (and even he was released after a little more than a year, with his sentence commuted to time served).

From 1947 to 1962, the authorities could claim bounty points on Scales, first as a fugitive, then as a defendant, and finally as a convict—and always as an avowed Communist deeply committed to winning equal rights for blacks and organized labor. Reactionary Southern leaders who considered all integrationists and trade unionists to be at least fellow travelers if not card-carrying reds must have looked thankfully upon this bird in hand; he was literally the only one they could point to in illustration of their specious claim. If Scales hadn't come along when he did, they would have had to invent him.

Outside the South, anticommunism had little directly to do with race. No doubt W. E. B. Du Bois and Paul Robeson gravitated to the Communist ideology at least in part because of their despair and disgust with American racism, but the U.S. authorities who hounded them probably would have been just as aggressive had the two been white men extolling the virtues of Marxist-Leninist ideology and Soviet policy.

Joe McCarthy showed no interest in race, consumed as he was with the persecution of anyone who didn't buy his brand of patriotic Americanism. William F. Buckley, Jr., coauthored a militantly pro-McCarthy book in 1954 that gave only the barest mention to race or the South. Even the House Un-American Activities Committee, long controlled by Dixie demagogues Martin Dies and John Rankin, was by the early 1950s a preserve of Midwestern Republicans and assorted other arch-conservatives who found nothing in the race relations of the South half as stimulating as the threat of subversive cells in Hollywood or Manhattan. And, with the United States at war against the international Communist menace in Korea, it was easy for the nation to let the South and its racial problems fall between the cracks, as had happened so many times before.

The national climate of reactionary anticommunism and rock-ribbed conservatism was all-pervasive in the early fifties. The American Medical Association fought tooth and nail against proposed health-care reforms, calling them "communistic attempts to force socialized medicine on doctors and their patients." The American Bar Association adopted resolutions in support of states' rights and segregation that could as easily have been written in Birmingham or Jackson as in Seattle or Cleveland. The Southern Newspaper Publishers Association, in opposing the United Nations Declaration on Human Rights as "a serious threat to the basic American freedoms of religion, speech, press, assembly, and petition," echoed the sentiments of the national assembly of publishers. The U.S. Chamber of Commerce, the National Association of Manufacturers, and numerous others were equally as intemperate in their pronouncements.

All of this conservative militancy played well in the South, particularly after the Republican victories of 1952. Since concern for the civil rights of black Americans was a long-expressed position of the Communist Party, it was a short and easy step from there for white Southerners to attack all civil rights advocates as reds. If you stood for anything the Communists were for, you were a fellow traveler or a party-liner; if you belonged to the NAACP—staunchly anticommunist though it was—you were a red or a criminal, or both. For conservative white Southerners, the rigid rules of order could be reduced to a simple litany: Subjugate the blacks and fight the unions, the welfare state, big government, higher taxes, and all things socialized. And if white supremacy alone was not enough to keep the blacks down and the whites unified, anticommunist white supremacy would surely do the trick.

One more significant reason for the potency of the anti-red offensive in the South was the fact that it energized some liberals and leftists almost as much as their conservative counterparts. The Socialist farm-union leaders, Howard Kester and H. L. Mitchell, had bitterly opposed the Communists back in the thirties; individuals and organizations as widely separated as Virginius Dabney and Ralph McGill, Howard Odum and Charles S. Johnson, Lillian Smith and Francis Pickens Miller, the CIO and the Americans for Democratic Action, expressed similar views through the forties and fifties. McGill savagely red-baited the Southern Conference Educational Fund in 1950, and the NAACP was caught up in the same reflex impulse to prove its own purity by being tough on radicals. The fact that all of these critics would themselves be branded as Communists by the far right was solid proof that the real litmus test was white supremacy; those who flunked it were dyed an unacceptable shade of pink, and that was that.

By 1951—an ominous year of heightened tensions in the South—the reinforced phenomenon of anticommunist white supremacy had come to full flower, and it had more thorns than a thistle. The Korean War alone would have been more than enough to keep the nation on edge, presenting as it did the emotional combination of heavy casualties, a frustrating stalemate, and President Truman's dismissal of his popular military commander, General Douglas MacArthur. But there was much more going on, from the continuing rampage of McCarthyism to the spy trials of Julius and Ethel Rosenberg to the indictment, trial, and acquittal of W. E. B. Du Bois on charges that he was a secret agent of a foreign power. (And if that still wasn't enough, you could turn on the television and watch the Senate hearings on organized crime, a daily drama skillfully directed by first-term senator Estes Kefauver of Tennessee.)

Such developments as these had consequences in the South, but they were lessened by the fact that the events themselves occurred elsewhere. Of far greater impact were those that happened inside the region. The token desegregation of the University of North Carolina that autumn brought to five the number of Southern states (plus six others on the region's border) where the color bar had been lowered; just since 1948, federal court rulings had ordered public universities in six states not to exclude black students because of their race, and that consistent judicial pattern would be continued until the last of the states—Georgia, Alabama, Mississippi, and South Carolina—were finally desegregated in the early 1960s.

No ugly incidents marred the advent of these changes in Texas, Virginia, Louisiana, and North Carolina in 1950 and 1951, but elsewhere in the South, the violence that was so often associated with racial matters continued to take its toll on all who were caught up in it, victims and perpetrators alike. Only one racial killing was officially classified as a lynching in 1951, and for the next three years after that, there were none—but numerous explosive acts of violence still claimed lives, and by far the most of them involved the deaths of blacks at the hands of whites.

Some of the most bizarre acts were official state executions. In Virginia, seven black men charged with raping a white woman were swiftly convicted, and after all appeals failed, the seven were electrocuted in the same week—four on one day and three on another. In Mississippi, a black man reportedly involved in a consensual relationship with a married white woman was tried three times for rape before the state supreme court got a conviction it could uphold. Two more years of legal pleadings drew national attention to the case before the defendant, Willie McGee, was put to death in a portable electric chair at the Jones County Courthouse in Laurel. Cheers went up from the crowd of about a thousand whites waiting outside; many more listened to a broadcast of the event on a statewide radio hookup.

The most shocking terrorist act of 1951 took place on Christmas night in Mims, Florida, a little town east of Orlando. Harry T. Moore, a schoolteacher and state director of the NAACP, died with his wife, Harriette, when a bomb planted under their house exploded. An FBI investigation turned up several suspects, but no one was ever prosecuted in the case. Almost forty years later, a former marine and Ku Klux Klansman told NAACP officials that he and other Klansmen had conspired with law-enforcement officials to plan and carry out the murder. One of the lawmen implicated was Lake County Sheriff Willis McCall, who had himself been tried and acquitted of murder a short time before in the suspicious shooting of two handcuffed black prisoners he was transporting to trial.

According to a subsequent report from the Southern Regional Council in Atlanta, the homes of forty black Southern families were bombed during 1951 and 1952. Some, like Harry Moore, were social activists whose work exposed them to danger, but most were either people who had refused to bow to racist convention, or were simply innocent bystanders, unsuspecting victims of random white terrorism. It was a perilous time to stand on the racial fault line in the South, and it was getting more dangerous by the day.

White people who dared to question the racial status quo were also at risk. Frank Graham and Dorothy Tilly were showered with verbal abuse and threats for years after they served on the President's Committee on Civil Rights. Lillian Smith was threatened so frequently from the mid-thirties on that she was finally able—some of the time, at least—to brush off anonymous hostility with aplomb. Hodding Carter kept a loaded gun in his desk at the *Delta Democrat-Times,* explaining that "Southerners will generally treat you politely until they make up their minds to kill you." Dozens of others were forced to the realization that it took enormous courage to risk your job, your health, your good standing in the community, or your very life by taking even mild exception to the ever-tightening white code of racial conduct.

And once more, anti-red was blended with anti-black. Time and time again in the fifties, people who had been active in the Southern Conference for Human Welfare years earlier had their liberalism thrown back at them with insinuations that they were "security risks," or somehow lacking in whatever it took to be loyal Americans. The radicals among them—Aubrey Williams, Myles Horton, Jim Dombrowski, and others—came to expect the slanderous accusations that were heaped upon them, but more moderately inclined people such as Francis Pickens Miller, C. Vann Woodward, Herman C. Nixon, and Philip Hammer hardly knew how to respond to such nonsense.

Democratic social reform in the South was being sacrificed on the altar of anticommunist white supremacy, and no force in or out of the region seemed strong enough—or concerned enough—to come to the aid of the reformers. In Washington, the Truman administration was fighting for its life against the conservative Republican insurgency, and no one on the President's staff was any longer giving much thought to race or the South. With the advent of the Eisenhower administration in 1953, Southerners of both races and black Americans in general would find themselves relegated to the lowest echelons of national interest and priority.

In New York, government agents were busy prosecuting W. E. B. Du Bois on a charge so manifestly weak that the judge issued a directed verdict of acquittal without even hearing the case for the defense. Harassment of the aged scholar got worse after that. His passport was invalidated, as was Paul Robeson's, and through most of the fifties, these two enormously talented and towering figures in American social history had to endure the shameful attempts of federal officials to discredit and silence them. Robeson lost his popularity, but never his artistic genius or his dignity. Du Bois finally renounced his U.S. citizenship in 1961, when he was ninety-three; two years later he died in Accra, Ghana, his adopted home, ending a singular career that had spanned three-quarters of a century.

Even white Southerners who left the region were not safe from attack. John Henry Faulk, a folksy humorist from Austin, Texas, built a career for himself on the CBS radio network with monologues that reminded listeners of Mark Twain and Will Rogers. But he was blacklisted by Aware, Incorporated, a right-wing snoop group in New York that was feeding malicious material to Joe McCarthy and the House Un-American Activities Committee. Fearful CBS executives ordered Faulk, a union member and a liberal, to apologize to his accusers and stop criticizing the anticommunist movement; when he refused, they fired him. Shut out of the industry and unable to find work for six years, he finally won a libel judgment against Aware.

The three-and-a-half-year period between the midterm elections in November 1950 and the U.S. Supreme Court's *Brown* decision in May 1954 was a disillusioning time for white and black Southerners who had come to see that far-reaching social reforms in the region were both necessary and inevitable. Those who had tried for so long to coax and nudge their region out of its reactionary racism didn't know—couldn't have known— that the last realistic hope for self-generated reform had gone up in smoke by the end of 1950. They kept on trying, and now and again they made some headway, but for all practical purposes there was not much left for anyone to do—except for those who remained in the center to choose sides. In the organizations and institutions from which liberal and progressive ideas and energy had been trickling for two decades, it was now harder than ever to see, hear, or feel a measurable degree of momentum for social change.

The Southern Regional Council, curiously enough, had a breakthrough on the racial front early in the new decade, finally coming down firmly on the side of absolute equality for all citizens in an open society. After eight years of debate and disagreement, the Council on December 12, 1951, adopted "a statement of policy and aims" that used the word *segregation* only once but made explicit the intent of the organization to work for the creation of a society in which racial discrimination no longer existed. The document, drafted by staff member Harold Fleming, pledged the members to seek this vision:

Hodding Carter, editor of the Delta Democrat-Times *in Greenville, Mississippi, at work in his office*

Arkansas Gazette *editor Harry S. Ashmore in the newsroom of the Little Rock paper*

Edwin R. Embree (left), director of the Julius Rosenwald Fund, being interviewed during the Race Relations Institute at Fisk University in 1947 by New York Times *reporter George Streator, a Nashville native and Fisk alumnus*

Left: *After half a century of prominence as a scholar and activist, W. E. B. Du Bois was internationally renowned, controversial—and still deeply engaged in intellectual and political issues.*

Right: *Benjamin E. Mays was forty-five years old when he returned to his native South in 1940 to begin a twenty-seven-year tenure as president of Morehouse College.*

John H. McCray, cofounder of the South Carolina Progressive Democratic Party in 1944 and editor of the Lighthouse & Informer in Columbia, speaking at a black church in the early 1950s

Two weeks after the first federal court ruling in the Clarendon County, South Carolina, school desegregation case in May 1951, the state NAACP honored the plaintiffs and others who had joined in the legal challenge to segregation. Taking part were (from left) Modjeska Simkins, J. W. Seals, S. J. McDonald (presenting citation), J. A. DeLaine (organizer of the Clarendon plaintiffs), lead plaintiff Harry Briggs, Sr. (receiving citation), John H. McCray, Flutie Boyd, and James Hinton, state NAACP president.

The Senate Judiciary Committee's Internal Security Subcommittee was closely identified with Mississippi's senior senator, James O. Eastland (left), throughout much of the 1950s and 1960s. Democrat-turned-Republican Strom Thurmond of South Carolina (right) was another of the Southerners who used the powers of congressional inquiry to attack advocates of desegregation in the South.

Senator Kenneth D. McKellar, Democrat of Tennessee (below), had been in Congress for more than forty years when he campaigned unsuccessfully for reelection in 1952. Tennessee Congressman Albert Gore, Sr., stayed on the road to wear out the aging incumbent in the Democratic primary.

After the Supreme Court outlawed school segregation and the Reverend Martin Luther King, Jr., emerged as the leader of the antisegregation movement in the South, billboards showing King at a "Communist Training School"—Highlander—were posted throughout the region. Among those in the photo with King were Aubrey Williams, Myles Horton, and Rosa Parks (first, second, and fourth from the right of the young minister, wearing dark tie, in front row).

James E. "Big Jim" Folsom, towering over his wife Jamelle and his "hillbilly band," the Strawberry Pickers, made a second successful run for the Alabama governor's office in the spring of 1954.

NAACP Legal Defense Fund lawyers and witnesses paused outside the federal courthouse in Richmond after the trial of the Prince Edward County, Virginia, school desegregation case in February 1952. Standing in front are local attorneys Spottswood W. Robinson (left) and Oliver W. Hill.

A week before the Supreme Court's Brown decision was handed down in May 1954, the Southern Regional Council convened a group of the region's progressives in Williamsburg, Virginia, to discuss affirmative responses to the court's anticipated ruling. Among those present were Grace T. Hamilton, Dorothy R. Tilly, Oliver W. Hill, and John A. Griffin (second, fourth, fifth, and sixth from left, front row); C. H. Parrish, Rufus Clement, Morris Abram, Brooks Hays, and Charles S. Johnson (second through sixth from left, middle row); and Harold Fleming, Philip G. Hammer, and George S. Mitchell (first, third, and sixth from left, back row).

President Dwight Eisenhower met with Walter White (right), Clarence Mitchell (center), and other NAACP officials at the White House in January 1954.

At a Washington social function in 1953, Supreme Court Justices Stanley F. Reed, William J. Brennan, and Tom Clark (from left), Justice William O. Douglas (right), and another listener enjoy a story by finger-pointing Justice Hugo L. Black. Southerners Reed, Clark, and Black stood with their colleagues in the unanimous and historic Brown decision outlawing segregation in 1954.

Rosa Parks and Myles Horton at the Highlander Folk School in August 1957. Mrs. Parks first attended a Highlander workshop in the summer of 1955, months before her altercation with a Montgomery, Alabama, bus driver precipitated a history-making boycott.

The South of the future, toward which our efforts are directed, is a South freed of stultifying inheritances from the past. It is a South where the measure of a man will be his ability, not his race; where a common citizenship will work in democratic understanding for the common good; where all who labor will be rewarded in proportion to their skill and achievement; where all can feel confident of personal safety and equality before the law; where there will exist no double standard in housing, health, education, or other public services; where segregation will be recognized as a cruel and needless penalty on the human spirit, and will no longer be imposed; where, above all, every individual will enjoy a full share of dignity and self-respect, in recognition of his creation in the image of God.

Several black members of the council's board—Benjamin Mays, Rufus Clement, Albert W. Dent, and others—had been pressing from the beginning for an unequivocal acknowledgment that segregation was the single most destructive obstacle in the South's path to parity, and must be eliminated. As the debate dragged on through the late forties and into the fifties, there was a gradual falling away by the defenders of segregation, almost all of whom were white. Immediately after the surviving majority, made up about equally of black and white members, had voted approval of the new statement of policy, Virginius Dabney resigned, acknowledging his inactive status over the past several years and saying that he simply didn't have time "to perform the duties expected of me." A little later on, former Virginia Governor Colgate W. Darden, Jr., then president of the University of Virginia, sent a check covering two years of unpaid dues along with his letter of resignation. More candidly than Dabney, Darden noted that "the Council is sympathetic to the abolition of segregation in the primary and secondary schools," and he was resigning because he could not support that view. Numerous others followed him out.

In coming to grips at last with the issue of segregation, the SRC had made an eleventh-hour choice to stand on the right side, as morality and pragmatism and history itself would eventually define right and wrong in this matter. The choice exacted a high price. The threadbare organization (its annual budget in 1950 was only $39,000—less than it had been five years earlier) had fewer than three thousand members, and almost half of them were delinquent dues-payers like Colgate Darden. The new president of the council, Marion A. Wright, a South Carolina attorney, faced the unenviable prospect of trying to rally a small and underpaid staff, a divided board, and a declining membership to overcome a budget deficit—and then to go into the cage against the segregationist lions.

Right-wing reactionaries stepped up their attacks on the SRC; high-powered snipers like Roy V. Harris of Augusta, Thomas Waring of the Charleston *News & Courier*, and James J. Kilpatrick of the Richmond *News Leader* blasted it as a "Communist-front organization" and a "haven for fellow-travelers." Even the Georgia attorney general and the state Democratic Party leadership would join Governor Herman Talmadge in accusing the council of engaging in "subversive activities." Just at the time when it was finally getting focused on its primary mission, the Southern Regional Council was being knocked back on its heels, and the attacks showed how vulnerable it was in the overheated climate of anti-red hysteria.

Every other reform-minded group in the region was similarly exposed. The Congress of Industrial Organizations had been openly committed to ending racial segregation when it emerged as a liberal alternative to the American Federation of Labor in the late 1930s. Now, though, it was drifting steadily to the right under the relentless bombardment of those who saw the push for racial equality as a Communist plot. By the mid-1950s, when the CIO and the AFL would paste over their differences and enter into a merger, liberal Southerners in the labor movement would be reined in and their ties to reformist organizations curtailed. Two of the most committed of them, Lucy Randolph Mason and Paul Christopher, would face constant pressure to resign their board posts in such groups as the Highlander Folk School and the Southern Conference Educational Fund.

Churches were just as rigid. Anticommunism came naturally to them, given the red party line of atheism and the brutal aggression of Soviet forces against the Catholic peoples of Eastern Europe. Religious groups in the United States seemed unable to separate the threat of Communist imperialism on the international scene from the demagogic exploitation of the "red menace" at home. As for the parallel but generally unrelated issue of social reform, it had become so controversial by the early 1950s that neither congregations nor denominations were eager to tackle it. The Federal Council of Churches and its successor, the National Council of Churches, kept on establishing study commissions and passing resolutions, but below that level there was even less expressed concern in, say, 1951, than there had been five years earlier.

Black churches had found little latitude for open opposition to Jim Crow segregation by 1950, but soon thereafter, the National Baptist denomination headquartered in Baton Rouge mounted a short-lived boycott of city buses in the Louisiana capital, presaging the more successful and historically pivotal bus boycott that would take hold in Montgomery, Alabama, in 1955. The white churches clearly were not ready for such direct action; consequently, individual white Southerners whose reform motivations were rooted in religious faith and belief were compelled to look outside their institutions for ways to express and live out their convictions.

The case of Claude Williams was perhaps the most extreme example. In his journeys across Tennessee, Arkansas, and Alabama, with a wartime sojourn in Detroit, controversy had dogged his every step. Many people, including some of his closest associates, thought of him as a shadow man, a radical activist if not a revolutionary, a Christian Socialist and, in spite of that, a Communist too, somehow. In the early 1950s, his Presbyterian ruling elders in Michigan chose inexplicably to press a number of charges against him, including "subversion and corruption of faith" and "membership in the Communist Party." In a bizarre inquisition that lasted for several days, Williams appeared alone and without counsel before a ten-member judicial commission, which declared him guilty as charged and defrocked him.

But he had already parted company with the Presbyterians by then, and was publishing cogent treatises on segregation and sundry other evils under the banner of something he called the People's Institute of Applied Religion. As far as anyone could tell, the "institute" was just Williams acting alone (his preferred modus operandi), mailing his broadsides from a rural box number outside Helena, Alabama, not far from Birmingham. If Claude Williams was a Communist, he was a cagey one; lifelong protester though he was, he advised his readers in 1948 to forget the Progressive Party and vote Democratic because "we can't afford the luxury of a protest vote."

The Highlander Folk School's ties to the CIO and the AFL were weakened considerably when anticommunist pressures were brought to bear on organized labor in the late 1940s. Myles Horton and his small staff, working with Aubrey Williams of the *Southern Farmer*, tried to build a long-term working relationship with the National Farmers' Union during those years, but that too had proved to be unfruitful by 1951. All the while, the Tennessee school had deepened its commitment to racial equality, and that presented yet another set of problems: The mere presence of African-Americans on the Monteagle campus was proof to many of Highlander's ties to communism.

By the end of 1952, the twenty-year-old institution faced a crisis of mission. Its work with industrial and agricultural unions was at a virtual standstill. To restore the school's sense of purpose and direction, Horton and George S. Mitchell, Highlander's board chairman (and also the executive director of the Southern Regional Council), led the way in planning a program of adult education to help prepare the South for a racially integrated society. From that point on, the durable little institution would invest most of its energy and its meager resources in the historic Southern struggle over desegregation of the public schools.

The Southern Conference Educational Fund had signed up for the same war. From its headquarters in New Orleans, the surviving stepchild of the late Southern Conference for Human Welfare girded for battle with about as much armor as Highlander had—precious little—but with the same intensity of feeling. Coming down from Mr. Jefferson's Virginia mountain after their ringing Declaration of Civil Rights in late 1948, the remnant of SCEF loyalists, led by James Dombrowski and Aubrey Williams, reaffirmed the organization's commitment to eliminating racial discrimination and focused its energies in particular on segregation in Southern schools and colleges.

Clark Foreman had left the Southern Conference and the South after the Henry Wallace debacle in 1948, and would stay gone. Moving in the opposite direction was Virginia Durr, another SCHW-SCEF stalwart; she and her lawyer husband, Clifford, returned to their native Alabama in the early 1950s. Cliff Durr started a law practice in Montgomery, and his wife renewed her interest in the work of Williams and Dombrowski in the SCEF—which had become, in the estimate of one historian, "the most militantly antisegregationist force in Southern life."

Williams was also living in Montgomery; Dombrowski was in New Orleans, George S. Mitchell was still at the Southern Regional Council in Atlanta, Myles Horton was on Monteagle mountain in Tennessee, and Lillian Smith was on Old Screamer in north Georgia. Most of the other white activists whose involvement in Southern social issues over the previous two decades had earned them reputations as radicals or leftists or liberals were no longer engaged in highly vocal or visible struggles with the right-wing defenders of the Southern Way of Life. The blacks who fought against discrimination either had to make common cause with the beleaguered whites or expose themselves to even greater peril in the state and local branches of the NAACP.

But the federal courts had all but destroyed the "separate but equal" myth in higher education, and now they were debating desegregation issues involving public elementary and secondary schools. The "invisible man" culture of segregation was cracking and crumbling in a thousand other facets of American life. The world was changing; by almost every sign and portent, it was becoming clear that segregation and white supremacy defined an unworkable way of life that would soon collapse. The white Southerners who fought for it, who vowed to defend it to the death, still held the whip hand in their states—and, to a large extent, in Congress as well. They had managed to silence almost everyone except the scattered remnant of radicals, but they could feel the rumble of the earth beneath their feet, and they were worried.

And so it happened that James O. Eastland, the senior senator from Mississippi and the ranking Democrat on the Senate Internal Security subcommittee, decided to bring a road show to New Orleans in March 1954, and summon his enemies for a command performance.

Jim Eastland was running for reelection in 1954, and he was fearful that the U.S. Supreme Court would declare momentarily that school segregation was unconstitutional. The very idea made his blood pressure rise. He needed a new club, a bludgeon—something he could inflict heavy damage with before his South got clobbered by the court and the Communists. He wanted to strike a blow for the cause of segregation—and in the process, grab a big win from the voters of Mississippi.

The subcommittee chairman, Republican Senator William Jenner of Indiana, announced in January that the Southern Conference Educational Fund, an alleged "subversive organization," would be the subject of a hearing conducted by Senator Eastland. The SCEF board of directors met in Atlanta in February and wrangled over defensive strategy. Whoever was called to testify, they agreed, should stoutly affirm his or her noninvolvement in any way with communism—but beyond that, some members wanted no one to take the Fifth Amendment protection against self-incrimination, while others wanted that choice to be left to each individual. No, said board member Benjamin Mays, that was too vague and evasive; it would invite unwarranted suspicion. The debate dragged on, and ended inconclusively, after which Mays told the others he was resigning. His departure was a loss the SCEF could ill afford; several other African-American members took their cue from the highly respected Atlantan and quit too.

In March, the subpoenas came—for Dombrowski, for Aubrey Williams, for board member Myles Horton, and for former board member Virginia Durr. (The speculation was that Eastland wanted to attack Durr, who was Supreme Court Justice Hugo Black's sister-in-law, as an indirect way of getting at Black on the eve of the dreaded ruling in the *Brown* case.) The confrontation was set for New Orleans. When the first act of the drama opened in a somber, mahogany-paneled hearing room on an upper floor of the U.S. Post Office on March 18, only Eastland and his staff were there as inquisitors—not Chairman Jenner or the other Republicans, not Democratic Senators John McClellan of Arkansas or Olin Johnston of South Carolina. Where was everybody? The answer seemed to be that this was Eastland's show to run as he wished. That he did in an imperious manner, informing the witnesses that he would "let you know what the rules are as we go along."

Dombrowski took the stand. He denied that he was or ever had been a

Communist, but beyond that he would say little (though he didn't take the Fifth Amendment). Eastland called two former Communists as witnesses. One of them, North Carolina–born Paul Crouch—not only an ex-red but an ex-convict, and now a "professional witness"—asserted that Dombrowski was indeed a closet Communist, and told of cell meetings they had allegedly attended together.

Then Virginia Durr was called. She allowed that she was indeed who she said she was, said she was married to Clifford Durr, said she wasn't a Communist, and then said, "That's all. From here on out, I'm standing mute." Eastland and his staff counsel plied her with questions, but she was a stone, coolly pausing now and then to take out a compact and powder her nose. In a written statement, she said she had "total and utter contempt for this Committee." (Later she would fume that Eastland was "as common as pig tracks.") The senator recalled Crouch, who claimed that Mrs. Durr had gotten government secrets from Eleanor Roosevelt and passed them on to a ring of Communist spies. The astonishing implication that the President's wife had betrayed her country sent a nervous buzz through the hearing room.

Aubrey Williams came next, with Clifford Durr as his attorney. Both men were in a state of extreme agitation, Durr for the outrageous accusation against his wife and Williams for his building animosity toward Eastland. The senator sensed this, and treaded cautiously. Williams said he was not and never had been a Communist; Crouch was called to allege unequivocally that he was. Williams dared him to repeat the charges outside the hearing room, saying, "I'll sue you for everything you've got." Then, in a momentary lapse of his control, Eastland waived the rules he had announced earlier and allowed Cliff Durr to cross-examine Crouch. Their rancorous exchange included Crouch's assertion that Durr himself had once been a red.

This went on for two days—firm denials of any Communist ties by all of the witnesses, sensational charges to the contrary by Crouch and his cohort, bullying tactics by Eastland and his chief counsel. On the third day, Horton was called to testify, and neither he nor the hotheaded senator were in any mood for each other. Right off the bat, Horton was asked if Jim Dombrowski was affiliated with Highlander; he replied that he'd like to explain why he didn't want to answer.

"Do you decline to answer the question?" Eastland demanded.

"Mr. Chairman, you listened to an ex-Communist who is a paid informer. Why won't you listen to the testimony of an ordinary American?"

"Answer my question. Do you decline to answer my question?"

"Mr. Chairman, I would like to state—"

"Do you mean to say that you refuse to answer?" Eastland summoned the marshals. "All right, take him out!"

Two plainclothes officers lifted Horton out of his seat and started for the door. "Mr. Chairman, am I an American citizen or not?" the witness cried. He was taken into the hallway and thrown down on the marble steps.

The hearing room was in an uproar. Eastland called Crouch once more, saying he would be the last witness. Crouch denied any intent to "attack the patriotism" of the Roosevelts or Justice Black, but went on to assert that Mrs. Durr "had full knowledge of the Communist conspiracy and its works when she allegedly persuaded Black to address the organizational meeting of the Southern Conference for Human Welfare in Birmingham in 1938."

The hired witness had planted the seeds of suspicion, as Eastland had clearly wanted. Just as the hearing was being gaveled to a conclusion, Cliff Durr lunged at Crouch in a rage. "You son of a bitch, I'll kill you for lying about my wife like that!" he shouted. The marshals quickly pulled him back, and as they did, Durr slumped to the floor, stricken by a mild heart attack.

In this explosive flash of emotion the drama came to a close. Eastland had threatened to hold the witnesses in contempt, but no such action was forthcoming. In the press, meanwhile, it was Eastland and Crouch, not the witnesses, who were held in contempt. Even the conservative Montgomery *Advertiser* said "the great Southern Commie hunt" was a bust, and the witnesses had been subjected to "character lynching." Although Eastland promised more hearings "to expose Communism in the South," there were to be no more. Paul Crouch was finished too, discredited as a government witness and shunted aside by the congressional investigative committees.

At first the Southern Conference Educational Fund and the Highlander Folk School and the individual witnesses appeared to have come out of the emotional proceedings in good shape. But their image as radical disturbers of the peace was enhanced, and in the tense atmosphere of the Cold War, that was a minus, not a plus. Both SCEF and Highlander would survive, but their effectiveness would always be clouded by unwarranted suspicions.

Even more dispiriting in the greater scheme of things was a dawning realization by 1954 that the progressive, reform-minded organizations and individuals of the South, few and scattered though they were, had too much competitive animosity for one another to gain any realistic chance of mounting a cooperative offensive against racial and regional inequality. On a personal level and as institutions, they were rivals—fighting for territory, for rank-and-file followers, for operating funds (which, incidentally, had to come from Northern liberals because Southerners had clearly shown they wouldn't support liberal reform efforts).

All of these well-intentioned Southerners, white and black—in SCEF, Highlander, the Southern Regional Council, the state-based NAACP branches, the press, the churches, the universities, the unions—were too divided to have a significant impact. The Communist Party's old United Front of the thirties was too fresh in the memories of some for them to consider joining any sort of united front themselves, by whatever name. No group and no individual was persuasive enough to summon everyone onto one ark to ride out the storm, lest they sink separately, one by one. By the early 1950s they all appeared to agree, finally, that segregation was the common enemy, but they still couldn't join forces to fight it. The fractious internal politics of race and reform—characterized by historian Numan V. Bartley as "the soft underbelly of Southern liberalism"—would become even more contentious in the future.

In a curious and ironic way, the composite profile of the liberals could be crudely compared to that of the Old South reactionaries on the other side: They were too male, too white, too middle class, too spooked by communism, too dependent on Yankees for their wherewithal—and, finally, too full of doubt that they could accomplish more as an integrated force for social change than as rival factions of true believers in their own righteousness.

3. *Tiptoeing and Whispering*

Controlling the institutions that were susceptible to political, economic, or social pressure was standard operating procedure for the long gray line of Dixie politicians who had kept the South in penury since the 1870s. But in the 1950s, even as social tension bred a fearful silence, the total domination they had previously enjoyed was no longer possible. Outside pressures were being felt now—national, even world pressures—and the scattered voices of dissent within the region did manage to filter through the magnolia curtain from time to time. Segregation was ever so gradually breaking down in the popular culture, as all Americans were reminded whenever they went to the movies or the ballpark, bought a magazine, listened to music, or turned on the television. (The visibility of Ralph

Ellison's *Invisible Man* was not only an affirmation of the book's honesty but a signal of changing times.)

The black minority's spreading mood of consensus was also apparent; hardly a man or woman among them didn't share in the firm determination to secure the same blessings of liberty and democracy that white Americans could claim as a birthright. There was measurable progress, too: The number of blacks registered to vote in the South had risen from a quarter of a million in 1944, when the white primary was outlawed, to a million in 1952—from five percent of the voting-age population to twenty percent. Furthermore, the same federal courts that had opened the voting booths to blacks—there being no such thing as separate but equal elections—were continuing to bring the U.S. Constitution to bear upon the inequitable and undemocratic actions of white lawmakers.

What had been set in motion over the previous twenty years couldn't be stalled at will, simply turned off like a light switch; it too had a certain self-generated energy and a constituency, just as the forces of segregation did. (If major-league baseball and the U.S. Army could clip the wings of Jim Crow, the argument went, why couldn't the rest of America?) By far the greatest number of Southern politicians were still openly on the side of white supremacy, but there were a few who looked beyond the present and saw the inevitability of change, and together with the small contingent of reformers outside the political arena, they were resourceful enough to make a contest of the mushrooming struggle over segregation.

Even though politicians seemed to generate the least amount of change, they were still the people to watch, if only because their greatest skill was in blocking change. In fact, when you review what went on in gubernatorial elections and in Southern statehouses during the first half of the 1950s, the standout feature is not militant racism and defiance, but do-nothing denial and caretaker protection of the status quo. The politicians made a big stink about communism and social equality from time to time, but they must not have believed their own talk—nor did their audiences pay much attention—because the political campaigns in the three or four years after the Graham and Pepper losses in 1950 were comparatively quiet and tame. If white Southerners were truly concerned that communism or integration was about to engulf them, they hardly gave a hint of it.

But it was not the presence of a liberal opposition to Jim Crow discrimination that made the early fifties a quiet time; more likely, it was the restored confidence of the reactionaries that they could stop any civil rights initiative in its tracks—in Congress, in the statehouses, or anywhere else. Their confidence was derived from the ease with which they defeated almost every single liberal initiative of President Truman's, just months after he had trounced them at the polls. To their surprise and delight, the Dixie bloc discovered that they didn't need a renegade party to get what they wanted; they could accomplish the same goals by joining forces with the Republicans—and by exposing the shallow commitment of Northern Democrats to civil rights and racial equality. The Dixiecrats were a one-issue, one-election fringe party doomed to failure—but the issues that energized them in 1948 were simply transplanted back into the two-party system in the years that followed, there to be reintroduced when they deemed the time to be right.

In only two or three gubernatorial elections during that period did winning candidates ride into office on an aggressive platform of white supremacy; most of the time, the race issue was ignored, as if it were a settled matter. In Mississippi, former governor Hugh L. White won an-other term in 1951 by defeating Paul B. Johnson, Jr., son of a former governor, in the Democratic primary runoff. White convinced a bare majority of fifty-one percent that "a vote for Johnson is a vote for the Truman crowd and civil rights." Both men testified to their deep faith in states' rights and segregation, but the more restrained Johnson said, "I don't want to win by making the Negro the whipping boy when he isn't even an issue in the race."

Governor Herman Talmadge of Georgia won another campaign against M. E. Thompson in a close 1950 primary in which Talmadge vowed to stifle black voting with restrictive new registration laws, and to bar the doors of all white schools to black applicants. He won the popular vote by a narrow 49-to-48 plurality, but the state's grossly inequitable county unit system gave him victory by a margin of almost three to one. By the time he left office in 1955, soon to embark on a new career as a U.S. senator, Talmadge was also an author. *You and Segregation*, his call to arms against "intermingling and intermarriage," told the white citizens of the South that they were a sovereign people, and if they would stand together against the Supreme Court, which had "violated the law," they could be "the Court of Last Resort," and their decision would be "the ruling ver-dict." That came closer to advocating the overthrow of the government by force and violence than any public utterance of a real Dixie red.

The only other aggressively segregationist candidate who even made it to the primary finals in those years was diehard Dixiecrat Ben Laney of Arkansas, who tried in 1950 to win another term as governor by unseating the incumbent, Sid McMath. Curiously, neither candidate had much to say about race. Arkansas didn't need an old-guard governor who was "bound up, body and soul, with the Dixiecrat movement," the moderately progressive and reform-minded McMath told the voters—and they agreed, giving him another two-year term by a wide margin. (In 1952, though, McMath lost in a runoff to conservative challenger Francis Cherry, and in 1954 he failed in an effort to unseat Senator John McClellan; it was also in 1954 that Arkansans elected an Ozark opportunist named Orval Faubus to his first term as governor.)

Elsewhere, the rabidly extreme candidates fared poorly. Bull Connor, the race-baiting Birmingham police commissioner, finished a distant sixth in Alabama's 1950 gubernatorial primary (although the winner, Gordon Persons, turned out to be another white supremacist). In Mississippi, a reactionary editor, Mary Cain, ran fifth in a 1951 contest for governor after she advocated closing the schools to avoid desegregation. White Southerners had already done too much for blacks, she said, and the time had come to get tough.

It was not yet the season for massive resistance, though; that disaster was still waiting to happen, down the road a piece. It wasn't the season for modest progress, either. This was the season to tiptoe and whisper, to close your eyes and cover your ears. In a match between two patrician gentlemen, John S. Battle defeated Francis Pickens Miller in the 1949 Virginia Democratic gubernatorial primary, after receiving the nod of old-guard Senator Harry Flood Byrd. Then Battle stood by helplessly in 1952 as Byrd, nemesis of all things progressive since the 1920s, cold-shouldered Adlai Stevenson and the Democrats, assuring victory in the state for Eisenhower and the Republicans. (Byrd also won his own race for reelection that year by handily defeating the luckless Francis Pickens Miller.)

In Texas, a latter-day Dixiecrat, Governor Allan Shivers, hopped on Ike's coattails in 1952 and thus ensured his own reelection and a Texas win for the general—but as in Arkansas and Virginia and elsewhere, race wasn't an important factor in the campaign. (Anticommunism was, though, and Shivers covered that base too, going out of his way to hail Joe McCarthy as a paragon of patriotic Americanism.) In Louisiana, Governor Robert F. Kennon also endorsed Ike. A right-wing tide was rising in the South, sure enough, but those who were swept along by it found no Communists in their path, and most of them wouldn't take the race issue seriously until after the Supreme Court had decided the school segregation cases.

Alabama, Florida, and North Carolina all elected soft-shell conservatives, not breast-beaters, as their governors in the years just prior to 1954. South Carolina replaced Strom Thurmond with ex–New Dealer James F. Byrnes—no classic demagogue in the Ben Tillman–Cole Blease tradition, but a more dignified Republicrat who considered white supremacy "the very soul of the South." Voters in the border state of Maryland twice elected a liberal Republican, Theodore McKeldin, and Kentucky also picked moderate leaders in the fifties—first Lawrence Weatherby and then A. B. "Happy" Chandler, the former governor, senator, and commissioner of baseball. In Frank G. Clement, Tennessee elected a sanctimonious orator with progressive instincts that pegged him a high notch above the Boss Crump surrogates who had run the state for so long. (Both Chandler and Clement would prove to be temperate and constructive leaders when the desegregation controversy surfaced in their states.)

Also on the side of the law, but handling (or mishandling) matters in his own inimitable way, would be Alabama's James E. Folsom. Big Jim's second turn as governor, from the campaign in 1954 to his waning days in office in January 1959, was a study in Southern eccentricity. He was a good-hearted, glad-handing populist sport with a genuine empathy for "the little man," white and black, and he built a huge following in Alabama that puzzled and frustrated the reactionary politicians who had seized control of the Democratic Party during the Dixiecrat revolt. The state's moderate senators, Lister Hill and John Sparkman, were closer to Folsom than to the arch-conservatives, but they were almost as wary of the governor, a man of exceptional entertainment value and few inhibitions.

Two weeks after his victory in the 1954 Democratic primary, the U.S. Supreme Court announced its decision in the school cases, and Folsom's path from that point on would be strictly an uphill struggle. He managed to avoid direct comment on the ruling for a while, but finally indicated his acceptance of it as the law of the land. By then, Alabama whites were rallying for another lost cause, and Folsom found himself increasingly vilified and isolated.

Typically, though, he kept on being Big Jim; it was the only role this irrepressible character knew how to play. When Harlem congressman Adam Clayton Powell, Jr., made a visit to Montgomery in the fall of 1955, Folsom sent his chauffeur out to meet him and bring him to the mansion for a drink. The image of these two roguish politicians sipping scotch with their feet up on the furniture was enough to drive most of the white citizens of Alabama over the edge; Southern hospitality was one thing, but this was outrageous. In 1956 the governor gave a quiet nod of approval to the Montgomery bus boycott and the desegregation-of the University of Alabama; in neither case was he openly supportive of the black cause, but considering the belligerent defiance of his successors in the office, the governor's acquiescent response was remarkable—and more than enough to burn a few more of his bridges. By the time his term was up, many of his white constituents had branded him as a traitor, and they were ready to run him out of the state.

In stark contrast to Folsom's personality and to his tempestuous second term was the reign of James F. Byrnes in South Carolina. During his long and lofty tenure in the three branches of the federal government, Byrnes had acquired the manipulative skills of a master politician and dressed them in the cool formality of a sophisticated diplomat. In 1950 he decided, at the age of sixty-eight, to offer his services to the voters as Strom Thurmond's successor in the governor's office. If I said the overwhelming preponderance of white voters were grateful to elect him and swear him in, that would be an extreme understatement; more precisely, they exhibited an eagerness to acclaim and anoint him.

To have so few of the stereotypical behavior traits that were a dead giveaway of the reactionary racists, Byrnes was disappointingly close to them in his thinking. He was a chronic, absolute, unquestioning believer in the natural inferiority of the African stock, and not even a paternalistic sense of compassion or fair play softened his views. Never an out-front motivator of the masses, he had quietly retired from the Truman administration in 1947, pleading poor health—and then had worked hard behind the scenes for the President's defeat. Byrnes was never an avowed Dixiecrat, but he was an unreconstructed closet Rebel in his heart of hearts, and the reason, pure and simple, was race.

During his four years as governor, he redirected a large portion of the state's education budget into a capital spending program for black schools, hoping desperately to ward off court-ordered desegregation; by any measure, the effort was a transparent failure. He endorsed Eisenhower in 1952 and every Republican candidate thereafter, until his death in 1972. With deep and unremitting bitterness, Byrnes became totally alienated from the U.S. Supreme Court and the national Democratic Party—institutions he had served ably and faithfully during his long and varied public life—and he remained forever unreconciled to them.

At the Southern Governors' Conference in Hot Springs, Arkansas, in November 1951, Byrnes was busily trying to coax his disaffected fellow governors into the Republican camp when a most remarkable thing happened. A white native of his own state, Greenvillian Harry S. Ashmore, then editor of the *Arkansas Gazette* in Little Rock, stood before a luncheon microphone at the invitation of the host governor, Sid McMath, to speak on race relations in the South. It was the first time that subject had ever been broached at the convocation of governors. The speech was not exactly a ringing declaration of war against segregation, but it was straightforward enough. The handwriting was on the wall, Ashmore told the stone-faced executives, and the same old negative response to every attempt at reform would no longer do:

> Some of us have suffered under the delusion that the South is the victim of an evil conspiracy, and that if we could only remove a few key men from power our troubles would be over. That is . . . dan-

gerous nonsense. For every genuine radical or cynical political opportunist who exploits the race issue for his own ends, there are ten
thousand sober, sincere, essentially conservative Americans who have
accepted the proposition set forth in the civil rights program proposed by President Truman and embodied in the platform of the
Republican Party. And the more we strike back in blind reaction to
their demands, the more convinced they become that we are all
misbegotten racists who will respond to nothing less than federal
coercion.

When he finished, Ashmore heard applause from Governor McKeldin
of Maryland, from McMath, and from a few renegade back-benchers in
the press. Georgia's Herman Talmadge had stalked out in the middle.
Jimmy Byrnes, asked for a reaction by Johnny Popham of the *New York
Times*, could only sputter in disbelief, "Why, I believe I know that boy's
family!"

And so, wrote Ashmore later, "the governors went forth to help pull
down their own temple—refusing to face the problem they themselves
counted as paramount, and worse still, trying to convince the world that
it didn't exist." Neither political party was prepared to confront the issue
of race, he concluded, yet, ironically, the positions of both had been
shaped by the South—by its "inaction in the days of grace, and by blind
defiance when time began to run out."

The Southern politicians in Congress eased through the early fifties
with much the same spirit of inaction as their office-holding brethren back
home. Most of them had been less visible in the Dixiecrat Party than were
the governors and state Democratic Party officials. After the movement's
crushing loss, though, it was the Southern delegations in Washington that
got revenge by destroying President Truman's legislative program—and
that proved once again, if any more proof was needed, that it was the
senators and congressmen who held the reins of power in the South.

They were much better at impeding change than leading it. Instead of
forging a new party, or even shifting their allegiance to an old one, they
hunkered down with their like-minded colleagues across the aisle, and on
the first day of the pivotal Eighty-second Congress in January 1951, they
displayed the strength, the will, and the parliamentary skill to take back
the political initiative they had all but lost to Truman and the liberal wing
of the Democratic Party.

Most political analysts and pundits were in agreement after 1948 that
the Southern white majority had three choices. The first—a separate

party—had already failed once, and none but the most unyielding white supremacists saw any future in it. The second—a merger with like-minded Republicans—was widely predicted. The third—a pragmatic accommodation with blacks in a broader and more progressive Democratic Party— was the hope of most blacks and many whites, but not enough to make it happen.

Realistically speaking, the proponents of social change were too few, too divided (not to say competitive, or even hostile toward one another), and too circumscribed by the superior numbers and rigidity of the opposition to have any serious prospect of gaining political power. Neither was the Dixiecrat remnant viable; it had dwindled to a few fanatics obsessed with fear and hatred of the black minority, and there were simply not enough of them at that time to sustain a disciplined movement. After the 1950 elections, when they suffered still more humiliation, the last survivors had to search for another strategy.

Between these two camps was the ruling white majority of conservative Southern Democrats. In truth, they were much closer to the Dixiecrats than to the liberals, and most of them would slide to the right as the middle eroded. They had a great deal in common with the Northern Republicans: Both were against the growth and centralization of federal power, against broadening the franchise, against federal solutions to most (but not all) social problems, against a "welfare state" to aid the poor, against any program that smacked of socialism or communism. The Southerners freely embraced the Republicans' obsessive anticommunism and put it to work for them; the Republicans in turn acquiesced in the states'-rights demands of the Southern bloc, knowing that their hidden agenda was to keep segregation and white supremacy. The understanding they reached made wholesale party-switching unnecessary; simply by agreeing to work together for mutual goals, the two conservative factions ensured that in the South—and to a large extent, in Congress— power would remain in the same ideological orbit and the same upper-class hands.

It was widely anticipated by those in the know that the two traditional parties were on the verge of a major realignment along liberal-conservative lines, with the Republicans embracing this anti-federalist, North-South union of upper-crust conservatives and the Democrats becoming the progressive party of labor, blacks, ethnics, urbanites, Jews, Catholics—in other words, the eclectic host of American liberals.

It never quite happened that way. Not for another twenty years would there be a significant number of Republicans elected to office in the South—and when a genuine two-party system was finally in place, it wouldn't be definable as a classic right-left split; there would be at least a hint of an ideological cross-section in each camp, reflecting to some extent the complex makeup of the national parties.

That Jimmy Byrnes and Harry Byrd could conspicuously spurn the Democrats in 1952 without being drummed out of the party showed not only how secure they were in their power but also how compatible the Democratic and Republican conservatives were in their thinking. Eisenhower won Texas, Florida, Virginia, and Tennessee, and he would add Louisiana to that list in 1956, but his success didn't do a thing for the Republican Party in the South.

Numbers would tell the story: None of the old Confederate states would elect a Republican governor until Winthrop Rockefeller of Arkansas and Florida's Claude Kirk won in 1966. State legislatures stayed Democratic too. In 1948 there was a grand total of 50 Republicans among 1,788 legislators in the eleven Southern states. That tiny fraction climbed to 62 the year Ike was elected; eight years later, it had slipped back to 60. (By 1972, though, almost 300 Southern Republicans would be serving in their state assemblies.)

Two east Tennessee Republicans were the only members of their party among 105 Southerners in the U.S. House of Representatives in 1948; there were 6 after the 1952 elections, but only 7 by 1960. Twelve years after that, GOP members would make up nearly one-third of the Southern bloc. No Republican would be elected to the Senate from a Southern state until John Tower of Texas won a special election in 1961. By 1972, 7 of the 22 Southerners would be Republicans—including South Carolina's Strom Thurmond, who finally switched parties in 1966.

The rise of Republicanism and of two-party politics in the South was not a direct outgrowth of the Dixiecrat rebellion or the Eisenhower victories, but a later phenomenon; it would have more to do with Barry Goldwater in defeat and Richard Nixon in victory than with Ike. In the pivotal and decisive years between 1948 and 1954, the South remained firmly in the grasp of the same ruling oligarchy that had dominated throughout the Jim Crow era (the same in spirit, if not in personalities). Having weathered the threat of a liberal breakout on civil rights, the Southern Democrats whose power base was on Capitol Hill returned to business as usual with a collective sigh of relief.

In a club where tradition reigned, seniority meant prominence, and a good many of the Southerners had it. Kenneth McKellar of Tennessee, Walter George of Georgia, and Tom Connally of Texas could count among them almost a hundred years of service in the Senate when they made their exits in the fifties. Harry Byrd of Virginia, Richard Russell of Georgia, Allen Ellender of Louisiana, and Lister Hill of Alabama had all been elected in the thirties, and all would serve for thirty years or more. Half a dozen others were elected in the war years, and most of them would still be there in the sixties or beyond: John McClellan and J. William Fulbright of Arkansas, Olin Johnston and Burnet R. Maybank of South Carolina, James Eastland of Mississippi, and Clyde R. Hoey of North Carolina. All of these men except Hill and Fulbright could fairly be called reactionary guardians of the old and inequitable Southern way of life, with its built-in advantages for white males of means; on the specific issue of racial equality, even Hill and Fulbright joined the others in their increasingly desperate effort to ward off change.

The postwar crop of Southern senators included a few more liberal or progressive thinkers. John Sparkman of Alabama was considered moderate enough to be Adlai Stevenson's running mate on the 1952 Democratic ticket. Estes Kefauver of Tennessee and Lyndon Johnson of Texas were destined to be high-visibility Southern moderates-cum-liberals from the day they got to the Senate in 1948, and the same was true of Albert Gore, Sr., chosen by Tennessee voters over Kenneth McKellar in 1952. Kerr Scott of North Carolina, who as governor had picked Frank Graham for the Senate in 1949, got the seat himself in 1954 after Willis Smith, the man who beat Graham, died of a heart attack. It was also in the mid-fifties that Herman Talmadge defeated Walter George in Georgia and Strom Thurmond won election in South Carolina with write-in votes after the sudden death of Burnet Maybank.

The Democrats had come out of the 1948 election with comfortable majorities in both houses of Congress, but the margins almost evaporated in 1950, and with Eisenhower's election in 1952, the Republicans narrowly took control of both the Senate and the House. It was an unhappy time of dissension and backbiting among the Democrats, punctuated by acrimonious quarrels rooted in race and ideology. But their ravenously ambitious and opportunistic young minority leader in the Senate, Lyndon Johnson, worked hard to pull the factions together—and to solidify his own base of power. In 1954 he would engineer a 67-to-22 vote of condemnation on Senator Joseph McCarthy that not a single Democrat would oppose. It was an unprecedented public judgment of the Club against one of its members—but by that time Truman was long gone, and with him had fled the last hope of progress on civil rights.

When the Democrats regained their one-vote advantage in the 1954 elections, Johnson became majority leader, and he would remain at the center of power in American politics for the rest of his career. By the late 1950s he would be a key figure—eventually *the* key figure—in the transformation of Congress from a citadel of white supremacy to a functioning institution of democratic government. But during his first four years in the Senate—which were also Truman's last four in the White House—Johnson was at least tolerant if not supportive of the Southern reactionaries who did the President in.

In the House of Representatives, there had been a scattering of New Deal liberals throughout the Roosevelt years. Most of the more progressive senators of the fifties had been House members in the thirties and forties—Kefauver and Gore, Hill and Sparkman, Fulbright and LBJ. Others stayed in the House—Sam Rayburn of Texas, Hale Boggs of Louisiana, Wilbur Mills and Brooks Hays of Arkansas, J. Percy Priest and Joe L. Evins of Tennessee. In the first decade following the war, such men as Robert E. Jones and Carl Elliott of Alabama, Jim Wright and Jack Brooks of Texas, Dante Fascell of Florida, and Frank E. Smith of Mississippi were a moderating influence in their delegations. Thomas G. Abernethy of Mississippi was certainly no left-winger, but he almost looked like one compared to the man he beat in 1952—the notorious John E. Rankin.

Nothing revolutionary came out of Congress in these years; in fact, very little that was evolutionary could be detected. No significant piece of the Truman civil rights package became law, and when groups and individuals interested in social reform looked to Washington for support and encouragement, they got little except more empty promises and calls for patience. The White House and the Democratic Party had failed to subdue their Southern reactionary wing or the far-right Republicans, and the smear tactics of Joe McCarthy and the red-hunters kept creative and progressive ideas bottled up for the duration of the Truman presidency.

Only in the federal courts did the ideals and principles of equal rights under the law move closer to reality. One of the great untold stories of the civil rights era, in fact, is that of the judges—white, upper-class, conservative Southern males, for the most part—who were appointed to district and appellate courts in the South over a thirty-year period by five Democratic and Republican presidents beginning with Franklin Roosevelt, and who honored the letter and spirit of their oath to uphold the Constitution and laws of the United States. Not all of the appointees were so virtuous, to be sure—but those who did summon the honesty and courage to follow the documents, regardless of their own private attitudes and biases, deserve recognition as stewards of the highest American ideals.

The twenty-year-long New Deal–Fair Deal era was drawing to a close in 1952 when Aubrey Williams went before the resolutions committee at the Democratic National Convention in Chicago to appeal for a strong, affirmative civil rights plank in the party platform. He found the conservatives to be openly hostile to his ideas, and the liberals to be nervously unsettled by them. The moment of opportunity had passed; the South and the nation had lost their last chance to orchestrate a voluntary social reformation.

Soon after his post-election honeymoon ended in 1949, Harry Truman must have found himself wondering why in the world he had decided to run for a full term of his own. Coming in for the fallen hero, FDR, had been a tough assignment, but the man from Missouri had performed admirably on the whole, and he could have bowed out in 1948 with the grateful thanks of the nation for a job well done. But later, looking back on his last four years in office, he could not have failed to see the frustrations and humiliations visited upon him by the arch-conservative Republicans and Southern Democrats who were his bitterest enemies.

On the surface, two issues and the men who symbolized them were Truman's undoing: Korea and communism, Douglas MacArthur and Joseph McCarthy. The Asian war and the imperious general's conduct of it were not problems of the President's making, but they were enough to give him ulcers. Domestic anticommunist hysteria whipped up by the unstable Wisconsin senator owed its origin in part to Truman's own authorization of loyalty oaths and investigative sweeps through the private lives of millions of citizens, and his regret of that made him hate "that son of a bitch McCarthy" all the more.

Everywhere the President turned, it seemed, these two willful and egotistical men were taunting him, defying him, thwarting his efforts to govern—MacArthur in the Pacific, or before a joint session of Congress, or in a ticker-tape parade on Broadway; McCarthy in the Senate, or in the papers, or on television. They were a double-scotch hangover that wouldn't go away, and the bourbon-sipping Truman was almost obsessed by them. It was frustrations of this sort that finally sapped his energy and his will. By November 1951 he had made up his mind not to run for reelection, and he announced the decision the following March, just as the primary season was heating up. Never in his last two years in office would his approval rating in the polls rise above thirty-two percent.

In point of fact, however, it wasn't these two men or the war or the red scare that got Truman in trouble in the South; it was his words and actions on the subject of race. The Southern members of Congress and their closest allies back home grew to hate the President for not behaving like a white supremacist, and it was they who joined with right-wing Republicans to shred his domestic agenda and generally to oppose his administration's initiatives both at home and abroad. They would not forgive him for creating the Committee on Civil Rights, or for heeding its recommendations and trying to implement many of them; they felt the same about his executive orders aimed at ending discrimination in the District of Columbia, in federal employment, and in the armed forces. Not even the morale-boosting unity and efficiency of the racially integrated military effort in Korea placated the diehard racists.

Harry Truman and his top presidential advisers had come to see that segregation and discrimination could not possibly be justified or sustained in the largest and most successful democratic nation of all time. In recognizing the inevitability of racial equality, they also acknowledged the rightness of it—socially and morally, politically and economically. And, not least, they understood the international propaganda value of it as well.

But in 1951, after six years on the job, the President was compelled to conclude (though not to concede) that he had lost the civil rights fight to a Congress that had neither the motivation, the will, the concern, nor the consensus to bring the country's behavior into harmony with its stated laws and ideals. It may have been that realization, as much as any other, that largely accounted for his unproductive last years in office, his low standing in the polls, and his decision to quit.

There was no shortage of Democrats who wanted to replace him. Estes Kefauver was already in the race, hoping to parlay his coonskin-cap folksiness and his freshly minted reputation as a TV crime-buster into a campaign that would play well in the South and elsewhere. Vice President Alben Barkley had aspirations, but he was thought to be too old. Richard Russell was touted as the man to carry the segregationist banner, but few fell in behind him. Former New York Governor Averell Harriman was briefly in the running too. But the man Truman finally favored—and the eventual winner, on the third ballot at the Chicago convention—was Governor Adlai M. Stevenson of Illinois. In a bid to hold the dissatisfied South, the party put Senator John Sparkman of Alabama on the ticket with him. Philosophically and temperamentally, both men were peaceable moderates who wanted to operate between the reactionary right and the liberal left. In stark contrast to the explosive 1948 campaign, it seemed this time that almost everyone was trying to avoid conflict—and no white Democrats anywhere wanted to talk about race.

The Republicans were in an ideological mood to pick their longtime right-wing leader, Senator Robert Taft of Ohio, but patriotism—and an insatiable passion for victory—turned them instead to the conquering hero of the war in Europe, General Dwight D. Eisenhower. In many ways, the grandfatherly Ike was the perfect candidate for these times. He was a man with no known views on public issues, no clearly articulated philosophy, no designated religion, and, best of all, no politics (he had never even voted). He was a genial, easygoing fellow with a quick grin and a somewhat simplistic approach to the problems of a deeply divided nation.

Reporters pulled from him the news that he was a fiscal conservative ("a Harry Byrd Republican"); he also came across as a peacemaker ("I will go to Korea") and a chairman-of-the-board type of manager. He was deferential to Congress, wary of Senator McCarthy, and favorably disposed only to the most limited and symbolic federal efforts to guarantee civil rights. (Earlier he had expressed doubts about the wisdom of desegregating the armed forces, testifying in 1949 to his personal belief that the branches of service were not ready—"spiritually, philosophically, or mentally"—for racial equality.)

With California Senator Richard M. Nixon as his vice-presidential choice, Eisenhower stuck to inoffensive generalities as much as he could, and left the low-road red-baiting to his Communist-hunting subordinate. A mean-spirited mood of nastiness crept into the campaign, thanks in part to the continuing accusations of McCarthy. At the expense of some personal honor, Eisenhower joined Nixon in endorsing the Wisconsinite's ends, if not his means. Even though McCarthy had slanderously cast suspicion on the loyalty of Ike's patron and wartime superior, General (and later Secretary of State) George C. Marshall, the presidential candidate refused to call the reckless senator's hand.

Almost every political advantage seemed to turn in Eisenhower's favor: Prosperity was not just around the corner but in plain view; unemployment was in the low single digits; a large majority of Americans seemed more comfortable and complacent than they had ever been; dissatisfied citizens kept quiet for fear of being branded as Communists. With a ten-to-one bulge in press endorsements, with plenty of money for television commercials, and with race and the South all but ignored as campaign issues, Ike breezed to an easy victory. His margin was more than six million popular votes, and 442 to 89 in the electoral count. Stevenson carried nine Southern and border states and lost all the rest, including his Illinois homeland.

When he took office in January 1953, President Eisenhower was about as far removed as he could possibly be from a conscious concern about the racial problems of the United States—or the broader social problems of the South. Not many others were thinking about these matters either, except the legal staff of the National Association for the Advancement of Colored People and a scattering of federal judges—and, of course, Southerners themselves, white and black. Like Harry Truman before him, Eisenhower had his hands full with Korea, with the aggressions of the Communist empire in other parts of the world, and with the fear of Communist infiltration at home.

Joe McCarthy was now Ike's cross to bear, and he chafed under the load. A year into the new administration, McCarthy picked a fight with the

U.S. Army—by no coincidence, the President's alma mater of sorts—and soon the senator was enticed into letting live television cameras broadcast his baritone accusations that the army was shot through with subversives and traitors. From late April until early June 1954, the Army-McCarthy hearings were the talk of the nation, a daily drama better by far than soap operas.

As a backdrop to this event, there was more discouraging news from overseas. Another Southeast Asian territory, the longtime French colony of Vietnam, was falling day by agonizing day into the hands of Communist-backed anticolonial forces. Through television reports, the American viewing public was introduced to the heroic but doomed defenders of a remote outpost called Dien Bien Phu.

And in the midst of all this came still another dramatic—though not unexpected—event: On May 17, 1954, the U.S. Supreme Court handed down its long-awaited decision in a cluster of school desegregation cases styled as *Brown* v. *Board of Education of Topeka.*

"One day it will be Monday," Ralph McGill had been telling his readers for some time now, and numerous others had said it too. It was customary for the court to issue rulings on the first workday of the week. This was the day that McGill and practically everyone else had been waiting for, some with fear and loathing, some with faith and hope.

4. *Courts of Last Resort*

"Black Monday," the segregationists would call it, with unintended irony: a dark and dreadful day for the forces of white supremacy. It was certainly that—but it was also a bright day of hope and promise for the ten million black Southerners and other Americans who had fought for an equal claim to the promises of the U.S. Constitution and the Bill of Rights.

In the most fundamental way, everything came together around this court decision, around the issue of race and education. For the past quarter of a century, Americans in general and Southerners in particular had been contending with one another over rights and privileges and responsibilities, over race and color, caste and class. They might have chosen another issue, such as the right to vote, as the primary vehicle for this monumental debate. They might have, but they didn't. Every American citizen had a direct interest in public education; millions of them saw it as the key to the future well-being of their families. The ballot was crucial, without a doubt, but education struck every chord on the scale: age, sex, race, religion, occupation, residence, language, nationality.

All the players were drawn into this game: the President, the federal judiciary, politicians at all levels of government, the universities, the schools with all their teachers and students, the churches, the press, business and labor, the legal profession, the NAACP, the Southern Regional Council and other social reform groups, the soon-to-be-founded white supremacist Citizens' Council and other resistance groups, Democrats and Republicans, conservatives and liberals, the reactionary right and the radical left, whites and blacks and all shades of color in between. Everybody.

When the New Deal liberals put race on the American agenda in the thirties, their faith was in economics. Recovery and growth would point the way to social reform, they said; if people have jobs and money, then nice houses and good health and educational opportunity will follow, and the problems of discrimination will disappear. In his turn, Harry Truman tried to effect a political solution, reasoning that if the government guaranteed the basic rights of all its people, the majority would see the fairness of that idea and rise to the challenge. Both initiatives helped, but neither brought an end to racism; in fact, though conditions did improve somewhat, the problems of racial discrimination were more divisive in 1952 than they had been in 1932.

The beginning of desegregation in higher education and the prospect of more in the lower schools introduced an educational solution to the problem of racial injustice. For the next quarter of a century or more, a substantial segment of the American population, particularly in the South, would work sacrificially to achieve this objective, while many more opposed it. John N. Popham of the *New York Times*, recalling years later his reporting on these efforts in the Southern states, would remember best "the dedicated people who had a transforming faith in the power of education."

Still, none of these strategies alone—economic, political, educational— would do as much to spark a new spirit of liberty in the United States as the federal courts and the church-based multitude of black Southerners did in the fifties and sixties. The other efforts were substantial and vital, and they would continue, but it would be the judicial and moral responses to segregation and white supremacy that would have the most pervasive and durable impact throughout the rest of the twentieth century.

The enormous symbolic and tactical importance of the Supreme Court's *Brown* decision in 1954 and the Montgomery bus boycott in 1955 could hardly be overstated; they would be hailed in the future as the two events that gave birth to the civil rights movement—and historical immortality to attorney Thurgood Marshall and the Reverend Martin Luther King, Jr.

(That "big bang" theory of movement history obscured some pivotal earlier events, though, as well as the heroic and prophetic acts of many individuals and groups in the previous generation—including those of Marshall and the National Association for the Advancement of Colored People.)

For three-quarters of a century, from Reconstruction to the 1950s, no racial development in the South sparked as much reaction, pro and con, as the *Brown* decision and the black nonviolent protest in Montgomery—the one predictable and inexorable, the other spontaneous and surprising, and both of them ultimately inevitable. Those who took an active interest in the world around them knew that *Brown* was imminent; they had seen it, or something like it, coming for a long time. It was like an earthquake or a hurricane: Your intelligence and your common sense told you it was bound to happen sooner or later, but it was still a profound shock when it finally hit.

Dozens of individuals—blacks and whites, and most of them Southern—had written or spoken prophetically on the future consequences of racial chauvinism. The immovable object of white supremacy and the irresistible force of racial equality had been on a collision course since the end of World War II—had been cemented in irreconcilable opposition, in fact, for centuries. Against all the progressive forces of change that had buffeted them from within and without since the early days of slavery, the ruling white oligarchs of the South had always reacted defiantly. Not even the Lost Cause and the lost war had been enough to dispel the myth of racial superiority and open the way for whites and blacks—and the South and the nation—to live with one another on an equal footing.

Now and again, a contrary voice of admonition had echoed through the Dixie wilderness as some troubled native son or daughter between the shades of alabaster and ebony dared to stand and speak from the heart. But too few heard, and fewer heeded. As the years and the opportunities slipped away, the paradox of better times obscured the problem of racial injustice, pushing it ever further back into the corners of life and memory. By 1950, relatively fewer African-American Southerners were lynched or terrorized or kept in peonage; relatively more of them voted and went to college and got good jobs. The South, white and black, had made economic, political, educational progress since the early thirties—but it still suffered grievously from the causes and effects of racial discrimination, and no amount of denial or finger-pointing at the North would make the problem disappear. Now, finally, forces beyond its control would compel the region to change.

Brown was the beginning of that next step, the start of a cure. After a generation of preliminaries, the main event was about to begin. Everything else had been Yesterday. *Brown* was Tomorrow.

In the closing chapters of *Simple Justice*, Richard Kluger's masterful retracing of the five cases that flowed to confluence in the U.S. Supreme Court as *Brown* v. *Board of Education*, the author recounted two remarkable expressions of unanimity that underscored the significance of the historic decision. The first was in the U.S. Senate, where on March 1, 1954, not a single member voted against the confirmation of Earl Warren as chief justice—a role the former California governor had already stepped into five months earlier, right after President Eisenhower awarded him an interim appointment to replace the deceased Fred M. Vinson.

The second unanimous vote was in the Supreme Court itself, where Chief Justice Warren patiently and diplomatically coaxed a wavering minority of his eight brethren to affirm without any dissenting voices their chief's opinion "that in the field of public education the doctrine of 'separate but equal' has no place." The decision, though stunning and momentous, was not unexpected—but virtually no one anticipated unanimity from the all-white, all-male court. Hugo L. Black of Alabama, Tom C. Clark of Texas, Stanley Reed of Kentucky, Sherman Minton, Harold H. Burton, Robert H. Jackson, Felix Frankfurter, William O. Douglas, and Earl Warren. *So say us all.*

Following the circuitous paths of all this litigation, I find myself wishing the title case had been *Briggs* v. *Elliott*, the South Carolina suit—or better yet, something like *DeLaine* v. *Clarendon County*, in honor of the Reverend Joseph A. DeLaine of Summerton, South Carolina, the one individual above all others most responsible for bringing this first of the five cases into court. It's not that the complaint of Oliver Brown and others against the school board of Topeka, Kansas, wasn't representative enough, or as much in need of redress; it's just that Kansas is a long way from the heart of Dixie, and the facts of that dispute seem less compelling, somehow, than those surrounding the Clarendon County drama, or the case from Prince Edward County, Virginia. (Two other lawsuits, one from Wilmington, Delaware, and the other from the District of Columbia, seemed to belong, with the Kansas case, closer to the periphery of the conflict—again, not because the facts weren't indicative of the problem, but because the places weren't as Southern or as symbolic of the central issue.)

Clarendon County in 1950 was a flat, dusty throwback to Yesterday's South, a sprawling rural patchwork of cottonfields and piney woods in the Carolina low country southeast of Columbia and north of Charleston. The population of 32,000 was almost three-fourths black; in the public schools, the ratio was higher still. There were only two towns of any size— Manning, the county seat, and Summerton. Most of the blacks and a good many of the whites were poor farmers who worked the land for the tiny white ruling class or served them in other capacities. Over two-thirds of the households in the county earned less than a thousand dollars in 1950.

Two-thirds of the county school budget was allocated to the schools that served white children, even though they made up just thirteen percent of the total enrollment. The whites were clustered in a dozen school buildings that bore no resemblance to the sixty ramshackle buildings, most of them one- or two-room structures, into which scores or hundreds of black children were crowded. The whites had buses, too, about thirty in all; the blacks walked, some more than five miles each way.

J. A. DeLaine was one of a handful of black citizens in the Summerton area who decided in the summer of 1947 that it would help a lot if the school board would provide them with a bus. They asked the board chairman, R. W. Elliott, a sawmill operator. His reply, later quoted by one of the men who went to see him, was "We ain't got no money to buy a bus for your nigger children." They asked the superintendent, L. B. McCord, a Presbyterian minister. His answer was a bit more polite, but just as unavailing. They wrote to the state superintendent of education and the U.S. Attorney General—and again, they got nowhere. Finally the black parents scraped up enough money to buy an old heap of a worn-out bus, but it broke down a lot, and the school board wouldn't even agree to put gas in it.

All of this deeply troubled J. A. DeLaine, a college-educated minister in the African Methodist Episcopal Church who served as pastor of two congregations and taught school during the week. He was almost fifty years old, and not at all eager to risk his teaching job or his health in a confrontation with the white authorities. But in Columbia that summer, he heard a speech by the Reverend James M. Hinton, president of the South Carolina NAACP, that seemed almost like a call from on high. Hinton was talking about racial discrimination in the public schools, and he specifically cited the lack of buses for black children. The NAACP needed some brave plaintiffs to attack these problems with them, he said. DeLaine took it upon himself to find such a person. He got Levi Pearson, a farmer in one of his churches, to sign a formal request for a bus. The white school officials ignored it. Then, in March 1948, the NAACP attorney in Columbia, Harold Boulware, filed a complaint in federal court in Pearson's name. The case was dismissed on a technicality. Soon thereafter, Pearson found that the white moneylenders and storekeepers in Clarendon County had cut off his credit.

A year went by. In the spring of 1949, DeLaine and Pearson met again with NAACP officials in Columbia, and this time Thurgood Marshall was there. He told them they had a good case, but they needed several plaintiffs, not just one, and they would have to stick together and stay the course. Back home, about three hundred frustrated but determined blacks had a meeting. They promised Joseph DeLaine that if he would lead them, they would follow. Putting aside his reluctance and hesitation, he finally accepted their call.

It cost him his teaching job quickly, but he knew that was coming. Then the school officials tried to lure him back and stop the legal wheels from turning, but it was too late for that. By November, DeLaine had secured the names of twenty people willing to sign on as plaintiffs in a new lawsuit. First among them, alphabetically, was Harry Briggs, a thirty-four-year-old navy veteran and father of four who worked at a filling station in Summerton. His name and that of the school board chairman would be paired in the title. The suit was filed later that month in the federal district court in Charleston—Judge J. Waties Waring's court. A year later, on November 17, 1950, Thurgood Marshall went before Judge Waring for a pretrial hearing. Three and a half years after R. W. Elliott first denied them a bus, the black petitioners of Clarendon County were about to get their day in court. It would be another three and a half years before justice was done in *Briggs* v. *Elliott*.

As the South Carolina case was moving by fits and starts toward the courtroom, Marshall and the NAACP Legal Defense Fund were struggling for consensus on matters of policy and strategy that would profoundly affect *Briggs* and all the other school cases. Throughout his twelve years as the association's legal director, Marshall had never faltered in his personal commitment to the long-term goal that his Howard University mentor, Charles H. Houston, had spelled out in 1935: "the abolition of all forms of segregation" in American law. But Marshall had grave doubts that the Supreme Court under Chief Justice Fred M. Vinson was ready to overturn *Plessy* v. *Ferguson's* "separate but equal" principle and declare that segregation itself was a violation of the equal rights provisions of the U.S. Constitution.

Marshall didn't want to gamble on that point and risk losing everything. The old strategy had been to compel the transgressors to pay the price of making separate equal, or else desegregate. The lawyers had pried open the graduate and professional schools of almost a dozen states with that approach, and those were gains they didn't want to jeopardize by trying to make segregation unlawful—and risk losing both the battle and the war in the process.

But others, led by Howard University law professor James M. Nabrit,

Jr., an old friend and colleague of Marshall's, were ready for a frontal attack on segregation—the Charles Houston vision—in part because the old approach was simply not working well enough or fast enough. Higher education was Exhibit A for that argument too: Only token desegregation was taking place in most graduate and professional schools; undergraduate programs generally weren't affected at all; and in five states—Mississippi, Alabama, Georgia, South Carolina, and Florida—higher education was still totally segregated. (In Florida, forty-three-year-old Virgil D. Hawkins's 1949 application to the state's only public law school was then in court—and would stay bottled up there for eight years.) Nabrit's position was to force the Supreme Court either to declare that segregation was unconstitutional or "take the blame if it dares to say to the entire world, '*Yes*, democracy rests on a legalized caste system; segregation of races is legal.' "

When these issues were thrashed out at an NAACP conference in June of 1950 (two months after Houston died of heart disease), Marshall came around to the conviction that they could attack segregation head-on without surrendering the minimum gain of separate-but-equal funding. At his urging, the NAACP board of directors approved a resolution making "education on a non-segregated basis" the primary goal to be sought by its attorneys. Thereafter, the Legal Defense Fund focused the lion's share of its resources on overturning the laws and practices governing racial segregation in public elementary and secondary schools.

Coming before Judge Waring in the pretrial hearing on the *Briggs* case that November, Marshall was playing his new policy close to the vest. If he were still suing for equalization of programs and funding, this would be the case and the court for it; the facts clearly supported his argument, and Judge Waring had certainly shown his belief in the principle of equity. But the rules of judicial procedure required a three-judge panel for cases questioning the constitutionality of state laws, and that could mean that Marshall would end up on the short end of a two-to-one decision. If he had to take that on appeal to the Supreme Court—and if they ruled against him on the constitutionality of segregation—he and his Clarendon County plaintiffs could come away with nothing, not even equalized funding.

While Marshall was pondering all this and trying to figure out how he could attack the legality of segregation itself and still keep the case in Waring's court, the judge surprised him by suggesting that he refile his complaint with an explicit claim that the Clarendon schools were unconstitutionally segregated. Apparently, Waring was eager to see the larger question raised in his court, even if two other judges less sympathetic to it than he were hearing it with him; Marshall, on the other hand, was just as eager to avoid a three-judge panel. Waring got it his way: The first suit was withdrawn, and a new one was filed a month later. The case was set for trial in May 1951.

By this time, Waties Waring and his wife were so estranged from their former friends and associates in Charleston that their contacts away from the courtroom were largely confined to their black friends in the city and those of both races who reached out to them from afar. Such was the hostility that flowed between the Warings and their enemies that neither side could any longer find a trace of virtue in the other. From both came such expressions of self-righteous certitude and hypersensitivity that it was hard to sort out fact from fiction. Would white Charlestonians have acted more charitably toward Waties Waring if he had ruled against segregation but never divorced his first wife? Would they have ostracized him if he had divorced but not ruled? Would Waring have changed his mind about white supremacy if he hadn't married Elizabeth Avery? The questions are intriguing, but unanswerable.

One thing was crystal clear, though: J. Waties Waring and his wife were outspokenly and unequivocally committed to the principle of racial equality, and their adversaries in the South Carolina power structure, from Governor Byrnes and former Governor Strom Thurmond to the judge's nephew Tom Waring at the Charleston *News & Courier*, were just as devoted to the cause of white supremacy. Having passed his seventieth birthday, the judge was looking beyond the *Briggs* case to the prospect of his retirement, and escape from his smothering isolation under a magnolia blanket. But first he hoped to "preach a sermon" in what was to be his last major ruling.

Riding south on the Atlantic Coast Line's overnight run from New York to Charleston, Thurgood Marshall was heading for the courtroom battle in *Briggs* v. *Elliott* in a mood of relaxed good humor that cloaked his nervous concern. This was the start, he knew, of another phase in the long struggle for racial equality. The odds were long, the stakes were enormous—and the first skirmish was going to take place in the historic city where Rebel gunners had fired the first shot of the Civil War.

"We joked a lot on that ride," psychologist Kenneth B. Clark would recall later. He was to be an expert witness, testifying to the psychological effects of segregation on black children. Robert L. Carter, the Legal Defense Fund's number-two lawyer, was also in the traveling party, and when the train pulled into Richmond early that evening, a fourth man joined them: thirty-four-year-old Spottswood W. Robinson III, a quiet, scholarly attorney who, with his partner, Oliver W. Hill, represented the NAACP in Virginia. One of the pleasures of this journey for the four men was the knowledge that their table in the dining car and their Pullman accommodations were rights and privileges the Legal Defense Fund had won for all Americans of color.

Just hours before Spottswood Robinson came to the train station on that May evening in 1951, he had been to the federal courthouse in Richmond to file suit in another case that would become a link in the *Brown* chain: *Davis* v. *County School Board of Prince Edward County.* Unlike the others, *Davis* originated not with adults but with students—the entire student body, in fact, of a black high school where painfully obvious inequities had been ignored for so long that it took a strike to get anybody's attention. The cool-headed organizer of the walkout, sixteen-year-old Barbara Rose Johns, was an inspiration to Robinson. So was the Reverend L. Francis Griffin, a Baptist minister and Prince Edward's answer to J. A. DeLaine down in Clarendon County. As the train rolled on across North Carolina, the Richmond attorney told his companions the essence of the story, and they talked about how the case might tie in with *Briggs*.

The South that passed by them in the darkness of that warm spring night was teetering like a blind man on a tightrope, unsure of the right steps to safety. Jimmy Byrnes, newly installed as South Carolina's governor, had already warned that his state would "abandon the public school system" before it would give up segregation, and that sentiment was echoed by his recently reelected Georgia neighbor, Governor Herman Talmadge. Congress had been stirred to a frenzy by Joe McCarthy's anti-red screed in the Senate and General MacArthur's sacking in Korea. Claude Pepper and Frank Graham were goners, Harry Truman was on a slippery slope, W. E. B. Du Bois was on trial in New York—and now these outsiders, these "colored lawyers from up North," were about to get up on the firing range in Charleston, South Carolina, and draw a bead on school segregation. When they stepped off the train into that venerable anteroom of the Old South, the NAACP team was as wary and circumspect as a diplomatic delegation to the camp of the enemy.

Though nothing especially dramatic would happen during the two-day trial, the cast of characters gave the event an air of drama and portent that raised it to the level of a morality play. There were, first of all, the lawyers: Marshall's Legal Defense Fund on one side, and on the other, a clever and skillful Charleston attorney named Robert McCormick Figg, Jr., a former prosecutor with political connections in high places (he had raised funds for Strom Thurmond's Dixiecrat adventure) and a long list of prominent clients in government. Assisting him was the leading attorney in Clarendon County, aristocratic S. Emory Rogers, a man with impressive credentials as both a student and a teacher of law in several top universities, North and South.

A number of expert witnesses had been sought by each side, but the ones who testified were less revealing of the South's state of mind regarding race than the ones who didn't appear. Robert Carter's search for a white social scientist from a Southern university turned up no one who would dare to criticize segregation from the stand; the closest he could get was a young Ohioan in the lower ranks of the University of Louisville's political science department, and he was an ineffective witness. Figg and Rogers went to Chapel Hill to plead with Howard Odum and Guy Johnson to appear for the defense, but neither would do it, though Figg did quote Odum in court, and the attorney later claimed that both of the University of North Carolina sociologists "felt very strongly that at the present time . . . it would be disastrous to force mixed schools" in the South.

The sitting judges were a study in themselves: J. Waties Waring, the "host" jurist—intense and determined, a besieged liberal prophet without honor in his own town; George Bell Timmerman, another South Carolina district judge—a segregationist without reservation or apology, and a certain vote for the defense; and the senior jurist, John J. Parker, chief judge of the Fourth Circuit Court of Appeals—a North Carolina Republican with more than twenty-five years on the bench. Back in 1930, the U.S. Senate had failed by just two votes to confirm Parker's nomination to the Supreme Court—partly because he was the nominee of an unpopular president, Herbert Hoover, and partly because of a skillful lobbying effort by Walter White, a rising young political activist on the staff of the NAACP. Ironically, Parker went on to compile an enviable record of fairness and moderation on the circuit court—consistently better than the man who got the Supreme Court seat he was denied.

The ubiquitous Johnny Popham of the *New York Times* was also in the Charleston courtroom, reporting for his paper, and so was Ted Poston of the New York *Post*. But of all the characters on this stage, none stood out more impressively than the throng of black citizens who came to listen and watch. J. A. DeLaine and Harry Briggs had left Summerton at dawn, leading a convoy of battered automobiles on the two-hour drive to Charleston. Other spectators joined them there to form a double line that began at the courtroom doors on the second floor of the Federal Building and wound along the hallway, down the stairs, out the front door, and around the corner of Broad and Meeting Streets in the heart of the old city. When the courtroom doors were opened, those at the head of the line filed through in orderly fashion, and the two hundred or so unsegregated spectator seats were quickly filled. Few whites other than participants and reporters were present in the small room; that privilege fell to the envoys of the aggrieved, and their silent witness was eloquent. It was as if, said Judge Waring later, "they had come there on a pilgrimage."

When the hearing opened, attorney Figg surprised the judges and the plaintiffs by conceding that "inequalities in the facilities, opportunities, and curricula of the schools of this district do exist." (They were not just unequal, he would say later—"they were very embarrassingly unequal.") The defense strategy began to unfold: concede inequality, point to the state's new plan to bolster spending on black schools, and plead for time to equalize facilities and resources; don't say *never*—say *not now*, and avoid saying *when;* and as for segregation, it had been the law for a long time (Congress itself had segregated the schools of the District of Columbia), so the lawyers saw that as a settled issue.

Thurgood Marshall had intended to use some of his time establishing proof of inequality; now he had no need to do that, and his plan of attack was diverted. Some of his witnesses were not yet present. Instead of taking the fight to his opponents, he had been thrown on the defensive by them. He finally recovered and finished strong, but the testimony was not persuasive, and the entire proceeding had an anticlimactic air.

The conclusion was probably foregone too. Timmerman was a sure vote for continuing segregation, Waring was equally as firm for ending it, and Judge Parker was not prepared to overrule the *Plessy* "separate but equal" standard. Three weeks later, on June 23, he issued the written opinion, Timmerman concurring: "If conditions have changed so that segregation is no longer wise, this is a matter for the legislatures and not the courts." The defendants were ordered to equalize educational facilities in Clarendon County "promptly."

Waties Waring's dissent was his swan song from the bench. The only question before the court was the doctrine of segregation, he declared. The Fourteenth Amendment was intended to guarantee the black minority their "full rights as citizens," but it was still an unkept promise. Segregation was harmful to white as well as black children. "Segregation in education can never produce equality. . . . *Segregation is per se inequality.*" The sermon he had hoped to preach didn't soar rhetorically, but it made the key point.

The embattled judge and his wife spent much of the rest of the summer away from Charleston. Waring's biographer, Tinsley Yarbrough, found in the couple's correspondence and other papers clear signs of their keen disappointment with the outcome of the hearing and with Marshall's "insufficiently militant" handling of the plaintiffs' case. By his own admission, Waties Waring was no longer an adjudicator but an advocate. "I've got a cause to live for and a job to do," he told a reporter from Ohio. "What can they do to me, at seventy-one, that would matter?" For their part, the Charlestonians who now detested him seemed only to wish he would go away.

He was only too happy to oblige them. On January 28, 1952, two days after he was eligible to retire with full salary, Judge Waring announced that he was leaving the bench. Less than a month later, he and his wife went by train to New York, there to live until the judge's death, in 1968. He would speak from time to time nostalgically about the beauty of Charleston, but he had nothing good to say about his adversaries there, nor they about him. His one and only return to the city of his birth was to be in a coffin. Fewer than a dozen whites would join the hundreds of black mourners at his funeral.

Conservative South Carolina hadn't been prodded to change its ways by Waring's withering blasts from the bench, and it wouldn't change much after he was gone. The long-suffering Reverend J. A. DeLaine took some comfort from Judge Waring's dissent and clung to the hope of further relief in the Supreme Court, but the Summerton minister's personal burden grew heavier in October 1951 when his home was destroyed by a fire of mysterious and suspicious origin. Later reports from Clarendon County promised that some new school facilities for black children would be in place by the fall of 1952. Judge Parker's ruling was appealed to the Supreme Court, which sent the case back for rehearing—but this time, Judge Waring would not be there to write a dissent.

John H. McCray, the combative editor of the *Lighthouse & Informer* in Columbia, understood better than most South Carolinians what the fuss over *Briggs* was all about. Shortly before the hearing, he had written that "the burning question" in the state was "whether or not segregation of the races in education shall be continued." The South had neither the capability nor the readiness to maintain two separate school systems, he declared. "It doesn't have the money to operate a first-class system for whites, let alone another for Negroes."

When blacks began to analyze their predicament in the postwar years, said McCray, they saw that their best chance was in the courts—and whatever progress they have made "has come as a direct appeal to the courts. . . . The political bosses of this state have never acted decently until and unless they had the club of a policeman over their head. . . . And the only policeman they fear is the federal courts." The *Briggs* case would give both races equality of opportunity, he predicted: "In the America for which we labor, fight and die today, there are no Negro, no white, no racial children. They are all just children, and any teacher not prepared to teach all of them isn't prepared to teach any of them."

After *Briggs*, McCray wrote that he had "a very strong feeling that when the case is finally decided, Judge Waring will be—once again—the man way ahead of the rest of the South."

Virginia's entry in the *Brown* derby, Prince Edward County, presented a good example of the honeycomb of subtle differences beneath the common stereotype of "the solid South." On the surface, this looked like just another isolated agricultural jurisdiction with a large black underclass and the usual patterns of garden-variety segregation. True enough, as far as it went—but Prince Edward was tobacco country, and that meant smaller farms and more individual landowners, black and white. The population was smaller, too, and more evenly divided, with about eight thousand whites and seven thousand blacks, and among the leading citizens of both races there were men and women of education and accomplishment, culture and refinement, manners and civility, who would have considered it positively un-Virginian to resort to violence and lawlessness over any matter of personal dispute.

The schools were every bit as segregated and unequal as Clarendon County's, and blacks didn't have the ballot (nor did all that many whites), and of course the churches and other institutions, including two colleges, were racially exclusive. But if there was any one symbol of the intangible quality of quiet dignity and self-respect that could be found among black citizens in Prince Edward County, it was this: The First Baptist Church on Main Street in Farmville, the county seat, was the leading *black* church; Farmville Baptist Church, one of the county's largest *white* congregations, anchored another block nearby on the same side of the downtown avenue. Never the twain did meet—but at least there was a twain, a semblance of separate equality.

And First Baptist had, in the Reverend L. Francis Griffin, a man who was in every respect the equal of Farmville's finest. A fourth-generation minister, he had grown up there under the watchful gaze of his father and a dynamic occasional visitor and sometime resident, the Reverend Vernon Johns. (The college- and seminary-trained Johns was a man of dazzling intellectual and oratorical skills who went on to serve the Dexter Avenue Baptist Church in Montgomery, Alabama, for almost a decade after World War II before leaving in 1954 to make way for a young seminary graduate, Martin Luther King, Jr.) The younger Griffin roamed afield to test his own wings in the late thirties, fought in Europe with an all-black tank battalion, and then went to college and into the ministry. He was thirty-two years old when the congregation at First Baptist called him in 1949 to fill his late father's shoes. Like so many black ex-GIs, he had seen enough of freedom to have an unquenchable thirst for it. As soon as he got settled, he organized a local chapter of the NAACP.

Farmville and Prince Edward County had been languishing in a sort of antebellum time warp until the postwar stirrings of social change jostled them awake. In the peculiarly elitist manner of so many Virginians, the community didn't even build a white high school until the 1920s (the wealthy had their children tutored at home, or sent them away for "finishing")—and for blacks, not until 1939. Robert R. Moton High, named for a native son who followed Booker T. Washington as the head of Tuskegee Institute, had room for 180 students when it opened; by 1950 its enrollment was almost triple that number, and youngsters were spilling out into a tacky string of poorly constructed temporary buildings—nothing more than tarpaper shacks.

It was this facility, so obviously and insultingly unequal to the high school for whites, that became the focal point in *Davis* v. *County School Board*. On a Monday morning in April 1951, a small group of students, led by Barbara Johns, staged a carefully planned assembly at which the entire student body of 450 rose up in protest and marched out on strike. The principal, M. Boyd Jones, was away from the school at the time, and no teachers prevented the walkout. Barbara Johns, a junior barely sixteen years old—and a niece of the Reverend Vernon Johns—was eloquent and persuasive in her assertion that the white authorities had never given them their fair share under the "separate but equal" formula, and never would unless forced.

It was all very orderly and dignified—and effective. Instantly, the attention of the entire community was riveted on the issue. New developments came in rapid-fire succession: The students called in L. Francis Griffin to advise them; he put them in touch with NAACP attorneys Oliver Hill and Spottswood Robinson in Richmond; hundreds of black residents met with the lawyers and student leaders, first at the high school and then at the Reverend Griffin's church; they endorsed a lawsuit attacking segregation; the all-white county school board fired Principal Jones and announced plans to build a new Moton High School; Barbara Johns's parents, fearing for her safety, sent her to live with her uncle Vernon in Montgomery; and the suit, *Davis* (first-named of the student plaintiffs) v. *County School Board of Prince Edward County*, was filed in federal court on May 23, 1951, five days before the *Briggs* trial was to begin in Charleston.

Pressure on black adults to intervene and defuse the protest was steady and intense. It surfaced briefly in Griffin's church that summer when some of his flock tried to remove him for his spirited encouragement of rebellion. He met the challenge with a thundering sermon. "I would sacrifice my job, money, and any property for the principles of right," he declared, "and I'm willing to die rather than let these children down. No one's going to scare me from my convictions by threatening my job. All who want me to stay as the head of this church, raise your hands." If there was a soul present who kept still, the record didn't show it.

The case came before a three-judge court in Richmond on February 25, 1952. The Prince Edward defense, bolstered by the participation of Virginia Attorney General J. Lindsay Almond, Jr., a former judge and congressman (and later to be the state's governor), took the same tack as the Clarendon lawyers: Plead no contest on the equality issue, promise to begin correcting the disparities, and defend segregation as customary, moral, and lawful. The plaintiffs, represented by NAACP attorneys Robert Carter, Oliver Hill, and Spottswood Robinson, managed to hold their own during the five days of sometimes tense and acrimonious exchanges, but they knew from the makeup of the bench that their chances of victory were slim to nonexistent.

The presiding judge was Armistead M. Dobie of the Fourth Circuit Court of Appeals, a former University of Virginia law school professor and dean. (He would also take part in the rehearing of the Clarendon case, replacing Judge Waring.) He had been a close colleague of Judge John Parker for more than a decade, and seldom voted contrary to him. The other two men hearing this case with Dobie were district judges in Virginia, and nothing in their past performances gave any hint of exceptionality.

In his summation, Attorney General Almond declared that Virginia would not follow a course of deliberate defiance if the courts eventually outlawed segregation—but, presuming to speak for "our people," he said segregation was "morally and legally defensible," and they would close down the public schools rather than be forced to integrate them. (Eight years later, it would be Governor Almond who did exactly that, ordering school closings in three Virginia cities before bowing to a federal judge's threatened contempt-of-court ruling against him; Prince Edward officials, meanwhile, would go on to close their school system and keep it closed for five years.)

It took Judge Dobie and his colleagues only a week to issue a unanimous ruling to the effect that segregation in Virginia schools rested on the mores and traditions of the people, and was legal and harmless—but it ought to be equal, according to the law, so Prince Edward County should work to make it so "with diligence and dispatch." No timetable was suggested.

The *Briggs* case was reheard in March, and this time all three judges sided with the defendants. Now Marshall and his Legal Defense Fund forces had stinging and unequivocal defeats from South Carolina and Virginia to take on appeal to the Supreme Court, along with three other more complex and ambiguous rulings from Kansas, Delaware, and the District of Columbia. As it neared adjournment in June 1952, the high court announced that it would hear arguments in two of the cases in the fall; then, in October, the pieces began to fall into place for a full-scale hearing and oral arguments on all five appeals beginning December 9. The five were bracketed as a single entry, arbitrarily given the name of the Kansas case, *Brown* v. *Board of Education of Topeka.*

As the showdown approached, intense pressure was building on all sides. South Carolina retained former Democratic presidential nominee John W. Davis—"the most accomplished and admired appellate lawyer in America," according to Richard Kluger—to join Robert Figg in the Clarendon defense. The lame-duck Truman administration, waiting for the January inauguration of Dwight Eisenhower, weighed in with a friend-of-the-court brief from the Attorney General's office; written by a veteran solicitor, Philip Elman, the document argued that the court should overturn the *Plessy* doctrine as a violation of the equal-rights provisions of the Constitution, and should give school districts "a reasonable period of time" to make "progressive adjustment to a non-segregated system." At the NAACP, Thurgood Marshall and the Legal Defense Fund staff worked frantically to hone their arguments for the coming drama before the Supreme Court.

Among those in the hushed audience that packed the courtroom for the three days of debate in December was the Reverend Joseph A. DeLaine—still waiting quietly, faithfully, for the complex and seemingly endless process to yield a wise answer, one worthy of a Solomon or a Moses. Fortunately, the South Carolina minister's patience was not exhausted.

After the hearing, the justices wrestled with the cases behind closed doors through the first six months of 1953; then, just before adjournment for the summer, they announced yet another postponement and the scheduling of more oral arguments in the fall, at which time Eisenhower's Attorney General, Herbert Brownell, would be asked to file a brief. (This he subsequently did, agreeing with his predecessor that segregation was inconsistent with the Constitution, but equivocating on the question of what the court should do about it.) In a stunning and disruptive turn of events, all sides in the vitally important school cases had yet another adjustment to make when Chief Justice Fred M. Vinson died suddenly of a heart attack in September. President Eisenhower, returning a campaign favor, named California's third-term governor, Earl Warren, to the top seat on the court.

Fresh troops would be recruited to help prepare for this last round of arguments. The NAACP's budget was seriously strained, but the association got a number of attorneys and scholars to assist voluntarily in the intensive effort. Among them were at least four Southern expatriates: Charles L. Black, a Texan turned Ivy League law professor; President Horace Mann Bond of Lincoln University in Pennsylvania, whose roots were in Kentucky and Tennessee; and two historians of national stature— Howard University's John Hope Franklin, an Oklahoma native and Fisk University alumnus, and C. Vann Woodward of Johns Hopkins University, an Arkansan with degrees from Emory and North Carolina. Black's strength was his expertise in legal theory; the other three drew upon their knowledge of educational and social history to draft background papers putting the school desegregation issue into historical context. No resident Southern scholars risked involvement with either side in the great debate.

And then, finally, the last three days of questions and answers and arguments rose to an oratorical cry and fell to a histrionic whisper in the marble mausoleum that housed the United States Supreme Court. When every man had had his say and Chief Justice Warren gaveled the last session to adjournment on December 9, 1953, both sides had some reason to hope that a five-to-four or six-to-three ruling would favor them. The combatants and the adjudicators—indeed, the South and the nation— would have five more months to ponder the question: Was the promise of equal justice under law, chiseled into the very stone above the Supreme Court's entrance, meant to be taken literally—or did it mean *separate* but equal justice under law?

For at least two years before the court's ruling in *Brown*, anyone who was paying the slightest attention to the daily news in the United States knew that a momentous decision was coming on the question of school segregation. Newspapers and magazines reported at length on the five cases as they made their way through the murky channels of judicial review. *The Saturday Evening Post* ran a major piece by Virginius Dabney ("Southern Crisis: The Segregation Decision") in one of its November 1952 editions. Hodding Carter's articles explaining the South (some critics would say he was defending it, others that he was attacking it) appeared frequently in the *Post, Look, Collier's,* and the Sunday magazine of the *New York Times,* and Ralph McGill's byline was likewise familiar in most of the same publications.

The Minneapolis *Tribune* sent a young black reporter, Carl T. Rowan— born and raised in rural Tennessee—on an investigative journey through the South in 1951, and his articles were foundation stones for a book, *South of Freedom.* Rowan also got national attention for a widely reprinted series he wrote in 1953, called "Jim Crow's Last Stand," about the five communities in which the pending school cases had originated.

The Southern press was not ignoring the issue, either, and for the most part its reporting, and even much of its editorial comment, was fair-minded and professional. When the South Carolina and Virginia defendants conceded in court that their separate black schools were manifestly unequal to those for whites and promised to correct the problem, the papers told their readers all about it. They reported, too, when state after state announced new funding plans aimed at convincing federal judges of their good intentions.

Surveying the states, some newspapers refined and updated their estimates of what it would take to equalize educational spending in the region (most now suggested a billion dollars minimum, and probably more). The Southern Regional Council in Atlanta made a detailed study of the problem, as did the Southern Regional Education Board, the Southern Conference Educational Fund, and other organizations. State and local school officials and politicians across the region clearly knew that a hard choice was looming before them: either to spend their way to equality with massive amounts of money they didn't have, or to consolidate their duplicative operations into unitary school systems serving both races.

If there was one aspect of this story the papers didn't really cover or analyze (neither the Southern press nor its upcountry counterparts), it was the extent to which the ruling elite of the region never seriously tried to deliver on either option. For all their talk, they couldn't summon the will, let alone the means, to equalize spending. There were too many reactionaries in power who believed in their hearts that blacks were too dumb to learn, that learning only ruined obedient laborers, that a little learning was a dangerous thing, and that whites ought to get the scarce resources in any case. And as for integration, well, there was just no way, they said; even if the double cost of maintaining segregation doomed the region to remain forever a poor stepchild of the affluent North, that would be better than letting all the flowers of white womanhood and girlhood be exposed to "social situations" with black males.

For a time after the Dixiecrat failure, this hard-core extremism seemed to be weakening. The churches were adopting resolutions of interracial brotherly love, and university students and faculty were expressing a high degree of receptivity to desegregation, and public opinion polls were showing an erosion of Jim Crow sentiment, especially among young Southern whites. But the tactic of red-baiting as a means of discrediting and isolating the advocates of racial equality also gained a new potency in the McCarthy era; it collared such organizations as the Southern Conference and the Highlander Folk School with the tag of extreme radicalism, and that severely limited their effectiveness. The same offensive smear was aimed at the NAACP, which was easily the most aggressive and effective organization working for racial equality in the South, but its Northern base made it less vulnerable to the Dixie reactionaries.

In spite of its middle-of-the-road caution, the Southern Regional Council was attacked too, and might have withered and died for want of funds and members had it not been for Atlanta's protective shield—that and a quarter-million-dollar grant from the Ford Foundation.

You had to experience Atlanta to get the full flavor of its uniqueness as an urban oasis in the Sahara of segregation. On the surface, blacks were still locked out of practically everything—but as Hylan Lewis, who was then on the social science faculty at Atlanta University, would explain it years later, "Atlanta was not a back-door city, like most places in the South. It was still segregated out front, but it had side doors and windows through which people of both races came and went." For a long time before the mid-fifties, Atlanta was a greenhouse of possibility.

It had the Atlanta University cluster of black colleges, plus Emory and Georgia Tech. It had the *Constitution* and Ralph McGill, the *Journal,* and the *Daily World,* with the Scott family and Bill Gordon. It had William Hartsfield, a progressive mayor. It had one of the nation's most active chapters of the American Veterans Committee, a biracial voice for reform. It had the Hungry Club, a black organization that welcomed white guests on its own terms, as equals. It had Protestants, Catholics, and Jews who were committed to racial equality. It had Grace Hamilton and the Urban League, and attorney A. T. Walden, and a strong NAACP chapter led by William Boyd and Clarence A. Bacote. It had some of the South's most influential women—Dorothy Tilly, Josephine Wilkins, Lucy Randolph Mason, and others. It had the Southern leaders of organized labor in the AFL and the CIO. It had the SRC, with its solid mix of the city's white and black progressives. And, to keep all this in realistic perspective, it also had Governor Herman Talmadge and a rural-dominated legislature adamantly opposed to social reform.

The Southern Regional Council saw itself as a forward-looking private agency faced with the necessity of building a progressive alliance in a region of reactionary resistance. The task had never been easy. The SRC had been trying for years to obtain a substantial grant from Ford, which, since the termination of the Rosenwald Fund, had been the philanthropic foundation most interested in Southern issues. For three years running, proposals from the Atlanta group had gone up to the foundation in New York, only to be rejected. Finally, in 1952, a small grant of $10,000 was received, and the following year the amount was raised to $25,000.

The foundation had two special-focus divisions by then: the Fund for the

Republic, which promoted the strengthening of democratic institutions, and the Fund for the Advancement of Education. In April 1954, the Fund for the Republic, having satisfied itself that the SRC was not an incubator for radical anarchists, made a major grant of $240,000 to the organization. (As one requirement, the council adopted an employee loyalty oath that summer—not only to satisfy the Ford Foundation, but also, its leaders explained, to protect itself from the red-hunters.)

Suddenly flush for the first time in its history, going all the way back to the origin of the Commission on Interracial Cooperation in 1919, the SRC quickly set about trying to make itself useful in the upcoming school desegregation effort. Just a week before the *Brown* decision was handed down, the council sponsored a four-day conference in Williamsburg, Virginia, as the first step in helping the South to adjust to the consequences of the ruling, whatever they turned out to be. Among the participants were George Mitchell, Harold Fleming, Dorothy Tilly, and Katherine Stoney of the SRC staff; Charles S. Johnson of Fisk and Rufus Clement of Atlanta University; Grace Hamilton of the Urban League; Emory University administrator John A. Griffin and old pro Will Alexander; Oliver Hill of the NAACP and Philip Hammer of the National Planning Association; labor leader Paul Christopher and Brooks Hays of Arkansas, the only member of Congress then in an active role in the SRC.

One other race-related project based in Atlanta and funded by Ford was launched in this period when everyone was waiting for the Supreme Court to rule. In the spring of 1953, the Fund for the Advancement of Education announced that it would sponsor a comprehensive study of segregated education to determine with some precision just how separate and how unequal the schools were. One of the greatest needs, said the fund's president, Owen J. Roberts—a retired justice of the Supreme Court himself—was for objective facts to help local school officials and citizens make wise decisions. The plan was to base the study at a major educational institution in the South, but by June of that year, no such base had been established.

Harry Ashmore, executive editor of the *Arkansas Gazette*, took a leave of absence from his paper to serve as director of the project (a role later characterized by one of his friends in the state legislature as tantamount to "running for son of a bitch without opposition"). The fund had offered "a blank check" to several Southern universities, Ashmore recalled later, but "the undertaking was so politically charged" that no institution, public or private, would accept the risk. There were many individual scholars who were willing and eager to take part, though, and Ashmore became, in effect, the managing editor, working out of Little Rock with a core staff based in Atlanta and a team of about forty social scientists and legal scholars scattered across the South and beyond.

The Ashmore Project, as it came to be called, was an accelerated exercise in statistical compilation, analysis, and interpretation—not to argue the case for or against segregation in public education, but to provide accurate and reliable information to those who would be debating the issue. No one knew when the decision would be rendered, but it was generally anticipated in the 1953–54 term of the court, and the Fund for the Advancement of Education wanted to release the findings of the study ahead of the ruling.

On the central staff, Ashmore had five colleagues: Phil Hammer of the National Planning Association's Atlanta-based Committee of the South; Harold Fleming of the SRC; Mozell C. Hill, chairman of the sociology department at Atlanta University; John A. Griffin of Emory; and Ruth A. Morton of the American Friends Service Committee. Their meetings and collateral sessions with the research scholars and with state school officials took place in an atmosphere of rising anxiety about the coming decision. Working feverishly, the staff assembled the essence of the research and fed it to Ashmore, who put the finishing touches on *The Negro and the School*. In the conclusion he wrote:

> In the long sweep of history the public school cases before the Supreme Court may be written down as the point at which the South cleared the last turning in the road to reunion—the point at which finally, and under protest, the region gave up its peculiar institutions and accepted the prevailing standards of the nation at large as the legal basis for its relationship with its minority race.

The University of North Carolina Press agreed to publish the book, and pulled out all the stops to rush it into print the following spring—less than a year after Ford hired Ashmore to pull it all together. The official publication date was pegged to fall somewhere between the availability of review copies in the latter part of April and the last day of the court's term in the middle of May. The chosen date for the book was Sunday, May 16, 1954.

At about ten minutes before one o'clock the next day, Washington time—high noon in much of the South—Chief Justice Earl Warren began reading the Supreme Court's decision in *Brown* v. *Board of Education*. It had been a well-kept secret until that morning; the press wasn't clued in, and even the justices' clerks weren't certain until the word spread just before the court convened. Soon, all of the clerks and staff attorneys were lining the alcove along the side of the ceremonial room, knowing that this was a rare moment.

Thurgood Marshall was there with some of his colleagues, anticipating a ruling on this, the last day of the court's term. J. A. DeLaine and Harry Briggs were somewhere in exile from Clarendon County, L. Francis Griffin was in Prince Edward County, and Barbara Johns was at her uncle Vernon's home in Montgomery, all unaware of what was happening in Washington. When Earl Warren started reading the long-awaited "judgment and opinion of the court," there was a rapt silence in the great hall.

It was the first major opinion rendered by the new Chief Justice, a man with no prior judicial experience. He had something that most of the others didn't have, though—political experience—and that was what rescued him and the court and the nation on this singular occasion. On assuming his duties the previous October, he had found four of the justices—Black, Douglas, Minton, and Burton—ready to overturn *Plessy* and decide the school cases in favor of the plaintiffs. The other four—Clark, Frankfurter, Jackson, and Reed—had a variety of reservations and doubts. Warren was the swing vote, and from the beginning he was firmly on the side of abandoning the separate-but-equal myth. But political instinct told him that a narrow decision on such a controversial issue wouldn't win popular support; what was needed was an overwhelming majority—a unanimous vote—to help the nation pull together.

After the second round of arguments in December, Warren began his low-key effort to win over the undecided members. Tom Clark came along first; having helped Truman desegregate the armed forces, he knew in his heart that segregation was wasteful, divisive, and ultimately indefensible. Then Felix Frankfurter joined the majority, believing as strongly as Warren that unanimity would greatly strengthen the nation's resolve to comply. Robert Jackson had a heart attack that fall, and some said it was the glimpse of his own mortality that brought him around; in any case, after he told Warren of his decision, he came directly from the hospital to be present and counted with the majority on May 17.

The last holdout was Stanley F. Reed, a seventy-year-old Kentuckian, born and raised in rural Mason County, on the south bank of the Ohio River, literally within sight of the Mason-Dixon fault line and the Yankee domain beyond, stretching away to the horizon. At Yale and Columbia and the University of Virginia, he had acquired a taste for both cultures, North and South. His faithful service as a government lawyer was rewarded when Franklin Roosevelt sent him up to the Supreme Court in 1938. Stan Reed proved to be a good and faithful servant of the New Deal philosophy—but that didn't extend to turning a venerable Southern tradition on its ear. Warren never pressured him, but they talked often, one to one.

Finally the Chief Justice gently told his colleague, "You're all by yourself in this now," and time was running out. Reed's heart was in the right place; his doubts were not about the rightness of the choice, but about how the South would receive it. It was not until the weekend before the decision was to be issued that Stanley Reed finally made up his mind.

The opinion itself was not a literary work of art. Warren wanted it to be nontechnical, nonemotional, nonrhetorical. Make it plain, simple, direct, and reasonably short, he decided; reach out to everybody with a statement of judicial moderation. It could have stood a little more punch, a few soaring phrases—and, some said, more law and less sociology. But the bottom line would have been the same: Racial segregation was inconsistent with the U.S. Constitution.

"We conclude," said the Chief Justice, reading from the printed text—and then, looking up at the audience, he added the word "unanimously," sending a ripple of electricity through the room—"that in the field of public education the doctrine of 'separate but equal' has no place. Separate educational facilities are inherently unequal." Waties Waring had used a slightly different phrase to say the same thing.

Thurgood Marshall had been expecting Justice Reed to dissent. "I watched his eyes as Warren read the opinion," Marshall recalled years later. "He was looking me right straight in the face too, because he wanted to see my reaction when I realized he hadn't written that dissent." The two men exchanged unsmiling, barely perceptible nods—silent expressions of mutual respect. Stanley Reed's clerk saw tears on the justice's cheeks as Warren concluded. Before he retired in 1957, the Kentuckian would classify *Brown* as probably "the most important decision in the history of the court."

The courage of the three Southerners—Reed, Tom Clark of Texas, and Hugo Black of Alabama—was fully recognized and appreciated by their six brethren. Black, the only Deep South native, the onetime Klansman, the court's senior member and most consistent liberal voice, would never again be welcomed with open arms to the land of his birth and upbringing.

To open the way for the momentous changes the decision would require, Warren invited the attorneys general of the Southern states to take part in hearings during the 1954–55 term of the court, and thus to have a hand in deciding how the ruling would be implemented.

President Eisenhower would finally say, much later, that he believed "the judgment of the court was right." But long before he got around to that, his refusal to endorse the decision publicly left the judges twisting slowly in the wind of increasingly hostile Southern opinion. Privately, the President told friends that appointing Warren to the court was the worst mistake he had ever made. At a White House dinner in the spring of 1954,

Ike had been overheard pressuring Warren to show some sympathy for the Southern whites who wanted to keep segregation. (Warren, the listener reported, bluntly told the President, "You mind your business and I'll mind mine.")

E. Frederic Morrow, a White House aide to Eisenhower and one of only a handful of black officials in the administration, characterized the President as "a gentle and noble man," but criticized his "failure to show strong moral leadership in the field of civil and human rights," and said he was "neither intellectually nor emotionally disposed to combat segregation." Morrow's assessment is at least tacitly acknowledged by Eisenhower's close associates and his biographers.

Into the void of presidential leadership would step the demagogues of Dixie, and in a short time the battle lines would be drawn again in the dirt by a small cadre of willful men intent on repeating the South's rebellious history. There would be only a handful of them at first: Herman Talmadge, Harry F. Byrd, James O. Eastland, and a few others. Talmadge charged that the court had "reduced our Constitution to a mere scrap of paper" by issuing "a bald political decree without basis in law," and that Georgians "cannot and will not" accept it. Eastland thundered that "the South will not abide by or obey this legislative decision by a political court." Byrd would soon become the father of a "massive resistance" movement that most Southern politicians found practically irresistible.

Governor Byrnes of South Carolina, describing himself as "shocked" by the decision, declined to repeat his earlier threat to close the state's schools—but wouldn't say, either, that South Carolinians would accept the ruling as the law of the land. Most of the Southern governors did say at least that much, though—"we are a law-abiding people, and we will approach this calmly and do our duty," or words to that effect.

Several major religious bodies in the region, including the Southern Baptist Convention, would endorse the ruling. Many of the largest and most influential daily newspapers across the South—from the Dallas *Morning News* to the Miami *Herald,* from the Louisville *Courier-Journal* to the Norfolk *Virginian-Pilot*—declared themselves editorially to be at least resigned to, if not positively accepting of, the verdict of the court. (The most extreme counterpoint came from Mississippi's Frederick Sullens, editor of the Jackson *Daily News;* in a black-bordered front-page editorial called "Blood on the White Marble Steps," he declared threateningly, "This is a fight for white supremacy . . . there will be no room for neutrals or non-combatants . . . if you are a member of the Caucasian race . . . You Are For Us Or Against Us.")

Ralph McGill was traveling in England when he received the news; back home, his *Constitution* and the *Journal* told their readers that Georgia was big enough to face this, never mind what Talmadge said. Hodding Carter wrote in the *Delta Democrat-Times:* "If ever a region asked for such a decree the South did through its shocking, calculated and cynical disobedience to its own state constitutions, which specify that separate school systems must be equal." In the Raleigh *News & Observer*, Jonathan Daniels predicted that the decision "will be met in the South with the good sense and the good will of the people of both races in a manner which will serve the children and honor America."

To W. E. B. Du Bois, the *Brown* ruling was a giant step toward "complete freedom and equality between black and white Americans." To Charles S. Johnson, it was "the most important national mandate on civil rights since the Emancipation Proclamation." Lillian Smith called it "every child's Magna Carta." In New York, Walter White was exuberant at an NAACP news conference, and Thurgood Marshall seemed content to let him have the spotlight. (To one reporter, though, Marshall did offer a prediction that school segregation would be eradicated within five years, and in less than ten years Jim Crow would be dead and buried forever.) Judge J. Waties Waring, now retired, gave the press a brief statement in praise of the court, but made no reference to the Charleston conflict or his part in it. That evening, he and his wife invited a few friends for a quiet celebration in their Manhattan apartment.

For the next several days, the Virginia and South Carolina newspapers would report and comment at length on the Supreme Court ruling. The decision itself was printed in full, and the reactions of scores of people were recorded, from governors and senators to school officials and people on the street. Virginius Dabney forecast in his *Times-Dispatch* editorial that the "truly historic decision" would take years to implement; he called on "men and women of good will in both races" to work it out. In the Richmond *News Leader*, editor James J. Kilpatrick declared, "We accept the Supreme Court's ruling. We do not accept it willingly, or cheerfully or philosophically. We accept it because we have to." In Charleston, *News & Courier* editor Thomas R. Waring concluded that the court "has cut deeply into the sinews of the Republic," and driven "another nail in the coffin of States' rights." He would keep up a fusillade of outrage and invective against the federal judiciary for months and years to come.

In all of the extended comments recorded by the press, not much was heard from the people whose courageous acts had forced the South and the nation to face up to the segregation issue. Neither L. Francis Griffin nor Barbara Johns was quoted prominently, and neither of them would live to see a fully integrated school system in Prince Edward County, Virginia; most of the whites there would retreat to private schools rather than submit to such a change. Likewise in Clarendon County, South

Carolina, school segregation would be perpetuated by the creation of private schools for whites, and black citizens would have little to show for their costly fight against white supremacy.

Most of the public praise and condemnation that Harry Briggs and J. A. DeLaine would get for having the temerity to stand up against racial discrimination had already come and gone when the Supreme Court decision vindicated their belief in the law. Their reward for such transcending faith would never be anything tangible, never much more than the thought, the abstract realization, that in some way they had helped others.

Briggs and DeLaine and most of the other plaintiffs in the school suit didn't remain long in Summerton, in Clarendon, in South Carolina, or even in the South. Some were driven out by hostility and threats, others by the lack of opportunity or by discouragement with the glacial pace of change. The Reverend DeLaine would continue his ministry in the North for a time, and then turn back toward home, living out his last years in North Carolina.

Harry Briggs finally settled in the Bronx and sent for his family; he and his wife raised their children there. Sometimes on the city's hard and forbidding streets, Briggs was like the protagonist in Ralph Ellison's *Invisible Man*—one anonymous immigrant among many, the product of a peasant culture, driven to nostalgic reminiscence and melancholy by the smell of a street vendor's baked Carolina yams.

Harry Briggs would never outlive his longing for the salt marshes and the sandy loam of the Carolina low country. What is more—and worse— neither he nor his brother in exile, Joseph DeLaine, would ever have the satisfaction of knowing the full measure of their gift to America, and to their native South.

Epilogue: There Comes a Time

When I picked up a *Courier-Journal* at the student cafeteria that Tuesday morning, I took a quick glance at the banner headline— SUPREME COURT BANS SCHOOL SEGREGATION—and then flipped to the sports section. Practically the entire front page was filled with stories about the court ruling, and I was curious enough to wonder vaguely what it all meant—but I had more important things on my mind. Just a week or so before, a twenty-five-year-old British physician named Roger Bannister had run a mile in less than four minutes. No one else had ever done that. His picture had been on page one, and the sports pages had told and retold the amazing story. I read it all avidly, thrilled by this singular act of athletic achievement.

This was my first and only year at Western Kentucky State College. I went into Harry Truman's desegregated army that summer, taking with me nothing but pleasant memories of my introduction to campus life—all the pretty girls, the good friends I had made, the great basketball team (and incidentally, one good professor, an English teacher who complimented my writing and encouraged me to think of becoming a journalist).

In that all-white environment, I never gave a moment's thought, one way or the other, to the matter of skin color. Segregation didn't restrict me in any way, so it was easy to accept things the way they were, to take my freedom for granted and not worry about anybody else's. I do remember, though, that when I was thrown together with many different kinds of people in the army, I sometimes felt vaguely defensive and inferior around strange-talking Yankees, who seemed a lot more weird and mystifying— and at times intimidating—than the black guys from Mississippi and Alabama.

Almost forty years later, when I went back to take a closer look at the May 1954 issues of the *Courier-Journal*, some of the stories I found seemed newly significant to me, like items from a time capsule or long-lost pieces of a jigsaw puzzle. They had been there all along, of course; I just hadn't paid any attention to them at the time.

For weeks before the *Brown* story broke, the paper was full of news and comment about Senator McCarthy's crusade against "subversives," and the fall of the French in Indochina. I could see in retrospect how tense and agitated people were about the perceived threat of communism, and how that caused them to tolerate and rationalize the most extreme abuses of civil rights and civil liberties. I could also see how fear and ignorance of "the red menace" played into the hands of the South's racist demagogues.

In the first two weeks of May, the paper virtually ignored the festering controversy over race and the schools; no one in Kentucky seemed all that concerned about it. On Sunday the sixteenth, Tarleton Collier of the *C-J* editorial staff had a long review of the just-released Harry Ashmore book, *The Negro and the Schools*. The next day, there was a page-one story about Carl and Anne Braden, a white couple identified as "active in the Progressive Party" (and, incidentally, both employed by the newspaper company); they had bought a house in a Louisville subdivision and transferred the title to a black couple. The all-white neighborhood was up in arms; six shots had been fired into the home, and a cross was burned outside. I hadn't even seen those stories the first time around.

On Tuesday's editorial page, the lengthy and favorable comment on *Brown* was altogether in keeping with the liberal opinions and beliefs long expressed by the *Courier-Journal's* president and editor, Barry Bingham, by its publisher, Mark Ethridge, and by Collier and the other opinion writers. The decision had been coming for a long time, they said, so no one should be surprised; besides, the outcome could hardly have been otherwise, given the language and spirit of the Constitution. Those in the Deep South who vowed defiance and threatened to abolish public education were entertaining "a mad and impossible idea." When they came to their senses, the editorial predicted, they would see that this was not the end of the world but the fulfillment of the democratic promise.

The names were all familiar to me now—Bingham, Ethridge, Collier, Ashmore. I knew who the Bradens were, too; he would be red-baited and railroaded to prison in the climate of hysteria that was then about to begin, and she would become a prime mover of the surviving remnant of radicals in the Southern Conference Educational Fund. These were just a few of the scores of people I had encountered along the road from Roosevelt to *Brown*.

As I examined this microfilmed artifact, I had a peculiar sensation of something akin to double vision. Through the eyes of a nineteen-year-old college freshman, I got a narrow, nearsighted view of Roger Bannister, the carefree "good old days" of my youth, and not much else—but with the perception of an older traveler in time, I found myself gazing back at a multitude of complex people and a parade of dramatic events spanning an entire generation of twentieth-century American life.

I was coming at last to my intended destination, to the end of my journey of discovery. There would be no definitive moment of finality, no tidy conclusion, nor had I expected one. If only history were that neat and clean. But it's not—it's a perpetual story, an unending saga of accidental and deliberate happenings, rolling like a mighty locomotive through time and space. I had climbed aboard the train in November 1932, when Franklin Roosevelt answered the call to save the nation, and with it the South; I was getting off in May 1954, just as the people of the region, white and black, were absorbing the news that Jim Crow, age fifty-eight, had been dealt a potentially fatal blow by the Supreme Court.

There was just enough time for one more look around—a fleeting glance backward, an anxious peek ahead—before we pulled into the station.

Through the remaining days of 1954, public opinion in the South was mixed but cautiously moderate, even quietly hopeful. In only four states— Mississippi, Georgia, South Carolina, and Virginia—were bluntly hostile and defiant words spoken by senators and governors in response to the *Brown* ruling, and even a few of them (for example, Governor Thomas B. Stanley of Virginia) showed some respect for "the edict of the court."

Two Tennessee writers, Wilma Dykeman and James Stokely, traveled through the region in the wake of the ruling and came home believing— later saying in their book, *Neither Black nor White*—that people of good will were out there, in every state, willing and ready to "do the right thing." Robert Penn Warren, once an ally of the reactionary Fugitive-Agrarians at Vanderbilt University and now a famous novelist and a teacher at Yale, made a Southern tour of his own and wrote a book about the journey that candidly explored the peril and promise of desegregation, and its inescapable necessity. Another native Southerner, the historian C. Vann Woodward, presented his revisionist account of "the strange career of Jim Crow" (which would soon be the title of his book on the subject) in a series of lectures at the University of Virginia in the fall of 1954, leaving some in his audience with the comforting thought that you didn't have to be a segregationist to be a good Southerner.

There were further promising signs. The Catholic bishops of the South issued pastoral letters instructing their churches and schools to eliminate segregation. Jewish organizations and many Protestant groups did like-wise. Token desegregation of public universities continued without inci-dent. Many people were saying positive things: This was democratic, it was Christian, it made economic and practical sense, it was good for our image abroad. In Atlanta, the Southern Regional Council, feeling vindi-cated and invigorated by the court's action, looked ahead to an era of growth and progress. In Nashville, a grant from the Ford Foundation's Fund for the Advancement of Education allowed a board of educators and newspaper editors to organize the Southern Education Reporting Service, an independent agency to monitor and document the school desegregation process.

But these tiny shoots of new growth heralded a false spring. The white South could perhaps have been persuaded to obey the law of the land, but it lacked the voices of responsible leadership to ensure that outcome. If its congressmen and senators were momentarily quiescent, they were not to be compliant, and soon they would spark an angry resistance. Governors, legislators, city and county politicians, and state and local school officials fell dutifully, often enthusiastically, in line with the Washington-based advocates of white power. Businessmen sounded the alarm, and labor officials echoed it. The bar associations of almost every Southern state and city failed to speak out in defense of the rule of law, and some even went so far as to condemn the Supreme Court and defy its ruling. With each passing day, more and more ministers and academicians and editors who dared to affirm the integrity of the federal judiciary were ostracized and silenced.

In the emotional years to come, only a relative handful of Southern newspapers—probably fewer than a dozen—would be able to sustain a clear, consistent editorial position in favor of obeying the law of the land, the implication of which was eventual integration and racial equality. By far the greater number would either join in the strident chorus of resistance or make a pretense of objectivity by defending the status quo against militant forces of the right and left. "In truth, all of them were devoted to sustaining the advantage of the upper-class white," said Johnny Popham of the *New York Times* in reflection. "Not even once a year, in a sort of lenten confessional, did the papers acknowledge how racially biased they were—and I'm talking about the papers of the North just as much as those in the South."

The Southern Education Reporting Service was illustrative of the glacial pace of social and cultural adjustment after *Brown*. In many ways, the SERS was on the leading edge of change in the region, and for almost twenty years it would be an invaluable source of reliable, balanced, ostensibly objective information on desegregation of schools and other institutions. But its board of directors was led in the beginning by Virginius Dabney of Richmond, a genteel segregationist, and Tom Waring of Charleston, a combative white supremacist. The board was biracial, and its leadership in future years was enlightened and progressive, and its professional staff turned out publications that were a model of evenhandedness. But Dabney and Waring saw to it from the start that the staff would be all-white. A research analyst from Fisk University who was slated for a staff position was never assigned an office—and thereafter, no other black professional or clerical employee would work for the SERS for more than a decade.

The vacuum of responsible moral and political leadership at the state and local levels reflected the void in Congress and in the White House, where President Eisenhower steadfastly refused to lend the weight of his office to the action of the Supreme Court. On numerous occasions, moderate and respected Southerners pleaded with the President, as Harold Fleming of the Southern Regional Council put it, "to exert his private and personal influence on the powerful Southern businessmen and politicians who were his close friends and fellow golfers and quail shooters." Far from doing that, the President told Virginius Dabney at a White House dinner in 1958 that he deplored the court decision and had gone "as far as I could" in trying to persuade the justices not to abandon the separate-but-equal doctrine.

Encouraged by official inaction and unofficial resistance at the highest level, a small group of middle- and upper-class whites in the Mississippi Delta organized the Citizens' Council in July 1954 to fight desegregation by whatever means they could muster. Within two years the movement had spread into every Southern state and some beyond, with the Black Belt regions of Mississippi, Alabama, Louisiana, South Carolina, and Virginia being the hotbeds. By 1957 these "country club" or "white collar" Klans (formally known as the Citizens' Councils of America), together with the more traditional KKK units and various other extremist groups, would boast of having more than a half-million dues-paying members. Whether or not the claim was valid, this much was surely true: The reactionary white South had developed a mass movement bigger by far than anything such liberal groups as the Southern Conference for Human Welfare and the Southern Regional Council could ever have imagined for themselves.

The period of adjustment that the Supreme Court had intended to hold out to the anxious South by delaying its implementation order in *Brown* proved to be more of an advantage for the segregationists than for the reformers. The plaintiffs wanted school desegregation to take place all at once in the 1955–56 school year; the defendant states didn't want it to happen at all, and didn't want the court to say specifically how or when they had to act. When the court finally spoke—unanimously once again—on May 31, 1955, it tried to draw a straight and narrow line of action somewhere between now and never. The schools were told to make "a prompt and reasonable start toward full compliance"; the lower courts would monitor "good faith implementation"; each system's performance would be judged on its merits; there would be no fixed deadlines, no timetable—just "all deliberate speed." At last the court had dropped the other shoe. It was a soft slipper, not a hobnail boot.

The next morning, James J. Kilpatrick of the Richmond *News Leader* fired the first volley in the war of massive resistance. He sneered at "that inept fraternity of politicians and professors known as the United States

Supreme Court"—they who "repudiated the Constitution, spit upon the Tenth Amendment, and rewrote the fundamental law of this land to suit their own gauzy concepts of sociology." He cautioned against open defiance of the court, saying that although "the idea [was] not without merit," it was "impossible of execution." No use to "enter upon anarchy" when indirect defiance would do just as well: The South should pursue "a long course of lawful resistance. . . . Let us pledge ourselves to litigate this thing for fifty years." The court had said "as soon as practicable"; that, said Kilpatrick, "means never at all."

That summer, outbursts of random violence against black Southerners spread ominously across the South, as had happened after the world wars. In Mississippi, four people were killed in separate incidents that amounted to nothing less than assassinations, lynchings. One of the victims, fourteen-year-old Emmett Till of Chicago, had been visiting relatives in Tallahatchie County. A young white woman claimed he got fresh with her. Two men, one of them the woman's husband, tortured and killed the boy, and threw his mutilated body into a river. After they had been acquitted by an all-white jury, the men told the whole story to maverick journalist William Bradford Huie, representing *Look* magazine. The case stirred the nation's conscience momentarily, but the attention span was short, and the South soon slipped again into the shadows, out of sight, out of mind.

The Washington journalist I. F. Stone summed up this latest manifestation of the American dilemma:

> There is a sickness in the South. . . . Mississippi went through the motions [of seeking justice], and the motions were enough to muffle the weak conscience of the northern white press. . . . Those whites in the South and in the North who would normally have moved to act have been hounded out of public life and into inactivity. To the outside world it must look as if the conscience of white America has been silenced, and the appearance is not too deceiving. Basically all of us whites, North and South, acquiesce in white supremacy, and benefit from the pool of cheap labor created by it. . . . The American Negro needs a Gandhi to lead him, and we need the American Negro to lead us.

Two months later, in Montgomery, Alabama, a black Gandhi with a voice like Southern thunder answered the call.

It was after the second *Brown* decision and the Till murder trial, but before the start of the Montgomery bus boycott, that the Southern Historical Association invited William Faulkner and Benjamin Mays, among others, to discuss the Supreme Court's school decisions at the group's annual meeting in November 1955. The SHA had overcome its traditional deference to segregation in recent years, and on this occasion—an integrated dinner meeting at the Peabody Hotel in Memphis—the historians interrupted Mays with prolonged applause several times as the Morehouse College president delivered an eloquent and impassioned "historical sermon" on the immorality of segregation.

The historians who were chiefly responsible for this session—Bell I. Wiley of Emory University, Thomas D. Clark of the University of Kentucky, Philip G. Davidson of the University of Louisville, and James W. Silver of the University of Mississippi—would long remember with special pride the appearance of both Mays and Faulkner, the latter by then a world-renowned author by virtue of his Nobel Prize. Later, when the South's cancerous racism had broken to the surface, the quiet Mississippian would speak with confused ambivalence about the South's crucible of race. But on this occasion, his brief remarks (and an appended passage he wrote later) were direct and to the point.

"To live anywhere in the world of A.D. 1955 and be against equality because of race or color," Faulkner declared, "is like living in Alaska and being against snow." The only faith "powerful enough to stalemate the idea of communism" is the belief in "individual human freedom and liberty and equality." The momentous question was "no longer of white against black," Faulkner asserted—it was the age-old question of slavery or freedom. It also had to do with repeating the mistakes of the past: "We accept insult and contumely and the risk of violence because we will not sit quietly by and see our native land, the South, not just Mississippi but all the South, wreck and ruin itself twice in less than a hundred years, over the Negro question." He concluded:

> We speak now against the day when our Southern people who will resist to the last these inevitable changes in social relations, will, when they have been forced to accept what they at one time might have accepted with dignity and goodwill, will say, "Why didn't someone tell us this before? Tell us this in time?"

Faulkner was not the first Southerner to "speak now" against white supremacy, and to prepare his listeners for a coming time when segregation would fail and the old social order would be swept aside for the new. He had found enough universal truths in the provincial lives of his fictional Mississippi characters to know that everything changes—that peace and prosperity, mobility and materialism, technology and population growth, and dozens of other factors beyond the control of any man, democrat or demagogue, will inevitably transform a society, ready or not. The segs weren't going to turn back the clock back to the nineteenth century any more than they were going to take Jackie Robinson and Willie Mays out of the lineup, or bar Ralph Bunche from the Harvard campus, or keep Thurgood Marshall from prosecuting Jim Crow, or take away Edith Mae Irby's University of Arkansas medical degree.

Benjamin Mays, standing on the shoulders of such giants as James Weldon Johnson and W. E. B. Du Bois, had been pointing to Jim Crow's judgment day since he assumed the presidency of Morehouse in 1940. Numerous other Southern progressives, including half a dozen or more who died in the mid-1950s, right around the time of *Brown*—Mary McLeod Bethune, Walter White, Osceola McKaine, Maury Maverick, Howard Odum, Charles S. Johnson—had found their own quite different and varied ways to "speak now" in admonition of and preparation for the inevitable demise of segregation, and they had gone on speaking until their voices faded away and new ones filled the silence. Johnson, in a *New York Times Magazine* article in September 1956, just a month before he died suddenly of a heart attack, took note of the thinning ranks of white liberal advocates of civil rights in the tense post-*Brown* atmosphere. The South, "provincial and isolationist to the core," would never reform voluntarily, he concluded—the courts would have to mandate it.

A month after Mays and Faulkner spoke to the historians, events in Montgomery hastened the day of racial justice that would eventually sweep over the South. There were heralds and antecedents to this drama: Two local organizations of black citizens—the Progressive Democratic Association, headed by E. D. Nixon, and the Women's Political Council, led by Jo Ann Robinson, had long been trying to combat racial discrimination in the city. Nixon, a former president of the Montgomery NAACP chapter, was a Pullman car porter with organizing skills he had learned from his revered labor union boss, A. Philip Randolph. Among Nixon's local friends were Aubrey Williams, the *Southern Farmer* publisher, and Clifford and Virginia Durr, the former New Deal attorney and his activist wife (all three of them having been in the news the previous year during their sensational clash with Senator James Eastland in New Orleans). Through Williams and the Durrs, Nixon had met Jim Dombrowski of the Southern Conference Educational Fund and Myles Horton of the Highlander Folk School. Highlander had started summer workshops on school desegregation in 1954, right after the *Brown* decision. The Montgomery NAACP wanted to send a delegate to Highlander the next year. They chose their youth director, Rosa Parks, a forty-two-year-old seamstress.

The rest of the story is now engraved in civil rights history. Rosa Parks was arrested on December 1, 1955, after she refused to obey a Montgomery bus driver's order to surrender her seat to a white person. (On two previous occasions that year, teenage black girls had been dragged from city buses and jailed for alleged violations of the segregation code.) E. D. Nixon was called, and he took Cliff and Virginia Durr with him when he went to the jail to post bail for Mrs. Parks. A boycott of the bus system was announced, and on Tuesday evening, December 5, a mass meeting was held at one of the city's black churches to organize a nonviolent Christian protest group called the Montgomery Improvement Association—the forerunner of the Southern Christian Leadership Conference. It was at that gathering that twenty-five-year-old Martin Luther King, Jr., the newly installed pastor of the Dexter Avenue Baptist Church, was chosen to lead the group, and it was there that he first galvanized and mobilized a following with eloquent, soaring rhetorical flourishes:

> If we are wrong—the Supreme Court of this nation is wrong. If we are wrong—God Almighty is wrong! If we are wrong—Jesus of Nazareth was merely a utopian dreamer and never came down to earth! If we are wrong—justice is a lie! And we are determined here in Montgomery to work and fight until justice runs down like water, and righteousness like a mighty stream!

On the wings of the biblical prophets, a new voice—young, black, and unmistakably Southern—was speaking against the day when a confused and divided South would face the inevitable demise of segregation uninformed and unprepared. For the next thirteen years, Martin Luther King would be the transcendent figure in a movement to liberate the soul of the South.

Having survived the shock of *Brown I* and *Brown II* and seen little in the way of actual school desegregation as a consequence, some of the South's political leaders believed that if they could put up a united front against the Supreme Court's decisions, they might be able to force a reversal. The idea for this "Solid South counterattack" originated with Senator Strom Thurmond of South Carolina in late 1955, after a second year of school openings had passed with only token desegregation in a scattered few communities, and white resistance arising in most of them.

Thurmond knew that segregation and white supremacy would soon fall if the old guard didn't throw everything it had against the reformers. He went first to the elder barons of the oligarchy—Harry Byrd of Virginia, Walter George and Richard Russell of Georgia—and found them willing and eager to help him draft what amounted to a proclamation of political war on the court. By the first week of February, they were passing around versions of their "Declaration of Constitutional Principles" and laying plans for a caucus of the entire Southern delegation in both houses.

The Byrd machine in Virginia was preparing for massive resistance to desegregation, drawing venom from the rhetoric of the nineteenth-century

South Carolina secessionist John C. Calhoun. Thurmond, a Calhoun devotee, was just as indignant as Harry Byrd about the court decree, and he
also sensed the political potency of the issue among his white constituents.
Thurmond and Byrd were the two principal phrasemakers for the early
drafts of the declaration, which was quickly dubbed "the Southern Manifesto." Richard Russell, showing a modicum of restraint, toned the document down a bit, and then Thurmond and Russell, joined by John Stennis
of Mississippi, J. William Fulbright of Arkansas, and Price Daniel of Texas,
wrote the final version, removing the references to "interposition" and
"nullification" (Calhounese for willful disobedience) and softening the
charge that the court's ruling was the judicial equivalent of an act of
treason.

And still the statement bristled with militant defiance. It declared that
the justices, "with no legal basis for such action," had proceeded "to exercise their naked judicial power and substituted their personal political and
social ideas for the established law of the land." The court was "destroying
the amicable relations" between the races; it had "planted hatred and suspicion where there [had] been heretofore friendship and understanding."
Uninvited "outside agitators" were "threatening immediate and revolutionary changes" that would "destroy the system of public education" and
"the dual system of government which has enabled us to achieve our greatness." They would not meekly accept these threats to their way of life, the
signees declared: "We pledge ourselves to use all lawful means to bring
about a reversal of this decision which is contrary to the Constitution."

This was the separation of the sheep from the goats. What the Walter
Georges of the South had been saying since the 1920s, the Harry Byrds
and Richard Russells since the 1930s, the Strom Thurmonds since the
1940s—and what the John C. Calhouns had said in the 1840s—was now to
be the blood oath of a Solid South in the 1950s: to stand and fight once
again for white supremacy, for "our dual system of government."

Every Southern member of Congress was under intense pressure to
sign the document. When Walter George read the Southern Manifesto in
the Senate chamber on March 12, 1956, it bore the signatures of 19 of the
22 Democratic senators from the eleven once-rebellious states. In the
House, 82 of the 106 Southerners also signed. The 24 representatives who
wouldn't join in this expression of massive resistance included 2 of the 7
Republicans (B. Carroll Reece and Howard H. Baker, Sr., both representing east Tennessee), and these Democrats: Dante Fascell of Florida;
J. Percy Priest and Joe L. Evins of Tennessee; Harold D. Cooley, Charles
B. Deane, and Thurmond Chatham of North Carolina; and 16 Texans led
by the House majority leader, Sam Rayburn.

The Senate majority leader, Lyndon B. Johnson of Texas, had ambitions that transcended the issue of the moment. He saw that it was "politically essential to separate himself from southern segregationists if he were going to run for President," his biographer Robert Dallek wrote. "In his view, the South could never come into the mainstream of American economic and political life until it freed itself from the burden of racial discrimination." Johnson was able to present himself as standing above the battle, not being asked to sign the manifesto because he had a "different responsibility" as Senate leader.

Two other Southern senators refused to sign: Estes Kefauver and Albert Gore of Tennessee. Kefauver was running for President again, as he had in 1952, and knew that he had to take a national stance. Gore, who was serving his first term, didn't claim to be a liberal trailblazer, but he saw the manifesto as "a dangerous and deceptive propaganda move which encouraged Southerners to defy the government." When Thurmond approached him on the Senate floor, Gore pushed the document back at him and turned away.

The bus boycott was then in a critical stage in Montgomery (Martin Luther King's house had been bombed), and in Tuscaloosa, white students and their off-campus supporters had rioted at the University of Alabama to protest the admission of a single black graduate student, twenty-six-year-old Autherine Lucy. She was expelled after she accused university officials of conspiring with the mob. In that fateful spring of 1956, the South and the nation careened past the last exit, on course for a collision that would be heard around the world.

The Southern governors in this crucial time were about evenly split— six who leaned to moderation, five hard-line segs—but even the best of them, LeRoy Collins of Florida, was at first displeased by the *Brown* decision, and only later came to see the necessity and the wisdom of it. "I had wanted the states and the Congress to meet their responsibility and abolish the laws on segregation," he would explain, "but they wouldn't do it. I finally saw that a Supreme Court ruling was the only way it would ever happen. Segregation was wrong—morally, legally, politically. It had to change. That it *should* change became deeply implanted in my soul and conscience when I was governor. I felt an enlargement of responsibility to all the people of Florida."

It was a feeling that no other governor in the region would be openly expressing by 1960. After more than half a century of politics as theater, as spectator sport staged by tin-pot dictators posing as statesmen, the South was still a rebellious colony, still isolated, impoverished, laggard, defensive, and sundered by race and class divisions. The better politicians who came along occasionally didn't last very long. Ellis Arnall was a one-term governor of Georgia; Jim Folsom won twice in Alabama, but wasn't effective; Sid McMath lost two races after serving four years as governor of Arkansas; Earl Long of Louisiana got put away in a mental institution. North Carolinians Charles Deane and Thurmond Chatham lost their seats in the House right after they refused to sign the Southern Manifesto; Frank E. Smith of Mississippi, Brooks Hays of Arkansas, and Carl Elliott of Alabama felt they had to sign in order to keep their seats in the House— and all of them eventually lost to more conservative challengers anyway. LeRoy Collins ran for the Senate eight years after he was governor of Florida, and lost to a Republican.

If there was ever a chance that a liberal or even moderate political spirit would take root in the South after World War II—and that possibility did seem to exist—it diminished rapidly with the crushing defeat of Claude Pepper and Frank Graham in 1950, the triumph of Dwight Eisenhower and Richard Nixon in 1952, the *Brown* decision in 1954, and Eisenhower's landslide reelection victory in 1956 (he won all but six states). With an overwhelming vote of confidence, Ike was encouraged to keep on standing aloof from the worsening racial and social problems of the South and the nation. In 1957 the rudderless ship of state finally drifted over the falls into a whirlpool of strife and violence, and Eisenhower, the reluctant warrior, had to send federal troops into Little Rock, Arkansas, to put down a calculated act of rebellion by the state's governor, Orval Faubus. In a classic exhibition of blind rage and futility, the South would thrash about for the next decade in self-destructive combat with its own national government. The sins of the fathers would be visited upon succeeding generations for the rest of the century.

From the smoldering ashes of the Dixiecrat defeat in 1948, a handful of reactionaries had fanned the sparks into a flaming new rebellion, one more lost cause to die for—the same cause of racial and regional chauvinism that had rallied their ancestors. The thin scattering of Southern liberals and progressives and moderates who opposed them had lost their last and only hope of a peaceful and voluntary social reformation. Realistically, they had never had the numbers, the discipline, the unity, or the fervor to pull it off. Their institutions—the church, the academy, the press, the unions, the corporations, the political parties—had failed to lead the way. The rest of the country had stood back—uninformed, unengaged, unconcerned—and waited for the South to do as it promised, to take care of its own problems, when they had been everybody's problems all along.

Perhaps *Brown* and Montgomery were inevitable; without them, we might never have avoided the full-scale outbreak of another civil war. Thurgood Marshall, Earl Warren, and Martin Luther King died for our sins.

So did Lillian Smith, and James Weldon Johnson, and Buck Kester, and H. L. Mitchell, and Mary McLeod Bethune, and Charlotte Hawkins Brown, and Frank Porter Graham, and Osceola McKaine, and John Henry McCray, and Jim Dombrowski, and Benjamin Mays, and Myles Horton, and Walter White, and Will Alexander, and Lucy Randolph Mason, and Charles S. Johnson, and Aubrey Williams, and Richard Wright, and all the other native sons and daughters who had qualified and testified as sage prophets of the Good South.

Ralph McGill was among them, too—a Tennessee country boy raised up among the common folk, proud of his heritage but mystified and troubled by the deep strain of racism that seemed to run in the blood. When he became the editor of the Atlanta *Constitution* in 1938, he was a mainstream white Southerner—paternalistic, progressive in the New Deal spirit, and conservatively accepting of the laws and mores and traditions of segregation. He attacked the Klan and the lynch mobs with a fury, but resisted federal solutions to violence and injustice, believing with a simple, patient faith that his people were decent and would right the wrongs. He quickly saw through Joe McCarthy, but not through his own hot-tempered tendency to red-bait Southerners who he felt were pushing too hard for reform.

He wasn't ready for *Brown*, but he never doubted for a minute that a nine-to-nothing Supreme Court ruling was the law of the land. The only way to resist that, he said, was "secession by armed force," a wayward strategy that had proved disastrously wrong the first time it was tried, and would be insanely wrong if tried again. So McGill stood for obeying the law, and when the middle ground had eroded away, he landed firmly on the "radical" side of law and order and nonviolence, the side of Martin Luther King and virtually all black Southerners, of most federal judges, of Thurgood Marshall and the NAACP, of Hodding Carter and Harry Ashmore and the tattered sprinkling of white liberals still fearless enough to stand up in their motherland and bear the brunt of white scorn and rage.

Reluctant though he was to play the role, Ralph McGill grew into it with an increasing sense of mission. His reputation spread. His front-page column in the *Constitution* was syndicated in the late 1950s, and soon the readers of more than three hundred papers were discovering him. He was always readable, often eloquent; for millions of people, white and black, in and out of the region, he became a symbol of reason and hope, the conscience of the white South. From the late fifties until his death in 1969, he spoke with unrestrained candor about the "chloroforming myths" of white supremacy: that violence was the doing of "outside agitators," or wasn't even happening at all; that "separate but equal" could or would ever be achieved; that the white South eventually would do right by its black minority freely and voluntarily, without external pressure; that the segregationists were the real persecuted minority, and that theirs was the legal and moral high ground. McGill knew better, and said so.

On February 10, 1959, the Atlanta editor came to Lexington for a major address at the University of Kentucky. As a publicist for my alma mater, I was assigned to meet him at the airport and be close at hand during his stay. It was a task I performed proudly, having found in his column a voice that captured my attention and won my admiration.

He was sixty years old. I was twenty-three. When I looked at him, I thought of my father—they could have worn the same suit and tie. (They would have found a lot to talk about, too: FDR, the Tennessee backcountry, the call of the open road, home cooking, good whiskey, faithful friends.) McGill seemed in person much like he sounded on the printed page—well-mannered and charming, tough and tender, easygoing but serious, a good storyteller and a good listener, sentimental and softhearted but capable of indignant outrage, a gentle man with a sense of humor and a distant air of melancholy. It had taken him a quarter of a century to cast his lot with the Southern advocates of racial and social equality, but for the decade he had left, he would hold fast to that ideal. McGill had his flaws, God knows—but the white South was flat out of saints. Now that I think of it, I wonder if perhaps it was his imperfections that endeared him to so many people. What he demonstrated, more than anything else, was the capacity of white Southerners to change, to repudiate racism and rise up to the standard of justice and equality so courageously sought by their black fellow citizens in the freedom movement sparked by *Brown* and Montgomery. That was Ralph McGill's real contribution, his basic message: If he could change, if he could do the right thing, maybe the rest of us could too.

That night in Lexington, he spoke about the discredited leadership of the South. Those who would close their schools had already closed their minds, he said. But they were wrong, and ultimately they would fail, for this too would pass; a new day was coming, and new leaders, white and black, were rising among the young: "To be a young Southerner in this day and age is the most delightful, mystical, and wonderful agony of all." The South was in desperate need of some truth, some honesty, some justice, he said. It had a long way to go. The journey would be difficult, but rewarding. The hour was late, and we needed to be about our task. This was the place to start—right here, right now.

He had his audience with him, hanging on every word. There was a sense of urgency in the message, and a tense current of wakening energy among those who heard it. I could feel the magnetic power of his voice, rolling like an altar call through the crowded, darkened auditorium.

"There comes a time," McGill said, "when you must stand and fight for what you believe, for what you know is right and true—or else tuck tail and run."

That time had come in Montgomery for Martin Luther King and the black American minority. Now, at last, it was also coming for Ralph McGill, for the white South—and for us all.

Sources, Resources, Credits, and Notes on Structure

In his monumental three-volume narrative history of the Civil War, Shelby Foote acknowledged the striving of both historians and novelists to recapture the drama of a given time by resurrecting the players after all the firsthand testimony has ended. Once the evidence is in, he said, "all else is speculation or sifting, an attempt to reconcile differences and bring order out of multiplicity." In the bibliographical notes of the trilogy, Foote described his own effort as a fusion of these two kinds of writing, fiction and nonfiction. "The point I would make," he declared,

> is that the novelist and the historian are seeking the same thing: the truth—not a different truth: the same truth—only they reach it, or try to reach it, by different routes. Whether the event took place in a world now gone to dust, preserved by documents and evaluated by scholarship, or in the imagination, preserved by memory and distilled by the creative process, they both want to tell us *how it was:* to re-create it, by their separate methods, and make it live again in the world around them. . . . Accepting the historian's standards without his paraphernalia, I have employed the novelist's methods without his license. Instead of inventing characters and incidents, I searched them out—and having found them, I took them as they were.

Foote went on to explain that he had used no material in his narrative "without the authority of documentary evidence which I consider sound," but he also said he had chosen to leave out footnotes in the belief that "they would detract from the book's narrative quality." In every detail, he said, "the book is as accurate as care and hard work could make it." And then, without further ado, he opened the way for his legions of diverse and unselfconsciously eloquent real-life characters to speak for themselves.

His narrative is its own impregnable defense; it is also my inspiration for attempting the work at hand. In a word, "Colonel" Foote gave me my marching orders—and though like every soldier of fortune I know that I am fully responsible for my own independent actions, I am nonetheless indebted to him for showing me an approach to this challenging task that is very much in keeping with my own ideas and instincts about writing.

I also recall with appreciation a useful distinction I once heard Foote make: between writers who want to know everything there is to know about a subject before they begin to write about it, and writers who choose a subject and shortly begin to write about it in order to plumb its mysterious depths, hoping to discover what it is that makes it so intriguing. That insight alone would have been enough to make me celebrate Shelby Foote as a writer. His unorthodox example gave me encouragement and a certain permission, if not authority, to undertake my own journey of discovery.

The further I went on this odyssey, the more I came to admire some of the Southern writers who had taken sizable risks in their attempts to tell us *how it was*. Several of the most celebrated and enduring nonfiction books about the South to come out of the 1930s and 1940s were characterized by an unconcealed personal perspective. Some of them excluded footnotes and endnotes; others had no bibliographical references at all, and a few even lacked an index—and yet they hold secure and permanent rank in the upper strata of Southern literature. Among these more or less unconventional works of remembrance and belief and history are W. J. Cash's *The Mind of the South*, Lillian Smith's *Killers of the Dream*, Richard Wright's *Black Boy*, Erskine Caldwell's *You Have Seen Their Faces*, James Agee's *Let Us Now Praise Famous Men*, Clarence Cason's *90° in the Shade*, Saunders Redding's *No Day of Triumph*, Stetson Kennedy's *Southern Exposure*, Zora Neale Hurston's *Dust Tracks on a Road*, and William Alexander Percy's *Lanterns on the Levee*.

All of these books were published between 1934 and 1949, and all retain to this day the enduring power to engage readers, provoke thought, stir emotions, and linger in the mind. As different as they are, each from the next, these memorable volumes are united by their common grounding in the viewpoints—the beliefs and convictions—of their authors; each book is made persuasive not by its particular point of view or the weight of its documentary evidence but by its revealed knowledge, its insight, its boldness, and the intensity and originality of its language.

With the inspiration of these and other works to sustain me, I have ventured to look with a fresh eye at the time of my own awakening in the South: the years from the mid-thirties, when I was born, to the mid-fifties, when I became an independent adult. In that generational span of almost a quarter of a century, the South was transformed from a feudalistic colonial province to an interdependent region within a modern nation. Living though I was in the midst of that quiet social revolution, I was almost completely oblivious of it. Now my curiosity has drawn me back into those times to search for a deeper understanding of them. This book is a summary of what I found.

Against the current of several contemporary trends—sanitized school textbooks, neo-orthodox and politically correct histories, ethnocentrism, and cultural balkanization—I have written a narrative interpretation of Southern social history in the mid-twentieth century that makes no attempt to hide my personal perspective. Descriptively, this is a subjective reconstruction of a fragment of the recent past in America, with all the limitations implied by that label. I have tried to establish at the beginning my claim to an opinion, and have gone on from there to draw informed but ultimately individual and personal conclusions about incidents and episodes, issues and people, the place and the times. Throughout, I have sought to make my account understandable, persuasive, and effective; that is the point of good writing. More than that, I have taken care to ensure, to the best of my ability, that what I have written is true, accurate, and fair. If I have succeeded in that, perhaps it will also be convincing—not as the one true story, but as one among many.

In the pages that follow, my purpose is to provide a general explanation of where and how and from whom I gathered the material for this composition, and to express my gratitude to those who helped me. Though it is true that writers—unlike, say, filmmakers or television producers—must finally follow a solo path in their creative endeavors, it is also true that a work of nonfiction such as this depends in large measure on the supporting efforts of countless others. For me to have undertaken this project alone would have been utterly impossible. From the first dawning of the idea that was to become the book, I began turning to outside sources—to scholars and other writers whose words I sought in conversations and interviews, to books and papers in libraries and archives, to friends and acquaintances and strangers who had personal knowledge of the subject and showed an interest in my questions.

This book is a synthesis, in the truest and fullest meaning of that term. It is a gathering-up of other people's words, written and oral, and a combining of those diverse statements with my own to produce a revised account—a reinterpretation—of a period in the South's past that is still near enough to us to be considered recent, if not contemporary. The gathering process has been long and eventful. In one sense, it began more than thirty-five years ago, when I returned from military duty overseas and discovered at college in Kentucky that I had a strong and abiding interest in the South and in social history. For almost a decade I whetted this appetite, exploring the field tentatively and indirectly through independent reading and occasional articles I managed to get published in newspapers and magazines. Then, in 1965, I joined the staff of an education and race-relations magazine based in Nashville. During six years in that job, followed by almost twenty-five more as a freelance writer living in Nashville, I have come to understand that just as I chose to stay in the South, the South has stayed in me as an absorbing personal and professional challenge.

But it was many years after I came to Nashville—in mid-1987, to be exact—that the idea for this particular book started to intrude upon my consciousness. That summer, I opened a file on the South of the 1940s and started systematically collecting materials and charting the locations and availability of a variety of resources: books, magazine and newspaper articles, audio and video recordings, archival papers, movies, music. By the spring of 1991, this casual and occasional search had become a more or less continuous pursuit (as well as a book under contract). It eventually took me to every Southern state, to half a dozen others beyond the region, and to the nation's capital. I was quickly relieved of the mistaken notion that this might be a largely unexplored period of Southern history; on the contrary, the time is rich with written and recorded and remembered accounts. Even so—in this as in all times past—there is a wealth of obscure and unfamiliar material waiting to be resurrected, and I find a special pleasure in blending and merging these known and unknown stories.

Libraries were my primary destination, but interviews were vitally important too. Various sources are noted below. I begin with the libraries, that most indispensable of institutions for all writers.

Libraries and Archives

For any writer of nonfiction to practice the craft without benefit of one or more supporting libraries seems utterly impossible to me. With its diverse resources and staff of skilled specialists, a good library is to a working writer what a strong theater company is to an actor, or a modern operating room to a surgeon, or a well-equipped garage to an auto mechanic: a proving ground where the practitioner's skill and instinct and judgment are brought to bear against a challenge, a problem, a puzzle, an unknown force. It is here that the creative strength and focused intelligence of the practitioner are repeatedly put to the test. As a professional writer, I know that each time I begin a new project, I must gain command of the relevant resources in this repository of knowledge or else face failure and defeat. Consequently, I spend a lot of time in libraries, and I owe a substantial debt to these institutions and the people who operate them.

Several dozen libraries (and many individual librarians, listed here in parentheses) have given me vital and essential support in this venture. Foremost among them are these:

Library of Congress, Washington—Social Science Division (Annette Hale and numerous others) and Division of Prints and Photographs (Mary Eisen).

Louis Round Wilson Library of the University of North Carolina at Chapel Hill—Southern Historical Collection (David Moltke-Hansen, Richard A. Shrader, and others), North Carolina Collection, and Photographic Services Section.

Jean and Alexander Heard Library of Vanderbilt University in Nashville—Reference Services (Anne Reuland and numerous others), Special Collections (Marice Wolfe, Sara Harwell), Government Documents (Larry Romans), Circulation (Clint Grantham), School of Law Library, Peabody College Library, and Blair School of Music Library.

The reference departments, special collections, archival collections, or photographic archives of the following:

Atlanta University (Wilson N. Flemister, Sr.)
Berea College, Berea, Kentucky (Shannon Wilson)
Census Bureau Library, Washington, D.C.
Duke University, Durham, North Carolina
Emory University, Atlanta, Georgia (Linda Matthews)
Fisk University, Nashville, Tennessee (Ann Allen Shockley, Beth M. Howse)
Florida State University, Tallahassee
Georgia State University, Atlanta (Robert C. Dinwiddie)
Howard University, Washington, D.C.
Louisiana State University, Baton Rouge
Memphis State University (Michele Fagan)
Mississippi State University, Starkville (Mattie Sink)
Murray State University, Murray, Kentucky
National Archives, Washington, D.C.—Still and Motion Picture Branches
Population Reference Bureau, Washington, D.C.
Tulane University, New Orleans, Louisiana
Tuskegee Institute, Tuskegee, Alabama
University of Alabama, Tuscaloosa
University of Arkansas, Fayetteville (Andrea Cantrell)
University of Chicago
University of Florida, Gainesville
University of Georgia, Athens
University of Kentucky, Lexington (Bill Cooper)
University of Louisville (James Anderson)
University of Mississippi, Oxford
University of South Carolina, Columbia (Thomas L. Johnson)
University of Tennessee, Knoxville
University of Texas, Austin
University of Virginia, Charlottesville
University of Wisconsin/Wisconsin Historical Society, Madison
Western Kentucky University, Bowling Green

The Tennessee State Library and Archives in Nashville (Wayne Moore and others) and the Metropolitan Nashville–Davidson County Public Library (Sally Raye and others) also gave me substantial assistance, as did the North Carolina Division of Archives and History (Steve Massengill), the Virginia State Library and Archives (John T. Kneebone, Edward D. C. Campbell), and similar libraries in Alabama, Arkansas, Georgia, Mississippi, and South Carolina. The Virginia Historical Society's Library (Charles F. Bryan and others) in Richmond was very supportive too, as were the South Carolina Historical Society (Stephen

Hoffius), the Tennessee Historical Society (Susan Gordon), several other state societies, and the Atlanta Historical Society.

The library of the Southern Regional Council in Atlanta was vitally important to me, not least for its extensive file of newspaper clippings from the 1940s (noted below under Periodicals). In a similar vein, I made use of monthly summaries of events and trends in race relations during the 1940s, compiled during that eventful decade by Fisk University's Social Science Institute. Bound volumes of these documents can be found at Fisk and in a few other university libraries around the South.

Certain specialized or private libraries were also particularly beneficial, including these:

The library of the Highlander Research and Education Center, New Market, Tennessee
Mercantile Library, St. Louis, Missouri (Charles Brown)
Harry Ransom Humanities Research Center, University of Texas, Austin
Schomburg Center for Research in Black Culture, New York City
Franklin D. Roosevelt Presidential Library, Hyde Park, New York
Harry S. Truman Presidential Library, Independence, Missouri
Dwight D. Eisenhower Presidential Library, Abilene, Kansas
Lyndon B. Johnson Presidential Library, Austin, Texas
Historical Office of the U.S. Senate (Donald A. Ritchie)

I also received assistance from the city libraries of Atlanta, Baltimore, Birmingham, Chattanooga, Charlotte, Charleston (South Carolina and West Virginia), Columbia, Dallas, Greenville (Mississippi and South Carolina), Jackson, Knoxville, Little Rock, Louisville, Macon, Montgomery, Memphis, San Antonio, Shreveport, Tampa, and Washington, D.C., as well as the public libraries of many smaller cities, including Athens, Columbia, and Crossville, Tennessee; Denton, Texas; Fayetteville, Arkansas; Hendersonville and Gastonia, North Carolina; Hopkinsville, Kentucky; Marion, Virginia; Monroe, Georgia; Minden, Louisiana; St. Augustine, Florida; Sumter, South Carolina; Tupelo, Mississippi; and Tuscaloosa, Alabama.

The libraries, clipping files, photography collections, research services, and reportorial-editorial staffs of a number of newspapers proved to be especially valuable to me. For their substantial efforts to provide assistance to me from these resources, I wish to thank Jim Auchmutey, Diane Hunter, Pam Prouty, and Celestine Sibley of the Atlanta *Journal & Constitution;* Dannye Romine and Lew Powell of the Charlotte *Observer;* Sharon Bidwell, Judith Egerton, and David Hawpe of the Louisville *Courier-Journal;* Kay Beasley, Eddie Jones, and Sally Moran of the Nashville *Banner;* Beverly Burnett, Dwight Lewis, Annette Morrison, and Frank Sutherland of the *Tennessean* in Nashville; Robert Hooker of the St. Petersburg *Times;* Leland Hawes of the Tampa *Tribune;* and Linton Weeks and Deborah Needleman of the Washington *Post.*

People and Institutions

I owe special thanks to a multitude of people who have helped me in large ways and small to bring this book to life. On a personal level, I speak first in praise of Ann Bleidt Egerton, whose encouragement and support and overarching generosity of spirit have always far exceeded whatever mutual obligations and expectations she and I might have attached to a long and happy marriage.

It has been my good fortune from the beginning of this project to have the collaboration and support of Ann Close, my editor at Alfred A. Knopf. In this and a previous book we produced together, her editorial contribution has been enormous. I am pleased and proud to acknowledge her unseen hand—the mark of a great editor—and to express my profound appreciation to her. Her assistant, Ann Kraybill, has also been extraordinarily helpful, and so, too, have production editor Dori Carlson, copy editor David Wade Smith, and art director Carol Carson.

In much the same way that many librarians have gone beyond the call of professional duty to support me in this venture, so have a large number of journalists, writers, historians, and other scholars. I wish in particular to express my grateful thanks to two of them, Bruce Clayton of Allegheny College in Pennsylvania and Steven A. Channing of Durham, North Carolina, who read the entire first draft of the manuscript as I was writing it and offered many critically important and useful suggestions (as well as personal support, friendship, and encouragement). Only those who have experienced the agony and ecstasy of bookmaking can fully appreciate what generous gifts these were. This book is far better than it could ever have been without them.

Several others read one or more chapters behind me, much to my benefit, and I wish to thank them publicly for their critiques. Among them were Frank Adams, David Britt, Leslie Dunbar (who read it all), Tony Dunbar, Paul Gaston, Raymond Gavins, Rose Gladney, Randy Greene, Jeff Norrell, Linda Rocawich, John Salmond, Adele Schweid, Richard Schweid, Sam B. Smith, Steve Suitts, and Roy Reed.

The generosity of the community of professional historians was further exemplified by five of its most respected senior members: Thomas D. Clark, John Hope Franklin, Dewey W. Grantham, George B. Tindall, and C. Vann Woodward. They not only gave me encouragement and wise counsel—and, in some cases, manuscript criticism—but also provided substantive information from their own experiences as active participants in the train of events about which I was writing. It has been my special pleasure to observe these noted scholars in three dimensions: as pick-and-shovel miners of the mother lode of the past, as observers of the continuous and exquisite realism of history, and as players on the stage of that unfolding drama. At every level, they have enlarged my understanding of Southern history and enriched my appreciation for the social and cultural diversity of the region.

I also wish to acknowledge, both here and in the dedication of this work, several men who in the years after World War II were central figures in an informal network of Southern journalists and others with modern and progressive ideas about the future of their native region. The late Ralph McGill was their elder statesman; his band of younger colleagues, later to refer to themselves jocularly as the Southern War Correspondents and Camp

Followers Association, included four charter members still active in the 1990s. Each of them sat for interviews with me and offered many expressions of encouragement and support as I went about the task of researching and writing this book. I express to Harry S. Ashmore, John A. Griffin, and John N. Popham my deepest appreciation and gratitude, and in the same spirit I honor the memory of Harold C. Fleming, who died in September 1992.

Motivated by their interest in the South and in this work, these and countless other professionals responded graciously when I turned to them for help. In like manner, a host of individuals from other walks of life went out of their way to be generous to me, not out of any professional or philosophical motivation, but simply because I asked. Some were old friends of mine, and others I had never met; they all responded unhesitatingly, without any thought or expectation of return. I have tried diligently to keep an accurate and unabridged list of these samaritans, but forgetfulness and human frailty have no doubt caused me to overlook a few. To one and all—friends and strangers, scriveners and scholars, named and nameless—I offer heartfelt thanks, credit, and praise. For whatever weaknesses this book proves to have, I accept full responsibility; for whatever strengths it reveals, I proudly and gratefully share the credit with all those named above and below:

Frank and Margaret Adams, Raymond Andrews, Raymond Arsenault, Beverly A. Asbury, Jim Auchmutey, Numan V. Bartley, Jack Bass, Kay Beasley, Ezme Bhan, Perry H. Biddle, Jr., Terry Birdwhistell, Staige Blackford, Nancy Blackwelder and Steve Oden, Erik Bledsoe, Julia Washington Bond, William Boozer, Clayton and Jowain Braddock, Anne Braden, Ella Brennan, Donna Brim, David and Mary Hart Britt, George Brosi, Bonnie Campbell, Edward D. C. Campbell, Robert F. Campbell, Webb Campbell, Will and Brenda Campbell, Buddy Carter, Dan T. Carter, Frances Neel Cheney, Al and Mary Ann Clayton, Paul and Ruth Clements, Alice Cobb, Roger and Cela Collins, Thomas L. Connelly, John F. Cooke, Bill Cooper, Jerry Cotten, Paula Covington, Edwin M. Crawford, Nathaniel A. Crippens, Joe Cumming, Bill and Paula Cunningham, Constance Curry, Patsy Curtis, Pete Daniel, Neil O. Davis, Lane Denson and Caroline Stark, Marcus DePietro, Harriet Doar, John Dorsey, Anthony P. Dunbar, Leslie Dunbar, Matthew Dunne.

Ambrose Easterly, Brooks Egerton, Graham Egerton and Anne Redfern, Judith Egerton, March Egerton, Charles Elder, Charles Elkins, Bill and Lucy Emerson, Eli N. Evans, Betsy Fels, William Ferris, Ginna Fleming, Genevieve Morrow Folger, John and Midge Folger, Jimmie Franklin, Sam H. Franklin, Catherine Fry, Gretchen Adams Fults, Betty Furstenberger, Frye Gaillard, Gail Galloway, Paul Gaston, Raymond Gavins, James E. Ghee, Jr., Rose Gladney, Randall E. Greene, Wayne Greenhaw, Anne Griffin, Larry Griffin, Alice E. Griffith, Alex Haley, Bob Hall, Jacqueline Dowd Hall, Tom T. Hall, Wade Hall, John Hamilton, Philip and Jane Ross Hammer, Leland Hawes, Joe and Betty Hendricks, Robert Herring, Roy B. Herron, Joe Hewgley and Rebecca Bain, Skip and Barnie Higgs, Fred Hobson, Helen Houston, Richard Howarth, William S. Howland, Jr., Nancy Rowe Hull, Robert Hull, F. Jack Hurley, Ben Hutcherson, Blyden Jackson, Art Jester, Clifford Johnson, Loyal Jones.

Carolyn King, Jack Temple Kirby, Lorene Wharton Kirby, John T. Kneebone, Clifford M. Kuhn, Calvin and Elizabeth Kytle, Jim Leeson, Joseph Logsdon, Sophie Lowe, Strawberry Luck, Ronni Lundy, Sharon Macpherson, Patrick E. McCauley, Marge Manderson, Bob and Elizabeth Mann, Frances Frank Marcus, Judi Marshall, Skip Mason, Anne and Jimmy McDaniel, Isaac McDaniel, Clifton Meador, Susan Mabry Menees, Beth Mercer, Jim Wayne Miller, Suzanne Morse and Ned Moomaw, Bill Moyers, Roy Neel, Margaret

Bleidt Newby, John T. Nixon, Rosalie V. Oakes, Grace Benedict Paine, Gary Parker, Joe Pennel, David Perry, James S. Pope, Jr., Frances Evans Popham, John N. Popham IV, Andrew Ramsey, Alice Randall, Tom Rankin, John Shelton Reed, Roy Reed, Carolyn and Frank Richardson, Anne Campbell Ritchie and Donald A. Ritchie, Linda Rocawich, Howard Romaine.

Del Sawyer, Jan Scanlan, Jim Schnur, Adele Mills Schweid and Bernie Schweid, Richard Schweid, Anne Firor Scott, Pam Seay, Margaret Shannon, Don Shoemaker, Celestine Sibley, Mike Sims, Claude Sitton, Charlie Slack, John Slate, Al Smith, Lee Smith and Hal Crowther, Sam and Sue Smith, W. O. and Kitty Smith, Ellen Spears, Vince Staten, James Still, Katherine Stoney, George C. Stoney, Howard G. Stovall, Jeffrey Stovall and Adria Bernardi, Thomas G. Stovall, Virginia and Tom Stovall, Steve Suitts, Patricia Sullivan, Jack Tarver, Pauline Testerman, Gertie Thomas, Patricia Thompson, Sue Thrasher, Marnette Trotter, Evelyn Wakefield, Ann Waldron, Ron Watson, Pat and Glenda Watters, Willis D. Weatherford, Jr., Linton and Jan Weeks, T. Weesner, Willoyd Wharton, Jim Whitehead, Eliot Wigginton, Teri Wildt, Randall Williams, Martin Williams, Miller Williams, Roger Williams, Phyllis Willis, Carolyn Wilson, Charles Reagan Wilson, Ashley Wiltshire and Susan Ford Wiltshire, Harmon Wray, Lawrence Wright, Michael Zibart.

A half-dozen or more institutions have helped to sustain this work with research grants and other favors large and small, in cash and in kind. For these manifestations of support I express my deep appreciation to Robert K. Hampton, Joel L. Fleishman, and other officers of the Kathleen Price and Joseph M. Bryan Family Foundation of Greensboro, North Carolina; Leslie Phillabaum, Catherine Fry, and others on the staff of the Louisiana State University Press in Baton Rouge; Rick Montague, Jack Murrah, and members of the staff of the Lyndhurst Foundation of Chattanooga, Tennessee; Jacqueline Dowd Hall, Pamela Dean, Jovita Flynn, Tracy E. K'Meyer, and Jackie Gorman of the Southern Oral History Program at the University of North Carolina in Chapel Hill; Steve Suitts and other members of the staff at the Southern Regional Council in Atlanta; Robert C. Vaughan and others on the staff of the Virginia Foundation for the Humanities and Public Policy in Charlottesville; and Charles F. Bryan and other staff members of the Virginia Historical Society in Richmond.

Interviews

During the course of my work in the South since the mid-1960s, I have interviewed a large number of people who were, or had been, involved in the public life of the region. Many of the earlier conversations were with individuals who are now deceased but who belong to the "cast of characters" in this book. Included on that "old list" of interviewees are the following people, almost all of whom I met and talked with between 1965 and 1990 at the locations noted in parentheses:

William C. Baggs (Tampa)
James F. Byrnes (Columbia, South Carolina)
A. B. "Happy" Chandler (Lexington, Kentucky)
James McBride Dabbs (Mayesville, South Carolina)
Robert B. Eleazer (Nashville)
Orval Faubus (Nashville)
Dagnall F. Folger (Asheville, North Carolina)

John Birks "Dizzy" Gillespie (Nashville)
Harry Golden (Tampa and Charlotte)
L. Francis Griffin (Farmville, Virginia)
Brooks Hays (Nashville)
Myles Horton (New Market, Tennessee)
Howard A. Kester (Black Mountain, North Carolina)
Benjamin E. Mays (Tampa)
Ralph McGill (Atlanta and Lexington, Kentucky)
C. A. "Pete" McKnight (Nashville)
H. L. Mitchell (Montgomery and Nashville)
Claude D. Pepper (Miami and Washington, D.C.)
Nelson Poynter (St. Petersburg)
Reed Sarratt (Nashville)
James W. Silver (Tampa)
Robert Penn Warren (Fairfield, Connecticut)

Of the interviews I conducted for this book in the 1990s—some in person, others by telephone—a substantial number were either not tape-recorded at all or were taped subject to certain restrictions. Included on that list were these individuals, at the places noted:

Ellis Arnall (Atlanta)
Alberta Johnson Bontemps (Nashville)
Will D. Campbell (Nashville)
Jimmy Carter (Plains, Georgia)
Frances Neel Cheney (Nashville)
Thomas D. Clark (Lexington, Kentucky)
Paul K. Conkin (Nashville)
Samuel DuBois Cook (New Orleans)
Pearl Sanders Creswell (Nashville)
Philip G. Davidson (Nashville)
John Dorsey (Nashville)
Gwen Duffey (Chapel Hill, North Carolina)
Wilma Dykeman (Newport, Tennessee)
Jean Fairfax (Phoenix)
Johnny Glustrum (Atlanta)
Dewey W. Grantham (Nashville)
Philip G. Hammer (Washington, D.C., and Tampa)
Minerva Johnson Hawkins (Nashville)
Oliver W. Hill (Richmond)
Blyden Jackson (Chapel Hill)
Edith Irby Jones (Houston)
Fletcher Knebel (Honolulu)
Eula McGill (Birmingham)
Sylvan Meyer (Dahlonega, Georgia)
Helen Hill Miller (Washington, D.C.)
W. E. Nash (Athens, Tennessee)
Rosalie Oakes (Arlington, Virginia)
Frances Freeborn Pauley (Atlanta)

Lester Persells (Atlanta)
Celestine Sibley (Atlanta)
Frank E. Smith (Jackson, Mississippi)
Stanton E. Smith (Chattanooga)
W. O. Smith (Nashville)
Katherine Stoney (San Francisco)
Robert A. Thompson (Atlanta)
George B. Tindall (Chapel Hill)
Molly Todd (Nashville)
Bonita Valien (Washington, D.C.)
Pat Watters (Atlanta)

The following interviews, all conducted in 1990 and 1991, were tape-recorded. A grant from the Bryan Family Foundation of Greensboro to the Southern Oral History Program of the University of North Carolina at Chapel Hill provided funds for transcription of the tapes. Both the tapes and the typescripts are in the Southern Historical Collection at UNC's Louis Round Wilson Library. After each person's name (and best-known identification during the time covered by this book), the date and place of the interview are noted:

Harry S. Ashmore (Arkansas editor); June 16, 1990, Atlanta
Daisy Bates (Arkansas editor); September 7, 1990, Little Rock
Gould Beech (Alabama editor); August 9, 1990, Magnolia Springs, Alabama
Betty Werlein Carter (Mississippi editor); September 6, 1990, Greenville, Mississippi
James P. Coleman (Mississippi governor); September 5, 1990, Ackerman, Mississippi
LeRoy Collins (Florida governor); April 13, 1990, Tallahassee, Florida
Virginius Dabney (Virginia editor); March 5, 1990, Richmond
Daniel Duke (Georgia prosecutor); August 22, 1990, Tyree, Georgia
Virginia Foster Durr (Alabama activist); February 6, 1990, Montgomery
William A. Emerson (Georgia journalist); November 29, 1990, Atlanta
Harold C. Fleming (Georgia activist); January 24, 1991, Washington, D.C.
John Hope Franklin (historian); July 27, 1990, Durham, North Carolina
William Gordon (Georgia journalist); January 19, 1991, Silver Spring, Maryland
John A. Griffin (Georgia academician); February 7, 1991, Atlanta
Grace Townes Hamilton (Georgia activist); May 10, 1990, Atlanta
Alexander Heard (North Carolina academician); July 18, 1991, Nashville
John E. Ivey (regional higher education); July 21, 1990, Chapel Hill
Guy B. Johnson (North Carolina sociologist); July 22, 1990, Chapel Hill
Lyman Johnson (Kentucky educator); July 12, 1990, Louisville
Charles M. Jones (North Carolina minister); July 21, 1990, Chapel Hill
Stetson Kennedy (Florida activist); April 11, 1990, Jacksonville
Calvin Kytle (Georgia journalist); January 19, 1991, Cabin John, Maryland
Hylan Lewis (Georgia academician); January 13, 1991, New York
Sidney S. McMath (Arkansas governor); September 8, 1990, Little Rock
John N. Popham III (regional journalist); July 9, 1990, Chattanooga
Edgar Ray (Florida journalist); April 10, 1990, New Smyrna Beach, Florida
Modjeska Simkins (South Carolina activist); May 2, 1990, Columbia, South Carolina
George C. Stoney (regional journalist); June 13, 1990, Nashville
Herman E. Talmadge (Georgia governor); November 8, 1990, Hampton, Georgia

Margaret Walker (Mississippi writer); June 7, 1991, High Hampton, North Carolina
C. Vann Woodward (historian); January 12, 1991, New Haven, Connecticut
Wilson W. Wyatt, Sr. (Kentucky politician); July 12, 1990, Louisville

This book is not an oral history but a synthesis of the written and spoken words of hundreds of people who lived and worked in the South between 1932 and 1955. The principal use I have made of all the interviews, whether tape-recorded or not, has been to corroborate and confirm information I collected from other sources. I have sparingly used direct quotations from the audiotapes; I regard them primarily as contemporary reflections on events that happened a long time ago, not as literal expressions of what these men and women thought and said in those earlier times. No one can fairly be called to recollect, literally and in detail, his or her exact words and actions a half-century after the fact.

Periodicals

H undreds of periodical publications—daily and weekly newspapers, monthly and quarterly magazines and journals, occasional and irregular newsletters, small-circulation broadsheets—published interesting and important social information about the South from the 1930s to the mid-1950s. The particular issues I consulted in the course of my research were of such number that specific citation here would require more space than I can justify. Listed below in alphabetical order are the titles of most of the periodicals from which I drew substantive information.

MAGAZINES

Alabama
American Mercury
American Veterans Committee Bulletin
Annals of the American Academy of Political and Social Science
Appalachian Heritage
Appalachian Journal
The Atlantic Monthly
Caralogue and *South Carolina Historical Magazine,* publications of the South Carolina
    Historical Society
Collier's
Common Ground
Council of the Southern Mountains publications
Crisis (National Association for the Advancement of Colored People)
Double Dealer
Ebony
Georgia Historical Quarterly
Harper's
Journal of American History
Journal of Negro Education
Journal of Negro History
Journal of Southern History
Life

Look
The Nation
Negro Digest
The New Republic
New South/South Today/Southern Voices/Southern Changes (Southern Regional Council)
Newsweek
The New Yorker
North Carolina Historical Review
Opportunity (National Urban League)
Phylon (Atlanta University Review of Race and Culture)
Reviewer
The Saturday Evening Post
Saturday Review
Scribner's (later *Century*)
Sewanee Review
Social Forces
South Atlantic Quarterly
South Today (formerly *North Georgia Review*, formerly *Pseudopodia*)
Southern Frontier (Commission on Interracial Cooperation)
Southern News Almanac
Southern Packet
Southern Patriot (Southern Conference for Human Welfare)
Southern Review
Southern Visions
Southwest Review
Survey Graphic
Tennessee Historical Quarterly
Time
Virginia Quarterly Review

NEWSPAPERS

The most influential black newspapers of this period were one daily, the Atlanta *Daily World,* and several large-circulation Northern weeklies, among them the *Amsterdam News* in New York, the Baltimore *Afro-American,* the Chicago *Defender,* and the Pittsburgh *Courier.* Within the South, the most important weeklies included the Louisville *Defender,* the Houston *Informer,* the Norfolk *Journal & Guide,* and the *Lighthouse & Informer* in Columbia, South Carolina; Birmingham, Little Rock, New Orleans, Jackson, Memphis, and most other large cities in the region also had black-owned weekly papers.

Northern and border-state daily newspapers provided much useful material. By far the most helpful to me were the Baltimore *Sun,* the *New York Times,* the Pittsburgh *Gazette,* the St. Louis *Post-Dispatch,* and the Washington *Post.* It is perhaps more than mere coincidence that these papers, together with black-owned publications such as the Baltimore *Afro-American,* the Chicago *Defender,* and the Pittsburgh *Courier,* showed more than a passing interest in the South and its social problems; not surprisingly, all of these newspapers had a strong representation of Southerners in their ranks, whether as reporters, editors, or publishers, and they never seemed to lose interest in the regional drama and its colorful cast of heroes and villains.

This was the last great moment of the print age, the golden twilight of press monopoly before the advent of television. Southern editors and publishers, no less than their Northern counterparts, enjoyed a degree of public stature (sometimes notoriety) that was destined not to survive for long in the video era. Personal journalism was still in vogue, as witness the front-page columns of Atlanta *Constitution* editor Ralph McGill, the statewide visibility and influence of arch-conservatives like Frederick Sullens of the Jackson *Daily News*, and such idiosyncratic periodicals as P. D. East's *Petal Paper* in south Mississippi and Harry Golden's *Carolina Israelite* in Charlotte. These are the major Southern dailies I turned to for coverage of social issues from the thirties to the mid-fifties:

Alabama:
    Birmingham *Age-Herald*
    Birmingham *News*
    Birmingham *Post*
    Montgomery *Advertiser*
    Montgomery *Journal*
Arkansas:
    Arkansas Gazette, Little Rock
    Arkansas Democrat, Little Rock
Florida:
    Florida Times-Union, Jacksonville
    Miami *Herald*
    Miami *News*
    Orlando *Sentinel*
    St. Petersburg *Times*
    Tampa *Times*
    Tampa *Tribune*
Georgia:
    Atlanta *Constitution*
    Atlanta *Georgian*
    Atlanta *Journal*
    Macon *News*
    Macon *Telegraph*
Kentucky:
    Louisville, Courier-Journal
Louisiana:
    Baton Rouge *Morning Advocate*
    New Orleans *Item*
    New Orleans *States*
    New Orleans *Times-Picayune*
Mississippi:
    Delta Democrat-Times, Greenville
    Jackson *Clarion-Ledger*
    Jackson *Daily News*
North Carolina:
    Charlotte *News*
    Charlotte *Observer*
    Greensboro *News*

Raleigh *News & Observer*
Winston-Salem *News-Journal*
South Carolina:
Charleston *News & Courier*
Columbia *Record*
The State, Columbia
Tennessee:
Chattanooga *News–Free Press*
Chattanooga *Times*
Memphis *Commercial Appeal*
Memphis *Press-Scimitar*
Nashville *Banner*
The Tennessean, Nashville
Texas:
Dallas *Morning News*
Dallas *Times-Herald*
Houston *Chronicle*
Houston *Post*
Virginia:
Norfolk *Virginian-Pilot*
Richmond *News Leader*
Richmond *Times-Dispatch*

CLIPPINGS—THE SOUTHERN REGIONAL
COUNCIL COLLECTION

From the time of its founding in 1944, the Southern Regional Council in Atlanta clipped and collected articles and editorials on a wide variety of topics of interest to the council staff and membership. Scores of daily and weekly newspapers, magazines, journals, and institutional publications were read and clipped on a regular basis, and the accumulated material was separated into broad categories and filed for future reference. As the years passed, the SRC clip files grew to enormous size; eventually it became necessary for the older material to be put away in storage outside the offices of the council.

In the fall of 1989, SRC executive director Steve Suitts and librarian Marge Manderson made arrangements for me to gain access to the 1944–54 clip files. Over a period of weeks and months, I gleaned from that cache of forgotten clippings a rare and absorbing picture of the South in its early postwar years of awakening to social change. To a degree that would have been impossible otherwise, I was able to focus on such things as elections and voting rights, political campaigns, state and local government, court decisions, labor organizing drives, racial violence, church and university developments, and numerous pivotal events and issues; what's more, I could see how the major stories were presented, not in one or three or a dozen newspapers but in forty or fifty, large and small, white and black, liberal and moderate and conservative.

The clippings—including hundreds of letters to the editors from readers—helped me to gauge how aware people were of the issues of the day, and how important they deemed them to be. I was also able to get from the newspaper accounts a clear sense of where the region's most influential leaders stood on those issues. So much detailed information on specific topics from a multiplicity of sources strongly reinforced the mass of material I obtained from other fields of research, and greatly increased my confidence to interpret this period of history, to form opinions and draw conclusions about it. Without the SRC clippings, I would have seen some events and issues through a glass darkly, and missed others altogether.

Photographic Credits

The task of assembling photographs to augment and bolster this narrative history proved to be much harder than I expected. Many subjects that I assumed would be preserved on film apparently are not. (To cite one surprising example, I have found no evidence that any photographs were made of the research team headed by Gunnar Myrdal that produced the monumental study of race relations *An American Dilemma* in 1944.) Some institutions, such as the Congress and the Supreme Court of the United States, have restricted the use of cameras during their formal sessions, and thus the record from these sources is barren. Newspapers might be thought to have the most extensive files of photographs, but these are generally not open to the public—and worse, many papers have thoughtlessly destroyed their old photo files in order to preserve space. The future prospects for an adequate photographic record are even more bleak: New electronic scanner technology is making archival negatives and prints obsolete. The time may be coming when it will be even harder to illustrate history than it is now.

All the more reason, then, to search exhaustively for the surviving record. The pictures reproduced in this book came from a wide variety of sources. I am especially grateful to Steve Oden, Donald A. Ritchie, Deborah Needleman, Bill Cooper, Mattie Sink, Stetson Kennedy, Wayne Moore, Wayne Greenhaw, and numerous others named in preceding pages for their invaluable help in locating, obtaining, and reproducing these materials.

Photographs following page 116

Florida agricultural workers (Photograph by Marion Post Wolcott, Farm Security Administration: Library of Congress)

Convict laborers (Photograph by Jack Delano, Farm Security Administration: Library of Congress)

Textile strike (Photograph by Jack Delano, Farm Security Administration: Library of Congress)

Southern Tenant Farmers Union leaders (STFU papers, Southern Historical Collection, University of North Carolina)

Southern Tenant Farmers Union sign-up (Photograph by Louise Boyle: STFU papers, Southern Historical Collection, University of North Carolina)

Providence Farm (Photograph reproduced from a 1980 monograph on Delta and Providence cooperative farms by Sam H. Franklin. Used with permission.)

W. D. Weatherford (Courtesy of W. D. Weatherford, Jr., through the Weatherford collection, Berea College Library)

Mechanical cotton picker (A. E. Cox collection, Mississippi State University Library)

Carter Glass, Tom Connally (Historical Office, U.S. Senate)

Huey Long (Historical Office, U.S. Senate)

Joseph T. Robinson (Historical Office, U.S. Senate)

Maury Maverick (Maverick papers, Center for American History, University of Texas)

Walter George, Richard Russell, Franklin D. Roosevelt (Historical Office, U.S. Senate)

Langston Hughes, Charles S. Johnson, E. Franklin Frazier (Courtesy of Mrs. Regina Andrews, through Special Collections, Fisk University)

Frank M. Davis (Photograph by Griffin J. Davis: Archives and Special Collections, Robert W. Woodruff Library, Atlanta University Center)

Thurgood Marshall, Donald Murray, Charles H. Houston (NAACP collection, Library of Congress)

Charlotte Hawkins Brown (North Carolina Division of Archives and History)

Claude Pepper (Historical Office, U.S. Senate)

Jessie Daniel Ames (Courtesy of Jacqueline Dowd Hall)

William H. Hastie (Photograph by Underwood & Underwood for the Washington *Post*)

Robert C. Weaver (Photograph by Underwood & Underwood for the Washington *Post*)

Martin Dies, Joe Starnes, J. B. Matthews (Photograph by Underwood & Underwood for the Washington *Star*. The *Star* collection, now the property of the Washington *Post*, is housed at the Martin Luther King Memorial Library in the District of Columbia Public Library System.)

Howard W. Odum (Odum papers, Southern Historical Collection, University of North Carolina)

Zora Neale Hurston (Photograph by Alan Lomax: Lomax collection, Library of Congress)

James Weldon Johnson (Beinecke Rare Book and Manuscript Library, Yale Collection of American Literature, Yale University)

H. L. Mencken (Still Pictures Branch, National Archives)

William Faulkner, Milton Abernethy (Courtesy of Wallace Kuralt, through the North Carolina collection, University of North Carolina)

Howard Kester (Kester papers, Southern Historical Collection, University of North Carolina)

H. L. Mitchell, Howard Kester, Norman Thomas (STFU papers, Southern Historical Collection, University of North Carolina)

Herman Clarence Nixon (Courtesy of Judge John T. Nixon)

Don West (Courtesy of Anthony P. Dunbar)

Eugene Talmadge (Atlanta *Journal and Constitution*)

Photographs following page 244

Harold Ickes, Marian Anderson (Photograph by Underwood & Underwood for the Washington *Post*)

James F. Byrnes swearing-in (Photograph by Harris & Ewing: Washington *Star* collection, District of Columbia Public Library)

Hattie Caraway (Historical Office, U.S. Senate)

Pat Harrison (Historical Office, U.S. Senate)

"Cotton Ed" Smith (South Caroliniana Library, University of South Carolina)

Lister Hill (Historical Office, U.S. Senate)

Harry F. Byrd (Photograph by Harris & Ewing: Washington *Star* collection, District of Columbia Public Library)

Richard Wright (Photograph by Gordon Parks, Office of War Information: Library of Congress)

Alfred A. Knopf and W. J. Cash (Charlotte *News* photograph, courtesy of Charles H. Elkins, Sr., and the Wake Forest University Library)

Virginius Dabney (*The March of Time:* Motion Pictures Branch, National Archives)

Gunnar Myrdal (Still Pictures Branch, National Archives)

Thomas Sancton (Photograph by Phil Johnson, New Orleans *Item:* Courtesy of Thomas Sancton)

Frank Porter Graham, Louise Charlton, Will W. Alexander (Archives and Special Collections, Robert W. Woodruff Library, Atlanta University Center)

A. Philip Randolph (Photograph by Gordon Parks, Office of War Information: Library of Congress)

Eugene Talmadge, Daniel Duke (Atlanta *Journal and Constitution*)

South Carolina Progressive Democratic Party (Chicago *Defender* photograph: South Caroliniana Library, University of South Carolina)

Ira De A. Reid, W. E. B. Du Bois (Archives and Special Collections, Robert W. Woodruff Library, Atlanta University Center)

Lillian Smith, Mary McLeod Bethune, Eleanor Roosevelt (Washington *Star* collection, District of Columbia Public Library)

FDR's funeral train (Atlanta *Journal and Constitution*)

Photographs following page 404

Ralph McGill, Carl Sandburg (Photograph by Kenneth Rogers for the Atlanta *Journal and Constitution Magazine*)

Lucy Randolph Mason, Paul Christopher (Southern Labor History Archives, Georgia State University)

Columbia, Tennessee, disturbance (Nashville *Banner*)

Athens, Tennessee, disturbance—two scenes (Nashville *Banner*)

Herman Talmadge bill-signing (Atlanta *Journal and Constitution*)

Isaac Woodard (Amsterdam *News* photograph: Georgia State University Archives)

Walter White, Albert Harris (South Caroliniana Library, University of South Carolina)

Klansman in robe (Stetson Kennedy papers, Georgia State University Library)

Ellis Arnall, Stetson Kennedy (Photograph by John DeBiase for the New York newspaper *PM:* Courtesy of Stetson Kennedy)

Paul Robeson (South Caroliniana Library, University of South Carolina)

Duke Ellington (Royal collection, Photographic Archives, Ekstrom Library, University of Louisville)

J. Waties Waring and friends (Waring papers, Moorland-Spingarn Research Center, Howard University Library)

Greenville, South Carolina, lynch trial (Photograph by Ed Clark: *Life* magazine)

Clark Foreman, John Henry Faulk, Henry Wallace, James Dombrowski (Faulk papers, Center for American History, University of Texas)

Frank Sinatra, Joe Louis, others (Archives and Special Collections, Robert W. Woodruff Library, Atlanta University Center)

Southern Conference for Human Welfare officers (*Southern Patriot,* February 1946: Tennessee State Library and Archives)

Monticello gathering (*Southern Patriot,* December 1948: Tennessee State Library and Archives)

J. William Fulbright (Historical Office, U.S. Senate)

Estes Kefauver (Historical Office, U.S. Senate)

Lyndon B. Johnson, Tom C. Clark (Lyndon Baines Johnson Library)

Francis Pickens Miller (Washington *Star* collection, District of Columbia Public Library)

E. H. Crump (Nashville *Tennessean*)

Truman Civil Rights Committee (Dorothy R. Tilly papers, Special Collections, Robert W. Woodruff Library, Emory University)

Truman and Barkley campaigning (Jonathan Daniels papers, Southern Historical Collection, University of North Carolina)

Truman speech to NAACP (Photograph by Abbie Rowe, National Park Service: Harry S. Truman Library)

Truman with Claude Pepper, George Smathers (U.S. Navy photograph: Harry S. Truman Library)

Blacks voting in Columbia (South Caroliniana Library, University of South Carolina)

Theodore S. Bilbo (Photograph by Harris & Ewing: Washington *Star* collections, District of Columbia Public Library)

Henry Wallace campaigning in the South (Memphis *Press-Scimitar* photograph: Special Collections, Memphis State University Library)

Dixiecrat convention (Courtesy of Stefan Lorant)

Strom Thurmond, Fielding Wright (Godwin Advertising collection, Mississippi State University)

Frank Porter Graham, Kerr Scott (Raleigh *News & Observer* photograph: North Carolina Division of Archives and History)

Frank Porter Graham campaigning (North Carolina Division of Archives and History)

Photographs following page 564

Harry Ashmore (Photograph by Rodney Dungan, Arkansas *Gazette:* Courtesy of Harry Ashmore)

Hodding Carter (Carter papers, Special Collections, Mississippi State University Library)

Edwin Embree, George Streator (Julius Rosenwald papers, Special Collections, Fisk University Library)

W. E. B. Du Bois (Photograph by Carl Van Vechten: Special Collections, Robert W. Woodruff Library, Atlanta University Center)

Benjamin E. Mays (Skip Mason, Digging It Up, Atlanta)

John H. McCray (South Caroliniana Library, University of South Carolina)

Clarendon County plaintiffs (South Caroliniana Library, University of South Carolina)

James O. Eastland, Strom Thurmond (Historical Office, U.S. Senate)

Kenneth D. McKellar (Nashville *Banner*)

Albert Gore, Sr. (Photograph by Joe Rudis: Nashville *Tennessean*)

Highlander billboard (Photograph by Dale Ernsberger: Nashville *Tennessean*)

James E. Folsom (Wayne Greenhaw and the Alabama Department of Archives and History)

Legal Defense Fund in Richmond (Courtesy of Oliver W. Hill)

Southern Regional Council (Photograph by Paul Christopher: Charles S. Johnson papers, Special Collections, Fisk University Library)

President Eisenhower, Walter White (Photograph by Harris & Ewing: Washington *Star* collection, District of Columbia Public Library)

Supreme Court justices (Special Collections, University of Kentucky Library)

Rosa Parks, Myles Horton (Nashville *Banner*)

Annotated Bibliography
Including Books, Dissertations and Theses,
Government Documents, and Reference Works

Abram, Morris B. *The Day Is Short: An Autobiography*. New York: Harcourt Brace Jovanovich, 1982.

Adams, Frank T. *Unearthing Seeds of Fire: The Idea of Highlander*. Winston-Salem: Blair, 1975. (On Myles Horton and the Highlander Folk School.)

———.*James Dombrowski: An American Heretic, 1897–1983*. Knoxville: University of Tennessee Press, 1992.

Ader, Emile B. *The Dixiecrat Movement: Its Role in Third Party Politics*. Washington, D.C.: Public Affairs Press, 1955. (A short and relatively contemporaneous analysis of why the Dixiecrats failed to capture the South.)

Agar, Herbert, and Allen Tate, eds. *Who Owns America? A New Declaration of Independence*. Boston: Houghton Mifflin, 1936. (Eight of the Vanderbilt Agrarians and thirteen others contributed to this follow-up of sorts to the 1930 Agrarian Manifesto.)

Agee, James, and Walker Evans. *Let Us Now Praise Famous Men*. Boston: Houghton Mifflin, 1941.

Allred, William Clifton, Jr. "The Southern Regional Council, 1943–1961." Master's thesis, Emory University, 1966.

Alsop, Joseph, and Turner Catledge. *The 168 Days*. Garden City, New York: Doubleday, Doran, 1938. (An account of the six-month struggle between FDR and Congress over the President's plan to enlarge the Supreme Court.)

Anderson, Jervis. *A. Philip Randolph: A Biographical Portrait*. New York: Harcourt Brace Jovanovich, 1973.

Anderson, Sherwood. *Puzzled America*. New York: Charles Scribner's Sons, 1935. Reprint, Mamaroneck, N.Y.: Paul P. Appel, 1970. (Sketches of America in the mid-1930s by the noted novelist-journalist-activist.)

Anderson, William. *The Wild Man of Sugar Creek: The Political Career of Eugene Talmadge*. Baton Rouge: Louisiana State University Press, 1975.

Angelou, Maya. *I Know Why the Caged Bird Sings*. New York: Random House, 1969. (The poet's autobiography, beginning with her growing-up years in rural Arkansas in the 1930s.)

Aptheker, Herbert, ed. *Against Racism: Unpublished Essays, Papers, Addresses, 1887–1961*. Amherst: University of Massachusetts Press, 1985.

Arnall, Ellis Gibbs. *The Shore Dimly Seen*. New York: Acclaim, 1946. (The Georgia governor's postwar vision of the South, largely ghost-written by journalist DeWitt Roberts.)

Arnow, Harriette. *The Dollmaker*. New York: Macmillan, 1954. (A novel about a Kentucky mountain family's experiences living and working in Detroit during World War II.)

Ashby, Warren. *Frank Porter Graham: Southern Liberal.* Winston-Salem: Blair, 1980.

Ashmore, Harry S. *An Epitaph for Dixie.* New York: W. W. Norton, 1958. (Early reporting and analysis of the civil rights struggle.)

———. *Hearts and Minds: The Anatomy of Racism from Roosevelt to Reagan.* New York: McGraw-Hill, 1982. Updated and revised, Cabin John, Md.: Seven Locks Press, 1988. (The revised edition has a different subtitle: *A Personal Chronicle of Race in America.*)

———. *Civil Rights and Wrongs: A Memoir of Race and Politics, 1944–1994.* New York: Pantheon, 1994.

Bailey, Thomas Pearce. *Race Orthodoxy in the South: And Other Aspects of the Negro Question.* New York: Neale, 1914.

Baldwin, Sidney. *Poverty and Politics: The Rise and Decline of the Farm Security Administration.* Chapel Hill: University of North Carolina Press, 1968.

Bardolph, Richard. *The Negro Vanguard.* New York: Rinehart, 1959. (Profiles and character sketches of prominent blacks in American history.)

———. *The Civil Rights Record: Black Americans and the Law, 1849–1970.* New York: Thomas Y. Crowell, 1970.

Barnard, William D. *Dixiecrats and Democrats: Alabama Politics, 1942–1950.* Tuscaloosa: University of Alabama Press, 1974.

Barnes, Catherine A. *Journey from Jim Crow: The Desegregation of Southern Transit.* New York: Columbia University Press, 1983.

Bartley, Numan V. *The Rise of Massive Resistance: Race and Politics in the South During the 1950's.* Baton Rouge: Louisiana State University Press, 1969.

———, ed. *The Evolution of Southern Culture.* Athens: University of Georgia Press, 1988.

Bartley, Numan V., and Hugh Davis Graham. *Southern Politics and the Second Reconstruction.* Baltimore: Johns Hopkins University Press, 1975.

Bass, Jack. *Unlikely Heroes: The Dramatic Story of the Southern Judges of the Fifth Circuit Who Translated the Supreme Court's Brown Decision into a Revolution for Equality.* New York: Simon and Schuster, 1981.

———. *Taming the Storm: The Life and Times of Judge Frank M. Johnson, Jr., and the South's Fight over Civil Rights.* New York: Doubleday, 1993.

Bass, Jack, and Walter DeVries. *The Transformation of Southern Politics: Social Change and Political Consequence Since 1945.* New York: Basic Books, 1976.

Bates, Daisy. *The Long Shadow of Little Rock.* New York: McKay, 1962. (Memoir of the 1950s racial crisis.)

Beckham, Sue Bridwell. *Depression Post Office Murals and Southern Culture: A Gentle Reconstruction.* Baton Rouge: Louisiana State University Press, 1989. (Public art in the New Deal era.)

Belfrage, Cedric. *South of God.* New York: Modern Age, 1941. (Biography of Claude Williams, a Southern white radical.)

Bendiner, Robert. *Just Around the Corner: A Highly Selective History of the Thirties.* New York: Harper & Row, 1967.

Bennett, Lerone, Jr. *Before the Mayflower: A History of the Negro in America, 1619–1964.* Chicago: Johnson, 1962. Revised edition, Baltimore: Penguin, 1966.

———. *Confrontation: Black and White.* Chicago: Johnson, 1965.

Bergreen, Lawrence. *James Agee: A Life.* New York: Dutton, 1984.

Berman, William C. *The Politics of Civil Rights in the Truman Administration.* Columbus: Ohio State University Press, 1970.

Bernstein, Carl. *Loyalties: A Son's Memoir*. New York: Simon and Schuster, 1989. (Concerning, in part, the virus of postwar anticommunism.)

Berry, Wendell. *The Hidden Wound*. Boston: Houghton Mifflin, 1970. (An essay on white attitudes about race by a Kentucky writer and farmer.)

Beth, Loren P. *John Marshall Harlan: The Last Whig Justice*. Lexington: University Press of Kentucky, 1992.

Bilbo, Theodore G. *Take Your Choice: Separation or Mongrelization*. Poplarville, Miss.: Dream House, 1947. (Self-published call to arms by the notoriously racist senator from Mississippi.)

Black, Earl. *Southern Governors and Civil Rights: Racial Segregation as a Campaign Issue in the Second Reconstruction*. Cambridge: Harvard University Press, 1976.

Black, Earl, and Merle Black. *Politics and Society in the South*. Cambridge: Harvard University Press, 1987.

———. *The Vital South: How Presidents Are Elected*. Cambridge: Harvard University Press, 1987.

Blair, Lewis H. *A Southern Prophecy: The Prosperity of the South Dependent upon the Elevation of the Negro*. Boston: Little, Brown, 1964. (An 1889 volume, edited with a new introduction by C. Vann Woodward.)

Bledsoe, Thomas. *Or We'll All Hang Separately: The Highlander Idea*. Boston: Beacon, 1969. (The earliest of several books about the Highlander Folk School in Tennessee.)

Bogardus, Ralph F., and Fred Hobson, eds. *Literature at the Barricades: The American Writer in the 1930s*. Tuscaloosa: University of Alabama Press, 1982. (Among the essays: Louis D. Rubin, Jr., on Southern literature and the depression, and Jack B. Moore on Richard Wright as a Southern writer.)

Bolte, Charles G. *The New Veteran*. New York: Reynal & Hitchcock, 1945. (This volume outlines the need for and aims of the American Veterans Committee.)

Bond, Horace Mann. *The Education of the Negro in the American Social Order*. New York: Prentice-Hall, 1934.

Bontemps, Arna. *Black Thunder*. New York: Macmillan, 1936. (novel)

———. *100 Years of Negro Freedom*. New York: Dodd, Mead, 1961.

Bourke-White, Margaret. *Portrait of Myself*. New York: Simon and Schuster, 1963. (This book deals in part with Bourke-White's marriage to Erskine Caldwell.)

Bowles, Billy, and Remer Tyson. *They Love a Man in the Country: Saints and Sinners in the South*. Atlanta: Peachtree, 1989. (Profiles of Southern political characters.)

Boyle, Sarah Patton. *The Desegregated Heart: A Virginian's Stand in Time of Transition*. New York: Morrow, 1962.

Braden, Anne. *The Wall Between*. New York: Monthly Review, 1958. (Anne and Carl Braden, white, and Charlotte and Andrew Wade, black, battle against segregated housing in Louisville, 1954.)

Brady, Tom P. *Black Monday*. Winona, Miss.: Association of Citizens' Councils, 1955. (A Mississippi circuit judge's thundering denunciation of the Supreme Court's school desegregation decision.)

Branch, Taylor. *Parting the Waters: America in the King Years, 1954–1963*. New York: Simon and Schuster, 1988.

Brinkley, David. *Washington Goes to War*. New York: Alfred A. Knopf, 1988. (The nation's capital in the 1940s.)

Brisbane, Robert H. *The Black Vanguard: Origins of the Negro Social Revolution, 1900–1960*. Valley Forge, Pa.: Judson, 1970.

Brooks, Thomas R. *Walls Come Tumbling Down: A History of the Civil Rights Movement, 1940–1970.* Englewood Cliffs, N.J.: Prentice-Hall, 1974.

Brown, Sterling A. *Southern Road.* New York: Harcourt, Brace, 1932. (A volume of poetry.)

Brown, Sterling A., Arthur P. Davis, and Ulysses Lee, eds. *The Negro Caravan: Writings by American Negroes.* New York: Dryden, 1941.

Buck, Pearl. *My Several Worlds.* New York: John Day, 1954. (The autobiography of the West Virginia–born, Virginia-educated author.)

Bunche, Ralph J. *The Political Status of the Negro in the Age of FDR.* Edited with an introduction by Dewey W. Grantham. Chicago: University of Chicago Press, 1973. (Previously unpublished working papers of Bunche, a principal investigator for Gunnar Myrdal on his *American Dilemma* project, 1938–1944.)

Burk, Robert Fredrick. *The Eisenhower Administration and Black Civil Rights.* Knoxville: University of Tennessee Press, 1984.

Burrows, Edward F. "The Commission on Interracial Cooperation, 1914–1944." Ph.D. diss., University of Wisconsin, 1955.

Byrnes, James F. *All in One Lifetime.* New York: Harper & Brothers, 1958. (An autobiography.)

Cable, George W. *The Silent South.* New York: Charles Scribner's Sons, 1885. (Early liberal thought on Southern social issues.)

Caldwell, Erskine. *Deep South: Memory and Observation.* New York: Weybright & Talley, 1968. (An autobiography, part of which was originally published in England under the title *In the Shadow of the Steeple.*)

Caldwell, Erskine, and Margaret Bourke-White. *You Have Seen Their Faces.* New York: Viking/Modern Age, 1937. (The depression-era South in words and photographs.)

Campbell, Edward D. C., Jr. *The Celluloid South: Hollywood and the Southern Myth.* Knoxville: University of Tennessee Press, 1981.

Campbell, Will D. *Brother to a Dragonfly.* New York: Seabury, 1977. (A Mississippi writer recounts the separate paths he and his brother took out of the depression and into recent times.)

———. *Providence.* Atlanta: Longstreet, 1992. (The story of Providence Cooperative Farm in Mississippi.)

Carawan, Guy, and Candie Carawan. *Voices from the Mountains.* New York: Alfred A. Knopf, 1975. (Life and struggle in the Appalachian South, captured in words, photographs, and songs.)

Carmer, Carl. *Stars Fell on Alabama.* New York: Farrar & Rinehart, 1934. Reprint, with a new introduction by J. Wayne Flynt, Tuscaloosa: University of Alabama Press, 1985. (A diplomatically critical portrait of the time and place.)

Caro, Robert A. *The Years of Lyndon Johnson.* 2 vols. New York: Alfred A. Knopf, 1982, 1990.

Carpenter, Ronnie J. "Hodding Carter, Jr., and the Race Issue." Master's thesis, Louisiana State University, 1983.

Carter, Dan T. *Scottsboro: A Tragedy of the American South.* Baton Rouge: Louisiana State University Press, 1969. Enlarged and revised edition, 1979.

Carter, Hodding. *The Winds of Fear.* New York: Farrar & Rinehart, 1944. (fiction)

———. *Southern Legacy.* Baton Rouge: Louisiana State University Press, 1950.

———. *Where Main Street Meets the River.* New York: Rinehart, 1953.

———. *First Person Rural.* Garden City, N.Y.: Doubleday, 1963.

Carter, Paul A. *The Decline and Revival of the Social Gospel: Social and Political Liberalism in American Protestant Churches, 1920–1940.* Ithaca, N.Y.: Cornell University Press, 1954.

Cash, W. J. *The Mind of the South.* New York: Alfred A. Knopf, 1941.

Cashman, Sean Dennis. *African-Americans and the Quest for Civil Rights, 1900–1990.* New York: New York University Press, 1991.

Cason, Clarence. *90° in the Shade.* Chapel Hill: University of North Carolina Press, 1934. Reissued, with a new introduction by J. Wayne Flynt, Tuscaloosa: University of Alabama Press, 1983. (Observations and interpretations by a sensitive native Alabamian.)

Catledge, Turner. *My Life and "The Times."* New York: Harper & Row, 1971. (A memoir by a Southerner and longtime managing editor of the *New York Times.*)

Caudill, Harry M. *Night Comes to the Cumberlands: A Biography of a Depressed Area.* Boston: Atlantic/Little, Brown, 1963.

Caute, David. *The Great Fear: The Anti-Communist Purge Under Truman and Eisenhower.* New York: Simon and Schuster, 1978.

Cayton, Horace, and George S. Mitchell. *Black Workers and New Unions.* Chapel Hill: University of North Carolina Press, 1939.

Chalmers, David M. *Hooded Americanism: The First Century of the Ku Klux Klan, 1865–1965.* Garden City, N.Y.: Doubleday, 1965.

Charters, Samuel, and Ann Charters. *The Poetry of the Blues.* New York: Oak, 1963. (Lyrics and social history, with photographs.)

Childers, James Saxon. *A Novel About a White Man and a Black Man in the Deep South.* New York: Farrar & Rinehart, 1936.

Clark, Septima. *Ready from Within: Septima Clark and the Civil Rights Movement.* Navarro, Calif.: Wild Trees, 1986.

Clark, Septima, with LeGette Blythe. *Echo in My Soul.* New York: E. P. Dutton, 1962. (The autobiography of a South Carolina educator and her part in the fight against segregation.)

Clark, Thomas D. *The Emerging South.* New York: Oxford University Press, 1961.

———. *The South Since Reconstruction.* Indianapolis: Bobbs-Merrill, 1973.

Clark, Thomas D., and Albert D. Kirwan. *The South Since Appomattox: A Century of Regional Change.* New York: Oxford University Press, 1967.

Clayton, Bruce. *W. J. Cash: A Life.* Baton Rouge: Louisiana State University Press, 1991.

Clayton, Bruce, and John A. Salmond, eds. *The South Is Another Land: Essays on the Twentieth-Century South.* Westport, Conn.: Greenwood, 1987. (Included are essays on James F. Byrnes, W. J. Cash, Lucy Randolph Mason, and documentary books of the Great Depression.)

Cliff, Michelle, ed. *The Winner Names the Age: A Collection of Writings by Lillian Smith.* New York: W. W. Norton, 1978.

Coan, Otis W., and Richard G. Lillard. *America in Fiction: An Annotated List of Novels That Interpret Aspects of Life in the United States.* Palo Alto, Calif.: Stanford University Press, 1941. (Short descriptive notes, but a very long and useful list of books, including many pertinent to the South.)

Cobb, James C. *The Selling of the South: The Southern Crusade for Industrial Development, 1936–1980.* Baton Rouge: Louisiana State University Press, 1982.

Cobb, James C., and Michael V. Namorato, eds. *The New Deal and the South.* Jackson: University of Mississippi Press, 1984. (Essays by Numan V. Bartley, Alan Brinkley, Pete Daniel, J. Wayne Flynt, Frank Freidel, Harvard Sitkoff.)

Cohodas, Nadine. *Strom Thurmond and the Politics of Southern Change.* New York: Simon and Schuster, 1993.

Coles, Robert. *Farewell to the South.* Boston: Atlantic/Little Brown, 1972. (Essays written by the noted Harvard psychiatrist during his fifteen years of working and living in the South.)

Collier, James Lincoln. *Duke Ellington.* New York: Oxford University Press, 1981.

Collier, Tarleton. *Fire in the Sky.* Boston: Houghton Mifflin, 1941. (fiction)

Collins, Charles Wallace. *Whither Solid South? A Study in Politics and Race Relations.* New Orleans: Pelican, 1947. (Scholarly underpinning for the white-supremacy argument.)

Conkin, Paul K. *Tomorrow a New World: The New Deal Community Program.* Ithaca, N.Y.: Cornell University Press, 1959. (The only complete tracing of "new communities" developed by the Farm Security Administration and other New Deal agencies in the prewar era, 1933–1942.)

———. *Gone with the Ivy: A Biography of Vanderbilt University.* Knoxville: University of Tennessee Press, 1985.

———. *The Southern Agrarians.* Knoxville: University of Tennessee Press, 1988.

Cook, Fred J. *The Nightmare Decade: The Life and Times of Senator Joe McCarthy.* New York: Random House, 1971.

Cooper, William J., Jr., and Thomas E. Terrill. *The American South: A History.* New York: Alfred A. Knopf, 1990.

Couch, W. T., ed. *Culture in the South.* Chapel Hill: University of North Carolina Press, 1934.

Couch, W. T., et al., eds. *These Are Our Lives.* Chapel Hill: University of North Carolina Press, 1939. (Personal histories of Southern working men and women in North Carolina, Tennessee, and Georgia, recorded and written by members of the Federal Writers' Project staff in the Southeast, under the direction of Couch.)

Couto, Richard. *Ain't Gonna Let Nobody Turn Me Round: The Pursuit of Racial Justice in the Rural South.* Philadelphia: Temple University Press, 1991.

Crossman, Richard, ed. *The God That Failed.* New York: Harper & Row, 1949. (Personal essays on their experiences with communism by six intellectuals, including Richard Wright.)

Cunningham, Bill. *Kentucky's Clark.* Kuttawa, Ky.: McClanahan, 1987. (Oral history interview and autobiographical remembrance by historian Thomas D. Clark.)

Dabbs, James McBride. *The Southern Heritage.* New York: Alfred A. Knopf, 1958.

———. *Civil Rights in Recent Southern Fiction.* Atlanta: Southern Regional Council, 1969.

———. *Haunted by God: The Cultural and Religious Experience of the South.* Richmond: John Knox, 1972.

Dabney, Virginius. *Liberalism in the South.* Chapel Hill: University of North Carolina Press, 1932.

———. *Below the Potomac: A Book About the New South.* New York: Appleton-Century, 1942.

———. *Across the Years: Memories of a Virginian.* Garden City, N.Y.: Doubleday, 1978.

Dalfiume, Richard M. *Desegregation of the U.S. Armed Forces: Fighting on Two Fronts, 1939–1953.* Columbia: University of Missouri Press, 1969.

Dallek, Robert. *Lone Star Rising: Lyndon Johnson and His Times, 1908–1960.* New York: Oxford University Press, 1991.

Daniel, Bradford, ed. *Black, White and Gray: Twenty-one Points of View on the Race Question.* New York: Sheed and Ward, 1964.

Daniel, Pete. *The Shadow of Slavery: Peonage in the South, 1901–1969.* Urbana: University of Illinois Press, 1972.

———. *Breaking the Land: The Transformation of Cotton, Tobacco, and Rice Cultures Since 1880.* Urbana: University of Illinois Press, 1985.

———. *Standing at the Crossroads: Southern Life in the Twentieth Century.* New York: Hill & Wang, 1986.

Daniels, Jonathan. *A Southerner Discovers the South.* New York: Macmillan, 1938.

———. *Tar Heels: A Portrait of North Carolina.* New York: Dodd, Mead, 1941.

———. *The Man of Independence.* Philadelphia: J. B. Lippincott, 1950. (A biography of Harry Truman.)

———. *The Time Between the Wars: Armistice to Pearl Harbor.* Garden City, N.Y.: Doubleday, 1966.

———. *White House Witness, 1942–1945.* Garden City, N.Y.: Doubleday, 1975.

Davis, Allison, and John Dollard. *Children of Bondage: The Personality Development of Negro Youth in the Urban South.* Washington, D.C.: American Council on Education, 1940.

Davis, Allison, Burleigh B. Gardner, and Mary R. Gardner. *Deep South: A Social Anthropological Study of Caste and Class.* Chicago: University of Chicago Press, 1941. (This study focuses on Natchez and Claiborne County, Mississippi.)

Davis, Frank Marshall. *I Am the American Negro.* Chicago: Black Cat Press, 1937. (A volume of poetry.)

———. *Livin' the Blues: Memoirs of a Black Journalist and Poet.* Edited, with an introduction by John Edgar Tidwell. Madison: University of Wisconsin Press, 1993. (A posthumous publication of the writer's autobiography.)

Dawson, Carl. *November 1948.* Charlottesville: University Press of Virginia, 1990.

Day, John F. *Bloody Ground.* New York: Doubleday, Doran, 1941. Reprint, with new commentary by Thomas D. Clark and Harry M. Caudill, Lexington: University Press of Kentucky, 1981. (Stark description of the Kentucky coalfields in the 1930s.)

Degler, Carl N. *Place Over Time: The Continuity of Southern Distinctiveness.* Baton Rouge: Louisiana State University Press, 1977.

———, ed. *The New Deal.* New York: Quadrangle, 1970.

Dies, Martin. *The Trojan Horse in America.* New York: Dodd, Mead, 1940. (An attack on communism, ghost-written by J. B. Matthews, a Kentucky native and former Communist who was chief investigator for the House Un-American Activities Committee.)

Dixon, Thomas. *The Flaming Sword.* Atlanta: Monarch, 1939. (The last of the propagandistic novels of a widely read North Carolina right-winger who also wrote *The Clansman,* on which the movie *Birth of a Nation* was based.)

Dollard, John. *Caste and Class in a Southern Town.* New Haven: Yale University Press, 1937. (A sociological study of a Mississippi Delta community—either Indianola or Greenwood.)

Donald, David Herbert. *Look Homeward: A Life of Thomas Wolfe.* Boston: Little, Brown, 1987.

Donovan, Robert J. *Eisenhower: The Inside Story.* New York: Harper & Brothers, 1956.

———. *Conflict and Crisis: The Presidency of Harry S Truman, 1945–1948.* New York: W. W. Norton, 1977.

Doyle, Don H. *Nashville Since the 1920s.* Knoxville: University of Tennessee Press, 1985.

Drake, St. Clair, and Horace R. Cayton. *Black Metropolis: A Study of Negro Life in a Northern City.* New York: Harcourt Brace, 1945. (Southern expatriate Richard Wright wrote the introduction to this study of Chicago.)

Duberman, Martin Bauml. *Paul Robeson.* New York: Alfred A. Knopf, 1988.

Du Bois, W. E. B. *The Souls of Black Folk: Essays and Sketches.* Chicago: A. C. McClurg, 1903.

————. *Black Folk, Then and Now: An Essay in the History and Sociology of the Negro Race.* New York: Henry Holt, 1939. Reprint, with a new introduction by Herbert Aptheker, Millwood, N.J.: Kraus-Thomson Organization, 1975.

————. *Dusk of Dawn: An Essay Toward an Autobiography of a Race Concept.* New York: Harcourt, Brace, 1940. Reprint, with a new introduction by Herbert Aptheker, Millwood, N.J.: Kraus-Thomson Organization, 1975.

————. *The Autobiography of W. E. B. Du Bois: A Soliloquy on Viewing My Life from the Last Decade of Its First Century.* New York: International, 1968. (Written in his ninetieth year and published five years after his death.)

Dunbar, Anthony P. *Against the Grain: Southern Radicals and Prophets, 1929–1959.* Charlottesville: University of Virginia Press, 1981. (Howard Kester, H. L. Mitchell, Claude Williams, Don West, and James Dombrowski are the principal figures in this work of social history/biography.)

Dunne, Gerald T. *Hugo Black and the Judicial Revolution.* New York: Simon and Schuster, 1977.

Durr, Virginia Foster. *Outside the Magic Circle.* Tuscaloosa: University of Alabama Press, 1985. (Autobiography of an Alabama liberal activist of the mid-twentieth century, edited by Hollinger F. Barnard.)

Dykeman, Wilma. *Prophet of Plenty: The First Ninety Years of W. D. Weatherford.* Knoxville: University of Tennessee Press, 1966.

Dykeman, Wilma, and James Stokely. *Neither Black nor White.* New York: Rinehart, 1957. (Early reporting and analysis of the Civil Rights Movement.)

————. *Seeds of Southern Change: The Life of Will Alexander.* Chicago: University of Chicago Press, 1962.

Eagles, Charles W. *Jonathan Daniels and Race Relations: The Evolution of a Southern Liberal.* Knoxville: University of Tennessee Press, 1982.

East, P. D. *The Magnolia Jungle: The Life, Times and Education of a Southern Editor.* New York: Simon and Schuster, 1960.

Egerton, John. *A Mind to Stay Here: Profiles from the South.* New York: Macmillan, 1970. (Howard Kester, James McBride Dabbs, and others.)

Eighmy, John Lee. *Churches in Cultural Captivity: A History of Social Attitudes of Southern Baptists.* Knoxville: University of Tennessee Press, 1972.

Eller, Ron D. *Miners, Millhands, and Mountaineers: Industrialization of the Appalachian South.* Knoxville: University of Tennessee Press, 1982.

Elliott, Carl, Sr., and Michael D'Orso. *The Cost of Courage: The Journey of an American Congressman.* New York: Doubleday, 1992. (Memoir of an Alabama moderate.)

Ellison, Ralph. *Invisible Man.* New York: Random House, 1952. (novel)

————. *Going to the Territory.* New York: Random House, 1986. (Essays and other nonfiction.)

Embree, Edwin R. *Brown America: The Story of a New Race.* New York: Viking, 1931.

————. *13 Against the Odds.* New York: Viking, 1944. (Short biographies of Mary M. Bethune, Richard Wright, Charles S. Johnson, Walter White, G. W. Carver, Langston Hughes, Marian Anderson, W. E. B. Du Bois, Mordecai Johnson, William Grant Still, A. Philip Randolph, Joe Louis, and Paul Robeson.)

Embree, Edwin R., and Julia Waxman. *Investment in People: The Story of the Julius*

Rosenwald Fund. New York: Harper & Brothers, 1949. (A retrospective assessment of the Rosenwald philanthropy, including a list of its 1,500 fellowship recipients.)

Emmerich, J. Oliver. *Two Faces of Janus: The Saga of Deep South Change.* Jackson: University and College Press of Mississippi, 1973.

Ethridge, Richard C. "Mississippi's Role in the Dixiecrat Movement." Ph.D. diss., Mississippi State University, 1971.

Evans, Eli N. *The Provincials: A Personal History of Jews in the South.* New York: Atheneum, 1973.

———. *The Lonely Days Were Sundays: Reflections of a Jewish Southerner.* Jackson: University Press of Mississippi, 1993.

Fabre, Michael. *The Unfinished Quest of Richard Wright.* New York: William Morrow, 1973.

Fadiman, Regina K. *Faulkner's "Intruder in the Dust": Novel into Film.* Knoxville: University of Tennessee Press, 1978.

Farmer, James. *Lay Bare the Heart: An Autobiography of the Civil Rights Movement.* New York: Arbor House, 1985. (The autobiography of the cofounder and director of the Congress of Racial Equality.)

Faulkner, William. *The Sound and the Fury.* New York: Random House, 1929. (Race, class, culture, family, and history are among the complex elements in this novel of the rural South, the fourth of about twenty fictional works by the Nobel Prize–winning Mississippi author between 1926 and 1959; among the others to probe these themes are *As I Lay Dying* [1930], *Light in August* [1932], *Absalom, Absalom!* [1936], *Go Down, Moses* [1942], and *Intruder in the Dust* [1948].)

Federal Writers' Project. *American Stuff: An Anthology of Prose and Verse by Members of the Federal Writers' Project, With Sixteen Prints by the Federal Arts Project.* New York: Viking, 1937. (Among the entries is Richard Wright's "The Ethics of Living Jim Crow.")

Ferrell, Robert H., ed. *Off the Record: The Private Papers of Harry S Truman.* New York: Harper & Row, 1980.

Ferris, William. *Blues from the Delta.* Garden City, N.Y.: Doubleday, 1978.

Fifteen Southerners. *Why the South Will Survive.* Athens: University of Georgia Press, 1981. (Scholars and writers, including Cleanth Brooks, John Shelton Reed, and Fred Hobson, examine their region a half-century after the Vanderbilt Agrarians.)

Fishel, Leslie H., Jr., and Benjamin Quarles, eds. *The Negro American: A Documentary History.* Glenview, Ill.: Scott, Foresman, 1967.

Fite, Gilbert C. *Cotton Fields No More: Southern Agriculture, 1865–1980.* Lexington: University Press of Kentucky, 1984.

Flamming, Douglas. *Creating the Modern South: Millhands and Managers in Dalton, Georgia, 1884–1984.* Chapel Hill: University of North Carolina Press, 1993.

Flynt, J. Wayne. *Dixie's Forgotten People: The South's Poor Whites.* Bloomington: Indiana University Press, 1979.

———. *Poor but Proud: Alabama's Poor Whites.* Tuscaloosa: University of Alabama Press, 1989.

Fontenay, Charles L. *Estes Kefauver: A Biography.* Knoxville: University of Tennessee Press, 1980.

Ford, Thomas R., ed. *The Southern Appalachian Region: A Survey.* Lexington: University of Kentucky Press, 1962. (A comprehensive social-cultural-historical study of the mountain region.)

Fowler, Hubert R. *The Unsolid South: Voting Behavior of Southern Senators, 1947–1960*. Tuscaloosa: University of Alabama Press, 1968.

Frank, John P. *Mr. Justice Black: The Man and His Opinions*. New York: Alfred A. Knopf, 1948.

Franklin, John Hope. *From Slavery to Freedom: A History of American Negroes*. New York: Alfred A. Knopf, 1947.

———. *The Militant South*. Cambridge: Harvard University Press, 1956.

———. *Race and History: Selected Essays, 1938–1988*. Baton Rouge: Louisiana State University Press, 1989.

Franklin, Sam H., Jr. "Early Years of the Delta Cooperative Farm and the Providence Cooperative Farm." Alcoa, Tenn.: Privately printed, 1980. (A remembrance of two interracial agricultural communities in Mississippi, 1939 to 1959, by one of the principals, a retired theologian.)

Frazier, E. Franklin. *The Negro Family in the United States*. Chicago: University of Chicago Press, 1939. (Numerous revised and expanded editions have been issued as *The Negro in the United States*.)

———. *Black Bourgeoisie: The Rise of a New Middle Class*. Glencoe, Ill.: Free Press, 1957.

Frazier, E. Franklin, and C. Eric Lincoln. *"The Negro Church in America" and "The Black Church Since Frazier."* New York: Schocken, 1974. (Combined reissue of Frazier's 1964 study and Lincoln's "sequel" based on his 1970 James Gray lectures at Duke University.)

Freidel, Frank. *F.D.R. and the South*. Baton Rouge: Louisiana State University Press, 1965.

Friedman, Leon, ed. *Southern Justice*. New York: Pantheon, 1965. (Lawyers' perspectives on judges, the courts, and the administration of justice in the South since World War II.)

Furguson, Ernest B. *Hard Right: The Rise of Jesse Helms*. New York: W. W. Norton, 1986.

Gaillard, Frye. *The Dream Long Deferred*. Chapel Hill: University of North Carolina Press, 1988. (The Charlotte, North Carolina, school desegregation story, with antecedents.)

Gallagher, Buell G. *Color and Conscience: The Irrepressible Conflict*. New York: Harper & Brothers, 1946.

Garfinkel, Herbert. *When Negroes March: The March on Washington Movement in the Organizational Politics for FEPC*. Glencoe, Ill.: Free Press, 1959.

Garrison, Joseph Yates. "Paul Revere Christopher: Southern Labor Leader, 1910–1974." Ph.D. diss., Georgia State University, 1976.

Garrow, David J. *Bearing the Cross: Martin Luther King, Jr., and the Southern Christian Leadership Conference*. New York: William Morrow, 1986.

Garson, Robert A. *The Democratic Party and the Politics of Sectionalism, 1941–1948*. Baton Rouge: Louisiana State University Press, 1974.

Gaston, Paul. *The New South Creed: A Study in Southern Mythmaking*. New York: Alfred A. Knopf, 1970.

Gavins, Raymond. *The Perils and Prospects of Southern Black Leadership: Gordon Blaine Hancock, 1884–1970*. Durham, N.C.: Duke University Press, 1977.

Gayle, Addison. *Richard Wright: Ordeal of a Native Son*. Garden City, N.Y.: Anchor/ Doubleday, 1980.

Gilliam, Dorothy Butler. *Paul Robeson: All-American*. Washington, D.C.: New Republic, 1976.

Gilpin, Patrick J. "Charles S. Johnson: An Intellectual Biography." Ph.D. diss., Vanderbilt University, 1973.

Gladney, Margaret Rose, ed. *How Am I to Be Heard? Letters of Lillian Smith*. Chapel Hill: University of North Carolina Press, 1993.

Glen, John M. *Highlander: No Ordinary School, 1932–1962.* Lexington: University Press of Kentucky, 1988.

Gloster, Hugh. *Negro Voices in American Fiction.* Chapel Hill: University of North Carolina Press, 1948.

Golden, Harry. *Carl Sandburg.* New York: World, 1961. (Golden, an adopted North Carolinian, formed a close friendship with Sandburg after the poet moved to the state in 1945.)

———. *The Right Time: An Autobiography.* New York: G. P. Putnam's Sons, 1969.

Goldfield, David R. *Promised Land: The South Since 1945.* Arlington Heights, Ill.: Harlan Davidson, 1987.

———. *Black, White and Southern: Race Relations and the Southern Culture, 1940 to the Present.* Baton Rouge: Louisiana State University Press, 1990.

Goldman, Eric F. *The Crucial Decade: America, 1945–1955.* New York: Alfred A. Knopf, 1959.

Goodman, Walter. *The Committee: The Extraordinary Career of the House Committee on Un-American Activities.* New York: Farrar, Straus & Giroux, 1968.

Gore, Albert. *Let the Glory Out: My South and Its Politics.* New York: Viking, 1972. (A memoir of the Tennessee senator's thirty-two years in Washington.)

Gossett, Thomas F. *Race: The History of an Idea in America.* Dallas: Southern Methodist University Press, 1963.

Goulden, Joseph C. *The Best Years, 1945–1950.* New York: Atheneum, 1976.

Grafton, Carl, and Anne Permaloff. *Big Mules and Branchheads: James E. Folsom and Political Power in Alabama.* Athens: University of Georgia Press, 1985.

Graham, Gene. *One Man, One Vote: "Baker v. Carr" and the American Levellers.* Boston: Atlantic Monthly Press/Little, Brown, 1972. (The background to reapportionment and voting rights.)

Graham, Hugh Davis. *Crisis in Print: Desegregation and the Press in Tennessee.* Nashville: Vanderbilt University Press, 1967.

———. *The Civil Rights Era: Origins and Development of National Policy, 1960–1972.* New York: Oxford University Press, 1990.

Grant, Nancy L. *TVA and Black Americans: Planning for the Status Quo.* Philadelphia: Temple University Press, 1990. (A critical assessment of the racial and social policies of the New Deal's most radical agency.)

Grantham, Dewey W. *The Democratic South.* Athens: University of Georgia Press, 1963. (A political history of the South in the twentieth century.)

———. *The United States Since 1945: The Ordeal of Power.* New York: McGraw-Hill, 1976. Expanded and updated edition under a new title, *Recent America: The United States Since 1945,* Arlington Heights, Ill.: Harlan Davidson, 1987.

———. *Southern Progressivism: The Reconciliation of Progress and Tradition.* Knoxville: University of Tennessee Press, 1983.

———. *The Life and Death of the Solid South: A Political History.* Lexington: University Press of Kentucky, 1988.

Graves, John Temple. *The Fighting South.* New York: G. P. Putnam's Sons, 1943. (A Birmingham journalist's wartime hearkening to old Southern verities that will make him, a thirties liberal, into a fifties reactionary.)

Green, Fletcher Melvin, ed. *Essays in Southern History.* Chapel Hill: University of North Carolina Press, 1949.

Green, George Norris. *The Establishment in Texas Politics: The Primitive Years, 1938–1957.* Westport, Conn.: Greenwood, 1979.

Green, Paul. *Out of the South: The Life of a People in Dramatic Form.* New York: Harper & Brothers, 1939. (Fifteen plays, including the Pulitzer Prize–winning *In Abraham's Bosom.*)

————. *The Hawthorn Tree: Some Papers and Letters on Life and the Theatre.* Chapel Hill: University of North Carolina Press, 1943.

Gregory, Ross. *America 1941: A Nation at the Crossroads.* New York: Free Press, 1989.

Grubbs, Donald. *Cry from the Cotton: The Southern Tenant Farmers' Union and the New Deal.* Chapel Hill: University of North Carolina Press, 1971.

Gunther, John. *Inside U.S.A.* New York: Harper & Brothers, 1947. (A sweeping postwar journalistic portrait of America's diversity, with plenty of Southern material included.)

Haas, Edward F. *DeLesseps S. Morrison and the Image of Reform: New Orleans Politics, 1946–1961.* Baton Rouge: Louisiana State University Press, 1974.

Halberstam, David. *The Fifties.* New York: Villard, 1993. (Social history viewed from a distance of four decades.)

Hall, Jacqueline Dowd. *Revolt Against Chivalry: Jessie Daniel Ames and the Women's Campaign Against Lynching.* New York: Columbia University Press, 1979.

Hall, Jacqueline Dowd, et al. *Like a Family: The Making of a Southern Cotton Mill World.* Chapel Hill: University of North Carolina Press, 1987.

Hall, Wade. *The Rest of the Dream: The Black Odyssey of Lyman Johnson.* Lexington: University Press of Kentucky, 1988. (The life and times of a Kentucky desegregation pioneer.)

Hamby, Alonzo L. *Beyond the New Deal: Harry S Truman and American Liberalism.* New York: Columbia University Press, 1973.

————. *Liberalism and Its Challengers: FDR to Reagan.* New York: Oxford University Press, 1985.

Hamilton, Virginia Van der Veer. *Lister Hill: Statesman from the South.* Chapel Hill: University of North Carolina Press, 1987.

Havard, William C., ed. *The Changing Politics of the South.* Baton Rouge: Louisiana State University Press, 1972. (A state-by-state assessment of the changing political scene, more than twenty years after V. O. Key's classic.)

Havard, William C., and Walter Sullivan, eds. *A Band of Prophets: The Vanderbilt Agrarians After Fifty Years.* Baton Rouge: Louisiana State University Press, 1982.

Haygood, Atticus G. *Our Brother in Black: His Freedom and His Future.* St. Louis: Advocate, 1881.

Hays, Brooks. *A Southern Moderate Speaks.* Chapel Hill: University of North Carolina Press, 1959.

Heard, Alexander. *A Two-Party South?* Chapel Hill: University of North Carolina Press, 1952. (An early political analysis of the rise of Republican power in the postwar South.)

Helm, MacKinley. *Angel Mo' and Her Son, Roland Hayes.* Boston: Atlantic Monthly Press/ Little, Brown, 1942. (An as-told-to autobiography of the noted concert singer, who was born, raised, and educated in the South.)

Hemenway, Robert E. *Zora Neale Hurston: A Literary Biography.* Champaign: University of Illinois Press, 1977.

Henderson, Harold Paulk. *The Politics of Change in Georgia: A Political Biography of Ellis Arnall.* Athens: University of Georgia Press, 1991.

Hendrickson, Paul. *Looking for the Light: The Hidden Life and Art of Marion Post Wolcott.* New York: Alfred A. Knopf, 1992.

Hentoff, Nat. *The Jazz Life.* New York: Dial, 1961. (This book covers, among other things, the Southern origins of the music.)

Hill, Herbert, ed. *Soon, One Morning: New Writing by American Negroes, 1940–1962.* New York: Alfred A. Knopf, 1966.

Hill, Samuel S., ed. *Encyclopedia of Religion in the South.* Macon, Ga.: Mercer University Press, 1984.

Hill, Samuel S., Edgar T. Thompson, et al. *Religion and the Solid South.* Nashville: Abingdon, 1972.

Hobson, Fred. *Serpent in Eden: H. L. Mencken and the South.* Chapel Hill: University of North Carolina Press, 1974.

———. *Tell About the South: The Southern Rage to Explain.* Baton Rouge: Louisiana State University Press, 1983. (The author probes the efforts of Southern writers down through the years to understand and interpret the mystique of their region.)

———, ed. *South Watching: Selected Essays by Gerald W. Johnson.* Chapel Hill: University of North Carolina Press, 1983.

Holt, Rackham. *Mary McLeod Bethune: A Biography.* Garden City, N.Y.: Doubleday, 1964.

Horton, Myles, with Judith Kohl and Herbert Kohl. *The Long Haul: An Autobiography.* New York: Doubleday, 1990.

Houser, Henry Paul. "The Southern Regional Council." Master's thesis, University of North Carolina, 1950.

Howe, Irving, and Lewis Coser. *The American Communist Party: A Critical History, 1919–1957.* Boston: Beacon, 1957.

Huey, Gary. *Rebel with a Cause: P. D. East, Southern Liberalism, and the Civil Rights Movement, 1953–1971.* Wilmington, Del.: Scholarly Resources, 1985. (The biography of an iconoclastic Mississippi journalist.)

Hughes, Langston. *The Big Sea: An Autobiography.* New York: Alfred A. Knopf, 1940. (An account of Hughes's early life.)

———. *I Wonder as I Wander: An Autobiographical Journey.* New York: Rinehart, 1956. (This volume covers the 1930s.)

Huie, William Bradford. *Mud on the Stars.* New York: L. B. Fischer, 1942. (Fiction set at the University of Alabama.)

———. *Ruby McCollum: Woman in the Suwannee Jail.* New York: E. P. Dutton, 1956. (Early "new journalism" about a black woman in Florida jailed for the murder of a white doctor.)

Humphrey, Hubert, ed. *Integration vs. Segregation.* New York: Thomas Y. Crowell, 1964. (Essays on race, edited by the liberal Minnesota senator.)

Humphrey, Seth K. *The Racial Prospect.* New York: Charles Scribner's Sons, 1920.

Hurley, F. Jack. *Portrait of a Decade: Roy Stryker and the Development of Documentary Photography in the Thirties.* Baton Rouge: Louisiana State University Press, 1972.

———. *Marion Post Wolcott: A Photographic Journey.* Albuquerque: University of New Mexico Press, 1989.

Hurston, Zora Neale. *Mules and Men.* Philadelphia: J. B. Lippincott, 1935. (Black folklore.)

———. *Dust Tracks on a Road.* Philadelphia: J. B. Lippincott, 1942. (An autobiography; the 1984 reprint contains chapters omitted from the original, and an introductory essay by Robert E. Hemenway.)

Jackson, Blyden. *The Waiting Years: Essays on American Negro Literature.* Baton Rouge: Louisiana State University Press, 1976.

Jackson, Walter A. *Gunnar Myrdal and America's Conscience: Social Engineering and Racial Liberalism, 1938–1987.* Chapel Hill: University of North Carolina Press, 1990.

Jacoway, Elizabeth, and David R. Colburn, eds. *Southern Businessmen and Desegregation.* Baton Rouge: Louisiana State University Press, 1982.

Jewel, Derek. *Duke.* New York: W. W. Norton, 1977. (A biography of Duke Ellington.)

Johnson, Charles S. *A Preface to Racial Understanding.* New York: Friendship, 1936.

————. *Growing Up in the Black Belt: Negro Youth in the Rural South.* New York: Schocken, 1941.

Johnson, Charles S., Edwin R. Embree, and W. W. Alexander. *The Collapse of Cotton Tenancy.* Chapel Hill: University of North Carolina Press, 1935.

Johnson, Charles S., *et al. To Stem This Tide: A Survey of Racial Tension Areas in the United States.* Boston: Pilgrim, 1943.

————. *Monthly Summary of Events and Trends in Race Relations.* Nashville: Social Science Institute, Fisk University. (Five bound volumes of monthly reports covering the years 1943–1948—a digest of articles, analysis, and opinion drawn from about five hundred publications.)

————. *Into the Main Stream: A Survey of Best Practices in Race Relations in the South.* Chapel Hill: University of North Carolina Press, 1947.

Johnson, Gerald W. *The Wasted Land.* Chapel Hill: University of North Carolina Press, 1938. (The South and the Great Depression.)

Johnson, James Weldon. *The Autobiography of an Ex-Coloured Man.* New York: Alfred A. Knopf, 1912. Reissued in 1927, with a new introduction by Carl Van Vechten. (Fiction loosely based on the author's experiences.)

————. *Along This Way.* New York: Viking, 1933. (An autobiography.)

————. *Negro Americans, What Now?* New York: Viking, 1934. (An unsentimental look back at the struggle for equality—and a realistic look at the future options facing black citizens.)

Johnson, Thomas L. "James McBride Dabbs: A Life Story." Ph.D. diss., University of South Carolina, 1980.

Johnston, Erle. *Mississippi's Defiant Years, 1953–1973: An Interpretive Documentary with Personal Experiences.* Forest, Miss.: Lake Harbor, 1990. (A candid and revealing "inside history" of massive resistance to desegregation in Mississippi, written by a former newspaper editor and political publicist who was an active participant in the resistance.)

Jones, Anne Goodwyn. *Tomorrow Is Another Day: The Woman Writer in the South, 1859–1936.* Baton Rouge: Louisiana State University Press, 1981.

Jordan, Clarence. *The Cotton Patch Version of Paul's Epistles.* New York: Association Press, 1968. (Jordan, a white Baptist Southerner who founded Koinonia Farm, an interracial cooperative community near Americus, Georgia, in 1942, published this colloquial paraphrase of a portion of the New Testament a year before he died at the age of fifty-seven; more of his rich, earthy translations of scripture into the Southern idiom were published posthumously, including *The Cotton Patch Version of Luke and Acts* [1969] and *The Cotton Patch Version of Matthew and John* [1970].)

Kearns, Doris. *Lyndon Johnson and the American Dream.* New York: Harper & Row, 1976.

Kelley, Robin D. G. *Hammer and Hoe: Alabama Communists During the Great Depression.* Chapel Hill: University of North Carolina Press, 1990.

Kendrick, Benjamin Burks, and Alex Mathews Arnett. *The South Looks at Its Past.* Chapel Hill: University of North Carolina Press, 1935.

Kennedy, Stetson. *Southern Exposure*. Garden City, N.Y.: Doubleday, 1946. (Postwar social criticism by a native Floridian.)

———. *I Rode with the Klan*. London: Arco, 1954. Reprint, as *The Klan Unmasked*, together with *Jim Crow Guide* (another Kennedy book published overseas in the 1950s), Boca Raton: Florida Atlantic University Press, 1990.

Kester, Howard. *Revolt Among the Sharecroppers*. New York: Covici-Friede, 1936. Reprint, New York: Arno Press and the *New York Times*, 1969.

Key, V. O., Jr., and Alexander Heard. *Southern Politics in State and Nation*. New York: Alfred A. Knopf, 1949.

Killens, John Oliver. *Black Man's Burden*. New York: Trident, 1965.

Killian, Lewis M. *White Southerners*. New York: Random House, 1970. Revised edition, Amherst: University of Massachusetts Press, 1985.

Kilpatrick, James Jackson. *The Southern Case for School Segregation*. New York: Crowell-Collier, 1962.

King, Richard H. *A Southern Renaissance: The Cultural Awakening of the American South, 1930–1955*. New York: Oxford University Press, 1980.

Kingsbury, Paul, and Alan Axelrod, eds. *Country: The Music and the Musicians*. New York: Abbeville/Country Music Foundation, 1988. (An illustrated history of country-and-Western music from its origins in the rural South of the 1920s.)

Kirby, Jack Temple. *Media-Made Dixie*. Baton Rouge: Louisiana State University, 1978. (The South as it appears in popular culture, especially the movies.)

———. *Rural Worlds Lost: The American South, 1920–1960*. Baton Rouge: Louisiana State University Press, 1987.

Kirby, John B. *Black Americans in the Roosevelt Era: Liberalism and Race*. Knoxville: University of Tennessee Press, 1980.

Klibaner, Irwin. *Conscience of a Troubled South: The Southern Conference Educational Fund, 1946–1966*. Brooklyn, N.Y.: Carlson, 1989.

Kluger, Richard. *Simple Justice: The History of "Brown v. Board of Education" and Black America's Struggle for Equality*. New York: Alfred A. Knopf, 1976. (Includes the text of the *Brown* decision and an index of principal related cases.)

Kneebone, John T. *Southern Liberal Journalists and the Issue of Race, 1920–1944*. Chapel Hill: University of North Carolina Press, 1985.

Krueger, Thomas A. *And Promises to Keep: The Southern Conference for Human Welfare, 1938–1948*. Nashville: Vanderbilt University Press, 1967.

Kuhn, Clifford M., Harlon E. Joye, and E. Bernard West. *Living Atlanta: An Oral History of the City, 1914–1948*. Athens: University of Georgia Press, 1990.

Lachicotte, Alberta. *Rebel Senator: Strom Thurmond of South Carolina*. New York: Devin-Adair, 1966.

Lacy, Leslie Alexander. *Cheer the Lonesome Traveler: The Life of W. E. B. Du Bois*. New York: Dial, 1970.

Lamon, Lester. *Blacks in Tennessee, 1791–1970*. Knoxville: University of Tennessee Press, 1981.

Landry, Stuart Omer. *The Cult of Equality: A Study of the Race Problem*. New Orleans: Pelican, 1945. (A white writer's brief for inequality.)

Lash, Joseph. *Dealers and Dreamers: A New Look at the New Deal*. Garden City, N.Y.: Doubleday, 1988.

Lawson, R. Alan. *The Failure of Independent Liberalism, 1930–1941*. New York: G. P. Putnam's Sons, 1971.

Lawson, Steven F. *Black Ballots: Voting Rights in the South, 1944–1969.* New York: Columbia University Press, 1976.

———. *Running for Freedom: Civil Rights and Black Politics in America Since 1941.* Philadelphia: Temple University Press, 1991.

Lemann, Nicholas. *The Promised Land: The Great Black Migration and How It Changed America.* New York: Alfred A. Knopf, 1991.

Lester, Jim. *A Man for Arkansas: Sid McMath and the Southern Reform Tradition.* Little Rock: Rose, 1976.

Lester, Julius, ed. *The Seventh Son: The Thought and Writings of W. E. B. Du Bois.* 2 vols. New York: Random House, 1971.

Leuchtenburg, William E. *Franklin D. Roosevelt and the New Deal, 1932–1940.* New York: Harper & Brothers, 1963.

———. *A Troubled Feast: American Society Since 1945.* Boston: Little, Brown, 1973.

Levy, Eugene, *James Weldon Johnson: Black Leader, Black Voice.* Chicago: University of Chicago Press, 1973.

Lewis, David Levering. *When Harlem Was in Vogue.* New York: Alfred A. Knopf, 1981. (A social history of the Harlem Renaissance.)

———. *W. E. B. Du Bois: Biography of a Race.* New York: Henry Holt, 1993.

Lewis, Hylan. *Blackways of Kent.* Chapel Hill: University of North Carolina Press, 1955. (A study of the black subculture in a small industrial town in the Carolina piedmont region.)

Liebling, A. J. *The Earl of Louisiana: The Liberal Long.* New York: Simon and Schuster, 1961.

Logan, Rayford W. *The Attitude of the Southern White Press Toward Negro Suffrage, 1932–1940.* Washington, D.C.: Foundation Publishers, 1940.

———. *The Betrayal of the Negro: From Rutherford B. Hayes to Woodrow Wilson.* New York: Collier, 1965. (Originally published in 1954 as *The Negro in American Life and Thought: The Nadir, 1877–1901.*)

———, ed. *What the Negro Wants.* Chapel Hill: University of North Carolina Press, 1944. (Fourteen essays by noted black conservatives, moderates, and liberals, including Mary M. Bethune, W. E. B. Du Bois, A. Philip Randolph, Frederick D. Patterson, and Langston Hughes.)

Logan, Rayford W., and Michael R. Winston, eds. *Dictionary of American Negro Biography.* New York: W. W. Norton, 1982.

Logue, Calvin M., ed. *Ralph McGill: Editor and Publisher.* 2 vols. Durham, N.C.: Moore, 1969. (A collection of the noted Atlanta journalist's writings.)

———, ed. *Southern Encounters: Southerners of Note in Ralph McGill's South.* Macon, Ga.: Mercer University Press, 1983.

Logue, Calvin M., and Howard Dorgan, eds. *The Oratory of Southern Demagogues.* Baton Rouge: Louisiana State University Press, 1981.

Lomax, Alan. *The Land Where the Blues Began.* New York: Pantheon, 1993.

Lomax, Louis E. *The Negro Revolt.* New York: Harper & Brothers, 1962. (An expatriate black Georgian's perspective on racial and social issues.)

Lorant, Stefan. *The Glorious Burden: The American Presidency.* New York: Harper & Row, 1968.

Loveland, Anne C. *Lillian Smith: A Southerner Confronting the South.* Baton Rouge: Louisiana State University Press, 1986.

Lumpkin, Katharine Du Pre. *The South in Progress.* New York: International, 1940. (A social scientist's measure of Southern maturation in the waning days of the depression.)

——. *The Making of a Southerner.* New York: Alfred A. Knopf, 1947. (A memoir.)

Lyons, Mary E. *Sorrow's Kitchen: The Life and Folklore of Zora Neale Hurston.* New York: Scribner's, 1990.

Mains, Frances Helen, and Grace Loucks Elliott. *From Deep Roots: The Story of the YWCA's Religious Dimensions.* New York: National Board of the YWCA, 1974.

Malone, Bill C. *Country Music, U.S.A.* Austin: University of Texas Press, 1968. Revised edition, 1985.

——. *Southern Music, American Music.* Lexington: University Press of Kentucky, 1979.

Manchester, William. *The Glory and the Dream: A Narrative History of America, 1932–1972.* Boston: Little, Brown, 1974.

Mangione, Jerre. *The Dream and the Deal: The Federal Writers' Project, 1935–1943.* Boston: Little, Brown, 1972.

Marable, Manning. *Race, Reform, and Rebellion: The Second Reconstruction in Black America, 1945–1982.* Jackson: University Press of Mississippi, 1984.

——. *W. E. B. Du Bois: Black Radical Democrat.* Boston: Twayne, 1986.

Marshall, F. Ray. *Labor in the South.* Cambridge: Harvard University Press, 1967.

Martin, Charles H. *The Angelo Herndon Case and Southern Justice.* Baton Rouge: Louisiana State University Press, 1976.

Martin, Harold H. *Ralph McGill, Reporter.* Boston: Atlantic/Little, Brown, 1973.

——. *Atlanta and Environs: 1940–1976.* Athens: University of Georgia Press/Atlanta Historical Society, 1987.

Martin, John Bartlow. *The Deep South Says "Never."* New York: Ballantine, 1957.

Martin, Roscoe C., ed. *TVA: The First Twenty Years.* Knoxville: University of Tennessee Press, 1956.

Mason, Lucy Randolph. *To Win These Rights: A Personal Story of the CIO in the South.* New York: Harper & Brothers, 1952.

Matthews, Donald R., and James W. Prothro. *Negroes and the New Southern Politics.* New York: Harcourt, Brace & World, 1966.

Maverick, Maury. *A Maverick American.* New York: Covici-Friede, 1937. (A memoir.)

Mays, Benjamin E. *Seeking to Be Christian in Race Relations.* New York: Friendship, 1957.

——. *Born to Rebel: An Autobiography.* New York: Charles Scribner's Sons, 1971.

Mays, Benjamin E., and Joseph William Nicholson. *The Negro's Church.* New York: Institute of Social and Religious Research, 1933. Reprint, New York: Negro Universities Press, 1969.

McCaughan, Richard B. *Socks on a Rooster: Louisiana's Earl K. Long.* Baton Rouge: Claitor's Book Store, 1967.

McCoy, Donald R., and Richard Ruetten. *Quest and Response: Minority Rights and the Truman Administration.* Lawrence: University Press of Kansas, 1973.

McCullers, Carson. *The Heart Is a Lonely Hunter.* Boston: Houghton Mifflin, 1940.

McCulloch, James E., ed. *Battling for Social Betterment: Proceedings of the Southern Sociological Congress, Memphis, Tennessee, May 6–10, 1914.* Nashville: Southern Sociological Congress, 1914.

McCullough, David. *Truman.* New York: Simon and Schuster, 1992.

McDonald, Michael J., and John Muldowny. *TVA and the Dispossessed: The Resettlement of Population in the Norris Dam Area.* Knoxville: University of Tennessee Press, 1982.

McDonough, Julia Anne. "Men and Women of Good Will: A History of the Commission on

Interracial Cooperation and the Southern Regional Council, 1919–1954." Ph.D. diss., University of Virginia, 1992.

McDowell, John Patrick. *The Social Gospel in the South: The Woman's Home Mission Movement in the Methodist Episcopal Church, South, 1886–1939*. Baton Rouge: Louisiana State University Press, 1982.

McGill, Ralph. *The South and the Southerner*. Boston: Atlantic/Little, Brown, 1963. (The region as its most famous journalist saw it in the last decade of a long career.)

———. *No Place to Hide: The South and Human Rights*. Edited, with an introduction by Calvin M. Logue. 2 vols. Macon, Ga.: Mercer University Press, 1984. (A compilation of McGill's journalistic essays and speeches.)

McLaurin, Ann Mathison. "The Role of the Dixiecrats in the 1948 Election." Ph.D. diss., University of Oklahoma, 1972.

McMillen, Neil R. *The Citizens' Council: A History of Organized Resistance to the Second Reconstruction*. Urbana: University of Illinois Press, 1971.

———. *Black Mississippians in the Age of Jim Crow*. Urbana: University of Illinois Press, 1990.

McWhiney, Grady. *Southerners and Other Americans*. New York: Basic Books, 1973.

Meltzer, Milton. *Langston Hughes: A Biography*. New York: Thomas Y. Crowell, 1968.

Mencken, H. L. *Prejudices, Second Series*. New York: Alfred A. Knopf, 1920. (This volume includes his South-bashing "Sahara of the Bozart" essay.)

Mezerik, A. G. *The Revolt of the South and West*. New York: Duell, Sloan & Pearce, 1946.

Michie, Allan A., and Frank Ryhlick. *Dixie Demagogues*. New York: Vanguard, 1939.

Miller, Douglas T., and Marion Nowak. *The Fifties: The Way We Really Were*. Garden City, N.Y.: Doubleday, 1977.

Miller, Francis Pickens. *Man from the Valley: Memoirs of a 20th Century Virginian*. Chapel Hill: University of North Carolina Press, 1971.

Miller, Jim, ed. *The Rolling Stone Illustrated History of Rock & Roll*. New York: Random House/Rolling Stone Press, 1976. Revised and updated, 1980.

Miller, Loren. *The Petitioners: The Story of the Supreme Court of the United States and the Negro*. New York: Pantheon, 1966.

Miller, Merle. *Plain Speaking: An Oral Biography of Harry S Truman*. New York: Berkley, 1973.

Miller, Robert Moats. *American Protestantism and Social Issues, 1919–1939*. Chapel Hill: University of North Carolina Press, 1958.

Miller, William D. *Mr. Crump of Memphis*. Baton Rouge: Louisiana State University Press, 1964.

Minton, John D. "The New Deal in Tennessee." Ph.D. diss., Vanderbilt University, Nashville, 1959.

Mitchell, Broadus, and George S. Mitchell. *The Industrial Revolution in the South*. Baltimore: Johns Hopkins University Press, 1930. Reprint, New York: AMS Press, 1969. (An early look at the coming of industry to the South.)

Mitchell, George S. *Textile Unionism and the South*. Chapel Hill: University of North Carolina Press, 1932.

Mitchell, H. L. *Mean Things Happening in This Land: The Life and Times of the Southern Tenant Farmers Union*. Montclair, N.J.: Allanheld, Osmun, 1979.

———, ed. *Roll the Union On: A Pictorial History of the Southern Tenant Farmers Union*. Chicago: Charles H. Kerr, 1987.

Moon, Bucklin, ed. *Primer for White Folks*. Garden City, N.Y.: Doubleday, Doran, 1945.

Moon, Henry Lee. *Balance of Power: The Negro Vote*. Garden City, N.Y.: Doubleday, 1949.

Moore, John L., ed. *Congressional Quarterly's Guide to U.S. Elections*. 2nd ed. Washington: Congressional Quarterly, 1985.

Morris, Aldon D. *The Origins of the Civil Rights Movement: Black Communities Organizing for Change*. New York: Free Press/Macmillan, 1984.

Morrison, Joseph L. *W. J. Cash, Southern Prophet: A Biography and a Reader*. New York: Alfred A. Knopf, 1967.

Morrow, E. Frederic. *Black Man in the White House: A Diary of the Eisenhower Years by the Administrative Officer for Special Projects, the White House, 1955–1961*. New York: Coward-McCann, 1963.

———. *Forty Years a Guinea Pig*. New York: Pilgrim Press, 1980.

Murray, Albert. *South to a Very Old Place*. New York: McGraw-Hill, 1971. (An expatriate goes home to Alabama and the South.)

Murray, Pauli. *Song in a Weary Throat: An American Pilgrimage*. New York: Harper & Row, 1987.

———, ed. *States' Laws on Race and Color*. Cincinnati: Woman's Division of Christian Service, Methodist Church, 1950.

Muse, Benjamin. *Ten Years of Prelude: The Story of Integration Since the Supreme Court's 1954 Decision*. New York: Viking, 1964. (Includes some earlier contextual history.)

Myrdal, Gunnar, et al. *An American Dilemma: The Negro Problem and Modern Democracy*. New York: Harper & Row, 1944. (The twentieth-anniversary edition [2 vols., New York: McGraw-Hill, 1964] includes a new preface by the author and a postscript by his principal assistant, Arnold Rose.)

Natanson, Nicholas. *The Black Image in the New Deal: The Politics of FSA Photography*. Knoxville: University of Tennessee Press, 1992.

National Emergency Council. *Report to the President on Economic Conditions in the South*. Washington: U.S. Government Printing Office, 1938.

Newby, I. A. *Jim Crow's Defense: Anti-Negro Thought in America, 1900–1930*. Baton Rouge: Louisiana State University Press, 1965.

Nichols, Charles H., ed. *Arna Bontemps–Langston Hughes Letters, 1925–1967*. New York: Dodd, Mead, 1980.

Nichols, Lee. *Breakthrough on the Color Front*. New York: Random House, 1954. (An examination of the desegregation of the armed forces.)

Nixon, Herman Clarence. *Forty Acres and Steel Mules*. Chapel Hill: University of North Carolina Press, 1938.

Norrell, Robert J. *Reaping the Whirlwind: The Civil Rights Movement in Tuskegee*. New York: Alfred A. Knopf, 1985.

O'Brien, Michael. *The Idea of the American South, 1920–1941*. Baltimore: Johns Hopkins University Press, 1979.

Odum, Howard W. *Southern Regions of the United States*. Chapel Hill: University of North Carolina Press, 1936. (Principally a social science text, this volume and an accompanying manual were intended as models for a redirection of public-policy social planning in which the focus would shift from the forty-eight separate states to six interrelated regions; the Southeast, as one of the six proposed regions, included ten of the eleven old Confederate states plus Kentucky, with Texas being part of the Southwest region.)

———. *Race and Rumors of Race*. Chapel Hill: University of North Carolina Press, 1943.

———. *The Way of the South: Toward the Regional Balance of America*. New York: Macmillan, 1947.

Osofsky, Gilbert, ed. *The Burden of Race: A Documentary History of Negro-White Relations in America*. New York: Harper & Row, 1967.

Ottley, Roi. *New World A-Coming: Inside Black America*. Boston: Houghton-Mifflin, 1943.

———. *Black Odyssey: The Story of the Negro in America*. New York: Charles Scribner's Sons, 1948.

———. *No Green Pastures*. New York: Charles Scribner's Sons, 1951.

Owsley, Frank L. *Plain Folk of the Old South*. Baton Rouge: Louisiana State University Press, 1949.

Painter, Nell Irvin. *The Narrative of Hosea Hudson: His Life as a Negro Communist in the South*. Cambridge: Harvard University Press, 1979.

Parks, Gordon. *A Choice of Weapons*. New York: Harper & Row, 1965. (A memoir of the black photographer-filmmaker, who got his start in the Farm Security Administration and the Office of War Information in the New Deal.)

Paschal, Andrew G., ed. *A W. E. B. Du Bois Reader*. New York: Macmillan, 1971.

Patterson, Haywood, and Earl Conrad. *Scottsboro Boy*. Garden City, N.Y.: Doubleday, 1950.

Pearce, John Ed. *Divide and Dissent: Kentucky Politics, 1930–1963*. Lexington: University Press of Kentucky, 1987.

Peavey, Charles D. *Go Slow Now: Faulkner and the Race Question*. Eugene: University of Oregon Press, 1971.

Peeks, Edward. *The Long Struggle for Black Power*. New York: Scribner's, 1971.

Peeler, David P. *Hope Among Us Yet: Social Criticism and Social Solace in Depression America*. Athens: University of Georgia Press, 1987.

Peirce, Neal R. *The Deep South States of America: People, Politics, and Power in Seven Deep South States*. New York: W. W. Norton, 1974. (Social-political profiles of Alabama, Arkansas, Florida, Georgia, Louisiana, Mississippi, and South Carolina, in the fashion of Gunther's *Inside U.S.A.*)

———. *The Border South States: People, Politics, and Power in the Five Border South States*. New York: W. W. Norton, 1975. (Another volume in the Peirce series covering all fifty states, this one includes Kentucky, North Carolina, Tennessee, Virginia, and West Virginia; Texas is included in *The Plains States of America*.)

Pells, Richard H. *Radical Visions and American Dreams: Cultural and Social Thought in the Depression Years*. New York: Harper & Row, 1973.

Peltason, J. W. *58 Lonely Men: Southern Federal Judges and School Desegregation*. New York: Harcourt, Brace & World, 1961. (University of Illinois Press paperback editions, published in the 1970s, include additional material.)

Pepper, Claude Denson, with Hays Gorey. *Pepper: Eyewitness to a Century*. San Diego: Harcourt Brace Jovanovich, 1987.

Percy, Walker. *Signposts in a Strange Land*. New York: Farrar, Straus & Giroux, 1991. (Essays and other previously unpublished nonfiction by the Mississippi-Louisiana novelist, collected and edited after the author's death, with an introduction by Patrick Samway.)

Percy, William Alexander. *Lanterns on the Levee: Recollections of a Planter's Son*. New York: Alfred A. Knopf, 1941. (A 1973 edition, published by Louisiana State University Press, contains a new introduction by the author's nephew, the novelist Walker Percy.)

Perrett, Geoffrey. *Days of Sadness, Years of Triumph: The American People, 1939–1945.* New York: Coward, McCann & Geoghegan, 1973.

Perry, Jennings. *Democracy Begins at Home: The Tennessee Fight on the Poll Tax.* Philadelphia: J. B. Lippincott, 1944.

Peterkin, Julia W., and Doris Ulmann. *Roll, Jordan, Roll.* New York: Ballou, 1933. (Text by Peterkin, with photographs by Ulmann.)

Pfeffer, Paula F. *A. Philip Randolph, Pioneer of the Civil Rights Movement.* Baton Rouge: Louisiana State University Press, 1990.

Pleasants, Julian M., and Augustus M. Burns III. *Frank Porter Graham and the 1950 Senate Race in North Carolina.* Chapel Hill: University of North Carolina Press, 1990.

Ploski, Harry A., and Roscoe C. Brown, Jr. *The Negro Almanac.* New York: Bellwether, 1966.

Polk, William T. *Southern Accent: From Uncle Remus to Oak Ridge.* New York: William Morrow, 1953.

Pope, Liston. *Millhands and Preachers.* New Haven: Yale University Press, 1942. (A study of the historical background and contemporary events surrounding the 1929 textile mill strike in Gastonia, North Carolina.)

Poston, Ted. *The Dark Side of Hopkinsville.* Edited and annotated by Kathleen A. Hauke. Athens: University of Georgia Press, 1991. (Short stories by a Kentucky-born New Dealer who became "the dean of black journalists.")

Powdermaker, Hortense. *After Freedom: A Cultural Study of the Deep South.* New York: Viking, 1939. (A social-anthropological study focused on Indianola, Mississippi.)

Powell, Richard J. *Homecoming: The Art and Life of William H. Johnson.* Washington, D.C.: National Museum of American Art/Smithsonian, 1991. (An obscure South Carolina primitive artist's work examined in the context of the culture from which he came.)

Powledge, Fred. *Free at Last? The Civil Rights Movement and the People Who Made It.* Boston: Little, Brown, 1991.

President's Commission on Higher Education. *Higher Education for American Democracy: The Report of the President's Commission on Higher Education.* Washington, D.C.: U.S. Government Printing Office, 1947. (The second of six parts in this study is titled "Equalizing and Expanding Individual Opportunity," and deals with the problems of segregation and discrimination.)

President's Committee on Civil Rights. *To Secure These Rights: The Report of the President's Committee on Civil Rights.* Washington, D.C.: U.S. Government Printing Office, 1947.

President's Committee on Equality of Treatment and Opportunity in the Armed Forces. *Freedom to Serve.* Washington, D.C.: U.S. Government Printing Office, 1950.

Raeburn, Ben, ed. *Treasury for the Free World.* New York: Arco, 1946. (Essays on postwar world freedom by about sixty authors, including Carl Sandburg and Gunnar Myrdal.)

Raines, Howell. *My Soul Is Rested: Movement Days in the Deep South Remembered.* New York: G. P. Putnam's Sons, 1977.

Rainey, Glenn W. "The Race Riot of 1906 in Atlanta." Master's thesis, Emory University, 1929.

Raper, Arthur F. *The Tragedy of Lynching.* Chapel Hill: University of North Carolina Press, 1933.

———. *Preface to Peasantry: A Tale of Two Black Belt Counties.* Chapel Hill: University of North Carolina Press, 1936. (This volume focuses on Greene and Macon counties in Georgia.)

Raper, Arthur F., and Ira De A. Reid. *Sharecroppers All.* Chapel Hill: University of North Carolina Press, 1941.

Raper, Arthur F., and Jack Delano. *Tenants of the Almighty.* New York: Macmillan, 1943. (A later look at Greene County, Georgia, with photographs by Delano.)

Record, Wilson. *The Negro in the Communist Party.* Chapel Hill: University of North Carolina Press, 1951.

―――. *Race and Radicalism: The NAACP and the Communist Party in Conflict.* Ithaca, N.Y.: Cornell University Press, 1964.

Redding, J. Saunders. *No Day of Triumph.* New York: Harper & Brothers, 1942. (A black writer's journey through the South.)

―――. *On Being Negro in America.* Indianapolis: Bobbs-Merrill, 1951. (Personal reflections.)

―――. *The Lonesome Road: The Story of the Negro's Past in America.* Garden City, N.Y.: Doubleday, 1958.

―――. *A Scholar's Conscience.* Lexington: University Press of Kentucky, 1992. (Selected writings, 1942–1977, from the pen of a perceptive critic of American and Southern history and culture; edited and introduced by Faith Berry.)

Reed, John Shelton. *The Enduring South: Subcultural Persistence in Mass Society.* Chapel Hill: University of North Carolina Press, 1972.

―――. *One South: An Ethnic Approach to Regional Culture.* Baton Rouge: Louisiana State University Press, 1982.

Reed, Linda. *Simple Decency and Common Sense: The Southern Conference Movement, 1938–1963.* Bloomington: Indiana University Press, 1991.

Robertson, Ben. *Red Hills and Cotton: An Upcountry Memory.* Columbia: University of South Carolina Press, 1942. Reprint, with a biographical sketch of the author by Wright Bryan, 1960.

Robinson, Jo Ann Gibson. *The Montgomery Bus Boycott and the Women Who Started It.* Knoxville: University of Tennessee Press, 1987. (Memoir by a leader of the Women's Political Council, an organization of Alabama that black women founded in 1946 to work for the eradication of race and gender discrimination.)

Roland, Charles P. *The Improbable Era: The South Since World War II.* Lexington: University Press of Kentucky, 1975.

Roller, David C., and Robert W. Twyman, eds. *The Encyclopedia of Southern History.* Baton Rouge: Louisiana State University Press, 1979.

Roosevelt, Eleanor. *This I Remember.* New York: Harper & Brothers, 1949. (A memoir.)

Roper, John Herbert. *C. Vann Woodward, Southerner.* Athens: University of Georgia Press, 1987.

Rosengarten, Theodore. *All God's Dangers: The Life of Nate Shaw.* New York: Alfred A. Knopf, 1974. (The real-life odyssey of Ned Cobb, an Alabama sharecropper.)

Rowan, Carl T. *South of Freedom.* New York: Alfred A. Knopf, 1952. (A black journalist's account of a journey through his native region.)

―――. *Breaking Barriers: A Memoir.* Boston: Little, Brown, 1991.

―――. *Dream Makers, Dream Breakers: The World of Justice Thurgood Marshall.* Boston: Little, Brown, 1993.

Rubin, Louis D., Jr. *A Gallery of Southerners.* Baton Rouge: Louisiana State University Press, 1982.

―――, ed. *The American South: Portrait of a Culture.* Baton Rouge: Louisiana State University Press, 1980. (Essays on the Southern mystique.)

Salmond, John A. *A Southern Rebel: The Life and Times of Aubrey Willis Williams, 1890–1965*. Chapel Hill: University of North Carolina Press, 1983.

———. *Miss Lucy of the CIO: The Life and Times of Lucy Randolph Mason, 1882–1959*. Athens: University of Georgia Press, 1988.

———. *Conscience of a Lawyer: Clifford J. Durr and American Liberties, 1899–1975*. Tuscaloosa: University of Alabama Press, 1990.

Sarratt, Reed. *The Ordeal of Desegregation: The First Decade*. New York: Harper & Row, 1966. (This volume focuses on public schools.)

Satterly, Kenneth R. "Donald Davidson, Southern Regionalism, and the TVA." Ph.D. diss., Brown University, 1973.

Scales, Junius Irving, and Richard Nickson. *Cause at Heart: A Former Communist Remembers*. Athens: University of Georgia Press, 1987.

Scott, Anne Firor. *The Southern Lady: From Pedestal to Politics, 1830–1930*. Chicago: University of Chicago Press, 1970.

Sellers, Charles G., ed. *The Southerner as American*. Chapel Hill: University of North Carolina Press, 1960. (Essays by Dewey W. Grantham, George B. Tindall, and others.)

Shannon, Jasper Berry. *Toward a New Politics in the South*. Knoxville: University of Tennessee Press, 1949.

Shapiro, Herbert. *White Violence and Black Response: From Reconstruction to Montgomery*. Amherst: University of Massachusetts Press, 1988.

Sherrill, Robert. *Gothic Politics in the Deep South: Stars of the New Confederacy*. New York: Grossman, 1968. (Journalistic profiles of Herman Talmadge, James Eastland, Strom Thurmond, and others.)

Shockley, Ann Allen. *Afro-American Women Writers, 1746–1933: An Anthology and Critical Guide*. Boston: G. K. Hall, 1988.

Shoemaker, Don, ed. *With All Deliberate Speed: Segregation-Desegregation in Southern Schools*. New York: Harper & Brothers, 1957. (An account, with some early history, of the Southern response to the Supreme Court's 1954 school desegregation decision.)

Shouse, Sarah Newman. *Hillbilly Realist: Herman Clarence Nixon of Possum Trot*. Tuscaloosa: University of Alabama Press, 1986.

Sikora, Frank. *The Judge: The Life & Opinions of Alabama's Frank M. Johnson, Jr.* Montgomery: Black Belt, 1992.

Simkins, Francis Butler. *The South Old and New: A History, 1820–1947*. New York: Alfred A. Knopf, 1947.

———. *A History of the South*. New York: Alfred A. Knopf, 1953.

Simpson, Lewis P., James Olney, and Jo Gulledge, eds. *The "Southern Review" and Modern Literature, 1935–1985*. Baton Rouge: Louisiana State University Press, 1988.

Sims, George E. *The Little Man's Big Friend: James E. Folsom in Alabama Politics, 1946–1958*. Tuscaloosa: University of Alabama Press, 1985.

Singal, Daniel Joseph. *The War Within: From Victorian to Modernist Thought in the South, 1919–1945*. Chapel Hill: University of North Carolina Press, 1982.

Sitkoff, Harvard. *A New Deal for Blacks: The Emergence of Civil Rights as a National Issue*. New York: Oxford University Press, 1978.

———. *The Struggle for Black Equality, 1954–1980*. New York: Hill & Wang, 1981.

Skaggs, William H. *The Southern Oligarchy: An Appeal on Behalf of the Silent Masses of Our Country Against the Despotic Rule of the Few*. New York: Devin-Adair, 1924. (A volume from the genre of calls to conscience by expatriate Southern whites.)

Smith, Bob. *They Closed Their Schools: Prince Edward County, Virginia, 1951–1964.* Chapel Hill: University of North Carolina Press, 1965.

Smith, Frank E. *Congressman from Mississippi.* New York: Pantheon, 1964. (The memoir of a Southern moderate lawmaker.)

Smith, Jessie Carney, ed. *Notable Black American Women.* Detroit: Gale Research, 1991.

———. *Epic Lives: One Hundred Black Women Who Made a Difference.* Detroit: Gale Research, 1993.

Smith, Lillian. *Strange Fruit.* New York: Harcourt, Brace & World, 1944. (A novel.)

———. *Killers of the Dream.* New York: W. W. Norton, 1949. Revised and enlarged edition, New York: Doubleday/Anchor, 1963.

———. *Now Is the Time.* New York: Dell, 1965. (Reflections on race and the South in light of *Brown v. Board of Education.*)

Smith, Stephen A. *Myth, Media, and the Southern Mind.* Fayetteville: University of Arkansas Press, 1985.

Sosna, Morton. *In Search of the Silent South: Southern Liberals and the Race Issue.* New York: Columbia University Press, 1977.

Southern, David W. *Gunnar Myrdal and Black-White Relations.* Baton Rouge: Louisiana State University Press, 1987.

Sprigle, Ray. *In the Land of Jim Crow.* New York: Simon and Schuster, 1949.

Steinbeck, John. *The Grapes of Wrath.* New York: Viking, 1939. (The modern classic novel depicting the odyssey of Oklahoma sharecroppers and tenant farmers.)

Sternsher, Bernard, ed. *The Negro in Depression and War: Prelude to Revolution, 1930–1945.* Chicago: Quadrangle, 1969.

Stone, I. F. *A Nonconformist History of Our Times: The War Years, 1939–1945.* Boston: Little, Brown, 1988. (A collection of the independent journalist's columns, one in a series of volumes that also includes *The Truman Era, 1945–1952* and *The Haunted Fifties, 1953–1963.*)

Stott, William. *Documentary Expression and Thirties America.* New York: Oxford University Press, 1973.

Strickland, Michael, Harry Davis, and Jeff Strickland, eds. *The Best of Ralph McGill: Selected Columns.* Atlanta: Cherokee, 1980.

Sugg, Redding S., and George Hilton Jones. *The Southern Regional Education Board: Ten Years of Regional Cooperation in Higher Education.* Baton Rouge: Louisiana State University Press, 1960.

Suggs, Henry Lewis, ed. *The Black Press in the South, 1865–1979.* Westport, Conn.: Greenwood, 1983.

Sullivan, Patricia Ann. "Gideon's Southern Soldiers: New Deal Politics and Civil Rights Reform, 1933–1948." Ph.D. diss., Emory University, 1983.

Talmadge, Herman E. *You and Segregation.* Birmingham: Vulcan, 1955. (A prominent Southern politician's impassioned defense of white supremacy in the aftermath of the *Brown* decision.)

———. *Talmadge: A Political Legacy, a Politician's Life.* Atlanta: Peachtree, 1987. (A memoir, written with Mark Royden Winchell.)

Taylor, Paul S., and Dorothea Lange. *An American Exodus: A Record of Human Erosion.* New York: Reynal & Hitchcock, 1939. (A depression-era documentary, with Lange's photographs.)

Taylor, Thomas E. "A Political Biography of Ellis Arnall." Master's thesis, Emory University, 1959.

Terkel, Studs. *Hard Times: An Oral History of the Great Depression*. New York: Pantheon, 1970.

———. *The Good War*. New York: Pantheon, 1984. (An oral history of World War II.)

———. *Race: How Blacks and Whites Think and Feel About the American Obsession*. New York: New Press, 1992.

Terrill, Tom E., and Jerrold Hirsch, eds. *Such as Us: Southern Voices of the Thirties*. Chapel Hill: University of North Carolina Press, 1978.

Tindall, George B. *The Emergence of the New South, 1913–1945*. Baton Rouge: Louisiana State University Press, 1967.

———. *The Disruption of the Solid South*. Athens: University of Georgia Press, 1972.

———. *The Ethnic Southerners*. Baton Rouge: Louisiana State University Press, 1976.

Tirro, Frank. *Jazz: A History*. New York: W. W. Norton, 1977.

Truman, Margaret. *Harry S Truman*. New York: William Morrow, 1973.

Turner, William H., and Edward J. Cabbell, eds. *Blacks in Appalachia*. Lexington: University Press of Kentucky, 1985.

Twelve Southerners. *I'll Take My Stand: The South and the Agrarian Tradition*. New York: Harper & Brothers, 1930.

Twitty, W. Bradley. *Y'all Come: "Big Jim" Folsom*. Nashville: Hermitage, 1962. (A biography of Alabama's postwar governor.)

Tygiel, Jules. *Baseball's Great Experiment: Jackie Robinson and His Legacy*. New York: Oxford University Press, 1983.

Ulanov, Barry. *Duke Ellington*. New York: Creative Age, 1946.

U.S. House of Representatives, 80th Congress, Committee on Un-American Activities. *Report on the Southern Conference for Human Welfare: Investigation of Un-American Activities in the United States*. Washington, D.C.: U.S. Government Printing Office, 1947.

U.S. Senate, 83rd Congress, Subcommittee to Investigate the Administration of the Internal Security Act, U.S. Senate Committee on the Judiciary. *Hearings on Subversive Influence in the Southern Conference Educational Fund: New Orleans, La., March 18–20, 1954*. Washington, D.C.: U.S. Government Printing Office, 1954.

Vance, Rupert B. *Human Geography of the South: A Study in Regional Resources and Human Adequacy*. Chapel Hill: University of North Carolina Press, 1932.

———. *All These People: The Nation's Human Resources in the South*. Chapel Hill: University of North Carolina Press, 1945.

Waldron, Ann. *Hodding Carter: The Reconstruction of a Racist*. Chapel Hill: Algonquin, 1993.

Walker, Margaret. *Richard Wright, Daemonic Genius: A Portrait of the Man, a Critical Look at His Work*. New York: Warner, 1988.

Warren, Robert Penn. *All the King's Men*. New York: Random House, 1946. (A novel inspired by the life of Huey Long.)

———. *Segregation: The Inner Conflict in the South*. New York: Random House, 1956.

———. *Who Speaks for the Negro?* New York: Random House, 1965.

Watters, Pat, and Reese Cleghorn. *Climbing Jacob's Ladder: The Arrival of Negroes in Southern Politics*. New York: Harcourt, Brace & World, 1967.

Weatherford, W. D. *Negro Life in the South: Present Conditions and Needs*. New York: Association Press, 1910.

Weatherford, W. D., and Charles S. Johnson. *Race Relations: Adjustment of Whites and Negroes in the United States*. Boston: D. C. Heath, 1934.

Weaver, Robert C. *Negro Labor: A National Problem.* New York: Harcourt, Brace, 1946.

Weglyn, Michi. *Years of Infamy: The Untold Story of America's Concentration Camps.* New York: William Morrow, 1976.

West, Don. *Clods of Southern Earth.* New York: Boni & Gaer, 1946. (A volume of poetry.)

Whisnant, David E. *Modernizing the Mountaineer: People, Power, and Planning in Appalachia.* Boone, N.C.: Appalachian Consortium, 1980.

———. *All That Is Native and Fine: The Politics of Culture in an American Region.* Chapel Hill: University of North Carolina Press, 1983. (Appalachian social history.)

White, Helen, and Redding S. Sugg, Jr., eds. *From the Mountain.* Memphis: Memphis State University Press, 1972. (An anthology of articles from the three Georgia magazines edited by Lillian Smith and Paula Snelling, 1936–1945, with an introduction by the book's editors, White and Sugg.)

White, Walter. *Rope and Faggot: A Biography of Judge Lynch.* New York: Alfred A. Knopf, 1929.

———. *A Rising Wind.* Garden City, N.Y.: Doubleday, Doran, 1945. (Seeing race and color as a postwar issue worldwide.)

———. *A Man Called White.* New York: Viking, 1948. (An autobiography.)

———. *How Far the Promised Land?* New York: Viking, 1955.

Wigginton, Eliot, ed. *Refuse to Stand Silently By: An Oral History of Grass Roots Activism in America, 1921–1964.* New York: Doubleday, 1991. (Based on interviews with dozens of people with ties to the Highlander Folk School in Tennessee.)

Wilkinson, J. Harvie. *Harry Byrd and the Changing Face of Virginia Politics, 1945–1966.* Charlottesville: University of Virginia Press, 1968.

Williams, Martin. *The Jazz Tradition.* New York: Oxford University Press, 1970. Revised and expanded, 1983.

Williams, Roger. *Sing a Sad Song: The Life of Hank Williams.* 2nd ed. Urbana: University of Illinois Press, 1981.

Williams, T. Harry. *Romance and Realism in Southern Politics.* Athens: University of Georgia Press, 1961.

———. *Huey Long.* New York: Alfred A. Knopf, 1969.

Williamson, Joel. *The Crucible of Race: Black-White Relations in the American South Since Emancipation.* New York: Oxford University Press, 1984. Condensed version, titled *A Rage for Order,* New York: Oxford, 1986.

Wilson, Charles Reagan, William Ferris, et al. *Encyclopedia of Southern Culture.* Chapel Hill: University of North Carolina Press, 1989.

Wolters, Raymond. *Negroes and the Great Depression: The Problem of Economic Recovery.* Westport, Conn.: Greenwood, 1970.

Woodward, C. Vann. *Origins of the New South, 1877–1913.* Baton Rouge: Louisiana State University Press, 1951.

———. *The Strange Career of Jim Crow.* New York: Oxford University Press, 1955. Revised, with a new preface by the author, 1966.

———. *The Burden of Southern History.* Baton Rouge: Louisiana State University Press, 1960. (Subsequent editions have included some revisions and additions.)

———. *American Counterpoint: Slavery and Racism in the North-South Dialogue.* Boston: Little, Brown, 1971. (Essays on race.)

———. *Thinking Back: The Perils of Writing History.* Baton Rouge: Louisiana State University Press, 1986. (Reflections on a long career by the best-known contemporary historian of the South.)

Woofter, Thomas J. *Southern Race Progress: The Wavering Color Line*. Washington, D.C.: Public Affairs Press, 1957.

Workman, William D., Jr. *The Case for the South*. New York: Devin-Adair, 1960. (A South Carolina editor's defense of segregation.)

Wright, Gavin. *Old South, New South: Revolutions in the Southern Economy Since the Civil War*. New York: Basic Books, 1986.

Wright, George C., and Martin G. White. *A History of Blacks in Kentucky: In Pursuit of Equality, 1890–1980*, vol. 2. Frankfort: Kentucky Historical Society, 1992.

Wright, Marion A., and Arnold Shankman. *Human Rights Odyssey*. Durham, N.C.: Moore, 1978.

Wright, Richard. *Uncle Tom's Children: Five Long Stories*. New York: Harper & Brothers, 1940. (An earlier edition, published in 1938, contained four novellas; this expanded version also includes "The Ethics of Living Jim Crow," Wright's clearly autobiographical sketch of a black youngster's life in Arkansas, Mississippi, and Memphis.)

———. *Native Son*. New York: Harper & Brothers, 1940. (A fictional account of a black migrant Southerner's undoing in the urban North.)

———. *12 Million Black Voices: A Folk History of the Negro in the United States*. New York: Viking, 1941. (An essay with Farm Security Administration photographs.)

———. *Black Boy: A Record of Childhood and Youth*. New York: Harper & Brothers, 1945. (Nonfictional remembrance and indictment.)

Wyatt, Wilson W. *Whistle Stops: Adventures in Public Life*. Lexington: University Press of Kentucky, 1985. (The autobiography of a New Deal–era politician from Louisville.)

Wynes, Charles E., ed. *Forgotten Voices: Dissenting Southerners in an Age of Conformity*. Baton Rouge: Louisiana State University Press, 1967.

Yarbrough, Tinsley E. *A Passion for Justice: J. Waties Waring and Civil Rights*. New York: Oxford University Press, 1987.

Young, James O. *Black Writers of the Thirties*. Baton Rouge: Louisiana State University Press, 1973.

Zangrando, Robert L. *The NAACP Crusade Against Lynching, 1909–1950*. Philadelphia: Temple University Press, 1980.

Zinn, Howard. *The Southern Mystique*. New York: Alfred A. Knopf, 1964.

———. *Postwar America: 1945–1971*. Indianapolis: Bobbs-Merrill, 1973.

———, ed. *New Deal Thought*. Indianapolis: Bobbs-Merrill, 1966.

Index

A NOTE ON THE TYPE

This book was set in Caledonia, a face designed by William Addison Dwiggins (1880–1956) for the Mergenthaler Linotype Company in 1939. It belongs to the family of types referred to by printers as "modern," a term used to mark the change in type styles that occurred around 1800. Caledonia was inspired by the Scotch types cast by the Glasgow typefounders Alexander Wilson & Sons circa 1833.

Composed by American-Stratford Graphic Services,
Brattleboro, Vermont
Printed and bound by Arcata Graphics,
Martinsburg, West Virginia
Designed by Peter A. Andersen